Texas
Real Estate
Principles
I&II

Rod M. Rodriguez, JD
Kathleen E. Terrell, CREI
Eddie Stockton, CREI
Kay Adams

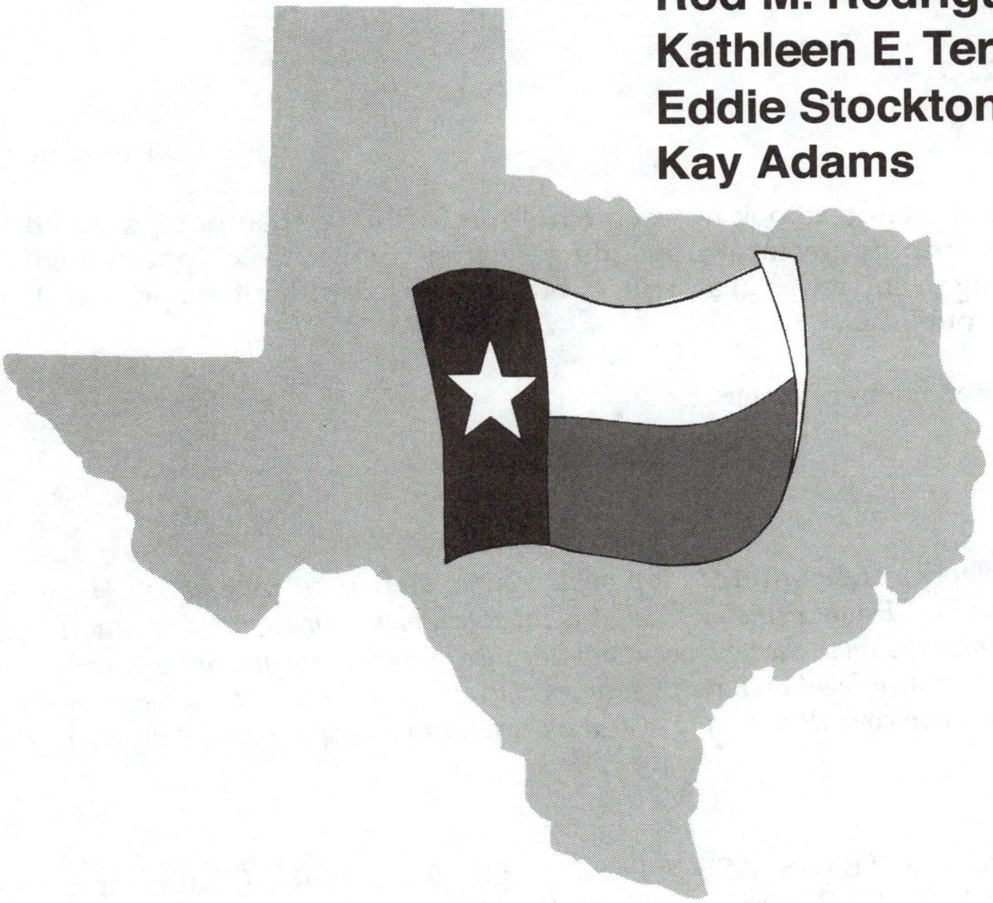

Richard Helgeson – Review Editor

Copyright 2007, First Edition
Educational Textbook Company, Inc.
P.O. Box 3597
Covina, California 91722
(626) 339-7733
(626) 332-4744 (Fax)
www.etcbooks.com or **www.etctextbooks.com**

Library of Congress Cataloging-in-Publication Data

Texas Real Estate Principles I&II - Rod M. Rodriguez, JD, Kathleen E. Terrell, Eddie Stockton, Kay Adams

ISBN 978-0-916772-91-8

Disclaimer: The authors have taken great care to provide accurate and current information. However, this textbook, "Texas Real Estate Principles I&II," is intended for informational and educational purposes only. The information in the textbook is not intended as a means of providing or replacing personal legal advice or as a legal opinion on any specific subjects, facts or circumstances. The authors urge the reader to consult with a lawyer with respect to any specific legal questions the reader may have.

Special thanks to the TEXAS ASSOCIATION OF REALTORS (TAR)® and the TEXAS REAL ESTATE COMMISSION (TREC) for allowing us to reprint their forms. Endorsement is not implied.

Preface

"You can't help but notice the immense size of this book — it had to be to contain all the immense talent who contributed to its creation." Walt Huber

In this first edition of *Texas Real Estate Principles I&II*, real estate publisher Walt Huber has brought together the remarkable talents and experience of instructors and authors Rod M. Rodriguez, Kathleen E. Terrell, Kay Adams, and Eddie Stockton. As such, it is the crown jewel in Educational Textbook Company's trilogy of Texas real estate textbooks. With this book, in combination with *Texas Real Estate Contracts* and *Texas Real Estate Agency*, we have fulfilled and surpassed the Texas Real Estate Commission's requirements for licensing in the great state of Texas.

Rodrigo (Rod) M. Rodriguez holds a Doctor of Jurisprudence degree from the University of Houston Law Center and a B.A. degree from St. Mary's University in San Antonio. A long-time practicing attorney, Rodriguez presently serves as professor of real estate at Collin County Community College in Plano, Texas. In addition to being a Texas real estate licensee, he is a member of the Texas Real Estate Teacher's Association, where he holds the Certified Real Estate Instructor (CREI) designation.

Kathleen E. Terrell is a past president of the Texas Real Estate Teacher's Association and a mortgage broker, real estate broker, and co-owner and administrator of "Real Estate Education Consultants," "P.R.E.P.A.R.E. Mortgage," and "PREPARE Real Estate." She holds a CREI designation and has been awarded accolades too numerous to list here, including winning the Educator of the year award by the Texas Association of REALTORS®.

Eddie Stockton is the king of real estate in Beaumont, Texas. He owns and operates one of the largest brokerages in the area and has been teaching for many years. He is well respected and admired by students and clients alike. He holds a CREI designation among others.

Kay Adams is a REALTOR® and instructor who has been an active member of the real estate profession for 30 years and in 3 states. She has worked as an agent, broker/owner, and manager of real estate companies. Since 1996 she has also worked as an owner and director of real estate schools, writing courses and as an instructor of real estate.

We owe a special debt of gratitude to Richard Helgeson, associate professor of Collin County Community College in Plano, Texas, without whom we could not have produced such an exceptional work. Richard is the owner/president of Parthenon Property Company and his vast knowledge in the area of Texas real estate, his eagle-eye editing, as well as his writing and rewrite skills were paramount to the quality of this book.

We appreciate the assistance of Bruce W. Davis, Ph.D., the Director of Test Development for PSI. PSI helps to maintain the relevancy and appropriate weighting of the testing topics and generally contributes to the quality of the real estate testing industry in the state of Texas and the rest of the country.

We'd like to thank Ed Doran, Sr. of Richland College for originally inspiring us to write this book.

Special thanks to the professionals who helped design and produce this book: Colleen Taber, executive editor; Rick Lee, pre-press editor and layout; Phillip Dockter, art director; and Melinda Winters, cover design.

Acknowledgments

Ed Doran, Sr.
Richland College
Dallas, Texas

Cullin Smith
Lamar Institute of Technology
Beaumont, Texas

Ken Combs, Professor
Del Mar College
Corpus Christi, Texas

Ken Trussell
Continuing Education for Licensing, Inc. (CELI)
Texas A&M University – Commerce
College Station, Texas

Jessica M. Rocha
Houston Community College
Houston, Texas

George Renfro
Bellaire, Texas

Dr. Christian Ashibuogwu
HCC Southwest
Houston, Texas

Greg Glenn
Real Estate Broker
Amarillo College

Richard Helgeson
Collin County Community College
Plano, Texas

Table of Contents

Chapter 1: Introduction To Real Estate 1

Chapter 2: Estates, Transfers, and Titles 39

Table of Contents

Table of Contents

Chapter 5:   Contracts   155

Table of Contents

Chapter 12: Financial Institutions   443

Chapter 13: Appraisal Basics   479

Chapter 16: Taxation of Real Estate 593

REALTORS®

I AM A TEXAS REALTOR®

I PLEDGE TO BE HONEST AND ALWAYS PUT MY CLIENT'S INTERESTS FIRST. I GO BEYOND WHAT THE LAW REQUIRES. I FIGHT FOR HOMEOWNERS' RIGHTS. MY CLIENTS HAVE A LOT AT STAKE. I OWE IT TO THEM TO BE MORE THAN JUST AN ORDINARY REAL ESTATE AGENT. I VOLUNTEER IN MY COMMUNITY BECAUSE I LIVE THERE, TOO. I WORK HARD TO CREATE OPPORTUNITIES FOR MORE PEOPLE TO AFFORD HOMES. I TAKE COURSES TO INCREASE MY EXPERTISE SO I CAN BETTER SERVE YOU. COMMERCIAL

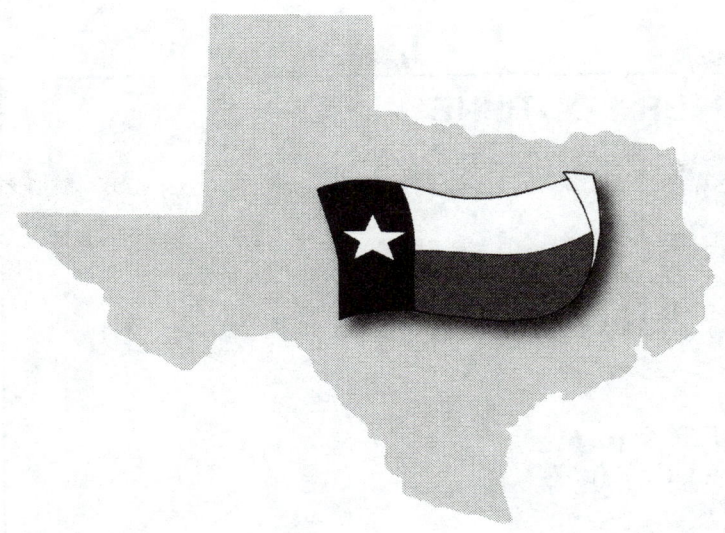

Chapter 1
Introduction to Real Estate

I. Texas: The Lone Star State

Texas is the land where battles have been fought, fortunes gambled, and destinies created.

A. AS BIG AS TEXAS

TEXAS. The very name evokes images of wide open spaces and expansive vistas. It also conjures up thoughts of big ranches, big oil and big business. From the mountains of far west Texas to the piney woods of east Texas, and from the plains of the panhandle to the gulf coast, Texas is as unique as its people and land.

Texas is the second largest state in size, with 267,277 square miles, and the second largest in population, with 23 million residents.

Texas occupies about seven percent of the total water and land area of the United States. Comprised of piney woods, prairie, marsh, plains, plateaus, mountains, and 367 miles of coastline, Texas possesses an incredibly rich heritage teeming with wildlife as diverse as the landscape.

More land is farmed in Texas than any other state.

1

CHAPTER 1 OUTLINE

Rivers and Streams

The State of Texas has approximately 3,700 streams, for a total length of approximately 80,000 miles. Among its major rivers are the following:

- The Rio Grande River
- Red River
- Colorado River
- Sabine River
- Pecos River
- Devils River
- Nueces River
- Guadalupe River

Approximately fourteen percent of United States farmland is located in Texas or roughly 131 million acres. Long considered to be the birthplace of American ranching, the King Ranch of south Texas is larger than the state of Rhode Island. In fact, Texas contains nearly as many cattle as people. Texas fueled the automobile age when crude oil gushed out of the ground in a small field known as Spindletop just outside of Beaumont in 1901. But a mere 60 years after that first gusher, Texas also helped rocket America's manned space program with the establishment of the Johnson Space Center just outside of Houston.

When the Republic of Texas was annexed to the United States in 1845, Texas retained control of its public lands. Today, the federal government owns only approximately 1.4 percent of Texas land, and the state government owns less than one percent.

Six Flags Over Texas

Texas has been under six national flags in its history since the first European exploration of the region by Cortez in 1519:

1. Spain, 1519-1685; 1690-1821;
2. France, 1685-1690;
3. Mexico, 1821-1836;
4. Texas as a Republic, 1836-1845;
5. Texas in the Confederacy, 1861-1865
6. Texas in the United States of America, 1845-1861, 1865 - Present.

Nearly 97 percent of Texas land is privately-owned.

B. A MELTING POT OF CULTURES AND IDEAS

Historically, Texas has been at the crossroads of several great cultures. First explored in the 1600s by the Spanish and French, and later settled by the Mexican and Texican colonists, these cultures have left their influence on local values, customs and laws which are still being felt to this very day. For example, present day marital property law can be traced back to its origins of Spanish/Mexican law, while elements of mineral and boundary law have their root in the early French adventurers who explored the Texas coast and the Mississippi River. A great many other laws are influenced by the **English Common Law**. Texas adopted common law as part of its system of justice when it became a state.

"Common law" is a body of law that originated in England and relies on custom and usage in the community and also gives weight to earlier, relevant court decisions (called precedents). "Statutory law," on the other hand, relies on the written law.

C. LAND OF OPPORTUNITY

Around 2040, Texas' two most populated areas, Houston-Baytown-Sugar Land and Dallas-Fort Worth, could hit ten million people. If projections prove true, Texas will have between 35.8 and 45.4 million residents in 2040.

Due to increased job opportunities, higher birthrates, immigration, and migration, Texas' population growth rate is expected to increase from its current 22.1 million residents to as many as 45 million by the year 2040. By then, the Houston and Dallas/Fort Worth Metroplex could see population more than double to more than 10 million residents in each metropolitan area, according to a recently published report in the

Real Estate Center at Texas A & M University (Real Estate Center). As its name implies, the Real Estate Center is the state-designated research center for real estate issues in Texas. It is considered to be one of the top "think-tanks" for real estate in the nation and is a top-notch resource for data about Texas real estate.

http://recenter.tamu.edu.
Texas A&M University (Real Estate Center)

Currently, the number of new houses and condominiums being constructed is low. As a result, the demand for housing is already outpacing supply.

Everything is Bigger in Texas!

II. The Real Estate Business in Texas

A. COST OF HOUSING

According to the Real Estate Center, nearly 240,000 residential units are sold in Texas each year, representing a dollar volume of nearly $40 billion, with the largest number of home sales in the Houston market followed next by the DFW Metroplex, Austin, and San Antonio areas. The state average sales price was $164,400+ with a median price of $129,700+. As a percentage, more Texas families could afford a median priced home as compared to the national average.

B. COST OF HOMEOWNERSHIP

Even though Texas ranks well in terms of housing affordability, a home purchase is still an expensive proposition. In the majority of cases, a home purchase will require a monthly payment consisting of a portion devoted just to the **PRINCIPAL** *(the repayment of the loan amount borrowed)* and an element of **INTEREST** *(being the rental portion devoted to the time value of money). Because this payment consists of principal and interest, it is generally known as a* **PI PAYMENT**. Typically, these types of payments equal 25 to 28 percent of a homeowner's monthly gross wages, however, creative loan products can alter this percentage significantly.

Many loan plans provide for the repayment of PITI (Principal, Interest, Taxes, and Insurance).

In those types of loans, the monthly payment consists not only of the principal and interest, but also of escrowed property **taxes** (the "T" element of the payment) and homeowner's **insurance** (the "I" portion of the monthly payment). Regardless of whether the homeowner makes a monthly PI payment or a PITI payment, the monthly payment is only part of the expense of homeownership. For this reason, first-time homebuyers should be aware that home repairs, maintenance, other improvements, as well as furnishings, and utility expenses are additional expenses that will contribute to the costs of homeownership.

A home is often the largest and most important purchase a person makes in his/her lifetime.

C. THE REAL ESTATE LICENSE ACT (TRELA)

In 1939, the Texas Legislature passed the state's first laws requiring real estate professionals to become licensed.

Under the Real Estate Dealer's License Act, professionals were required to be licensed with the Texas Secretary of State's office. In 1949, the law was amended, turning licensing over to the newly created **Texas Real Estate Commission (TREC)**. *In its present form, the state's licensing law is known as THE REAL ESTATE LICENSE ACT (TRELA)* and is codified in Title 7 of the Texas Occupations Code, Section 1101, which is detailed later in this book.

In reviewing the law, it's important to understand at the outset the relationship between the Texas Real Estate Commission and the Texas Legislature. The role of the Texas Legislature is to enact new laws and amend existing laws including those dealing with real estate. The Texas Legislature, by enacting TRELA, created TREC and charged it with the responsibility of administering the provisions of TRELA including the licensing and discipline of real estate salespersons and brokers. The Legislature also gave TREC the authority to adopt rules which govern the day-to-day operations of licensees. Texas licensees must be careful to obey not only the provisions of TRELA, but also those regulations adopted by TREC.

The Texas Legislature created the licensing laws. In so doing, they created the Texas Real Estate Commission (TREC), which regulates the activities of brokers and salespersons, as well as other real estate professionals, by administering TRELA.

D. TEXAS REAL ESTATE COMMISSION (TREC)

The Texas Real Estate Commission administers the provisions of The Real Estate License Act (TRELA).

By law, the Commission is comprised of nine members, including six broker members and three members of the general public. All members are appointed by the governor with the advice and consent of the Texas Senate. The commissioners, in turn, hire an administrator who oversees a staff of 100+ who deal with everything from licensing and education to enforcement and discipline. The most current and accurate information regarding the Commission's duties and functions can be found at the agency website (see page 8).

E. PROFESSIONS IN REAL ESTATE

As will be explained in later chapters, a real estate license is required in Texas when representing another person for a fee or valuable consideration. In other words, if you do any of the acts enumerated in The Real Estate License Act as "acts of a broker," for a fee or valuable consideration, for another person, you must have a real estate license. A real estate education can open other doors and create numerous opportunities. Here's a sampling of related occupational areas where a real estate education might prove valuable:

- Construction
- Title insurance and escrow

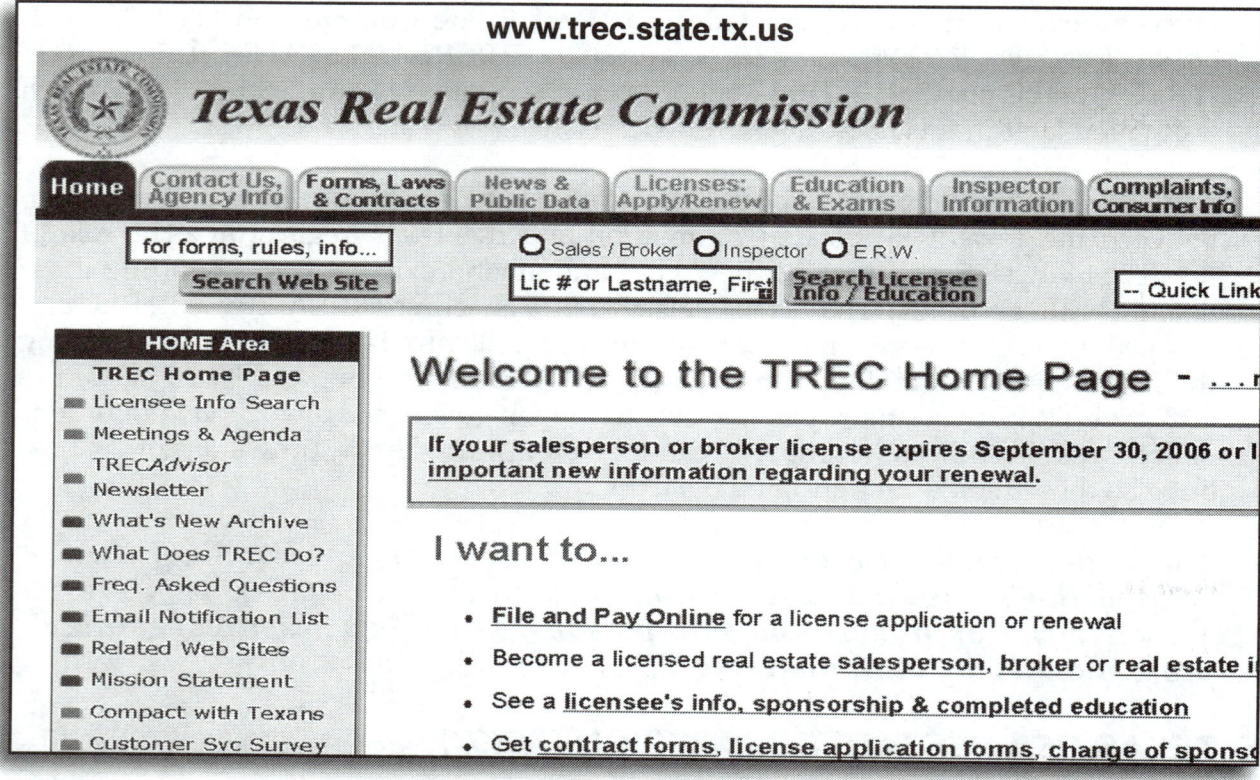

www.trec.state.tx.us

Texas Real Estate Commission

| Home | Contact Us, Agency Info | Forms, Laws & Contracts | News & Public Data | Licenses: Apply/Renew | Education & Exams | Inspector Information | Complaints, Consumer Info |

for forms, rules, info...   ○ Sales / Broker ○ Inspector ○ E.R.W.

Search Web Site   Lic # or Lastname, First   Search Licensee Info / Education   -- Quick Link

HOME Area
TREC Home Page
▪ Licensee Info Search
▪ Meetings & Agenda
TRECAdvisor
▪ Newsletter
▪ What's New Archive
▪ What Does TREC Do?
▪ Freq. Asked Questions
▪ Email Notification List
▪ Related Web Sites
▪ Mission Statement
▪ Compact with Texans
▪ Customer Svc Survey

Welcome to the TREC Home Page - ...

If your salesperson or broker license expires September 30, 2006 or l
important new information regarding your renewal.

I want to...

- **File and Pay Online** for a license application or renewal
- Become a licensed real estate **salesperson**, **broker** or **real estate i**
- See a **licensee's info, sponsorship & completed education**
- Get **contract forms**, **license application forms**, **change of sponso**

TEXAS REAL ESTATE COMMISSION (TREC)

The Texas Real Estate Commission (TREC) is on the Internet. They supply all of the information necessary on obtaining and maintaining a Texas Real Estate Salesperson or Broker license.

TREC is constantly improving its website and adding valuable services to be accessed via the Internet. You can now conduct many licensing transactions online, including:

1. Access testing information
2. Apply for salesperson or broker license
3. Salesperson and broker license renewals
4. File mailing address changes
5. Access documents relating to broker sponsorship

In addition, the *TREC Advisor*, an award-winning publication for licensees, is now available exclusively online.

- Residential and commercial lending
- Urban planning
- Property development
- Real estate appraisal
- Surveying
- Property tax appeals
- Property and casualty insurance
- Corporate real estate acquisition
- Residential property inspection
- Building code inspectors
- Real estate education and research
- Real estate accounting
- Alternative dispute resolution

Having a real estate education opens many occupational doors.

F. BROKERAGE

Brokerage operation is the area most people think about when they think of real estate as a profession.

BROKERAGE *is the business of representing buyers, sellers, landlords, and tenants with the goal of completing real estate transactions and earning a commission.*

In Texas, the entry level license is the **REAL ESTATE SALESPERSON**. The educational and eligibility requirements for a salesperson's license will be explained in later chapters. *With sufficient additional experience and education, a salesperson may take the state* **BROKER LICENSE EXAMINATION**. Until such time as a salesperson becomes a broker, state law requires that all salespersons must be sponsored by a broker.

COMMISSIONS *may be paid as a percent of the sales price, flat fee, or any other amount agreed upon between the broker and seller or buyer.* The broker is free to negotiate the compensation to his or her salespeople and will generally identify a payment structure to a salesperson at the time the salesperson interviews for a position with the brokerage. The broker is responsible for paying his or her sponsored salespersons their part of any commissions, without deductions for federal income taxes or social security.

Commissions paid to brokers are fully negotiable and must be so stated in the agreements between the broker and the client. These agreements are usually prepared by the broker.

Commissions that real estate brokers receive vary in amount. Here is an example to illustrate how to figure a commission: If a home sells for $500,000 and the broker involved in the sale receives a 6% commission, he/she would collect a total of $30,000 ($500,000 x .06), which the broker then splits with the salesperson. Salesperson and

broker commission splits are negotiable and are commensurate with the experience and clientele base a salesperson possesses.

Brokerage requires well-trained individuals who can work within the bounds of the law, are self-motivated and disciplined, with a good work ethic, excellent people skills, and the ability to place the needs of their clients above their own.

Increasingly, sophisticated clients are also looking for tech-savvy real estate professionals who are familiar with computer applications and the Internet.

III. The Nature of Real and Personal Property

Property can be classified into two types: real property (immovable) and personal property (movable), which is sometimes called "chattel."

LAND consists of the surface of the earth, that which is below the surface to the center of the earth, and the airspace above the surface of the earth.

REAL ESTATE consists of land PLUS all items attached to the land by man (improvements).

REAL PROPERTY consists of land and real estate PLUS the "bundle of legal rights."

Ownership of real property, which is also referred to as "realty," is much more than simply possessing land. It also involves possessing certain legal rights which accompany ownership.

A. REAL PROPERTY

"Real property" is the right or legal interest that a person has in the land or anything attached to the land.

REAL PROPERTY is legally defined as:

1. *The actual land itself including the surface, subsurface, and air rights, along with*
2. *anything that is permanently attached or affixed to the land, together with*
3. *anything incidental or appurtenant to the land, including the rights of ownership.*

1. Land

LAND ownership is commonly thought of as owning the surface of the earth; in other words, the ground upon which we walk and build. But ownership also gives us rights to the airspace that is above our land and extends below our land to the center of the earth (see **Figure 1-1**).

An AIRSPACE is the right to the use of the airspace above the surface of the earth. It is real property. In reality, the courts have restricted, to a reasonable height, the right

Figure 1-1

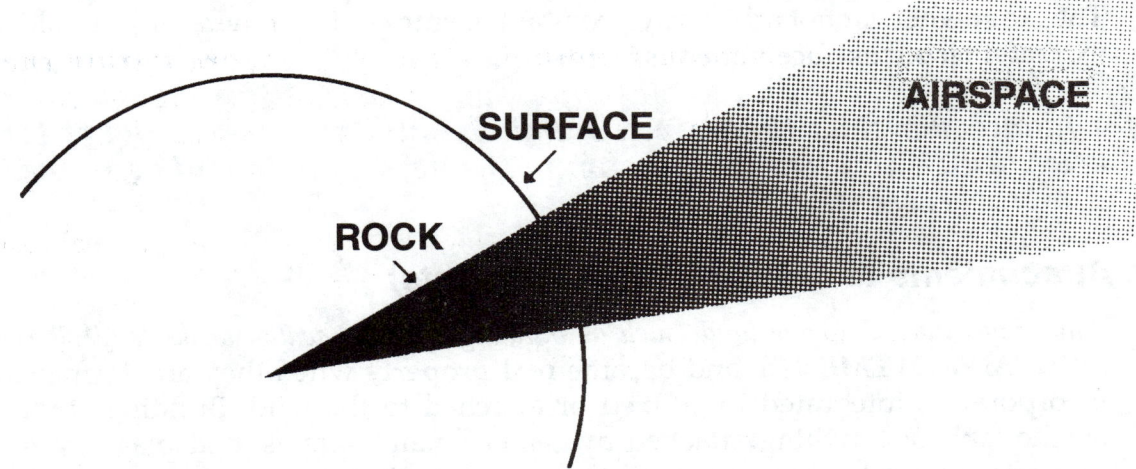

of the property owner to use this space. An example for allowing only **reasonable use** of airspace is the need for airlines to have public "air highways" to provide us with transportation.

This airspace above the ground can be leased or sold in the same manner that mineral rights can be leased or sold. Airspace is an effective way to fully utilize the prime construction sites in many of our larger cities by building "up" instead of "out."

In several major Texas cities, private property owners often negotiate airspace rights with local municipal authorities in order to build skybridges or skywalks over downtown city streets.

Condominiums are another example of airspace use. Inside a *CONDOMINIUM, one only owns the airspace (area within the finished walls). The owner also owns a fractional share of the entire project (COMMON AREA).* Each owner may use the airspace within his or her unit in any manner he or she wishes, unless it violates the bylaws of the homeowners' association.

Generally, all that is beneath the surface of the earth belongs to the owner as real property, unless it has been previously reserved by a prior owner, such as mineral, oil, or gas rights.

MINERAL RIGHTS are solids, liquids, and gases, such as coal, oil, or natural gas, that are a part of the real property, but can be removed. A landowner may sell or lease the oil and gas rights to an oil company, for example, while retaining the surface and air rights. The holder of the oil and gas rights would have reasonable access

to their minerals and the use of the landowner's surface rights, however written arrangements with payment for damage would be a part of the entry agreement. The landowner cannot arbitrarily prohibit the entry of the mineral rights holder to extract their subsurface minerals.

If a landowner sells the property and retains the mineral rights for himself/herself through a provision in the deed, this would be termed a "mineral reservation."

2. Attachments to the Land (Improvements)

Anything attached to the land, such as buildings, fences, walls, walks, and slabs, are called **IMPROVEMENTS**, *and become* **real property** *when they are permanently incorporated, integrated in, affixed or attached to the land. Buildings that rest on the land or anything attached by cement, nails, screws, and plaster are real property, as is a load bearing wall that supports the upper part of a structure. If their removal causes damages, they have been annexed to the land.*

Real property is the land and anything attached to the land (called "improvements"). Natural growth vegetation (vegetation attached by roots) is real property as are industrial crops produced by labor and industry until they are severed, mortgaged, or sold.

a. Incidental or Appurtenant to the Land

Anything that is incidental or appurtenant to the land is real property.

APPURTENANT *means attached to and running with the land.* Certain things that are a part of the land must be sold with the land or else the usefulness of the land is reduced. For example, some small communities own shares of stock in their mutual water companies that supply them with water. When the land is sold, the shares in the water company go with the land. Easements that allow the use of someone else's land, such as a driveway to enter your land, also go with the land being sold if it is the only way to access the land.

Appurtenant means ownership "runs with the land"; it transfers automatically, without the need of a separate conveyance.

b. Immovable by Law

That which by law is considered immovable is real property.

Legally, established crops and trees are a part of the land. This vegetation is termed **FRUITS OF NATURE.** *Cultivated vegetables or fruits are considered emblements, or* **FRUITS OF LABOR** *and thus personal property. Trees are sold with the land,* however, they may be separated from the land and sold to a different buyer. The exception would then be written in a contract of sale for these items before the land is sold.

The removal of an item which causes real property to become personal property is called **SEVERANCE**. *The addition of personal property which causes that personal property to become real property is called* **ATTACHMENT**.

3. The Bundle of Legal Rights

In the historical legal sense, property refers to "all the rights" or interests one has in the "thing" owned, rather than the thing itself. Commonly referred to as a "bundle of rights," some of these rights include possession, enjoyment, control, and disposition (see **Figure 1-2**).

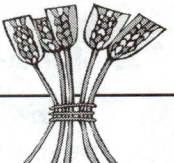

Figure 1-2   **Bundle of Rights Theory**

The bundle of rights theory views property ownership rights as a large "bundle of sticks," where each "stick" is a property right. Individually, these rights represent various, specific forms of ownership; the more of these you hold the more completely you own the property. So if you lease the property to someone, you give up one of your "sticks"—the right of possession—for a period of time. The basic rights of ownership include the following:

1. **Possession** – the right to occupy, rent, or keep others out.
2. **Enjoyment** – the right to legal "peace of mind" without the interference from past owners and others; to use the property in any legal matter.
3. **Exclusion** – the right to exclude whomever the owner pleases.
4. **Control** – the right to control any and all activities occurring on the property.
5. **Disposition** – the right to transfer all or part of your property to others as you see fit.

Within these rights are included further rights: to mortgage, lease or license, cultivate or mine, will, dedicate or give away, share, trade, or exchange.

All of your ownership rights are, of course, subject to governmental limitations and restrictions, and the rights others may hold.

B. FIXTURES

FIXTURES *are items of personal property that are attached to, or incorporated into the land (and improvements) in such a manner so as to become real property.*

As a real estate licensee, it is important to understand this area of law because it is the source of many disputes among parties when buying and selling real property.

Traditionally, the courts use these four tests to determine if an item is a fixture:

1. Annexation
2. Adaptation
3. Intention
4. Agreement

Note: No single element will be determinative. All four elements have to be considered as a whole.

1. Manner of Annexation

If an item can be removed by simply being unplugged, it is probably personal property. On the other hand, if it is attached by cement, plaster, screws, nails or plumbing, it is probably real property. If removal of an item would leave permanent damage or an unusable area, it is surely real property. A rug lying in a living room would be considered personal property; carpet affixed to the floor would be considered real property.

Cost, size and time installed are NOT tests in determining if something is a fixture.

2. Adaptation or Modification of the Item

The second test involves how the item of personal property has been adapted or modified for ordinary use in connection with the land. For example, a microwave oven can be manufactured so that it sits on a tabletop. Thus, it will be considered to be personal property. However, if it is designed so that it is wall mounted, complete with screw holes, then it's probably a fixture.

3. Intention of the Parties

Assume that a home seller has installed some wall mounted surround sound speakers as part of an expensive home theater system. Should a dispute arise concerning whether these speakers are considered fixtures (and thus considered part of the real property being sold), the court might very well consider the possible intention of the seller when he/she installed the speakers. If the court determines that the seller intended the speakers to match the audio and video equipment, it might conclude that the speakers are personal property. But if the court finds that the seller intended them to match the acoustics of this particular room, it might rule that the speakers should remain with the house.

The intention of the person attaching the personal property to the land is an important consideration to a court of law.

4. The Existence of an Agreement Between the Parties

The courts will be heavily influenced by whether there exists any type of agreement between the parties regarding the items.

It is always best to "get it in writing" when dealing with fixtures.

Although the standard TREC contracts contain a section listing many fixtures as being a part of the property to be sold, don't assume that the contract mentions every single one of them. Remember Murphy's Law—anything that can go wrong, will go wrong!

When assisting the clients or customers, as the agent, you should be very specific and clearly identify each item which is to be excluded or remain with the sale. Remember: if in doubt, put it in writing!

The four tests stated above are used to determine facts and the facts are what the courts use to settle disputes.

C. TRADE FIXTURES (Used in Business)

TRADE FIXTURES are personal property used in the normal course of business, such as shelving or refrigeration units. A tenant may remove any trade fixture he or she installed, provided the real property is left in the same condition as he or she found it. A written agreement for removal and repair to original condition may be written by the parties or legal counsel. In this sense, trade fixtures are an exception to the rules of personal property.

Tenants own trade fixtures (built-in business furniture), so that they are removed by tenants when they leave. Any damage caused by these removals must be repaired by the tenant.

Even though tenants normally retain ownership of trade fixtures, it's possible that a landlord may legally claim the fixtures, especially if the tenant has vacated the premises owing rent. In this case, most commercial leases provide for the landlord to claim a lien on the tenant's property in order to secure the unpaid rent. Likewise,

if a tenant does not remove a trade fixture at the end of the lease, the trade fixture is considered to have been abandoned and becomes property of the landlord.

D. WATER RIGHTS

Water rights are an extremely important right related to land ownership. It is important to note that water rights do not always relate to the ownership of water itself but rather to the reasonable **use** of water.

1. Littoral Rights

LITTORAL RIGHTS refer to the water rights held by an owner of land bordering a lake or large body of water. Thus under littoral rights, an owner of land may make reasonable use of the non-flowing body of water which touches their land.

2. Riparian Rights

Under *RIPARIAN RIGHTS, the right of reasonable use is given to the landowner adjoining a river stream or water course.* The extent of the riparian rights enjoyed may depend on whether the river can be classified as navigable or non-navigable. *For non-navigable water, landowners may own to the **MID-POINT OF THE BODY OF WATER,** whereas for navigable water a landowner may own to the **MEAN VEGETATION LINE.***

"Littoral rights" refer to the water rights held by a landowner adjoining a lake or other large body of water. "Riparian rights," on the other hand, refer to the water rights held by an owner adjoining a river or stream.

3. Surface Water Rights in Texas

Although riparian rights are still followed in many other states, today they are practically non-existent in Texas.

Under state law, all surface water flowing in every stream, river, lake, including floodwater, storm water and accumulated rainwater, belongs to the state of Texas. This ownership extends to all water flowing into the state as well.

In most cases, the right to divert state-owned water for private consumption is granted only with the permission of the state. The *TEXAS COMMISSION ON ENVIRONMENTAL QUALITY is the agency charged with issuing and transferring water permits.*

As a result of a historic drought, the Texas Legislature in 1967 was forced to re-evaluate the rights of all water users in the state. Under the **Water Rights Adjudication Act**, all water rights holders were required to have their water rights determined by the courts by means of "Certificates of Adjudication." Furthermore, anyone seeking water rights after 1969 would be required to obtain a permit from the state.

Buyers seeking to purchase farm and ranch property should inquire whether a water permit is necessary. If so, an attorney can help with acquiring or transferring the permit.

4. Underground Water Rights in Texas

Unlike surface water which is owned by the state of Texas, underground water follows a different rule.

Much of the state's underground water is contained in nine large aquifers that supply 97% of the ground water used in Texas. An *AQUIFER is an underground formation of permeable rock material that holds large quantities of water.* Sometimes underground water will percolate to the surface. *PERCOLATING WATER generally refers to underground water that seeps up through the soil, resulting in a spring.* Much underground water is also potable. *POTABLE WATER refers to water that is suitable for human consumption.* In fact, the City of San Antonio relies on artesian wells fed by several aquifers as its primary source of public drinking water.

Since 1904, Texas courts have recognized that, under "the rule of capture," landowners may, with certain exceptions, "capture" as much underground water as they are able to pump without liability to any neighbor whose wells may be depleted in the process.

Presently, Texas remains one of the last, if not the last, western state to follow this rule of law. But the rule has come under fire in recent years for promoting uncontrolled pumping at a time when the state's underground water resources are stretched thin. To counter this effect, the legislature has created a number of water conservation districts which impose pumping limits over underground water.

5. Texas Open Beach Law

Under Texas law, all beaches are open to the public as a public easement. Legally, the beach begins at the low tide line of the shoreline facing the Gulf of Mexico and continues to the clearly identified vegetation line.

Under state law, there can be no obstruction of any kind or placement of structures on the public beach easement. Unfortunately, natural forces, such as hurricanes, can serve to shift beach areas. If the vegetation line changes through erosion, avulsion, or accretion, a neighboring owner's property line will change accordingly.

Texas homeowners who now find themselves living on a newly formed beach because of hurricane forces can be sued by the state of Texas and forced to move their homes or face having them torn down.

E. CLASSES OF REAL PROPERTY

Real property may be classed by the uses it or its improvements provide. **The highest value of the property is directly influenced by the highest utility of the improvements**. The zoning of a property is not always the indicator of its classification. The five classes are identified as follows:

1. Residential Property

RESIDENTIAL PROPERTY is any property used as housing. This would include single detached homes, townhomes, condominiums, cooperatives, manufactured housing, apartments, and modular homes.

2. Commercial Property

COMMERCIAL PROPERTY is defined as office or retail space. The types of property improvements would include high-rise office structures, detached office buildings, office parks and complexes as well as condominium office developments. Retail property would include shopping centers, malls, outlet centers, restaurants, fast food chains and food courts.

3. Industrial Property

INDUSTRIAL PROPERTY includes properties where manufacturing and distribution are the primary operation. Warehousing, self-storage, document storage, wholesale meat operations, chemical facilities, and utility generation are examples of the industrial sector.

4. Agricultural Property

AGRICULTURAL PROPERTY includes raw land held for future development, as well as many different types of farms or ranches. Crop farming, plus specific farming such as game, fish, and specialty food, including crawfish, alligator, and emu, would be examples of agricultural categories.

5. Specific Purpose Property

The improvements dictate the use of *SPECIFIC PURPOSE PROPERTY, which would include structures such as bowling alleys, places of worship, schools, cinemas, water or theme parks, and one-use structures in general.*

F. PERSONAL PROPERTY

PERSONAL PROPERTY is any property that is "movable" and cannot be properly classified under the definition of real property. Items such as clothes, furniture, and automobiles are tangible and easily movable.

Personal property can also be documents that represent value, such as stocks, bonds, leases, or promissory notes. Personal property can be sold, can be used as security for a debt, or can be changed into real property by becoming "affixed" to the land. Another term for personal property is **personalty**.

Personal property is "movable," like a refrigerator, washer, or dryer. The seller takes his/her personal property, unless negotiated otherwise. Any personal property meant to be included in the sale should be written in the contract.

*When buying personal property, your receipt is called a **BILL OF SALE**. The Bill of Sale states that the goods have been paid for and that no outstanding loans exist on the personal property.* It is always considered good practice to obtain a Bill of Sale.

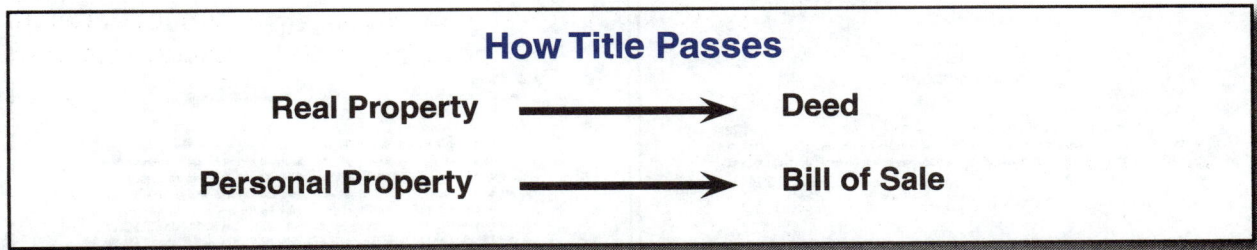

Figure **1-3** shows examples of a typical deed and bill of sale.

IV. Legal Descriptions of Real Estate

In order to sell or convey real property in Texas, it is always necessary to describe the property in such a way so that it cannot be possibly confused with another tract.

A. COMMON STREET ADDRESS IS LEGALLY INSUFFICIENT

Legally, a common address will be insufficient to describe real property. A *COMMON ADDRESS is the address that is used for mail delivery, or the address posted on the property.* For example, let us assume that you live at "732 Elm Street, Houston, Texas." There may be several "Elm Streets" in Houston. Does the street run north and south or east and west? What are the boundaries of the property? What if the mailing address is

Figure 1-3

GF No. 123456

CASH WARRANTY DEED

The State of Texas   )
County of Longhorn   )   **KNOW ALL MEN BY THESE PRESENTS:**

    That Greatbig Homes, L.P., a Texas limited partnership (hereinafter called "Grantor," whether one or more, masculine, feminine or neuter) for and in consideration of the sum of Ten Dollars ($10.00) and other good and valuable consideration, the receipt and sufficiency of which are hereby acknowledged, in hand paid by Henry Homebuyer (hereinafter called "Grantee," whether one or more, masculine, feminine or neuter,) for which no lien is retained either express or implied, has **Granted, Sold and Conveyed,** and by these presents does **Grant, Sell and Convey,** unto the said Grantee all that certain real property located in Longhorn County, Texas, and described as follows:

        Lot 8, Block 10 of Happy Trails Estates, an addition to the City of Cowboy, Longhorn County, Texas, according to the map thereof recorded in Volume 422, Page 1604, Map Records, Longhorn County, Texas,

together with all the improvements thereon, if any, and all right, title and interest in and to adjacent sidewalks, streets, roads, alleys and rights of way.

    This Deed is executed and delivered subject to all easements, reservations, conditions, covenants and restrictive covenants as the same appear of record in the Office of the County Clerk of the county and state aforesaid.

    TO HAVE AND TO HOLD the above-described premises, together with all and singular the rights and appurtenances thereto in anywise belonging unto the said Grantee, his, her, or its successors, heirs, and assigns, as the case may be, forever; and Grantor does hereby bind Grantor and Grantor's successors, heirs, executors and administrators, as the case may be, to **WARRANT AND FOREVER DEFEND** all and singular the said premises unto the said Grantee and Grantee's successors, heirs and assigns, as the case may be, against every person whomsoever lawfully claiming, or to claim the same, or any part thereof.

    Executed this _____ day of _____, _____.

                    Greatbig Homes, L.P.,
                    a Texas limited partnership
                    By: Greatbig Homes, Inc. a Texas
                    corporation, its General Partner

                    _____

ACKNOWLEDGMENT

STATE OF TEXAS   )
COUNTY OF LONGHORN   )

    This instrument was acknowledged before me on the _____ day of _____, 2006, by James Greatbig, President and authorized officer of Greatbig Homes, Inc., a Texas corporation, general partner of Greatbig Homes, L.P., a Texas limited partnership, on behalf of said partnership.

                    _____
                          Notary Public

BILL OF SALE

State of Texas   )
County of Longhorn   )   KNOW ALL MEN BY THESE PRESENTS:

    That the undersigned, Sam Seller, (hereinafter known as Seller) being the owner, and possessor of the items of personal property described herein, for and in consideration of the sum of SIX HUNDRED DOLLARS AND NO/100, ($600.00), of which the entire sum has actually been paid this date, and other good and valuable consideration, in hand paid to the undersigned by Ben Buyer (hereinafter known as Buyer), the receipt and sufficiency of which is hereby acknowledged by the Seller, has BARGAINED, SOLD, and DELIVERED, and by these presents does hereby BARGAIN, SELL, and DELIVER unto the said Buyer the items of personal property described as follows:

    Maytag Washing Machine (Serial Number 1234567)
    Maytag Electric Dryer (Serial Number 765432)
    Whirlpool Side by Side Refrigerator (Model HB-4, Serial Number 8473463)

    This property is sold AS-IS and WITHOUT WARRANTY OF ANY KIND.

    Seller represents to Buyer that he is the owner of the above-described personal property, that he has the sole right to sell and deliver the same to the Buyer, and that such personal property is unencumbered by any debt or lien. Seller does hereby bind Seller, Seller's heirs, executors, administrators and assigns to forever warrant and defend the title to the said personal property against every person whomsoever lawfully claiming, or to claim the same, or any part thereof.

    Executed this _____ day of _____, _____

              _____
              Sam Seller

"P.O. Box 1234"? Does that tell where the property is located? As is clearly evident, a common address does not give all the information needed to properly describe or locate a property.

A legal description, on the other hand, is much more precise than a common address and will be acceptable to the courts. With a *LEGAL DESCRIPTION, a tract of land can be uniquely described so that it can definitely be located and even physically staked out if necessary.* The ability to locate the specific property described is evidence of the adequacy of the legal description.

In Texas, every parcel of land must be legally described. If the property is to be sold, financed or leased, a recognized legal description is required. A street address and apartment number may be used in a residential lease, however.

B. ROLE OF THE SURVEYOR

Historically, surveyors have been instrumental in literally mapping out the new territory of our infant nation. From the earliest of colonial times, surveyors have applied their skill and knowledge to laying out land, taking measurements, and building maps so that tracts of land can be easily located by written means. Using instruments considered crude by today's standards, early surveyors laid out our cities and mapped out our westward expansion.

Three Elements of a Full Survey

1. **Survey** – provides the legal description of the property.
2. **Survey Sketch** – provides the legal description and shows the location and dimensions of the property.
3. **Improvement Survey** – is a survey sketch which shows the location, size, and dimensions of buildings on the parcel.

In Texas, surveyors are regulated by the *TEXAS BOARD OF PROFESSIONAL LAND SURVEYING.* Generally, the board registers professional land surveyors who conduct land boundary and property surveys for the general public. It also licenses state land surveyors who conduct surveys on state or public lands and the board certifies surveyors-in-training. In Texas, professional surveying requires special knowledge of math and science along with a keen understanding of the laws relating to the measurement or location of points, lines, angles, elevations, natural and man-made features located on the earth's surface, below the surface, or even underwater, so as to enable the surveyor to establish boundary lines of individual tracts of land or even entire subdivisions. There is little wonder that the science of establishing boundary lines begins with the surveyor.

Professional surveyors in Texas are required to be licensed and/or registered.

C. METHODS OF DESCRIBING REAL PROPERTY

The three methods of legally describing real property are:

1. Metes and bounds
2. Platted subdivision, lot and block
3. U.S. Government Survey

Although all three methods are commonly used throughout the United States as a means of describing real estate, only the first two are used in Texas. As will be seen later in this chapter, the U.S. Government Survey method is not used in Texas. But despite this, all three methods of legally describing real estate share a common denominator: all three methods are initially established with the help of a surveyor.

1. Metes and Bounds

METES AND BOUNDS (measuring boundaries) is among the oldest of description methods and involves identifying (describing) property by its boundaries, distances, and angles from a given starting point, or **POINT OF BEGINNING (POB)**, *until it returns to the POB. Hence, it is a description of the perimeter of a parcel.*

a. Surveyor's Compass

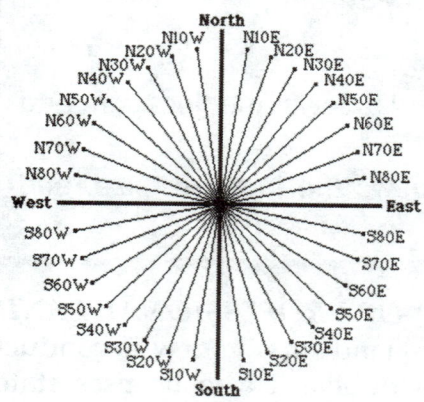

This method of describing property involves a series of distances and directions using a special surveyor's compass.

The surveyor establishes the legal description by beginning at a known point, then tracing the perimeter of the subject property, recording a series of distances and directions until closing the figure by returning to the starting point.

b. Reference Points

In the past, surveyors often used natural objects as a starting point in their descriptions. A *MONUMENT is a fixed object and point set in the earth by surveyors to establish land locations and indicate where the surveyor would take directional changes.* Monuments in older surveys could have been trees, boulders, and intersections of roadways. For example, an old surveyor's report might have read:

"Starting at the old oak tree at the stream, go 300 feet north along the river bed, then make a 90 degree turn and proceed 100 feet to the old hickory stump, then go 300 feet south to the ash tree, then go west 100 feet to the point of the beginning."

The weakness of this type of description is that when natural objects are used as starting points, there is a chance that time, or man may move or destroy these objects. Along a stream or river, the amount of land owned may change by accretion (gradual addition) or erosion (gradual wearing away). However, when the natural objects are replaced with more permanent monuments, the strength of this boundary measuring system can be easily seen.

BENCHMARKS are permanent monuments from which modern surveys are usually based.

Often, but not always, benchmarks are embedded in sidewalks or in streets. Many benchmarks also contain additional *altitude and elevation information (DATUM)* from which heights and water depths can be measured or calculated.

c. Everyday Issues

Consider, for example, this modern day hypothetical example of a metes and bounds legal description using precise direction measurements and updated monuments:

BEGINNING at a found iron rod for the Southeast corner of said Block 114;

THENCE in a Northerly direction along the East line of said Block 114 a distance of 780.30 feet to a found iron rod marking the South line of Main Street; and being a point for corner;

THENCE in a Westerly direction along the South line of Main Street; a distance of 270.60 feet to a point for corner;

THENCE in a Southerly direction along a line parallel to the East line of said Block 114, a distance of 780.30 feet to a point for corner, said point being on the South line of said Block 114;

THENCE in an Easterly direction along said line a distance of 270.60 feet to the Point of BEGINNING and containing 4.85 acres, more or less.

This is how this description might be drawn:

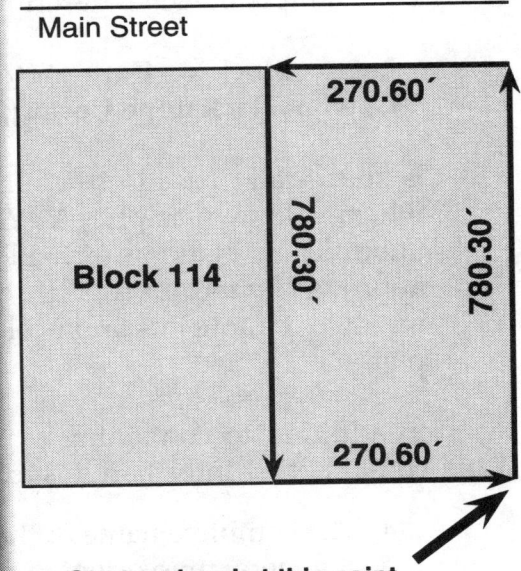

This description serves as an excellent reminder that when buying or selling real estate described with a metes and bounds description, real estate professionals should exercise caution for two important reasons. First, in attempting to set or offer an exact price for land, a broker/salesperson should be wary in making assumptions about the quantity of land with the metes and bounds description method because of the "more or less" possibilities.

Although a seller's existing deed may reference a number of acres more or less, there is no guarantee of the size of the tract without a formal survey certified by a surveyor.

Secondly, many modern metes and bounds descriptions are exceedingly long and complicated. Legal accuracy will often require detailed descriptions requiring several pages, depending on the size and shape of the parcel.

Brokers and salespersons should avoid manually retyping long legal descriptions.

A typographical error here by a well intentioned salesperson could result in an erroneous legal description further resulting in litigation. This is a risk best avoided by merely "cutting and pasting" an existing metes and bounds description into a sales contract.

2. Platted Subdivision, Lot and Block

In Texas, legal descriptions are also established by reference to a subdivision plat. For example the legal description of:

Lot 5, Block 6, Happy Homeowner's Estates Subdivision, City of Cowboy, Jackalope County, Texas

is specifically based on a survey map of the Happy Homeowner's subdivision which is known as plat. A *PLAT is essentially a survey map of an entire subdivision.* Subdivision plats are considered legal documents and must first be generally approved by the appropriate city or county government whenever land is divided into two or more lots or parcels. **Figure 1-4** shows a portion of a typical subdivision plat.

In addition to containing a survey map of the subdivision, plats must usually contain other information such as:

1. The complete name of the subdivision;
2. A general map orientation showing north and the map scale;
3. A metes and bounds description of the subdivision boundaries;

Figure 1-4

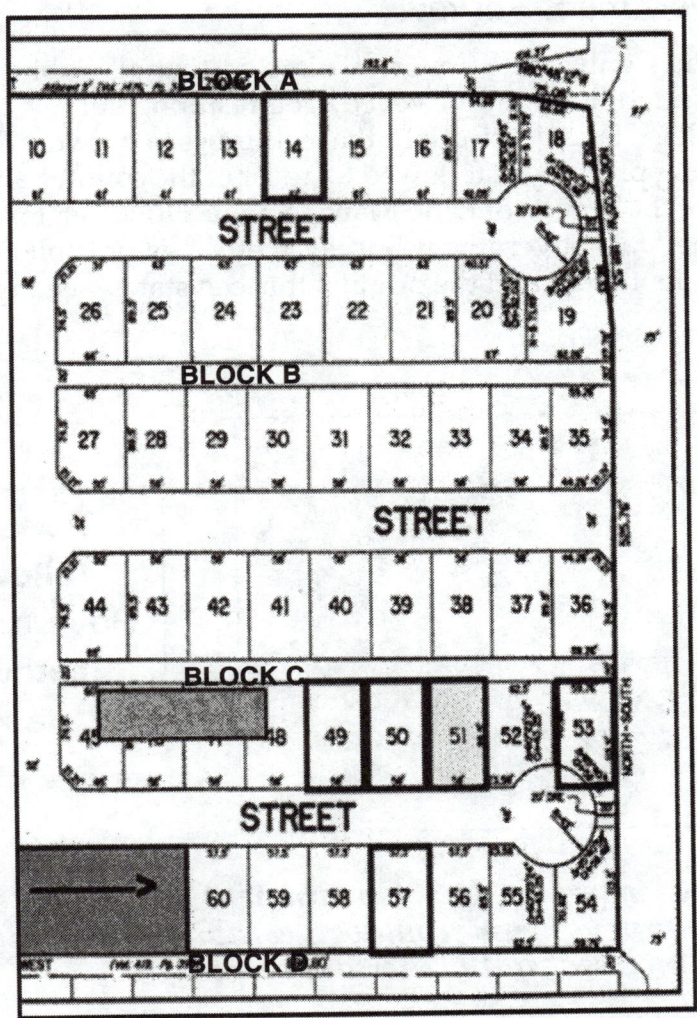

4. Identification of all streets, driveways, alleys, lots and blocks, and easements;
5. A public dedication statement of the subdivision's streets, easements and parks for the general public use;
6. An approval statement by the local municipality;
7. A surveyor's certificate; and
8. A notary statement which will be necessary for public filing.

The approved subdivision map is recorded at the County Clerk's office of the county where the property is located, and is given a book and page number.

Once a plat is recorded, all future transactions can be referenced to that map. In Texas, most residential property is based on a recorded subdivision plat.

3. U.S. Government Survey

In 1785, the Continental Congress directed that all public lands within the then existing United States be surveyed. The resulting survey created a checkerboard pattern of legal land descriptions that continues to this very day. Today, this method of describing property is followed by most of the country and continues under the direction of the Bureau of Land Management. However, for historical and political reasons the U.S. Government Survey method is not followed in Texas, Hawaii, Kentucky, Tennessee and the original thirteen states (see **Figure 1-5**).

Figure 1-5

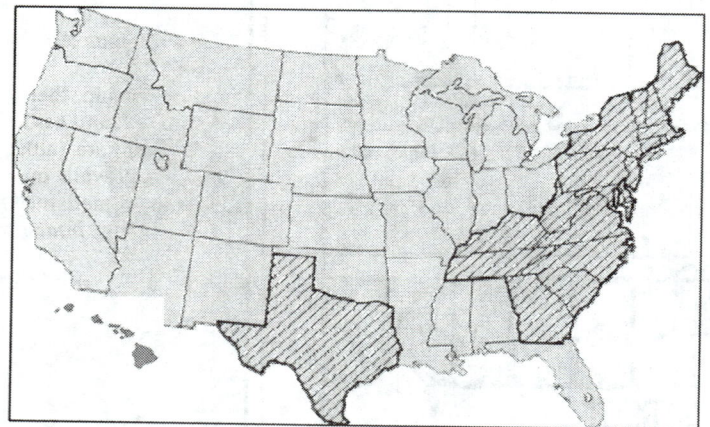

Texas does not follow the U.S. Government Survey method of legal description.

In those states where the U.S. Government Survey method is followed, all property surveys begin from well established starting points where "base lines" intersect with "meridian lines."

a. Base Lines and Meridians

A **BASE LINE** *is a horizontal line that runs east and west from a designated starting point.* Each base line is marked in six-mile increments. *Every six-mile increment is called a RANGE and each range is six miles in width.* It is possible to move east or west a designated number of ranges from any starting point.

MERIDIAN LINES *are vertical lines that run north and south from a designated starting point. Meridians are also marked off in increments of six miles each, but each increment north or south on a meridian is called a TOWNSHIP or TIER.*

b. Tiers, Ranges, and Townships

Each rectangular survey grid consists of a series of lines that run parallel to the principal meridian and the base line, at intervals of six miles (see **Figure 1-6**). *The east-west lines (running parallel to the base line) are called TIER LINES.*

Figure 1-6

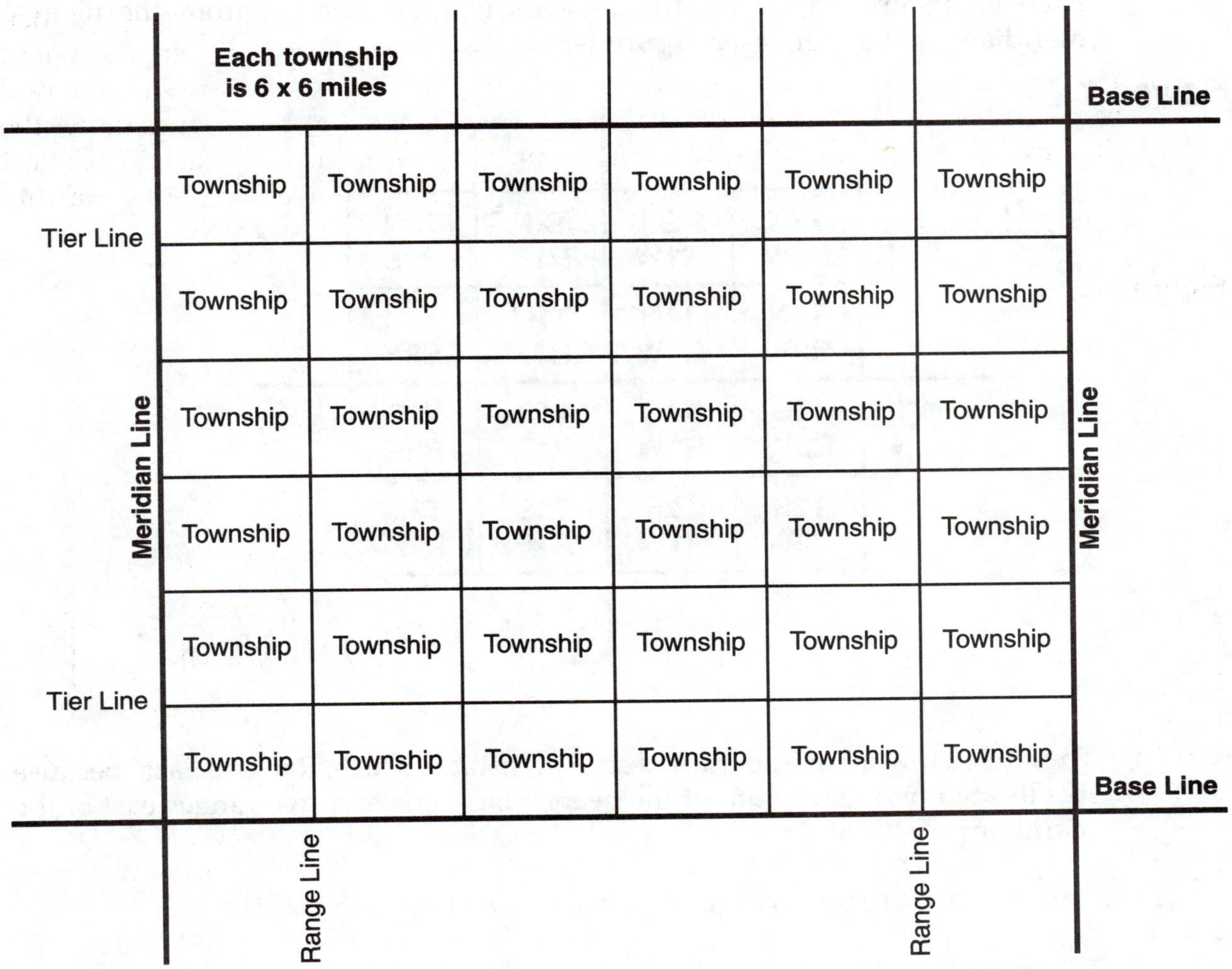

	Each township is 6 x 6 miles						Base Line
Tier Line	Township	Township	Township	Township	Township	Township	
	Township	Township	Township	Township	Township	Township	
Meridian Line	Township	Township	Township	Township	Township	Township	Meridian Line
	Township	Township	Township	Township	Township	Township	
Tier Line	Township	Township	Township	Township	Township	Township	
	Township	Township	Township	Township	Township	Township	Base Line

Range Line   *Range Line*

The north-south lines (parallel to the principal meridian) are referred to as **RANGE LINES.**

"Township lines" divide the land into a series of east-west strips, called tiers. "Range lines" divide the land into north-south strips called ranges.

Where a tier intersects with a range, the result is a six miles by six miles square of land known as a **TOWNSHIP.**

Don't confuse these townships with municipal towns. Townships are main divisions under the U.S. Government Survey System and they each contain 36 square miles.

c. Locating Townships

Each township can be identified by its relative position from the nearest meridian and base line (see **Figure 1-7**).

Figure 1-7

T2N R2W	T2N R1W	T2N R1E	T2N R2E
T1N R2W	T1N R1W	T1N R1E	T1N R2E
T1S R2W	T1S R1W	T1S R1E	T1S R2E
T2S R2W	T2S R1W	T2S R1E	T2S R2E

The circled township is identified as "Township 2 South, Range 2 East" because it is located two tiers south of the nearest base line and two ranges east of the meridian.

To locate a township, work backwards on the description.

When reading a description, read it from right to left. A verbal interpretation of the above description would read: "Starting from the Base Line and Meridian, go two ranges east and two townships south." You have located the township in which the property is located.

d. Sections

Each township is divided into 36 sections. A section is one mile square of land, which is 640 acres. There are 36 sections in a township (see **Figure 1-8**).

These sections are numbered in sequential order starting at the upper right-hand corner, as illustrated in Figure 1-8. Since each township is 6 miles square and consists of 36 sections, each section measures one mile square. *Furthermore, since Section 16 was originally set aside under the law for school purposes, it is commonly known as the SCHOOL SECTION.*

Figure 1-8

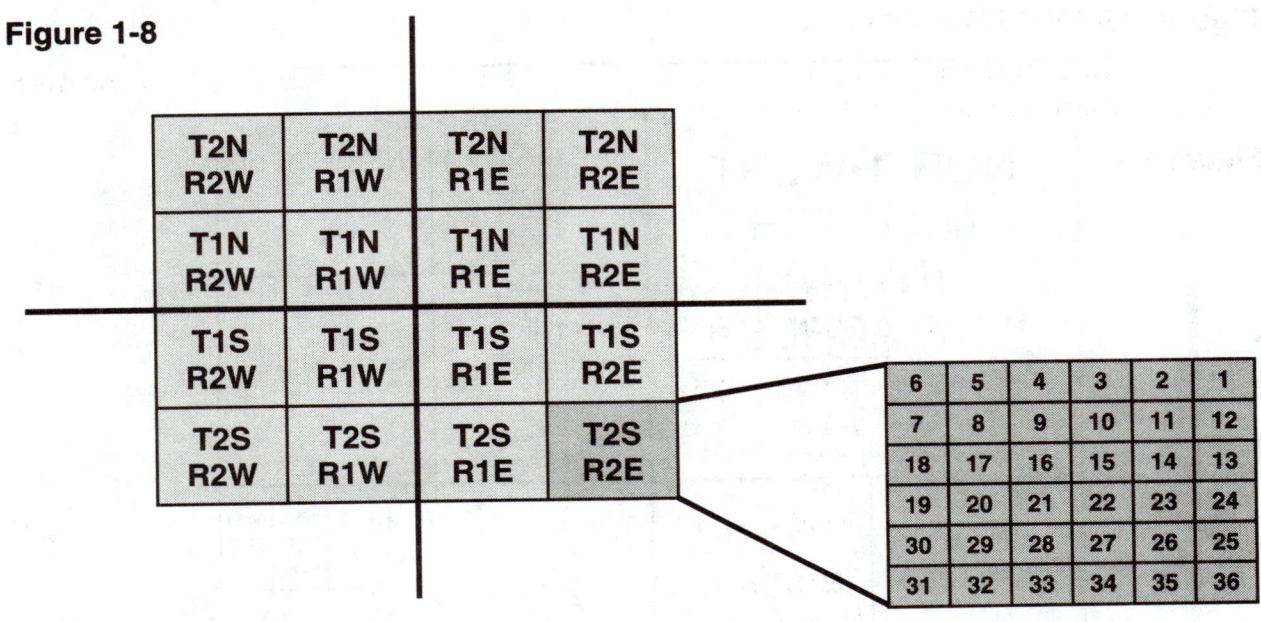

**Each township
contains 36 numbered sections**

Continuing with our previous example, if we wanted to locate section 29 as shown in Figure 1-8, the complete description would read:

Section 29, Township 2 South, Range 2 East

e. Working Within Sections

As stated above, each section measures one mile square and consists of 640 acres. A section can be broken down into halves or quarters. **Figure 1-9** shows a number of ways that a typical section can be further divided.

> 1 Section = 640 acres
> ½ Section = 320 acres
> ¼ Section = 160 acres, etc.

For example, the complete description thus far for the **northwest** quarter of section 29 would read:

NW ¼ of Section 29, Township 2 South, Range 2 East

Quarter sections can be broken down further into halves or quarters.

For example, the description of the northeast quarter of the northeast quarter of section 29 would read:

NE ¼ of the NE ¼ of Section 29, Township 2 South, Range 2 East

Figure 1-9

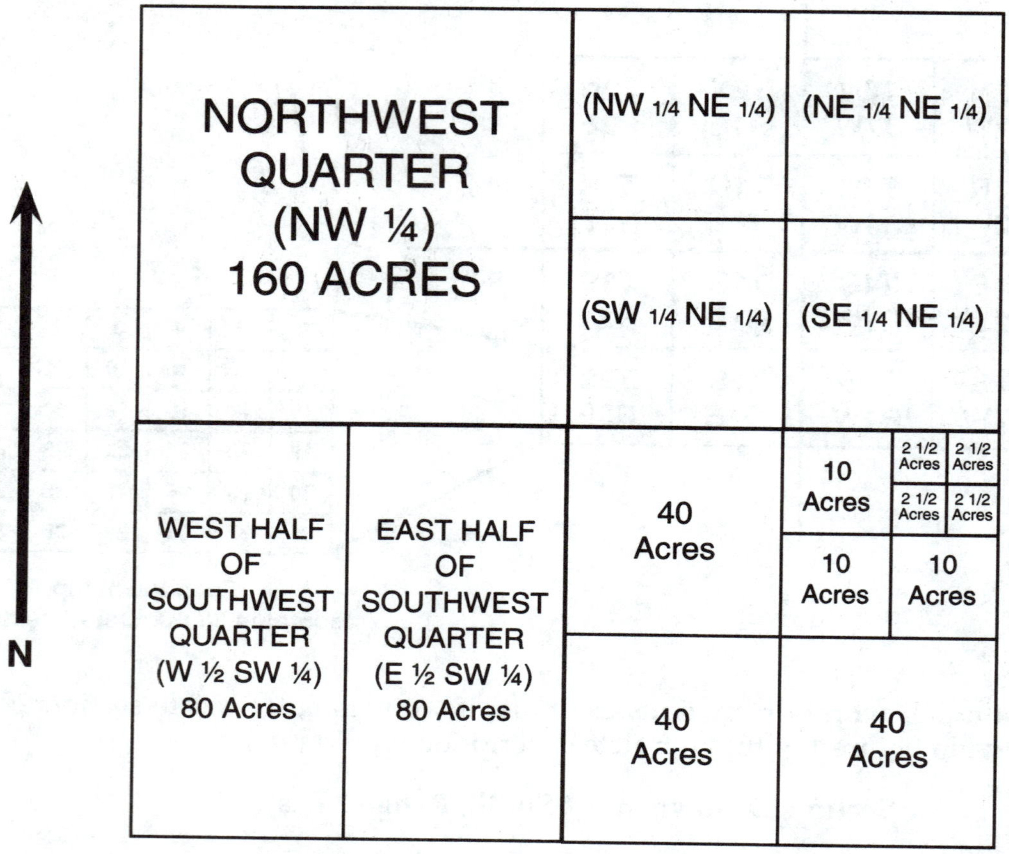

NORTHWEST QUARTER (NW ¼) 160 ACRES		(NW ¼ NE ¼)	(NE ¼ NE ¼)
		(SW ¼ NE ¼)	(SE ¼ NE ¼)
WEST HALF OF SOUTHWEST QUARTER (W ½ SW ¼) 80 Acres	EAST HALF OF SOUTHWEST QUARTER (E ½ SW ¼) 80 Acres	40 Acres	10 Acres / 2 1/2 Acres 2 1/2 Acres / 2 1/2 Acres 2 1/2 Acres ; 10 Acres / 10 Acres
		40 Acres	40 Acres

N

This procedure can continue until the property is completely described.

f. Calculating Acreage

Suppose you are given the following legal description:

The NE ¼ of the NE ¼ of the NE ¼ of the NE ¼ of Section 29

It is easy to calculate how many acres are within this tract by doing some simple multiplication and remembering that each section contains 640 acres.

First, remember that the word "of" when used in word problems means to multiply. Thus, this description can be "mathematically" translated into the following equation:

¼ times ¼ times ¼ times ¼

Fractions are multiplied across, thus, $\dfrac{1 \text{ times } 1 \text{ times } 1 \text{ times } 1}{4 \text{ times } 4 \text{ times } 4 \text{ times } 4} = \dfrac{1}{256}$

As a result, the legal description is for a tract of land which contains 1/256 of 640 acres. By dividing 640 acres by 256, we get the answer of 2.5, which means that our legal description *(NE ¼ of the NE ¼ of the NE ¼ of the NE ¼ of Section 29)* contains 2.5 acres of land. Further calculations can then be made based on this result, if necessary.

For example, a question might ask how many square feet are contained within this 2.5 acre tract. Or another question might ask what is the price per square foot if the entire tract sells for a given sales price.

See **Figure 1-10** for a handy reference table and **Figure 1-11** for related math problems.

Figure 1-10

REFERENCE TABLE

One **ACRE** is 43,560 square feet.

One **SQUARE ACRE** is 208.71 feet on each side, but this number is generally rounded off to 209 feet.

One **MILE** is 5,280 feet long.

One **SQUARE MILE** contains 640 acres.

One **SECTION** is one square mile.

One **TOWNSHIP** (standard) is six miles square (36 square miles).

One **COMMERCIAL ACRE** is an acre minus any required public dedications.

One **ROD** is 16.5 feet long (5.5 yards).

Figure 1-11

How Do You Find The Dimensions Of An Acre?

An **ACRE** *is an area of land that contains 43,560 square feet.* So, if the area of a lot has more than 43,560 square feet, there is more than an acre of land. On the other hand, if there is less than 43,560 square feet in a lot, it is smaller than an acre.

AREA *is a definite amount of space within a shape.* In America, area is usually measured in square feet, but may also be measured in square yards or square meters in other parts of the world. Most test questions about area refer to a rectangular or square shape. The area of a rectangular or square shape is obtained by multiplying length x (times) width. The answer is in square feet. The area of a square lot 100 feet x 100 feet is 10,000 square feet.

Example (1): How many acres is a parcel of land that measures 330 feet by 660 feet?

Answer:

Area   =   Length x Width
217,800   =   330 feet x 660 feet

Note: 1 acre = 43,560 square feet

$\dfrac{217,800}{43,560}$ =   **5 ACRES** (Round if necessary)

Example (2): If an acre is divided into four equal lots, with each lot placed parallel to the other and having a depth of 240 feet, what is the width of each lot?

Answer:

Area   =   Length x Width
43,560   =   240 feet (x 4 lots)   x ? feet
43,560   =   960 feet   x ? feet

$\dfrac{43,560}{960}$ =   **45.375 feet wide (Round to 45.4 feet wide)**

See Chapter 17 for more math problems.

V. CHAPTER SUMMARY

Texas is the second largest state in terms of population and the second in terms of size. It joined the union in 1845 but was able to retain control of its public lands. Today, Texas is 97 percent privately owned. Legally, Texas follows the English-based common law system of justice as is followed in the majority of the other states, but it retains elements of Spanish, Mexican, and French law, particularly in the area of marital property rights.

Based upon the national average, housing is considered to be affordable in Texas and as a result, presents many opportunities for real estate professionals. In Texas, real estate professionals are governed by the **Texas Real Estate Commission (TREC)**. The Commission did not enact the state licensing laws. The Texas Legislature enacted the licensing laws beginning in 1939 and in the process created TREC. Today, a real estate education is an essential element towards obtaining a salesperson or broker license and can open the door to other real estate related careers. In Texas, brokers and salespersons are compensated by means of a commission, which is fully negotiable.

Real property is generally immovable, passed by deed, and includes the right or interests in the 1) land; 2) anything permanently attached or affixed to the land; 3) anything incidental or appurtenant to the land; and 4) that which is immovable by law. Anything attached to the land (like fences, walls, etc.) becomes real property when they are permanently incorporated or integrated in, affixed, or attached to the land (called **improvements**). Land ownership is not only the surface of the earth but the **airspace** above it and that which is below, like mineral rights. Real property can be thought of as consisting of a **bundle of rights**, which includes the rights of possession, enjoyment, exclusion, control, and disposition.

A **fixture** is an item of personal property that is attached to or incorporated into the land in such a way as to become real property. The tests for fixture are: method of attachment, adaptation, intention, and agreement. **Trade fixtures** are personal property used in the normal course of business, such as shelving or refrigeration units, which can be removed by commercial tenants, who are responsible for any damage caused by their removal.

Ownership of real estate also carries certain water rights. **Littoral rights** are the rights of persons who own land adjacent to a large body of water such as a lake. **Riparian rights** pertain to the rights of someone living next to a river or stream. If the water way is classified as navigable, the property line may extend only to the mean vegetation line of the water way, otherwise, the owner's property may extend to the midpoint of the stream. **In Texas, the state owns all surface water**. For underground water, the landowner may own all the water he is able to "capture" by means of pumping.

However, state created underground water conservation districts are increasingly limiting the amount of water that private landowners are able to pump. Finally, under Texas law, all beaches are open to the public. The beach area is considered as covering the area of land facing the Gulf of Mexico and extending from the low tide line to the line of vegetation. If a hurricane moves the shoreline so that an owner finds himself/ herself now on the public beach, the state of Texas may force the owner to move the house or face having it torn down.

The classes of real property are **residential, commercial, industrial, agricultural,** and **specific purpose**.

Personal property is movable, like a refrigerator or a washing machine, but can include **emblements** (annually harvested crops) and some substances beneath the land, like **oil and minerals** when they have been removed from the land. Anything that is **appurtenant** to the land means it runs with the land and must be sold with the land. An example is an easement appurtenant. While **title** to real property is commonly passed with a **deed**, title to personal property is passed with a **bill of sale**.

Every parcel of land must be properly described and identified. The three methods of identification include the Metes and Bounds method, the Platted Subdivision, Lot and Block method, and the U.S. Government Survey method. The U.S. Government Survey method is not used in Texas. **Metes and Bounds** is the method of identifying a property in relationship to its boundaries, distances, and angles from a **Point of Beginning. Lots, Blocks, and Tracts** make up subdivisions, which are recorded on a **Subdivision Map** in the County Clerk's Office. **Sections** and **Townships** are used in the **Government Survey System** (rectangular survey system) to identify public and private lands. This system uses **base lines** (running east and west) and **meridian lines** (running north and south), as well as defining townships (36-square-mile sections of land, where each section is 640 acres).

Introduction to Real Estate

VI. TERMINOLOGY

A. Acre
B. Airspace
C. Base Lines
D. Bill of Sale
E. Bundle of Rights
F. Commission
G. Condominium
H. Emblements

I. Fixtures
J. Meridian Lines
K. Metes and Bounds
L. Personal Property
M. Plat
N. Potable Water
O. Range
P. Real Property

Q. Mineral Reservation
R. Riparian Rights
S. Section
T. Texas Real Estate Commission
U. Township
V. Trade Fixtures

1.____ A column of land six miles wide, determined by a government survey, running in a north-south direction, lying east or west of a principal meridian.
2.____ Personal property that has become permanently attached to the land or improvements that are legally treated as real property; examples: plumbing fixtures, or built in range, etc..
3.____ Personal property used in a business, attached to the property, but removable by the tenant.
4.____ A structure of two or more units where the interior airspace of each unit is individually owned; the balance of land and improvements is owned in common by all the owners.
5.____ Imaginary north-south lines used in U.S. government surveys.
6.____ Property that is movable and not real property.
7.____ A written instrument that passes title of personal property from vendor (seller) to the vendee (buyer).
8.____ An amount, usually a percentage, paid to a broker as compensation for his or her services.
9.____ A legal description of land, setting forth all the boundary lines with their terminal points and angles.
10.____ All of the legal rights relevant to ownership of property including rights of use, possession, encumbering and disposition.
11.____ In the survey of public lands, a territorial subdivision six miles long, six miles wide and containing 36 sections, each one square mile.
12.____ Land, improvements, items permanently attached to the land, appurtenances and that which is immovable by law.
13.____ The state agency that licenses salespersons and brokers.
14.____ An area of land equaling 43,560 square feet, or a tract about 208.71 feet square.
15.____ The right of a landowner, whose land borders a stream or waterway, to use and enjoy the water, provided such use does not injure the rights of other owners.
16.____ A square of land (U.S. Government Survey) that contains 640 acres and is one square mile.
17.____ The means by which a seller may retain the mineral rights, while selling the surface estate..
18.____ The reasonable space above a parcel or in a condominium; the cubic area of a space within the walls of a condominium.
19.____ Imaginary east-west lines that intersect meridian lines to form a starting point for the measurement of land.
20.____ Water that is suitable for human consumption.
21.____ Crops (produced on leased land by a tenant farmer) from an annual cultivation considered personal property.
22.____ A survey map of an entire subdivision.

Answers to the matching terminology are found on page 713.

VII. MULTIPLE CHOICE

1. How many square miles are there in a section?
    a. 6
    b. 9
    c. 4
    d. 1

2. Which of the following are considered improvements?
    a. Buildings
    b. Fences
    c. A concrete drainage ditch
    d. All of the above

3. What is the term used when mineral rights are retained by the seller in the deed?
    a. Mineral allotment
    b. Mineral reservation
    c. Equitable retainage
    d. Personalty exclusion

4. The number of acres in a section of land is:
    a. 240.
    b. 360.
    c. 120.
    d. 640.

5. The bundle of legal rights includes all the following, except:
    a. possession.
    b. enjoyment.
    c. avulsion.
    d. disposition.

6. Which of the following properties would be an example of a specific use property?
    a. A donut shop
    b. A frame and front-end shop
    c. A movie theater
    d. A factory

7. A landowner may claim a "riparian right" to what substance on, under or adjacent to his or her land?

  a. Water
  b. Silver
  c. Gold
  d. None of the above

8. Emblements are considered:

  a. annually cultivated crops by tenant farmers.
  b. designs on houses.
  c. transfer of ownership documents.
  d. none of the above.

9. The commission paid for the sale of a condominium is:

  a. 6%.
  b. 10%.
  c. set by law.
  d. fully negotiable.

10. The address posted on a property is the:

  a. legal address.
  b. common address.
  c. assessor's address.
  d. lot, block, and tract address.

ANSWERS: 1. d; 2. d; 3. b; 4. d; 5. c; 6. c; 7. a; 8. a; 9. d; 10. b

THE GREAT TEXAS
COASTAL BIRDING
TRAIL

SITE UTC-052

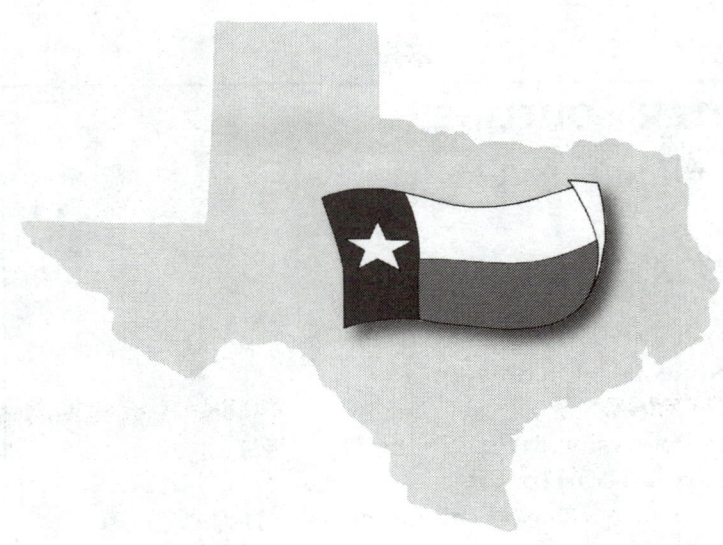

Chapter 2
Estates, Transfers, and Titles

The previous chapter explained the differences between real and personal property. This chapter illustrates the types of estates (ownership) that you may have, the ways in which you can hold title and the methods of transferring real property.

I. Estate Ownership

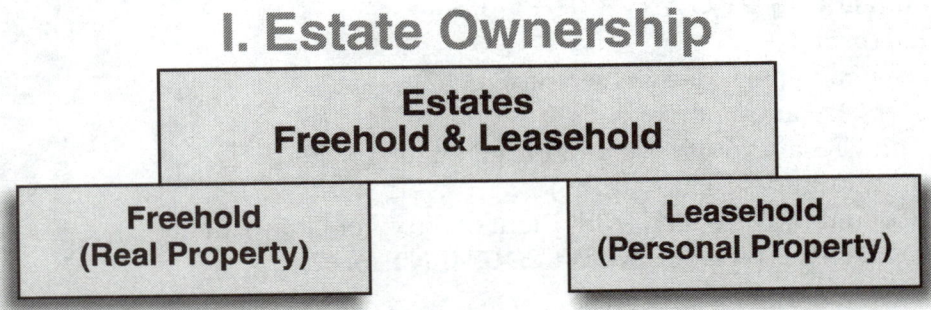

A. ESTATES (OWNERSHIP)

An *ESTATE is an interest, share, right or equity in real estate that varies from the minimal right of a renter to the maximum right of a full owner.*

Estates are either (1) **freehold** or (2) **leasehold**, depending upon the degree of ownership and the duration of interest. Freehold estates are real property and less-than-freehold estates are personal property. Less-than-freehold estates come with certain rights for the use of real property.

CHAPTER 2 OUTLINE

B. FREEHOLD ESTATE (Convey Ownership)

Freehold estates are 1) fee simple estates or 2) life estates.

These freehold estates are the greatest degree of ownership you can have under the law (see **Figure 2-1**).

Figure 2-1

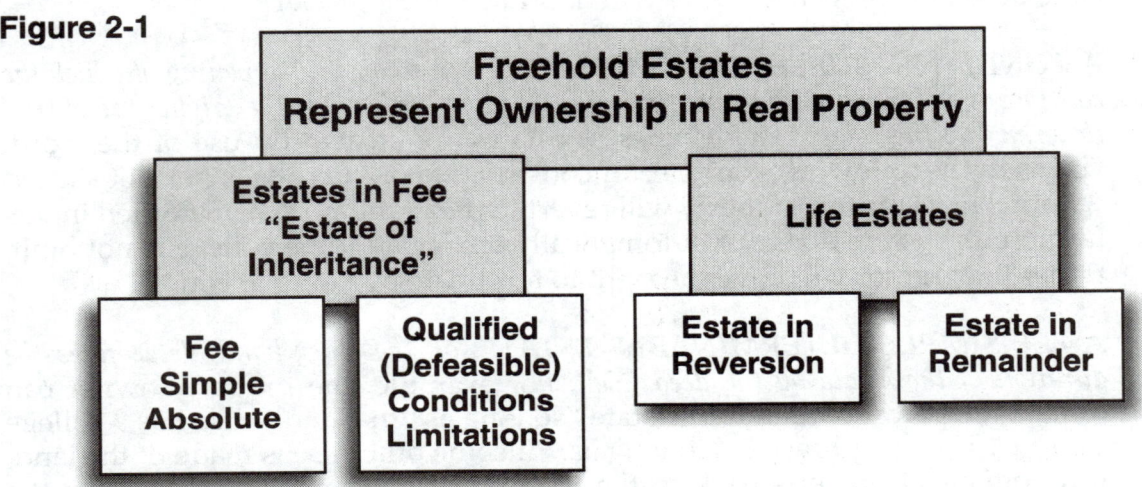

A freehold estate is a right to title to land.

1. Estates in Fee

Fee simple (paramount and superior title) is the most interest (greatest) one can hold; it is of "indefinite duration" (perpetual), "freely transferable," and "inheritable" (referred to as an estate of inheritance).

A fee simple estate is the most complete form of ownership and the most common in Texas. This can be referred to as fee, fee ownership, or fee simple. *FEE SIMPLE means an owner has transferred all rights of a property to a new owner for an indefinite duration of time (perpetual).* All transfers are assumed to be fee simple unless the grant part of the deed limits, by the use of conditions, the property's use.

a. Conditions That Restrict a Fee Estate (Fee Simple Defeasible)

A FEE SIMPLE DEFEASIBLE ESTATE (or qualified fee estate) is a fee estate that can be lost or defeated by the happening of some event after the initial agreement. It is subject to particular limitations imposed by the grantor of the estate. **Breaking any condition of the transfer may be grounds for terminating or revoking the property transfer.**

There are three categories of conditions: 1) condition precedent; 2) condition subsequent; and 3) determinable.

In the case of a **CONDITION PRECEDENT**, *title will not take effect until a condition is performed*. For example, a property owner will give the state a parcel of land on the condition that the state agrees to build a college on the site. If the state does not agree, the owner will not transfer the property.

A **CONDITION SUBSEQUENT** *is a future event upon the happening of which the contract is no longer binding on the parties. It gives the grantor the "right of re-entry" to terminate the estate.* These types of estates are created by use of the word, "if" as in the following example, "if construction of the college has not started within five years, the property will revert to the grantor." When worded in this fashion, the estate does not automatically terminate if the college is not built, rather the grantor will have the right to terminate by going to court.

A **FEE SIMPLE DETERMINABLE ESTATE**, *on the other hand, determines the duration of the estate by the deed itself*. For example, the property owner can donate the parcel of land to the state "so long as" the land is used as a college campus. The key phrase is "so long as." If some other use is made of the land, it automatically reverts back to the grantor, or someone else named by the grantor. There is no need to go to court in order to exercise the right as under a fee simple subject to condition subsequent.

A "fee simple defeasible estate" is an estate that can be defeated if a condition placed upon the estate is violated.

For example, if a person takes title subject to a condition that liquor NOT be served on the premises, and then turns around and breaks this promise, the previous title holder has grounds to reclaim title through a court action.

A fee simple defeasible estate, with a condition (precedent or subsequent) hanging over it, has less value than a fee simple estate.

Defeasible Fee Type	When Reversion Occurs
Fee Simple Determinable	Reversion (ownership returns to grantor) automatically happens when a stated condition has occurred.
Fee Simple Subject to Condition Subsequent	Reversion happens only when the grantor exercises a right of re-entry by going to court.

2. Life Estate (Ownership for Someone's Lifetime)

"Life estate" and "fee simple" are the two types of freehold estates.

A **LIFE ESTATE** *is an ownership interest in real property that only exists for the life of any designated person or persons (often the grantee).* The usual intent of this type of estate is to provide a lifetime residence for an individual. A life estate can be created by either a will or a deed.

A "life estate" is a freehold estate with a limited duration based upon someone's lifetime. This can be the lifetime of the person granting the estate or any other person so designated. The term "pur autre vie" refers to the "life of another."

When that designated person dies, the estate reverts back to the original owner. A person holding a life estate is free to lease the property to someone else, but this lease is also subject to the lifetime limitation. If the designated person dies, the estate ends and all rights, including any tenant rights, revert back to the original owner.

The owner of a life estate CANNOT grant more rights than he/she holds. A life tenant may lease the property to someone, but the lease terminates when the life estate ends.

The life tenant usually has certain interests and obligations as long as the life estate is in effect. The life tenant:

1. has the right of physical possession of the property;
2. has the right to all rents and profits, but this terminates when the life estate holder dies;
3. can usually lease the property, but not beyond the time frame of the life estate;
4. is obligated to keep the property in good repair, although he or she is not required to make improvements;
5. may not damage or destroy any permanent part of the property to the detriment of succeeding interests; and
6. is usually responsible for all annual costs and expenses.

Ownership reverts (returns) to the grantor when the life estate holder dies.

The party (grantor) granting a life estate is said to hold an **ESTATE IN REVERSION**.

Consider the following case/example.

Juan conveys a house to Tom by means of a life estate measured by Tom's lifetime. After Tom takes ownership he decides to rent it to Liz. Liz is living in the house when Tom dies unexpectedly. When this happens, ownership reverts automatically to Juan.

If an owner granting a life estate names another person to receive title upon the death of the current life estate holder, that other person claims an **ESTATE IN REMAINDER**. The holder of an estate in remainder or estate in reversion has no right to the use and enjoyment of the property until the current life tenant dies.

An uncle deeds his property to his niece, but reserves the right to live there until he dies. This is "reserving a life estate." Always talk to a tax advisor before deeding over any property!

Because a life estate may have some unusual and unexpected tax consequences, it's always wise to consult with a tax professional before conveying property by means of a life estate.

3. Homestead (Legal Life Estate)

In Texas, a homestead is considered to be a "legal life estate" because it is created by law. The Texas Constitution allows Texas residents the right to have a home that is free from the reach of creditors except for those types specifically described by law. Generally speaking, the homestead is free from forced sale, except for the mortgage, property taxes, home equity loans, or other types of creditors as specifically named. This means that if, for example, a judgment is taken by a credit card company against a homeowner, the credit card company will not be able to foreclose against the homestead property.

In Texas, a homestead is a form of life estate by virtue of the Texas Constitution.

C. LEASEHOLD ESTATE (Convey Only Possession to Real Property)

A **LEASEHOLD ESTATE** *is a personal right to the use of real property for a period of time.* It is more commonly referred to as a "lease" or "rental agreement," which gives tenants various rights to use real property for a specified period (see **Figure 2-2**).

The lease or rental agreement is personal property because there is no true ownership in the property. The tenant only has possession of the property.

Figure 2-2

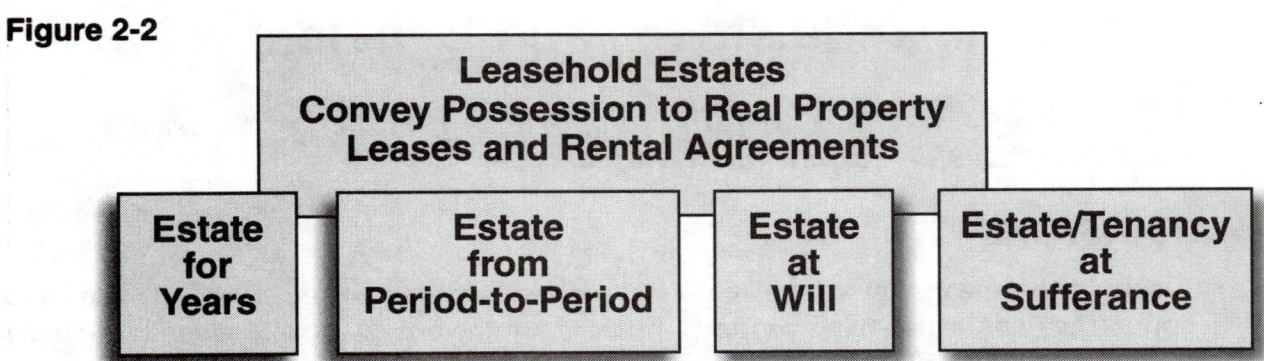

The lease is the personal property of the lessee (renter).

1. Estate For Years (Lease for a Fixed Term)

An **ESTATE FOR YEARS** *is a lease for a fixed period of time, agreed to in advance. This period can be from a few days up to several years. No notice to terminate is necessary.*

A lease for a definite period of time, regardless of the length, is called an estate for years.

2. Estate From Period-To-Period (Lease is Periodically Renewable)

An **ESTATE FROM PERIOD-TO-PERIOD** *is a renewable agreement to rent or lease a property for a period of time, where the rental or lease amount is fixed at an agreed to sum per week, month, or year. A notice to terminate must be given.*

Under Texas law, the amount of advance notice needed to terminate this type of lease must be equal, at a minimum, to the rental payment period unless otherwise stated in the lease. For example, to terminate a month-to-month lease, the termination notice must be given 30 days in advance, unless the lease states otherwise.

3. Estate At Will (Lease at the Will of Both Parties)

An **ESTATE AT WILL** *is a rental agreement that can be terminated by either party at any time.*

4. Estate At Tenancy/Sufferance

An **ESTATE AT TENANCY/SUFFERANCE** *occurs when the person renting or leasing a particular property remains after the expiration of the stated term.*

The four main types of leasehold estates are explained in further detail in Chapter 8.

II. Acquisitions and Transfers

"Acquisition" means to acquire, buy, or pull in, whereas "alienation" means to transfer, sell, or push away.

A. TRANSFERS

A sale is the means by which real estate is usually transferred. A sale is the most familiar way of transferring property, but it is not the only way. The seven basic ways to transfer real property are:

1. Deed
2. Will
3. Probate
4. Intestate succession (no will)
5. Accession
6. Occupancy
7. Dedication

Figure 2-3 illustrates the seven methods of transferring real property.

Figure 2-3

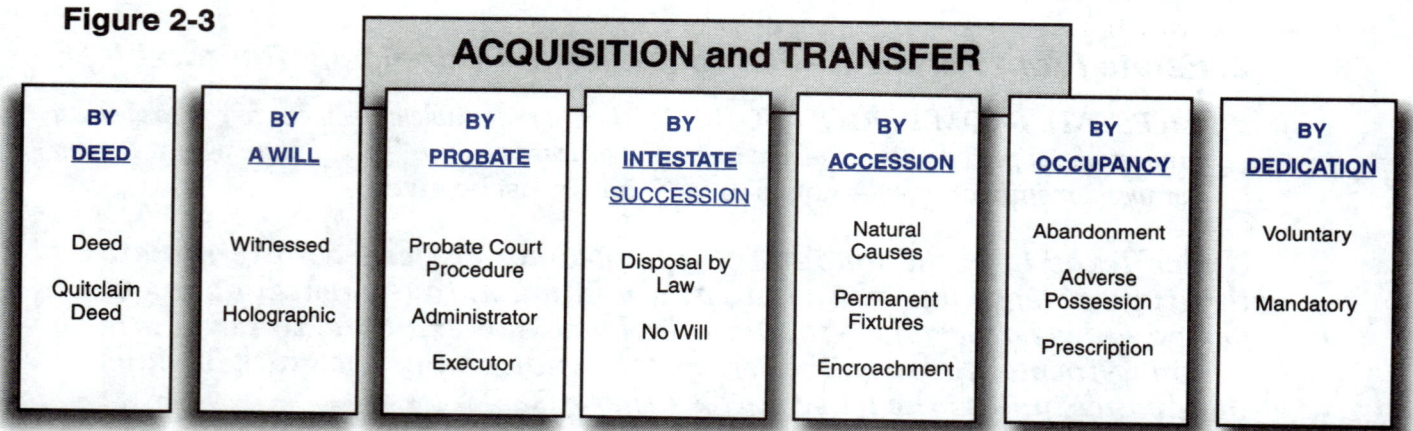

1. Transfer by Deed

The deed is NOT the title, but rather the document that is used to convey title.

The most common method of acquiring title to a property is by deed transfer. In Texas, the **DEED** *is the document used to effect the transfer of title to property from one person to another.* A **DEED** *is a written instrument that conveys and evidences title.*

The *GRANTOR* *(seller) is the person who grants property or property rights*. The *GRANTEE* *(buyer) is the person to whom the grant is made*. A grantee cannot be a fictitious person (i.e., Batman or Catwoman), but it can be a busines or legal entity (i.e., Microsoft, Inc.).

A **VALID DEED** has all the following eight essential elements:

1. It must be in writing to be enforceable.
2. The parties must be properly identified.
3. Grantor must be competent to convey real property.
4. The property must be adequately described (usually with a legal description).
5. There must be a granting clause (action clause).
6. It must be signed by the granting party (grantor).
7. The grantee must be capable of holding title to real property (living).
8. A deed does not take effect until it is delivered and accepted.

In Texas, a deed commonly used to pass title is the *GENERAL WARRANTY DEED*. *It is called a general warranty deed because of the warranties or promises that it contains* (see **Figure 2-4**).

In Texas, a general warranty deed offers the grantee the most protection: "covenant of siesin" and "covenant against encumbrances."

The warranties, which are not expressly written into the deed itself, but are implied, include two basic warranties:

1. *COVENANT OF SIESIN, in which the grantor warrants that he/she is the owner of the property and has the right to sell it;* and
2. *COVENANT AGAINST ENCUMBRANCES, in which the grantor warrants that the property is free from any liens or encumbrances except those specified in the deed.*

A key legal element of the General Warranty Deed is the grantor's promise to "warrant and forever defend" the grantee's ownership against anyone in the entire history of ownership. From the grantee's perspective, this is a good promise to have from the grantor. However, another popular type of Texas deed places limits on this promise.

A *SPECIAL WARRANTY DEED is very similar to a general warranty deed with one major exception. While a grantor under a general warranty deed promises to protect the grantee from any and all challengers in the chain of title, the grantor in the special warranty deed only promises to protect the grantee's title from anything the grantor might have done while he/she held title to the property (i.e., encumbered the property in some way).*

Figure 2-4

GENERAL WARRANTY DEED

THE STATE OF TEXAS   §

                         §   KNOW ALL MEN BY THESE PRESENTS:

COUNTY OF LONGHORN   §

THAT THE UNDERSIGNED, Sam Seller, hereinafter referred to as "Grantor", whether one or more, for in consideration of the sum of TEN DOLLARS ($10.00) cash, and other good and valuable consideration in hand paid by the Grantee, herein named, the receipt and sufficiency of which is hereby fully acknowledged and confessed, has GRANTED, SOLD and CONVEYED, and by these presents does hereby GRANT, SELL and CONVEY unto Henry Homebuyer, herein referred to as "Grantee", whether one or more, the real property described as follows:

Lot 10, Block 4, Lovely Country Estates, County of Longhorn, Cowboy, Texas.

This conveyance, however, is made and accepted subject to any and all validly existing encumbrances, conditions and restrictions, relating to the hereinabove described property as now reflected by the records of the County Clerk of Longhorn County, Texas.

TO HAVE AND TO HOLD the above described premises, together with all and singular the rights and appurtenances thereto in anywise belonging unto the said Grantee, Grantee's heirs, executors, administrators, successors and/or assigns forever; and Grantor does hereby bind Grantor, Grantor's heirs, executors, administrators, successors and/or assigns to WARRANT AND FOREVER DEFEND all and singular the said premises unto the said Grantee, Grantee's heirs, executors, administrators, successors and/or assigns, against every person whomsoever claming or to claim the same or any part thereof.

Current ad valorem taxes on said property having been prorated, the payment thereof is assumed by Grantee.

EXECUTED this _____ day of _____, 20xx .

_____
Sam Seller, a single man

Grantee's Address:
105 Main Drive.
Cityview, Texas 77777

Despite this legal limitation, special warranty deeds are common in Texas and typically used by sellers who have owned the property for a very short time, such as new homebuilders or lenders who have foreclosed.

While a warranty deed typically contains express words of "grant" and implied warranties, a Quitclaim Deed contains neither. A *QUITCLAIM DEED is a document that transfers all the present rights or interest that a person may have in a property, without any warranty, title, or interest.*

A quitclaim deed can convey absolute ownership or only such title as one may hold. If there is no ownership interest, then nothing can be acquired. For example, in the right case, it might be perfectly legal and appropriate to give a quitclaim deed in a major downtown office building even if the grantor is not sure he/she owns any part of it.

Read the quitclaim deed in **Figure 2-5**. Note that there are no warranties. This deed is used primarily to clear a cloud on title from the records. A *CLOUD ON TITLE is a claim, encumbrance or condition that impairs the title to real property until removed or eliminated, as, for example, through a quitclaim deed or a quiet title legal action.*

Commonly Used Texas Deeds

General Warranty Deed – In addition to conveying the property, this grantor promises to protect the grantee against any claim occurring within the entire chain of title.

Special Warranty Deed – This deed will also convey title, but the grantor only promises to protect the grantee from claims arising as a result of the grantor's ownership.

Bargain and Sale Deed (also known as Deeds Without Warranty) – This deed conveys property but contains absolutely no promises or warranties of any type.

Trustee's Deed – This deed is given by a trustee to the purchaser at a foreclosure sale.

Sheriff's Deed – Typically, this deed is given to the purchaser at a court ordered sale.

Quitclaim Deed – A quitclaim deed purports to pass whatever right, title, and interest the grantor has in the property, and nothing more.

Figure 2-5

QUITCLAIM DEED

THE STATE OF TEXAS   §

                            §   KNOW ALL MEN BY THESE PRESENTS:

COUNTY OF COWBOY   §

  THAT THE UNDERSIGNED, William B. Travis, hereinafter referred to as "Grantor", whether one or more, for in consideration of the sum of TEN AND NO/100 DOLLARS ($10.00) in hand paid by Grantee herein named, and other good and valuable consideration, the receipt and sufficiency of which is hereby acknowledged, has QUITCLAIMED, and by these presents does QUITCLAIM unto David Crockett of the County of Bexar and State of Texas, herein referred to as "Grantee", whether one or more, the real property described on attached Exhibit "A".

  TO HAVE AND TO HOLD all of Grantor's right, title and interest in and to the above described premises unto the said Grantee, Grantee's heirs, administrators, executors, successors and/or assigns forever; so that neither Grantor nor Grantor's heirs, administrators, executors, successors and/or assigns shall have, claim or demand any right or title to the aforesaid property, premises or appurtenances or any part thereof.

  EXECUTED this _____ day of _____, 20xx .

      _____

        William B. Travis

Grantee's Address:

One Alamo Place
San Antonio, Texas 78888

A *QUIET TITLE ACTION is a court proceeding to remove a cloud on title to real property*. It is usually a minor defect that requires a quitclaim deed before a title insurance company will clear the transfer. A quitclaim deed is often used in divorce actions, so that one party may have clear title.

Quitclaim deeds make NO "covenants" (promises); they guarantee nothing. These documents only convey whatever rights the grantor may have.

To be effective, a deed must be delivered by the grantor and accepted by the grantee.

The following are the three basic methods of delivery:

1. *MANUAL DELIVERY is a direct transfer of the deed from the grantor to the grantee.*
2. *DELIVERY THROUGH RECORDING is the act of putting the title of record in the grantee's name at the county clerk's office.* The grantee must have agreed to the recording. Recording is perfomed in the county where the property is located.
3. *CONDITIONAL DELIVERY requires that a specific event take place before title can be passed, and must be passed through a third party, such as an escrow agent.*

A deed delivered by "grantor to grantee" with a condition involved is a manual delivery, NOT a conditional delivery, because there is no third party involved.

DEEDS OF TRUST ARE MORTGAGE INSTRUMENTS

A deed of trust is a form of deed, but, as its name implies, it conveys a limited interest to a trustee who holds it in trust, that is to say conditionally, for the benefit of a lender.

In Texas, if a homebuyer must finance any portion of the purchase price, a deed of trust is used to secure payment of a promissory note by creating a lien on the property and giving the trustee the power to foreclose in the event of a default.

But if the homebuyer successfully pays off his or her loan, the beneficiary need only release the lien by means of an appropriately named release of lien instrument.

As a result, a deed of trust is more in the nature of a mortgage instrument rather than a deed.

2. Transfer by Will (Testate)

A **WILL** *is a document, created by a person, stating how that person's property is to be conveyed or distributed upon his or her death.* It also leaves instructions as to the disposition of the body upon death. This is known as dying **TESTATE**, *which means having made and left a valid will.* A **TESTATOR** *(referring to a male) or* **TESTATRIX** *(referring to a female) is one who makes a will. To* **BEQUEATH** *is to transfer personal property by will; to* **DEVISE** *is to transfer real property by will.*

There are two types of wills that can legally dispose of real and personal property:

1. Witnessed will (typed)
2. Holographic will (handwritten)

A **WITNESSED WILL** *is a typed document usually prepared by an attorney, dated, signed by the property owners and declared to be a will by at least two witnesses (three signatures total).*

A **HOLOGRAPHIC WILL** *is entirely handwritten by the owner, dated and signed.* Since it is in the owner's own handwriting, no other formalities and no witnesses are required.

A **CODICIL** *is a change made to a will before the maker's death.*

A holographic will signed with an "X" must be witnessed.

Note: A **REVOCABLE INTER VIVOS (LIVING) TRUST** *is a trust that is effective during the life of the owner, rather than upon his or her death.* It can eliminate probate (to prove a will) cost and serve the same function as a will. A trust consists of real and/or personal property (the *trust corpus*), which is held by a trustee for the benefit of certain named beneficiaries. It is revocable at the discretion of the benefactor (owner), but becomes fully enforceable upon that person's death. There can be a considerable estate tax savings under this arrangement, depending on the size of the estate. At the very least, a revocable living trust protects the interests of everyone involved while avoiding the time and expense of probate. This type of trust is, however, rather complicated to set up, so an attorney specializing in this field should be consulted.

3. Transfer by Probate (Probate Court Approval)

PROBATE *is a court procedure to determine a will's validity, any creditors' claims, and establish the identity of the beneficiaries.*

After a person dies, an **administrator (male)** or **administratrix (female)** is appointed by the court to temporarily take possession of the property until probate is finalized. If the will has appointed a particular person to administer the estate, that person is known as an **executor** (male) or an **executrix** (female).

Note: Wills and living trusts are legal devices for transferring property at death. To protect yourself, have an attorney draw up a will or living trust that reflects your desires. You may also leave your own handwritten (holographic) will but it could be risky if not done correctly.

4. Transfer by Intestate Succession (Inheritance)

If there is no will, the procedure used for transferring the deceased's property to his or her heirs is called INTESTATE SUCCESSION. This is usually accomplished through state laws known as the laws of descent and distribution. These laws provide for the disposition of the property. The rules for dividing the property are complex and depend upon the relationship of the kin. Here are just a few:

Community Property:

If the decedent (deceased person) leaves a spouse and no children or if all children are of this marriage, then all community property goes to the surviving spouse.

But if the decedent leaves a spouse and children from a prior marriage, then half goes to the spouse with the remainder to the children.

Separate Property:

If there is a surviving spouse and children, 1/3 life estate to spouse and 2/3 to children.

If there is no surviving spouse, but there are children, separate property is divided equally among the children.

If there is no surviving spouse and no children, then all to his/her parents according to the Texas laws of descent and distribution.

ESCHEAT is the term used if there is no will and there are no heirs; the property passes to the state of Texas. See Chapter 15 for a further explanation of how escheat works in Texas.

Individuals do NOT acquire property by escheat. If there are NO heirs and NO will, property passes to the state of Texas. If you don't want the State of Texas deciding for you how your property should be divided upon your death, then write a will.

5. Transfer by Accession (Natural Forces)

ACCESSION occurs when an owner acquires title to additional land by natural causes, that is, additions to the property by natural growth. The addition to land from natural causes, such as earthquakes, volcanoes, or the action of moving water is known as ACCRETION. For example, a river over time may slowly deposit soil on one of its banks. *These deposits of earth made through the natural action of water, called ALLUVIUM,* become the real property of the landowner who holds title to the river bank. *AVULSION is the sudden, violent tearing away of land by, for example, a raging river impacted by a storm.* Title to that land is lost by the property owner.

Permanent fixtures attached to the land or buildings by residential tenants must be left with the building. Any improvements that are mistakenly placed on the property must also remain. *Placement of improvements and permanent fixtures on property that does not legally belong to the person who placed them is called ENCROACHMENT.*

6. Transfer by Occupancy

Ownership of real property, or the use of real property, can be gained through three types of occupancy:

    a. Abandonment
    b. Adverse Possession
    c. Prescription (by use)

a. Abandonment

ABANDONMENT is the relinquishing of a right or interest with the intention of never again reclaiming it. One cannot acquire title to abandoned real property without court action, but a landlord can acquire possession of a property that is left (abandoned) by a tenant simply by gaining full control of the property. In the case of a lease, a financially troubled tenant might negotiate a release or abandon the property, thereby forfeiting part of the deposit.

b. Adverse Possession

ADVERSE POSSESSION is acquiring title to another's property through continuous, open, and notorious occupancy under a claim of title. It is a legal way to acquire title without a deed.

Title may be obtained through adverse possession only if certain conditions are met:

1. **Open and notorious occupancy** – The adverse possessor must live on, or openly use, the property in such a way that the titled owners might easily detect his or her presence.

2. **Uninterrupted continuous use** – The adverse possessor must use the property continuously.
3. **Claim of title (color of title)** – The adverse possessor must have some reasonable claim of right or color of title (perhaps a defective written instrument) as a basis for his or her assertion. For example, a person could claim that his uncle gave the property to him before he died, but the deed is missing.
4. **Hostile** – The adverse possessor must possess the property in a manner legally hostile to the legal owner, that is, without his or her permission or any rental payment (consideration).

There are a number of ways that an owner can prevent the effects of adverse possession. One way may be to eject the claimant from the land thereby depriving him/her of physical possession. Another way is to simply give the possessor permission to be there which destroys the element of hostility.

In either case, the true owner of the property can defend his/her ownership by taking action to prevent the adverse possessor from meeting all of the required elements of adverse possession.

Under the principle of *TACKING, it may be possible for someone to claim adverse possession by combining his/her period of possession with that of a predecessor.* Suppose, for example, a law requires a claimant to occupy the land for five years before he/she is entitled to full ownership. If the claimant acquires possession from someone who has occupied the land for four years, the claimant need only occupy the same land for another year in order to meet the requirements under the five-year statute, assuming, of course, that all other requirements are met.

In order to utilize the principle of tacking, there must be a direct and uninterrupted connection between the claimant and his/her predecessor.

Although it may sound harsh to divest someone of ownership due to another person's actions, there's a good legal reason for adverse possession.

Adverse possession is designed to legally settle property ownership claims where the possessor has come onto and occupied the property by peaceable means while the true owner, who could have discovered the occupant, has done nothing to stop it.

An adverse possessor is not the same as a trespasser. A trespasser comes onto a property with no right of possession whatsoever. An adverse possessor, on the other hand, comes onto the property under a belief that the property is his/hers.

In Texas, claims of adverse possession are determined by means of a court proceeding based upon a law that requires the true owner to take action within 3, 5, 10, or 25 years depending on the statute used.

Each statute has other unique requirements which must also be met. For example, one statute requires the possessor to pay property taxes, while another statute places limits on the size of the tract that may be claimed. But regardless of the law used, the courts will require substantial proof before awarding ownership to the adverse possessor. To obtain fee simple title, the claim must be determined and decreed by a court.

Adverse possession is NOT possible against public or government lands, but only against privately owned lands.

c. Prescription

PRESCRIPTION refers to an easement, not ownership, that is to say, the right to use another's land, which in Texas can be obtained through ten years of continuous use. It is similar in concept to adverse possession with the main difference being that only the use of the property will be legally obtained.

To acquire property by prescription means to acquire the use of the property. It does not refer to acquiring ownership.

7. Transfer by Dedication

DEDICATION is the gift (appropriation) of land, by its owner, for some public use. To be fully dedicated, the land must be accepted for such use by authorized public officials. Dedication may be either (1) voluntary or (2) mandated by statute.

A developer may often "dedicate land" for a street, a school, or even a park.

III. Title (Forms of Ownership)

A. TITLE

TITLE is the right to ownership of land and the evidence of that ownership. There are four distinct methods of holding title. **Figure 2-6** displays the four ways a person, or persons, may hold title to real property and whether a single title holder has the right to will or sell his or her share independent of the other owners. *VESTING is the placing of a person's (or persons') name on the deed and the description of the method by which that person will hold title.*

Figure 2-6	**Methods of Holding Title (Vesting) Concurrently or in Severalty**		
MAY A SINGLE TITLE HOLDER TRANSFER THE PROPERTY BY:		**WILL?**	**SALE?**
SEVERALTY ("Sole Ownership")		YES	YES
TENANCY IN COMMON		YES	YES
JOINT TENANCY WITH RIGHT OF SURVIVORSHIP		NO	YES
COMMUNITY PROPERTY		YES	NO
COMMUNITY PROPERTY WITH RIGHT OF SURVIVORSHIP		NO	NO

Vesting is the method by which one holds title. A deed to a legal or business entity is valid; a deed to a fictitious person is void.

1. Severalty (Separate Ownership)

SEVERALTY is the sole and separate ownership of property by one individual or by a corporation. The word "severed" means to sever; to cut off or separate. The name severalty is misleading; it means "single."

Title can be held by a corporation (legal person) or individual (natural person). Severalty means ownership by "only one."

Obviously ownership by severalty includes a single person who is purchasing a home alone. But since Texas is a community property state, ownership by severalty could also include property owned by a spouse. Here are the rules for when one spouse may own separate property:

1. Property acquired before (or after marriage);
2. Property acquired during marriage by gift, devise (by will), or descent (by inheritance);
3. Property acquired during marriage due to a personal injury claim (except for loss of earning capacity during marriage); and
4. Property acquired pursuant to the terms of a prenuptial agreement.

While the "proceeds" from the sale of separate property remain separate property, "income" from separate property becomes community property.

This may help better explain this concept. Suppose a father gave his daughter an apple tree as a pre-wedding gift. Since the tree was acquired before marriage, it is clearly her separate property. If, during marriage, the woman sells her tree, the

sales proceeds remain as her separate property. But if she were to keep the tree and the tree yields a large harvest of apples, then the income from the sales of the apples becomes community property.

Obviously, this can quickly become a complex area. If the parties have questions, they should consult with an attorney. In no event should you ever offer an answer to a legal question. Doing so may cause you to lose your license and expose you to liability even if your answer is correct. In short, it's not worth it.

Property held by corporations is also owned in severalty, as if by a single individual. A **CORPORATION** *is a body of persons treated by law as a single "legal person," having a personality and existence distinct from that of its shareholders.* A corporation can go on forever; it does not die.

Examples to show ownership by severalty are:

1. as a natural person, a real person

> **Mary Smith, a single woman**
> **Mary Smith, an unmarried woman**
> **Jim Smith, a single man**

2. or as a legal person; charter granted by the state

> **Urban Analysis Inc., a Texas corporation**

3. Sometimes married people wish to keep ownership to certain properties as separate property (in severalty). They may then use the phrase:

> **Mary Smith, a married woman, as her sole and separate property**
> **Jim Smith, a married man, as his sole and separate property**

2. Tenancy In Common

Two or more people hold ownership concurrently, with the right to individually possess, will, or sell. While each person holds an undivided interest, this does NOT necessarily mean that each share is of equal size.

When two or more people own property together with the right to will or sell it (however, without survivorship rights or community property rights), it is called **TENANCY IN COMMON**. *If there is no other agreement, they will each share an equal interest in the property. All tenants in common have "unity of possession," which means they each have the right to occupy the property. Often, the property is rented to one of the owners or to a tenant. Tenancy in common gives all owners a share of the income and expenses of the property. An example of the wording illustrating this would be:*

Jim Smith and Fred Jones, as tenants in common

Each owner may sell or transfer his or her interest separately from the others.

For example, assume that four people own equal, undivided shares in a building. Any co-owner may sell his/her undivided interest without restriction. And upon the death of each co-owner, that owner's share will pass to his/her heirs.

If the owners do not agree on the ownership or management, and persistent disagreements exist, it would probably be best to sell the property and divide the profits accordingly. *If an agreement cannot be reached by the owners, the parties can ask a court to physically divide the property so that each owner receives a portion of the property in severalty. This is known as a* **PARTITION ACTION**. It is obviously better for the owners to sell the property themselves, as attorney's fees and court costs would be involved. Furthermore, the court would probably sell the land at a lower price to expedite the sale.

3. Joint Tenancy With Right of Survivorship

JOINT TENANCY occurs when two or more people have identical interests in the whole property with the same right of possession and the right of survivorship. If one of the joint tenancy owners should die, his or her interest is then split evenly with the surviving owners. Joint tenancy can never be willed.

Joint tenants have the right of "survivorship." A joint tenancy interest CANNOT be willed.

When a joint tenancy is established, there are four necessary unities (T-Tip):

T 1. Title – All owners are granted title by the same instrument.
T 2. Time – All owners obtain title at the same time.
I 3. Interest – All owners share an equal interest.
P 4. Possession – All owners have an equal right to possess the property.

To create joint tenancy, there must be intention by the owners. The deed must be in writing and contain the phrase:

"as joint tenants" or "in joint tenancy"

If it does not "state" that it is a joint tenancy, joint tenancy does not exist. Here's an example of how it would be used:

Jim Smith and Fred Jones, as joint tenants

If one of the parties should die, the property is automatically transferred to the remaining parties without having to go through the court procedure known as

PROBATE (to prove a will). The transferred portion conveys the ownership and all debts on the property at the moment of death. Upon death, that debt does not transfer to the surviving joint tenants until it is foreclosed. Although probate costs may be avoided in joint tenancy, the surviving owners may end up paying higher income taxes later.

A lien placed on one joint tenant's interest does not sever a joint tenancy until the debt is foreclosed. Until then, surviving joint tenants are not liable to creditors of a deceased joint tenant.

A joint tenant can sell or transfer his or her ownership interest. Any portion of joint tenancy transferred or sold to a nonowner will bring the nonowner into tenancy in common with the other owners, who remain as joint tenants. If A, B, and C own a property together and C sells his interest to D, then D gets only the tenancy in common interest with A and B (who continue to be joint tenants).

Because a corporation could, conceivably, go on forever, it is not permitted to enter into joint tenancies. Such a situation would give corporations an unfair survivorship advantage.

4. Community Property

In contrast to separate property, COMMUNITY PROPERTY refers to all the other property acquired by a husband and wife during their marriage. This includes any conversions from separate to community property that the parties brought into the marriage and then converted to community property.

Here are some examples of how community property might be designated on a deed:

Jim Smith and Mary Smith, husband and wife
Jim Smith, et. ux., Mary Smith
Mary Smith and Jim Smith, wife and husband

In Texas, both husband and wife must sign all documents necessary to convey homestead property, even if the homestead property is the separate property of one of the parties. Failure to do so, though not illegal, will certainly complicate the sale. Moreover, the proceeds from the sale of homestead property are exempt from the reach of creditors for a period of six months after the date of sale.

Salespeople should make certain that both husband and wife sign all real estate documents such as listing agreements, sales contracts, closing statements and the deed if the property being transferred is homestead property.

The right to manage the community property is shared by both the husband and wife except for those assets under the direct control of one spouse, such as personal earnings. But once personal earnings, for example, are mixed with other jointly controlled community property, the separately managed property loses its distinction.

Questions about marital debts should be directed to an attorney, as this issue is quite complex.

Do NOT advise a buyer how to hold title—that is giving legal advice. How a person holds title has a big impact upon income tax planning and estate planning.

5. Community Property With Right of Survivorship

In 1987, Texas voters approved an amendment to the Texas Constitution which allows married couples to hold title to real and personal property as community property with right of survivorship. *COMMUNITY PROPERTY WITH RIGHT OF SURVIVORSHIP transfers ownership to the remaining spouse automatically at death, bypassing completely the probate process.* This means that if community property is designated as having rights of survivorship, it need never even be mentioned in a will. It will pass automatically.

For this to occur, the law requires that the spouses execute a written agreement among themselves, which describes the community property to be subject to survivorship. The statute strongly suggests that the agreement should use the following phrases:

"with right of survivorship";
"will become the property of the survivor";
"will vest in and belong to the surviving spouse"; or
"shall pass to the surviving spouse."

This agreement is revocable by the parties and other than creating rights of survivorship upon the death of one of the spouses has no effect on the ownership or management of community property.

Creating survivorship property rights could have some federal income tax consequences. As a result, it's always a good idea to meet with a tax professional before creating these rights.

IV. Recording and Acknowledgment

A deed does NOT have to be "acknowledged" or "recorded" to be valid, although it is very wise to do both.

A. RECORDING

RECORDING is the legal process of making an instrument an official part of the records of a county, after it has been acknowledged. Instruments that affect real property are legal documents, such as deeds, deeds of trust, mortgages, and liens. Recording gives constructive notice of the existence and content of these instruments to the public.

CONSTRUCTIVE NOTICE is notice presumed by law to have been acquired by a person and thus imputed to that person. Any recorded notice that can be obtained from the county clerk's office can be considered constructive notice (and therefore public knowledge).

ACTUAL NOTICE is knowing (or one's responsibility for knowing) that a transaction has taken place. If you have found, for example, that someone other than the owner is living in a house you are buying, you should have been aware of the existence of a signed lease. This is actual notice, whereas public records are representative of constructive notice. The act of taking possession (holding an unrecorded deed) gives constructive notice.

The recording process is a privilege rather than a legal requirement. You may record an acknowledged instrument at any time. However, failure to utilize the privilege of recording at the earliest possible date can result in a question of legal or rightful title. **If the same property is sold to more than one party, the individual who has recorded first will usually be recognized as the rightful owner.** Therefore, time of recording is very important to a bona fide purchaser who is protected only if he or she records first.

If there are NO prior arrangements, the deed having priority is the one recorded first (so long as the owner had no constructive or actual notice of the rights of others).

In order to establish priority, the documents affecting real property must be recorded by the county clerk in the county where the property is located. If the property is located in two counties, it should be recorded in both counties.

B. PRIORITY OF RECORDING

Under the recording system in Texas, "The first in time is the first in right." If an owner sells his or her house twice, the first deed recorded would be considered the valid deed. This person must not have knowledge of the rights of the other party. This is the reward granted in Texas for recording any real estate transaction. However, there are four exceptions to the rule that protects a person from later recordings. They are:

1. Government liens, property taxes, and special assessments
2. Actual or constructive notice of another person's prior rights
3. Mechanic's liens
4. Agreements to the contrary (subordination agreements)

A *SUBORDINATION AGREEMENT is an agreement among two or more creditors made for the purpose of rearranging the order of priority.*

C. ACKNOWLEDGMENT (or Notary)

All documents must be written in the English language and acknowledged before they are recorded by the county clerk.

ACKNOWLEDGMENT refers to a signed or verbal statement by the named person that he or she has signed that document of his or her own free will, in other words, that person "acknowledges" his or her signature. This acknowledgment must be performed in the presence of a witness, usually a notary public, authorized by law to witness acknowledgments. See **Figure 2-7** for an example of an acknowledgment for an individual.

Figure 2-7

> The State of Texas,
> County of _____,
>
>   "Before me _____ (here insert the name and character of the officer) on this day personally appeared _____, known to me (or proved to me on the oath of _____ or through _____ (description of identity card or other document)) to be the person whose name is subscribed to the foregoing instrument and acknowledged to me that he executed the same for the purposes and consideration therein expressed.
>
>   (Seal) "Given under my hand and seal of office this _____ day of _____ _____, A.D., _____."

Additionally, instruments regarding real property must meet two other technical requirements before they can be recorded.

First, the mailing address of each grantee must appear on the instrument or on a separate page attached to the document. The reason for this is quite simple. This is

so the county clerk will know where to mail the deed, for example, after it's been recorded.

Secondly, all documents executed on or after January 1, 2004 which transfer real property must contain the following statement in 12 point uppercase letters:

NOTICE OF CONFIDENTIALITY RIGHTS: IF YOU ARE A NATURAL PERSON, YOU MAY REMOVE OR STRIKE ANY OF THE FOLLOWING INFORMATION FROM THIS INSTRUMENT BEFORE IT IS FILED FOR RECORD IN THE PUBLIC RECORDS: YOUR SOCIAL SECURITY NUMBER OR YOUR DRIVER'S LICENSE NUMBER.

The failure of an instrument to contain this wording will not invalidate the document.

A deed does NOT have to be acknowledged to be valid, but must be acknowledged to be recorded.

A **NOTARY PUBLIC** *is a person who is authorized by the Secretary of State to witness the acknowledgment of documents.* All notarized documents must be authenticated with a notary seal that clearly shows when embossed, stamped or printed on a document:

1. the words, "Notary Public, State of Texas" around a star of five points;
2. the notary public's name; and
3. the date the notary public's commission expires.

An embossed seal is not required when transmitting electronically filed documents, however, the other notary requirements will have to appear on the page.

Within the state of Texas, other officers may acknowledge a document. They include: a clerk of a district court, a judge or clerk of a county court.

A Texas notary public who holds himself/herself out as "notario publico" faces criminal prosecution because of the confusion it may cause within the Spanish speaking population.

In Mexico, *notario publicos* are required to be Mexican attorneys and are authorized by law to assist in title transfers, payment of taxes, and legal disputes. If a Texas notary public advertises in Spanish, the ad must contain the following disclaimer:

I AM NOT AN ATTORNEY LICENSED TO PRACTICE LAW IN TEXAS AND MAY NOT GIVE LEGAL ADVICE OR ACCEPT FEES FOR LEGAL ADVICE.

VERIFICATION *is an oath or affirmation made before a notary public that the content of an instrument is true.* Notices of completion, non-responsibility and the statements used in filing a mechanic's lien are among instruments that must be verified rather than simply acknowledged.

An *AFFIRMATION is a solemn and legally binding declaration made by a person whose religious or other beliefs prohibit the taking of an oath.*

An *AFFIDAVIT is a written statement of circumstances, submitted under verification.*

D. DUTY OF RECORDER

The *COUNTY CLERK is the official recorder of each county as established by the Texas Constitution.* The clerk is required by law to promptly record, in sequential order, all recordable real property records and maintain an index of records organized alphabetically by the name of the grantor and grantee.

In some counties, this index is kept in hard bound books, but in larger counties this index is maintained on a computerized system. Either way, these indexes are open to the public and fully searchable.

While all counties accept filing of documents in person, some will accept filing electronically. If a county is equipped to allow for electronic filing of documents, the following persons may do so:

1. Texas licensed attorneys
2. Banks and other financial institutions
3. A federal agency
4. Persons licensed as mortgage lenders
5. Title companies
6. State agencies

With access to a grantor-grantee index in every county, nearly anyone can establish a chain of title. However, since these are legal documents, the interpretation of documents and opinions of title should be done by legal professionals.

E. DO NOT GIVE LEGAL ADVICE

A real estate salesperson or broker may not give legal advice, as the law is a highly complex and specialized profession that requires years of preparation and training. In the state of Texas, only a licensed attorney who is a member of the State Bar of Texas is allowed to practice law. A broker cannot give legal advice, unless he or she is also an attorney, and must realize the truth in the saying: "A man who is his own lawyer has a fool for a client."

Unless a real estate salesperson or broker is licensed to practice law, he or she may never give legal advice. To do so is a ground of license suspension/revocation and may subject the licensee to court action by the State Bar of Texas.

V. CHAPTER SUMMARY

An **estate** is an interest, share, right or equity in real estate, and can be either **freehold** (real property) or **leasehold** (personal property). A freehold estate includes fee estates or life estates.

A **fee simple** is the most complete form of ownership as it is of indefinite duration, freely transferable, and inheritable. If a **condition precedent** (before) or **condition subsequent** (future) **condition** is attached to a property's use, it is a **fee simple defeasible estate**.

A **life estate** is a **freehold estate** with a limited duration based upon someone's lifetime, with the property reverting back to the original owner (who holds an **estate in reversion**) upon the death of the life estate holder. If someone other than the owner is to receive title, that person is said to hold an **estate in remainder**.

A property owner may reserve a life estate for the duration of his or her lifetime. Although the estate is deeded to a designated party, he or she doesn't take possession until the death of the owner. In Texas, a homestead is a legal life estate.

A **lease** or **rental agreement** is a leasehold estate, where the tenant is given rights to use the real property for a period of time. It's personal property because no real ownership exists. An **estate for years** is a lease for a fixed period of time, agreed to in advance. Other leasehold estates include **estates from period-to-period**, **estates at will**, and **estates at sufferance**.

Property can be sold or transferred by: 1) **deed**, 2) **will** (witnessed or holographic), 3) **probate** (after death through the courts), 4) **intestate succession** (no will, divided among family or state), 5) **accession** (land increases through natural causes), 6) **occupancy** (**abandonment, adverse possession,** and **prescription**), and 7) **dedication** (gift to public).

A **deed** is a document that transfers title (evidence of the right to possess property). The method (tenancy) under which you hold that title is called **vesting**. The methods of **tenancy** include **severalty, tenants in common, joint tenancy with right of survivorship, community property,** and **community property with right of survivorship**.

Although **severalty** means separate ownership, title can be held by an individual or a corporation and can be willed or sold. When two or more people own property concurrently, it is called a **tenancy in common**, and it too can be willed or sold (although there are no survivorship or community property rights).

If there is the right of survivorship it is called **joint tenancy**, and that title cannot be willed. The four unities for joint tenancy are: 1) **title**, 2) **time**, 3) **interest**, and 4) **possession** (Remember: "T-TIP").

Community property refers to all the property acquired by a husband and wife during their marriage and it can be willed, but if no heir exists, it goes to the remaining spouse. **Community property with right of survivorship** is created by means of a written agreement and allows the property to pass to the surviving spouse without probate administration.

All deeds must be **acknowledged** (witnessed by a notary public) to be recorded, and are not valid unless recorded with the county. **Generally, the deed recorded first has priority over any that follow**.

VI. TERMINOLOGY

A. Abandonment
B. Accession
C. Actual Notice
D. Adverse Possession
E. Affirmation, Affidavit, Verification
F. Community Property
G. Condition Precedent
H. Condition Subsequent
I. Constructive Notice
J. Dedication
K. Delivery

L. Encroachment
M. Escheat
N. Freehold Estate
O. General and Limited Partnerships
P. General Warranty Deed
Q. Holographic Will
R. Intestate Succession
S. Joint Tenancy
T. Life Estate
U. Notary Public
V. Prescription

W. Probate
X. Quitclaim Deed
Y. Recording
Z. Remainder
AA. Reversion
BB. Severalty
CC. Tenancy in Common
DD. Witnessed Will

1.____ The giving of private land by its owner for a public use; most commonly, the developer who gives it to a city.

2.____ The reverting of private property to the state when there are no valid heirs.

3.____ A deed where the grantor protects the grantee's title against anyone else in the history of ownership.

4.____ An estate of indeterminable duration, e.g., fee simple or life estate.

5.____ Undivided ownership of a property interest by two or more persons, each of whom has a right to an equal share in the interest and a right of survivorship.

6.____ It is notice that is actually and expressly given or implied.

7.____ A person authorized by the state to witness the signatures of persons executing documents, sign the certificate and affix the official seal.

8.____ An event that must happen before title is passed.

9.____ Documents filed with the County clerk in such a way as are considered open notice to the world.

10.____ Co-ownership of property by two or more persons who hold undivided interest, without right of survivorship. The interests need not be equal.

11.____ An unlawful intrusion onto another's property by making improvements to real property, e.g., a swimming pool built across a property line.

12.____ The intentional and voluntary relinquishment of any ownership interest (such as an easement) or possession of real property.

13.____ The means of acquiring interests in land, usually an easement, by continued use.

14.____ A condition attached to an estate whereby the estate is defeated or changed through the failure or non-performance of the condition.

15.____ A process of law by which the state lays out the correct succession of inheritance when a person dies without leaving a valid will.

16.____ Many different types of statements made before a professional witness.

17.____ An estate that reverts back to the grantor after the life of the tenant expires.

18.____ The court procedure of proving that a will is valid.

19.____ A method of acquiring title to real property, through possession of the property for a statutory period under certain conditions, by a person other than the owner.

20.____ A deed to relinquish any interest in property which the grantor may have, without any warranty of title or interest.

21.____ An estate that is transferred to a third party (anyone other than the grantor) upon the death of the life estate holder.

22.____ A formal expression of a person's desires, witnessed by others, as to the disposition of his or her property after death.

23.____ Property acquired by husband and/or wife during marriage that is not acquired as separate property.

24.____ An estate of a single entity held by a single person alone.

25.____ An estate or interest in real property that is held for the duration of the life of some certain person. It may be the person holding title to the estate or some other person.

26.____ A handwritten expression of a person's desires as to the disposition of their property after death.

27.____ Placing a document in the official records of the county.

28.____ The act of receiving a deed.

29.____ The acquiring of additional property.

VII. MULTIPLE CHOICE

1. The most complete form of land ownership is:
    a. fee simple.
    b. estate for years.
    c. estate at will.
    d. none of the above.

2. The two types of freehold estates are:
    a. life estate and estate at will.
    b. fee simple and life estate.
    c. fee simple and estate for years.
    d. fee qualified and estate at will.

3. A lease for a fixed period of time, agreed to in advance and requiring NO notice of termination is called a(n):
    a. estate for years.
    b. estate from period-to-period.
    c. estate at sufferance.
    d. perpetual estate.

4. A lease for a period of time that is renewable and requires a notice of termination is called a(n):
    a. life estate.
    b. estate for years.
    c. estate from period-to-period.
    d. estate in reversion.

5. A deed must be signed by:
    a. the grantee.
    b. both the grantor and grantee.
    c. neither if the grantee takes possession.
    d. the grantor of the property.

6. A holographic will that is signed with an "X":
    a. is not legal.
    b. must be reviewed by an attorney.
    c. requires no other formalities to be legal.
    d. must be witnessed.

7. A legal way to acquire title without a deed is through:

    a. adverse possession.
    b. prescription.
    c. encroachment.
    d. dedication.

8. Smart, Black, and Curtis have a joint tenancy. Curtis sells his interest to Jones. A short time later, Smart dies. What method of co-ownership do Black and Jones have?

    a. Joint tenancy
    b. Tenancy in common
    c. Tenancy in partnership
    d. Severalty

9. Frank and Margaret Sharp purchased an income producing property through broker Finch. The Sharps asked Finch how they should hold title. Finch suggested they hold title as tenants in common. Finch's advice is:

    a. legal as long as the buyers asked him.
    b. legal as long as community property is not involved.
    c. legal if Finch is a member of NAR.
    d. against the law; Finch is not an attorney.

10. Frank is a life estate holder. He leases the property to Mary for a five-year period. After two years of the lease, Frank dies. The original grantor orders Mary to move out. Mary's lease was:

    a. not legal to begin with.
    b. legal and valid until Frank's death.
    c. legal and valid for the full five years.
    d. valid only if confirmed by the administrator of the deceased's will.

ANSWERS: 1. a; 2. b; 3. a; 4. c; 5. d; 6. d; 7. a; 8. b; 9. d; 10. b

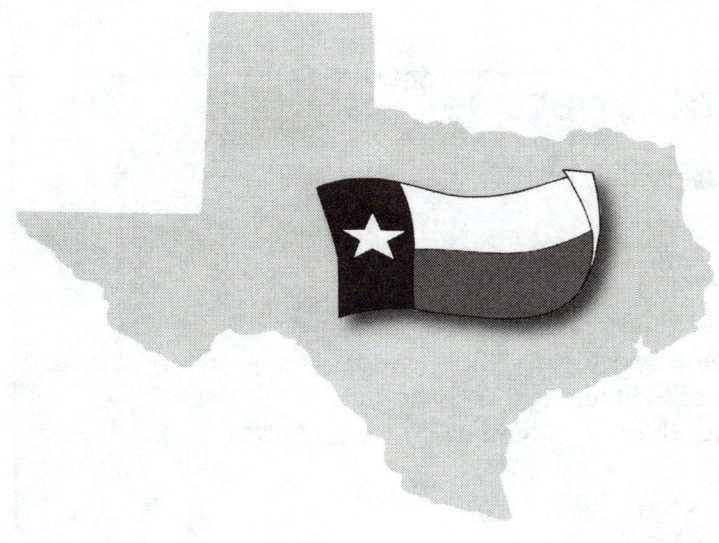

Chapter 3
Encumbrances

I. Encumbrances – An Overview

An encumbrance burdens the property (affects or limits title) by either:

*   *1) money owed (liens) or*
*   *2) items that affect the physical use of the property (non-money).*

The term encumbrance is usually new to the beginner in real estate. An *ENCUMBRANCE is a right or interest in real property held by someone other than an owner or tenancy interest.* It is a burden to the property that limits its use and may lessen its value. The two main types of encumbrances, shown in **Figure 3-1** and **Figure 3-3**, are: (1) liens and (2) items that affect the physical condition or use of the property. All liens are encumbrances but not all encumbrances are liens.

While an encumbrance does not constitute ownership, ownership is affected by and subject to encumbrances.

An owner typically encumbers his/her own property by means of one or more voluntary liens (money owed). *When the owner pays off the indebtedness related to that lien, the owner is entitled to a release or a* ***RELEASE OF LIEN****.*

CHAPTER 3 OUTLINE

Figure 3-1

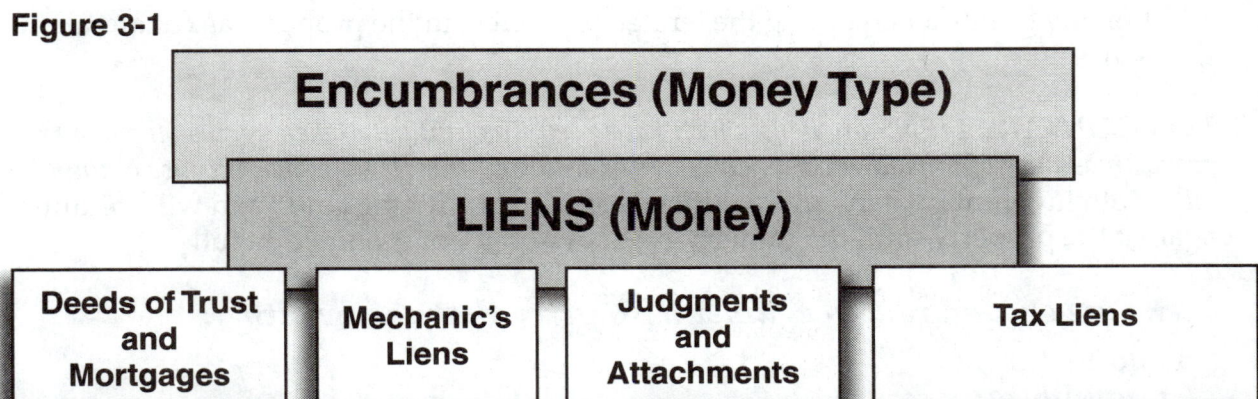

Encumbrances (Money Type)

LIENS (Money)

| Deeds of Trust and Mortgages | Mechanic's Liens | Judgments and Attachments | Tax Liens |

Occasionally an owner may encumber more than one lot under a single lien, known as a BLANKET LIEN. A blanket lien covers all properties much like a blanket covers a bed. For example, a homebuilder may grant a blanket lien to a lender to secure the indebtedness related to purchasing all of the lots in a particular subdivision. As each house is completed and sold, the homebuilder pays the lender for that particular lot. In return, the lender issues a *PARTIAL RELEASE OF LIEN, which releases that portion of the blanket lien which has been paid off.*

Regardless of whether a single lien covers one property or multiple properties, a lien (money owed) will usually contain a "release clause" so that the lien or a portion of a lien will be released when certain conditions are met, such as the full payment of all sums due.

II. Liens (Money Owed)

Liens ("money owed") are money encumbrances.

A *LIEN is an encumbrance whereby the subject property secures the payment of a debt or the discharge of an obligation.* It is money owed for one reason or another on a property. Real property liens include mortgage liens, tax liens, special assessment liens, mechanic's liens, judgment liens, and attachments.

Liens are either:

1. voluntary or involuntary, and
2. specific or general.

A. VOLUNTARY AND INVOLUNTARY LIENS

VOLUNTARY LIENS are liens voluntarily granted by the owner in favor of a lender who has typically loaned money related to the property. The owner agrees to repay the loan and

additionally grants a lien giving the lender an interest in the property as collateral for the loan.

INVOLUNTARY LIENS are liens which have been involuntarily taken against the owner's property because of unpaid government taxes or resulting from legal action because of unpaid bills. Both involuntary liens and voluntary liens "run with the land" and will continue against the property until the underlying debt is paid, or assumed in full.

Liens are encumbrances against a property that can be either:
   1) voluntary, or
   2) involuntary.

B. SPECIFIC AND GENERAL LIENS

SPECIFIC LIENS are liens against specifically named property. Generally speaking, specific liens result from unpaid property taxes or from a typical mortgage situation where the seller or the lender takes a lien against a purchaser's residence to secure the repayment of the purchase loan.

GENERAL LIENS are liens against generally all the owner's property, no matter where it is located. Unpaid federal income taxes and judgment liens can become a general lien on all real property.

C. DEED OF TRUST (Security Device – Voluntary and Specific)

A *DEED OF TRUST is the most commonly used device for creating a lien against residential property in Texas. Specifically, it is a written instrument that makes real property collateral for a loan.* The debt, on the other hand, is created by the promissory note that accompanies the deed of trust.

A deed of trust typically involves three parties: the *GRANTOR (typically the owner),* the *TRUSTEE, who receives and holds a limited interest in trust,* and the *BENEFICIARY (usually the lender) for whose benefit the trustee serves.* The deed of trust not only pledges (hypothecates) the property as collateral, or security, for the note but it also contains a *POWER OF SALE, entitling the beneficiary to order the property be sold in the event of a default of the loan.* While the deed of trust is the usual security device for residential property in Texas, many other states, especially eastern states, use a document called a **mortgage**. But regardless of whether the document used is a deed of trust or a mortgage, both documents have the effect of claiming a mortgage on real property. See Chapter 12 for details on deeds of trust and mortgages.

Deeds of trust, as mainly used in Texas, and mortgages, as used in many other states, are "security devices" that make property security for the debt. The accompanying "promissory note" is the evidence of the debt.

D. MECHANIC'S LIENS (Involuntary and Specific)

MECHANIC'S LIENS (sometimes referred to as Mechanic's and Materialman liens, or just M&M liens) are liens that may be involuntarily taken against a property by a person who labors, specially fabricates material, or furnishes labor or material for construction, repair or even demolition of a house, building or improvement. By law, the lien is to secure the payment for unpaid labor and/or services and attaches to the owner's house, building, fixtures, or improvements. Once in place, a mechanic's lien places a cloud upon the owner's title and entitles the lien holder to file suit to foreclose upon the lien.

Like all other liens, Texas law entitles the holder of a mechanic's lien to foreclose on the property if the lien is not paid.

1. Priority and Commencement of the Lien

Lien priority is typically an important consideration for any lien holder because lien priority often determines who will get paid first in the event of a property foreclosure.

Lien holders want to be first in priority.

Under Texas law, a mechanic's lien will "relate back" to the date that construction was first commenced or materials were originally delivered to the jobsite.

In some cases, the relation-back may actually pre-date a mortgage lien, thus giving a mechanic's lien a first priority.

As a tool to help establish this date, Texas law permits the contractor and the owner to voluntarily file an **"affidavit of commencement"** with the county clerk of the county in which the work is to be performed or materials supplied. If the parties agree to file this affidavit, it must be filed no later than 30 days after the work begins or the materials are delivered.

The commencement date contained in the affidavit will be considered evidence of the inception date of the mechanic's lien for priority purposes.

Lien priority is a serious issue with lien holders. Although it is not required by law, the filing of an affidavit of commencement will help establish the date by which the lien legally commences even if the lien is created months later.

2. Liens of an Original Contractor (Non-Residential Contracts)

*An **ORIGINAL CONTRACTOR** is defined as a person who contracts directly with a property owner or through his/her representative.* In many cases, this will be the general

Contrary to popular belief, Texas contractors do not file actual Mechanic's Lien documents. Instead, they file "affidavits" which set out what work was done and how much the contractor is still owed. If these affidavits are timely prepared and filed they will serve as an involuntary lien upon the property.

contractor who, upon securing the job, orders the materials and hires the subcontractors to do the actual work.

In order to create a lien upon property, the unpaid original contractor must file an affidavit with the county clerk in the county where the subject property is located.

Within 5 days of recording the affidavit, the original contractor must mail a copy of the affidavit to the property owner by registered or certified mail.

In lien law, timing is critical. Texas law provides strict deadlines by which an original contractor must file the affidavit in relation to the date when the contractor's indebtedness accrues. A miscalculation of dates could invalidate the lien.

3. Liens of Subcontractors

Unlike original (general) contractors who typically enter into agreements directly with the homeowner, **SUBCONTRACTORS** *(generally called "SUBS")* rarely *contract with property owners. They are, instead, hired by original contractors and usually dependent upon them for payment.*

Although an unpaid "sub" may seek legal recourse against a recalcitrant original contractor, Texas law recognizes that a sub's greatest weapon may be in seeking payment from funds still in the hands of the property owner.

As a result, state law has given subcontractors two powerful and distinct methods to secure payment: the fund trapping lien and statutory retainage.

FUND TRAPPING *is the practice of requiring the property owner to withhold funds directly from the original contractor but for the benefit of the unpaid subcontractors. For this type of lien to apply, state law requires subcontractors to timely send a notice letter to the property owner and/or the original contractor stating that the subcontractor has not been paid and authorizing the property owner to withhold funds which would be normally due to the original contractor.*

If the subcontractor fails to timely provide the notice letter, the property owner will not be held responsible for failing to withhold.

In addition, the law also affords additional protection to the subcontractor by means of **STATUTORY RETAINAGE**, *whereby all property owners are required to hold* back or retain 10% of the contract amount (or value of the work then completed) for 30 days after the work is completed. An owner who fails or refuses to retain could face a lien from the subcontractor against the home, building, fixtures or improvements against all related properties.

> **Statutory Retainage** – A law that requires all property owners to hold back or retain 10% of the contract amount (or value of the work then completed) for 30 days after the work is completed.

Both the "fund trapping lien" and "statutory retainage" represent potential sources of recovery for the unpaid subcontractor. However, these may be of no practical benefit to the sub if the property owner has already completely paid the original contractor.

4. Residential Construction Projects

Special rules apply for mechanic's liens placed on homestead property. Under the law, **RESIDENTIAL CONSTRUCTION PROJECTS** *are defined as projects for the construction or repair of a new or existing residence, including improvements related to the residence.* Before a residential construction contract is signed by the owner, the original contract must provide to the owner a disclosure notice as shown in **Figure 3-2**.

Although the law requires that this disclosure be provided to an owner, the failure to do so will not invalidate a mechanic's lien.

Under Texas law, four conditions must first be met before a contractor can place a lien on homestead property:

1. There must be a written contract which contains all the terms of the agreement;
2. The contract must be signed before the material is furnished or the labor is performed;
3. If the owner is married, the contract must be signed by both spouses; and
4. The contract must be filed for record with the county clerk of the county where the property is located.

Texas law also requires that as a condition of final payment under a residential construction contract, the original contractor must, when the final payment is made, execute and deliver to the property owner an affidavit stating that the original contractor has paid all persons who have supplied labor or materials (known as a "Final Bills-Paid" affidavit).

Figure 3-2

Disclosure Statement Required for Residential Construction Contracts
Texas Property Code §53.255

KNOW YOUR RIGHTS AND RESPONSIBILITIES UNDER THE LAW. You are about to enter into a transaction to build a new home or remodel existing residential property. Texas law requires your contractor to provide you with this brief overview of some of your rights, responsibilities, and risks in this transaction.

CONVEYANCE TO CONTRACTOR NOT REQUIRED. Your contractor may not require you to convey your real property to your contractor as a condition to the agreement for the construction of improvements on your property.

KNOW YOUR CONTRACTOR. Before you enter into your agreement for the construction of improvements to your real property, make sure that you have investigated your contractor. Obtain and verify references from other people who have used the contractor for the type and size of construction project on your property.

GET IT IN WRITING. Make sure that you have a written agreement with your contractor that includes: (1) a description of the work the contractor is to perform; (2) the required or estimated time for completion of the work; (3) the cost of the work or how the cost will be determined; and (4) the procedure and method of payment, including provisions for statutory retainage and conditions for final payment. If your contractor made a promise, warranty, or representation to you concerning the work the contractor is to perform, make sure that promise, warranty, or representation is specified in the written agreement. An oral promise that is not included in the written agreement may not be enforceable under Texas law.

READ BEFORE YOU SIGN. Do not sign any document before you have read and understood it. NEVER SIGN A DOCUMENT THAT INCLUDES AN UNTRUE STATEMENT. Take your time in reviewing documents. If you borrow money from a lender to pay for the improvements, you are entitled to have the loan closing documents furnished to you for review at least one business day before the closing. Do not waive this requirement unless a bona fide emergency or another good cause exists, and make sure you understand the documents before you sign them. If you fail to comply with the terms of the documents, you could lose your property. You are entitled to have your own attorney review any documents. If you have any question about the meaning of a document, consult an attorney.

GET A LIST OF SUBCONTRACTORS AND SUPPLIERS. Before construction commences, your contractor is required to provide you with a list of the subcontractors and suppliers the contractor intends to use on your project. Your contractor is required to supply updated information on any subcontractors and suppliers added after the list is provided. Your contractor is not required to supply this information if you sign a written waiver of your rights to receive this information.

MONITOR THE WORK. Lenders and governmental authorities may inspect the work in progress from time to time for their own purposes. These inspections are not intended as quality control inspections. Quality control is a matter for you and your contractor. To ensure that your home is being constructed in accordance with your wishes and specifications, you should inspect the work yourself or have your own independent inspector review the work in progress.

MONITOR PAYMENTS. If you use a lender, your lender is required to provide you with a periodic statement showing the money disbursed by the lender from the proceeds of your loan. Each time your contractor requests payment from you or your lender for work performed, your contractor is also required to furnish you with a disbursement statement that lists the name and address of each subcontractor or supplier that the contractor intends to pay from the requested funds. Review these statements and make sure that the money is being properly disbursed.

(continued)

CLAIMS BY SUBCONTRACTORS AND SUPPLIERS. Under Texas law, if a subcontractor or supplier who furnishes labor or materials for the construction of improvements on your property is not paid, you may become liable and your property may be subject to a lien for the unpaid amount, even if you have not contracted directly with the subcontractor or supplier. To avoid liability, you should take the following actions:

(1) If you receive a written notice from a subcontractor or supplier, you should withhold payment from your contractor for the amount of the claim stated in the notice until the dispute between your contractor and the subcontractor or supplier is resolved. If your lender is disbursing money directly to your contractor, you should immediately provide a copy of the notice to your lender and instruct the lender to withhold payment in the amount of the claim stated in the notice. If you continue to pay the contractor after receiving the written notice without withholding the amount of the claim, you may be liable and your property may be subject to a lien for the amount you failed to withhold.

(2) During construction and for 30 days after final completion, termination, or abandonment of the contract by the contractor, you should withhold or cause your lender to withhold 10 percent of the amount of payments made for the work performed by your contractor. This is sometimes referred to as "statutory retainage." If you choose not to withhold the 10 percent for at least 30 days after final completion, termination, or abandonment of the contract by the contractor and if a valid claim is timely made by a claimant and your contractor fails to pay the claim, you may be personally liable and your property may be subject to a lien up to the amount that you failed to withhold.

If a claim is not paid within a certain time period, the claimant is required to file a mechanic's lien affidavit in the real property records in the county where the property is located. A mechanic's lien affidavit is not a lien on your property, but the filing of the affidavit could result in a court imposing a lien on your property if the claimant is successful in litigation to enforce the lien claim.

SOME CLAIMS MAY NOT BE VALID. When you receive a written notice of a claim or when a mechanic's lien affidavit is filed on your property, you should know your legal rights and responsibilities regarding the claim. Not all claims are valid. A notice of a claim by a subcontractor or supplier is required to be sent, and the mechanic's lien affidavit is required to be filed, within strict time periods. The notice and the affidavit must contain certain information. All claimants may not fully comply with the legal requirements to collect on a claim. If you have paid the contractor in full before receiving a notice of a claim and have fully complied with the law regarding statutory retainage, you may not be liable for that claim. Accordingly, you should consult your attorney when you receive a written notice of a claim to determine the true extent of your liability or potential liability for that claim.

OBTAIN A LIEN RELEASE AND A BILLS-PAID AFFIDAVIT. When you receive a notice of claim, do not release withheld funds without obtaining a signed and notarized release of lien and claim from the claimant. You can also reduce the risk of having a claim filed by a subcontractor or supplier by requiring as a condition of each payment made by you or your lender that your contractor furnish you with an affidavit stating that all bills have been paid. Under Texas law, on final completion of the work and before final payment, the contractor is required to furnish you with an affidavit stating that all bills have been paid. If the contractor discloses any unpaid bill in the affidavit, you should withhold payment in the amount of the unpaid bill until you receive a waiver of lien or release from that subcontractor or supplier.

OBTAIN TITLE INSURANCE PROTECTION. You may be able to obtain a title insurance policy to insure that the title to your property and the existing improvements on your property are free from liens claimed by subcontractors and suppliers. If your policy is issued before the improvements are completed and covers the value of the improvements to be completed, you should obtain, on the completion of the improvements and as a condition of your final payment, a 'completion of improvements' policy endorsement. This endorsement will protect your property from liens claimed by subcontractors and suppliers that may arise from the date the original title policy is issued to the date of the endorsement.

A contractor signing such an affidavit will be held personally liable for any loss or damage resulting from false or incorrect information and may even face a criminal penalty of a jail term of not more than 1 year.

The Texas mechanic's lien statutes are a complicated area of law. As always, it's best to seek competent legal advice when dealing with contractor's liens.

E. PROPERTY TAX LIENS (Specific Liens)

If property taxes are not paid, a court could order the property foreclosed.

Under the Texas Constitution, unpaid AD VALOREM (property) taxes can result in foreclosure against the taxpayer's property even if it is the taxpayer's homestead.

Unpaid taxes will result in a lien on property as of January 1 of the year they are due and such a lien will take priority against most other liens including mortgage liens.

If the property is foreclosed and sold at a court ordered tax sale, the taxpayer may still be able to repurchase his or her property even after the property is sold.

Under the taxpayer's **STATUTORY RIGHT OF REDEMPTION**, *Texas law provides that the taxpayer may repurchase the property for up to 2 years following the tax sale by reimbursing the purchaser for the bid price, the cost of all taxes paid including penalties and interest, deed recording fees, and a state imposed "redemption premium" of 25% per year.*

Because mortgage lenders stand a very real risk of having their liens defeated by unpaid taxes, home lenders will insist that all property taxes are current when the property is initially acquired and while the property is being financed. They will usually require payments into an escrow account from which the taxes will be paid.

F. JUDGMENTS (Involuntary and General Liens)

A **JUDGMENT** *is a court decision determining the rights of the parties involved and the amount of compensation. A judgment can be appealed.*

For a judgment to become a lien, an **ABSTRACT OF JUDGMENT**, *or formal filing of the judgment*, must be recorded. The judgment then becomes a lien upon all nonexempt property of the debtor. It also becomes a lien on all future property he or she later acquires until the lien is paid. A judgment lien is good for ten years. So, if any property is transferred within this ten-year period, the lien must first be paid off. Under additional court action, the judgment holder may be able to force the debtor to sell the real property to pay off the lien.

A judgment is a general and involuntary lien against all real property owned by the judgment debtor in the county in which the judgment is recorded. Once recorded, it is normally valid for 10 years.

1. Execution of Judgment

Judgments are usually enforced by means of a **WRIT OF EXECUTION**, *which is a court order to sell property to satisfy a judgment*. But not all property can be sold. Texas law spells out which property is exempt from execution. For example, as will be explained later in this chapter, Texas homestead property is exempt from execution by judgment holders except for eight specifically named types of creditors. However, aside from homestead property, most other real property can be sold to satisfy a judgment.

2. Termination of Judgment Lien

Most judgment liens are terminated by the satisfaction of the judgment.

SATISFACTION OF JUDGMENT *is a document indicating that a judgment has been paid in full or part. The judgment may be compensation made by the payment of money or the return of property*. A notice that the judgment has been satisfied should be filed with the clerk of the court. It clears the lien from the record. Sometimes certain properties may be released from the judgment, but only with the judgment holder's consent. This partial release enables an owner to sell a property to satisfy a part of the judgment. A judgment may also be terminated if a bond is posted or if the judge grants a new trial.

Satisfaction of judgment clears the lien from the record.

G. ATTACHMENT (Court–Seized Property)

An **ATTACHMENT** *is a process of the law that creates a lien on real and personal property. It gives custody of property to the courts to assure payment of a pending lawsuit in that county*. This is to assure that there will be enough property to satisfy the judgment should the plaintiff prevail. The **PLANTIFF** *is the person filing a court action to obtain an attachment lien*. The **DEFENDANT** *is the person who is being sued*.

Attachment is available only in connection with an existing lawsuit and in Texas is only available upon certain grounds, such as, for example, where the defendant is about to remove property from the state, the defendant is in hiding, or the defendant has hidden property from his creditors. Although an attachment will create a lien on much of the defendant's property, it will not create a lien against the homestead.

Once a judge issues the attachment, it becomes a lien on real property when it is recorded with the county clerk. Use of the attachment lien is not very common because there are many rules and formalities involved in obtaining this type of lien. This is another area that requires the help of an attorney. The important thing to remember about an attachment lien is that it does exist, and can be a lien on real property.

An attachment is a special judicial remedy available in limited circumstances in connection with a pending lawsuit. When successfully used, it creates a specific and involuntary lien on a defendant's property.

H. COMMERCIAL BROKER AND APPRAISER LIEN
(Involuntary and Specific Lien)

Texas commercial real estate brokers and appraisers are also legally entitled by statute to place liens on commercial real estate in order to protect earned, but unpaid real estate commissions of at least $2,500. For purposes of the lien statutes, commercial real estate is broadly defined to include all real property except for residential or farm and ranch property.

In order to claim a lien on commercial property, a broker's commission must first be "earned" as defined under the law and the broker or appraiser must file a notice of lien.

A commission is considered legally earned when an event occurs under the commission agreement that defines when the commission is earned or when the person who is obligated to pay the commission enters into a purchase contract or lease, whichever is earlier.

The notice of lien must be signed by the broker or the broker's representative, filed with the county clerk and thereafter mailed to the commercial property owner and the prospective buyer, tenant and escrow agent, as may be applicable.

The broker's lien will attach to the property once the notice is filed and will continue until such time as a court orders the lien discharged, the commission is paid, or, as in the case of a pending real estate closing, an escrow account is established or an indemnity bond is posted.

I. LIS PENDENS ("Lawsuit is Pending")

LIS PENDENS is the recording of a notice with the county clerk's office warning all persons that a lawsuit is pending concerning a particular property. Texas law allows lis pendens to be filed during a pending lawsuit involving title to real estate or even during the enforcement of an encumbrance involving real property. When recorded, a lis pendens is notice to the world of its contents and places a cloud on the title of the subject property. As a practical matter, the property may not be marketable until the lis pendens is removed.

A lis pendens is notice of a pending lawsuit that affects title or possession of real property (clouds title) and remains on the public record until judgment is rendered or it is otherwise removed.

III. Items That Affect Physical Use (Non-Money Encumbrances)

A. ITEMS THAT AFFECT PHYSICAL USE

ITEMS THAT AFFECT PHYSICAL USE are non-money encumbrances that affect the physical use of real property. They include: easements, building restrictions, zoning and encroachments, which are conditions that limit the physical use of the property (see **Figure 3-3**).

Figure 3-3

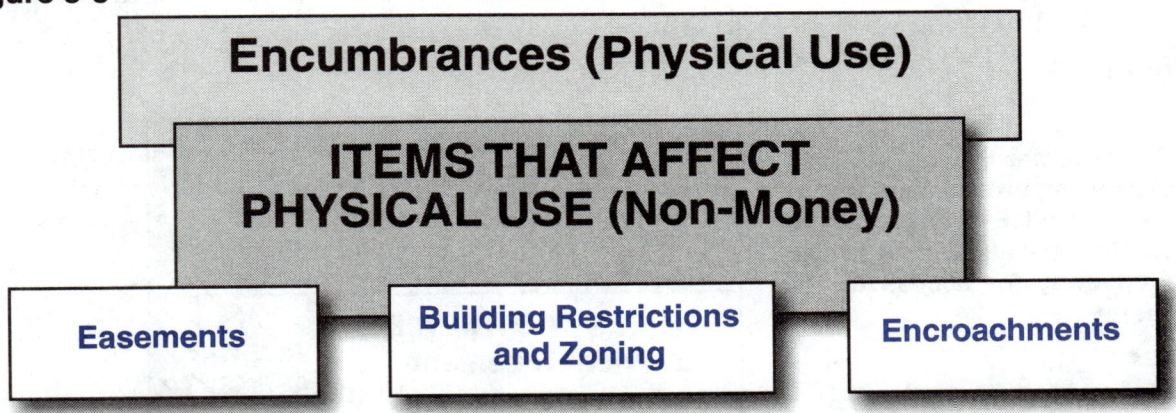

Some encumbrances affect the physical use of the property. They are:

1. Easements
2. Building Restrictions and Zoning
3. Encroachments
4. Leases (see Chapter 8).

1. Easements (The Right to Use Another Person's Land)

An easement is an interest in another's land; it is a right. Easements are non-money encumbrances; they are NOT liens. Land that is burdened with an easement is said to be "encumbered."

An *EASEMENT* is an interest in land owned by another person consisting in the right to use or control the land, or an area above or below it, for a specific, limited purpose. The right to enter is called *INGRESS* and the right to exit is *EGRESS*. Easements are of two types: (1) easements appurtenant and (2) easements in gross.

An easement is the right to use another's land. It is a right, interest or privilege, but NOT an estate.

a. Easement Appurtenant (Runs With the Land)

An easement is said to be appurtenant, which means the easement "belongs to" or "runs with the land." (Easements are non-exclusive, meaning the owner can still use the land.) The new buyer would have the "same rights" to the easement as did the seller.

An *EASEMENT APPURTENANT* is an easement "created for and beneficial to" the owner of adjoining or attached lands. An easement is real property, not personal property, but it is not an estate. In this case there are two parcels of land, with one owner giving another owner an easement. The *DOMINANT TENEMENT* is the land that obtains the benefits of an easement. **Figure 3-4** is an illustration of a driveway easement. Owner A's land is the dominant tenement and Owner B's land is the servient tenement.

Figure 3-4

Property owner B owns the land the easement crosses but cannot block or hinder in any way the right of property owner A to use the driveway for access to his property.

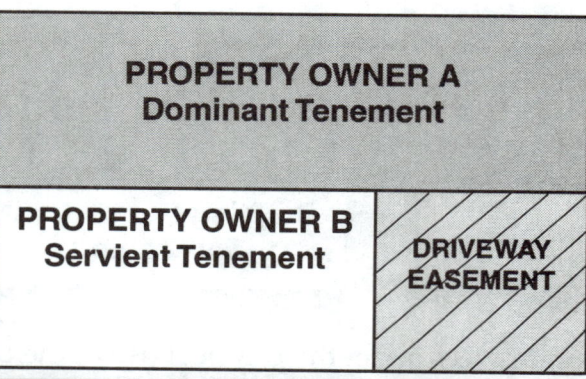

The dominant tenement is the land that benefits; the owner is the party who can terminate the easement, which does not expire for non-use.

A *SERVIENT TENEMENT is the land that gives the easement (use of the land) for the benefit of another.* The appurtenant easement belongs to the land and is transferred with the land. This easement cannot be transferred separately from the land.

> The **SERVIENT TENEMENT** is the land on which the easement is located. It can thus be said that the servient tenement "serves" the dominant tenement.

The owner of the servient tenement CANNOT revoke the easement; it must "serve" the dominant tenement, even if not used.

b. Easement in Gross (Does Not Benefit Adjoining Landowner)

An example of an easement in gross would be an easement for the telephone company (utility company) to enter the property to run telephone lines. Easements in gross do NOT benefit adjoining lands.

An *EASEMENT IN GROSS is not attached to any particular land or dominant tenement.* It is an easement created for the benefit of others who do not own adjoining or attached lands. It is a personal property right. Even though it is a personal right, there are still servient tenements. An example of an easement in gross would be a utility company obtaining the right to run natural gas lines across your land. In this instance your land would become a servient tenement.

An easement that does not specify a special area for a right-of-way is also valid. *A property owner could give the right to cross his/her land and not limit how or where a person would have to cross. This is known as an UNLOCATED EASEMENT.*

c. Creation of an Easement

Easements are created in three basic ways:

1. Express Grant (in writing)
2. Implication of Law (implied easement)
3. Long Use (prescription)

IN WRITING (RESERVED), AS IN A DEED OR CONTRACT. If a property is transferred as part of the deed, an easement appurtenant to the land would be included in the grant. The same thing is accomplished by transferring a property, but reserving an easement over the land. A written contract can create an easement between the parties. For legal protection, this contract should be acknowledged and recorded.

IMPLICATION OF LAW (IMPLIED EASEMENT). If an easement is implied in a transfer, or if it is necessary for use of the land, then the easement is said to be implied by law. The right to use the land for obtaining minerals implies that you have the right of surface entry in order to extract the minerals.

If surface entry is denied to someone with an implied easement, the damaged party should file a quiet title action in court to perfect title.

EASEMENT BY NECESSITY *(involving landlocked property) is an easement that is absolutely necessary for access.* If a person is sold property that landlocks that person, he or she may acquire an easement by necessity. When the grantor transfers a portion of his or her land that leaves the grantee totally surrounded by the grantor (transferor), the grantor can be forced to give an easement of access to the grantee. An easement by necessity does not have to be the most convenient way of entering the property. If the grantee later acquires another access to his or her property, the easement by necessity is then terminated.

LONG USE (EASEMENT BY PRESCRIPTION). Prescription is an easement to continue using land by virtue of having used it for a long period of time.

In Texas, a prescriptive easement can be obtained after ten years of uninterrupted use of another's land. There is no confrontation with the owner or property tax payments required.

Possession for ten continuous years can create a prescriptive easement, as long as there is:

1. open and notorious use;
2. uninterrupted use for five out of the ten years;
3. hostile (without permission of the owner); and
4. under a claim of right or color of title.

Easements by prescription are without the permission of the landowner.

d. Transfer of an Easement

Easements are transferred automatically if they are easements appurtenant. Easements in gross can be transferred only by express agreement, providing the easement is not made to a specific individual. An easement should be recorded. If it is not recorded, and the purchaser does not have knowledge of an easement, then the easement may not be considered to have been transferred with the property.

e. Termination of an Easement

Easements may be terminated in several ways:

1. **EXPRESS RELEASE** – Any written agreement can terminate an easement, but the usual form is a quitclaim deed. The servient tenement is the only one that could benefit from the termination of an easement.

2. **MERGER OF DOMINANT AND SERVIENT TENEMENTS** – An easement is automatically terminated when the dominant and servient tenements merge into a common, or single, ownership. The easement can be created again if any part of the property is later transferred to a "separate owner."

3. **EXCESSIVE USE** – The courts have held that excessive use of an easement that increases the burden on the servient tenement may be forfeited through a court injunction. If the dominant tenement refuses to correct the excessive use, and misuses of the easement can be established, the easement can be terminated. An example would be a dominant tenement owner allowing the entire neighborhood to use the easement as a through-street.

4. **ABANDONMENT AND NON-USE** – If there is an obvious intent of an easement holder to abandon his or her easement, then that person may lose the easement through court action. Because abandonment requires proof of intent, mere non-use may be insufficient.

Proving that an easement has been abandoned may be difficult because proof of "intent to abandon" will be required. As a practical matter, this type of proof may be hard to come by.

5. **DESTRUCTION OF SERVIENT TENEMENT** – When a governing body, by exercising the right of eminent domain, takes servient tenement property for its own use, the dominant tenement easement is considered automatically terminated.

f. Compare with License

A *LICENSE is the revocable permission to enter a licensor's land to do something that would otherwise be illegal, such as parking your car on your neighbor's driveway. Like an easement, a license is a right to use someone else's property, however, unlike an easement, a license can be revoked.*

To sum up:

- Easements are a right to use land (NOT an estate in land).
- Easements are NOT liens, they are encumbrances.
- Easements are usually created by deed or prescription.
- Easements are classified as appurtenant or in gross.

2. Building Restrictions (CC&Rs) and Zoning

These restrictions can be categorized as: 1) "private deed restrictions," such as those placed on a property by the grantor or developer, or 2) "public restrictions," such as city zoning laws. The restrictions that are the most restrictive will always control the use of the property.

PRIVATE DEED RESTRICTIONS *limit the use or occupancy of the land.* A typical restriction would be to limit the types of buildings on a given piece of land to single-family residences. Also, a restriction might require future construction to meet specific standards. For example, all houses erected on a property must be at least 5,000 square feet. Another example might be a setback requirement, which would require any structure to be set back a certain number of feet from the street or adjoining property.

There are three types of private building restrictions: Covenants, Conditions, and Restrictions (CC&Rs). They are usually included in the deed at the time the property is subdivided, or may be created by a written contract and are listed in the recorded declaration of restrictions. Their main purpose is to keep use of the land uniform throughout certain tracts of land. Subdivisions and condominiums usually include deed restrictions as a method to promote the aesthetics and economics of the project. These private deed restrictions and bylaws are usually recorded separately, and are only referenced in the original grant deeds.

Private restrictions are written agreements to establish private land use controls which are part of a developer's general plan.

a. Covenants (Promise Broken, Sue for Damages)

A **COVENANT** *is a clause in a contract that obligates or restricts the parties, and, if broken, can result in a legal action.* For instance, a property could sell with a covenant stating that the property shall never be used to sell alcoholic beverages. If the covenant is broken, the usual court remedy would be an action for money damages. A court may also grant an injunction requiring compliance with the covenant.

A condo association CANNOT prohibit the placing of a "for sale" sign (a restraint of trade), but can dictate the size, color, and location of sign.

b. Conditions (More Stringent than Breaking a Covenant – Can Lose Title)

CONDITIONS *are promises to do or not to do something, the failure of which may terminate the contract.* **The penalty for not following the set conditions is the reversion of the property to the grantor.** This penalty is so stiff that most courts will treat a condition as a covenant unless the terms are clearly stated in the deed or other contract. For a complete discussion of conditions, see Chapter 5.

The private enforcement of deed restrictions is extremely important in Houston, as it is the largest city in the nation without zoning.

c. Governmental Restrictions (Zoning)

PUBLIC RESTRICTIONS are limits made by governmental agencies, usually by cities and counties, in the form of zoning.

"Public restrictions" promote health, safety, morals, and general welfare of the public. This is the use of police power.

PRIVATE RESTRICTIONS are made by the present or previous landowners and are created only for their benefit. On the other hand, ZONING RESTRICTIONS are created by and for the benefit of the general public to insure its health, safety, comfort, and morals.

Cities and counties can divide land into districts for control over local property through local laws that enforce zoning, building codes, and other subdivision land use regulations.

ZONING is the restriction on the use of private property by the local government agency. Zoning dictates how the property can be used, the setbacks required and the height limit on any structures.

Private restrictions, on the other hand, are placed on the property by the grantor or developer.

If there are two restrictions, the most restrictive of the two will take precedence.

For example, if a developer sets a deed restriction of 15,000 square feet to a lot but zoning only allows 10,000 square feet per lot, the zoning is more restrictive and would prevail.

d. Race Restrictions (Illegal)

In 1948, the United States Supreme Court in the landmark case of *Shelley v. Kraemer* ruled that restrictive covenants based upon race violated the Fourteenth Amendment to the Constitution.

In addition, Texas law also prohibits property restrictions based upon race.

> If a restriction that affects real property, or a provision in a deed that conveys real property or an interest in real property... prohibits the use by or the sale, lease or transfer to a person because of race, color, religion or national origin, the provision or restriction is void.
>
> **§ 5.026 – Texas Property Code**

Texas law instructs courts to dismiss any suit, or any part of a suit, that seeks to enforce such a void provision.

Race restrictions on a property by a grantor (past or present) are unenforceable and illegal.

3. Encroachments

As stated earlier, an *ENCROACHMENT is the wrongful, unauthorized placement of improvements or permanent fixtures on property by a non-owner of that property.* It is similar to *TRESPASS in that a trespass is the wrongful entry onto a person's property by a person,* while an encroachment is the wrongful entry by someone's property.

If one neighbor builds a driveway over another neighbor's property, it is considered an encroachment.

Often fences, walls or buildings may extend over the recognized boundary line. However, the encroachment could also consist of invading vegetation such as the limbs or roots of a tree or even grasses.

In Texas, a property owner faced with an encroachment may take the following action:

1. In some cases, physically remove the encroachment (for example, trim the offending branches from a neighbor's tree);
2. Request a court order to enjoin (stop) the encroachment;
3. Sue for money damages; and/or
4. Sue for trespass to try title to determine the title of the encroaching property.

Regardless of which legal remedy is pursued, an encroachment will legally limit the use of your property.

When buying a house, it's always a good idea to purchase title insurance to guard against defects or problems with title. However, it is important to remember that the standard Texas title insurance policy will not cover against encroachments unless such coverage is specifically requested, a survey is supplied to the title company, and an additional premium is paid.

IV. Your Residence as Homestead
(Protects Against Many Types of Creditors)

Although a homestead is not an encumbrance, it is appropriately discussed at this point because of the protection it provides to Texas homeowners. A *HOMESTEAD is a special provision under the Texas Constitution that allows homeowners to protect their homes from forced sale to satisfy their debts, within certain limits.* This protection extends to all debts **except** for the following:

1. The unpaid purchase price remaining;
2. Taxes due on the property;
3. A lien based on the partition (division) of the property due to a court order;
4. The refinancing of a lien against the homestead;
5. An unpaid mechanic's or materialman's lien against the homestead;
6. A home equity loan;
7. A reverse mortgage (a special type of mortgage loan available to homeowners who are, or whose spouses are 62 years of age or older); and
8. The conversion or refinance of a personal property lien on a manufactured home to that of a lien on real property.

Additionally, Texas law allows homeowners' associations to conduct foreclosure sales of homestead property in certain situations. Under the Texas Residential Property Owner's Protection Act, a mandatory owners' association may foreclose a lien against delinquent homeowners only if the association is authorized to collect regular or special assessments. Following a foreclosure sale, a homeowner then has 180 days to redeem the homestead property by repaying all assessments with interest, along with other costs incurred by the association.

Upon the sale of the homestead, the proceeds of sale are exempt from seizure for six months after the date of sale.

A. LIMITS OF THE TEXAS HOMESTEAD

For purposes of a rural home, a family (husband and wife) may claim a homestead not to exceed 200 acres, within one or more parcels, including all improvements thereon. For a single adult, the rural homestead is 100 acres together with all improvements.

For purposes of an urban home, the homestead, regardless of whether for a family or single adult, is limited to only 10 acres together with all improvements. A homestead is considered to be urban if:

1. The property is located within a municipality or its extra-territorial jurisdiction, or a platted subdivision; and

2. The property is served by police and fire protection and any three of the following services provided by a municipality:

   a. electric
   b. natural gas
   c. sewer
   d. storm sewer; and
   e. water

You may have only one homestead at any given time.

B. DECLARATION OF HOMESTEAD

In order to claim the protections offered by the homestead laws, a Texas resident need do nothing at all. These are protections guaranteed to all residents under the Texas Constitution.

Although it is not required, a Texas resident may voluntarily designate a particular tract or tracts as his/her homestead by filing a DESIGNATION OF HOMESTEAD with the county clerk.

A Designation of Homestead must be signed, acknowledged before a notary, and recorded to be valid. A Designation of Homestead must contain the following elements:

1. A legal description of the subject property;

2. A statement by the claimant that the subject property is designated as his or her homestead;

3. The name of the current owner of the subject property; and

4. If the property is a rural homestead, the number of acres designated as the homestead.

Often, a mortgage company will require a homeowner to execute a Designation of Homestead at or prior to closing. Although this serves to protect the homeowner from the forced sale of the home by other creditors, it also serves to protect the collateral interest of the mortgage company.

C. DISTINGUISHED FROM A HOMESTEAD TAX EXEMPTION

Many Texas taxing jurisdictions grant a homestead property exemption to persons and families who occupy their own homes. However, this is not the same as the homestead protection granted under the Texas Constitution. These are two distinct concepts.

A homestead exemption for property tax purposes merely means that the taxpayer may receive a reduction on taxes because he or she is living in his or her own home before January 1. A constitutional homestead, on the other hand, means that the home is exempt from forced sale, except for those specific circumstances previously listed.

Unfortunately, many people are under the impression that if they somehow lose their tax exemption, they have lost their constitutional homestead status. This is simply not true.

A person might temporarily lose his or her homestead tax exemption by forgetting to file a Homestead Exemption Application with the local appraisal district office. This can be easily rectified by filing the form at no cost to the taxpayer. However, terminating the homestead protection guaranteed by the Texas Constitution is quite another thing.

D. TERMINATION OF HOMESTEAD

A homestead may be terminated by various means. While the mere removal or destruction of any dwellings located upon the subject property will not terminate a homestead, a sale or other conveyance of the property will.

Under very limited circumstances, a homestead may also be terminated by means of **abandonment**. The reason for abandoning a homestead is to allow the homeowner the privilege of obtaining another homestead on a new residence.

If a homestead claimant is married, the homestead cannot be abandoned without the consent of the claimant's spouse.

Finally, if the person claiming a homestead dies, that does not terminate the homestead rights of the surviving spouse. Under the law, the surviving spouse may continue to enjoy the benefits of homestead protection for so long as he or she chooses to occupy the property as a homestead.

V. CHAPTER SUMMARY

An **encumbrance** is a burden to a property that limits its use by either: 1) **money owed (liens)** or 2) **items that affect the physical use of the property (non-money)**. All liens are "encumbrances," but not all encumbrances are liens. A **blanket lien** is a voluntary lien placed over more than one property, and usually has a partial release clause for one or more of the parcels.

A **lien** is a document that uses a property to secure the payment of a debt or the discharge of an obligation. Liens may be **voluntary** or **involuntary**. They may also be **specific** or **general**.

Deeds of trust are the security devices that make real property security for a debt in Texas, and are considered personal property. The accompanying **promissory note** is the evidence of the debt.

If the people who supply labor or materials for construction on a property are not paid, they can claim a **mechanic's lien** against that the owner's property. It is a specific and involuntary lien, and once fixed can have priority over all other liens except property taxes. Before claiming a mechanic's lien, an **original contractor** must first file an **affidavit** with the county clerk setting forth a description of the unpaid work or materials provided.

In order for a contractor to gain a priority over non-tax liens, it is important to establish the **starting date** of the work or materials supplied. An **Affidavit of Commencement** should be recorded by the owner and contractor within 30 days of commencement of the work. For residential construction contracts, Texas law also requires that as a condition of final payment, the original contractor must, when the final payment is made, execute and deliver to the property owner a **Final Bills-Paid affidavit**.

Property taxes and mechanic's liens are **specific liens**, meaning against just one property, whereas income taxes and judgments are **general liens**, covering all the properties of an owner. A judgment is a general and involuntary lien against all real property in the county in which the judgment is recorded, and is good for ten years. A **satisfaction of judgment** is made by payment of money or return of property and clears the lien from the record.

An **attachment** (lien) creates a specific and involuntary lien on one property to assure payment of a pending lawsuit. A **lis pendens** is a notice of a pending lawsuit that affects title (clouds title) and remains on the public record until judgment is rendered or suit is dismissed. If a person does not pay off a judgment, he or she may be forced to sell the property under a court order called a **writ of execution**.

Items that affect physical use of a property are **non-money encumbrances** and include: 1) easements, 2) restrictions, 3) encroachments, and 4) leases.

An **easement** is the right to enter, use and exit another person's land for certain purpose. If it runs with the land it is an **easement appurtenant**. The **dominant tenement** is the land that benefits from the easement that the **servient tenement** gives up. An **easement in gross** benefits others who do not own adjoining or attached lands (like a utility company running a gas line across a property).

Easements can be created by: 1) deed (writing), 2) implication of law (implied easement or easement by necessity), or 3) prescription (long use). They can also be terminated in several ways, including: 1) express release, 2) merger of dominant and servient tenements, 3) excessive use, 4) abandonment and non-use, and 5) destruction of servient tenement.

Restrictions can be private deed restrictions, or public restrictions. **Covenants, conditions, and restrictions (CC&Rs)** are private building restrictions. **Public restrictions** are limits made by governmental agencies and are meant to promote health, safety, morals, and general welfare of the public (police power). **Zoning** is a public restriction dictating how property can be used. An **encroachment** is the wrongful, unauthorized placement of improvements or permanent fixtures on a property by a non-owner.

A **homestead** is not an encumbrance. Homestead laws are a provision of the Texas Constitution that allows homeowners to protect their homes from forced sale from all creditors except for the following: the unpaid purchase price remaining, unpaid property taxes, a court ordered partition lien, the refinancing of the homestead, unpaid mechanic's liens, a reverse mortgage, and converted manufactured home liens.

A homestead may be terminated by: 1) abandonment or 2) the sale of the homesteaded property. While death may terminate the rights of the homestead claimant, this does not terminate the rights of the surviving spouse in the family homestead.

VI. TERMINOLOGY

A. Abandonment
B. Abstract of Judgment
C. Affidavit of Commencement
D. Attachment
E. Blanket Encumbrance
F. Conditions
G. Covenant
H. Declaration of Homestead
I. Deed of Trust
J. Dominant Tenement
K. Easement

L. Easement Appurtenant
M. Easement in Gross
N. Encroachment
O. Encumbrance
P. Fund Trapping
Q. General Lien
R. Homestead
S. Lien
T. Lis Pendens
U. Materialman
V. Mechanic's Lien

W. Mortgage
X. Release of Lien
Y. Restrictions
Z. Servient Tenement
AA. Specific Lien
BB. Statutory Retainage
CC. Subs
DD. Writ of Execution

1. ____ A non-revocable right, limited to a specific use, that one party has in the land of another.

2. ____ A constitutional protection of a home from the claims of certain creditors and judgment lien holders.

3. ____ Anything that affects or limits the fee simple title to, or value of, property, e.g., mortgages or easements.

4. ____ A voluntary affidavit which helps establish the start date of a construction project for lien priority purposes.

5. ____ A limitation on the use of real property. These limitations fall into two general classifications - public and private. Zoning ordinances are public, while a clause in the deed requiring the roof to be made of Spanish red title would be a private limitation.

6. ____ The process by which real or personal property is seized by the court for the purpose of assuring payment.

7. ____ A form of encumbrance that usually makes specific property security for the payment of a debt.

8. ____ Discharge of a Deed of Trust from the public record upon payment of the debt.

9. ____ A limiting restriction stating that upon the happening or not happening of some stated event, the estate shall be changed in some manner.

10. ____ A clause in a contract obligating or restricting the parties, that, if broken, can result in legal action.

11. ____ A law that requires all property owners to hold back or retain 10% of the contract amount for 30 days after the work is completed.

12. ____ An instrument commonly used outside of Texas, especially the eastern states, by which residential property is hypothecated to secure the payment of a debt.

13. ____ Subcontractors.

14. ____ A recorded document of the essential provisions of a court judgment which creates a lien.

15. ____ A lien, created by statute, which exists against real property in favor of persons who have performed work or furnished materials for the improvement of real property.

16. ____ A legal document used in Texas by which a borrower pledges certain real property as collateral for the repayment of a loan. In addition to the borrower and the lender, there is a third party to the transaction known as a trustee.

17. ____ A voluntary affidavit that designates a particular tract or tracts as a person's homestead in Texas.

18. ____ A lien covering more than one property of the borrower.

19. ____ A statute which requires property owners to hold back or retain 10% of the contract price (or value of the work completed) for 30 days after the work is completed in order to protect subcontractors.

20. ____ A method of terminating a homestead which requires the consent of the spouse.
21. ____ A person who supplies materials to a property for purposes of construction, repair or even demolition.
22. ____ Improvements which overlap onto the property of another.
23. ____ An easement for the benefit of the owner of an adjacent parcel of land.
24. ____ Real property that benefits from an easement.
25. ____ A writ to carry out a court order, usually arising from a judgment.
26. ____ A property that is burdened by an easement held by an adjoining landowner.
27. ____ An easement for the benefit of a person or utility company rather than for the benefit of adjacent landowners.
28. ____ A notice filed or recorded for the purpose of warning all persons that the title to certain real property is in litigation.
29. ____ A lien such as a tax lien or judgment lien that attaches to all property of the debtor rather than a specific property.
30. ____ A lien that attaches to a specific property rather than all the property of the debtor.

VII. MULTIPLE CHOICE

1. A mechanic's lien is:
   - a. a general lien.
   - b. a voluntary lien.
   - c. a non-money encumbrance.
   - d. created by affidavit.

2. Unpaid property taxes may result in a(n):
   - a. voluntary lien.
   - b. attachment lien.
   - c. specific lien.
   - d. general lien.

3. An easement appurtenant:
   - a. runs with the land.
   - b. cannot be transferred.
   - c. has a separate conveyance.
   - d. does not benefit the adjoining land.

4. If you fail to pay a subcontractor and he or she claims a mechanic's lien, the lien is:
   - a. specific.
   - b. general.
   - c. voluntary.
   - d. both a and b.

5. Homesteads allow homeowners, in some cases, to protect their homes from forced:
   - a. robbery.
   - b. sale to pay debts.
   - c. condemnation.
   - d. eminent domain.

6. A post judgment sale CANNOT be the result of a(n):
   - a. judgment.
   - b. court action.
   - c. writ of execution.
   - d. easement.

7. Which of the following is true with regard to a homestead?

    a. A homestead will not protect forced sale due to unpaid property taxes
    b. It is guaranteed as a matter of law
    c. One property at a time can be homesteaded
    d. All of the above

8. A document using property to secure the payment of debt is called a:

    a. lien.
    b. cloud on title.
    c. grant deed.
    d. reconveyance.

9. Which of the following would be considered a voluntary lien?

    a. Special assessment
    b. Tax lien
    c. Attachment
    d. Deed of trust

10. A Texas broker may claim a lien:

    a. on commercial property.
    b. by filing a broker's lien with the county clerk.
    c. for work performed and materials supplied.
    d. for an unpaid commission that is yet to be earned.

ANSWERS: 1. d; 2. c; 3. a; 4. a; 5. b; 6. d; 7. d; 8. a; 9. d; 10. a

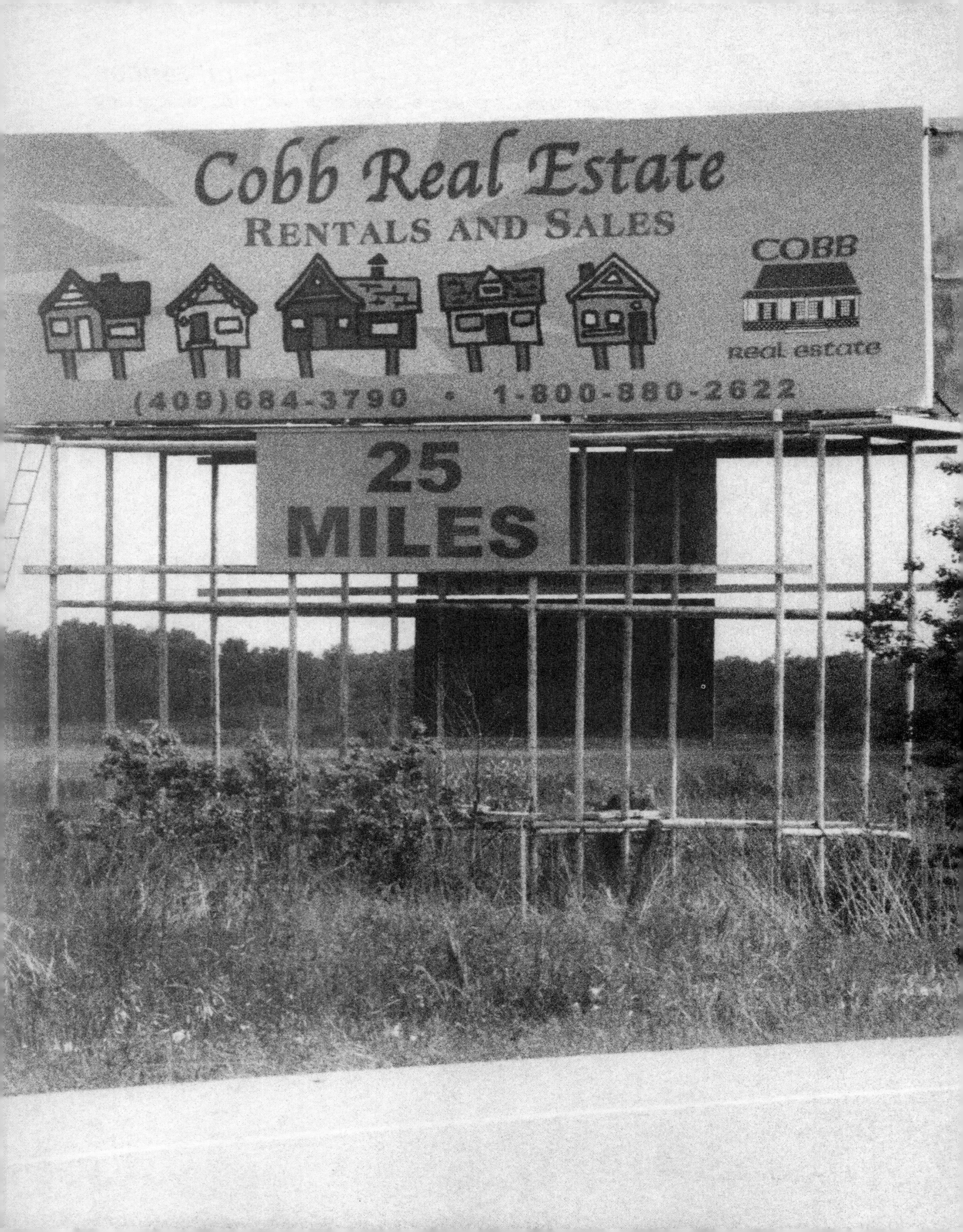
Cobb Real Estate
RENTALS AND SALES
COBB
real estate
(409)684-3790 • 1-800-880-2622
25
MILES

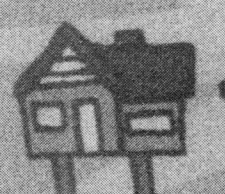

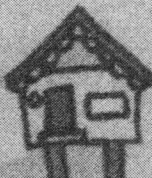

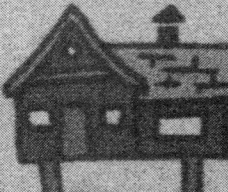

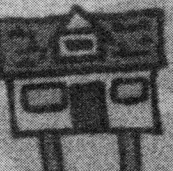

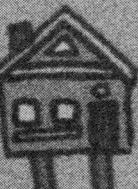

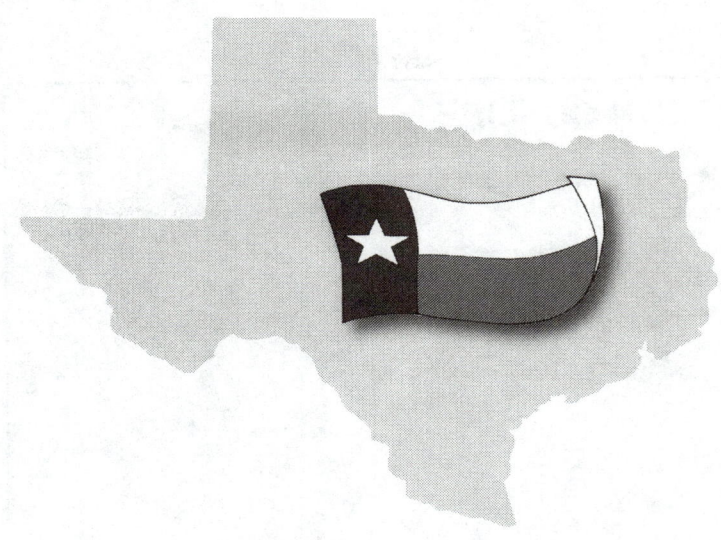

Chapter 4
Agency and Its Responsibility

I. Introduction

A. AGENCY DEFINED

AGENCY is that special relationship which results from one person (the principal) consenting that another person (the agent) act on his behalf and be subject to his/her control. This relationship also requires that the agent agree to act for the principal.

For an agency relationship to be formed, both elements of the principal-agent definition must be met; otherwise no agency status can exist. There must be a delegation of authority by the principal which is communicated to the agent, and an acceptance of that authority by the agent which is communicated back to the principal. Under the law of agency, there is no required form for the principal's designation of authority, but what is critical is that the delegation and acceptance be clear and definite.

Agency law consists of the common law, state statutes, and the rules of the Texas Real Estate Commission that govern this complex relationship between principal and agent. Although the rules of the commission are not laws, the courts have held that the rules have the force of law for Texas real estate licensees.

CHAPTER 4 OUTLINE

In a transaction where real estate licensees are used, it is the broker who serves as agent. Other licensees may perform most of the work, but in reality they work for the broker. These other licensees act in the name of and for the benefit of their sponsoring broker.

1. Agent

An *AGENT is the person who agrees to act for a principal.* The agent is given authority from the principal.

2. Principal

The *PRINCIPAL is the person who wishes for someone to act on his/her behalf. From the viewpoint of the agent, this person is also known as the CLIENT.* On the one hand, if the principal is a buyer, then the agent represents the buyer. On the other hand, if the principal is the seller, the agent represents the seller.

3. Customer

A *CUSTOMER is a third party who falls outside of the principal-agent relationship.* If the agent represents the seller, for example, a customer would be any third party who is interested in the property. A customer could also be a person represented by another agent.

B. LEGAL EFFECT OF AN AGENCY RELATIONSHIP

A principal who delegates authority to an agent is bound by an agent's authorized actions. For example, suppose that a factory owner authorizes its sales manager to negotiate and sign a contract to deliver a truck load of widgets. The sales manager's signature on the contract binds the factory owner to the terms of the agreement, just as though the owner had signed it himself. However, as will be discussed below, while most Texas real estate agents are authorized to act on behalf of a buyer or seller, they are typically not authorized to enter into contracts on behalf their clients.

Not only will an agent's acts be binding on the principal, but an agent's *wrongful acts* can be attributed to the principal as well, so that the principal may be legally responsible.

Yet another legal effect of the agency relationship is that the knowledge of the agent can be credited to the principal. Suppose that a third party discloses an important item of information to an agent. The principal may then be held to have known it, regardless of whether the agent actually passed the information along to the principal. *In other words, to tell the agent is to tell the principal.*

Agency status connotes much more than having one person act for another. Once this relationship is established, the law creates certain duties and obligations, and imposes upon the parties consequences for their actions regardless of whether the result was intended.

C. TYPES OF AGENTS

Agents may be classified according to the scope of authority the principal has conferred upon the agent. An agent may be one of three types: universal, general, or special agent.

1. Universal Agents

A *UNIVERSAL AGENT has the authority to perform every type of transaction that a principal may lawfully delegate to the agent.* This is a very broad grant of authority, for it delegates all decision-making authority to the agent. *Typically, this is done through a signed document known as a POWER OF ATTORNEY. The person granted the authority is called an ATTORNEY-IN-FACT.*

A good example of this type of agency relationship would be when an elderly parent wishes that his adult child manage all of his personal and financial affairs. To do so, the parent, as principal, signs a power of attorney which authorizes his adult child as the agent to act for him and in his place. The power of attorney contains the language which spells out the scope of the agent's authority.

2. General Agents

Like a universal agent, a general agent is authorized to act on behalf of a principal; however, here the *GENERAL AGENT can only perform acts specifically designated by the principal.* Under a general agency, the agent may take all appropriate actions necessary to accomplish the designated act even if these actions are not spelled out.

A good example of this type of agency is the relationship between a broker and an associated salesperson. The salesperson has the authority to represent the broker in a wide range of activities, but only in connection with real estate brokerage activities that the broker permits.

3. Special Agents

A *SPECIAL AGENT has even more limited authority than the general agent. Here, the authority granted is restricted only to the acts permitted by the principal and is very limited in scope of authority.* In the real estate field, special agents cannot typically enter into any contracts on behalf of the principal.

A prime example of special agency is the listing agreement under which brokers operate. Listing agreements only delegate to the agent the authority to market and sell the property, but nothing more. In this case, the sole job of the licensee is to offer the property for sale and to bring offers to the owner. The agent typically does not have authority to accept any contract offer on behalf of the principal.

C. TYPICAL AGENCY RELATIONSHIPS WITHIN A REAL ESTATE TRANSACTION

It is possible to have as many as four agency relationships within a single real estate transaction. Assuming that the buyer and the seller each have their own real estate agents, there are two special agency relationships present. Assuming further that each broker-agent employs a sales associate, two other general agency relationships are present. Altogether there may be up to four agency relationships within any given real estate transaction. These relationships will be detailed later in the chapter.

With so many relationships possible within a given transaction, it is important to understand how these relationships are legally formed and terminated.

II. How Agency is Created

An agency relationship can be created in one of several ways. For example, a principal may directly authorize an agent to act on his/her behalf. This is the way that most agency relationships are created. But agency authority can also be given even after the agent has acted. In either case, the principal intentionally consents to the actions taken.

On the other hand, an agency relationship can also exist, even if unintended, if innocent third parties have been led to believe that the agent is authorized to act on behalf of the principal when in fact the agent is not so authorized.

It is important to remember that the promise of, or payment of, a commission is never a factor in determining whether an agency relationship has been created.

A. EXPRESS AGENCY

An *EXPRESS AGENCY relationship is created when the agency is expressly created between the parties either orally or in writing*. There is clear understanding of the terms of the agency relationship.

1. Written Agreements

A written real estate listing agreement is not only a good example of how an express agency agreement is created but it is also the preferred manner of creating agency relationships.

a. Between Brokers and Sellers

The Texas Association of REALTORS® (TAR) has created a number of agency contracts for use by its members. **Figure 4-1** shows the TAR Residential Real Estate Listing Agreement, Exclusive Right to Sell, which is intended only for TAR members and their seller/landlord clients. Use of these forms by any other person is strictly prohibited without the express consent of the TAR.

b. Between Brokers and Buyers

By the same token, brokers who wish to represent residential buyers and tenants may also enter into express agency agreements. A complete buyer's representation agreement will be shown later in this chapter.

c. Between Brokers and Associates

TAR has additionally prepared a written contract form for creating an agency relationship between broker and sales associates. This will also be discussed later in this chapter.

2. Oral Agreements

While agency may be created by an express oral communication, this is extremely risky for real estate licensees. First of all, it is difficult to prove the existence of an oral agreement in a court of law. But more importantly, as will be seen in Chapter 6 in The Real Estate License Act, a written commission agreement is legally necessary to enforce payment in a court of law.

If an agency relationship is created only orally, the broker will still be required to perform carefully and competently regardless of his/her ability to get paid.

B. IMPLIED AGENCY

An agency relationship can also be implied without the necessity of an express agreement. In this case, implied agency is inferred *by the conduct of the parties.* However, as stated above, because a written agreement is necessary for an agent to enforce a commission payment, this method of agency holds risk for the agent.

Gratuitous Agency is not a form of agency relationship, but rather describes an agency relationship that is formed as a favor or without compensation for the agent.

This holds risk for the agent because he/she will be held to the same standard of care and responsibility as if he/she had been fully compensated.

C. AGENCY BY RATIFICATION

An agency relationship can also be created when a principal gives "after the fact" approval to something that was originally done without authorization. As stated above, normally agency relationships are established

TEXAS ASSOCIATION OF REALTORS®

RESIDENTIAL REAL ESTATE LISTING AGREEMENT
EXCLUSIVE RIGHT TO SELL

USE OF THIS FORM BY PERSONS WHO ARE NOT MEMBERS OF THE TEXAS ASSOCIATION OF REALTORS® IS NOT AUTHORIZED.
©Texas Association of REALTORS®, Inc. 2003

1. PARTIES: The parties to this agreement (this Listing) are:

Seller: _____

_____

Address: _____
City, State, Zip: _____
Phone: _____ Fax: _____
E-Mail: _____

Broker: _____
Address: _____
City, State, Zip. _____
Phone: _____ Fax: _____
E-Mail: _____

Seller appoints Broker as Seller's sole and exclusive real estate agent and grants to Broker the exclusive right to sell the Property.

2. PROPERTY: "Property" means the land, improvements, and accessories described below, except for any described exclusions.

   A. <u>Land:</u> Lot_____, Block_____, _____
_____ Addition, City _____,
in _____ County, Texas known as _____
_____ (address/zip code),
or as described on attached exhibit. *(If Property is a condominium, attach Condominium Addendum.)*

   B. <u>Improvements:</u> The house, garage and all other fixtures and improvements attached to the above-described real property, including without limitation, the following permanently installed and built-in items, if any: all equipment and appliances, valances, screens, shutters, awnings, wall-to-wall carpeting, mirrors, ceiling fans, attic fans, mail boxes, television antennas and satellite dish system and equipment, heating and air-conditioning units, security and fire detection equipment, wiring, plumbing and lighting fixtures, chandeliers, water softener system, kitchen equipment, garage door openers, cleaning equipment, shrubbery, landscaping, outdoor cooking equipment, and all other property owned by Seller and attached to the above-described real property.

   C. <u>Accessories:</u> The following described related accessories, if any: window air conditioning units, stove, fireplace screens, curtains and rods, blinds, window shades, draperies and rods, controls for satellite dish system, controls for garage door openers, entry gate controls, door keys, mailbox keys, above-ground pool, swimming pool equipment and maintenance accessories, and artificial fireplace logs.

   D. <u>Exclusions:</u> The following improvements and accessories will be retained by Seller and excluded: _____
_____

   E. <u>Owners' Association:</u> The property ❏ is ❏ is not subject to mandatory membership in an owners' association.

(TAR-1101) 10-16-03   Initialed for Identification by Broker/Associate _____ and Seller _____, _____   Page 1 of 8

3. **LISTING PRICE:** Seller instructs Broker to market the Property at the following price: $_____ (Listing Price). Seller agrees to sell the Property for the Listing Price or any other price acceptable to Seller. Seller will pay all typical closing costs charged to sellers of residential real estate in Texas (seller's typical closing costs are those set forth in the residential contract forms promulgated by the Texas Real Estate Commission).

4. **TERM:**

   A. This Listing begins on _____ and ends at 11:59 p.m. on _____.

   B. If Seller enters into a binding written contract to sell the Property before the date this Listing begins and the contract is binding on the date this Listing begins, this Listing will not commence and will be void.

5. **BROKER'S FEE:**

   A. <u>Fee</u>: When earned and payable, Seller will pay Broker a fee of:

   ☐ (1) _____% of the sales price.

   ☐ (2) _____.

   B. <u>Earned</u>: Broker's fee is earned when any one of the following occurs during this Listing:
      (1) Seller sells, exchanges, options, agrees to sell, agrees to exchange, or agrees to option the Property to anyone at any time on any terms;
      (2) Broker individually or in cooperation with another broker procures a buyer ready, willing, and able to buy the Property at the Listing Price or at any other price acceptable to Seller; or
      (3) Seller breaches this Listing.

   C. <u>Payable</u>: Once earned, Broker's fee is payable either during this Listing or after it ends at the earlier of:
      (1) the closing and funding of any sale or exchange of all or part of the Property;
      (2) Seller's refusal to sell the Property after broker's fee has been earned;
      (3) Seller's breach of this Listing; or
      (4) at such time as otherwise set forth in this Listing.

   Broker's fee is <u>not</u> payable if a sale of the Property does not close or fund as a result of: (i) Seller's failure, without fault of Seller, to deliver to a buyer a deed or a title policy as required by the contract to sell; (ii) loss of ownership due to foreclosure or other legal proceeding; or (iii) Seller's failure to restore the Property, as a result of a casualty loss, to its previous condition by the closing date set forth in a contract for the sale of the Property.

   D. <u>Other Fees</u>:

      (1) <u>Breach by Buyer Under a Contract</u>: If Seller collects earnest money, the sales price, or damages by suit, compromise, settlement, or otherwise from a buyer who breaches a contract for the sale of the Property entered into during this Listing, Seller will pay Broker, after deducting attorney's fees and collection expenses, an amount equal to the lesser of one-half of the amount collected after deductions or the amount of the Broker's Fee stated in Paragraph 5A. Any amount paid under this Paragraph 5D(1) is in addition to any amount that Broker may be entitled to receive for subsequently selling the Property.

      (2) <u>Service Providers</u>: If Broker refers Seller or a prospective buyer to a service provider (for example, mover, cable company, telecommunications provider, utility, or contractor) Broker may receive a fee from the service provider for the referral. Any referral fee Broker receives under this Paragraph 5D(2) is in addition to any other compensation Broker may receive under this Listing.

(3) <u>Transaction Fees or Reimbursable Expenses</u>: _____

_____

_____ .

E. <u>Protection Period</u>:

(1) "Protection period" means that time starting the day after this Listing ends and continuing for _____ days. "Sell" means any transfer of any interest in the Property whether by oral or written agreement or option.

(2) Not later than 10 days after this Listing ends, Broker may send Seller written notice specifying the names of persons whose attention was called to the Property during this Listing. If Seller agrees to sell the Property during the protection period to a person named in the notice or to a relative of a person named in the notice, Seller will pay Broker, upon the closing of the sale, the amount Broker would have been entitled to receive if this Listing were still in effect.

(3) This Paragraph 5E survives termination of this Listing. This Paragraph 5E will not apply if:
   (a) Seller agrees to sell the Property during the protection period;
   (b) the Property is exclusively listed with another broker who is a member of the Texas Association of REALTORS® at the time the sale is negotiated; and
   (c) Seller is obligated to pay the other broker a fee for the sale.

F. <u>County</u>: All amounts payable to Broker are to be paid in cash in _____

_____ County, Texas.

G. <u>Escrow Authorization</u>: Seller authorizes, and Broker may so instruct, any escrow or closing agent authorized to close a transaction for the purchase or acquisition of the Property to collect and disburse to Broker all amounts payable to Broker under this Listing.

6. LISTING SERVICES:

❏ A. Broker will file this Listing with one or more multiple listing services (MLS) by the earlier of the time required by MLS rules or 5 days after the date this Listing begins. Seller authorizes Broker to submit information about this Listing and the sale of the Property to the MLS.

<u>Notice</u>: MLS rules require Broker to accurately and timely submit all information the MLS requires for participation including sold data. Subscribers to the MLS may use the information for market evaluation or appraisal purposes. Subscribers are other brokers and other real estate professionals such as appraisers and may include the appraisal district. Any information filed with the MLS becomes the property of the MLS for all purposes. **Submission of information to MLS ensures that persons who use and benefit from the MLS also contribute information.**

❏ B. Broker will not file this Listing with a Multiple Listing Service (MLS) or any other listing service.

7. ACCESS TO THE PROPERTY:

A. <u>Authorizing Access</u>: Authorizing access to the Property means giving permission to another person to enter the Property, disclosing to the other person any security codes necessary to enter the Property, and lending a key to the other person to enter the Property, directly or through a keybox. To facilitate the showing and sale of the Property, Seller instructs Broker to:
   (1) access the Property at reasonable times
   (2) authorize other brokers, their associates, inspectors, appraisers, and contractors to access the Property at reasonable times; and
   (3) duplicate keys to facilitate convenient and efficient showings of the Property.

B. <u>Scheduling Companies</u>: Broker may engage the following companies to schedule appointments and to authorize others to access the Property: _____ .

C. <u>Keybox:</u> **A keybox is a locked container placed on the Property that holds a key to the Property. A keybox makes it more convenient for brokers, their associates, inspectors, appraisers, and contractors to show, inspect, or repair the Property. The keybox is opened by a special combination, key, or programmed device so that authorized persons may enter the Property, even in Seller's absence. Using a keybox will probably increase the number of showings, but involves risks (for example, unauthorized entry, theft, property damage, or personal injury). Neither the Association of REALTORS® nor MLS requires the use of a keybox.**

    (1) Broker ❑ is ❑ is not authorized to place a keybox on the Property.

    (2) If a tenant occupies the Property at any time during this Listing, Seller will furnish Broker a written statement (for example, TAR No. 1411), signed by all tenants, authorizing the use of a keybox or Broker may remove the keybox from the Property.

D. <u>Liability and Indemnification:</u> When authorizing access to the Property, Broker, other brokers, their associates, any keybox provider, or any scheduling company are not responsible for personal injury or property loss to Seller or any other person. Seller assumes all risk of any loss, damage, or injury. **Except for a loss caused by Broker, Seller will indemnify and hold Broker harmless from any claim for personal injury, property damage, or other loss.**

8. **COOPERATION WITH OTHER BROKERS:** Broker will allow other brokers to show the Property to prospective buyers. Broker will offer to pay the other broker a fee as described below if the other broker procures a buyer that purchases the Property.

A. <u>MLS Participants:</u> If the other broker is a participant in the MLS in which this Listing is filed, Broker will offer to pay the other broker:
    (1) if the other broker represents the buyer: _____% of the sales price or $_____; and
    (2) if the other broker is a subagent: _____% of the sales price or $_____.

B. <u>Non-MLS Brokers:</u> If the other broker is not a participant in the MLS in which this Listing is filed, Broker will offer to pay the other broker:
    (1) if the other broker represents the buyer: _____% of the sales price or $_____; and
    (2) if the other broker is a subagent: _____% of the sales price or $_____.

9. **INTERMEDIARY:** *(Check A or B only.)*

❑ A. <u>Intermediary Status:</u> Broker may show the Property to interested prospective buyers who Broker represents. If a prospective buyer who Broker represents offers to buy the Property, Seller authorizes Broker to act as an intermediary and Broker will notify Seller that Broker will service the parties in accordance with one of the following alternatives.

    (1) If a prospective buyer who Broker represents is serviced by an associate other than the associate servicing Seller under this Listing, Broker may notify Seller that Broker will: (a) appoint the associate then servicing Seller to communicate with, carry out instructions of, and provide opinions and advice during negotiations to Seller; and (b) appoint the associate then servicing the prospective buyer to the prospective buyer for the same purpose.

    (2) If a prospective buyer who Broker represents is serviced by the same associate who is servicing Seller, Broker may notify Seller that Broker will: (a) appoint another associate to communicate with, carry out instructions of, and provide opinions and advice during negotiations to the prospective buyer; and (b) appoint the associate servicing the Seller under this Listing to the Seller for the same purpose.

    (3) Broker may notify Seller that Broker will make no appointments as described under this Paragraph 9A and, in such an event, the associate servicing the parties will act solely as Broker's intermediary representative, who may facilitate the transaction but will not render opinions or advice during negotiations to either party.

❑ B. <u>No Intermediary Status</u>: Seller agrees that Broker will not show the Property to prospective buyers who Broker represents.

Notice: If Broker acts as an intermediary under Paragraph 9A, Broker and Broker's associates:
* may not disclose to the prospective buyer that Seller will accept a price less than the asking price unless otherwise instructed in a separate writing by Seller;
* may not disclose to Seller that the prospective buyer will pay a price greater than the price submitted in a written offer to Seller unless otherwise instructed in a separate writing by the prospective buyer;
* may not disclose any confidential information or any information Seller or the prospective buyer specifically instructs Broker in writing not to disclose unless otherwise instructed in a separate writing by the respective party or required to disclose the information by the Real Estate License Act or a court order or if the information materially relates to the condition of the property;
* may not treat a party to the transaction dishonestly; and
* may not violate the Real Estate License Act.

10. **CONFIDENTIAL INFORMATION:** During this Listing or after it ends, Broker may not knowingly disclose information obtained in confidence from Seller except as authorized by Seller or required by law. Broker may not disclose to Seller any confidential information regarding any other person Broker represents or previously represented except as required by law.

11. **BROKER'S AUTHORITY:**

A. Broker will use reasonable efforts and act diligently to market the Property for sale, procure a buyer, and negotiate the sale of the Property.

B. In addition to other authority granted by this Listing, Broker may:
   (1) advertise the Property by means and methods as Broker determines, including but not limited to creating and placing advertisements with interior and exterior photographic and audio-visual images of the Property and related information in any media and the Internet;
   (2) place a "For Sale" sign on the Property and remove all other signs offering the Property for sale or lease;
   (3) furnish comparative marketing and sales information about other properties to prospective buyers;
   (4) disseminate information about the Property to other brokers and to prospective buyers, including applicable disclosures or notices that Seller is required to make under law or a contract;
   (5) obtain information from any holder of a note secured by a lien on the Property;
   (6) accept and deposit earnest money in trust in accordance with a contract for the sale of the Property;
   (7) disclose the sales price and terms of sale to other brokers, appraisers, or other real estate professionals;
   (8) in response to inquiries from prospective buyers and other brokers, disclose whether the Seller is considering more than one offer, provided that Broker will not disclose the terms of any competing offer unless specifically instructed by Seller;
   (9) advertise, during or after this Listing ends, that Broker "sold" the Property; and
   (10) place information about this Listing, the Property, and a transaction for the Property on an electronic transaction platform (typically an Internet-based system where professionals related to the transaction such as title companies, lenders, and others may receive, view, and input information).

C. Broker is not authorized to execute any document in the name of or on behalf of Seller concerning the Property.

(TAR-1101) 10-16-03   Initialed for Identification by Broker/Associate _____ and Seller _____, _____   Page 5 of 8

12. SELLER'S REPRESENTATIONS: Except as provided by Paragraph 15, Seller represents that:
   A. Seller has fee simple title to and peaceable possession of the Property and all its improvements and fixtures, unless rented, and the legal capacity to convey the Property;
   B. Seller is not bound by a listing agreement with another broker for the sale, exchange, or lease of the Property that is or will be in effect during this Listing;
   C. any pool or spa and any required enclosures, fences, gates, and latches comply with all applicable laws and ordinances;
   D. no person or entity has any right to purchase, lease, or acquire the Property by an option, right of refusal, or other agreement;
   E. there are no delinquencies or defaults under any deed of trust, mortgage, or other encumbrance on the Property;
   F. the Property is not subject to the jurisdiction of any court;
   G. all information relating to the Property Seller provides to Broker is true and correct to the best of Seller's knowledge; and
   H. the name of any employer, relocation company, or other entity that provides benefits to Seller when selling the Property is: _____.

13. SELLER'S ADDITIONAL PROMISES: Seller agrees to:
   A. cooperate with Broker to facilitate the showing, marketing, and sale of the Property;
   B. not rent or lease the Property during this Listing without Broker's prior written approval;
   C. not negotiate with any prospective buyer who may contact Seller directly, but refer all prospective buyers to Broker;
   D. not enter into a listing agreement with another broker for the sale, exchange, or lease of the Property to become effective during this Listing;
   E. maintain any pool and all required enclosures in compliance with all applicable laws and ordinances;
   F. provide Broker with copies of any leases or rental agreements pertaining to the Property and advise Broker of tenants moving in or out of the Property;
   G. complete any disclosures or notices required by law or contract to sell the Property; and
   H. amend any applicable notices and disclosures if any material change occurs during this Listing.

14. LIMITATION OF LIABILITY:

   A. If the Property is or becomes vacant during this Listing, Seller must notify Seller's casualty insurance company and request a "vacancy clause" to cover the Property. Broker is not responsible for the security of the Property nor for inspecting the Property on any periodic basis.

   B. **Broker is not responsible or liable in any manner for personal injury to any person or for loss or damage to any person's real or personal property resulting from any act or omission not caused by Broker's negligence, including but not limited to injuries or damages caused by:**
     (1) other brokers, their associates, inspectors, appraisers, and contractors who are authorized to access the Property;
     (2) acts of third parties (for example, vandalism or theft);
     (3) freezing water pipes;
     (4) a dangerous condition on the Property; or
     (5) the Property's non-compliance with any law or ordinance.

   C. **Seller agrees to protect, defend, indemnify, and hold Broker harmless from any damage, costs, attorney's fees, and expenses that:**
     (1) are caused by Seller, negligently or otherwise;
     (2) arise from Seller's failure to disclose any material or relevant information about the Property; or
     (3) are caused by Seller giving incorrect information to any person.

15. SPECIAL PROVISIONS:

16. DEFAULT: If Seller breaches this Listing, Seller is in default and will be liable to Broker for the amount of the Broker's fee specified in Paragraph 5A and any other fees Broker is entitled to receive under this Listing. If a sales price is not determinable in the event of an exchange or breach of this Listing, the Listing Price will be the sales price for purposes of computing Broker's fee. If Broker breaches this Listing, Broker is in default and Seller may exercise any remedy at law.

17. MEDIATION: The parties agree to negotiate in good faith in an effort to resolve any dispute related to this Listing that may arise between the parties. If the dispute cannot be resolved by negotiation, the dispute will be submitted to mediation. The parties to the dispute will choose a mutually acceptable mediator and will share the cost of mediation equally.

18. ATTORNEY'S FEES: If Seller or Broker is a prevailing party in any legal proceeding brought as a result of a dispute under this Listing or any transaction related to or contemplated by this Listing, such party will be entitled to recover from the non-prevailing party all costs of such proceeding and reasonable attorney's fees.

19. ADDENDA AND OTHER DOCUMENTS: Addenda that are part of this Listing and other documents that Seller may need to provide are:

[X] A. Information About Brokerage Services;
☐ B. Seller Disclosure Notice (§5.008, Texas Property Code);
☐ C. Seller's Disclosure of Information on Lead-Based Paint and Lead-Based Paint Hazards (required if Property was built before 1978);
☐ D. MUD, Water District, or Statutory Tax District Disclosure Notice (Chapter 49, Texas Water Code);
☐ E. Request for Information from an Owners' Association;
☐ F. Request for Mortgage Information;
☐ G. Information about On-Site Sewer Facility;
☐ H. Information about Special Flood Hazard Areas;
☐ I. Condominium Addendum to Listing;
☐ J. Keybox Authorization by Tenant;
☐ K. Seller's Authorization to Release and Advertise Certain Information; and
☐ L. _____
_____.

20. AGREEMENT OF PARTIES:

A. <u>Entire Agreement</u>: This Listing is the entire agreement of the parties and may not be changed except by written agreement.

B. <u>Assignability</u>: Neither party may assign this Listing without the written consent of the other party.

C. Binding Effect: Seller's obligation to pay Broker an earned fee is binding upon Seller and Seller's heirs, administrators, executors, successors, and permitted assignees.

D. Joint and Several: All Sellers executing this Listing are jointly and severally liable for the performance of all its terms.

E. Governing Law: Texas law governs the interpretation, validity, performance, and enforcement of this Listing.

F. Severability: If a court finds any clause in this Listing invalid or unenforceable, the remainder of this Listing will not be affected and all other provisions of this Listing will remain valid and enforceable.

G. Notices: Notices between the parties must be in writing and are effective when sent to the receiving party's address, fax, or e-mail address specified in Paragraph 1.

21. ADDITIONAL NOTICES:

A. Broker's fees or the sharing of fees between brokers are not fixed, controlled, recommended, suggested, or maintained by the Association of REALTORS®, MLS, or any listing service.

B. Fair housing laws require the Property to be shown and made available to all persons without regard to race, color, religion, national origin, sex, disability, or familial status. Local ordinances may provide for additional protected classes (for example, creed, status as a student, marital status, sexual orientation, or age).

C. Seller may review the information Broker submits to an MLS or other listing service.

D. Broker advises Seller to remove or secure jewelry, prescription drugs, and other valuables.

E. Statutes or ordinances may regulate certain items on the Property (for example, swimming pools and septic systems). Non-compliance with the statutes or ordinances may delay a transaction and may result in fines, penalties, and liability to Seller.

F. If the Property was built before 1978, Federal law requires the Seller to: (1) provide the buyer with the federally approved pamphlet on lead poisoning prevention; (2) disclose the presence of any known lead-based paint or lead-based paint hazards in the Property; (3) deliver all records and reports to the buyer related to such paint or hazards, and (4) provide the buyer a period up to 10 days to have the Property inspected for such paint or hazards.

G. Broker cannot give legal advice. READ THIS LISTING CAREFULLY. If you do not understand the effect of this Listing, consult an attorney BEFORE signing.

Broker's Printed Name	License No.	Seller	Date
By:			
Broker's Associate's Signature	Date	Seller	Date

before the agent performs the duties of the relationship, however, a principal's consent can be given after the agent has already acted. By approving the unauthorized action, the principal is legally accepting the benefits associated with the representation.

If an agency relationship is created by ratification, the legal consequences are just the same as if the action has been authorized beforehand by means of a written agreement.

D. OSTENSIBLE AGENCY (Agency by Estoppel)

OSTENSIBLE AGENCY is an agency relationship created by law where the words and actions of a licensee demonstrate to third parties that the licensee is apparently (ostensibly) working for a party and the party fails or refuses to correct this mistaken impression. In such a case, the party is legally barred (ESTOPPED) from later denying that such an agency relationship existed.

III. How an Agency Relationship is Terminated

Once an agency relationship is created, an agent becomes authorized to act on behalf of a principal. Such authority will continue until such time as the agency relationship is terminated.

Termination of Agency

By Act of the Parties

1. Accomplishment of Purpose
2. Expiration of Term
3. Mutual Agreement
4. Renunciation by the Agent
5. Revocation by the Principal
6. Abandonment by the Agent

By Operation of Law

1. Death of Party
2. Property Destroyed
3. Illegality
4. Bankruptcy of the Owner

A. TERMINATION BY ACT OF THE PARTIES

1. Accomplishment of Purpose

An agency relationship will terminate once its purpose has been accomplished.

For example, a homeowner hires an agent to help sell his home. When the house sells, the agency relationship is over. Accomplishment of purpose is perhaps the most common reason for agency termination.

2. Expiration of Term

When an agreement specifies that the agency relationship is for a limited term, the agency ends automatically when the term expires. In Texas, a real estate listing agreement must have a date of expiration. If it does not have one, there may not be an enforceable listing agreement and the licensee has exposed himself/herself to disciplinary actions by TREC for the improper listing agreement.

3. Mutual Agreement

An agency is a consensual relationship, which means that it is based on the mutual consent of both parties. If both the principal and the agent want to end the agency, they can agree to terminate at any point.

4. Renunciation by the Agent

The agent may **renounce** his/her agency at any time by refusing to act or notifying the principal that he will not act. Obviously, if the agent informs the principal that he/she will no longer act, the principal's authority is effectively terminated, thus ending the agency.

5. Revocation by the Principal

Just as an agent may renounce agency, a principal may terminate the relationship as well. *However, when a principal unilaterally terminates the relationship, it is known as REVOCATION OF AUTHORITY.*

6. Abandonment by the Agent

Having agreed to represent the principal, the agent must then do exactly that. The agent's **abandonment** of the agency's objectives will result in the termination of the agency relationship. This may occur when an agent, for example, accepts a listing, but fails to follow through with any of the steps necessary to sell the property.

B. TERMINATION BY OPERATION OF LAW

1. Death or Incapacity

The death or legal incapacity of either the principal or the agent serves to terminate the agency relationship. *INCAPACITY refers to a person's lack of intelligent understanding as the result of insanity or mental impairment.*

2. Destruction of the Property

The agency will also be terminated if the subject matter of the relationship is destroyed. For example, several investors own a luxury condominium. If the condo

is totally destroyed in a fire, there is no condo to sell; thus any agency agreement in existence to sell the property is terminated.

3. Illegality

An agency relationship cannot be formed for an illegal purpose, nor can it be formed for a purpose which will become illegal.

4. Bankruptcy of the Owner

If a person files for bankruptcy relief, all assets and liabilities must be fully disclosed to the court. A bankruptcy trustee may then be appointed to help liquidate (sell) assets and/or reorganize the affairs of the debtor. If a trustee is appointed, federal law gives the trustee has broad authority to continue or even reject pending contracts, including real estate brokerage agreements, as the trustee may see fit or necessary.

Just because an agency relationship is terminated does not mean that an agent's duty to his/her principal terminates.

As the next section will show, some agent duties may survive the agency relationship.

IV. Agency Responsibilities

A. FIDUCIARY RESPONSIBILITIES

Once formed, the connection between principal and agent is a fiduciary relationship with the agent fulfilling the role of fiduciary. A *FIDUCIARY is someone who acts for the benefit of another in a relationship founded on trust, confidence, integrity, and fidelity.* As a result, a relationship based on these standards is a higher relationship than just a business transaction between buyer and seller.

The starting point for understanding the duties owed by an agent to the principal is the common law.

COMMON LAW is the body of law that relies on custom and usage in the community and also gives weight to earlier, relevant court decisions (precedent). It developed in England and constitutes the basis for the legal systems of most of the states in the United States.

The common law fiduciary duties that an agent owes the principal can be remembered by the words OLD CAR.

Obedience to Instructions
Loyalty to Principal
Disclosure of Material Information
Confidentiality of Information
Accounting of Money and Property
Reasonable Care, Skill, and Diligence

1. Obedience to Instruction

An agent owes the principal obedience in order to carry out the principal's instructions, and may be held liable for any loss caused by the material failure to obey them. However, an agent has no duty to follow the principal's instructions if those instructions require the agent to do anything illegal. For example, if a seller instructs an agent not to show his/her home to minorities, the agent should tell his/her principal that he/she will not follow the instructions due to their illegal nature and advise the principal to conform to the law. If the principal refuses to change, the agent should withdraw from the agency relationship.

2. Loyalty to Principal

An agent owes the principal the duty of loyalty to put the principal's interest above his/her own or above the interest of anyone else. In other words, the agent must faithfully serve the principal.

3. Disclosure of Material Information

An agent is required to disclose to his/her principal any material information that affects the subject matter of the agency. Under this duty, a seller's agent, for example, would be required to disclose to his/her principal the following facts:

1. The true value of the property and anything that might affect its value;
2. All offers to purchase;
3. The identity of the purchaser;
4. The purchaser's financial condition (if known);
5. Any relationship between the purchaser and the broker; and
6. Any commission splitting arrangements with other brokers.

4. Confidentiality of Information

Out of loyalty to the principal, the agent must never reveal any confidential information to others, nor take advantage of it for himself/herself. This duty will survive the termination of the agency relationship. There are no other duties which survive the termination of agency.

5. Accounting of Money and Property

An agent also owes a duty to account to the principal for all money and property belonging to the principal that comes into the agent's possession.

6. Reasonable Care, Skill, and Diligence

Real estate agents are under a duty to be competent and hold expertise as real estate professionals. This means that an agent is supposed to make a reasonably diligent effort to achieve the principal's goals such as, for example:

1. Negotiating contract terms as required by the principal;
2. Properly completing the sales contract or lease agreement;
3. Competently marketing the subject property or searching for suitable properties; and
4. Becoming and remaining knowledgeable of local market conditions.

However, the duty of reasonable care does **not** include:

1. Offering advice which the agent knows to be inaccurate;
2. Giving complex financial advice to principals; or
3. Providing legal advice (unless the agent is licensed to practice law).

In addition to the common law (OLD-CAR) duties, Texas real estate licensees are also subject to the rules of the Texas Real Estate Commission. The first five rules of the commission constitute the **Canons of Professional Ethics** which all licensees are obligated to follow (see **Figure 4-2**).

The Canons of Professional Ethics require fidelity, integrity, and competency by all licensees on behalf of the principal being served.

B. DUTIES TO THIRD PARTIES

As was first explained above, a customer is a third party who falls outside of the principal-agent relationship. Even so, the common law, the provisions of The Real Estate License Act (TRELA), and the rules of the real estate commission require Texas licensees to treat all persons with whom the agent comes into contact fairly and honestly. This goes for customers and clients alike.

The rules of the real estate commission provide additional guidance as to what fairness and honesty should mean for a Texas real estate licensee.

1. Duty of Fairness to Third Parties

The rules of the commission make it clear that although the number one obligation of an agent is to his/her client, the agent also owes duties of fairness to third parties.

Figure 4-2

RULES OF THE TEXAS
REAL ESTATE COMMISSION

§531

CHAPTER 531 CANONS OF PROFESSIONAL ETHICS AND
CONDUCT FOR REAL ESTATE LICENSEES

§531.1. Fidelity. *[Adopted January 1, 1976; amended February 23, 1998]* A real estate broker or salesperson, while acting as an agent for another, is a fiduciary. Special obligations are imposed when such fiduciary relationships are created. They demand:

(1) that the primary duty of the real estate agent is to represent the interests of the agent's client, and the agent's position, in this respect, should be clear to all parties concerned in a real estate transaction; that, however, the agent, in performing duties to the client, shall treat other parties to a transaction fairly;

(2) that the real estate agent be faithful and observant to trust placed in the agent, and be scrupulous and meticulous in performing the agent's functions;

(3) that the real estate agent place no personal interest above that of the agent's client.

§531.2. Integrity. *[Adopted January 1, 1976; amended February 23, 1998]* A real estate broker or salesperson has a special obligation to exercise integrity in the discharge of the licensee's responsibilities, including employment of prudence and caution so as to avoid misrepresentation, in any wise, by acts of commission or omission.

§531.3. Competency. *[Adopted January 1, 1976; amended February 23, 1998]* It is the obligation of a real estate agent to be knowledgeable as a real estate brokerage practitioner. The agent should:

(1) be informed on market conditions affecting the real estate business and pledged to continuing education in the intricacies involved in marketing real estate for others;

(2) be informed on national, state and local issues and developments in the real estate industry; and

(3) exercise judgment and skill in the performance of the work.

§§531.10-531.17. Minimum Appraisal Standards. *[Repealed March 1, 1991]*

§531.18. Consumer Information Form 1-1. *[Adopted February 1, 1990; amended November 1, 1991; Ref: §1101.202(a)(2)]*

(a) The Texas Real Estate Commission adopts by reference Consumer Information Form 1-1 approved by the Texas Real Estate Commission in 1991. This document is published by and available from the Texas Real Estate Commission, P.O. Box 12188, Austin, Texas 78711-2188.

(b) Each real estate inspector or active real estate broker licensed by the Texas Real Estate Commission shall display Consumer Information Form 1-1 in a prominent location in each place of business the broker or inspector maintains.

§531.19. Discriminatory Practices. *[Adopted February 19, 1990; Ref: AG OP.JM-1093]* No real estate licensee shall inquire about, respond to or facilitate inquiries about, or make a disclosure which indicates or is intended to indicate any preference, limitation or discrimination based on the following: race, color, religion, sex, national origin, ancestry, familial status, or handicap of an owner, previous or current occupant, potential purchaser, lessor, or potential lessee of real property. For the purpose of this section, handicap includes a person who had, may have had, has, or may have AIDS, HIV-related illnesses, or HIV infection as defined by the Centers for Disease Control of the United States Public Health Service.

1

> ... the primary duty of the real estate agent is to represent the interests of the agent's client, and the agent's position, in this respect, should be clear to all parties concerned in a real estate transaction; that, however, the agent, in performing duties to the client, shall treat other parties to a transaction fairly. ...
>
> ***TREC Rule 531.1***

2. Duty of Integrity to Third Parties

The same duty of integrity that a licensee owes to his/her client is expected to be exercised for the benefit of third parties.

> A real estate broker or salesperson has a special obligation to exercise integrity in the discharge of the licensee's responsibilities, including employment of prudence and caution so as to avoid misrepresentation, in any wise, by acts of commission or omission.
>
> ***TREC Rule 531.2***

3. Duty to be Knowledgeable to All Parties

Under the commission rules, a licensee's skill, judgment and knowledge should be used for clients and third parties alike.

> It is the obligation of a real estate agent to be knowledgeable as a real estate brokerage practitioner. The agent should:
>
> (1) be informed on market conditions affecting the real estate business and pledged to continuing education in the intricacies involved in marketing real estate for others;
> (2) be informed on national, state, and local issues and developments in the real estate industry; and
> (3) exercise judgment and skill in the performance of the work.
>
> ***TREC Rule 535.3***

4. Duty to Avoid Misrepresentation to Third Parties

The law imposes upon licensees an on-going duty to avoid misrepresentations and exposes the wrongdoer to significant legal liability. Accordingly, this commission rule simply reinforces existing law.

> A licensee has a duty to convey accurate information to members of the public with whom the licensee deals.
>
> ***TREC Rule 535.156(d)***

5. Duty to Disclose Self Dealing

A licensee is also under a special duty to disclose to third parties when he/she is buying or selling real estate on his/her own account.

A licensee must never engage in a real estate transaction for himself/herself unless this fact is clearly disclosed to all concerned.

A licensee, when engaging in a real estate transaction on his or her own behalf, or on behalf of a business entity in which the licensee is more than a 10% owner, is obligated to inform any person with whom the licensee deals that he or she is a licensed real estate broker or salesperson acting on his or her own behalf either by disclosure in any contract of sale or rental agreement, or by disclosure in any other writing given prior to entering into any contract of sales or rental agreement.

A licensee shall not use the licensee's expertise to the disadvantage of a person with whom the licensee deals.

TREC Rule 535.144

Figure 4-3 summarizes the responsibilities that agents owe to their clients and customers.

Figure 4-3

Broker's Duties, Rights, and Responsibilities

To Clients	To Customers
Fiduciary Duties	Duty of Truthfulness
Obedience	Fairness
Loyalty	Integrity
Disclosure	Be Knowledgeable
Confidentiality	Avoid Misrepresentations
Accounting	Disclose Self dealing
Reasonable Care	
Plus Duty of Truthfulness	

V. Agency Types

There are four basic types of agency relationships that can be created under Texas law. They are:

1. **Seller Agency** – when the broker represents the seller/landlord.
2. **Buyer Agency** – when the broker represents the buyer/tenant.
3. **Intermediary Practice** – when the broker acts as Intermediary.
4. **Subagency** – when the broker works with another broker, usually the seller's broker, and represents that broker's client.

These four types of agency relationships are described in a TREC form known as **Information About Brokerage Services (IABS)** (see **Figure 4-4**).

The Real Estate License Act (TRELA) requires licensees to provide the information contained on the IABS form to an unrepresented party or proposed party at the time of the licensee's "first substantive dialogue" with that party. TRELA defines when the "first substantive dialogue" occurs.

...**"substantive dialogue"** means a meeting or written communication that involves a substantive discussion relating to specific real estate property. The term does not include:

(1) a meeting that occurs at a property that is held open for any prospective buyer or tenant; or
(2) a meeting or written communication that occurs after the parties to a real estate transaction have signed a contract to sell, buy, or lease the real property concerned.

TRELA § 1101.558(a)

The IABS form is not required to be given if the proposed transaction is only for a lease of one year or less. Nor is the IABS form required to be given if the party is represented by another license holder.

The following describes the four types of agency relationships.

A. BROKER REPRESENTS THE SELLER/LANDLORD (Seller's Agency)

Seller's agency refers to the agency relationship that results when an agent represents a person who wishes to sell or lease his/her property. As stated previously, it's best to establish this agency relationship by means of an express written agreement that clearly specifies how and when a commission will be earned. The three basic types of listing agreements are: 1) the exclusive right to sell listing agreement; 2) the exclusive agency listing agreement; and 3) the open listing agreement.

Figure 4-4

Approved by the Texas Real Estate Commission for Voluntary Use

Texas law requires all real estate licensees to give the following information about brokerage services to prospective buyers, tenants, sellers and landlords.

Information About Brokerage Services

Before working with a real estate broker, you should know that the duties of a broker depend on whom the broker represents. If you are a prospective seller or landlord (owner) or a prospective buyer or tenant (buyer), you should know that the broker who lists the property for sale or lease is the owner's agent. A broker who acts as a subagent represents the owner in cooperation with the listing broker. A broker who acts as a buyer's agent represents the buyer. A broker may act as an intermediary between the parties if the parties consent in writing. A broker can assist you in locating a property, preparing a contract or lease, or obtaining financing without representing you. A broker is obligated by law to treat you honestly.

IF THE BROKER REPRESENTS THE OWNER:
The broker becomes the owner's agent by entering into an agreement with the owner, usually through a written - listing agreement, or by agreeing to act as a subagent by accepting an offer of subagency from the listing broker. A subagent may work in a different real estate office. A listing broker or subagent can assist the buyer but does not represent the buyer and must place the interests of the owner first. The buyer should not tell the owner's agent anything the buyer would not want the owner to know because an owner's agent must disclose to the owner any material information known to the agent.

IF THE BROKER REPRESENTS THE BUYER:
The broker becomes the buyer's agent by entering into an agreement to represent the buyer, usually through a written buyer representation agreement. A buyer's agent can assist the owner but does not represent the owner and must place the interests of the buyer first. The owner should not tell a buyer's agent anything the owner would not want the buyer to know because a buyer's agent must disclose to the buyer any material information known to the agent.

IF THE BROKER ACTS AS AN INTERMEDIARY:
A broker may act as an intermediary between the parties if the broker complies with The Texas Real Estate License Act. The broker must obtain the written consent of each party to the transaction to act as an intermediary. The written consent must state who will pay the broker and, in conspicuous bold or underlined print, set forth the broker's obligations as an intermediary. The broker is required to treat each party honestly and fairly and to comply with The Texas Real Estate License Act. A broker who acts as an intermediary in a transaction:

(1) shall treat all parties honestly;
(2) may not disclose that the owner will accept a price less than the asking price unless authorized in writing to do so by the owner;
(3) may not disclose that the buyer will pay a price greater than the price submitted in a written offer unless authorized in writing to do so by the buyer; and
(4) may not disclose any confidential information or any information that a party specifically instructs the broker in writing not to disclose unless authorized in writing to disclose the information or required to do so by The Texas Real Estate License Act or a court order or if the information materially relates to the condition of the property.

With the parties' consent, a broker acting as an intermediary between the parties may appoint a person who is licensed under The Texas Real Estate License Act and associated with the broker to communicate with and carry out instructions of one party and another person who is licensed under that Act and associated with the broker to communicate with and carry out instructions of the other party.

If you choose to have a broker represent you,
you should enter into a written agreement with the broker that clearly establishes the broker's obligations and your obligations. The agreement should state how and by whom the broker will be paid. You have the right to choose the type of representation, if any, you wish to receive. Your payment of a fee to a broker does not necessarily establish that the broker represents you. If you have any questions regarding the duties and responsibilities of the broker, you should resolve those questions before proceeding.

Real estate licensee asks that you acknowledge receipt of this information about brokerage services for the licensee's records.

Buyer, Seller, Landlord or Tenant   Date

Texas Real Estate Brokers and Salespersons are licensed and regulated by the Texas Real Estate Commission (TREC). If you have a question or complaint regarding a real estate licensee, you should contact TREC at P.O. Box 12188, Austin, Texas 78711-2188 or 512-465-3960.

01A   TREC No. OP-K

These listing agreements are summarized in **Figure 4-5**.

Figure 4-5

Listing Type	How Commission is Paid
1. **Exclusive Right to Sell**	A single broker has the exclusive right to sell this property. As a result, the broker will be entitled to a commission *regardless* of whether the broker or owner sells the property.
2. **Exclusive Agency**	Here, the broker is the exclusive agent for the seller. The owner may sell, but the broker will be entitled to a commission only if he/she is successful in selling the property.
3. **Open Listing**	Several brokers are given the non-exclusive right to sell the property. The first successful broker is entitled to a commission unless the owner sells the property.

1. Exclusive Right To Sell Listing Agreement (Commission Paid If Either Owner Or Broker Sell)

The most common type of listing is the exclusive right to sell listing. The exclusive right to sell listing entitles the listing broker named in the contract to a commission even if the owner sells the property. Since the listing broker has the exclusive right to sell, there is no reason for another broker to attempt to find a buyer unless the listing broker will give part of the commission to the other broker who found a buyer. As a result, an exclusive right to sell is the most favorable listing agreement for the broker.

2. Exclusive Agency (No Commission if Owner Sells)

The exclusive agency listing is a listing providing that the specified broker has the right to be the only agent, other than the owner, to sell the property during a specified period. The owner, however, still has the right to sell the property independently without paying a commission to the listing broker.

3. Open Listing (Unilateral, Non-Exclusive Contract)

An open listing is a unilateral, non-exclusive listing agreement where the owner tells a group of brokers that he/she will pay a commission to any successful selling broker. Since the owner also retains the right to sell the property himself/herself, if the owner sells the property he or she is not required to pay a commission.

B. BROKER REPRESENTS THE BUYER (Buyer's Agency)

In a buyer agency, the buyer is the *principal* and the broker is the *agent*. From the viewpoint of the broker, the buyer is the client while it the seller who is the customer. The TAR **Residential Buyer/Tenant Representation Agreement** is shown in **Figure 4-6**.

Buyer's agency has the effect of "evening out the playing field" when it comes to client representation. This means that both sellers (including landlords) as well as buyers (including tenants) will be represented by agents who are obligated to provide them with the full array of OLD-CAR fiduciary duties. The buyer does not incur any costs. His/her broker agent is paid by the listing broker out of that broker's share.

C. BROKER ACTS AS INTERMEDIARY
(Represents Both Buyer and Seller)

The practice of a single agent representing the interests of both the buyer and seller at the same time has always been legally problematic because of the obvious conflict of interest. However, by following the exact requirements of the law, a single broker may legally act as an "impartial" intermediary, negotiating a transaction "between" two parties.

1. Only a Broker May Serve as Intermediary

At the very heart of intermediary practice is the role of the Intermediary. Under The Real Estate License Act, only brokers may serve as Intermediary. By law the Intermediary serves both the seller and the buyer.

2. Both Sides Must Give Their Written Consent

The very first step in creating an intermediary relationship is to obtain the permission of the buyer (or tenant) and seller (or landlord). The license act, among other things, provides that written consent may be contained within the written listing or buyer's representation agreement provided that:

- the agreement state the source of any expected compensation to the broker, and
- the agreement disclose to the parties those Intermediary activities which are prohibited by law.

Figure 4-6

TEXAS ASSOCIATION OF REALTORS®
RESIDENTIAL BUYER/TENANT REPRESENTATION AGREEMENT
USE OF THIS FORM BY PERSONS WHO ARE NOT MEMBERS OF THE TEXAS ASSOCIATION OF REALTORS® IS NOT AUTHORIZED.
©Texas Association of REALTORS®, Inc. 2006

1. **PARTIES:** The parties to this agreement are:

Client: _____

Address: _____
City, State, Zip: _____
Phone: _____ Fax: _____
E-Mail: _____

Broker: _____
Address: _____
City, State, Zip: _____
Phone: _____ Fax: _____
E-Mail: _____

2. **APPOINTMENT:** Client grants to Broker the exclusive right to act as Client's real estate agent for the purpose of acquiring property in the market area.

3. **DEFINITIONS:**
    A. *"Acquire"* means to purchase or lease.
    B. *"Closing"* in a sale transaction means the date legal title to a property is conveyed to a purchaser of property under a contract to buy. "Closing" in a lease transaction means the date a landlord and tenant enter into a binding lease of a property.
    C. *"Market area"* means that area in the State of Texas within the perimeter boundaries of the following areas:_____
    _____
    _____
    _____

    D. *"Property"* means any interest in real estate including but not limited to properties listed in a multiple listing service or other listing services, properties for sale by owners, and properties for sale by builders.

4. **TERM:** This agreement commences on _____ and ends at 11:59 p.m. on _____.

5. **BROKER'S OBLIGATIONS:** Broker will: (a) use Broker's best efforts to assist Client in acquiring property in the market area; (b) assist Client in negotiating the acquisition of property in the market area; and (c) comply with other provisions of this agreement.

6. **CLIENT'S OBLIGATIONS:** Client will: (a) work exclusively through Broker in acquiring property in the market area and negotiate the acquisition of property in the market area only through Broker; (b) inform other brokers, salespersons, sellers, and landlords with whom Client may have contact that Broker exclusively represents Client for the purpose of acquiring property in the market area and refer all such persons to Broker; and (c) comply with other provisions of this agreement.

7. **REPRESENTATIONS:**
    A. Each person signing this agreement represents that the person has the legal capacity and authority to bind the respective party to this agreement.
    B. Client represents that Client is not now a party to another buyer or tenant representation agreement with another broker for the acquisition of property in the market area.

(TAR-1501) 4-14-06   Initialed for Identification by: Broker/Associate _____, and Client _____, _____   Page 1 of 4

C. Client represents that all information relating to Client's ability to acquire property in the market area Client gives to Broker is true and correct.

D. Name any employer, relocation company, or other entity that will provide benefits to Client when acquiring property in the market area: _____.

8. **INTERMEDIARY:** *(Check A or B only.)*

☐ A. <u>Intermediary Status</u>: Client desires to see Broker's listings. If Client wishes to acquire one of Broker's listings, Client authorizes Broker to act as an intermediary and Broker will notify Client that Broker will service the parties in accordance with one of the following alternatives.

(1) If the owner of the property is serviced by an associate other than the associate servicing Client under this agreement, Broker may notify Client that Broker will: (a) appoint the associate then servicing the owner to communicate with, carry out instructions of, and provide opinions and advice during negotiations to the owner; and (b) appoint the associate then servicing Client to the Client for the same purpose.

(2) If the owner of the property is serviced by the same associate who is servicing Client, Broker may notify Client that Broker will: (a) appoint another associate to communicate with, carry out instructions of, and provide opinions and advice during negotiations to Client; and (b) appoint the associate servicing the owner under the listing to the owner for the same purpose.

(3) Broker may notify Client that Broker will make no appointments as described under this Paragraph 8A and, in such an event, the associate servicing the parties will act solely as Broker's intermediary representative, who may facilitate the transaction but will not render opinions or advice during negotiations to either party.

☐ B. <u>No Intermediary Status</u>: Client does not wish to be shown or acquire any of Broker's listings.

Notice: If Broker acts as an intermediary under Paragraph 8A, Broker and Broker's associates:
- may not disclose to Client that the seller or landlord will accept a price less than the asking price unless otherwise instructed in a separate writing by the seller or landlord;
- may not disclose to the seller or landlord that Client will pay a price greater than the price submitted in a written offer to the seller or landlord unless otherwise instructed in a separate writing by Client;
- may not disclose any confidential information or any information a seller or landlord or Client specifically instructs Broker in writing not to disclose unless otherwise instructed in a separate writing by the respective party or required to disclose the information by the Real Estate License Act or a court order or if the information materially relates to the condition of the property;
- shall treat all parties to the transaction honestly; and
- shall comply with the Real Estate License Act.

9. **COMPETING CLIENTS:** Client acknowledges that Broker may represent other prospective buyers or tenants who may seek to acquire properties that may be of interest to Client. Client agrees that Broker may, during the term of this agreement and after it ends, represent such other prospects, show the other prospects the same properties that Broker shows to Client, and act as a real estate broker for such other prospects in negotiating the acquisition of properties that Client may seek to acquire.

10. **CONFIDENTIAL INFORMATION:**

A. During the term of this agreement or after its termination, Broker may not knowingly disclose information obtained in confidence from Client except as authorized by Client or required by law. Broker may not disclose to Client any information obtained in confidence regarding any other person Broker represents or may have represented except as required by law.

B. Unless otherwise agreed or required by law, a seller or the seller's agent is not obliged to keep the existence of an offer or its terms confidential. If a listing agent receives multiple offers, the listing agent is obliged to treat the competing buyers fairly.

(TAR-1501) 4-14-06   Initialed for Identification by: Broker/Associate _____, and Client _____, _____   Page 2 of 4

11. BROKER'S FEES:

A. <u>Commission</u>: The parties agree that Broker will receive a commission calculated as follows: (1) ____% of the gross sales price if Client agrees to purchase property in the market area; and (2) if Client agrees to lease property in the market a fee equal to *(check only one box)*: ❑ _____% of one month's rent or ❑ ____% of all rents to be paid over the term of the lease.

B. <u>Source of Commission Payment</u>: Broker will seek to obtain payment of the commission specified in Paragraph 11A first from the seller, landlord, or their agents. If such persons refuse or fail to pay Broker the amount specified, Client will pay Broker the amount specified less any amounts Broker receives from such persons.

C. <u>Earned and Payable</u>: A person is not obligated to pay Broker a commission until such time as Broker's commission is *earned and payable*. Broker's commission is *earned* when: (1) Client enters into a contract to buy or lease property in the market area; or (2) Client breaches this agreement. Broker's commission is *payable*, either during the term of this agreement or after it ends, upon the earlier of: (1) the closing of the transaction to acquire the property; (2) Client's breach of a contract to buy or lease a property in the market area; or (3) Client's breach of this agreement. If Client acquires more than one property under this agreement, Broker's commissions for each property acquired are earned as each property is acquired and are payable at the closing of each acquisition.

D. <u>Additional Compensation</u>: If a seller, landlord, or their agents offer compensation in excess of the amount stated in Paragraph 11 (including but not limited to marketing incentives or bonuses to cooperating brokers) Broker may retain the additional compensation in addition to the specified commission. Client is not obligated to pay any such additional compensation to Broker.

E. <u>Acquisition of Broker's Listing</u>: Notwithstanding any provision to the contrary, if Client acquires a property listed by Broker, Broker will be paid in accordance with the terms of Broker's listing agreement with the owner and Client will have no obligation to pay Broker.

F. In addition to the commission specified under Paragraph 11, Broker is entitled to the following fees.
   (1) <u>Construction</u>: If Client uses Broker's services to procure or negotiate the construction of improvements to property that Client owns or may acquire, Client ensures that Broker will receive from Client or the contractor(s) at the time the construction is substantially complete a fee equal to:
   _____.
   (2) <u>Service Providers</u>: If Broker refers Client or any party to a transaction contemplated by this agreement to a service provider (for example, mover, cable company, telecommunications provider, utility, or contractor) Broker may receive a fee from the service provider for the referral.
   (3) <u>Other</u>: _____
   _____
   _____.

G. <u>Protection Period</u>: "Protection period" means that time starting the day after this agreement ends and continuing for _____ days. Not later than 10 days after this agreement ends, Broker may send Client written notice identifying the properties called to Client's attention during this agreement. If Client or a relative of Client agrees to acquire a property identified in the notice during the protection period, Client will pay Broker, upon closing, the amount Broker would have been entitled to receive if this agreement were still in effect. This Paragraph 11G survives termination of this agreement. This Paragraph 11G will not apply if Client is, during the protection period, bound under a representation agreement with another broker who is a member of the Texas Association of REALTORS® at the time the acquisition is negotiated and the other broker is paid a fee for negotiating the transaction.

H. <u>Escrow Authorization</u>: Client authorizes, and Broker may so instruct, any escrow or closing agent authorized to close a transaction for the acquisition of property contemplated by this agreement to collect and disburse to Broker all amounts payable to Broker.

I. <u>County</u>: Amounts payable to Broker are to be paid in cash in _____ County, Texas.

(TAR-1501) 4-14-06   Initialed for Identification by: Broker/Associate _____, and Client _____, _____   Page 3 of 4

12. MEDIATION: The parties agree to negotiate in good faith in an effort to resolve any dispute that may arise related to this agreement or any transaction related to or contemplated by this agreement. If the dispute cannot be resolved by negotiation, the parties will submit the dispute to mediation before resorting to arbitration or litigation and will equally share the costs of a mutually acceptable mediator.

13. DEFAULT: If either party fails to comply with this agreement or makes a false representation in this agreement, the non-complying party is in default. If Client is in default, Client will be liable for the amount of compensation that Broker would have received under this agreement if Client was not in default. If Broker is in default, Client may exercise any remedy at law.

14. ATTORNEY'S FEES: If Client or Broker is a prevailing party in any legal proceeding brought as a result of a dispute under this agreement or any transaction related to this agreement, such party will be entitled to recover from the non-prevailing party all costs of such proceeding and reasonable attorney's fees.

15. LIMITATION OF LIABILITY: Neither Broker nor any other broker, or their associates, is responsible or liable for Client's personal injuries or for any loss or damage to Client's property that is not caused by Broker. Client will hold broker, any other broker, and their associates, harmless from any such injuries or losses. Client will indemnify Broker against any claims for injury or damage that Client may cause to others or their property.

16. ADDENDA: Addenda and other related documents which are part of this agreement are:

- ☒ Information About Brokerage Services
- ☐ Protecting Your Home from Mold
- ☐ Information Concerning Property Insurance
- ☐ General Information and Notice to a Buyer
- ☐ Protect Your Family from Lead in Your Home
- ☐ Information about Special Flood Hazard Areas
- ☐ For Your Protection: Get a Home Inspection
- ☐ _____

17. SPECIAL PROVISIONS:

18. ADDITIONAL NOTICES:

A. Broker's fees and the sharing of fees between brokers are not fixed, controlled, recommended, suggested, or maintained by the Association of REALTORS® or any listing service.

B. Broker's services are provided without regard to race, color, religion, national origin, sex, disability or familial status.

C. Broker is not a property inspector, surveyor, engineer, environmental assessor, or compliance inspector. Client should seek experts to render such services in any acquisition.

D. If Client purchases property, Client should have an abstract covering the property examined by an attorney of Client's selection, or Client should be furnished with or obtain a title policy.

E. Buyer may purchase a residential service contract. Buyer should review such service contract for the scope of coverage, exclusions, and limitations. The purchase of a residential service contract is optional. There are several residential service companies operating in Texas.

F. Broker cannot give legal advice. This is a legally binding agreement. **READ IT CAREFULLY.** If you do not understand the effect of this agreement, consult your attorney **BEFORE** signing.

_____	_____	_____	_____
Broker's Printed Name	License No.	Client	Date
By:_____		_____	_____
Broker's Associate's Signature	Date	Client	Date

(TAR-1501) 4-14-06

These prohibited activities mean that an Intermediary may **not**:

(1) disclose to the buyer or tenant that the seller or landlord will accept a price less than the asking price, unless otherwise instructed in a separate writing by the seller or landlord;

(2) disclose to the seller or landlord that the buyer or tenant will pay a price greater than the price submitted in a written offer to the seller or landlord, unless otherwise instructed in a separate writing by the buyer or tenant;

(3) disclose any confidential information or any information a party specifically instructs the broker or salesperson in writing not to disclose, unless:
(A) the broker or salesperson is otherwise instructed in a separate writing by the respective party;
(B) the broker or salesperson is required to disclose the information by this chapter or a court order; or
(C) the information materially relates to the condition of the property;

(4) treat a party to a transaction dishonestly; or

(5) violate this chapter [The Real Estate License Act].

TRELA § 1101.651(d)

3. An Intermediary May Make Appointments

Although an Intermediary must act fairly and impartially with respect to each client, the law also recognizes that there are times when the parties will want preferential advice or opinions in connection with the transaction. Under the law, this may occur when the Intermediary makes **appointments** by assigning associates to provide additional assistance to each of the parties. While an Intermediary is not obligated to make appointments, if an associate is appointed for one party, another associate must be appointed for the other party.

Typically, an appointee can assist his/her assigned party in a number of ways. This includes:

1. Communicating with a party,
2. Carrying out that party's instructions,
3. Providing opinions to a party, and
4. Offering advice to a party.

When appointments are made, the Intermediary must retain his/her neutrality between the parties and prevent the flow of any confidential information from one side to the other. In this sense, the Intermediary acts a "firewall" between the two sides.

D. BROKER ACTS AS SUBAGENT

SUBAGENCY is a form of agency where the seller's agent works or "cooperates" with a licensee in another office in order to represent the seller. The statutory definition of a subagent is shown at the right.

> "Subagent" means a license holder who: (A) represents a principal through cooperation with and the consent of a broker representing the principal; and (B) is not sponsored by or associated with the principal's broker.
>
> ***TRELA § 1101.002(8)***

Under this form of agency practice, the subagent is usually aligned with the seller so that the subagent owes OLD-CAR duties to the seller. The buyer, on the other hand, is the subagent's customer, meaning that the subagent owes the buyer only duties of fairness and honesty. *Unfortunately, this rather unique working arrangement might lead a buyer to falsely believe that a subagent is working for him/her, when in fact, the subagent is really an agent of the seller. When this occurs, it is known as ACCIDENTAL DUAL AGENCY*, and may lead to substantial legal problems for the licensee involved.

Subagency is diminishing in use due to the popularity of buyer's agency as well as a general reluctance by listing agents to incur potential liability related to subagency.

VI. Liability for Misconduct

This section explains some of the more commonly known state and federal statutes which give rise to legal liability for misconduct.

A. THE REAL ESTATE LICENSE ACT (TRELA)

Under The Real Estate License Act, a licensee can face disciplinary action for acts of misconduct, whether done intentionally or intentionally. Section 1101.652 of TRELA, which is shown in Chapter 6, lists the grounds for license suspension/revocation. However, in addition to disciplinary action, TRELA also allows for the imposition of other enforcement actions against licensees. These include:

1. Administrative penalty,
2. Court injunctions,
3. State civil penalty, and
4. Criminal prosecution.

Additionally, TRELA has established a large recovery fund which is intended to reimburse persons who have successfully sued licensees, but are unable to collect. **The Texas Real Estate Recovery Trust Account** is administered by TREC to reimburse persons who have been harmed by acts of brokers, salespersons, other real estate licensees, and their agents. The account is further described in Chapter 6.

B. TEXAS DECEPTIVE TRADE PRACTICES CONSUMER PROTECTION ACT (DTPA)

The *TEXAS DECEPTIVE TRADE PRACTICES CONSUMER PROTECTION ACT (DTPA) was enacted in 1973 and is intended to be liberally construed so as to allow persons to file suit against unscrupulous business owners.* The law permits consumers to file lawsuits based upon false oral or written representations that arise in connection with contracts. Likewise, consumers may sue where any of the following events constitute a producing cause of economic damages or damages for mental anguish:

1. The use or employment by any person of a false, misleading or deceptive act or practice that is (1) specifically listed on the so-called **"Laundry List"** as will be detailed later in this chapter; and (2) relied on by the consumer to the consumer's detriment;

2. Breach of an express or implied warranty; or

3. Any unconscionable action or a course or action by any person.

"**Unconscionable** action or course or action" means an act or practice which, to a consumer's detriment, takes advantage of the lack of knowledge, ability, experience, or capacity of the consumer to a grossly unfair degree.

Texas Business and Commerce Code § 17.45(5)

---

1. Scope of Coverage

Under the law, consumers, as that term is defined, may bring suit for unlawful business practices. A *CONSUMER is defined as someone who seeks or acquires, through purchase or lease, any goods or services.* The term "services" includes brokerage services and applies to persons who are buying or just looking to buy real property.

2. Exclusion for Professional Services

Under the law, "professional services" are exempted. Under the DTPA, a professional service is defined as a service essentially providing "advice, judgment, opinion, or similar professional skill." However, even if the service provided by the broker falls within the professional services definition, this exemption, as it relates to the real estate industry, will not apply to:

- An express misrepresentation of a material fact that cannot be characterized as advice, judgment, or opinion;

- An unconscionable action or course of action that cannot be characterized as advice, judgment, or opinion; or

- Breach of an express warranty that cannot be characterized as advice, judgment or opinion.

3. The "Laundry List"

At the very heart of the DTPA are 27 practices which have been specifically declared "False, Misleading, or Deceptive" under the law. These illegal practices are often referred to as the "Laundry List." Of the list of 27 unlawful practices, these are the ones that relate to the real estate industry:

- Causing confusion or misunderstanding as to the source, sponsorship, approval, or certification of goods or services;
- Causing confusion or misunderstanding as to affiliation, connection, or association with, or certification by, another;
- Representing that goods or services have sponsorship, approval, characteristics, ingredients, uses, benefits, or quantities which they do not have or that a person has a sponsorship, approval, status, affiliation, or connection which he does not;
- Representing that goods are original or new if they are deteriorated, reconditioned, reclaimed, used, or secondhand;
- Representing that goods or services are of a particular standard, quality, or grade, or that goods are of a particular style or model, if they are of another;
- Disparaging the goods, services, or business of another by false or misleading representation of facts;
- Advertising goods or services with intent not to sell them as advertised;
- Making false or misleading statements of fact concerning the reasons for, existence of, or amount of price reductions;
- Representing that an agreement confers or involves rights, remedies, or obligations which it does not have or involve, or which are prohibited by law;
- Knowingly making false or misleading statements of fact concerning the need for parts, replacement, or repair service;
- Misrepresenting the authority of a salesman, representative or agent to negotiate the final terms of a consumer transaction;
- Representing that work or services have been performed on, or parts replaced in, goods when the work or services were not performed or the parts replaced;
- Failing to disclose information concerning goods or services which was known at the time of the transaction if such failure to disclose such information was intended to induce the consumer into a transaction into which the consumer would not have entered had the information been disclosed; and
- Taking advantage of a disaster declared by the governor by: selling or leasing fuel, food, medicine, or another necessity at an exorbitant or excessive price; or demanding an exorbitant or excessive price in connection with the sale or lease of fuel, food, medicine, or another necessity.

4. Required Settlement Offer

As a strict requirement of filing suit, the DTPA requires that the consumer give the accused written notice 60 days prior to the filing of suit. The law also gives the business person the right to request in writing the inspection of any goods that may become the subject of the suit. The purpose of the notice is to try to weed out frivolous complaints as well as to try to promote settlement of disputes before resorting to the court system.

Under the law this notice *must* contain the following elements:

1. Details regarding the specific complaint;
2. The amount of economic damages;
3. The damages for mental anguish; and
4. Expenses reasonably incurred by the consumer, including attorney's fees.

A business person who does not receive the notice prior to the filing of suit is entitled to ask the court to **ABATE** *(stop)* the suit until such time as the notice is given.

C. TEXAS REAL ESTATE FRAUD ACT

Another basis of liability for real estate licensees is under the Texas Real Estate Fraud Act which is located in Chapter 27 of the Texas Business and Commerce Code. Under the right set of circumstances, an injured party might bring a lawsuit based on both the Real Estate Fraud Act <u>and</u> the DTPA.

Under the act, the term "fraud" is statutorily defined as:

(1) false representation of a past or existing material fact, when the false representation is
  (A) made to a person for the purpose of inducing that person to enter into a contract; and
  (B) relied on by that person in entering into that contract; or
(2) false promise to do an act, when the false promise is
  (A) material;
  (B) made with the intention of not fulfilling it;
(C) made to a person for the purpose of inducing that person to enter into a contract; and
  (D) relied on by that person in entering into that contract.

Texas Business and Commerce Code § 27.01

For example, assume that a broker is showing some homes to a first-time homebuyer. In order to induce the client to make an offer, the broker falsely tells the client that he'd better act quickly because she has two other clients who are making offers on this same property tomorrow. If the client relies on the false representation and makes an offer to buy the property, the broker could face civil liability under the Texas Real Estate Fraud Act.

Under this law, a plaintiff (a person who files a lawsuit) who can prove fraud under either definition is entitled to recover **actual damages** under the act. However, if the plaintiff can prove that the fraud occurred and the defendant had "actual awareness" of the misrepresentation, then the plaintiff can also recover exemplary damages under the law. *EXEMPLARY DAMAGES are money damages which are typically very large and intended to "make an example" of the wrongdoer.*

D. FEDERAL ANTITRUST LAWS

The term "antitrust" refers to a group of federal laws which were enacted to prevent unfair competition by big corporations and large business interests. Over the years, the courts have refined the reach of these laws to cover the following types of practices:

1. Agreements in unreasonable restraint of trade;
2. Unfair methods of competition; and
3. Business practices that tend to monopolize commerce.

Under the federal antitrust laws, the following are examples of practices which are considered illegal.

Price Fixing – These include illegal agreements or understandings among businesses to establish or fix the price of goods or services.

In the real estate business, an example of this type of practice would include an agreement among brokerage firms to set the commission rate that is charged to the public within a local community.

Boycotts – This practice involves an agreement, motivated by anti-competitive reasons, among business leaders to deal with a particular competitor by denying the competitor a source of clients or access to a needed service.

In the real estate business, an example of this type of practice would include an agreement among brokerage firms to set the commission rate that is charged to the public within a local community.

Market Division – This consists of agreements among business competitors to divide a sales territory or allocate customers among themselves, thereby decreasing business competition.

An example here would include an illegal agreement among large brokerage firms to carve up a community and assign a firm to each sector so that only one firm could solicit customers in that area.

Tie-in Sales – Under this practice, a business sells a product or service to a consumer on the condition that a second product or service be purchased as well.

In the real estate field, this might include a situation where a broker advertises extremely low commission rates for sellers but later informs clients that the low rate is strictly on the condition that the same broker be allowed to represent the client as a buyer but for a much higher commission charge.

Penalties for violating the federal antitrust laws can be severe. Violations of the law are punishable by both civil and criminal sanctions. Corporations can be assessed a criminal fine of no more than $10,000,000. Individuals can face a fine of up to $370,000 and 3 years in prison.

VII. The Broker-Salesperson Relationship

Agency law not only applies to the relationship between brokers and clients, but also between brokers and salespersons. A salesperson must formally associate with a licensed broker if the salesperson intends to work in the brokerage business. In that respect, it is a relationship required by TRELA but guided by the terms a private agreement.

A. BROKER ASSOCIATION REQUIRED BY LAW

Under The Real Estate License Act, a Texas real estate broker is authorized to perform a wide range of brokerage activities such as sales, rentals, and exchanges of investment property. But the law also provides that licensed salespersons can only perform the same acts if they are formally "associated" with and are acting for a broker. This is what is meant by a salesperson being sponsored by a broker. Thus, a salesperson's legal ability to perform brokerage services is directly and entirely dependent upon a relationship with a sponsoring broker.

Sponsorship is normally accomplished by submitting to the commission a Salesperson Sponsorship Form signed by both the broker and the salesperson. Once the sponsorship form has been received by the real estate commission, the commission is required by law to deliver the salesperson license to the sponsoring broker, where it must be kept under the broker's custody and control.

B. NATURE OF RELATIONSHIP

Brokerage firm owners have a choice in manner and form of the business relationship with their sponsored licensees. This relationship may be formed as independent contractors or as employees. This makes a difference when it comes to issues of control and federal taxation. As a general rule, licensees whose function is to sell are usually treated as independent contractors, while support staff and management staff are typically employees.

1. **Employees** work for employers and have duties and designated hours which place them under the direct control and supervision of the employer. As a general rule, employers must withhold income taxes, withhold and pay Social Security and Medicare taxes, and pay unemployment taxes on wages paid to an employee. The failure to do so may result in substantial penalties by the IRS for the employer.

Withholding income and F.I.C.A. taxes from wages paid another person is considered evidence of employment.

TREC Rule § 535.35

---

2. **Independent contractors**, on the other hand, are not under the direct supervision of an employer. They do their job in the manner they wish. They set their own hours of work, prospect for business in the way they wish, solicit the neighborhoods where they wish to specialize, and are asked by their broker simply to bring deals that close and generate commissions. Thus their approach to work is not subject to the direct supervision of another person. The broker pays the associate his/her share of the commission check when earned and does not withhold any money for payment of taxes or Social Security taxes. It becomes the obligation of the independent contractor to pay to the government all sums due.

Figure 4-7 is the TAR Independent Contractor Agreement For Sales Associate.

C. BROKER'S RESPONSIBILITY

Just as the principal is legally responsible for the acts of the agent, a broker is legally responsible for the acts of his/her sponsored agents. Under TRELA, a broker is responsible, not only for his/her own actions, but also for the actions of any associates.

A licensed broker is liable to:

- the [real estate] commission,
- the public, and
- the broker's clients

for any conduct engaged in under [the License Act] by the broker or by a salesperson associated with or acting for the broker.

TRELA § 1101.803

Is the broker required to supervise the sponsored salesperson(s)? Surprisingly, the answer is "no." Under the commission rules, a sponsoring broker always remains liable for the acts of the salesperson regardless of whether the salesperson is supervised.

Figure 4-7

TEXAS ASSOCIATION OF REALTORS®

INDEPENDENT CONTRACTOR AGREEMENT FOR SALES ASSOCIATE

USE OF THIS FORM BY PERSONS WHO ARE NOT MEMBERS OF THE TEXAS ASSOCIATION OF REALTORS® IS NOT AUTHORIZED.
©Texas Association of REALTORS®, Inc. 1998

1. **PARTIES:** The parties to this agreement are _____ (Broker) and
    _____ (Associate).

2. **TERM:** This agreement commences on _____ (Commencement Date)
    and continues until such time as either party terminates this agreement in accordance with Paragraph 21.

3. **DEFINITIONS:**

    A. *"Brokerage services"* means assistance and services to prospects that are reasonably necessary to negotiate and bring about the successful closing of transactions for the sale, purchase, or lease of real estate.

    B. *"Broker's office"* means Broker's place or places of business at or through which the brokerage services will be provided under this agreement, located at _____
    _____ .

    C. *"Files"* means any documents, instruments, contracts, written agreements, memorandum, books, publications, records, cards, correspondence, computer data and any other data related to Broker's real estate business. The term "files" ☐ includes ☐ excludes   Associate's prospect lists.

    D. *"Prospect"* means a buyer, prospective buyer, seller, prospective seller, landlord, prospective landlord, tenant, or prospective tenant of real estate or a client or customer of Broker or Associate.

    E. *"Real estate business"* means all business related to the acts of a real estate broker as defined by Section 2(2) of the Real Estate License Act, Article 6573a, Texas Civil Statutes.

    F. *"Special expenses"* means expenses that Broker incurs for _____
    _____
    (for example, franchise fees, E & O premiums, transaction fees, desk fees, etc).

4. **BEST EFFORTS:** Associate will use Associate's best professional efforts to: (1) solicit listings and prospects for Broker's real estate business; and (2) provide brokerage services to prospects procured by or assigned to Associate.

5. **EXCLUSIVE ASSOCIATION:** Associate will perform the services contemplated by this agreement exclusively for Broker. Associate may not engage in the brokerage of businesses or in the management of property without Broker's knowledge and written consent.

6. **LEGAL AND ETHICAL COMPLIANCE:** When delivering brokerage services to prospects and when otherwise performing under this agreement, the parties agree to comply with all applicable laws and standards of practice, including but not limited to the Real Estate License Act (Art. 6573a, VTCS), the Rules of the Texas Real Estate Commission (22 TAC), the Code of Ethics of the National Association of REALTORS®, the by-laws of the national, state, and applicable local associations of REALTORS®, any rules or regulations of any listing service to which the parties may subscribe, and any standards or policies that Broker adopts.

7. **LICENSES AND TRADE ASSOCIATIONS:**

    A. Broker's License and Membership Status: Broker is a licensed real estate broker in the State of Texas and is a member of the National Association of REALTORS®, the Texas Association of REALTORS®, and the following local association(s) of REALTORS®: _____ . Broker will maintain Broker's license and REALTOR® membership status active and in good standing at all times while this agreement is in effect.

    B. Associate's License and Membership Status: Associate is a licensed real estate ☐ salesman ☐ broker   in the State of Texas. Associate ☐ is ☐ will become   a member of the National Association of REALTORS®, the Texas Association of REALTORS®, and the following local association(s) of REALTORS®: _____
    _____ . Associate will maintain Associate's license and REALTOR® membership status active and in good standing at all times while this agreement is in effect.

(TAR-2301) 10-19-98   Initialed for Identification by Associate _____ and Broker _____   Page 1 of 6

8. INDEPENDENT CONTRACTOR:

A. <u>Contractor</u>: Associate is an independent contractor and is not Broker's employee. Broker will not withhold any amounts for taxes from the fees paid to Associate under this agreement. Broker will not pay any amounts for unemployment compensation or worker's compensation for Associate.

B. <u>Statement of Understanding</u>: On or about the first day of _____ of each calendar year this agreement is in effect, Associate will execute and deliver to Broker a Statement of Understanding, a copy of which is attached to this agreement.

C. <u>Not a Partnership</u>: This agreement does not create a partnership between the parties. Except as provided in this agreement, neither party is liable to the other party for any expense or obligation incurred by the other party.

9. ASSOCIATE'S AUTHORITY:

A. <u>Signing Brokerage Service Agreements</u>: On Broker's behalf and in accordance with any standards and policies Broker adopts, Associate may sign listing agreements, buyer or tenant representation agreements, and commission agreements.

B. <u>Submission of Agreements</u>: All listings, representation agreements, commission agreements, and other agreements for brokerage services that Associate procures or signs must be taken in the name of Broker and must be submitted to Broker within _____ days after the listing, representation agreement, or other agreement is taken by Associate.

C. <u>Cancellations</u>: Associate may not cancel or compromise any agreement to which Broker is a party without Broker's written approval.

D. <u>Other Agreements</u>: Unless specifically authorized by this agreement or by Broker in writing, Associate may not bind or obligate Broker to any agreement or relationship.

E. <u>Brokerage Services</u>: Associate may, on Broker's behalf, provide brokerage services to prospects.

10. FILES: In any transaction related to Broker's real estate business in which Associate is involved, Associate must maintain a file at Broker's office that contains all documents, contracts, agreements, disclosures, correspondence, data, and other information related to the transaction.

11. OWNERSHIP OF LISTINGS AND REPRESENTATION AGREEMENTS: All listings, representation agreements, commission agreements, and other agreements for brokerage services in which Broker is named as a party are owned exclusively by Broker.

12. RECEIPT OF MONEY BY ASSOCIATE:

A. <u>Compliance with Contracts</u>: Associate must promptly deposit all checks or funds Associate receives in trust for others in accordance with the contracts under which the checks or funds are received. Associate may not maintain a separate trust, escrow, or management account for real estate business purposes.

B. <u>Receipt of Brokerage Fees</u>: Associate must deliver any compensation for brokerage services received from any client, customer, escrow agent, title company, prospect, or any other person to Broker for disbursement in accordance with this agreement. Unless otherwise authorized by Broker, Associate may not accept any check made payable to Associate from any client, customer, escrow agent, title company, prospect, or any other person with whom Associate may deal in a matter related to Broker's real estate business.

13. FACILITIES: For use related to Broker's real estate business, Broker will furnish to Associate the following office facilities at Broker's office:

Use of the office facilities lies at Associate's discretion. Performance of this agreement does not require Associate to be present in Broker's office.

14. ADVERTISING: All advertising related to Broker's real estate business, including brokerage services performed by Associate, may be placed only by Broker or only with Broker's knowledge and consent. Broker will, at Broker's discretion, include Associate's name in such advertising when appropriate. Associate will not cause any advertisement that is related to Broker's real estate business to be published without Broker's prior knowledge and consent.

15. ASSIGNMENT OF PROSPECTS:

A. _Definition_: Under this Paragraph 15, _"assign"_ means to appoint an associate to deal with a prospect on Broker's behalf.

B. _Prospects Procured by Associate_: Broker gives to Associate the right, together with Broker, to deal with prospects that Associate procures and with prospects that Broker assigns to Associate.

C. _Prospects Procured by Broker_: Broker retains the right and sole discretion to assign leads and prospects that are procured by Broker through Broker's real estate business to any of Broker's associates as Broker determines appropriate.

D. _Reassignments_: Broker may reassign a prospect with whom Associate deals to another associate if: (1) Broker determines that a reassignment of the prospect is necessary for the orderly operation of Broker's real estate business; (2) Associate is not capable of continuing to service the prospect; or (3) this agreement terminates. This provision applies to all prospects, regardless of who procured the prospect.

E. _No Interference_: Associate may not interfere with any assignments or reassignments of prospects or leads that Broker may make.

16. ASSOCIATE'S FEES:

A. _Brokerage Fees are Paid to Broker_: All fees and compensation that Broker or Associate earn for providing brokerage services to prospects (for example, fees earned under listing agreements, buyer or tenant representation agreements, agreements between brokers, etc.) are payable to and belong to Broker.

B. _Amount of Associate's Fees_: Broker will pay Associate fees for the brokerage services that Associate provides under this agreement at the rates or in the amounts specified in the attached fee schedule.

C. _When Associate's Fees are Earned and Payable_: Associate's fees under this agreement are earned at the time that the Broker's fees under the applicable agreements for brokerage services are earned. Associates fees under this agreement are payable when Broker receives Broker's fees under the applicable agreements for brokerage services, unless the fees are subject to arbitration or litigation.

D. _Disputes Between Associates_: If another associate(s) of Broker claims a fee from a transaction for which Associate also claims a fee, the amount of the fee payable to Associate will be divided between Associate and the other associate(s) claiming the fee in accordance with an agreement between them, or if no such agreement is reached, by arbitration. Before disbursing any fee Broker may require written authorization from any associates claiming the fee. Associate agrees not to hold Broker liable for holding, in trust, any disputed funds between associates.

E. _Delinquent Brokerage Fees_: Broker is not liable to Associate for any fees not collected from a prospect. Broker retains complete discretion to enforce or not enforce any agreement for brokerage services contemplated by this agreement.

F. _Bonuses_: Associate may not accept any fee, bonus, or other compensation directly. All fees, bonuses, and other compensation must be paid to Broker for distribution in accordance with this agreement. Unless otherwise agreed in writing between the parties to this agreement, bonuses will be considered as part of the gross compensation Broker receives under the applicable agreements for brokerage services and will be disbursed in accordance with the attached fee schedule.

G. _Fees Upon Reassignment of Prospects_: If Broker reassigns a prospect with whom Associate deals to another associate or if Broker reassigns a prospect with whom another associate deals to Associate, Broker will pay Associate: (1) a fee in accordance with the attached fee schedule if the fee schedule specifically addresses reassignments of prospects; or (2) a fee that Broker determines to be equitable if the fee schedule does not specifically address reassignments of prospects.

H. _Assignment of Fees_: Associate may not assign any interest in fees or compensation due under this agreement to any other person.

17. EXPENSES:

A. _No Liability for Another's Expense_: Unless the parties agree otherwise, Broker is not liable for any expense incurred by Associate. Unless the parties agree otherwise, Associate is not liable to Broker for the expenses for the office facilities that Broker will provide under this agreement.

    B.   Special Expenses: Special expenses will be:

        ☐ (1) deducted from the gross fees that Broker receives under agreements for brokerage services and paid to the providers of the special services before calculating Associate's fees payable under this agreement.

        ☐ (2) invoiced to Associate by Broker and will become payable upon receipt of the invoice.

    C.   License and Membership Fees: Each party is responsible to pay all their respective license and membership fees. Associate must immediately reimburse Broker any fee, expense, or penalty that Broker incurs as a result of the parties' association or Associate's failure to maintain Associate's license or REALTOR® membership status as required by this agreement.

    D.   Automobile Expenses: Associate will furnish his or her own automobile and pay all such expenses. Broker is not liable or responsible for Associate's automobile or its expenses. Associate must maintain liability and property damage insurance satisfactory to Broker and must name Broker as an additional insured in any such policy. At Broker's request, Associate must deliver satisfactory evidence of the insurance required by this agreement.

    E.   Other Expenses: Associate is responsible for all of Associate's expenses necessary to perform the services required of Associate under this agreement, including but not limited to, license fees, association dues, entertainment costs, club dues, mobile phone expenses, education expenses, computer service access charges, periodical expenses, and other related expenses. Although not obligated to do so, if Broker pays any such expense for or on behalf of Associate, Associate will reimburse Broker such amount upon demand.

18. OFFSET: Broker retains the right of offset for all purposes. Broker may deduct amounts Associate owes Broker from any amounts Broker owes to Associate under this agreement.

19. DEFENSE OF DISPUTES AND LITIGATION:

    A.   Cooperation: If a dispute, litigation, or complaint against Broker or Associate occurs in a transaction in which Associate is involved and which is related to Broker's real estate business, the parties will cooperate fully with each other in defending the action.

    B.   Mutual Defense: Broker and Associate will share all expenses and costs related to defend any dispute, litigation, or complaint in the same proportion as they would share the fee resulting from the transaction as if there were no dispute, litigation, or complaint if: (1) both Broker and Associate are named as defendants or respondents to the dispute, litigation, or complaint; and (2) neither Broker nor Associate objects to a mutual defense of the dispute, litigation, or complaint.

    C.   Defense Management in a Mutual Defense: If the parties mutually defend a dispute, litigation, or complaint, Broker maintains sole discretion to: (1) determine whether to defend or compromise the dispute, litigation, or complaint; (2) employ attorneys or other experts; (3) direct the course of any defense strategy; and (4) determine the terms and conditions of any compromise or settlement, provided that Broker may not obligate Associate to pay anything of value without Associate's written consent.

    D.   Right to Separate Defense: If either party determines that it cannot mutually defend a dispute, litigation, or complaint with the other party, each party will be responsible for its own costs to defend the dispute, litigation, or complaint from the time one party notifies the other of such a determination.

    E.   Liability for Damages: Except as provided in Paragraph 19F, each party is responsible for the payment of any amounts for which it is found liable. The sharing of defense costs provided in this Paragraph 19 does not apply to the payment of damages for which a party is found liable by a court of law, arbitrator, or state agency.

    F.   Reimbursement and Indemnity: If Broker is found to be liable by a court, arbitrator, or state agency as a result of Associate's negligence, misrepresentations, fraud, false statements, or violation of the Real Estate License Act, Associate will indemnify and reimburse Broker all such amounts and all attorney's fees, costs, and other expenses necessary to defend the action including those defense costs that were previously shared under this Paragraph 19.

    G.   Survival: This Paragraph 19 survives termination of this agreement.

20. PROSECUTION OF CLAIMS: For all matters related to Broker's real estate business, Broker retains sole discretion to prosecute, complain, compromise, or settle any claim that Broker may have against any other person, including but not limited to other brokers and Broker's or Associate's clients, customers, and prospects.

21. TERMINATION:

A. <u>Either Party May Terminate</u>: Either party may terminate this agreement, with or without cause, by providing written notice to the other party.

B. <u>Entitlement to Fees</u>: Termination of this agreement does not divest the rights of the parties to any fees earned before the termination is effective.

C. <u>Services to Prospects</u>: Upon termination of this agreement, all negotiations and other brokerage services with prospects commenced by Associate before termination will be assumed by Broker. Associate will cooperate with Broker to provide for an orderly transition and assumption of such services by Broker.

D. <u>Associate's Obligations Upon Termination</u>: At the time this agreement terminates, Associate must: (1) cease all negotiations and other dealings that concern Broker's real estate business commenced by Associate before this agreement terminates; (2) provide Broker a written list of all current listings and pending sales and leases; (3) turn over to Broker all files related to Broker's real estate business that Associate may have or control; and (4) turn over to Broker all Broker's personal property including but not limited to keysafes, signs, equipment, supplies, manuals, forms and keys.

E. <u>Files</u>: Associate may not remove any files related to Broker's real estate business from Broker's office without Broker's prior knowledge and consent. Associate is entitled to copies of relevant documents concerning pending transactions in which Associate has a bona fide interest. Broker will not unreasonably withhold copies of such documents.

22. CONFIDENTIALITY OF BUSINESS OPERATIONS:

A. <u>Files:</u> The parties agree that all files related to Broker's real estate business are Broker's confidential business property.

B. <u>Prospects and Operations</u>: Unless required by law or expressly permitted by Broker, Associate may not furnish any person engaged in the real estate business with information about: (1) Broker's prospects or Broker's relationship with any prospects; or (2) Broker's policies and business operations. This provision survives termination of this agreement.

23. NOTICES:
All notices under this agreement must be in writing and are effective when hand-delivered, mailed, sent by facsimile transmission, or sent by electronic mail from one party to the other.

24. SPECIAL PROVISIONS:

25. AGREEMENT OF THE PARTIES:

A. <u>Addenda</u>: Attached to and incorporated into this agreement are: (1) the Fee Schedule dated _____ _____; (2) the Statement of Understanding; and (3)_____ _____ _____.

Independent Contractor Agreement between _____ and _____

B. <u>Entire Agreement</u>: This document contains the entire agreement between the parties and may not be changed except by written agreement.

C. <u>No Assignment</u>: Neither party may assign this agreement or any interest in this agreement without the written consent of the other party.

D. <u>Heirs and Successors</u>: The parties' obligations under this agreement and the parties' entitlement to any compensation or reimbursement under this agreement inures to the benefit of the respective party's successors, permitted assigns, heirs, executors, and administrators.

E. <u>Controlling Law</u>: The laws of the State of Texas govern the interpretation, validity, performance, and enforcement of this agreement.

F. <u>Severable Clauses</u>: If any clause in this agreement is found to be invalid or unenforceable by a court of law, the remainder of this agreement will not be affected and all other provisions of this agreement will remain valid and enforceable.

G. <u>Waiver</u>: Waiver of any provision in this agreement by any party is effective only if the waiver is in writing. A waiver, whether in writing or otherwise, may not be construed as a waiver of any subsequent breach or failure of the same provision or any other provision of this agreement.

This is intended to be a legally binding agreement. READ IT CAREFULLY. If you do not understand the effect of this agreement, consult your attorney BEFORE signing.

_____	_____
Associate's Name Printed (as appears on license)	Broker's Name Printed License No.
	By: _____
_____	_____
Associate's Signature Date	Signature Date
_____	_____
Social Security Number License No. & Expiration Date	Title
_____	_____
Home Address	Office Address
_____	_____
City, State, Zip Code	City, State, Zip Code
_____	_____
Home Phone E-mail	Office Phone E-mail

VIII. CHAPTER SUMMARY

Agency is a special relationship which results when one person (the principal) gives another person (the agent) authority to act on his/her behalf. This relationship also requires that the agent accept this grant of authority.

In a Texas real estate transaction, the **principal** is thought of as the buyer (landlord) or the seller (tenant) of real property. In this context, another name for the principal is **client**. A **customer** is a third party who falls outside of the principal-agent relationship. A customer can be someone who is entirely unrepresented or a person who is represented by another broker.

An agency relationship is legally important because a principal will be held responsible for the acts of his/her agent. Additionally, anything an agent is told can be attributed to the principal.

The three types of agents are: 1) **universal agent** (holds the broadest range of authority), 2) **general agent** (can perform a wide range of activities limited to a specific purpose), and 3) **special agent** (authority is restricted to given task). Most real estate agents are special agents. Additionally, special agents may not normally accept offers or sign contracts on behalf of their clients.

An agency relationship may be created by various means. It can be created by: 1) an oral or written agreement of the parties (**express agency**), 2) by the conduct of the parties (**implied agency**), 3) approval of an act by the principal that was performed on his/her behalf after the act was performed (**ratification**), or 4) when innocent third parties are allowed to believe that an agency relationship exists, when it has not been formally created (**ostensible agency**). For Texas real estate licensees, the best way to form an agency relationship is with an express, written agreement because it allows the agent to sue the client for an unpaid commission.

An agency relationship can be terminated by **act of the parties** (purpose accomplished, expiration of term, mutual agreement, renunciation by agent, revocation by principal, or abandonment by agent). It can also be terminated by **operation of law** (the death of a party, the subject property is destroyed, illegality, or the bankruptcy of the owner).

An agency relationship is a **fiduciary relationship**, which is a special relationship founded on **trust, confidence, integrity,** and **fidelity**. As a fiduciary, an agent owes the principal the duty of obedience to instruction, loyalty, the duty to disclose material information, confidentiality, the duty to account for all money and property, and the duty of reasonable care, skill, and diligence. Only the duty of confidentiality will survive the agency relationship. An agent will also owe duties of **fairness** and **honesty** to all individuals, clients, and customers alike.

A Texas real estate agent can find himself/herself in one of four types of agency relationship. The agent can work for a seller, a buyer, intermediary practice, or as a subagent. As a seller's agent, an agent can work under an exclusive right to sell, exclusive agency, or an open listing. Under all three, a seller may attempt to sell his/her own home but under an exclusive right to sell, the agent will be entitled to a commission regardless of who sells the property.

Intermediary practice was created by the Texas Legislature and permits Texas brokers to represent a buyer and seller at the same time. Under the law, only brokers can serve as intermediaries, if the parties so authorize, but the broker must remain fair and impartial with respect to both sides. In order to give each side the benefit of an agent's advice or opinion, an intermediary may appoint associates to assist each party. The intermediary may not appoint himself/herself to either party and must remember to remain neutral with respect to both sides.

A licensee can face legal liability for misconduct. Some of the laws that give rise to civil and criminal liability are **The Real Estate License Act**, the **Texas Deceptive Trade Practices Consumer Protection Act (DTPA)**, the **Texas Real Estate Fraud Act**, and the federal antitrust laws.

Finally, it must also be remembered that agency relationships exist within the context of the broker-salesperson relation. Texas law requires that all salespersons must be **associated** or **sponsored** by an active broker before engaging in the brokerage business. However, Texas law does not govern the nature of the actual business relationship between these two parties. Usually, most brokers will associate with salespersons as **independent contractors** rather than **employees**. Independent contractors are paid on the results they achieve and when they are paid, the contractors are responsible for the payment of their own income taxes.

IX. TERMINOLGY

A. Agent
B. Antitrust
C. Appointee
D. Client
E. Customer
F. Exclusive Agency
G. Exclusive Right to Sell
H. Express Agency

I. Express Agreement
J. Fiduciary
K. General Agent
L. Implied Agency
M. Intermediary
N. Intermediary Practice
O. Open Listing
P. Ostensible Agency

Q. Principal
R. Ratification
S. Renunciation of Authority
T. Revocation of Authority
U. Special Agent
V. Subagent
W. Unintended Dual Agency
X. Universal Agent

1. ___ Someone who acts for the benefit of another in a relationship founded on trust, confidence, integrity and fidelity.

2. ___ A person for whom action is to be taken in an agency relationship.

3. ___ A person who accepts a designation of authority by agreeing to act for the principal.

4. ___ A third party to whom the agent owes duties of fairness and honesty.

5. ___ An agent's principal.

6. ___ An agent who is empowered by the principal to do any/all lawful actions on behalf of the principal.

7. ___ An agent who is authorized to perform acts of a very limited nature such as, for example, selling a house pursuant to a listing agreement.

8. ___ An agent who is authorized to perform acts within a limited range and scope of an on-going nature. An example is the broker-associate relationship.

9. ___ Agency which is created by means of written or oral means.

10. ___ Agency which is created by the conduct or behavior of the parties rather than by an express agreement.

11. ___ The approval of a previous act or statement.

12. ___ An agent's rejection of authority.

13. ___ A principal's taking back of authority previously granted to an agent.

14. ___ An agency relationship recognized by law when a third-party believes that a particular person is acting as an agent for someone else.

15. ___ An agreement or contract that has been put into words, either written or spoken.

16. ___ A type of listing agreement where a broker is appointed as the exclusive agent for the seller. Under this type of agreement, the broker will not be entitled to a commission if the seller is successful in selling his/her own property.

17. ___ A type of listing agreement where the broker is appointed as the exclusive agent for the seller. Under this type of agreement, the broker will be entitled to a commission regardless of whether the seller or the broker sells the subject property.

18. ___ An authorization by an owner granted to one or more brokers to sell a particular property. Under this type of agreement, the owner may continue to sell and market his/her property, but the successful selling broker will be entitled to a commission.

19. ___ An agency relationship created pursuant to the provisions of The Real Estate License Act whereby one agent represents multiple parties in the same real estate transaction.

20. ___ Under intermediary practice, a broker who undertakes to simultaneously represent both parties in the same real estate transaction. Only a broker can be an intermediary.

21. ___ A real estate licensee associated with a broker who, with the knowledge and consent of the parties, is appointed by an intermediary to specifically represent one party to a real estate transaction.

22. ___ An unintended, and unauthorized relationship that results when a real estate licensee attempts or inadvertently attempts to represent both parties to a real estate transaction without their full knowledge and consent.

23. ___ A broker who represents a principal through cooperation with and the consent of a broker representing the principal; and (B) is not sponsored by or associated with the principal's broker.

24. ___ Federal laws which prohibit monopolies, unfair competition, and agreements which unreasonably restrain of trade by corporations and other large business interests.

X. MULTIPLE CHOICE

1. An agent may be defined as a person who:
    a. acts on behalf of another.
    b. acts on behalf of customer.
    c. is compensated as a salesperson.
    d. any of the above.

2. The client is the:
    a. buyer.
    b. customer.
    c. broker.
    d. principal.

3. The customer is:
    a. the buyer.
    b. the seller.
    c. the broker.
    d. a third party outside of a principal-agent relationship who receives services from an agent.

4. An agency agreement can be created by:
    a. express agreement.
    b. implied agreement.
    c. ratification.
    d. all of the above.

5. When a party approves of an act that was previously done without authority this creates:
    a. express agency.
    b. special agency.
    c. agency by ratification.
    d. agency by implication.

6. Which of the following are fiduciary duties owed by the agent to a principal?
    a. Obedience to instructions
    b. Disclosure of material information
    c. Accounting of money
    d. All of the above

7. Brokers owe:
    a. fiduciary duties to clients.
    b. duties of fairness to customers.
    c. duties of truthfulness to clients.
    d. all of the above.

8. The intermediary is:
    a. the licensee appointed by the buyer and the licensee appointed by the seller.
    b. an associate of the broker.
    c. a broker.
    d. any licensed person associated with the sale.

9. An appointee is:
    a. an associate of the broker selected by the parties.
    b. an associate of the broker selected by the broker.
    c. required to be a salesperson.
    d. required to be a broker.

10. If a subagent represents a seller:
    a. the buyer is unrepresented.
    b. the buyer is owed duties of truthfulness and honesty.
    c. the seller is owed OLD-CAR duties.
    d. all of the above.

ANSWERS: 1. a; 2. d; 3. d; 4. d; 5. d; 6. c; 7. d; 8. c; 9. b; 10. d

Agency and Its Responsibility

153

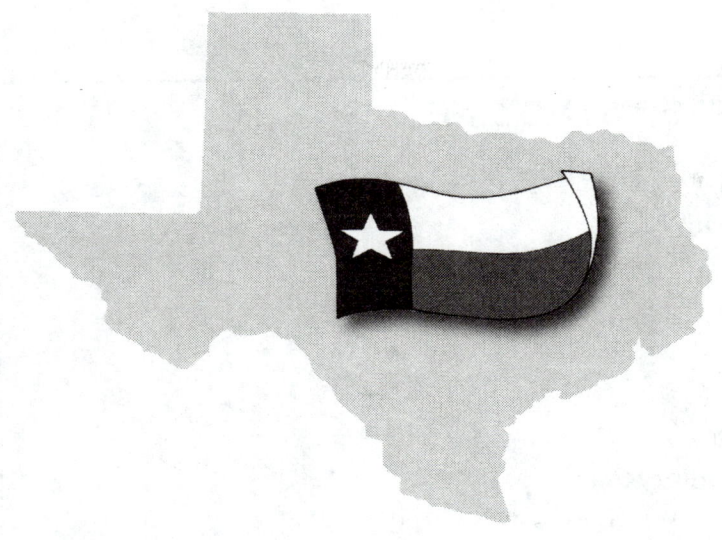

Chapter 5
Contracts

I. Contracts in General

Few areas of knowledge are as important to the real estate broker as the laws surrounding contracts. The wording of the contract not only serves to evidence the promises made by the parties, but also serves to outline their duties, obligations and responsibilities towards one another. In short, the entire real estate transaction is guided by the terms of the contract.

Because a real estate transaction is governed by the contract, it is important to understand the basic rules that govern the creation, life, and death of a contract.

This chapter will: 1) explain the essential elements necessary to create a legally binding contract; 2) illustrate in a general manner the important parts of Texas real estate contract forms promulgated by The Texas Real Estate Commission (TREC) as well as those created by the Texas Association of REALTORS® (TAR) and the addenda that accompany them; and 3) provide information on laws governing the use of contract forms by real estate licensees.

CHAPTER 5 OUTLINE

I. CONTRACTS IN GENERAL (p. 155)
  A. Classification of Contracts (p. 159)
    1. Valid (p. 159)
    2. Voidable (p. 159)
    3. Void (p. 160)
    4. Unenforceable (p. 160)
  B. Life of a Contract (p. 160)
    1. Phase 1 – Negotiation (p. 160)
    2. Phase 2 – Performance (Executory Stage) (p. 160)
    3. Phase 3 – Completed Performance (Fully Executed) (p. 160)

II. ELEMENTS OF A CONTRACT (p. 161)
  A. Competent Parties (p. 162)
    1. Minors (p. 162)
    2. Incompetents (p. 162)
    3. Parties Under the Influence of Alcohol or Drugs (p. 163)
  B. Mutual Consent (p. 163)
    1. The Offer (p. 163)
    2. Acceptance (p. 164)
    3. Termination of an Offer (p. 165)
    4. Genuine Consent or Acceptance (Contract is Void or Voidable by Victim) (p. 165)
  C. Legal Purpose (p. 166)
  D. Consideration (Anything of Value) (p. 166)
  E. Legal Description (p. 167)
  F. Agreement in Writing and Signed By the Parties (Real Estate Contracts) (p. 167)
    1. Parol Evidence Rule (p. 167)

III. PERFORMANCE, DISCHARGE, AND BREACH OF CONTRACT (p. 168)
  A. Performance of a Contract (p. 168)
  B. Discharge of a Contract (p. 169)
    1. Full Performance (p. 169)
    2. Substantial Performance (p. 169)
    3. Partial Performance (p. 169)
    4. Impossibility of Performance (p. 170)
    5. Agreement Between the Parties (p. 170)
    6. Operation of Law (p. 170)
    7. Breach (Nonperformance) (p. 170)

IV. REMEDIES FOR A BREACH OF CONTRACT (p. 171)
  A. Acceptance of Breach (p. 171)
  B. Unilateral Rescission (p. 171)
  C. Action for Dollar Damages (p. 172)
  D. Specific Performance (p. 172)

www.trec.state.tx.us
Texas Real Estate Commission
www.texasrealtors.com
Texas Association of Realtors®

A *CONTRACT is an agreement to do or not to do a certain act or service*. Every contract consists of a promise or a set of promises that are enforceable by law. These promises may be created in two ways, either in an express manner or in an implied manner.

An *EXPRESS CONTRACT is an agreement that is made either orally or in writing*. Listing agreements, sales contracts, and leases that are made in writing or orally, are all express contracts.

> *Real estate contracts may be either oral (ill-advised and likely unenforceable) or in writing. Any important contract should be written, even if not required by law. In Texas, because of the Statute of Frauds, a contract for the sale of real estate must be in writing to be enforceable. Only in the very rarest of circumstances will an oral contract for the sale of real estate be enforced.*

The Statute of Frauds requires certain contracts to be in writing to be enforceable. These include:

✔ Contracts for the sale of real estate

✔ Leases for longer than one year

✔ Agreements which cannot be performed within one year

✔ Agreements where a commission is to be paid for the sale or purchase of oil or gas mining leases or royalties, minerals or mineral interests

---

An *IMPLIED CONTRACT is created when an agreement is made based upon acts and/or conduct (implication) rather than by words*. For example, suppose you entered a hardware store where you had an account, picked up an $8 paint brush, and waved it at the clerk as you departed. The clerk, judging from your conduct, would assume that you wanted the paint brush charged to your account and would bill you accordingly. An implied contract may have been formed.

> *A contract may be formed by the express words of the parties or as a result of their actions.*

A *BILATERAL CONTRACT is a promise made by one party in exchange for the promise of another party*. It is **a promise for a promise**. For instance, a homeowner offers to sell his house for $200,000. The seller is actually promising to deliver the title. If a buyer accepts the offer, the buyer promises to pay $200,000 at the closing. The contract is thus based upon the seller making a promise to the buyer and the buyer making a promise to the seller.

*When only one party makes a promise for an act of another, the agreement is called a **UNILATERAL CONTRACT**. It is **a promise for an act**.* If someone acts upon an offer, the one making the offer is obligated to complete his or her promise. However, the person performing the act in the unilateral contract is not bound to act. Therefore, if he/she never "acts," no contract is formed. For example, suppose that instead of offering to sell his home, a seller offers a buyer an option to purchase his home for $200,000 at the end of one year. Only the buyer is required to do anything. A contract will only be formed if the buyer acts by exercising the option.

A Multiple Listing Service (MLS) property listing is an example of the unilateral contract among members of the service. The listing broker makes the offer of co-brokerage (along with the commission split) to the other broker member who successfully brings the buyer to contract with the listing broker's seller. This offer then becomes bilateral between brokers when performed.

A contract may be either bilateral (the exchange of a promise for a promise) or unilateral (the exchange of a promise for an act). The exchange of the two mutually binding promises is referred to as the "consideration" in a contract.

A. CLASSIFICATION OF CONTRACTS

Contracts may be classified in any of these four ways:

1. Valid

A *VALID CONTRACT is binding and enforceable in a court of law.* It has met all of the essential elements of a valid contract. (The elements of a contract are shown in Figure 5-1.)

Performance is expected, or legal action can be filed if a breach of the valid contract by one of the parties occurs.

2. Voidable

A *VOIDABLE CONTRACT is valid on its face, but one or more of the parties may elect to rescind or affirm it.*

A contract signed under duress is voidable. Likewise, a contract signed by someone under the age of 18 (minor) in Texas is voidable by the person who is under 18.

3. Void

A contract that is VOID has no legal force or effect. The contract did not meet the requirements of a valid contract. It is a null and void.

In a void contract, at least one of the essential elements of a contract is lacking. Therefore, a contract was never created in the first place.

4. Unenforceable

An *UNENFORCEABLE CONTRACT has met the requirements to become a contract, but cannot be enforced in a court of law.* For example, in Texas a contract for the sale of real estate or for the lease of real estate for more than a year that is not in writing is unenforceable according to the Statute of Frauds. Likewise, an oral promise by the seller to pay a commission to the listing broker is also unenforceable.

B. LIFE OF A CONTRACT

Contract Phases
● Pre-contract negotiation
● Contract performance
● Completed contract

A contract exists only when an offer is made, the offer accepted, and acceptance by the offeree is communicated back to the offeror. Then, if the essentials of a valid contract have all been met, the parties have created a legally binding agreement called a "contract." A contract has three basic phases.

1. Phase 1 – Negotiation

This is the negotiation period. During this period the buyer and seller discuss the possibility of a contract. If there is mutual interest between the parties, then an offer, or perhaps several offers, can be made. The offer becomes a contract when accepted, provided that all the other elements necessary for the creation of a contract are present.

2. Phase 2 – Performance (Executory Stage)

This is the performance stage of the contract. An *EXECUTORY CONTRACT is a legal agreement, the provisions of which have yet to be completely fulfilled.* A residential sales contract is executory until, at closing, the payment is made and title is transferred. Then it becomes executed.

3. Phase 3 – Completed Performance (Fully Executed)

This stage occurs after a contract has been completely performed. An *EXECUTED CONTRACT is one that has either been discharged or performed.*

This term should not be confused with the execution of a contract. To **EXECUTE A CONTRACT** *is to sign a contract*, while the **EXECUTION OF A CONTRACT** *is the act of performing or carrying out the contract.*

A contract to be performed is called "executory"; a completely performed contract has been "executed."

The legal right to bring an action regarding the contract is ended when the statute of limitations, in the particular state where the contract was formed, runs out. In Texas, the statute of limitations period for enforcing most written contracts is set by state law at four years.

II. Elements of a Contract

To be considered a valid real estate contract, the agreement must contain the following required elements (see **Figure 5-1**):

Figure 5-1

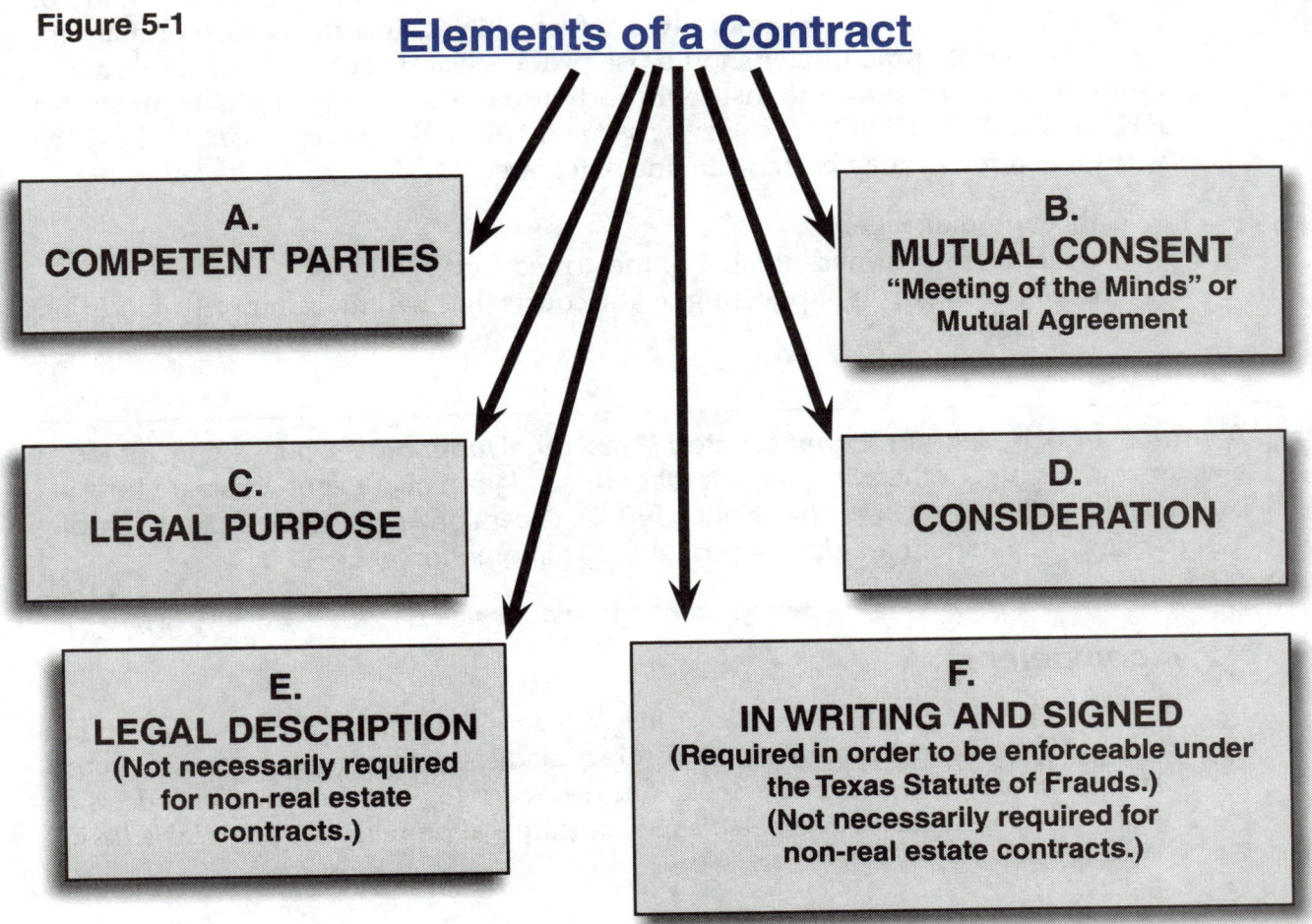

Elements of a Contract

A. COMPETENT PARTIES

B. MUTUAL CONSENT
"Meeting of the Minds" or Mutual Agreement

C. LEGAL PURPOSE

D. CONSIDERATION

E. LEGAL DESCRIPTION
(Not necessarily required for non-real estate contracts.)

F. IN WRITING AND SIGNED
(Required in order to be enforceable under the Texas Statute of Frauds.)
(Not necessarily required for non-real estate contracts.)

These are the four elements of any contract: 1) competent parties, 2) legal purpose, 3) consideration, and 4) mutual consent. For contracts involving the sale of real estate, two additional requirements should be met: 5) legal description, and 6) the agreement in writing and signed by the parties (to be enforceable).

A. COMPETENT PARTIES

For any contract to be valid, there must be two or more parties who have the legal capacity to contract. Generally, anyone is capable of contracting, with the exception of: 1) minors (for some purposes); 2) persons held to be legally "incompetent"; and 3) parties under the influence of alcohol or drugs, who may be held to be legally incapable of forming a contract. That is, they may be found to have been incapable of having the ability to form "contractual intent."

1. Minors

A **MINOR** *is a person under the age of eighteen.* A minor may contract with others in the sale of real estate, however, the contract may be voidable by the minor and not be enforceable against the minor. It is enforceable against the person of majority age. A real estate practitioner should use prudence and caution when choosing to represent another person to insure the individual has the capacity to contract. An **EMANCIPATED MINOR** *is one who has the contractual rights of an adult.* The three ways that a minor may become emancipated are:

1. through marriage,
2. a member or former member of the armed forces, and/or
3. declared to be self-supporting by the courts (has had their minority condition removed).

A minor who has been "emancipated" has legal capacity. Once emancipated, always emancipated, otherwise, a contract or deed signed by a minor would generally be voidable at the election of the minor. Certain exceptions exist for the purchase of "necessities." Any minor can acquire property by gift or inheritance.

2. Incompetents

An **INCOMPETENT** *is a person who is judged to be of unsound mind.* Such a person has no capacity (power) to contract; any contract made is void from its inception. In real estate transactions with incompetents, it is necessary to have the guardian's decision approved by the court. Incompetents may acquire real property by gift or inheritance.

Both minors and incompetents may acquire real property by gift or inheritance.

3. Parties Under the Influence of Alcohol or Drugs

Similarly, contracts with persons under the influence of alcohol or drugs at the time the contract was created may be voidable if it is determined that the drugs/alcohol prevented the person from appreciating or understanding the nature of his/her acts. However, the courts may not allow disaffirmance if it is found that the person willingly or voluntarily entered into the state of inebriation.

Contracts with persons under the influence of alcohol or drugs may be voidable.

B. MUTUAL CONSENT

Mutual consent is an offer by one party and acceptance by the other party.

The second contract requirement, **MUTUAL CONSENT,** *refers to a "meeting of the minds" by all parties of the contract elements.* This means that the parties will have to agree on all terms and conditions. This is usually accomplished though the process known as "offer and acceptance."

1. The Offer

An **OFFER** *expresses a person's willingness to enter into a contract under specified terms.* The **OFFEROR (an "OR" always gives)** *is the person who has made the offer, and the* **OFFEREE (an "EE" always receives)** *is the person to whom the offer has been made.* The offer made by the

> **Offeror** – The person who makes the offer.
>
> **Offeree** – The person who receives the offer.

offeror must be communicated to the offeree. Every offer must have contractual intent. **CONTRACTUAL INTENT** *exists when a party communicates an offer to another with the intention of forming a binding contract.* For example, a social invitation to attend a party is not meant to be a contract and therefore lacks contractual intent. Likewise, an advertisement in the newspaper to sell a home or a "listing" placed in the MLS is not normally an offer, but merely an invitation to deal.

Generally, an offeror may withdraw his/her offer at any time prior to receiving communication of its acceptance. Communication of the withdrawal may be done in writing, orally, by mail, or in some cases, registered mail. However, if the offer was made in writing, then generally, it should be withdrawn in writing.

Finally, an offer must be definite and certain in its terms. *DEFINITE AND CERTAIN means that the precise acts to be performed must be clearly stated.* A court can neither create contracts for parties nor fix the terms and conditions of any contract.

An *AMBIGUOUS CONTRACT is one in which the language in the contract is reasonably capable of being understood in more than one sense.* For example, assume that a homeowner hires a painter to paint his front room. However, the house in question has two front rooms. What room is to be painted? If there is ambiguity in a contract, the courts will construe the contract most strictly against the party who prepared it. This legal doctrine is frequently referred to as "the doctrine of construction against the maker."

By the same token, contracts cannot be based upon illusory promises. An *ILLUSORY CONTRACT is one that contains a purported promise that actually promises nothing because it leaves to the one making the promise the choice of performance or nonperformance.* For example, a person states, "I'll sell you my house at a good price, but only if I feel like it." In this case, the contract is unenforceable because there is no actual requirement upon the promisor that anything be done as the promisor has an alternative which, if taken, will render the promisee nothing.

An "illusory contract" appears to be a contract but it is NOT because it is based on a meaningless promise, so it is unenforceable.

2. Acceptance

ACCEPTANCE is the consent to all of the terms of the offer by the offeree. Acceptance of an offer must be in the manner specified in the offer, but if no particular manner of acceptance is specified, then acceptance may be made by any reasonable or usual mode.

If a valid offer is accepted by the offeree and valid acceptance properly communicated to the offeror, the accepted offer becomes a legally binding contract, provided all of the essentials of a valid contract have been met. Should the buyer or seller now die, there may still be a legally binding contract.

In contracts for the sale of real estate, silence by the offeree cannot be interpreted as an acceptance of an offer because acceptance must be communicated. One cannot say "If I do not hear from you in 10 days, the offer will be considered accepted." There must be a communicated acceptance of an offer in writing.

Acceptance must be absolute and unqualified. If it modifies the terms of the offer, it becomes a counter offer. A *COUNTER OFFER is the rejection of an original offer and the proposal of a new offer.* The offeree rejects the offer then becomes the offeror of the counter offer. **Once there is a counter offer, the previous offer is automatically terminated and cannot later be accepted.** To have the original offer later accepted after having been rejected, it would have to be proposed again.

Once there is a counter offer, the previous offer is **automatically terminated** and cannot later be accepted.

3. Termination of an Offer

The hope of the offeror is that the other party will accept the offer as written, and that a contract will be formed. However, a high percentage of initial offers are rejected. Six ways an offer can terminate include:

1. **Lapse of Time.** The offer is terminated if the offeree fails to accept within a prescribed period.

2. **Communication of Revocation.** An offer may be withdrawn or revoked at any time before the offeree has communicated his or her acceptance.

3. **Failure of Offeree to Fulfill a Condition.** If a specified condition must be satisfied in a prescribed manner for the offer to be considered accepted and a contract formed and that condition is not met, then the offer is terminated.

4. **Rejection.** If the offer is rejected, it is terminated.

5. **Death or Insanity of the Offeror or Offeree.** This would void the offer. The death of the offeror or offeree constitutes a revocation of the offer—the offer dies with the death of the offeror or offeree. However, once a contract is formed, death may have a different result on the continued enforceability of the contract.

6. **Illegality of Purpose.** If the conditions or the purpose of a contract are illegal, then the contract is void even if accepted. The contract is null and void. If an offer is made that incorporates an illegal purpose, it cannot result in a contract, even if the offeree accepts.

4. Genuine Consent or Acceptance (Contract is Void or Voidable by Victim)

The final requirement for mutual consent is that the offer and acceptance must be given freely. If not, the contract is void or voidable by the party being coerced, menaced or fraudulently induced into a contract. Genuine consent does not exist if any of the following conditions are present:

1. *FRAUD occurs when a person misrepresents a material fact, knowing it is not true, and intends that other person rely on that misrepresentation or is recklessly indifferent to the truth or falsity of the representation.* The contract is void or voidable, depending on the degree of fraud.

2. *MISTAKE exists when both parties are mistaken as to the matter of the agreement, or where the subject matter of the contract ceases to exist.* A mistake is also void or voidable. **Example:** The buyer offers to buy the seller's mountain cabin, but neither party knows it has burned down.

3. *DURESS is the unlawful attempt to coerce a person to perform an act against his or her will by force.* **Example:** If one person holds a gun to another person's head, and forces him/her to sign a contract at gunpoint, the contract is unenforceable against the one under duress.

4. *MENACE is a threat to commit unlawful violent injury to a person and/or his or her character as a party to the contract.*

5. *UNDUE INFLUENCE occurs when a person in a position of authority or special trust and confidence uses that authority to an unfair advantage.* This can occur especially when there is a relationship between the parties that is close or confidential (e.g. attorney-client, agent-client, and trustee-beneficiary). When it is proved that a person has signed a contract because he/she has been unduly influenced, the contract can be voided by that person.

If a contract was entered into under pressure, as with duress, menace, and undue influence, it is voidable by the person who was pressured to sign.

C. LEGAL PURPOSE

A contract that forces one to break the law is void.

A contract must be legal in its formation and operation. **Both the consideration and its objective must also be lawful.** The objective refers to what the contract requires the parties to do or not to do. If the contract consists of a single objective that is unlawful in whole or in part, then the contract is void. If there are several objectives, the contract is normally valid as to those parts that are lawful. The law will not enforce an illegal contract. **Example:** An owner of a building under construction enters into a contract to bribe a building inspector. The contract is void because it is for an illegal purpose.

D. CONSIDERATION (Anything of Value)

VALUABLE CONSIDERATION in a contract is anything of value given by one party to another party to make the agreement binding. A valid contract must have sufficient consideration, which is any amount of valued consideration. Consideration need not be money. It may: (1) benefit the person making the contract or another person; (2) be a loss suffered or agreed to be suffered; or (3) be an agreement not to bring a legal suit. If the price paid is a promise, consideration may be a promise for a promise. The important point is that the consideration must be of *some* value.

Payment of money is NOT needed as consideration. It can also be a benefit, like the performance of an act or the nonperformance (forbearance) of an act.

Some types of contracts require that consideration consist of a real amount of money, instead of a nominal amount of, for example, $1.00. In such contracts, courts have ruled the condition of adequate consideration must be met for those contracts to be enforceable. Other contracts, without such a condition, are enforceable no matter what the consideration is, as long as it is agreed on by all parties.

A contract based on unlawful consideration is void.

> Consideration must be something of value given by one person in exchange for something of value from another person. Consideration need not be equal, but it must be bargained for.

E. LEGAL DESCRIPTION

In order to constitute a valid writing under the statute of frauds, the agreement must contain an adequate description of the property to be sold.

F. AGREEMENT IN WRITING AND SIGNED BY THE PARTIES (Real Estate Contracts)

All contracts may be oral, except those specifically required by the Statute of Frauds to be in writing. A contract for the sale of personal property can be oral or written, but in Texas, according to the Statute of Frauds, most real estate contracts must be in writing to be enforceable.

> Personal property contracts, like rental agreements, for one year or less, need NOT be in writing. Any contract that cannot be performed **within a year from the date of signing** must be in writing to be enforceable.

1. Parol Evidence Rule

PAROL EVIDENCE refers to prior oral or written agreements of the parties, or even oral agreements concurrent (contemporaneous) with a written contract. Under the "parol evidence rule," a contract expressed in writing is intended to be a complete and final expression of the rights and duties of the contracting parties. The parol evidence rule means that prior oral or written agreements or additional writings of the parties **cannot** be introduced as evidence to contradict or modify the terms of the written contract. The courts, however, will permit such outside evidence to be

The **parol evidence rule** means that prior oral or written agreements or additional writings of the parties **cannot** be introduced as evidence to contradict or modify the terms of the written contract.

introduced when the written contract is incomplete, ambiguous, or it is necessary to show that the contract is not enforceable because of mistake or fraud.

All of the addenda used with the contract are considered part of the agreement between the parties to the contract and are not included under the parol evidence rule as "additional writings."

Rarely will the courts allow prior "oral parts or an entire oral contract" to be substituted for a later written contract.

III. Performance, Discharge, and Breach of Contract

*Acts described in a contract must be performed in a **TIMELY MANNER** (within time limits described in the contract).* Most contracts are properly performed and discharged without any legal complications. If difficulties do arise, the parties, either by themselves, or with the aid of legal counsel, usually work out an agreeable settlement. If there is no settlement, the courts are available for the resolution of any contractual conflicts.

A. PERFORMANCE OF A CONTRACT

PERFORMANCE is the successful completion of a contractual duty, usually resulting in the performer's release from any past or future liability. Sometimes with performance of a contract, one of the parties would prefer to drop out of the picture without terminating the contract. He or she may, under proper circumstances, accomplish this by assignment. An *ASSIGNMENT is the transfer of a person's right in a contract to another party.* An assignment happens when the *ASSIGNOR, the party to the original contract, transfers his or her rights in the contract to another party, called an ASSIGNEE.*

Generally speaking, any contract, unless it calls for some personal service, can be assigned if the contract does not state otherwise.

If the assignee does not perform, the assignor remains liable (secondary liability) for the contract. Listings are not assignable because they are personal service contracts.

Time is often significant in a contract and is usually stated in the contract. By statute, if no time is specified for the performance of an act, a reasonable time is allowed. If an act, by its nature, can be done instantly (such as the payment of money) it must be done. Generally speaking, if the last day for the performance of an act falls upon a holiday or weekend, the period is extended to include the next business day.

REVOCATION is the canceling of an offer to contract by the offeror.

B. DISCHARGE OF A CONTRACT

The *DISCHARGE OF A CONTRACT occurs when the contract has been terminated.* Contracts can be discharged in many ways, from the extreme of full performance (which is the usual pattern) to breach of contract (nonperformance). **Figure 5-2** illustrates these extremes and the variety of possibilities that may exist between them. A brief description of these possibilities follows.

Figure 5-2

Discharge of a Contract

- ✔ Full Performance
- ✔ Substantial Performance
- ✔ Partial Performance
- ✔ Impossibility of Performtmance
- ✔ Agreement Between the Parties
- ✔ Operation of Law
- ✔ Breach (Nonperformance)

1. Full Performance

The contract is completed according to the terms specified in the original agreement.

2. Substantial Performance

Sometimes the parties may agree to discharge a contract when the contract has almost, but not entirely, been completed. For example, a builder and a homeowner may agree that a new home will be substantially completed when the city issues a certificate of occupancy. Even though there may be a few cosmetic issues left to resolve, the parties can agree that the homeowners can take delivery at that time. Thus, although the home is not 100% completed, the parties agree that their contract will be discharged upon substantial performance.

3. Partial Performance

If both parties agree to the value of the work partially completed, the contract is discharged. This agreement should be in writing. However, if a dispute arises, the courts will determine the obligations of the defaulting party. Damages are one of the hardest things to prove, and the courts usually lean towards the non-defaulting party. A judge will most likely award the non-defaulting party any amount of money necessary to complete the contract.

4. Impossibility of Performance

Under certain circumstances, the contract, for one reason or another, may be impossible to perform. An obvious example is where a carpenter can no longer renovate a house because it was destroyed by fire. In such a case, the impossibility of performance excuses performance.

5. Agreement Between the Parties

If a contract is not completed, the parties may agree that some other action needs to be taken. For example, the parties may agree to a different type of manner of performance. Legally speaking, an *ACCORD is the agreement by the parties to perform differently*, and the *SATISFACTION is the fulfillment of that agreement*.

By the same token, the parties may also agree to a *MUTUAL RESCISSION, where the parties agree to suspend performance and thus cancel the contract*.

In some cases, the original contracting party may want to drop out of the contract completely. This can be done by novation. A *NOVATION is the substitution or exchange (by mutual agreement of the parties) of a new obligation or contract for an existing one with intent to cancel the old contract*. Since it is a new contract, it requires consideration and the other essentials of a valid contract.

Novation replaces the old contract with a new contract.

6. Operation of Law

Whenever a contract or parts of a contract become illegal or some law prevents performance, the contract is discharged by operation of law. For example, a factory owner contracts to purchase raw material from a foreign nation. After the contract has been signed, but before delivery can take place, the United States bars all trading with that country. Contract performance is thus excused through operation of law. The federal bankruptcy laws may also excuse performance in certain situations.

7. Breach (Nonperformance)

A *BREACH is the failure to perform a contract, in part or in whole, without legal excuse.* This is the nonperformance by one of the contracting parties.

The most common breaches, from the real estate broker's point of view, are: (1) the buyer who decides not to buy after signing the sales contract; or (2) the seller who decides not to sell after signing the sales contract. In either case, the breach may occur in one of two ways.

A *MATERIAL BREACH occurs when one party wrongfully fails or refuses to perform a material element of the contract.* For example, a buyer fails or refuses to attend the closing of a sale of a residence. An *ANTICIPATORY BREACH is a breach that occurs before performance is required.* For example, the day before a closing is to occur a buyer phones the seller and states that he simply will not attend the closing. In either case, the non-breaching party is excused from further performance and may pursue remedies for breach of contract.

IV. Remedies for Breach of a Contract

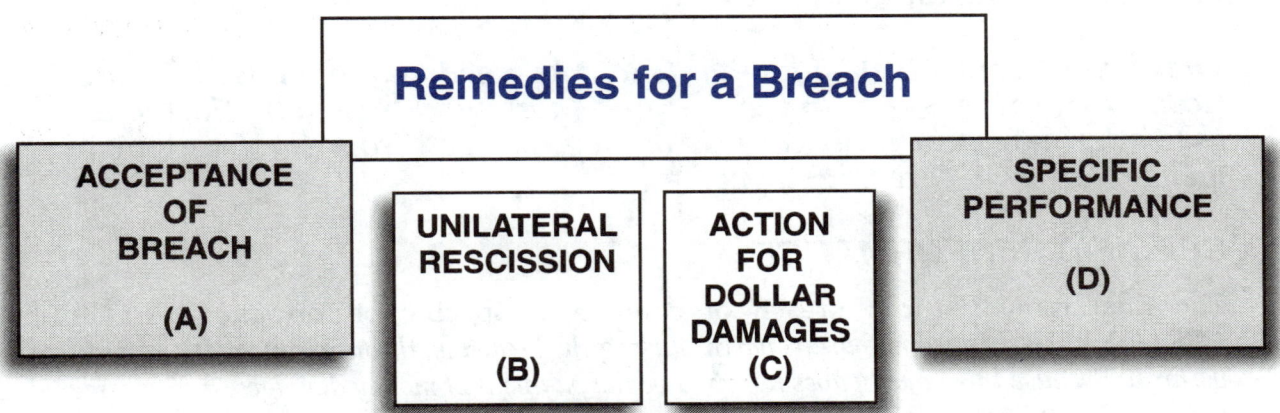

A breach of contract occurs when one party fails to perform his or her contractual obligations. Upon a party's wrongful breach, the non-defaulting party may be entitled to a variety of remedies.

A. ACCEPTANCE OF BREACH

A discharge of a contract may be simply the acceptance of the breach. In an *ACCEPTANCE OF BREACH, the wronged party does not pursue legal action.* Sometimes he or she may feel that the damages recoverable are too limited to justify litigation. Perhaps the person considers the other party judgment-proof, which means that the other party does not have enough assets available to satisfy a judgment. Moreover, the legal cost of a lawsuit, the time, the effort, and the psychological effect may not be worth the possible outcome.

B. UNILATERAL RESCISSION

In a *UNILATERAL RESCISSION the wronged party (1) discloses the wrong and (2) everything of value is restored to the offended party.* The legal grounds for a rescission are: fraud, mistake, duress, menace, undue influence, and faulty consideration. Rescission is possible when the contract is unlawful for causes not apparent on its face, when the parties are not equally at fault, or when the public interest would be hurt. Minors or incompetents may generally rescind their contracts.

C. ACTION FOR DOLLAR DAMAGES

An *ACTION FOR DOLLAR DAMAGES occurs when a court suit for a breach requests payment of a fixed amount of money as compensation. This is sometimes referred to as a LEGAL REMEDY.*

If a party to a contract causes you to lose money, it is only fair for you to receive compensation. In most purchase contracts, there is usually a *LIQUIDATED DAMAGES AGREEMENT which sets, in advance, a specified amount of money as compensation if there is a breach.* This clause is used because it is usually impractical or difficult to determine the actual damages caused by a breach.

The Texas residential sales contract, as used by most real estate licensees, provides that in the event of a wrongful breach by the buyer, the seller may retain all earnest money received from the buyer as a measure of liquidated damages.

D. SPECIFIC PERFORMANCE

The final remedy for a breach of contract is specific performance. *SPECIFIC PERFORMANCE means that the party causing the breach is, through court action, forced to perform. Because this remedy does not involve the payment of money damages, it is considered to be an EQUITABLE REMEDY.*

For the most part, courts are skeptical of forcing a person to sell their real property and as a result this type of remedy is seldom used. Therefore, courts will consider this action only if dollar damages cannot provide an adequate remedy. If specific performance is ordered, the remedy must be mutual. That is, neither party to a contract can be compelled specifically to perform unless the other party has performed or is also specifically compelled to perform.

Remember, as a Texas real estate licensee, you should never offer legal advice to a party concerning the desirability or undesirability of specific performance as a remedy unless you are also a licensed attorney in Texas.

V. Texas Real Estate Contracts

Listing agreements, buyer representation agreements, real estate sales contracts, option agreements, and contracts for deed, leases, and escrow agreements are the most commonly used written agreements by brokers and salespersons.

A. PROMULGATED CONTRACT FORMS

The Texas Real Estate Broker-Lawyer Committee was established by The Real Estate License Act (TRELA) to draft and revise standard contract forms to be used by licensees in real estate transactions.

The Texas Real Estate Commission (TREC) may approve or promulgate a contract form or addendum drafted by the Broker-Lawyer Committee. Once *PROMULGATED by the commission, the use of that form by a licensee for a particular transaction becomes mandatory subject to certain exceptions as noted below.*

1. Exceptions

A licensee must use promulgated forms when negotiating contracts binding the sale, exchange, option, lease, or rental of any interest in real property with the following exceptions:

1. Transactions in which the licensee is functioning solely as a principal, not as an agent;
2. Transactions in which an agency of the United States government requires a different form to be used;
3. Transactions for which a contract form has been prepared by the property owner or prepared by an attorney and required by the property owner;
4. Transactions for which no standard contract form has been promulgated by the Texas Real Estate Commission, and the licensee uses a form prepared by an attorney at law licensed by this state and approved by the attorney for the particular kind of transactions involved or prepared by the Texas Real Estate Broker-Lawyer Committee and made available for trial use by licensees with the consent of the Texas Real Estate Commission.

TREC promulgated contract forms are intended for use only by real estate licensees who are trained in their correct use. However, these forms are available for use by the general public, including nonlicensed buyers and sellers. As mistakes in the use of these forms may result in financial loss or an unenforceable contract, nonlicensees who use these forms are advised to contact a real estate licensee or an attorney for assistance on the TREC website.

B. THE REAL ESTATE SALES CONTRACT

The most important document in the transfer of real estate is the *REAL EATATE SALES CONTRACT (One to Four Family Residential Contract), which sets forth all the details of the agreement between the buyer and seller and establishes their legal rights and obligations.*

The sales contract serves as the blueprint for the real estate transaction.

1. Offer and Acceptance

A "meeting of the minds" is accomplished by the process of offer and acceptance—an essential element of a valid sales contract.

The broker presents to the seller a signed **offer** stating the price and conditions under which the prospective buyer will purchase the property. If the seller agrees to the offer exactly as it was made and signs the offer, the offer has been **accepted**. Once the appropriate **notification of acceptance** has been communicated to the buyer, the contract becomes valid and binding on the buyer and seller.

A *COUNTER OFFER is any attempt by the seller to change the terms proposed by the buyer.* It is a rejection of the original offer and the proposal of a new offer.

In a counter offer, the offeree becomes the offeror. The negotiation of a sales contract may involve several counter offers.

A seller's acceptance of an offer must be a "mirror image" of the buyer's offer. Changing any terms in the acceptance makes it a counter offer. An offer or counter offer may be withdrawn at any time before it has been accepted. An offer or counter offer is not considered to be accepted until the offeror has been notified of the other party's acceptance.

2. Earnest Money Deposits

When making an offer to purchase real estate, many buyers put down an *EARNEST MONEY DEPOSIT, which is a cash deposit that gives evidence of the buyer's intent to carry out the terms of the contract.*

Earnest money deposits are never required under the law, but if used, the final amount of the deposit necessary to create a contract is made by mutual agreement of the buyer and seller. The earnest money check is not deposited until an offer is accepted and notification of acceptance is given to the other party. After the offer is accepted, the broker must deposit the earnest money by the close of the second working day after the effective (execution) date of the contract, or by the time specified in the contract between the parties.

Generally, earnest money is held by a title insurance company or similar institution. If it is held by a broker, it must be held in a special trust or escrow account. A broker must maintain full, complete, and accurate records of all earnest money deposits, and a broker's license may be suspended or revoked for failure to account properly for such deposits.

3. Broker's Authority (No Legal Advice)

A licensed real estate broker is not authorized to practice law; that is, to prepare legal documents such as deeds and mortgages. According to the Rules of the Texas Real Estate Commission, a licensee may fill in forms approved and promulgated by the commission (or otherwise permitted by these rules) for the negotiation of real estate transactions.

The Rules of the Texas Real Estate Commission make it clear that a licensee shall add or delete factual statements and business details to the contract as may be desired by the parties, so long as the licensee does not engage in the unauthorized practice of law. Factual statements and business details go to the heart of the bargain and are an expression of what the parties will or will not do with respect to their agreement. Blank lines and check boxes are purposely written into the contract form so that the real estate licensee may complete these provisions in the manner as the principals may direct. If the parties to the contract agree to make a change to the already existing contract, the TREC amendment form may be used to accomplish the changes they desire. The amendment document becomes a part of the existing original contract and changes only the items agreed to in the amendment. All other items in the original contract remain in force and effect.

Advising your client as to how to take title in a real estate transaction is considered giving legal advice. If not a licensed attorney, you could face: 1) suspension or revocation of your real estate license; 2) a lawsuit from the State Bar of Texas; and/or 3) liability in a civil lawsuit brought by your client.

C. TREC RESIDENTIAL SALES CONTRACT (Form 20-7)

The most frequently used real estate contract in Texas is the **One to Four Family Residential Contract (Resale)**, which is TREC form 20-7 (see **Figure 5-3**). This form is to be used for the sale or purchase of a residential property of one to four units. It is NOT for the sale of condominiums, newly constructed, "to be" constructed, or "under construction" homes. Instead, it is to be used only for the resale of residences.

1. Paragraph Breakdown

The following is a breakdown of the TREC form 20-7 sales contract, paragraph by paragraph.

Paragraph 1 – Parties: identifies the seller and buyer as well as establishes the intent to sell and to buy.

Paragraph 2 – Property: sets forth the legal description and thus identifies the property to be sold by this contract; lists fixtures that are a part of the property.

Figure 5-3

02-13-06

PROMULGATED BY THE TEXAS REAL ESTATE COMMISSION (TREC)
ONE TO FOUR FAMILY RESIDENTIAL CONTRACT (RESALE)

NOTICE: Not For Use For Condominium Transactions

1. PARTIES: _____ (Seller) agrees to sell and convey to _____ (Buyer) and Buyer agrees to buy from Seller the Property described below.

2. PROPERTY:
  A. LAND: Lot _____ Block _____, _____ Addition, City of _____, County of _____, Texas, known as _____ (address/zip code), or as described on attached exhibit.
  B. IMPROVEMENTS: The house, garage and all other fixtures and improvements attached to the above-described real property, including without limitation, the following **permanently installed and built-in items,** if any: all equipment and appliances, valances, screens, shutters, awnings, wall-to-wall carpeting, mirrors, ceiling fans, attic fans, mail boxes, television antennas and satellite dish system and equipment, heating and air-conditioning units, security and fire detection equipment, wiring, plumbing and lighting fixtures, chandeliers, water softener system, kitchen equipment, garage door openers, cleaning equipment, shrubbery, landscaping, outdoor cooking equipment, and all other property owned by Seller and attached to the above described real property.
  C. ACCESSORIES: The following described related accessories, if any: window air conditioning units, stove, fireplace screens, curtains and rods, blinds, window shades, draperies and rods, controls for satellite dish system, controls for garage door openers, entry gate controls, door keys, mailbox keys, above ground pool, swimming pool equipment and maintenance accessories, and artificial fireplace logs.
  D. EXCLUSIONS: The following improvements and accessories will be retained by Seller and removed prior to delivery of possession: _____
  _____.

The land, improvements and accessories are collectively referred to as the "Property".

3. SALES PRICE:
  A. Cash portion of Sales Price payable by Buyer at closing................. $ _____
  B. Sum of all financing described below (excluding any loan funding fee or mortgage insurance premium)... $ _____
  C. Sales Price (Sum of A and B)...................................... $ _____

4. FINANCING: The portion of Sales Price not payable in cash will be paid as follows: (Check applicable boxes below)
  ❑ A. THIRD PARTY FINANCING: One or more third party mortgage loans in the total amount of $ _____ (excluding any loan funding fee or mortgage insurance premium).
    (1) Property Approval: If the Property does not satisfy the lenders' underwriting requirements for the loan(s), this contract will terminate and the earnest money will be refunded to Buyer.
    (2) Financing Approval: (Check one box only)
      ❑ (a) This contract is subject to Buyer being approved for the financing described in the attached Third Party Financing Condition Addendum.
      ❑ (b) This contract is not subject to Buyer being approved for financing and does not involve FHA or VA financing.
  ❑ B. ASSUMPTION: The assumption of the unpaid principal balance of one or more promissory notes described in the attached TREC Loan Assumption Addendum.
  ❑ C. SELLER FINANCING: A promissory note from Buyer to Seller of $ _____, secured by vendor's and deed of trust liens, and containing the terms and conditions described in the attached TREC Seller Financing Addendum. If an owner policy of title insurance is furnished, Buyer shall furnish Seller with a mortgagee policy of title insurance.

5. EARNEST MONEY: Upon execution of this contract by both parties, Buyer shall deposit $ _____ as earnest money with _____, as escrow agent, at _____ (address). Buyer shall deposit additional earnest money of $ _____ with escrow agent within _____ days after the effective date of this contract. If Buyer fails to deposit the earnest money as required by this contract, Buyer will be in default.

6. TITLE POLICY AND SURVEY:
  A. TITLE POLICY: Seller shall furnish to Buyer at ❑ Seller's ❑ Buyer's expense an owner policy of title insurance (Title Policy) issued by _____ (Title Company) in the amount of the Sales Price, dated at or after closing, insuring Buyer

Initialed for identification by Buyer _____ _____ and Seller _____ _____   TREC NO. 20-7 against loss under the provisions of the Title Policy, subject to the promulgated exclusions (including existing building and zoning ordinances) and the following exceptions:

(1) Restrictive covenants common to the platted subdivision in which the Property is located.
(2) The standard printed exception for standby fees, taxes and assessments.
(3) Liens created as part of the financing described in Paragraph 4.
(4) Utility easements created by the dedication deed or plat of the subdivision in which the Property is located.
(5) Reservations or exceptions otherwise permitted by this contract or as may be approved by Buyer in writing.
(6) The standard printed exception as to marital rights.
(7) The standard printed exception as to waters, tidelands, beaches, streams, and related matters.
(8) The standard printed exception as to discrepancies, conflicts, shortages in area or boundary lines, encroachments or protrusions, or overlapping improvements. Buyer, at Buyer's expense, may have the exception amended to read, "shortages in area".

B. COMMITMENT: Within 20 days after the Title Company receives a copy of this contract, Seller shall furnish to Buyer a commitment for title insurance (Commitment) and, at Buyer's expense, legible copies of restrictive covenants and documents evidencing exceptions in the Commitment (Exception Documents) other than the standard printed exceptions. Seller authorizes the Title Company to deliver the Commitment and Exception Documents to Buyer at Buyer's address shown in Paragraph 21. If the Commitment and Exception Documents are not delivered to Buyer within the specified time, the time for delivery will be automatically extended up to 15 days or the Closing Date, whichever is earlier.

C. SURVEY: The survey must be made by a registered professional land surveyor acceptable to the Title Company and any lender. (Check one box only)

☐ (1) Within _____ days after the effective date of this contract, Seller shall furnish to Buyer and Title Company Seller's existing survey of the Property and a Residential Real Property Affidavit promulgated by the Texas Department of Insurance (Affidavit). If the existing survey or Affidavit is not acceptable to Title Company or Buyer's lender, Buyer shall obtain a new survey at ☐ Seller's ☐ Buyer's expense no later than 3 days prior to Closing Date. If Seller fails to furnish the existing survey or Affidavit within the time prescribed, Buyer shall obtain a new survey at Seller's expense no later than 3 days prior to Closing Date.

☐ (2) Within _____ days after the effective date of this contract, Buyer shall obtain a new survey at Buyer's expense. Buyer is deemed to receive the survey on the date of actual receipt or the date specified in this paragraph, whichever is earlier.

☐ (3) Within _____ days after the effective date of this contract, Seller, at Seller's expense shall furnish a new survey to Buyer.

D. OBJECTIONS: Buyer may object in writing to defects, exceptions, or encumbrances to title: disclosed on the survey other than items 6A(1) through (7) above; disclosed in the Commitment other than items 6A(1) through (8) above; or which prohibit the following use or activity: _____
_____ .
Buyer must object not later than (i) the Closing Date or (ii) _____ days after Buyer receives the Commitment, Exception Documents, and the survey, whichever is earlier. Buyer's failure to object within the time allowed will constitute a waiver of Buyer's right to object; except that the requirements in Schedule C of the Commitment are not waived. Provided Seller is not obligated to incur any expense, Seller shall cure the timely objections of Buyer or any third party lender within 15 days after Seller receives the objections and the Closing Date will be extended as necessary. If objections are not cured within such 15 day period, this contract will terminate and the earnest money will be refunded to Buyer unless Buyer waives the objections.

E. TITLE NOTICES:
(1) ABSTRACT OR TITLE POLICY: Broker advises Buyer to have an abstract of title covering the Property examined by an attorney of Buyer's selection, or Buyer should be furnished with or obtain a Title Policy. If a Title Policy is furnished, the Commitment should be promptly reviewed by an attorney of Buyer's choice due to the time limitations on Buyer's right to object.
(2) MANDATORY OWNERS' ASSOCIATION MEMBERSHIP: The Property ☐ is ☐ is not subject to mandatory membership in an owners' association. If the Property is subject to mandatory membership in an owners' association, Seller notifies Buyer under §5.012, Texas Property Code, that, as a purchaser of property in the residential community in which the Property is located, you are obligated to be a member of the owners' association. Restrictive covenants governing the use and occupancy of the Property and a dedicatory instrument governing the establishment, maintenance, and operation of this residential community have been or will be recorded in the Real Property Records of the county in which the Property is located. Copies of the restrictive covenants and dedicatory instrument may be obtained from the county clerk. You are obligated to pay

Initialed for identification by Buyer_____ _____ and Seller _____ _____   TREC NO. 20-7

assessments to the owners' association. The amount of the assessments is subject to change. Your failure to pay the assessments could result in a lien on and the foreclosure of the Property. If Buyer is concerned about these matters, the TREC promulgated Addendum for Property Subject to Mandatory Membership in an Owner's Association should be used.

(3) STATUTORY TAX DISTRICTS: If the Property is situated in a utility or other statutorily created district providing water, sewer, drainage, or flood control facilities and services, Chapter 49, Texas Water Code, requires Seller to deliver and Buyer to sign the statutory notice relating to the tax rate, bonded indebtedness, or standby fee of the district prior to final execution of this contract.

(4) TIDE WATERS: If the Property abuts the tidally influenced waters of the state, §33.135, Texas Natural Resources Code, requires a notice regarding coastal area property to be included in the contract. An addendum containing the notice promulgated by TREC or required by the parties must be used.

(5) ANNEXATION: If the Property is located outside the limits of a municipality, Seller notifies Buyer under §5.011, Texas Property Code, that the Property may now or later be included in the extraterritorial jurisdiction of a municipality and may now or later be subject to annexation by the municipality. Each municipality maintains a map that depicts its boundaries and extraterritorial jurisdiction. To determine if the Property is located within a municipality's extraterritorial jurisdiction or is likely to be located within a municipality's extraterritorial jurisdiction, contact all municipalities located in the general proximity of the Property for further information.

(6) PROPERTY LOCATED IN A CERTIFICATED SERVICE AREA OF A UTILITY SERVICE PROVIDER: Notice required by §13.257, Water Code: The real property, described in Paragraph 2, that you are about to purchase may be located in a certificated water or sewer service area, which is authorized by law to provide water or sewer service to the properties in the certificated area. If your property is located in a certificated area there may be special costs or charges that you will be required to pay before you can receive water or sewer service. There may be a period required to construct lines or other facilities necessary to provide water or sewer service to your property. You are advised to determine if the property is in a certificated area and contact the utility service provider to determine the cost that you will be required to pay and the period, if any, that is required to provide water or sewer service to your property. The undersigned Buyer hereby acknowledges receipt of the foregoing notice at or before the execution of a binding contract for the purchase of the real property described in Paragraph 2 or at closing of purchase of the real property.

(7) PUBLIC IMPROVEMENT DISTRICTS: If the Property is in a public improvement district, §5.014, Property Code, requires Seller to notify Buyer as follows: As a purchaser of this parcel of real property you are obligated to pay an assessment to a municipality or county for an improvement project undertaken by a public improvement district under Chapter 372, Local Government Code. The assessment may be due annually or in periodic installments. More information concerning the amount of the assessment and the due dates of that assessment may be obtained from the municipality or county levying the assessment. The amount of the assessments is subject to change. Your failure to pay the assessments could result in a lien on and the foreclosure of your property.

7. PROPERTY CONDITION:
A. ACCESS,INSPECTIONS AND UTILITIES: Seller shall permit Buyer and Buyer's agents access to the Property at reasonable times. Buyer may have the Property inspected by inspectors selected by Buyer and licensed by TREC or otherwise permitted by law to make inspections. Seller at Seller's expense shall turn on existing utilities for inspections.

B. SELLER'S DISCLOSURE NOTICE PURSUANT TO §5.008, TEXAS PROPERTY CODE (Notice): (Check one box only)
  ☐ (1) Buyer has received the Notice.
  ☐ (2) Buyer has not received the Notice. Within _____ days after the effective date of this contract, Seller shall deliver the Notice to Buyer. If Buyer does not receive the Notice, Buyer may terminate this contract at any time prior to the closing and the earnest money will be refunded to Buyer. If Seller delivers the Notice, Buyer may terminate this contract for any reason within 7 days after Buyer receives the Notice or prior to the closing, whichever first occurs, and the earnest money will be refunded to Buyer.
  ☐ (3) The Seller is not required to furnish the notice under the Texas Property Code.

C. SELLER'S DISCLOSURE OF LEAD-BASED PAINT AND LEAD-BASED PAINT HAZARDS is required by Federal law for a residential dwelling constructed prior to 1978.

D. ACCEPTANCE OF PROPERTY CONDITION: Buyer accepts the Property in its present condition; provided Seller, at Seller's expense, shall complete the following specific repairs and treatments:_____
_____

E. LENDER REQUIRED REPAIRS AND TREATMENTS: Unless otherwise agreed in writing, neither party is obligated to pay for lender required repairs, which includes treatment for wood destroying insects. If the parties do not agree to pay for the lender required repairs or treatments, this contract will terminate and the earnest money will be refunded to Buyer. If the cost of lender required repairs and treatments exceeds 5% of the Sales Price, Buyer may terminate this contract and the earnest money will be refunded to Buyer.

F. **COMPLETION OF REPAIRS AND TREATMENTS:** Unless otherwise agreed in writing, Seller shall complete all agreed repairs and treatments prior to the Closing Date. All required permits must be obtained, and repairs and treatments must be performed by persons who are licensed or otherwise authorized by law to provide such repairs or treatments. At Buyer's election, any transferable warranties received by Seller with respect to the repairs and treatments will be transferred to Buyer at Buyer's expense. If Seller fails to complete any agreed repairs and treatments prior to the Closing Date, Buyer may do so and receive reimbursement from Seller at closing. The Closing Date will be extended up to 15 days, if necessary, to complete repairs and treatments.

G. **ENVIRONMENTAL MATTERS:** Buyer is advised that the presence of wetlands, toxic substances, including asbestos and wastes or other environmental hazards, or the presence of a threatened or endangered species or its habitat may affect Buyer's intended use of the Property. If Buyer is concerned about these matters, an addendum promulgated by TREC or required by the parties should be used.

H. **RESIDENTIAL SERVICE CONTRACTS:** Buyer may purchase a residential service contract from a residential service company licensed by TREC. If Buyer purchases a residential service contract, Seller shall reimburse Buyer at closing for the cost of the residential service contract in an amount not exceeding $_____. Buyer should review any residential service contract for the scope of coverage, exclusions and limitations. **The purchase of a residential service contract is optional. Similar coverage may be purchased from various companies authorized to do business in Texas.**

8. **BROKERS' FEES:** All obligations of the parties for payment of brokers' fees are contained in separate written agreements.

9. **CLOSING:**
   A. The closing of the sale will be on or before _____, 20_____, or within 7 days after objections made under Paragraph 6D have been cured or waived, whichever date is later (Closing Date). If either party fails to close the sale by the Closing Date, the non-defaulting party may exercise the remedies contained in Paragraph 15.
   B. At closing:
      (1) Seller shall execute and deliver a general warranty deed conveying title to the Property to Buyer and showing no additional exceptions to those permitted in Paragraph 6 and furnish tax statements or certificates showing no delinquent taxes on the Property.
      (2) Buyer shall pay the Sales Price in good funds acceptable to the escrow agent.
      (3) Seller and Buyer shall execute and deliver any notices, statements, certificates, affidavits, releases, loan documents and other documents required of them by this contract, the Commitment or law necessary for the closing of the sale and the issuance of the Title Policy.
   C. Unless expressly prohibited by written agreement, Seller may continue to show the Property and receive, negotiate and accept back up offers.
   D. All covenants, representations and warranties in this contract survive closing.

10. **POSSESSION:** Seller shall deliver to Buyer possession of the Property in its present or required condition, ordinary wear and tear excepted: ❑ upon closing and funding ❑ according to a temporary residential lease form promulgated by TREC or other written lease required by the parties. Any possession by Buyer prior to closing or by Seller after closing which is not authorized by a written lease will establish a tenancy at sufferance relationship between the parties. **Consult your insurance agent prior to change of ownership and possession because insurance coverage may be limited or terminated. The absence of a written lease or appropriate insurance coverage may expose the parties to economic loss.**

11. **SPECIAL PROVISIONS:** (Insert only factual statements and business details applicable to the sale. TREC rules prohibit licensees from adding factual statements or business details for which a contract addendum, lease or other form has been promulgated by TREC for mandatory use.)

Initialed for identification by Buyer_____ _____ and Seller _____ _____   TREC NO. 20-7

12. SETTLEMENT AND OTHER EXPENSES:
    A. The following expenses must be paid at or prior to closing:
       (1) Expenses payable by Seller (Seller's Expenses):
         (a) Releases of existing liens, including prepayment penalties and recording fees; release of Seller's loan liability; tax statements or certificates; preparation of deed; one-half of escrow fee; and other expenses payable by Seller under this contract.
         (b) Seller shall also pay an amount not to exceed $ _____ to be applied in the following order: Buyer's Expenses which Buyer is prohibited from paying by FHA, VA, Texas Veterans Housing Assistance Program or other governmental loan programs, and then to other Buyer's Expenses as allowed by the lender.
       (2) Expenses payable by Buyer (Buyer's Expenses):
         (a) Loan origination, discount, buy-down, and commitment fees (Loan Fees).
         (b) Appraisal fees; loan application fees; credit reports; preparation of loan documents; interest on the notes from date of disbursement to one month prior to dates of first monthly payments; recording fees; copies of easements and restrictions; mortgagee title policy with endorsements required by lender; loan-related inspection fees; photos; amortization schedules; one-half of escrow fee; all prepaid items, including required premiums for flood and hazard insurance, reserve deposits for insurance, ad valorem taxes and special governmental assessments; final compliance inspection; courier fee; repair inspection; underwriting fee; wire transfer fee; expenses incident to any loan; and other expenses payable by Buyer under this contract.
    B. Buyer shall pay Private Mortgage Insurance Premium (PMI), VA Loan Funding Fee, or FHA Mortgage Insurance Premium (MIP) as required by the lender.
    C. If any expense exceeds an amount expressly stated in this contract for such expense to be paid by a party, that party may terminate this contract unless the other party agrees to pay such excess. Buyer may not pay charges and fees expressly prohibited by FHA, VA, Texas Veterans Housing Assistance Program or other governmental loan program regulations.

13. PRORATIONS: Taxes for the current year, interest, maintenance fees, assessments, dues and rents will be prorated through the Closing Date. The tax proration may be calculated taking into consideration any change in exemptions that will affect the current year's taxes. If taxes for the current year vary from the amount prorated at closing, the parties shall adjust the prorations when tax statements for the current year are available. If taxes are not paid at or prior to closing, Buyer shall pay taxes for the current year.

14. CASUALTY LOSS: If any part of the Property is damaged or destroyed by fire or other casualty after the effective date of this contract, Seller shall restore the Property to its previous condition as soon as reasonably possible, but in any event by the Closing Date. If Seller fails to do so due to factors beyond Seller's control, Buyer may (a) terminate this contract and the earnest money will be refunded to Buyer (b) extend the time for performance up to 15 days and the Closing Date will be extended as necessary or (c) accept the Property in its damaged condition with an assignment of insurance proceeds and receive credit from Seller at closing in the amount of the deductible under the insurance policy. Seller's obligations under this paragraph are independent of any other obligations of Seller under this contract.

15. DEFAULT: If Buyer fails to comply with this contract, Buyer will be in default, and Seller may (a) enforce specific performance, seek such other relief as may be provided by law, or both, or (b) terminate this contract and receive the earnest money as liquidated damages, thereby releasing both parties from this contract. If, due to factors beyond Seller's control, Seller fails within the time allowed to make any non-casualty repairs or deliver the Commitment, or survey, if required of Seller, Buyer may (a) extend the time for performance up to 15 days and the Closing Date will be extended as necessary or (b) terminate this contract as the sole remedy and receive the earnest money. If Seller fails to comply with this contract for any other reason, Seller will be in default and Buyer may (a) enforce specific performance, seek such other relief as may be provided by law, or both, or (b) terminate this contract and receive the earnest money, thereby releasing both parties from this contract.

16. MEDIATION: It is the policy of the State of Texas to encourage resolution of disputes through alternative dispute resolution procedures such as mediation. Any dispute between Seller and Buyer related to this contract which is not resolved through informal discussion ❑ will ❑ will not be submitted to a mutually acceptable mediation service or provider. The parties to the mediation shall bear the mediation costs equally. This paragraph does not preclude a party from seeking equitable relief from a court of competent jurisdiction.

17. ATTORNEY'S FEES: The prevailing party in any legal proceeding related to this contract is entitled to recover reasonable attorney's fees and all costs of such proceeding incurred by the prevailing party.

Initialed for identification by Buyer_____ _____ and Seller _____ _____   TREC NO. 20-7

18. ESCROW:
   A. ESCROW: The escrow agent is not (i) a party to this contract and does not have liability for the performance or nonperformance of any party to this contract, (ii) liable for interest on the earnest money and (iii) liable for the loss of any earnest money caused by the failure of any financial institution in which the earnest money has been deposited unless the financial institution is acting as escrow agent.
   B. EXPENSES: At closing, the earnest money must be applied first to any cash down payment, then to Buyer's Expenses and any excess refunded to Buyer. If no closing occurs, escrow agent may require payment of unpaid expenses incurred on behalf of the parties and a written release of liability of escrow agent from all parties.
   C. DEMAND: Upon termination of this contract, either party or the escrow agent may send a release of earnest money to each party and the parties shall execute counterparts of the release and deliver same to the escrow agent. If either party fails to execute the release, either party may make a written demand to the escrow agent for the earnest money. If only one party makes written demand for the earnest money, escrow agent shall promptly provide a copy of the demand to the other party. If escrow agent does not receive written objection to the demand from the other party within 15 days, escrow agent may disburse the earnest money to the party making demand reduced by the amount of unpaid expenses incurred on behalf of the party receiving the earnest money and escrow agent may pay the same to the creditors. If escrow agent complies with the provisions of this paragraph, each party hereby releases escrow agent from all adverse claims related to the disbursal of the earnest money.
   D. DAMAGES: Any party who wrongfully fails or refuses to sign a release acceptable to the escrow agent within 7 days of receipt of the request will be liable to the other party for liquidated damages of three times the amount of the earnest money.
   E. NOTICES: Escrow agent's notices will be effective when sent in compliance with Paragraph 21. Notice of objection to the demand will be deemed effective upon receipt by escrow agent.

19. REPRESENTATIONS: Seller represents that as of the Closing Date (a) there will be no liens, assessments, or security interests against the Property which will not be satisfied out of the sales proceeds unless securing payment of any loans assumed by Buyer and (b) assumed loans will not be in default. If any representation of Seller in this contract is untrue on the Closing Date, Seller will be in default.

20. FEDERAL TAX REQUIREMENTS: If Seller is a "foreign person," as defined by applicable law, or if Seller fails to deliver an affidavit to Buyer that Seller is not a "foreign person," then Buyer shall withhold from the sales proceeds an amount sufficient to comply with applicable tax law and deliver the same to the Internal Revenue Service together with appropriate tax forms. Internal Revenue Service regulations require filing written reports if currency in excess of specified amounts is received in the transaction.

21. NOTICES: All notices from one party to the other must be in writing and are effective when mailed to, hand-delivered at, or transmitted by facsimile or electronic transmission as follows:

To Buyer at: _____	**To Seller** at: _____
_____	_____
_____	_____
_____	_____
Telephone: (____) _____	Telephone: (____) _____
Facsimile: (____) _____	Facsimile: (____) _____
E-mail: _____	E-mail: _____

Initialed for identification by Buyer_____ _____ and Seller _____ _____   TREC NO. 20-7

22. AGREEMENT OF PARTIES: This contract contains the entire agreement of the parties and cannot be changed except by their written agreement. Addenda which are a part of this contract are (Check all applicable boxes):

☐ Third Party Financing Condition Addendum

☐ Seller Financing Addendum

☐ Loan Assumption Addendum

☐ Buyer's Temporary Residential Lease

☐ Seller's Temporary Residential Lease

☐ Addendum for Sale of Other Property by Buyer

☐ Addendum for Seller's Disclosure of Information on Lead-based Paint and Lead-based Paint Hazards as Required by Federal Law

☐ Addendum for Property Subject to Mandatory Membership in an Owners' Association

☐ Environmental Assessment, Threatened or Endangered Species and Wetlands Addendum

☐ Addendum for "Back-Up" Contract

☐ Addendum for Coastal Area Property

☐ Addendum for Property Located Seaward of the Gulf Intracoastal Waterway

☐ Addendum for Release of Liability on Assumption of FHA, VA, or Conventional Loan Restoration of Seller's Entitlement for VA Guaranteed Loan

☐ Other (list): _____

_____

23. TERMINATION OPTION: For nominal consideration, the receipt of which is hereby acknowledged by Seller, and Buyer's agreement to pay Seller $_____ (Option Fee) within 2 days after the effective date of this contract, Seller grants Buyer the unrestricted right to terminate this contract by giving notice of termination to Seller within _____ days after the effective date of this contract. If no dollar amount is stated as the Option Fee or if Buyer fails to pay the Option Fee within the time prescribed, this paragraph will not be a part of this contract and Buyer shall not have the unrestricted right to terminate this contract. If Buyer gives notice of termination within the time prescribed, the Option Fee will not be refunded; however, any earnest money will be refunded to Buyer. The Option Fee ☐will ☐will not be credited to the Sales Price at closing. **Time is of the essence for this paragraph and strict compliance with the time for performance is required.**

24. CONSULT AN ATTORNEY: Real estate licensees cannot give legal advice. READ THIS CONTRACT CAREFULLY. If you do not understand the effect of this contract, consult an attorney BEFORE signing.

Buyer's
Attorney is: _____

Telephone: (____) _____

Facsimile: (____) _____

E-mail: _____

Seller's
Attorney is: _____

Telephone: (____) _____

Facsimile: (____) _____

E-mail: _____

**EXECUTED the _____day of _____, 20____ (EFFECTIVE DATE).
(BROKER: FILL IN THE DATE OF FINAL ACCEPTANCE.)**

_____
Buyer

_____
Buyer

_____
Seller

_____
Seller

TREC NO. 20-7

BROKER INFORMATION AND RATIFICATION OF FEE

Listing Broker has agreed to pay Other Broker _____ of the total sales price when Listing Broker's fee is received. Escrow Agent is authorized and directed to pay Other Broker from Listing Broker's fee at closing.

Other Broker	License No.	Listing Broker	License No.

represents ☐ Buyer only as Buyer's agent
☐ Seller as Listing Broker's subagent

represents ☐ Seller and Buyer as an intermediary
☐ Seller only as Seller's agent

Associate   Telephone

Broker's Address

City   State   Zip

Facsimile

Email Address

Listing Associate   Telephone

Listing Associate's Office Address   Facsimile

City   State   Zip

Email Address

Selling Associate   Telephone

Selling Associate's Office Address   Facsimile

City   State   Zip

Email Address

OPTION FEE RECEIPT

Receipt of $_____ (Option Fee) in the form of _____ is acknowledged.

Seller or Listing Broker   Date

CONTRACT AND EARNEST MONEY RECEIPT

Receipt of ☐ Contract and ☐ $_____ Earnest Money in the form of _____ is acknowledged.

Escrow Agent: _____ Date: _____

By: _____

Address

City   State   Zip

Email Address

Telephone (_____) _____

Facsimile: (_____) _____

TREC NO. 20-7

Paragraph 3 – Sales Price: establishes the cash down, loan amount, and sales price.

Paragraph 4 – Financing: stipulates the source of borrowed funds (details of the financing are specified in a Third Party Financing Condition Addendum, Loan Assumption Addendum, or Seller Financing Addendum).

Paragraph 5 – Earnest Money: specifies the amount of earnest money, if any, and identifies the escrow agent.

Paragraph 6 – Title Policy and Survey: identifies which party is to pay for the title policy: notes the exceptions to title if a title policy is furnished; stipulates requirements for a title commitment: provides survey options; specified procedures for a buyer to object to documents required in this paragraph and includes required notices to buyers.

Paragraph 7 – Property Condition: specifies a buyer's right to have the property inspected; provides for delivery of the Seller's Disclosure of Property Condition form and inspection for lead-based paint hazards; specifies any limitations on the buyer's acceptance of property condition; establishes procedures for completion of repairs; and includes other notices to the buyer.

Paragraph 8 – Brokers' Fees: notes that payments of brokers' fees are described in separate written agreements.

Paragraph 9 – Closing: establishes the target date for closing of the sale and identifies buyer and seller responsibilities at closing.

Paragraph 10 – Possession: specifies when the buyer may take possession of the property.

Paragraph 11 – Special Provisions: clarifies any business details of the sale not covered by the provisions of the printed earnest money contract form and not included in another TREC form; cannot include items that may constitute unauthorized practice of law

Paragraph 12 – Settlement and Other Expenses: identifies which party is to pay a specific expense at closing.

Paragraph 13 – Proration: specifies which items are to be prorated and fixes the timing of such proration through the day of closing; provides for an adjustment of the tax proration after closing, when necessary.

Paragraph 14 – Casualty Loss: identifies which party is to bear the risk of loss prior to closing and addresses the results of any such loss.

Paragraph 15 – Default: specifies the remedies available to each party in the event the other party breaches the contractual agreements.

Paragraph 16 – Mediation: offers the choice of mediation as a means to resolve disputes.

Paragraph 17 – Attorney's Fees: specifies that the prevailing party will be entitled to legal fees and all costs incurred by the prevailing party.

Paragraph 18 – Escrow: specifies the conditions under which the escrow agent agrees to be the holder of the earnest money and stipulates how such money is to be handled in the event the transaction does not close.

Paragraph 19 – Representations: lists statements made by the seller as to the status of the property and affords certain protections to the buyer should these statements prove false.

Paragraph 20 – Federal Tax Requirements: outlines the procedures to be followed by the buyer if the seller is a "foreign person," as defined by applicable law.

Paragraph 21 – Notices: states requirements for delivery of notices affecting the contract.

Paragraph 22 – Agreement of Parties: clarifies the understanding that no other agreements are to be relied on and identifies any TREC addenda or other forms to be a part of this contract.

Paragraph 23 – Termination Option: provides the buyer with an unrestricted right to terminate the contract, for a specified fee within a specified number of days after the effective date; specifies whether the option fee will be applied to the purchase price.

Paragraph 24 – Consult an Attorney: provides notice to both parties that real estate licensees cannot give legal advice and advises both parties to seek legal counsel for advice.

2. Final Acceptance

Final acceptance of the sales contract is accomplished by the completion of the last two sections on page 7 of the 8-page TREC form 20-7, the One to Four Family

Residential Contract (Resale). These two sections (which are not numbered, but fall under paragraph 24 of the contract) include the **Effective Date** and **Signature Lines**.

a. Effective Date

When the buyer and seller have reached mutual agreement as to the terms and both sign the contract form, *the broker fills in this date of execution line, which becomes the EFFECTIVE DATE OF THE CONTRACT.*

b. Signature Lines

Generally, all parties to the contract, or their designated agents, must sign the TREC form 20-7 in order for an enforceable contract to be formed. Until that time, the document may be considered to represent an offer in the near final stages of negotiation.

The **UNIFORM ELECTRONIC TRANSACTIONS ACT (UETA)** *gives electronic contracts and signatures the same legal status as paper signatures and contracts, as long as certain requirements are met.*

Because UETA is relatively new, title companies and mortgage lenders may insist on pen and ink signed contracts before issuing a title commitment or processing a loan application.

3. Last Page of the Sales Contract 20-7 (Page 8)

The contract that has been formed between the buyer and the seller includes everything *above* the signature lines at the bottom of page 7. The last page of the TREC form 20-7 (page 8) is NOT a part of the agreement between the buyer and seller, but is used as a convenience for notification of Seller's Receipt of the Option Fee, Broker Information and Ratification of Fee, and Receipt by the escrow agent of the earnest money and a copy of the contract.

a. Option Fee

The seller's signature is an acknowledgment that he/she has received the option fee and acknowledges the amount that was received.

b. Broker Information and Ratification of Fee

The Listing Broker acknowledges that he/she has agreed to pay the "Other Broker" (if any) a percentage of the Sales Price "when Listing Broker's fee is received." The Title Company is authorized by the Listing Broker in this paragraph to pay the Other Broker his/her portion of the commission at the time of closing.

c. Receipt

After a contract has been formed, Paragraph 5 "Earnest Money" requires that the buyer deposit the earnest money with the escrow agent named in that paragraph. In addition, the title company requires that the sales contract be deposited with them. The *RECEIPT is an acknowledgment from the escrow agent that both the earnest money and the contract have been deposited with them.* The escrow agent may notify the listing broker of the deposit of both the money and the contract. However, the listing broker should follow-up with the escrow agent to insure the buyer has deposited the earnest money as agreed. The buyer representative or the buyer should ask the escrow officer for the signed receipt on the buyer's copy or his/her broker's copy of the contract at the time the earnest money and contract are delivered to the escrow agent to insure there is evidence that the deposit was made in a timely manner. Paragraph 5 of the TREC form 20-7 states: "If Buyer fails to deposit the earnest money as required by this contract, Buyer will be in default."

D. OTHER PROMULGATED-APPROVED FORMS

In addition to the One to Four Family Residential Contract (Resale), the Texas Real Estate Commission has promulgated and approved a number of forms for use by Texas real estate licensees. These forms can be broadly classified as follows:

1. Other real estate contracts (condominiums, new home construction, farm and ranch, etc).
2. Addenda related to the property (third party financing, lead-based paint, etc).
3. Forms related to the transaction (Information about Brokerage Services, temporary residential lease, various notices, etc.).

As a real estate student, you will learn how and when to use the proper TREC forms in the Law of Contracts course you will have to take as a Texas pre-licensing requirement. (This information may be found in our companion textbook, *Texas Real Estate Contracts, 2nd ed.,* by Walt Huber and Rod Rodriguez, J.D.) In the meantime, **Figure 5-4** lists the forms that are presently approved/promulgated by TREC.

E. OPTION CONTRACTS

Another type of real estate contract is an option contract. An *OPTION CONTRACT is the right to purchase a property upon specified terms within a specific time period.*

Option contracts usually require the payment of separate consideration in order to legally prevent the offeror from withdrawing the offer of the option. Without this consideration, the optionor will be free to withdraw the offer of the option.

Figure 5-4 **TREC Approved/Promulgated Forms**
www.trec.state.tx.us/formslawscontracts/default.asp

TREC #	Form Caption
9-6	Unimproved Property Contract
10-4	Addendum for Sale of Other Property by Buyer
11-5	Addendum for "Back-Up" Contract
12-1	Addendum for Release of Liability on Assumption of FHA, VA or Conventional Loan, Restoration of Seller's Entitlement for VA Guaranteed Loan
15-3	Seller's Temporary Residential Lease
16-3	Buyer's Temporary Residential Lease
20-7	One to Four Family Residential Contract (Resale)
23-6	New Home Contract (Incomplete Construction
24-6	New Home Contract (Completed Construction)
25-5	Farm and Ranch Contract
26-4	Seller Financing Addendum
28-0	Environmental Assessment, Threatened or Endangered Species, and Wetlands Addendum
30-5	Residential Condominium Contract (Resale)
32-0	Condominium Resale Certificate
33-0	Addendum for Coastal Area Property
34-1	Addendum for Property Located Seaward of the Gulf Intracoastal Waterway
36-4	Addendum for Property Subject to Mandatory Membership in an Owners' Association
37-2	Subdivision Information, Including Resale Certificate for Property Subject to Membership in a Property Owners' Association
38-1	Notice of Termination of Contract
39-6	Amendment to Contract
40-2	Third Party Financing Condition Addendum
41-0	Loan Assumption Addendum
42-0	Notice Pursuant to Third Party Financing Condition Addendum
OP-C	Notice to Prospective Buyer
OP-H	Seller's Disclosure of Property Condition
OP-I	Texas Real Estate Consumer Notice Concerning Hazards or Repairs
OP-K	Information About Brokerage Services
OP-L	Lead-Based Paint Addendum

An option contract to purchase CANNOT be revoked by the optionor. If he/she attempted to revoke, he/she could be forced to sell the property through a lawsuit for specific performance. However, the optionor cannot compel the optionee to exercise his/her right to purchase.

> An **OPTIONOR** is typically a property owner who gives an interested buyer or tenant an exclusive right to purchase or lease a property.
>
> An **OPTIONEE** is a potential buyer or prospective tenant who purchases an agreed-to amount of time to buy or not buy a specific property upon set terms.

The optionee does not have to go through with the purchase but, generally speaking, to exercise the option, the optionee must exercise his/her option rights within the time period specified or lose the right. The option money is not refunded whether he/she buys or not. It is negotiable as to whether the option fee could be credited to the sales price at closing.

If the optionee decides to buy the property during his/her option period, the optionor must sell. In this case, the exercised option will become the sales contract and both parties are bound by its terms.

The optionee may also secure another buyer for the property and sell his/her option to another party during its term. Thus, all rights and interests may be transferred without the consent of the optionor, unless stated otherwise.

If an optionee has, for example, a one-year recorded option, and after six months decides not to exercise his/her option, the property owner should see to it that a quitclaim deed is recorded as a precaution so that the option might be removed from the records. As stated earlier, a quitclaim deed is a deed that will convey without warranty any claim of title or whatever interest, if any, the grantor has or may have in the property to the grantee.

> An agent who exercises an option to buy his/her own listing has a conflict of interest. If any questions are raised about the fairness of the transaction, issues of who established the sales price for the home, and what facts were used to determine value, will be among the many areas of concern.
>
> Brokers are bound by the requirements of the law and the rules of the real estate commission to look out for the best interest of their clients and to place their clients' interest above that their own.

1. Option Contract Distinguished from Option Provision

Traditionally, an option was normally purchased to take a property off the open market while not binding the optionee to complete the purchase. However,

Paragraph 23, "Termination Option" of the TREC form 20-7 One to Four Family Residential Contract (Resale), is an example of a different type of option agreement contained entirely within the regular sales contract form.

In this form of option, the buyer pays the Option Fee (consideration) **for the unrestricted right to terminate the contract** within the specified period of time written into the paragraph. If the buyer determines he/she does not want to purchase the home, for any reason, during that time period, he/she may terminate the contract without default and receive his/her earnest money back. In Paragraph 23, the right is a right to terminate instead of a right to purchase. In this case, the buyer is already contractually bound to purchase the property and what he/she is buying in this paragraph is an option to get out of the binding contract for any reason and not be in default.

VI. CHAPTER SUMMARY

A **contract** is an agreement to do or not to do a certain act or service. It can be **express** (oral or written) or **implied** (created by acts or conduct). A **bilateral contract** is a based upon a promise made by one party in exchange for the promise of another party. A typical real estate transaction is an example of a bilateral contract where the seller promises to convey title while the buyer promises to pay the required consideration On the other hand, a **unilateral contract** is a promise made in exchange for an act, such as the promise of a property owner to convey title only if the buyer exercises an option to purchase within one year.

A **valid** contract is binding and enforceable on both parties, while a **voidable** contract may be disavowed by either party. It is possible to have a contract that is both valid and voidable at the same time. On the other hand, a **void** contract refers to an agreement where no contract exists because it does not contain all the required elements.

There are generally three phases of a contract: **negotiation, performance,** and **completion**. If some provision of a contract is not yet fulfilled, it's called an **executory contract**. If the contract has been discharged or fully performed, it's considered an **executed contract**.

The six essential elements of a valid real estate contract are:

1. Competent Parties
2. Mutual Consent
3. Legal Purpose
4. Consideration
5. Legal Description
6. Written and Signed

An **offer** expresses a person's willingness to enter into a contract under specified terms. Every offer must be made by the **offeror** with the intent of forming a binding contract although it is permitted for a buyer to withdraw an offer before it is accepted. If the offer is rejected and a new offer is proposed by the **offeree**, it is known as a **counter offer** and automatically terminates the previous offer.

The offeree now becomes the offeror for purposes of making the counter offer. Even if the offer is accepted, if any of the following conditions exist, a contract may become void or voidable:

1. Fraud
2. Mistake
3. Duress
4. Menace
5. Undue Influence

Generally speaking, a contract may be oral or written, but the **Texas Statute of Frauds** requires real estate contracts to be in writing in order to be enforceable. In addition, contracts which cannot be completed within one year of signing, such as a long-term lease, must also be in writing to be enforceable.

A contract can be discharged by various means. First, the parties may discharge the contract by **full**, **substantial**, or **partial performance**. A contract may also be discharged because something has occurred which makes it impossible to perform the contract or because some law prevents performance. The parties may also choose an alternate means of terminating their original contract. For example, they may agree to a different type of outcome than what was originally anticipated (**accord** and **satisfaction**), or they may agree to enter into an entirely new agreement. But a contract may also be discharged simply because one of the parties breaches the agreement. The remedies for **breach of contract** include **acceptance of breach, unilateral rescission, action for money damages**, and **specific performance**.

The **Texas Real Estate Commission (TREC)** has promulgated and approved various forms for use by real estate licensees. Contract forms and related addenda are initially prepared and reviewed by the **Texas Broker-Lawyer Committee**. If the commission promulgates a form, the use of that form for a particular transaction becomes mandatory for use by real estate licensees unless the form falls into one of four exceptions. In using promulgated forms, real estate licensees are limited to completing forms by adding or deleting factual statements and business details as may be desired by the parties. In no event should licensees attempt to practice law. The practice of law by unlicensed individuals may result in the suspension/revocation of a real estate license, a lawsuit from the State Bar of Texas, and legal liability from the client.

An **option contract** is another type of real estate contract. Under an option contract, the **optionor** (seller) gives the **optionee** (the buyer) the exclusive right to buy during a specified period in exchange for payment of consideration. An option contract is similar to the option provision contained in the standard TREC residential sales contract in that for the duration of the option period the seller may not revoke his/her promise to sell. However, an option contract is distinguishable from an option provision in that the option contract is used to purchase real estate while the **option provision** is used in a contract to cancel the sale for any reason whatsoever.

VII. TERMINOLOGY

A. Acceptance
B. Assignee
C. Assignment
D. Assignor
E. Bilateral Contract
F. Breach
G. Competent Parties
H. Consideration
I. Contract For Real Estate
J. Counter Offer
K. Covenant

L. Dollar Damages
M. Execute
N. Executory Contract
O. Fraud, Duress, Menace
P. Implied Contract
Q. Incompetent
R. Liquidated Damages
S. Minors
T. Mutual Consent
U. Novation
V. Offeree

W. Offeror
X. Option
Y. Optionee
Z. Optionor
AA. Rescission
BB. Specific Performance
CC. Undue Influence
DD. Unilateral Contract
EE. Valid Contract
FF. Void Contract

1. _____ A court action to compel the performance of an agreement, e.g., sale of real property.
2. _____ Anything given or promised by a party to induce another to enter into a contract.
3. _____ A contract in which something remains to be done by one or both the parties.
4. _____ A right given, for consideration, to purchase a property upon specified terms within a specified time period, without obligating the party to purchase the property.
5. _____ A written proposal to purchase real property upon stated terms and conditions, accompanied by a deposit toward the purchase price, which becomes the contract for the sale of the property upon acceptance.
6. _____ All persons under 18 years of age.
7. _____ The act of agreeing or consenting to the terms of an offer, thereby establishing "the meeting of the minds" that is an essential element of a contract; genuine assent from both parties.
8. _____ One who assigns his or her right in a contract.
9. _____ A person to whom property or interests therein shall have been assigned.
10. _____ One who is mentally incapable of managing or taking care of self or property and therefore cannot enter into a contract without a guardian.
11. _____ A promise not to do a particular act.
12. _____ The substitution or exchange of a new contract for an old one by the mutual agreement of the parties.
13. _____ A transfer by a person of that person's rights under a contract.
14. _____ An agreement to do or not to do a certain thing. It must have at least six essential elements: competent parties, mutual consent, legal purpose, consideration, agreement in writing and signed (to be enforceable under the Statute of Frauds) and legal description.

15. ____ A binding contract created by the actions of the principals rather than by written or oral agreement.
16. ____ A contract under which only one party expressly makes a promise.
17. ____ A contract which has no legal force or binding effect.
18. ____ One making an offer.
19. ____ One to whom an offer is made.
20. ____ Voluntarily agreeing to the price and terms of an offer. Offer and acceptance create a contract.
21. ____ An offer in response to an offer.
22. ____ Failure to perform a contract, in whole or part, without legal excuse.
23. ____ Annulling a contract and placing the parties to it in a position as if there had not been a contract.
24. ____ A definite amount of damage, set forth in a contract, to be paid by the party breaching the contract. A predetermined estimate of actual damages from a breach.
25. ____ One who, for consideration, receives an option.
26. ____ One who, for consideration, gives an option.
27. ____ A contract under which the parties expressly enter into mutual promises.
28. ____ An action that abandons all other remedies and simply asks for money.
29. ____ Influence used to destroy the will of another so that any decision is not his or her free act.
30. ____ To complete a contract by signing it.
31. ____ Deceptive or threatening statements or acts used to wrongfully obtain acceptance of a contract.
32. ____ Individuals who have a legal capacity to contract, as opposed to minors, convicts, and incompetents.

VIII. MULTIPLE CHOICE

1. A contract that is created by acts and conduct, rather than by words, is known as a(n):
    a. bilateral agreement.
    b. unilateral contract.
    c. expressed contract.
    d. implied contract.

2. An agreement that fails to contain all the essential elements of a contract is:
    a. valid.
    b. void.
    c. voidable.
    d. all of the above.

3. Misrepresentation of a material fact that is known to be false is called:
    a. mistake.
    b. duress.
    c. fraud.
    d. undue influence.

4. A contract that has not been fully performed is called a(n):
    a. accord and satisfaction.
    b. novation contract.
    c. executed contract.
    d. executory contract.

5. An counter offer has the effect of:
    a. amending the original offer.
    b. terminating the original offer.
    c. modifying the original offer.
    d. no effect on the original offer.

6. Which of the following can terminate an original offer?
    a. Counter offer
    b. Lapse of time
    c. Withdrawal before acceptance
    d. All of the above

7. A bilateral contract is a(n):

    a. promise for an act.
    b. promise for a promise.
    c. implied contract.
    d. contract made in writing.

8. Another name for a lawsuit seeking liquidated damages as a remedy for breach of contract is a(n):

    a. action for dollar damages.
    b. unilateral rescission.
    c. specific performance.
    d. acceptance of breach.

9. A contract that contains purported promises that actually promises nothing is called a(n):

    a. implied contract.
    b. illusory contract.
    c. partially completed contract.
    d. emancipated contract.

10. Which of the following do the courts consider to be grounds for emancipation?

    a. Married minors
    b. Minors serving in the armed forces
    c. Court-declared self-supporting minors
    d. All of the above

ANSWERS: 1. d; 2. b; 3. c; 4. d; 5. b; 6. d; 7. b; 8. a; 9. b; 10. d

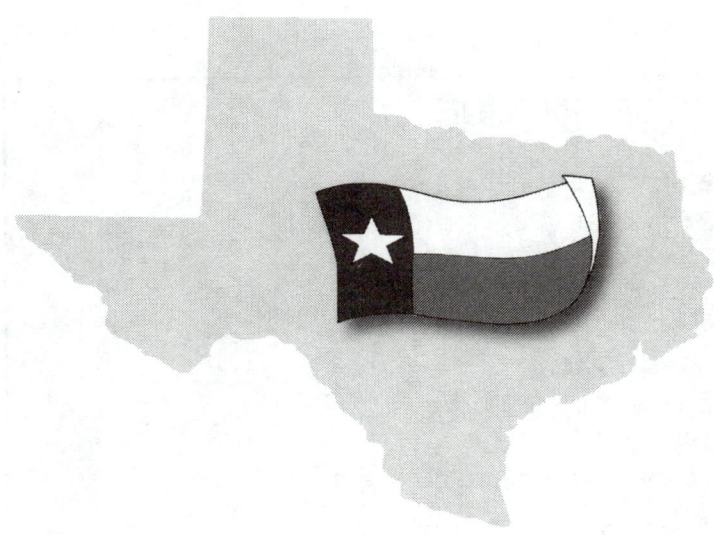

Chapter 6
The Real Estate License Act (TRELA)

I. An Overview of the Law

Real estate professionals in Texas have been licensed since 1939 when regulation was authorized under the Real Estate Dealer's License Act through the Texas Secretary of State's office. Ten years later, the law was amended and renamed as **The Real Estate License Act (TRELA)**. As part of the reorganization, in 1949 the legislature created a special agency known as the **Texas Real Estate Commission (TREC)** to administer and oversee the provisions of the license act. Since then the law has been amended numerous times so as to increase the scope and authority of the commission. Today, TREC has broad regulatory authority over many areas of real estate (see box).

TRELA further expands the scope of the commission by authorizing it to enact rules and regulations. The rules of the Texas Real Estate Commission are published in the Texas Administrative Code. While they are not published in this chapter, they can be found on the TREC website.

www.trec.state.tx.us
Texas Real Estate Commission

CHAPTER 6 OUTLINE

The Texas Real Estate Commission protects consumers by regulating:

- Real estate brokerage professionals (brokers and salespersons, and residential rental locators),
- Real estate property inspectors,
- Easement and right of way agents,
- Residential service (home warranty) companies, and
- Entities offering time share interests.

As a future Texas real estate licensee, you should become familiar with the Rules of the Texas Real Estate Commission because they supplement the law by governing the day-to-day activities of licensees. The courts have ruled that for licensing purposes, the rules of the commission hold the force of law.

As a state agency, the Texas Real Estate Commission is a member of **ARELLO, the Association of Real Estate License Law Officials,** an international association of real estate regulators. The mission of ARELLO is to support the public interest by assisting real estate regulators worldwide in the flow of ideas and information regarding real estate brokerage regulation.

The current licensing act, found in the Texas Occupations Code, is broadly organized in 17 subchapters that govern education of real estate professionals, licensing requirements and procedures, prohibited practices, and licensee discipline. The law additionally outlines the duties and responsibilities of the Texas Real Estate Commission and the Broker-Lawyer Committee, as well as to detail the provisions of the Real Estate Recovery Trust Account.

The legislature passed the license act to protect consumers, establish standards of conduct for licensees, and to professionalize the real estate industry. It may be considered to be a body of law under constant change.

The primary purpose of The Real Estate License Act (TRELA) is to protect real estate consumers in Texas.

It's important for all licensees to read and understand the law. To clarify how the law may apply under a specific set of factual circumstances, it's recommended that even licensees with a thorough familiarity of TRELA seek out the advice of an attorney.

II. The Real Estate License Act
(Chapter 1101 Texas Occupations Code)

Chapter 1101 of the Texas Occupations Code details the laws of TRELA that pertain to real estate brokers and salespersons.

A. SUBCHAPTER A. GENERAL PROVISIONS

The first subchapter of the law sets the groundwork by establishing important and key terms that will be followed throughout the licensing act such as the definitions of broker, salesperson, residential rental locator and subagent. Equally important is the section which describes those persons or transactions which are exempt from licensure.

§ 1101.001. SHORT TITLE.
This chapter may be cited as The Real Estate License Act.

§ 1101.002. DEFINITIONS.
In this chapter:

(1) "Broker":
- (A) means a person who, in exchange for a commission or other valuable consideration or with the expectation of receiving a commission or other valuable consideration, performs for another person one of the following acts:
  - (i) sells, exchanges, purchases, or leases real estate;
  - (ii) offers to sell, exchange, purchase, or lease real estate;
  - (iii) negotiates or attempts to negotiate the listing, sale, exchange, purchase, or lease of real estate;
  - (iv) lists or offers, attempts, or agrees to list real estate for sale, lease, or exchange;
  - (v) appraises or offers, attempts, or agrees to appraise real estate;
  - (vi) auctions or offers, attempts, or agrees to auction real estate;
  - (vii) deals in options on real estate, including buying, selling, or offering to buy or sell options on real estate;
  - (viii) aids or offers or attempts to aid in locating or obtaining real estate for purchase or lease;
  - (ix) procures or assists in procuring a prospect to effect the sale, exchange, or lease of real estate; or
  - (x) procures or assists in procuring property to effect the sale, exchange, or lease of real estate; and
- (B) includes a person who:
  - (i) is employed by or for an owner of real estate to sell any portion of the real estate; or

      (ii)   engages in the business of charging an advance fee or contracting to collect a fee under a contract that requires the person primarily to promote the sale of real estate by:

         (a)   listing the real estate in a publication primarily used for listing real estate; or

         (b)   referring information about the real estate to brokers.

(2) "Certificate holder" means a person registered under Subchapter K.

(3) "Commission" means the Texas Real Estate Commission.

(4) "License holder" means a broker or salesperson licensed under this chapter.

(5) "Real estate" means any interest in real property, including a leasehold, located in or outside this state. The term does not include an interest given as security for the performance of an obligation.

(6) "Residential rental locator" means a person who offers for consideration to locate a unit in an apartment complex for lease to a prospective tenant. The term does not include an owner who offers to locate a unit in the owner's complex.

(7) "Salesperson" means a person who is associated with a licensed broker for the purpose of performing an act described by Subdivision (1).

(8) "Subagent" means a license holder who:

    (A)   represents a principal through cooperation with and the consent of a broker representing the principal; and

    (B)   is not sponsored by or associated with the principal's broker.

> The statutory definition of a broker is very broad. It includes a broad range of real estate related activities which are performed in exchange or in anticipation of a commission or other valuable consideration. A salesperson is a person associated with a broker and as a result a salesperson may perform the same duties as a broker. However, as will be noted later, a salesperson may not earn a commission directly. Salespersons may earn commissions only through their brokers, for they represent their brokers in their transactions.

§ 1101.003. CORE REAL ESTATE COURSES.

(a) For purposes of this chapter, "core real estate courses" include:

  (1) agency law, which includes the following topics:

    (A)   the relationship between a principal and an agent;

    (B)   an agent's authority;

    (C)   the termination of an agent's authority;

    (D)   an agent's duties, including fiduciary duties;

    (E)   employment law;

    (F)   deceptive trade practices;

    (G)   listing or buying representation procedures; and

    (H)   the disclosure of agency;

  (2) contract law, which includes the following topics:

    (A)   elements of a contract;

    (B)   offer and acceptance;

    (C)   statute of frauds;

    (D)   remedies for breach, including specific performance;

    (E)   unauthorized practice of law;

    (F)   commission rules relating to use of adopted forms; and

    (G)   owner disclosure requirements;

(3) principles of real estate, which includes:

    (A)   an overview of:

        (i)   licensing as a broker or salesperson;

        (ii)   ethics of practice as a license holder;

        (iii)   titles to and conveyance of real estate;

        (iv)   legal descriptions;

        (v)   deeds, encumbrances, and liens;

        (vi)   distinctions between personal and real property;

        (vii)   appraisal;

        (viii) finance and regulations;

        (ix)   closing procedures; and

        (x)   real estate mathematics; and

    (B)   at least three hours of classroom instruction on federal, state, and local laws relating to housing discrimination, housing credit discrimination, and community reinvestment;

(4) property management, which includes the following topics:

    (A)   the role of a property manager;

    (B)   landlord policies;

    (C)   operational guidelines;

    (D)   leases;

    (E)   lease negotiations;

    (F)   tenant relations;

    (G)   maintenance;

    (H)   reports;

    (I)   habitability laws; and

    (J)   the Fair Housing Act (42 U.S.C. Section 3601 et seq.);

(5) real estate appraisal, which includes the following topics:

    (A)   the central purposes and functions of an appraisal;

    (B)   social and economic determinants of the value of real estate;

    (C)   appraisal case studies;

    (D)   cost, market data, and income approaches to value estimates of real estate;

    (E)   final correlations; and

    (F)   reporting;

(6) real estate brokerage, which includes the following topics:

    (A)   agency law;

    (B)   planning and organization;

    (C)   operational policies and procedures;

    (D)   recruitment, selection, and training of personnel;

    (E)   records and control; and

    (F)   real estate firm analysis and expansion criteria;

(7) real estate finance, which includes the following topics:

    (A)   monetary systems;

    (B)   primary and secondary money markets;

    (C)   sources of mortgage loans;
    (D)   federal government programs;
    (E)   loan applications, processes, and procedures;
    (F)   closing costs;
    (G)   alternative financial instruments;
    (H)   equal credit opportunity laws;
    (I)   community reinvestment laws, including the Community Reinvestment Act of 1977 (12 U.S.C. Section 2901 et seq.); and
    (J)   state housing agencies, including the Texas Department of Housing and Community Affairs;

(8) real estate investment, which includes the following topics:
    (A)   real estate investment characteristics;
    (B)   techniques of investment analysis;
    (C)   the time value of money;
    (D)   discounted and nondiscounted investment criteria;
    (E)   leverage;
    (F)   tax shelters depreciation; and
    (G)   applications to property tax;

(9) real estate law, which includes the following topics:
    (A)   legal concepts of real estate;
    (B)   land description;
    (C)   real property rights and estates in land;
    (D)   contracts;
    (E)   conveyances;
    (F)   encumbrances;
    (G)   foreclosures;
    (H)   recording procedures; and
    (I)   evidence of titles;

(10) real estate marketing, which includes the following topics:
    (A)   real estate professionalism and ethics;
    (B)   characteristics of successful salespersons;
    (C)   time management;
    (D)   psychology of marketing;
    (E)   listing procedures;
    (F)   advertising;
    (G)   negotiating and closing;
    (H)   financing; and
    (I)   Subchapter E, Chapter 17, Business & Commerce Code; and

(11) real estate mathematics, which includes the following topics:
    (A)   basic arithmetic skills and review of mathematical logic;
    (B)   percentages;
    (C)   interest;
    (D)   the time value of money;
    (E)   depreciation;
    (F)   amortization;
    (G)   proration; and
    (H)   estimation of closing statements.

(b) The commission may designate a course as an equivalent of a course listed in Subsection (a).

(c) The commission by rule may prescribe:

    (1) the content of the core real estate courses listed in Subsection (a); and

    (2) the title and content of additional core real estate courses.

The above section outlines a list of the core real estate courses which are applicable to obtaining a real estate license. A later section will explain exactly which and how many courses are actually needed for licensing. This list is by no means exhaustive because the law allows TREC to develop additional core courses as may be necessary.

---

§ 1101.004. ACTING AS BROKER OR SALESPERSON.

A person acts as a broker or salesperson under this chapter if the person, with the expectation of receiving valuable consideration, directly or indirectly performs or offers, attempts, or agrees to perform for another person any act described by Section 1101.002(1), as a part of a transaction or as an entire transaction.

§ 1101.005. APPLICABILITY OF CHAPTER.

This chapter does not apply to:

    (1) an attorney licensed in any state;

    (2) an attorney-in-fact authorized under a power of attorney to conduct a real estate transaction;

    (3) a public official while engaged in official duties;

    (4) an auctioneer licensed under Chapter 1802 while conducting the sale of real estate by auction if the auctioneer does not perform another act of a broker or salesperson;

    (5) a person acting under a court order or the authority of a will or written trust instrument;

    (6) a person employed by an owner in the sale of structures and land on which structures are located if the structures are erected by the owner in the course of the owner's business;

    (7) an on-site manager of an apartment complex;

    (8) an owner or the owner's employee who leases the owner's improved or unimproved real estate;

    (9) a partnership or limited liability partnership acting as a broker or salesperson through a partner who is a licensed broker; or

    (10) a transaction involving:

        (A)   the sale, lease, or transfer of a mineral or mining interest in real property;

        (B)   he sale, lease, or transfer of a cemetery lot; or

        (C)   the lease or management of a hotel or motel.

        (D)   the sale of real property under a power of sale conferred by a deed of trust or other contract lien.

This section outlines those parties and/or transactions for which no real estate license is needed to sell in Texas. For example, a person serving as county sheriff does not need to hold a real estate license to sell real property under a tax sale. As later sections will explain, only brokers may legally earn real estate commissions.

§ 1101.0055. NONAPPLICABILITY OF LAW GOVERNING CANCELLATION OF CERTAIN TRANSACTIONS.

A service contract that a license holder enters into for services governed by this chapter is not a good or service governed by Chapter 39, Business & Commerce Code.

§ 1101.006. APPLICATION OF SUNSET ACT.

The Texas Real Estate Commission is subject to Chapter 325, Government Code (Texas Sunset Act). Unless continued in existence as provided by that chapter, the commission is abolished and this chapter and Chapter 1102 expire September 1, 2007.

Like all state agencies, TREC is subject to review under the state Sunset Act. The Sunset Act is a law providing for a periodic review by all state agencies, commissions, and boards for the purpose of evaluating purpose and effectiveness by the Texas Sunset Commission. By law, TREC will expire on September 1, 2007 unless legislatively continued beyond that date.

B. SUBCHAPTER B. THE TEXAS REAL ESTATE COMMISSION

This subchapter describes the composition and make up of members serving on the Texas Real Estate Commission. Described here will be the provisions of law dealing with eligibility, gubernatorial appointment and term of office of the TREC commissioners as well as how the TREC presiding officer is selected.

§ 1101.051. COMMISSION MEMBERSHIP.

(a) The Texas Real Estate Commission consists of nine members appointed by the governor with the advice and consent of the senate as follows:

(1) six members who have been engaged in the brokerage business as licensed brokers as their major occupation for the five years preceding appointment; and

(2) three members who represent the public.

(b) Each member of the commission must be a qualified voter.

(c) Appointments to the commission shall be made without regard to the race, color, disability, sex, religion, age, or national origin of the appointee.

TREC consists of 9 members: 6 brokers and 3 public members. They are appointed by the governor.

§ 1101.052. PUBLIC MEMBER ELIGIBILITY.

A person is not eligible for appointment as a public member of the commission if the person or the person's spouse:

(1) is registered, certified, or licensed by an occupational regulatory agency in the real estate industry;

(2) is employed by or participates in the management of a business entity or other organization regulated by the commission or receiving funds from the commission;

(3) owns or controls, directly or indirectly, more than a 10 percent interest in a business entity or other organization regulated by the commission or receiving funds from the commission; or

(4) uses or receives a substantial amount of tangible goods, services, or funds from the commission, other than compensation or reimbursement authorized by law for commission membership, attendance, or expenses.

§ 1101.053. MEMBERSHIP AND EMPLOYEE RESTRICTIONS.

(a) In this section, "Texas trade association" means a nonprofit, cooperative, and voluntarily joined statewide association of business or professional competitors in this state designed to assist its members and its industry or profession in dealing with mutual business or professional problems and in promoting their common interest.

(b) A state elected president, president-elect, vice president, or secretary-treasurer, employee, or paid consultant of a Texas trade association in the real estate industry may not be a commission member and may not be a commission employee who is exempt from the state's position classification plan or is compensated at or above the amount prescribed by the General Appropriations Act for step 1, salary group A17, of the position classification salary schedule.

(c) A person who is the spouse of an officer, manager, or paid consultant of a Texas trade association in the real estate industry may not be a commission member and may not be a commission employee who is exempt from the state's position classification plan or is compensated at or above the amount prescribed by the General Appropriations Act for step 1, salary group A17, of the position classification salary schedule.

(d) A person may not serve as a commission member or act as the general counsel to the commission if the person is required to register as a lobbyist under Chapter 305, Government Code, because of the person's activities for compensation on behalf of a profession related to the operation of the commission.

§ 1101.054. OFFICIAL OATH.

Not later than the 15th day after the date of appointment, each appointee must take the constitutional oath of office.

§ 1101.055. TERMS; VACANCY.

(a) Commission members serve staggered six-year terms, with the terms of three members expiring January 31 of each odd-numbered year.

(b) If a vacancy occurs during a member's term, the governor shall appoint a person to fill the unexpired term.

§ 1101.056. OFFICERS.

(a) The governor shall designate a commission member who is a licensed broker as presiding officer. The presiding officer serves in that capacity at the pleasure of the governor.

(b) At a regular meeting in February of each year, the commission shall elect an assistant presiding officer and secretary from its membership.

§ 1101.057. GROUNDS FOR REMOVAL.

(a) It is a ground for removal from the commission that a member:

(1) does not have at the time of appointment the qualifications required by Section 1101.051(a) or (b) or 1101.052;

(2) does not maintain during service on the commission the qualifications required by Section 1101.051(a) or (b) or 1101.052;

(3) violates a prohibition established by Section 1101.053;

(4) cannot, because of illness or disability, discharge the member's duties for a substantial part of the member's term; or

(5) is absent from more than half of the regularly scheduled commission meetings that the member is eligible to attend during each calendar year, unless the absence is excused by majority vote of the commission.

(b) The validity of an action of the commission is not affected by the fact that it is taken when a ground for removal of a commission member exists.

(c) If the administrator has knowledge that a potential ground for removal of a commission member exists, the administrator shall notify the presiding officer of the commission of the ground. The presiding officer shall notify the governor that a potential ground for removal exists.

§ 1101.058. PER DIEM; REIMBURSEMENT.

A commission member is entitled to receive:

(1) $75 for each day the member performs the member's official duties; and

(2) reimbursement for actual and necessary expenses incurred in performing the member's official duties.

C. SUBCHAPTER C. ADMINISTRATOR AND OTHER COMMISSION PERSONNEL

It's a big job to regulate thousands of real estate licensees. That's why the law allows TREC to hire an administrator to run the day to day affairs of the real estate commission.

§ 1101.101. ADMINISTRATOR AND OTHER PERSONNEL.

(a) The commission may appoint an administrator.

(b) The commission may designate a subordinate officer as assistant administrator to act for the administrator in the administrator's absence.

(c) The commission may employ other subordinate officers and employees necessary to administer and enforce this chapter and Chapter 1102, including a general counsel, attorneys, investigators, and support staff.

(d) The commission shall determine the salaries of the administrator, officers, and employees of the commission. The amounts of the salaries may not exceed the amounts specified by the General Appropriations Act.

> To carry out the duties of the commission, the agency employs nearly 100 staff members who are organized in sections or divisions including enforcement, licensing, education, and communications.

§ 1101.102. DIVISION OF RESPONSIBILITIES.

The commission shall develop and implement policies that clearly define the respective responsibilities of the commission and the commission staff.

§ 1101.103. CODE OF ETHICS; STANDARDS OF CONDUCT.

Each member, officer, employee, and agent of the commission is subject to the code of ethics and standards of conduct imposed by Chapter 572, Government Code.

§ 1101.104. QUALIFICATIONS AND STANDARDS OF CONDUCT INFORMATION.

The commission shall provide, as often as necessary, to its members and employees information regarding their:

(1) qualifications for office or employment under this chapter and Chapter 1102; and

(2) responsibilities under applicable laws relating to standards of conduct for state officers or employees.

§ 1101.105. CAREER LADDER PROGRAM; PERFORMANCE EVALUATIONS.

(a) The administrator or the administrator's designee shall develop an intra-agency career ladder program. The program must require intra-agency postings of all nonentry level positions concurrently with any public posting.

(b) The administrator or the administrator's designee shall develop a system of annual performance evaluations. All merit pay for commission employees must be based on the system established under this subsection.

§ 1101.106. EQUAL EMPLOYMENT OPPORTUNITY POLICY; REPORT.

(a) The administrator or the administrator's designee shall prepare and maintain a written policy statement to ensure implementation of an equal employment opportunity program under which all personnel transactions are made without regard to race, color, disability, sex, religion, age, or national origin. The policy statement must include:

(1) personnel policies, including policies relating to recruitment, evaluation, selection, appointment, training, and promotion of personnel;

(2) a comprehensive analysis of the commission workforce that meets federal and state guidelines;

(3) procedures by which a determination can be made of significant underuse in the commission workforce of all persons for whom federal or state guidelines encourage a more equitable balance; and

(4) reasonable methods to appropriately address those areas of underuse.

(b) A policy statement prepared under Subsection (a) must:

(1) cover an annual period;

(2) be updated at least annually; and

(3) be filed with the governor.

(c) The governor shall deliver a biennial report to the legislature based on the information received under Subsection (b). The report may be made separately or as a part of other biennial reports made to the legislature.

D. SUBCHAPTER D. COMMISSION POWERS AND DUTIES

Remember that TREC did not enact The Real Estate License Act. So while the Texas legislature can take responsibility for creating TRELA, it is the job of TREC to administer and oversee the provisions of the license act. This portion of the law spells out TREC's statutory duties.

§ 1101.151. GENERAL POWERS AND DUTIES OF COMMISSION.

(a) The commission shall:

    (1) administer this chapter and Chapter 1102;

    (2) adopt rules and establish standards relating to permissible forms of advertising by a license holder acting as a residential rental locator;

    (3) maintain a registry of certificate holders; and

    (4) design and adopt a seal.

(b) The commission may:

    (1) adopt and enforce rules necessary to administer this chapter and Chapter 1102;

    (2) establish standards of conduct and ethics for persons licensed under this chapter and Chapter 1102 to:

        (A)   fulfill the purposes of this chapter and Chapter 1102; and

        (B)   ensure compliance with this chapter and Chapter 1102; and

    (3) authorize specific employees to conduct hearings and issue final decisions in contested cases.

To assist in the administration of The Real Estate License Act, the legislature has given TREC rule-making authority. TREC rules operate within the confines of the law and govern much of the day to day activity of the agency. TREC rules can be found at Title 22, Part 23 of the Texas Administrative Code, beginning at Chapter 531. They can also be accessed through the Texas Secretary of State's Office located at:

http://info.sos.state.tx.us/

---

§ 1101.152. FEES.

(a) The commission shall charge and collect the following fees:

    (1) for filing an original application for a broker license, not more than $100;

    (2) for annual renewal of a broker license, not more than $100;

    (3) for filing an original application for a salesperson license, not more than $75;

    (4) for annual renewal of a salesperson license, not more than $50;

    (5) for annual registration, $80;

    (6) for an application for a license examination, not more than $100;

    (7) for filing a request for a branch office license, not more than $20;

    (8) for filing a request for a change of place of business, change of name, return to active status, or change of sponsoring broker, not more than $20;

    (9) for filing a request to replace a lost or destroyed license or certificate of registration, not more than $20;

    (10) for filing an application for approval of an education program under Subchapter G, not more than $400;

    (11) for annual operation of an education program under Subchapter G, not more than $200;

    (12) for filing an application for approval of an instructor of core real estate courses, not more than $40;

    (13) for transcript evaluation, $20;

    (14) for preparing a license or registration history, not more than $20; and

    (15) for filing an application for a moral character determination, not more than $50.

(b) The commission may set and collect reasonable fees to implement the continuing education requirements for license holders, including the following fees:

(1) for an application for approval of a continuing education provider, not more than $400;

(2) for an application for approval of a continuing education course of study, not more than $100;

(3) for an application for approval of an instructor of continuing education courses, not more than $40; and

(4) or attendance at a program to train instructors of a continuing education course prescribed under Section 1101.455, not more than $100.

(c) Notwithstanding Subsection (a), if the commission issues an original inactive salesperson license under Section 1101.363(b) to a salesperson who is not sponsored by a licensed broker and the salesperson is subsequently sponsored by a licensed broker, the commission may not charge:

(1) the salesperson a fee for filing a request to place the salesperson license on active status; or

(2) the broker a fee for filing a request to sponsor the salesperson.

> TREC is authorized to charge two types of fees: fixed and "not to exceed" fees. For example, by law TREC must charge new potential applicants $20 when evaluating educational transcripts. But TREC is also authorized to charge, for example, not more than $75 for filing an original application for a salesperson's license. Thus, while the legislature has placed a statutory limit on how much can be charged, the actual filing fee will be determined on an annual basis based upon the budgetary needs of the agency.

§ 1101.153. FEE INCREASE.

(a) The fee for filing an original application for an individual broker license and the fee for annual renewal of an individual broker license is the amount of the fee set by the commission under Section 1101.152 and a fee increase of $200.

(b) Of each fee increase collected under Subsection (a), $50 shall be deposited to the credit of the foundation school fund and $150 shall be deposited to the credit of the general revenue fund.

§ 1101.154. ADDITIONAL FEE: TEXAS REAL ESTATE RESEARCH CENTER.

(a) The fee for the issuance or renewal of a:

(1) broker license is the amount of the fee set under Sections 1101.152 and 1101.153 and an additional $20 fee;

(2) salesperson license is the amount of the fee set under Section 1101.152 and an additional $17.50 fee; and

(3) certificate of registration is the amount of the fee set under Section 1101.152 and an additional $20 fee.

(b) The commission shall transmit quarterly the additional fees collected under Subsection (a) to Texas A&M University for deposit in a separate banking account that may be appropriated only to support, maintain, and carry out the purposes, objectives, and duties of the Texas Real Estate Research Center.

TREC maintains a statutory relationship with the Texas Real Estate Research Center (now known as the Real Estate Center) at Texas A & M University. Created in 1971, the Real Estate Center is the nation's largest publicly funded research and education center devoted to real estate issues. The bulk of its annual funding is based on the provisions of this section.

§ 1101.155. RULES RELATING TO CONTRACT FORMS.

(a) The commission may adopt rules in the public's best interest that require license holders to use contract forms prepared by the Texas Real Estate Broker-Lawyer Committee and adopted by the commission.

(b) The commission may not prohibit a license holder from using for the sale, exchange, option, or lease of an interest in real property a contract form that is:

    (1) prepared by the property owner; or

    (2) prepared by an attorney and required by the property owner.

(c) A listing contract form adopted by the commission that relates to the contractual obligations between a seller of real estate and a license holder acting as an agent for the seller must include:

    (1) a provision informing the parties to the contract that real estate commissions are negotiable; and

    (2) a provision explaining the availability of Texas coastal natural hazards information important to coastal residents, if that information is appropriate.

This section of the law establishes the basic conditions under which licensees may use contract forms which have been adopted by TREC. This provision is further explained in the Law of Contracts course.

§ 1101.156. RULES RESTRICTING ADVERTISING OR COMPETITIVE BIDDING.

(a) The commission may not adopt a rule restricting advertising or competitive bidding by a person regulated by the commission except to prohibit a false, misleading, or deceptive practice by the person.

(b) The commission may not include in rules to prohibit false, misleading, or deceptive practices by a person regulated by the commission a rule that:

    (1) restricts the use of any advertising medium;

    (2) restricts the person's personal appearance or use of the person's voice in an advertisement;

    (3) relates to the size or duration of an advertisement used by the person; or

    (4) restricts the person's advertisement under a trade name.

By law, TREC is statutorily barred from making rules regarding advertising, unless the rule is designed to prohibit misleading or deceptive advertising.

§ 1101.157. SUBPOENA AUTHORITY.

(a) The commission may request and, if necessary, compel by subpoena:

    (1) the attendance of witnesses for examination under oath; and

    (2) the production for inspection and copying of records, documents, and other evidence relevant to the investigation of an alleged violation of this chapter.

(b) A subpoena may be issued throughout the state and may be served by any person designated by the commission.

(c) If a person fails to comply with a subpoena issued under this section, the commission, acting through the attorney general, may file suit to enforce the subpoena in a district court in Travis County or in the county in which a hearing conducted by the commission may be held.

(d) The court shall order compliance with the subpoena if the court finds that good cause exists to issue the subpoena.

> TREC has the power to issue subpoenas. A subpoena is a legal command to appear before TREC. As this section explains, if a person, who is served with a subpoena, refuses to comply, he or she can be legally compelled to comply with the subpoena.

E. SUBCHAPTER E. PUBLIC INTEREST INFORMATION AND COMPLAINT PROCEDURES

Since TREC is a public agency, it's important for consumers to know what the agency does and how it works. It's also important for consumers to know how to file complaints against licensees for acts of misconduct.

§ 1101.201. PUBLIC INTEREST INFORMATION.

(a) The commission shall prepare information of public interest describing the functions of the commission and the procedures by which complaints are filed with and resolved by the commission.

(b) The commission shall make the information available to the public and appropriate state agencies.

§ 1101.202. COMPLAINTS.

(a) The commission by rule shall establish methods by which consumers and service recipients are notified of the name, mailing address, and telephone number of the commission for the purpose of directing a complaint to the commission. The commission may provide for that notice:

    (1) on each application for a license or certificate of registration or written contract for services of a person regulated under this chapter or Chapter 1102;

    (2) on a sign prominently displayed in the place of business of each person regulated under this chapter or Chapter 1102;

    (3) in a bill for services provided by a person regulated under this chapter or Chapter 1102;

    (4) in conjunction with the notice required by Section 1101.615; or

(5) to be prominently displayed on the Internet website of a person regulated under this chapter or Chapter 1102.

(b) The commission shall provide to a person who files a complaint with the commission relating to a license holder and to the license holder against whom the complaint is filed:

(1) an explanation of the remedies that are available to the person under this chapter; and

(2) information about appropriate state or local agencies or officials with whom the person may file a complaint.

> Chapter 1102, which is not covered in this book, refers to the part of the law where Real Estate Inspectors are licensed and regulated by the commission.

§ 1101.203. COMPLAINT INFORMATION.

(a) The commission shall maintain an information file about each complaint filed with the commission that the commission has authority to resolve.

(b) If a written complaint is filed with the commission that the commission has authority to resolve, the commission, at least quarterly and until final disposition of the complaint, shall notify the parties to the complaint of the status of the complaint unless the notice would jeopardize an undercover investigation authorized under Section 1101.204.

§ 1101.204. COMPLAINT INVESTIGATION AND DISPOSITION.

(a) The commission may, on its own motion, investigate the actions and records of a license holder.

(b) The commission shall investigate the actions and records of a license holder if:

(1) a person submits a signed, written complaint; and

(2) the complaint and any evidence presented with the complaint provide reasonable cause for an investigation.

(c) The commission may not conduct an investigation of a person licensed under this chapter or Chapter 1102 in connection with a complaint submitted later than the fourth anniversary of the date of the incident that is the subject of the complaint.

(d) The commission shall promptly provide a written notice to a person licensed under this chapter or Chapter 1102 who is the subject of an investigation unless after deliberation the commission decides against notification.

(e) Notwithstanding any other provision of this chapter, an undercover or covert investigation may not be conducted unless the commission expressly authorizes the investigation after considering the circumstances and determining that the investigation is necessary to implement this chapter.

(f) An investigation or other action against a person licensed under this chapter or Chapter 1102 may not be initiated on the basis of an anonymous complaint.

(g) The commission may authorize a commission employee to file a signed, written complaint against a person licensed under this chapter or Chapter 1102 and to conduct an investigation if:

(1) a judgment against the person has been paid from the real estate recovery trust account under this chapter or the real estate inspection recovery fund under Chapter 1102;

(2) the person is convicted of a criminal offense that may constitute grounds for the suspension or revocation of the person's license;

(3) the person fails to honor a check issued to the commission;

(4) the person fails to complete required continuing education within the period prescribed by commission rules adopted under Section 1101.457; or

(5) the person fails to provide, within a reasonable time, information requested by the commission in connection with an application to renew a license.

> While TREC may conduct an investigation of licensees based on its own information, it must investigate when it receives a signed, written complaint from a member of the public which creates a reasonable basis for an investigation. By law, TREC may not investigate complaints older than four years from the date of the alleged activity.

§ 1101.205. COMPLAINT INVESTIGATION OF CERTIFICATE HOLDER.

The commission shall investigate a signed complaint received by the commission that relates to an act of a certificate holder or a person required to hold a certificate under Subchapter K.

> TREC may also investigate the activities of certificate holders. Certificate holders do not hold traditional real estate licenses, but they are regulated nonetheless under the provisions beginning at §1101.501.

§ 1101.206. PUBLIC PARTICIPATION.

(a) The commission shall develop and implement policies that provide the public with a reasonable opportunity to appear before the commission and to speak on any issue under the commission's jurisdiction.

(b) The commission shall prepare and maintain a written plan that describes how a person who does not speak English or who has a physical, mental, or developmental disability may be provided reasonable access to the commission's programs.

F. SUBCHAPTER F. TEXAS REAL ESTATE BROKER-LAWYER COMMITTEE

The Texas Real Estate Broker-Lawyer Committee assists the commission by drafting and reviewing real estate contracts and addenda for use in Texas. Once approved by TREC, however, these standardized contract forms are required for use by all licensees.

§ 1101.251. DEFINITION OF COMMITTEE.

In this subchapter, "committee" means the Texas Real Estate Broker-Lawyer Committee.

§ 1101.252. COMMITTEE MEMBERSHIP.

(a) The Texas Real Estate Broker-Lawyer Committee consists of 13 members appointed as follows:

(1) six members appointed by the commission;

(2) six members of the State Bar of Texas appointed by the president of the state bar; and

(3) one public member appointed by the governor.

(b) Appointments to the committee shall be made without regard to the race, creed, sex, religion, or national origin of the appointee.

> The Texas Broker-Lawyer Committee consists of 13 members: 6 appointed by TREC, 6 appointed by the president of the State Bar of Texas, and one public member appointed by the governor.

§ 1101.253. TERMS; VACANCIES.

(a) Committee members serve staggered six-year terms, with the terms of two commission appointees and two State Bar of Texas appointees expiring every two years and the term of the public member expiring every six years.

(b) A committee member shall hold office until the member's successor is appointed.

(c) If a vacancy occurs during a member's term, the entity making the original appointment shall appoint a person to fill the unexpired term.

§ 1101.254. POWERS AND DUTIES.

(a) In addition to other delegated powers and duties, the committee shall draft and revise contract forms that are capable of being standardized to expedite real estate transactions and minimize controversy.

(b) The contract forms must contain safeguards adequate to protect the principals in the transaction.

G. SUBCHAPTER G. ACCREDITATION AND APPROVAL OF REAL ESTATE EDUCATIONAL PROGRAMS AND COURSES OF STUDY

By law, TREC may approve and accredit education programs offered by real estate education providers. In addition, TREC may approve the individual courses offered by providers which are necessary for licensing.

§ 1101.301. ACCREDITATION OF PROGRAMS AND COURSES OF STUDY.

(a) The commission, as necessary for the administration of this chapter and Chapter 1102, may:

(1) establish standards for the accreditation of educational programs or courses of study in real estate and real estate inspection conducted in this state, excluding programs and courses offered by accredited colleges and universities;

(2) establish by rule reasonable criteria for the approval of real estate and real estate inspection courses; and

(3) inspect and accredit real estate and real estate inspection educational programs or courses of study.

(b) The commission shall determine whether a real estate or real estate inspection course satisfies the requirements of this chapter and Chapter 1102.

§ 1101.302. BOND REQUIRED.

(a) In this section, "educational institution" means a school, excluding an accredited college or university, authorized by the commission under this chapter to offer a real estate or real estate inspection educational program or course of study.

(b) An educational institution shall maintain a corporate surety bond or other security acceptable to the commission that is:

   (1) in the amount of $10,000;

   (2) payable to the commission; and

   (3) for the benefit of a party who suffers damages caused by the failure of the institution to fulfill obligations related to the commission's approval.

§ 1101.303. APPROVAL OF CONTINUING EDUCATION PROVIDER OR COURSE OF STUDY.

(a) If the commission determines that an applicant for approval as a continuing education provider satisfies the requirements of this subchapter and any rule adopted under this subchapter, the commission may authorize the applicant to offer continuing education for a two-year period.

(b) If the commission determines that an applicant for approval of a continuing education course of study satisfies the requirements of this subchapter and any rule adopted under this subchapter, the commission may authorize the applicant to offer the course of study for a two-year period.

H. SUBCHAPTER H. LICENSE REQUIREMENTS

This subchapter outlines the requirements for obtaining a broker's or salesperson's license in Texas.

§ 1101.351. LICENSE REQUIRED.

(a) Unless a person holds a license issued under this chapter, the person may not:

   (1) act as or represent that the person is a broker or salesperson; or

   (2) act as a residential rental locator.

(b) An applicant for a broker or salesperson license may not act as a broker or salesperson until the person receives the license evidencing that authority.

(c) A licensed salesperson may not act or attempt to act as a broker or salesperson unless the salesperson is associated with a licensed broker and is acting for that broker.

> This section establishes the basic proposition that, unless exempted by law, a person must hold a Texas real estate license to work as a broker, salesperson or residential rental locator. Furthermore, an applicant cannot work as such unless and until the person actually receives his/her license from the commission. All salespersons must be formally associated with a broker before they can begin performing acts of a licensee.

§ 1101.352. LICENSE APPLICATION.

(a) Each applicant for a broker or salesperson license must submit an application on a form prescribed by the commission.

(b) Each applicant for a broker or salesperson license must disclose in the license application whether the applicant has:

(1) entered a plea of guilty or nolo contendere to a felony; or

(2) been convicted of a felony and the time for appeal has elapsed or the judgment or conviction has been affirmed on appeal.

(c) The disclosure under Subsection (b) must be provided even if an order has granted community supervision suspending the imposition of the sentence.

Application information and even the forms may be found on the TREC website at:

www.trec.state.tx.us/formslawspubs/forms/forms-r.e.app.asp

The applicant can also apply online at:

www.trec.state.tx.us/licenses/default.asp

Before making an application, TREC must first evaluate the potential applicant's real estate education. This is accomplished by submitting to TREC a Request for Evaluation of Education Documents. Upon formal approval, a person may then apply for a license.

---

§ 1101.353. MORAL CHARACTER DETERMINATION.

(a) If before applying for a license under this chapter a person requests that the commission determine whether the person's moral character complies with the commission's moral character requirements for licensing under this chapter and pays the fee prescribed by Section 1101.152, the commission shall make its determination of the person's moral character.

(b) Not later than the 30th day after the date the commission makes its determination, the commission shall notify the person of the determination.

(c) If a person applies for a license after receiving notice of a determination, the commission may conduct a supplemental moral character determination of the person. The supplemental determination may cover only the period after the date the person requests a moral character determination under this section.

(d) The commission may issue a provisional moral character determination. The commission by rule shall adopt reasonable terms for issuing a provisional moral character determination.

As the next section will soon explain, applicants for a real estate license must prove they are honest, trustworthy and are persons of integrity. As a result, potential applicants who have been previously convicted of certain felonies and misdemeanors may be barred from applying for a real estate license. This section allows concerned individuals to have a moral character determination made *in advance* to determine if their criminal history will prevent them from making an application for a license.

---

§ 1101.354. GENERAL ELIGIBILITY REQUIREMENTS.

To be eligible to receive a license under this chapter, a person must:

(1) at the time of application:

(A) be at least 18 years of age;

    (B)   be a citizen of the United States or a lawfully admitted alien; and

    (C)   be a resident of this state;

(2) satisfy the commission as to the applicant's honesty, trustworthiness, and integrity;

(3) demonstrate competence based on an examination under Subchapter I [the section of this chapter dealing with examinations];

(4) complete the required courses of study, including any required core real estate courses prescribed under this chapter; and

(5) complete at least:

    (A)   three classroom hours of course work on federal, state, and local laws governing housing discrimination, housing credit discrimination, and community reinvestment; or

    (B)   three semester hours of course work on constitutional law.

This section outlines the key eligibility requirements in order to obtain a Texas real estate license. Unless a person meets these basic requirements, he/she is not eligible for a license.

---

§ 1101.355. ADDITIONAL GENERAL ELIGIBILITY REQUIREMENTS FOR CERTAIN BUSINESS ENTITIES.

(a) To be eligible for a license under this chapter:

    (1) a corporation must designate one of its officers as its agent for purposes of this chapter; and

    (2) a limited liability company must designate one of its managers as its agent for purposes of this chapter.

(b) A corporation or limited liability company may not act as a broker unless the entity's designated agent is a licensed broker according to the commission's records.

§ 1101.356. BROKER LICENSE: EXPERIENCE AND EDUCATION REQUIREMENTS.

(a) An applicant for a broker license must provide to the commission satisfactory evidence that the applicant:

    (1) has had at least two years of active experience in this state as a license holder during the 36 months preceding the date the application is filed; and

    (2) has successfully completed at least 60 semester hours, or equivalent classroom hours, of postsecondary education, including:

        (A)   at least 18 semester hours or equivalent classroom hours of core real estate courses; and

        (B)   at least 42 hours of core real estate courses or related courses accepted by the commission.

(b) Subsection (a) does not apply to an applicant who, at the time of application, is licensed as a real estate broker by another state that has license requirements comparable to the requirements of this state.

(c) An applicant for a broker license who is licensed as a salesperson and is subject to the annual education requirements prescribed by Section 1101.454 must provide to the commission satisfactory evidence that the applicant has satisfied the requirements of that section. The hours completed under Section 1101.454 shall be applied to the number of hours required of the applicant under Subsection (a)(2) of this section.

This section of law establishes that a salesperson may not apply for a broker's license until he/she has held an active salesperson's license for at least two years out of the previous 36 months and fulfilled additional educational requirements.

§ 1101.357. BROKER LICENSE: ALTERNATE EXPERIENCE REQUIREMENTS FOR CERTAIN APPLICANTS.

An applicant for a broker license who does not satisfy the experience requirements of Section 1101.356 must provide to the commission satisfactory evidence that:

(1) the applicant:

(A) is a licensed real estate broker in another state;

(B) has had at least two years of active experience in that state as a licensed real estate broker or salesperson during the 36 months preceding the date the application is filed; and

(C) has satisfied the educational requirements prescribed by Section 1101.356; or

(2) the applicant was licensed in this state as a broker in the year preceding the date the application is filed.

§ 1101.358. SALESPERSON LICENSE: EDUCATION REQUIREMENTS.

(a) An applicant for a salesperson license must provide to the commission satisfactory evidence that the applicant has completed at least 14 semester hours, or equivalent classroom hours, of postsecondary education, including:

(1) at least four semester hours of core real estate courses on principles of real estate;

(2) at least two semester hours of each of the following core real estate courses:

(A) agency law;

(B) contract law; and

(C) one additional core real estate course; and

(3) at least four hours of core real estate courses or related courses.

(b) The commission shall waive the education requirements of Subsection (a) if the applicant has been licensed in this state as a broker or salesperson within the year preceding the date the application is filed.

(c) If an applicant for a salesperson license was licensed as a salesperson within the year preceding the date the application is filed and the license was issued under the conditions prescribed by Section 1101.454, the commission shall require the applicant to provide the evidence of successful completion of education requirements that would have been required if the license had been maintained without interruption during the preceding year.

§ 1101.359. ALTERNATE EDUCATION REQUIREMENTS FOR CERTAIN LICENSE HOLDERS.

An applicant for a broker license who is not subject to the education requirements of Section 1101.356(a)(2) and an applicant for a salesperson license who is not subject to the education requirements of Section 1101.358 or 1101.454 must provide to the commission satisfactory evidence that the applicant has completed the number of classroom hours of continuing education that would have been required for a timely renewal under Section 1101.455 during the two years preceding the date the application is filed.

Applicants for a Texas salesperson's license must have a minimum of 14 semester hours (210 classroom hours computed at the rate of 15 classroom hours for each semester hour) before they may take the salespersons exam. These courses consist of specific core courses (Principles of Real Estate, the Law of Agency, and the Law of Contracts), and other unspecified core courses. Refer back to §1101.003 for a complete list of core courses.

This statute also allows applicants to use up to 4 semester hours of "related" real estate courses in place of the undesignated core courses. TREC maintains and publishes a list of acceptable related courses on its website at:

www.trec.state.tx.us/education/related.asp

§ 1101.360. ELIGIBILITY REQUIREMENTS FOR CERTAIN NONRESIDENT APPLICANTS.

(a) A resident of another state who is not a licensed real estate broker and who was formerly licensed in this state as a broker or salesperson may apply for a license under this chapter not later than the first anniversary of the date of the expiration of the former license.

(b) A nonresident applicant is subject to the same license requirements as a resident. The commission may refuse to issue a license to a nonresident applicant for the same reasons that it may refuse to issue a license to a resident applicant.

(c) A nonresident applicant must submit with the application an irrevocable consent to a legal action against the applicant in the court of any county in this state in which a cause of action may arise or in which the plaintiff may reside. The action may be commenced by service of process or pleading authorized by the laws of this state or by delivery of process on the administrator or assistant administrator of the commission. The consent must:

(1) stipulate that the service of process or pleading is valid and binding in all courts as if personal service had been made on the nonresident in this state;

(2) be acknowledged; and

(3) if made by a corporation, be authenticated by its seal.

(d) A service of process or pleading served on the commission under this section shall be by duplicate copies. One copy shall be filed in the commission's office, and the other copy shall be forwarded by registered mail to the last known principal address recorded in the commission's records for the nonresident against whom the process or pleading is directed.

(e) A default judgment in an action commenced as provided by this section may not be granted:

(1) unless the commission certifies that a copy of the process or pleading was mailed to the defendant as provided by Subsection (d); and

(2) until the 21st day after the date the process or pleading is mailed to the defendant.

§ 1101.361. ADDITIONAL ELIGIBILITY REQUIREMENTS FOR CERTAIN NONRESIDENT APPLICANTS.

(a) Notwithstanding Section 1101.360, a nonresident applicant for a license who resides in a municipality whose boundary is contiguous at any point with the boundary of a municipality in this state is eligible to be licensed under this chapter in the same manner as

a resident of this state if the nonresident has been a resident of that municipality for at least the 60 days preceding the date the application is filed.

(b) A person licensed under this section shall maintain at all times a place of business in the municipality in which the person resides or in the municipality in this state that is contiguous to the municipality in which the person resides. The place of business must meet all the requirements of Section 1101.552. A place of business located in the municipality in which the person resides is considered to be in this state.

(c) A person licensed under this section may not maintain a place of business at another location in this state unless the person complies with Section 1101.356 or 1101.357.

§ 1101.362. WAIVER OF LICENSE REQUIREMENTS: PREVIOUS LICENSE HOLDERS.

The commission by rule may waive some or all of the requirements for a license under this chapter for an applicant who was licensed under this chapter within the six years preceding the date the application is filed.

§ 1101.363. ISSUANCE OF LICENSE.

(a) The commission shall issue an appropriate license to an applicant who meets the requirements for a license.

(b) The commission may issue an inactive salesperson license to a person who applies for a salesperson license and satisfies all requirements for the license. The person may not act as a salesperson unless the person is sponsored by a licensed broker who has notified the commission as required by Section 1101.367(b). Notwithstanding Section 1101.367(b), the licensed broker is not required to pay the fee required by that subsection.

(c) A license remains in effect for the period prescribed by the commission if the license holder complies with this chapter and pays the appropriate renewal fees.

> Assuming that an applicant has met all the requirements, the commission is required by law to issue a license. When an applicant first receives a salesperson's license it will be an **inactive** license until the commission receives a Salesperson Sponsorship form with the appropriate fee. Recall that under § 1101.351(c), a salesperson may not perform the acts of a broker, i.e. sell real estate, until this formal broker-salesperson association is complete.

§ 1101.364. DENIAL OF LICENSE.

(a) The commission shall immediately give written notice to the applicant of the commission's denial of a license.

(b) Before the applicant may appeal under Section 1101.658, the applicant must file, not later than the 10th day after the date the applicant receives the notice, an appeal requesting a time and place for a hearing before the commission. If the applicant fails to request a hearing as provided by this subsection, the commission's decision becomes final and is not subject to judicial review.

(c) The commission shall:

(1) set a time and place for the hearing not later than the 30th day after the date the commission receives the appeal; and

(2) give notice of the hearing to the applicant before the 10th day preceding the date of the hearing.

(d) The hearing may be continued from time to time with the consent of the applicant.

(e) After the hearing, the commission shall enter an appropriate order.

> Should TREC deny a person a license, the unsuccessful applicant may appeal this decision by filing an appeal with the commission within 10 days of the rejection notice. Failure to request an appeal will render the decision as final and not even the courts will be able to overturn the denial.

§ 1101.365. PROBATIONARY LICENSE.

(a) The commission may issue a probationary license.

(b) The commission by rule shall adopt reasonable terms for issuing a probationary license.

§ 1101.366. INACTIVE LICENSE: BROKER.

(a) The commission may place on inactive status the license of a broker if the broker:

    (1) is not acting as a broker;

    (2) is not sponsoring a salesperson; and

    (3) submits a written application to the commission before the expiration date of the broker's license.

(b) The commission may place on inactive status the license of a broker whose license has expired if the broker applies for inactive status on a form prescribed by the commission not later than the first anniversary of the expiration date of the broker's license.

(c) A broker applying for inactive status shall terminate the broker's association with each salesperson sponsored by the broker by giving written notice to each salesperson before the 30th day preceding the date the broker applies for inactive status.

(d) A broker on inactive status:

    (1) may not perform any activity regulated under this chapter; and

    (2) must pay annual renewal fees.

(e) The commission shall maintain a list of each broker whose license is on inactive status.

(f) The commission shall remove a broker's license from inactive status if the broker:

    (1) submits an application to the commission;

    (2) pays the required fee; and

    (3) submits proof of attending at least 15 classroom hours of continuing education as specified by Section 1101.455 during the two years preceding the date the application under Subdivision (1) is filed.

§ 1101.367. INACTIVE LICENSE: SALESPERSON.

(a) When the association of a salesperson with the salesperson's sponsoring broker terminates, the broker shall immediately return the salesperson license to the commission. A salesperson license returned under this subsection is inactive.

(b) The commission may remove a salesperson license from inactive status under Subsection (a) if, before the expiration date of the salesperson license, a licensed broker files a request with the commission advising the commission that the broker assumes sponsorship of the salesperson, accompanied by the appropriate fee.

(c) As a condition of returning to active status, an inactive salesperson whose license is not subject to the annual education requirements of Section 1101.454 must provide to the commission proof of attending at least 15 hours of continuing education as specified by

Section 1101.455 during the two years preceding the date the application to return to active status is filed.

Should the broker-salesperson relationship terminate for any reason, the broker is required to immediately send the salesperson's license to the commission where it will stay until it is reissued to a new broker. As stated before, a salesperson may not perform acts of a licensee with an inactive license.

I. SUBCHAPTER I. EXAMINATIONS

As stated in the previous subchapter of the law, an applicant must be determined competent in real estate knowledge before a license can be issued. This portion of the law governs how competency is determined so as to protect consumers.

§ 1101.401. EXAMINATION REQUIRED.

(a) The competency requirement prescribed under Section 1101.354(3) shall be established by an examination prepared or contracted for by the commission.

(b) The commission shall determine the time and place in the state for offering the examination.

(c) The examination must be of sufficient scope in the judgment of the commission to determine whether a person is competent to act as a broker or salesperson in a manner that will protect the public.

(d) The examination for a salesperson license must be less exacting and less stringent than the broker examination.

(e) The commission shall provide each applicant with study material and references on which the examination is based.

(f) An applicant must satisfy the examination requirement not later than six months after the date the license application is filed.

Competency is determined by a license examination. The broker's exam will be harder than the salespersons exam. Before any examination the commission will send to each applicant study material known as a Candidate Information Brochure (CIB).

---

§ 1101.402. WAIVER OF EXAMINATION.

The commission shall waive the examination requirement for an applicant for:

(1) a broker license if:
  (A) the applicant was previously licensed in this state as a broker; and
  (B) the application is filed before the first anniversary of the expiration date of that license; and

(2) a salesperson license if:
  (A) the applicant was previously licensed in this state as a broker or salesperson; and

(B) the application is filed before the first anniversary of the expiration date of that license.

§ 1101.403. ADMINISTRATION OF EXAMINATION; TESTING SERVICE.

(a) The commission shall administer any examination required by this chapter or Chapter 1102 unless the commission enters into an agreement with a testing service to administer the examination.

(b) The commission may accept an examination administered by a testing service if the commission retains the authority to establish the scope and type of the examination.

(c) The commission may negotiate an agreement with a testing service relating to examination development, scheduling, site arrangements, administration, grading, reporting, and analysis.

(d) The commission may require a testing service to:

(1) correspond directly with license applicants regarding the administration of the examination;

(2) collect fees directly from applicants for administering the examination; or

(3) administer the examination at specific locations and specified frequencies.

(e) The commission shall adopt rules and standards as necessary to implement this section.

Once a license application has been accepted by TREC, the applicant will be directed to contact the testing service to make arrangements for taking the exam. There are testing centers located throughout the state.

Hint: since the testing service will require applicants to show a government issued photo ID as a condition of admission, the name on the ID should exactly match the name appearing on the application form.

§ 1101.404. EXAMINATION RESULTS.

(a) Not later than the 30th day after the date an examination is administered, the commission shall notify each examinee of the results of the examination. If an examination is graded or reviewed by a national testing service, the commission shall notify each examinee of the results of the examination not later than the 14th day after the date the commission receives the results from the testing service.

(b) If the notice of the results of an examination graded or reviewed by a national testing service will be delayed for more than 90 days after the examination date, the commission shall notify each examinee of the reason for the delay before the 90th day.

The examination is typically administered on computer which means that the results should be made available to the applicant as soon as the test is completed. The test is given in two parts and the applicant must pass both parts in order to obtain a license. Under TREC rules, examination questions are highly confidential and disclosing test questions could expose an applicant, a licensee or education provider to stiff penalties.

(c) If requested in writing by a person who fails an examination, the commission shall provide to the person an analysis of the person's performance on the examination.

§ 1101.405. REEXAMINATION.

An applicant who fails an examination may apply for reexamination by filing a request accompanied by the proper fee.

There is no limit as to how many times an applicant may retake the license examination. However, under the terms of each application, the applicant must pass both parts of the exam within six months.

J. SUBCHAPTER J. LICENSE RENEWAL

Once a real estate license has been obtained, it must be continually renewed. As this subchapter explains, renewal will include the payment of a renewal fee and answering some questions about criminal history, but it may also include taking additional real estate education courses or periodic refresher courses as a condition of renewal.

§ 1101.451. LICENSE EXPIRATION.

(a) The commission may issue or renew a license for a period not to exceed 24 months.

(b) The commission by rule may adopt a system under which licenses expire on various dates during the year. The commission shall adjust the date for payment of the renewal fees accordingly.

(c) For a year in which the license expiration date is changed, renewal fees payable shall be prorated on a monthly basis so that each license holder pays only that portion of the fee that is allocable to the number of months during which the license is valid. On renewal of the license on the new expiration date, the total renewal fee is payable.

(d) A renewal fee for a license under this chapter may not exceed, calculated on an annual basis, the amount of the sum of the fees established under Sections 1101.152, 1101.154, and 1101.603.

Initially, a newly licensed salesperson who has taken the minimum number of course hours will receive a license term of one year. After the salesperson has completed the full educational requirement as will be detailed later, the license will be renewed for a two-year period.

License renewal is now conducted online through the TREC web page.

---

§ 1101.452. INFORMATION REQUIRED FOR LICENSE RENEWAL.

(a) To renew an active license that is not subject to the annual education requirements of Section 1101.454, the license holder must provide to the commission proof of compliance with the continuing education requirements of Section 1101.455.

(b) Each applicant for the renewal of a license must disclose in the license application whether the applicant has:

(1) entered a plea of guilty or nolo contendere to a felony; or

(2) been convicted of a felony and the time for appeal has elapsed or the judgment or conviction has been affirmed on appeal.

(c) The disclosure under Subsection (b) must be provided even if an order has granted community supervision suspending the imposition of the sentence.

> Assuming that a salesperson has met the educational requirement contained in §1101.454, the licensee is then subject to Mandatory Continuing Education (MCE) as a condition of license renewal. In addition, upon each renewal, the licensee must disclose whether he/she has pled guilty, nolo contendre (no contest), or been found guilty of any type of felony.

§ 1101.453. ADDITIONAL RENEWAL REQUIREMENTS FOR CERTAIN BUSINESS ENTITIES.

(a) To renew a license under this chapter:

(1) a corporation must designate one of its officers as its agent for purposes of this chapter; and

(2) a limited liability company must designate one of its managers as its agent for purposes of this chapter.

(b) A corporation or limited liability company may not act as a broker unless the entity's designated agent is a licensed broker according to the commission's records.

§ 1101.454. SALESPERSON LICENSE RENEWAL.

(a) An applicant applying for the first renewal of a salesperson license must provide to the commission satisfactory evidence of completion of at least 18 semester hours, or equivalent classroom hours, of postsecondary education, including 14 hours of core real estate courses.

(b) The commission may not waive the requirements for renewal under this section.

> If a person has completed the minimum number of hours necessary to obtain his/her sales license, then the salesperson must complete the remainder of the required 18 semester hours no later than his/her first annual renewal. This means that assuming that a salesperson obtained his/her sales license with 14 semester hours, he/she will have exactly one year, or no later than his/her first annual renewal, to complete another 4 semester hours as a condition of keeping his/her license.
>
> A much easier way to meet this requirement is to complete all 18 semester hours before taking the licensing exam.

§ 1101.455. CONTINUING EDUCATION REQUIREMENTS.

(a) In this section, "property tax consulting laws and legal issues" includes the Tax Code, preparation of property tax reports, the unauthorized practice of law, agency law, tax law, law relating to property tax or property assessment, deceptive trade practices, contract forms and addendums, and other legal topics approved by the commission.

(b) A license holder who is not subject to the annual education requirements of Section 1101.454 must attend during the term of the current license at least 15 classroom hours of continuing education courses approved by the commission.

(c) The commission by rule may:

  (1) prescribe the title, content, and duration of continuing education courses that a license holder must attend to renew a license; and

  (2) approve as a substitute for the classroom attendance required by Subsection (b):

    (A) relevant educational experience; and

    (B) correspondence courses.

(d) In addition, the commission may approve supervised video instruction as a course that may be applied toward satisfaction of the classroom hours of continuing education courses required by Subsection (b).

(e) At least six of the continuing education hours required by Subsection (b) must cover the following legal topics:

  (1) commission rules;

  (2) fair housing laws;

  (3) Property Code issues, including landlord-tenant law;

  (4) agency law;

  (5) antitrust laws;

  (6) Subchapter E, Chapter 17, Business & Commerce Code;

  (7) disclosures to buyers, landlords, tenants, and sellers;

  (8) current contract and addendum forms;

  (9) unauthorized practice of law;

  (10) case studies involving violations of laws and regulations;

  (11) current Federal Housing Administration and Department of Veterans Affairs regulations;

  (12) tax laws;

  (13) property tax consulting laws and legal issues; or

  (14) other legal topics approved by the commission.

(f) The remaining nine hours may be devoted to other real estate-related topics approved by the commission.

(g) The commission may consider courses equivalent to those described by Subsections (e) and (f) for continuing education credit.

(h) The commission shall automatically approve the following course as courses that satisfy the mandatory continuing education requirements of Subsection (f):

  (1) core real estate courses; and

  (2) real estate-related courses approved by the State Bar of Texas for minimum continuing legal education participatory credit.

(i) The commission may not require an examination for a course under this section unless the course is a correspondence course or a course offered by an alternative delivery system, including delivery by computer.

(j) Daily classroom course segments must be at least one hour and not more than 10 hours.

After a salesperson has completed the 18 semester hour basic educational requirement it's time to move on to Mandatory Continuing Education or MCE. Under this section, nearly all licensees (except for those as detailed in the next section) must complete a TREC approved 15-hour classroom course as a condition of license renewal. MCE courses are generally offered by local real estate boards, community colleges and private real estate schools.

As will be seen in a later section of the law, the failure to timely complete MCE requirements will not only result in a license non-renewal, but it will also subject the licensee to disciplinary action by TREC.

§ 1101.456. EXEMPTION FROM CONTINUING EDUCATION REQUIREMENTS FOR CERTAIN BROKERS.

Notwithstanding any other provision of this chapter, a broker who, before October 31, 1991, qualified under former Section 7A(f), The Real Estate License Act (Article 6573a, Vernon's Texas Civil Statutes), as added by Section 1.041, Chapter 553, Acts of the 72nd Legislature, Regular Session, 1991, for an exemption from continuing education requirements is not required to comply with the mandatory continuing education requirements of this subchapter to renew the broker's license.

Under a special 1991 law, brokers in certain Texas counties could apply for a special exemption from MCE provisions. As a result, some brokers today are not required to attend continuing education courses. Unless a broker received that special exemption in 1991, there is no other way that a licensee can avoid the MCE requirement as a condition of license renewal.

§ 1101.457. DEFERRAL OF CONTINUING EDUCATION REQUIREMENTS.

(a) The commission by rule may establish procedures under which an applicant may have the applicant's license issued, renewed, or returned to active status before the applicant completes continuing education requirements.

(b) The commission may require an applicant under this section to:

(1) pay an additional fee, not to exceed $200; and

(2) complete the required continuing education not later than the 60th day after the date the license is issued, renewed, or returned to active status.

K. SUBCHAPTER K. CERTIFICATE REQUIREMENTS

In Texas, persons who buy or sell easements or rights-of-way for compensation are required to either hold real estate licenses or be registered with the real estate commission. Because these registration requirements are located here in Subchapter K of the law, these registrants are often simply called Subchapter K Registrants or certificate holders.

§ 1101.501. CERTIFICATE REQUIRED.

A person may not sell, buy, lease, or transfer an easement or right-of-way for another, for compensation or with the expectation of receiving compensation, for use in connection with telecommunication, utility, railroad, or pipeline service unless the person:

(1) holds a license issued under this chapter; or

(2) holds a certificate of registration issued under this subchapter.

§ 1101.502. ELIGIBILITY REQUIREMENTS FOR CERTIFICATE.

(a) To be eligible to receive a certificate of registration or a renewal certificate under this subchapter, a person must be:

(1) at least 18 years of age; and

(2) a citizen of the United States or a lawfully admitted alien.

(b) To be eligible to receive a certificate of registration or a renewal certificate under this subchapter, a corporation, limited liability company, partnership, limited liability partnership, or other entity must designate as its agent one of its officers, partners, or managers who is registered under this subchapter.

§ 1101.503. ISSUANCE OF CERTIFICATE.

(a) The commission shall issue a certificate of registration to an applicant who meets the requirements for a certificate of registration.

(b) The certificate remains in effect for the period prescribed by the commission if the certificate holder complies with this chapter and pays the appropriate renewal fees.

§ 1101.504. CERTIFICATE EXPIRATION.

The duration, expiration, and renewal of a certificate of registration are subject to the same provisions as are applicable under Section 1101.451 to the duration, expiration, and renewal of a license.

§ 1101.505. DENIAL OF CERTIFICATE.

The denial of a certificate of registration is subject to the same provisions as are applicable under Section 1101.364 to the denial of a license.

§ 1101.506. CHANGE OF ADDRESS.

Not later than the 10th day after the date a certificate holder moves its place of business from a previously designated address, the holder shall:

(1) notify the commission of the move; and

(2) obtain a new certificate of registration that reflects the address of the new place of business.

§ 1101.507. DISPLAY OF CERTIFICATE.

A certificate holder shall prominently display at all times the holder's certificate of registration in the holder's place of business.

L. SUBCHAPTER L. PRACTICE BY A LICENSE HOLDER

Among other topics, this section establishes some basic representational issues such as the minimum level of services that every agent owes his/her client and how an agent may legally serve both parties.

§ 1101.551. DEFINITIONS.

In this subchapter:

(1) "Intermediary" means a broker who is employed to negotiate a transaction between the parties to a transaction and for that purpose may act as an agent of the parties.

(2) "Party" means a prospective buyer, seller, landlord, or tenant or an authorized representative of a buyer, seller, landlord, or tenant, including a trustee, guardian, executor, administrator, receiver, or attorney-in-fact. The term does not include a license holder who represents a party.

> The term "Intermediary" is a special term under Texas law. It specifically refers to a broker who seeks to legally represent both buyer and seller within the same transaction. The term never refers to a salesperson. Other sections of the law, which will be studied in greater detail in the Law of Agency, will explain exactly how this type of representation may be done within the confines of the law.

§ 1101.552. FIXED OFFICE REQUIRED; CHANGE OF ADDRESS; BRANCH OFFICES.

(a) A resident broker shall maintain a fixed office in this state. The address of the office shall be designated on the broker's license.

(b) Not later than the 10th day after the date a broker moves from the address designated on the broker's license, the broker shall submit an application, accompanied by the appropriate fee, for a license that designates the new location of the broker's office. The commission shall issue a license that designates the new location if the new location complies with the requirements of this section.

(c) A broker who maintains more than one place of business in this state shall obtain a branch office license for each additional office maintained by the broker by submitting an application, accompanied by the appropriate fee.

(d) A nonresident licensed broker is not required to maintain a place of business in this state.

> Brokers who maintain more than one place of business are required to have a branch office license for each location.

§ 1101.553. DISPLAY OF LICENSE.

A residential rental locator shall prominently display in a place accessible to clients and prospective clients:

(1) the locator's license;

(2) a statement that the locator is licensed by the commission; and

(3) the name, mailing address, and telephone number of the commission as provided by Section 1101.202(a).

§ 1101.554. CUSTODY OF SALESPERSON LICENSE.

(a) The commission shall deliver or mail each salesperson license to the broker with whom the salesperson is associated.

(b) The broker shall keep the license under the broker's custody and control.

> While residential rental locators are required by law to publicly display their licenses, brokers are only required to keep the licenses of their sponsored salespersons under their custody and control.

§ 1101.555. NOTICE TO BUYER REGARDING ABSTRACT OR TITLE POLICY.

When an offer to purchase real estate in this state is signed, a license holder shall advise each buyer, in writing, that the buyer should:

(1) have the abstract covering the real estate that is the subject of the contract examined by an attorney chosen by the buyer; or

(2) be provided with or obtain a title insurance policy.

Licensees are required to advise each purchaser in writing to have the abstract reviewed by an attorney or to obtain a title insurance policy. Title policies and abstracts of title are more fully discussed in Chapter 10.

Fortunately, the promulgated TREC contracts contain this advisory language as part of their standard provisions so that the licensee normally never has to worry about it. However, since licensees are allowed under certain circumstances to use non-promulgated contract forms, licensees will need to provide this disclaimer when using other forms. As later sections in this chapter will point out, the failure to give this notice may not only result in license suspension but may also prevent recovery of an unpaid sales commission.

---

§ 1101.556. DISCLOSURE OF CERTAIN INFORMATION RELATING TO OCCUPANTS.

Notwithstanding other law, a license holder is not required to inquire about, disclose, or release information relating to whether:

(1) a previous or current occupant of real property had, may have had, has, or may have AIDS, an HIV-related illness, or an HIV infection as defined by the Centers for Disease Control and Prevention of the United States Public Health Service; or

(2) a death occurred on a property by natural causes, suicide, or accident unrelated to the condition of the property.

§ 1101.557. ACTING AS AGENT; REGULATION OF CERTAIN TRANSACTIONS

(a) A broker who represents a party in a real estate transaction or who lists real estate for sale under an exclusive agreement for a party is that party's agent.

(b) A broker described by Subsection (a):

(1) may not instruct another broker to directly or indirectly violate Section 1101.652(b)(22);

(2) must inform the party if the broker receives material information related to a transaction to list, buy, sell, or lease the party's real estate, including the receipt of an offer by the broker; and

(3) shall, at a minimum, answer the party's questions and present any offer to or from the party.

(c) for the purposes of this section:

(1) a license holder who has the authority to bind a party to a lease or sale under a power of attorney or a property management agreement is also a party to the lease or sale;

(2) an inquiry to a person described by Section 1101.005(6) about contract terms or forms required by the person's employer does not violate Section 1101.652(b)(32) if the person does not have the authority to bind the employer to the contract; and

(3) the sole delivery of an offer to a party does not violate Section 1101.652(b)(22) if:

(A) the party's broker consents to the delivery;

(B) a copy of the offer is sent to the party's broker, unless a governmental agency using a sealed bid process does not allow a copy to be sent; and

(c) the person delivering the offer does not engage in anther activity that directly or indirectly violates Section 1101.652(b)(22).

> This section lays out a minimum level of service that all brokers owe to their clients.

§ 1101.558. REPRESENTATION DISCLOSURE.

(a) In this section, "substantive dialogue" means a meeting or written communication that involves a substantive discussion relating to specific real property. The term does not include:

(1) a meeting that occurs at a property that is held open for any prospective buyer or tenant; or

(2) a meeting or written communication that occurs after the parties to a real estate transaction have signed a contract to sell, buy, or lease the real property concerned.

(b) A license holder who represents a party in a proposed real estate transaction shall disclose, orally or in writing, that representation at the time of the license holder's first contact with:

(1) another party to the transaction; or

(2) another license holder who represents another party to the transaction.

(c) A license holder shall provide to a party to a real estate transaction at the time of the first substantive dialogue with the party the written statement prescribed by Subsection (d) unless:

(1) the proposed transaction is for a residential lease for not more than one year and a sale is not being considered; or

(2) the license holder meets with a party who is represented by another license holder.

(d) The written statement required by Subsection (c) must be printed in a format that uses at least 10-point type and read as follows:

"Before working with a real estate broker, you should know that the duties of a broker depend on whom the broker represents. If you are a prospective seller or landlord (owner) or a prospective buyer or tenant (buyer), you should know that the broker who lists the property for sale or lease is the owner's agent. A broker who acts as a subagent represents the owner in cooperation with the listing broker. A broker who acts as a buyer's agent represents the buyer. A broker may act as an intermediary between the parties if the parties consent in writing. A broker can assist you in locating a property, preparing a contract or lease, or obtaining financing without representing you. A broker is obligated by law to treat you honestly.

"IF THE BROKER REPRESENTS THE OWNER: The broker becomes the owner's agent by entering into an agreement with the owner, usually through a written listing agreement, or by agreeing to act as a subagent by accepting an offer of subagency from the listing broker. A subagent may work in a different real estate office. A listing broker or subagent can assist the buyer but does not represent the buyer and must place the interests of the owner first. The buyer should not tell the owner's agent anything the buyer would not want the owner to know because an owner's agent must disclose to the owner any material information known to the agent.

"IF THE BROKER REPRESENTS THE BUYER: The broker becomes the buyer's agent by entering into an agreement to represent the buyer, usually through a written buyer representation agreement. A buyer's agent can assist the owner but does not represent the owner and must place the interests of the buyer first. The owner should not tell a buyer's agent anything the owner would not want the buyer to know because a buyer's agent must disclose to the buyer any material information known to the agent.

"IF THE BROKER ACTS AS AN INTERMEDIARY: A broker may act as an intermediary between the parties if the broker complies with The Real Estate License Act. The broker must obtain the written consent of each party to the transaction to act as an intermediary. The written consent must state who will pay the broker and, in conspicuous bold or underlined print, set forth the broker's obligations as an intermediary. The broker is required to treat each party honestly and fairly and to comply with The Real Estate License Act. A broker who acts as an intermediary in a transaction: (1) shall treat all parties honestly; (2) may not disclose that the owner will accept a price less than the asking price unless authorized in writing to do so by the owner; (3) may not disclose that the buyer will pay a price greater than the price submitted in a written offer unless authorized in writing to do so by the buyer; and (4) may not disclose any confidential information or any information that a party specifically instructs the broker in writing not to disclose unless authorized in writing to disclose the information or required to do so by The Real Estate License Act or a court order or if the information materially relates to the condition of the property. With the parties' consent, a broker acting as an intermediary between the parties may appoint a person who is licensed under The Real Estate License Act and associated with the broker to communicate with and carry out instructions of one party and another person who is licensed under that Act and associated with the broker to communicate with and carry out instructions of the other party.

"If you choose to have a broker represent you, you should enter into a written agreement with the broker that clearly establishes the broker's obligations and your obligations. The agreement should state how and by whom the broker will be paid. You have the right to choose the type of representation, if any, you wish to receive. Your payment of a fee to a broker does not necessarily establish that the broker represents you. If you have any questions regarding the duties and responsibilities of the broker, you should resolve those questions before proceeding."

(e) The license holder may substitute "buyer" for "tenant" and "seller" for "landlord" as appropriate in the written statement prescribed by Subsection (d).

> This section legally establishes several agency law disclosures for real estate licensees. The long written disclosure contained in this section is available for use by licensees as a separate TREC form. This form is shown in Chapter 4 under Figure 4-4.

§ 1101.559. BROKER ACTING AS INTERMEDIARY.

(a) A broker may act as an intermediary between parties to a real estate transaction if:
  (1) the broker obtains written consent from each party for the broker to act as an intermediary in the transaction; and

(2) the written consent of the parties states the source of any expected compensation to the broker.

(b) A written listing agreement to represent a seller or landlord or a written agreement to represent a buyer or tenant that authorizes a broker to act as an intermediary in a real estate transaction is sufficient to establish written consent of the party to the transaction if the written agreement specifies in conspicuous bold or underlined print the conduct that is prohibited under Section 1101.651(d).

(c) An intermediary shall act fairly and impartially. Appointment by a broker acting as an intermediary of an associated license holder under Section 1101.560 to communicate with, carry out the instructions of, and provide opinions and advice to the parties to whom that associated license holder is appointed is a fair and impartial act.

> This section details how an intermediary relationship is created and describes the duties of an Intermediary.

§ 1101.560. ASSOCIATED LICENSE HOLDER ACTING AS INTERMEDIARY.

(a) A broker who complies with the written consent requirements of Section 1101.559 may appoint:

(1) a license holder associated with the broker to communicate with and carry out instructions of one party to a real estate transaction; and

(2) another license holder associated with the broker to communicate with and carry out instructions of any other party to the transaction.

(b) A license holder may be appointed under this section only if:

(1) the written consent of the parties under Section 1101.559 authorizes the broker to make the appointment; and

(2) the broker provides written notice of the appointment to all parties involved in the real estate transaction.

(c) A license holder appointed under this section may provide opinions and advice during negotiations to the party to whom the license holder is appointed.

§ 1101.561. DUTIES OF INTERMEDIARY PREVAIL.

(a) The duties of a license holder acting as an intermediary under this subchapter supersede the duties of a license holder established under any other law, including common law.

(b) A broker must agree to act as an intermediary under this subchapter if the broker agrees to represent in a transaction:

(1) a buyer or tenant; and

(2) a seller or landlord.

M. SUBCHAPTER M. REAL ESTATE RECOVERY ACCOUNT

The real estate commission administers two large recovery funds that may be used to compensate judgment holders who have been harmed by the acts of licensees. One recovery fund involves real estate inspectors, while the other fund, described below, involves brokers and salespersons.

§ 1101.601. REAL ESTATE RECOVERY TRUST ACCOUNT.

(a) The commission shall maintain a real estate recovery trust account to reimburse aggrieved persons who suffer actual damages caused by an act described by Section 1101. 602 committed by:

    (1) a license holder;

    (2) a certificate holder; or

    (3) a person who does not hold a license or certificate and who is an employee or agent of a license or certificate holder.

(b) The license or certificate holder must have held the license or certificate at the time the act was committed.

> The recovery fund is only available to persons who have been harmed by acts of a broker, salesperson, certificate holder or employee thereof. Moreover, the fund is intended to compensate for actual damages suffered.

§ 1101.602. ENTITLEMENT TO REIMBURSEMENT.

An aggrieved person is entitled to reimbursement from the trust account if a person described by Section 1101.601 engages in conduct described by Section 1101.652(a)(3) or (b) or 1101.653(1), (2), (3), or (4).

§ 1101.603. PAYMENTS INTO TRUST ACCOUNT.

(a) In addition to other fees required by this chapter, an applicant for an original license must pay a fee of $10.

(b) In addition to other fees required by this chapter, an applicant for an original certificate of registration or renewal certificate must pay a fee of $50.

(c) The commission shall deposit to the credit of the trust account:

    (1) fees collected under Subsections (a) and (b); and

    (2) an administrative penalty collected under Subchapter O for a violation by a person licensed as a broker or salesperson.

(d) An administrative penalty collected under Subchapter O for a violation by a person who is not licensed under this chapter or Chapter 1102 shall be deposited to the credit of the trust account or the real estate inspection recovery fund, as determined by the commission.

(e) On a determination by the commission at any time that the balance in the trust account is less than $1 million, each license holder at the next license renewal must pay, in addition to the renewal fee, a fee that is equal to the lesser of $10 or a pro rata share of the amount necessary to obtain a balance in the trust account of $1.7 million. The commission shall deposit the additional fee to the credit of the trust account.

(f) To ensure the availability of a sufficient amount to pay anticipated claims on the trust account, the commission by rule may provide for the collection of assessments at different times and under conditions other than those specified by this chapter.

§ 1101.604. MANAGEMENT OF TRUST ACCOUNT.

(a) The commission shall hold money credited to the trust account in trust to carry out the purpose of the trust account.

(b) Money credited to the trust account may be invested in the same manner as money of the Employees Retirement System of Texas, except that an investment may not be made that would impair the liquidity necessary to make payments from the trust account as required by this subchapter.

(c) Interest from the investments shall be deposited to the credit of the trust account.

(d) If the balance in the trust account on December 31 of a year is more than the greater of $3.5 million or the total amount of claims paid from the trust account during the preceding four fiscal years, the commission shall transfer the excess amount of money in the trust account to the credit of the general revenue fund.

§ 1101.605. DEADLINE FOR ACTION; NOTICE TO COMMISSION.

(a) An action for a judgment that may result in an order for payment from the trust account may not be brought after the second anniversary of the date the cause of action accrues.

(b) When an aggrieved person brings an action for a judgment that may result in an order for payment from the trust account, the license or certificate holder against whom the action is brought shall notify the commission in writing of the action.

> For purposes of making a claim against the recovery fund, this section establishes that the time limit for filing lawsuits is two years from when the claim arises.

§ 1101.606. CLAIM FOR PAYMENT FROM TRUST ACCOUNT.

(a) An aggrieved person who obtains a court judgment against a license or certificate holder for an act described by Section 1101.602 may, after final judgment is entered, execution returned nulla bona, and a judgment lien perfected, file a verified claim in the court that entered the judgment.

(b) After the 20th day after the date the aggrieved person gives written notice of the claim to the commission and judgment debtor, the person may apply to the court that entered the judgment for an order for payment from the trust account of the amount unpaid on the judgment. The court shall proceed promptly on the application.

§ 1101.607. ISSUES AT HEARING.

At the hearing on the application for payment from the trust account, the aggrieved person must show:

(1) that the judgment is based on facts allowing recovery under this subchapter;

(2) that the person is not:

    (A) the spouse of the judgment debtor or the personal representative of the spouse; or

    (B) a license or certificate holder who is seeking to recover compensation, including a commission, in the real estate transaction that is the subject of the application for payment;

(3) that, according to the best information available, the judgment debtor does not have sufficient attachable assets in this or another state to satisfy the judgment;

(4) the amount that may be realized from the sale of assets liable to be sold or applied to satisfy the judgment; and

(5) the balance remaining due on the judgment after application of the amount under Subdivision (4).

> In order to make a claim against the recovery fund, a person as defined in §1101.601 must first file a lawsuit against the licensee and not against TREC. Moreover, the person must win the suit and the licensee must have no funds to pay the judgment.

§ 1101.608. COMMISSION RESPONSE.

(a) On receipt of notice under Section 1101.606 and the scheduling of a hearing, the commission may notify the attorney general of the commission's desire to enter an appearance, file a response, appear at the hearing, defend the action, or take any other action the commission considers appropriate.

(b) The commission and the attorney general may act under Subsection (a) only to:

    (1) protect the trust account from spurious or unjust claims; or

    (2) ensure compliance with the requirements for recovery under this subchapter.

(c) The commission may relitigate in the hearing any material and relevant issue that was determined in the action that resulted in the judgment in favor of the aggrieved person.

§ 1101.609. COURT ORDER FOR PAYMENT.

The court shall order the commission to pay from the trust account the amount the court finds payable on the claim under this subchapter if at a hearing the court is satisfied:

    (1) of the truth of each matter the aggrieved person is required by Section 1101.607 to show; and

    (2) that the aggrieved person has satisfied each requirement of Sections 1101.606 and 1101.607.

TREC does not decide on its own who it will pay from the recovery fund. Instead, the court that originally heard the lawsuit against the licensee must enter an order directing TREC to pay from the recovery fund.

---

§ 1101.610. PAYMENT LIMITS; ATTORNEY'S FEES.

(a) Payments from the trust account for claims, including attorney's fees, interest, and court costs, arising out of a single transaction may not exceed a total of $50,000, regardless of the number of claimants.

(b) Payments from the trust account for claims based on judgments against a single license or certificate holder may not exceed a total of $100,000 until the license or certificate holder has reimbursed the trust account for all amounts paid.

(c) If the court finds that the total amount of claims against a license or certificate holder exceeds the limitations in this section, the court shall proportionately reduce the amount payable on each claim.

(d) A person receiving payment from the trust account is entitled to receive reasonable attorney's fees in the amount determined by the court, subject to the limitations prescribed by this section.

Payments from the recovery fund are not unlimited. The maximum payment is $50,000 for a single transaction and $100,000 for all claims against a single licensee. Remember that, in all cases, the recovery must be for actual damages sustained that are evidenced by a judgment.

---

§ 1101.611. APPLICATION OF JUDGMENT RECOVERY.

An aggrieved person who receives a recovery on a judgment against a single defendant before receiving a payment from the trust account must apply the recovery first to actual damages.

§ 1101.612. SUBROGATION.

(a) The commission is subrogated to all rights of a judgment creditor to the extent of an amount paid from the trust account, and the judgment creditor shall assign to the commission all right, title, and interest in the judgment up to that amount.

(b) The commission has priority for repayment from any subsequent recovery on the judgment.

(c) The commission shall deposit any amount recovered on the judgment to the credit of the trust account.

> Subrogation means that if the real estate commission is ordered to pay a claim to a judgment holder, it will have the right to reimbursement from the judgment debtor.

§ 1101.613. EFFECT ON DISCIPLINARY PROCEEDINGS.

(a) This subchapter does not limit the commission's authority to take disciplinary action against a license or certificate holder for a violation of this chapter or a commission rule.

(b) A license or certificate holder's repayment of all amounts owed to the trust account does not affect another disciplinary proceeding brought under this chapter.

§ 1101.614. WAIVER OF RIGHTS.

An aggrieved person who does not comply with this subchapter waives the person's rights under this subchapter.

§ 1101.615. NOTICE TO CONSUMERS AND SERVICE RECIPIENTS.

(a) Each license and certificate holder shall provide notice to consumers and service recipients of the availability of payment from the trust account for aggrieved persons:

(1) in conjunction with the notice required by Section 1101.202;

(2) on a written contract for the license or certificate holder's services;

(3) on a brochure that the license or certificate holder distributes;

(4) on a sign prominently displayed in the license or certificate holder's place of business;

(5) in a bill or receipt for the license or certificate holder's services; or

(6) in a prominent display on the Internet website of a person regulated under this chapter.

(b) The notice must include:

(1) the commission's name, mailing address, and telephone number; and

(2) any other information required by commission rule.

> TREC has produced a form for the purpose as described in this section. It is shown in Figure 6-1.

N. SUBCHAPTER N. PROHIBITED PRACTICES AND DISCIPLINARY PROCEEDINGS

This subsection spells out prohibited activity applicable to all real estate licensees. Under this subchapter, violations of law may subject licensees to disciplinary action, such as license suspension or

Figure 6-1

THIS FIRM IS

LICENSED AND REGULATED

BY THE

TEXAS REAL ESTATE

COMMISSION (TREC)

TREC ADMINISTERS TWO RECOVERY FUNDS

WHICH MAY BE USED TO SATISFY JUDGMENTS

AGAINST INSPECTORS AND REAL ESTATE

LICENSEES INVOLVING A VIOLATION OF THE LAW.

COMPLAINTS OR INQUIRIES SHOULD

BE DIRECTED TO

TEXAS REAL ESTATE COMMISSION
P.O. BOX 12188
AUSTIN, TEXAS 78711-2188

(512) 465-3960

Consumer Information Form 1-1 (8-91)

revocation, from the Texas Real Estate Commission. However, later subchapters make it clear that legally prohibited activity could give rise to other serious consequences such as lawsuits, penalties, and even criminal prosecution.

§ 1101.651. CERTAIN PRACTICES PROHIBITED.

(a) A licensed broker may not pay a commission to or otherwise compensate a person directly or indirectly for performing an act of a broker unless the person is:

(1) a license holder; or

(2) a real estate broker licensed in another state who does not conduct in this state any of the negotiations for which the commission or other compensation is paid.

(b) A salesperson may not accept compensation for a real estate transaction from a person other than the broker with whom the salesperson is associated or was associated when the salesperson earned the compensation.

(c) A salesperson may not pay a commission to a person except through the broker with whom the salesperson is associated at that time.

(d) A broker and any broker or salesperson appointed under Section 1101.560 who acts as an intermediary under Subchapter L may not:

(1) disclose to the buyer or tenant that the seller or landlord will accept a price less than the asking price, unless otherwise instructed in a separate writing by the seller or landlord;

(2) disclose to the seller or landlord that the buyer or tenant will pay a price greater than the price submitted in a written offer to the seller or landlord, unless otherwise instructed in a separate writing by the buyer or tenant;

(3) disclose any confidential information or any information a party specifically instructs the broker or salesperson in writing not to disclose, unless:

(A) the broker or salesperson is otherwise instructed in a separate writing by the respective party;

(B) the broker or salesperson is required to disclose the information by this chapter or a court order; or

(C) the information materially relates to the condition of the property;

(4) treat a party to a transaction dishonestly; or

(5) violate this chapter.

> This section establishes some ground rules with respect to the payment of commissions and intermediary practice. First, it sets out the basic principle that commissions on the sale of real estate may be only earned by licensed brokers. A broker may also pay a commission to his/her sponsored salesperson or another real estate broker.
>
> A second principle contained in this section involves confidential information given to an Intermediary.

§ 1101.652. GROUNDS FOR SUSPENSION OR REVOCATION OF LICENSE.

(a) The commission may suspend or revoke a license issued under this chapter or take other disciplinary action authorized by this chapter if the license holder:

(1) enters a plea of guilty or nolo contendere to or is convicted of a felony in which fraud is an essential element, and the time for appeal has elapsed or the judgment or conviction has been affirmed on appeal, without regard to an order granting community supervision that suspends the imposition of the sentence;

(2) procures or attempts to procure a license under this chapter for the license holder or a salesperson by fraud, misrepresentation, or deceit or by making a material misstatement of fact in an application for a license;

(3) engages in misrepresentation, dishonesty, or fraud when selling, buying, trading, or leasing real property in the name of:

    (A) the license holder;

    (B) the license holder's spouse; or

    (C) a person related to the license holder within the first degree by consanguinity;

(4) fails to honor, within a reasonable time, a check issued to the commission after the commission has sent by certified mail a request for payment to the license holder's last known business address according to commission records;

(5) fails or refuses to produce on request, for inspection by the commission or a commission representative, a document, book, or record that is in the license holder's possession and relates to a real estate transaction conducted by the license holder;

(6) fails to provide, within a reasonable time, information requested by the commission that relates to a formal or informal complaint to the commission that would indicate a violation of this chapter;

(7) fails to surrender to the owner, without just cause, a document or instrument that is requested by the owner and that is in the license holder's possession;

(8) fails to use a contract form required by the commission under Section 1101.155;

(9) fails to notify the commission, not later than the 30'th day after the date of a final conviction or the entry of a plea of nolo contrendre, that the person has been convicted of or entered a plea of nolo contendre to a felony or a criminal offense involving fraud; or

(10) disregards or violates this chapter.

(b) The commission may suspend or revoke a license issued under this chapter or take other disciplinary action authorized by this chapter if the license holder, while acting as a broker or salesperson:

(1) acts negligently or incompetently;

(2) engages in conduct that is dishonest or in bad faith or that demonstrates untrustworthiness;

(3) makes a material misrepresentation to a potential buyer concerning a significant defect, including a latent structural defect, known to the license holder that would be a significant factor to a reasonable and prudent buyer in making a decision to purchase real property;

(4) fails to disclose to a potential buyer a defect described by Subdivision (3) that is known to the license holder;

(5) makes a false promise that is likely to influence a person to enter into an agreement when the license holder is unable or does not intend to keep the promise;

(6) pursues a continued and flagrant course of misrepresentation or makes false promises through an agent or salesperson, through advertising, or otherwise;

(7) fails to make clear to all parties to a real estate transaction the party for whom the license holder is acting;

(8) receives compensation from more than one party to a real estate transaction without the full knowledge and consent of all parties to the transaction;

(9) fails within a reasonable time to properly account for or remit money that is received by the license holder and that belongs to another person;

(10) commingles money that belongs to another person with the license holder's own money;

(11) pays a commission or a fee to or divides a commission or a fee with a person other than a license holder or a real estate broker or salesperson licensed in another state for compensation for services as a real estate agent;

(12) fails to specify a definite termination date that is not subject to prior notice in a contract, other than a contract to perform property management services, in which the license holder agrees to perform services for which a license is required under this chapter;

(13) accepts, receives, or charges an undisclosed commission, rebate, or direct profit on an expenditure made for a principal;

(14) solicits, sells, or offers for sale real property by means of a lottery;

(15) solicits, sells, or offers for sale real property by means of a deceptive practice;

(16) acts in a dual capacity as broker and undisclosed principal in a real estate transaction;

(17) guarantees or authorizes or permits a person to guarantee that future profits will result from a resale of real property;

(18) places a sign on real property offering the real property for sale or lease without obtaining the written consent of the owner of the real property or the owner's authorized agent;

(19) offers to sell or lease real property without the knowledge and consent of the owner of the real property or the owner's authorized agent;

(20) offers to sell or lease real property on terms other than those authorized by the owner of the real property or the owner's authorized agent;

(21) induces or attempts to induce a party to a contract of sale or lease to break the contract for the purpose of substituting a new contract;

(22) negotiates or attempts to negotiate the sale, exchange, or lease of real property with an owner, landlord, buyer, or tenant with knowledge that that person is a party to an outstanding written contract that grants exclusive agency to another broker in connection with the transaction;

(23) publishes or causes to be published an advertisement, including an advertisement by newspaper, radio, television, the Internet, or display, that misleads or is likely to deceive the public, tends to create a misleading impression, or fails to identify the person causing the advertisement to be published as a licensed broker or agent;

(24) withholds from or inserts into a statement of account or invoice a statement that the license holder knows makes the statement of account or invoice inaccurate in a material way;

(25) publishes or circulates an unjustified or unwarranted threat of a legal proceeding or other action;

(26) establishes an association by employment or otherwise with a person other than a license holder if the person is expected or required to act as a license holder;

(27) aids, abets, or conspires with another person to circumvent this chapter;

(28) fails or refuses to provide, on request, a copy of a document relating to a real estate transaction to a person who signed the document;

(29) fails to advise a buyer in writing before the closing of a real estate transaction that the buyer should:
- (A) have the abstract covering the real estate that is the subject of the contract examined by an attorney chosen by the buyer; or
- (B) be provided with or obtain a title insurance policy;

(30) fails to deposit, within a reasonable time, money the license holder receives as escrow agent in a real estate transaction:
- (A) in trust with a title company authorized to do business in this state; or
- (B) in a custodial, trust, or escrow account maintained for that purpose in a banking institution authorized to do business in this state;

(31) disburses money deposited in a custodial, trust, or escrow account, as provided in Subdivision (30), before the completion or termination of the real estate transaction;

(32) discriminates against an owner, potential buyer, landlord, or potential tenant on the basis of race, color, religion, sex, national origin, or ancestry, including directing a prospective buyer or tenant interested in equivalent properties to a different area based on the race, color, religion, sex, national origin, or ancestry of the potential owner or tenant; or

(33) disregards or violates this chapter.

> All licensees should familiarize themselves with this long section because it lists the grounds for license suspension or revocation. License suspension means that a licensee, although permitted to retain his/her license, will be barred from using the license for a specified period of time. License revocation, on the other hand, means that the license is revoked or withdrawn completely by the real estate commission.

§ 1101.653. GROUNDS FOR SUSPENSION OR REVOCATION OF CERTIFICATE.
The commission may suspend or revoke a certificate of registration issued under this chapter if the certificate holder:
- (1) engages in dishonest dealing, fraud, unlawful discrimination, or a deceptive act;
- (2) makes a misrepresentation;
- (3) acts in bad faith;
- (4) demonstrates untrustworthiness;
- (5) fails to honor, within a reasonable time, a check issued to the commission after the commission has mailed a request for payment to the certificate holder's last known address according to the commission's records;
- (6) fails to provide to a party to a transaction a written notice prescribed by the commission that:
  - (A) must be given before the party is obligated to sell, buy, lease, or transfer a right-of-way or easement; and
  - (B) contains:
    - (i) the name of the certificate holder;
    - (ii) the certificate number;
    - (iii) the name of the person the certificate holder represents;
    - (iv) a statement advising the party that the party may seek representation from a lawyer or broker in the transaction; and

    (v)   a statement generally advising the party that the right-of-way or easement may affect the value of the property; or

(7) disregards or violates this chapter or a commission rule relating to certificate holders.

> This section only applies to the acts of a certificate holder as that term is defined in Subchapter K.

§ 1101.654. SUSPENSION OR REVOCATION OF LICENSE OR CERTIFICATE FOR UNAUTHORIZED PRACTICE OF LAW.

(a) The commission shall suspend or revoke the license or certificate of registration of a license or certificate holder who is not a licensed attorney in this state and who, for consideration, a reward, or a pecuniary benefit, present or anticipated, direct or indirect, or in connection with the person's employment, agency, or fiduciary relationship as a license or certificate holder:

    (1) drafts an instrument, other than a form described by Section 1101.155, that transfers or otherwise affects an interest in real property; or

    (2) advises a person regarding the validity or legal sufficiency of an instrument or the validity of title to real property.

(b) Notwithstanding any other law, a license or certificate holder who completes a contract form for the sale, exchange, option, or lease of an interest in real property incidental to acting as a broker is not engaged in the unauthorized or illegal practice of law in this state if the form was:

    (1) adopted by the commission for the type of transaction for which the form is used;

    (2) prepared by an attorney licensed in this state and approved by the attorney for the type of transaction for which the form is used; or

    (3) prepared by the property owner or by an attorney and required by the property owner.

> The commission may also suspend/revoke a real estate license if the licensee is found to be drafting legal documents or giving legal advice without being a licensed attorney. Additionally, the real estate licensee may face action from the State Bar of Texas.

§ 1101.655. REVOCATION OF LICENSE OR CERTIFICATE FOR CLAIM ON ACCOUNT.

(a) The commission may revoke a license or certificate of registration issued under this chapter if the commission makes a payment from the real estate recovery trust account to satisfy all or part of a judgment against the license or certificate holder.

(b) The commission may probate an order revoking a license under this section.

(c) A person is not eligible for a license or certificate until the person has repaid in full the amount paid from the account for the person, plus interest at the legal rate.

§ 1101.656. ADDITIONAL DISCIPLINARY AUTHORITY OF COMMISSION.

(a) In addition to any other authority under this chapter, the commission may suspend or revoke a license, place on probation a person whose license has been suspended, or reprimand a license holder if the license holder violates this chapter or a commission rule.

(b) The commission may probate a suspension, revocation, or cancellation of a license under reasonable terms determined by the commission.

(c) The commission may require a license holder whose license suspension or revocation is probated to:

(1) report regularly to the commission on matters that are the basis of the probation;

(2) limit practice to an area prescribed by the commission; or

(3) continue to renew professional education until the license holder attains a degree of skill satisfactory to the commission in the area that is the basis of the probation.

> The Texas Real Estate Commission has options available to it other than license suspension and revocation. Depending on the circumstances, the commission may place a licensee under probation, official supervision, or even issue a reprimand.

§ 1101.657. HEARING.

(a) If the commission proposes to suspend or revoke a person's license or certificate of registration, the person is entitled to a hearing before the commission or a hearings officer appointed by the commission.

(b) The commission shall adopt procedures by which all decisions to suspend or revoke a license or certificate are made by or are appealable to the commission.

(c) Except as provided by Subsection (d), the commission shall prescribe the time and place of the hearing.

(d) This subsection applies only to a hearing relating to a proposal to suspend or revoke a person's license or certificate of registration for a violation of Section 1101.652(a)(3) or (b). The hearing shall be held, if the license holder requests, in the county in which the principal place of business of the license holder is located, or, if the license holder is not a resident, the hearing may be held in any county in this state.

(e) A hearing under this section is governed by the contested case procedures under Chapter 2001, Government Code.

> In all cases where the licensee is facing suspension/revocation on grounds of allegedly violating §1101.652(a)(3) or (b) the licensee is entitled to an administrative agency hearing.

§ 1101.658. APPEAL.

(a) A person aggrieved by a ruling, order, or decision of the commission is entitled to appeal to a district court in the county in which the administrative hearing was held.

(b) An appeal is governed by the procedures under Chapter 2001, Government Code.

> A licensee who has received an adverse ruling from TREC is also entitled to appeal the decision to the courts. The right of judicial review is not automatic, however. The licensee must first exhaust all hearing avenues at the agency level, including requesting a rehearing before the actual TREC board, before he/she will be entitled to bring suit in state district court.

O. SUBCHAPTER O. ADMINISTRATIVE PENALTY

The enforcement power of TREC reaches far beyond real estate licensees. Under this subchapter of the law, TREC may impose special agency administrative penalties against persons involved in unlicensed real estate activity.

§ 1101.701. IMPOSITION OF ADMINISTRATIVE PENALTY.

The commission may impose an administrative penalty on a person who violates this chapter or a rule adopted or order issued by the commission under this chapter.

§ 1101.7015. DELEGATION OF ADMINISTRATOR'S AUTHORITY.

The commission may authorize the administrator to delegate to another commission employee the administrator's authority to act under this subchapter.

§ 1101.702. AMOUNT OF PENALTY.

(a) The amount of an administrative penalty may not exceed $1,000 for each violation. Each day a violation continues or occurs may be considered a separate violation for purposes of imposing a penalty if the commission determines that the person charged:

(1) engaged in an activity for which a broker or salesperson license is required without holding a license; and

(2) was not licensed by the commission as a broker or salesperson at any time in the four years preceding the date of the violation.

(b) In determining the amount of the penalty, the administrator shall consider:

(1) the seriousness of the violation, including the nature, circumstances, extent, and gravity of the prohibited acts;

(2) the history of previous violations;

(3) the amount necessary to deter a future violation;

(4) efforts to correct the violation; and

(5) any other matter that justice may require.

> The administrative penalty can be rather steep; up to $1,000 per day for each day the violation continues.

§ 1101.703. REPORT AND NOTICE OF VIOLATION AND PENALTY.

(a) If, after investigation of a possible violation and the facts relating to that violation, the administrator determines that a violation has occurred, the administrator may issue a violation report stating:

(1) the facts on which the determination is based; and

(2) the administrator's recommendation on the imposition of the administrative penalty, including a recommendation on the amount of the penalty.

(b) Not later than the 14th day after the date the report is issued, the administrator shall give written notice of the report to the person charged with the violation. The notice must:

(1) include a brief summary of the charges;

(2) state the amount of the recommended penalty; and

(3) inform the person of the person's right to a hearing on the occurrence of the violation, the amount of the penalty, or both.

§ 1101.704. PENALTY TO BE PAID OR HEARING REQUESTED.

(a) Not later than the 20th day after the date the person receives the notice under Section 1101.703, the person may:

(1) accept the administrator's determination, including the recommended administrative penalty; or

(2) request in writing a hearing on the determination.

(b) If the person accepts the administrator's determination, the commission by order shall approve the determination and order payment of the recommended penalty.

§ 1101.705. HEARING; DECISION BY COMMISSION.

(a) If the person requests a hearing or fails to timely respond to the notice, the administrator shall set a hearing and give notice of the hearing to the person.

(b) A hearings examiner designated by the administrator shall conduct the hearing. The hearings examiner shall:

(1) make findings of fact and conclusions of law; and

(2) promptly issue to the commission a proposal for decision regarding the occurrence of the violation and the amount of any proposed administrative penalty.

(c) Based on the findings of fact, conclusions of law, and proposal for decision of the hearings examiner, the commission by order may determine that:

(1) a violation occurred and impose an administrative penalty; or

(2) a violation did not occur.

(d) A proceeding under this section is subject to Chapter 2001, Government Code.

(e) The commission may authorize the hearings examiner to conduct the hearing and enter a final decision.

§ 1101.706. NOTICE OF ORDER.

The administrator shall give notice of the commission's order to the person. The notice must:

(1) include the findings of fact and conclusions of law, separately stated;

(2) state the amount of any penalty imposed;

(3) inform the person of the person's right to judicial review of the order; and

(4) include other information required by law.

§ 1101.707. OPTIONS FOLLOWING DECISION: PAY OR APPEAL.

(a) Not later than the 30th day after the date the commission's order becomes final, the person shall:

(1) pay the administrative penalty; or

(2) file a petition for judicial review with a district court in Travis County contesting the fact of the violation, the amount of the penalty, or both.

(b) Within the 30-day period, a person who acts under Subsection (a)(2) may stay enforcement of the penalty by:

(1) paying the penalty to the administrator for placement in an escrow account;

(2) giving the administrator a supersedeas bond in a form approved by the administrator that:

(A) is for the amount of the penalty; and

(B) is effective until judicial review of the order is final; or

(3) filing with the administrator an affidavit of the person stating that the person is financially unable to pay the penalty and is financially unable to give the supersedeas bond.

(c) A person who fails to take action as provided by this section waives the right to judicial review of the commission's order.

§ 1101.708. COLLECTION OF PENALTY.

If the person does not pay the administrative penalty and the enforcement of the penalty is not stayed, the administrator may refer the matter to the attorney general for collection of the penalty.

§ 1101.709. REMITTANCE OF PENALTY AND INTEREST.

(a) If after judicial review the administrative penalty is reduced or is not upheld by the court, the administrator shall:

(1) remit the appropriate amount, plus accrued interest, to the person if the person paid the penalty; or

(2) execute a release of the bond if the person gave a supersedeas bond.

(b) Interest accrues under Subsection (a)(1) at the rate charged on loans to depository institutions by the New York Federal Reserve Bank. The interest shall be paid for the period beginning on the date the penalty is paid and ending on the date the penalty is remitted.

P. SUBCHAPTER P. OTHER PENALTIES AND ENFORCEMENT PROVISIONS

If license suspension/revocation and administrative penalties are insufficient, this subchapter of the law allows TREC to assert other enforcement options against licensees and unlicensed persons.

§ 1101.751. INJUNCTIVE ACTION BROUGHT BY COMMISSION.

(a) In addition to any other action authorized by law, the commission may bring an action in its name to enjoin a violation of this chapter or a commission rule.

(b) To obtain an injunction under this section, the commission is not required to allege or prove that:

(1) an adequate remedy at law does not exist; or

(2) substantial or irreparable damage would result from the continued violation.

> This section refers to injunctive action brought in the name of TREC, as opposed to the next section which refers to injunctive action brought in the name of the state of Texas. Injunctive action refers to a court action for an injunction which is an order of a court seeking to stop a specifically named activity from continuing.

§ 1101.752. ADDITIONAL INJUNCTIVE AUTHORITY.

(a) In addition to any other action authorized by law, the commission, acting through the attorney general, may bring an action to abate a violation or enjoin a violation or potential violation of this chapter or a commission rule if the commission determines that a person has violated or is about to violate this chapter.

(b) The action shall be brought in the name of the state in the district court in the county in which:

(1) the violation occurred or is about to occur; or

(2) the defendant resides.

(c) An injunctive action may be brought to abate or temporarily or permanently enjoin an act or to enforce this chapter.

(d) The commission is not required to give a bond in an action under Subsection (a), and court costs may not be recovered from the commission.

(e) If the commission determines that a person has violated or is about to violate this chapter, the attorney general or the county attorney or district attorney in the county in which the violation has occurred or is about to occur or in the county of the defendant's residence may bring an action in the name of the state in the district court of the county to abate or temporarily or permanently enjoin the violation or to enforce this chapter. The plaintiff in an action under this subsection is not required to give a bond, and court costs may not be recovered from the plaintiff.

TREC, acting through the Texas Attorney General, may bring this injunctive action to not only stop present illegal activity, but also illegal activity which is *about* to occur.

§1101.753. CIVIL PENALTY FOR CERTAIN VIOLATIONS BY BROKER, SALESPERSON, OR CERTIFICATE HOLDER.

(a) In addition to injunctive relief under Sections 1101.751 and 1101.752, a person who receives a commission or other consideration as a result of acting as a broker or salesperson without holding a license or certificate of registration under this chapter is liable to the state for a civil penalty of not less than the amount of money received or more than three times the amount of money received.

(b) The commission may recover the civil penalty, court costs, and reasonable attorney's fees on behalf of the state.

(c) The commission is not required to give a bond in an action under this section, and court costs may not be recovered from the commission.

Under this section, persons who illegally receive a sales commission are liable to the state of Texas for a penalty of up to three times the amount wrongfully collected.

§ 1101.754. PRIVATE CAUSE OF ACTION FOR CERTAIN VIOLATIONS BY BROKER, SALESPERSON, OR CERTIFICATE HOLDER.

(a) A person who receives a commission or other consideration as a result of acting as a broker or salesperson without holding a license or certificate of registration under this chapter is liable to an aggrieved person for a penalty of not less than the amount of money received or more than three times the amount of money received.

(b) The aggrieved person may file suit to recover a penalty under this section.

Persons who illegally collect real estate commissions are also liable to the harmed consumer by means of a private lawsuit for up to three times the amount wrongfully collected.

§ 1101.755. APPEAL BOND EXEMPTION.

The commission is not required to give an appeal bond in an action to enforce this chapter.

§ 1101.756. GENERAL CRIMINAL PENALTY.

(a) A person commits an offense if the person willfully violates or fails to comply with this chapter or a commission order.

(b) An offense under this section is a Class A misdemeanor.

> This section makes it a criminal offense for either a licensee or an unlicensed person to disregard any provision of The Real Estate License Act or any TREC order. Under the Texas Penal Code a conviction of a Class A misdemeanor carries a range of punishment of up to a $4,000 fine and/or a jail term of up to 1 year. In Texas, criminal matters are usually prosecuted by the local district or county attorney.

§ 1101.757. CRIMINAL PENALTY FOR CERTAIN VIOLATIONS BY RESIDENTIAL RENTAL LOCATOR.

(a) A person commits an offense if the person engages in business as a residential rental locator in this state without a license issued under this chapter.

(b) An offense under this section is a Class A misdemeanor.

§ 1101.758. CRIMINAL PENALTY FOR CERTAIN VIOLATIONS BY BROKER, SALESPERSON, OR CERTIFICATE HOLDER.

(a) A person commits an offense if the person acts as a broker or salesperson without holding a license under this chapter or engages in an activity for which a certificate of registration is required under this chapter without holding a certificate.

(b) An offense under this section is a Class A misdemeanor.

> This section applies potential criminal liability against persons who engage in unlicensed broker activity.

Q. SUBCHAPTER Q. GENERAL PROVISIONS RELATING TO LIABILITY ISSUES

The final subchapter of the license act mainly deals with various aspects of liability or legal responsibility. It also sets out the legal elements for a broker filing a suit to recover an unpaid sales commission.

§ 1101.801. EFFECT OF DISCIPLINARY ACTION ON LIABILITY.

Disciplinary action taken against a person under Section 1101.652 does not relieve the person from civil or criminal liability.

> This section makes it clear that consequences for illegal activity will not necessarily stop with TREC disciplinary action. The person may still face additional civil and/or criminal liability.

§ 1101.802. LIABILITY RELATING TO HIV INFECTION OR AIDS.

Notwithstanding Section 1101.801, a person is not civilly or criminally liable because the person failed to inquire about, make a disclosure relating to, or release information relating to whether a previous or current occupant of real property had, may have had, has, or may have AIDS, an HIV-related illness, or HIV infection as defined by the Centers for Disease Control and Prevention of the United States Public Health Service.

§ 1101.803. GENERAL LIABILITY OF BROKER.

A licensed broker is liable to the commission, the public, and the broker's clients for any conduct engaged in under this chapter by the broker or by a salesperson associated with or acting for the broker.

> This section underscores a basic principle that a broker is legally responsible to TREC, the public in general, and especially his/her clients for the acts of a sponsored salesperson.

§ 1101.804. LIABILITY FOR PROVIDING CERTAIN INFORMATION.

A license holder or nonprofit real estate board or association that provides information about real property sales prices or the terms of a sale for the purpose of facilitating the listing, selling, leasing, financing, or appraisal of real property is not liable to another person for providing that information unless the disclosure of that information is specifically prohibited by statute.

> This section provides that if a licensee, for example, uses information for the purposes of selling or leasing property, the licensee will not be held legally liable, unless there is a law which expressly prohibits the disclosure of the information.

§ 1101.805. LIABILITY FOR MISREPRESENTATION OR CONCEALMENT.

(a) In this section, "party" has the meaning assigned by Section 1101.551.

(b) This section prevails over any other law, including common law.

(c) This section does not diminish a broker's responsibility for the acts or omissions of a salesperson associated with or acting for the broker.

(d) A party is not liable for a misrepresentation or a concealment of a material fact made by a license holder in a real estate transaction unless the party:

  (1) knew of the falsity of the misrepresentation or concealment; and

  (2) failed to disclose the party's knowledge of the falsity of the misrepresentation or concealment.

(e) A license holder is not liable for a misrepresentation or a concealment of a material fact made by a party to a real estate transaction unless the license holder:

  (1) knew of the falsity of the misrepresentation or concealment; and

  (2) ailed to disclose the license holder's knowledge of the falsity of the misrepresentation or concealment.

(f) A party or a license holder is not liable for a misrepresentation or a concealment of a material fact made by a subagent in a real estate transaction unless the party or license holder:

(1) knew of the falsity of the misrepresentation or concealment; and

(2) failed to disclose the party's or license holder's knowledge of the falsity of the misrepresentation or concealment.

This section provides that party to a transaction (for example, a buyer, seller, etc.) will not be legally liable to a licensee, for a misrepresentation or concealment of a material fact unless that party knew about the misrepresentation/concealment and failed to disclose it. The same thing applies if the licensee makes the misrepresentation or concealment instead of the party.

A "material fact," while not defined, is meant to be some critical fact about the property which would influence someone to buy or not to buy it.

§ 1101.806. LIABILITY FOR PAYMENT OF COMPENSATION OR COMMISSION.

(a) This section does not:

(1) apply to an agreement to share compensation among license holders; or

(2) limit a cause of action among brokers for interference with business relationships.

(b) A person may not maintain an action to collect compensation for an act as a broker or salesperson that is performed in this state unless the person alleges and proves that the person was:

(1) a license holder at the time the act was commenced; or

(2) an attorney licensed in any state.

(c) A person may not maintain an action in this state to recover a commission for the sale or purchase of real estate unless the promise or agreement on which the action is based, or a memorandum, is in writing and signed by the party against whom the action is brought or by a person authorized by that party to sign the document.

(d) A license holder who fails to advise a buyer as provided by Section 1101.555 may not receive payment of or recover any commission agreed to be paid on the sale.

This section applies when a licensed broker is attempting to sue a party in order to collect a sales commission. Essentially, a broker must prove at a minimum that:

1. he/she held a valid real estate license at the time of the transaction,
2. that he/she holds a writing promising to pay a sales commission, and
3. he/she gave the notice dealing with abstract of title/title insurance as required by §1101.555.

This section does not apply to an agreement or lawsuit among brokers concerning the payment of a shared commission.

XII. CHAPTER SUMMARY

The Real Estate License Act (TRELA) was enacted to protect Texas consumers and to establish uniform professional standards for real estate professionals. In 1949 the legislature created the **Texas Real Estate Commission (TREC)** which today regulates the activities of brokers, salespersons, residential rental locators, property inspectors, easement or right of way agents, residential service companies and entities which offer time share interests in Texas.

Under The Real Estate License Act, a broker is very broadly defined so as to include a person who, in exchange for a commission or the expectation of receiving a commission or other valuable consideration, may engage in a number of real estate related activities such as the **selling, leasing,** or the **exchange** of real estate. A **salesperson** is a person formally associated with a **broker** and by virtue of that association may perform the acts of a broker. A **residential rental locator** is a person who, for consideration, offers to locate units in an apartment complex for tenants.

The license act lists a group of individuals and transactional events for which no real estate license is needed. A person acting under a court order is exempt from the licensing provisions of the act as is a person employed by the owner in the business of selling of structure and land such as homebuilder. Transactions involving the sale of cemetery lots and hotel rooms are also exempt.

The Texas Real Estate Commission consists of nine members appointed by the governor. Six members must be brokers and three are public members who are appointed for six year staggered terms. The commission administers the license act and sets policy, but the daily operation of the commission is run by the administrator. Among the commission's many duties is the ability to adopt rules, maintain list of all licensees, establish standards of conduct, and investigate complaints against licensees.

The law also establishes a statutory relationship between the real estate commission and the **Real Estate Center** at Texas A&M University. The Real Estate Center is an education and research center funded mainly by fees collected by real estate licensees.

To be eligible to receive a real estate license in Texas, potential applicants must be at least 18 years of age, a citizen of the United States or a lawfully admitted alien, a resident of the state of Texas, satisfy the commission of the applicant's honesty, trustworthiness and integrity, satisfy the educational requirements, and demonstrate the applicant's competency by passing the licensing exam.

The real estate license examination is administered by a private testing service under contract with the real estate commission. The test is given by computer and the licensee must pass both parts of the examination. A licensee who misses one or both parts of the test may retake as many times a necessary. However, each application is only open for a six-month period.

For persons applying on and after January 1, 2006, the minimum requirement of certain designated core and related courses is 14 semester hours (210 classroom hours).

For those salespersons renewing for the first time on or after January 1, 2006, the law requires the salesperson to have completed 18 semester hours no later than the first annual renewal.

After a salesperson completes the the required 18 semester hour educational requirement, he/she becomes subject to the continuing education requirements. **Mandatory Continuing Education (or MCE)** is required for all salespersons who have completed SAE and for all brokers who did not become exempt under the provisions of a 1991 law. For each renewal term, which is now two years, the licensee must have 15 classroom hours of instruction of selected real estate issues including six hours in legal topics.

XIII. TERMINOLOGY

A. Administrative Penalty
B. Administrator
C. Broker
D. Broker-Lawyer Committee
E. Certificate Holder
F. Core Real Estate Courses
G. Hearing
H. Inactive License
I. Injunction
J. Intermediary
K. License Revocation

L. License Suspension
M. Mandatory Continuing Education (MCE)
N. On-Site Apartment Manager
O. Party
P. Real Estate Center
Q. Real Estate Mathematics
R. Recovery Trust Account
S. Residential Rental Locator
T. Salesperson
U. Subpoena

V. Subrogation
W. Substantive Dialog
X. Sunset Act
Y. Texas Real Estate Commission

1. ____ A person, who, in exchange for a commission or other valuable consideration, can engage in a wide variety of real estate activities such as the sale, rental or exchange of real estate.

2. ____ A real estate licensee associated with a broker. Also the entry level license in the real estate sales profession.

3. ____ A real estate licensee who works as an apartment locator for prospective tenants.

4. ____ A group of educational courses which are considered by law to be essential to real estate licensing.

5. ____ A state law that periodically reviews every state agency in order to determine its usefulness and whether the agency could continue.

6. ____ A special 13-member committee of the Texas Real Estate Commission charged with the responsibility of drafting and reviewing real estate contract forms for use by Texas licensees.

7. ____ The Texas agency established in 1949 to administer the provisions of The Real Estate License Act.

8. ____ The person in charge of the day-to-day operations of the Texas Real Estate Commission.

9. ____ A licensee-funded research and education center established at Texas A & M University.

10. ____ Education consisting of 15 hours each license term for those brokers who are not exempt from the requirements of continuing education and for all salespersons who have completed the annual educational requirements.

11. ____ An official status that allows salespersons and brokers to hold a real estate license but does not permit the licensee to perform duties associated with that license.

12. ____ A legal command to appear.

13. ____ One of the categories of persons who are exempt from the licensing provisions of The Real Estate License Act.

14. ____ One of the core courses established under The Real Estate License Act.

15. ____ A person who buys, sells or otherwise transfers easements and rights of way for compensation and who holds a certificate of registration with TREC.

16. ____ A real estate broker who seeks to represent both a buyer and seller within the same real estate transaction.

17. ____ As used in this chapter, a prospective buyer, seller, landlord or tenant in a real estate transaction.

18. ____ A meeting or written communication between a real estate licensee and a party to transaction that involves a substantive discussion relating to specific real property.

19. ____ A large fund established by state law and administered by TREC to compensate persons harmed by acts of a real estate licensee, a certificate holder, or their employee.

20. ___ Disciplinary activity by the real estate commission where the licensee is prohibited from using his/her license for a specified period of time.
21. ___ Disciplinary action taken by the Texas Real Estate Commission to revoke or take back a real estate license.
22. ___ A court order requiring someone to cease a particular act.
23. ___ A principle of law that entitles someone who has paid a claim on behalf of someone to seek reimbursement against the party for whose benefit the claim was paid.
24. ___ A monetary fee, penal in nature, that may be imposed by TREC against an unlicensed person who violates The Real Estate License Act, a TREC rule or TREC order.
25. ___ A public proceeding usually before a judge or hearings officer where formal allegations are presented, evidence is introduced, testimony heard, and arguments made.

XIV. MULTIPLE CHOICE

1. Which of the following is NOT an eligibility requirement for obtaining a Texas real estate license?
    a. A resident of the state of Texas
    b. A citizen of the US or lawfully admitted alien
    c. At least 21 years of age
    d. Honest and trustworthy

2. The longest period of time that TREC may issue a license is:
    a. 6 months under a probationary license.
    b. 18 months.
    c. 1 year.
    d. 2 years.

3. TREC may not investigate complaints submitted later than:
    a. 2 years from the date of the incident complaint.
    b. 4 years from the date of the incident complaint.
    c. the statute of limitations period for the complained of offense.
    d. there is no time limit for TREC investigations.

4. For which of the following is a real estate license not needed?
    a. A person acting under a court order who sells real property.
    b. A person who, for consideration, offers to find tenants in an apartment complex.
    c. A person who, for consideration, offers to procure sales prospects.
    d. A person, who, for consideration, lists property for sale.

5. The membership of TREC consists of:
   a. 3 brokers and 6 public members.
   b. 6 brokers and 3 public members.
   c. 6 members appointed by the governor, 6 members appointed by the State Bar of Texas and 1 public member.
   d. 6 brokers and 6 public members.

6. As of January 1, 2006, the total number of semester hours that a salesperson is required to complete before being eligible for mandatory continuing education is:
   a. 270 classroom hours.
   b. 10 semester hours.
   c. 18 semester hours.
   d. none of the above.

7. By law, TREC is barred from adopting rules regarding:
   a. the use of contract forms.
   b. the designation of additional core courses.
   c. advertising by brokers unless to prohibit misleading advertising.
   d. the administration of the license act.

8. By law, TREC will be abolished if not continued no later than:
   a. January 1, 2007.
   b. September 1, 2007.
   c. January 15, 2008.
   d. none of the above.

9. TREC has been given all of the following duties by the Texas legislature, except for:
   a. subpoena power.
   b. rulemaking power.
   c. power to set certain fees.
   d. power to require property owners to use TREC approved forms.

10. A salesperson cannot sell real estate in Texas until he/she:
    a. is associated with a broker.
    b. holds an active broker's license.
    c. holds an inactive salesperson's license.
    d. applies to take the salespersons examination.

ANSWERS: 1. c; 2. d; 3. b; 4. a; 5. b; 6. c; 7. c; 8. b; 9. d; 10. a

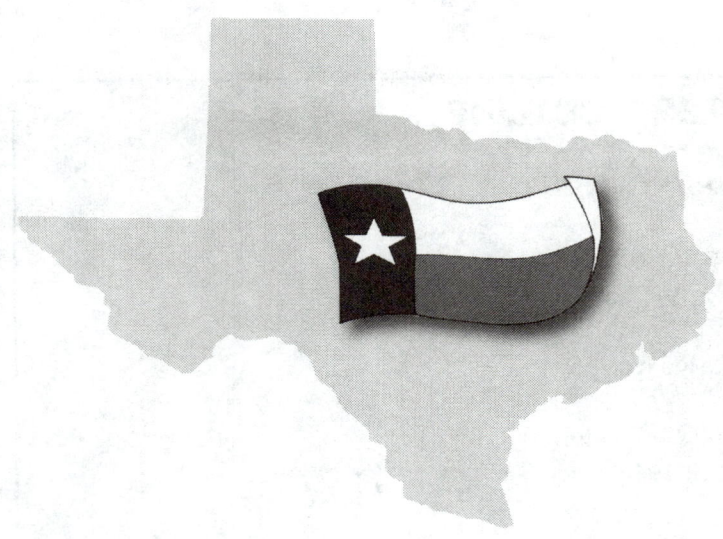

Chapter 7
Fair Housing Laws & Related Practices

I. Introduction to Fair Housing

A. WHAT IS FAIR HOUSING?

During the course of a day, a typical real estate agent will come into contact with a number of individuals looking to buy, sell, rent or lease real estate. Some of these individuals may have strong feelings about where they want to live and who their neighbors should be. Consider the following examples:

A landlord refuses to rent an apartment to an immigrant couple because he doesn't think they'll fit in with the rest of the residents.

An elderly seller is reluctant to accept an offer from a minority buyer for fear of what his long-time neighbors "will think."

A real estate broker hopes to attract a particular type of homebuyer by placing a newspaper ad stating that the home is located next to a Catholic Church.

Each of these situations involves an example of illegal housing discrimination.

CHAPTER 7 OUTLINE

> VI. CHAPTER SUMMARY (p. 287)
> VII. TERMINOLOGY (p. 289)
> VIII. MULTIPLE CHOICE (p. 291)

While the illegality of these practices might not seem obvious at first, it's clear that the housing choices of a potential purchaser or renter are **purposely being limited**. Thus, they are considered illegal under the fair housing laws.

We are all born as unique individuals. In fact, we are taught from early childhood to recognize racial, ethnic, and even religious differences. But to deny or to limit a person's housing choices based on those differences is discrimination. The fair housing laws make it

> Fair housing laws refer to various federal, state and local laws which have been enacted to prohibit discrimination in the housing market and related fields.

abundantly clear that housing discrimination is intolerable, illegal, and violations will hold severe consequences for real estate licensees.

B. WHY STUDY FAIR HOUSING LAWS?

Understanding the fair housing laws is more than just good business for brokers and salespersons, it's the law. As this chapter will later explain, violations of fair housing laws will have significant consequences for real estate licensees such as license suspension/revocation, as well as expose the real estate professional to civil liability. It is for this reason that Texas law requires all applicants for a salesperson's license to have at least three hours of classroom instruction on federal, state, and local laws relating to housing and housing credit discrimination.

II. Federal Fair Housing Laws

A. THE CIVIL RIGHTS ACT OF 1866

1. Origins of the Fair Housing Laws

The oldest of the federal fair housing laws is the Civil Rights Act of 1866.

Following the Civil War, Congress proposed a new amendment to the Constitution that would totally outlaw slavery in all states. In 1865, the Thirteenth Amendment to the Constitution was officially ratified by the states. Section 2 of this amendment gave Congress the right to pass any additional legislation necessary to prohibit any vestiges of slavery. It was against this backdrop that the Civil Rights Act of 1866 was enacted.

In its original form, the law read as follows:

Be it enacted by the Senate and House of Representatives of the United States of America in Congress assembled, that all persons born in the United States and not subject to any foreign power...shall have the same right, in every State and Territory in the United States, to make and enforce contracts, ... to inherit, purchase, lease, sell, hold, and convey real and personal property, and to full and equal benefit of all laws and proceedings for the security of person and property, as is enjoyed by white citizens....

2. Scope of Law

As one of the first civil rights laws passed by Congress, this was a "race-based" statute in the truest sense of the word. By this law, Congress intended that persons of all races should own and enjoy real property in the same manner as white citizens. But more than a hundred years following the passage of this significant civil rights legislation, it took a court decision to finally clarify the scope and extent of this statute.

3. Significant Decision: *Jones v. Mayer*

In the landmark case of *Jones v. Mayer*, the Supreme Court of the United States in 1968 upheld the Civil Rights Act of 1866 and in the process reaffirmed for all Americans that racial discrimination in housing is illegal without exception. The case details are presented in **Figure 7-1**.

In issuing its decision, **the Supreme Court declared that despite its age, the Civil Rights Act of 1866 remains valid law**. Moreover, this statute remains an important element of housing anti-discrimination legislation to this very day.

This case also demonstrates that to protect your legal rights under the Civil Rights Act of 1866, it is necessary to file a lawsuit in federal court.

B. TITLE VIII OF THE CIVIL RIGHTS ACT OF 1968 (THE FAIR HOUSING ACT)

1. Scope of Law

> It is the policy of the United States to provide, within constitutional limitations, for fair housing throughout the United States.
>
> **42 United States Code § 3601**

While the 1866 law was designed to combat discrimination solely on the basis of race, the Fair Housing Act (formally known as Title VIII of the Civil Rights Act of 1968) was intended to fight discrimination on a broader front. In fact, by enacting this legislation, Congress intended that this law serve as a statement of national policy.

Figure 7-1

Joseph Lee Jones v. Alfred H. Mayer Co.
(United States Supreme Court, 1968)

Facts: In 1965 Joseph Lee Jones and his wife Barbara Jo Jones were attempting to purchase a home from the Alfred H. Mayer Co. in the Paddock Woods community near St. Louis. According to the lawsuit filed, the homebuilder and the salesperson refused to consider Jones' application to purchase a house and to enter into a contract for the sale of a house and lot, because "Joseph Lee Jones is a Negro, and it is Defendants' general policy not to sell said houses and lots to Negroes". The lawsuit asked for $50 ordinary damages, $10,000 punitive damages, and injunctive relief.

As basis for the lawsuit, the Jones' relied on the provision of the Civil Rights Act of 1866 which reads in part:

All citizens of the United States shall have the same right, in every State and Territory, as is enjoyed by white citizens thereof to inherit, purchase, lease, sell, hold, and convey real and personal property.

The United States District Court dismissed the lawsuit and the court of appeals agreed, saying that the Civil Rights Act of 1866 really only applied to racial discrimination by the federal government. Both courts agreed that the case here involved only the rights of *private* individuals and, as a result, the 1866 law did not apply. Not to be deterred, the Jones family pursued the case to the United States Supreme Court.

Issue: Among the key issues considered by the Supreme Court was whether the Civil Rights Act of 1866 applied to acts of private racial discrimination in the purchase of real property.

Holding: The Supreme Court reversed the rulings of the district court and court of appeals. The high court concluded that the Civil Rights Act of 1866 does indeed apply to all racial discrimination, private as well as public, in the sale or rental of property, and that the statute, thus construed, is a valid exercise of the power of Congress to enforce the Thirteenth Amendment which outlawed slavery.

Discussion: In writing for the majority, Justice Stewart traced the history of the Civil Rights Act of 1866 back to the Thirteenth Amendment which barred slavery and gives Congress the right to pass appropriate enforcing legislation. The Civil Rights Act of 1866 was such a valid exercise of legislation and it attempted to improve the lives of black citizens in a post Civil War America in a way that the Thirteenth Amendment could not have done by itself.

In ruling that the Civil Rights Act of 1866 applies to all forms of racial discrimination he wrote:

At the very least, the freedom that Congress is empowered to secure under the Thirteenth Amendment includes the freedom to buy whatever a white man can buy, the right to live wherever a white man can live. If Congress cannot say that being a free man means at least this much, then the Thirteenth Amendment made a promise the Nation cannot keep.

So whatever happened to Mr. and Mrs. Jones? It's been reported that after the Supreme Court established the law in their favor, the case was sent back to the district court so that the original lawsuit could be tried. According to some accounts, the case was never tried because the homebuilder offered the Jones family an out of court cash settlement. Thus, we'll never know how *Jones v. Mayer* might have turned out upon a retrial.

Under the 1968 statute, housing discrimination is barred on the basis of:

Race – This means whether a person is white, African American, etc.

Color – This refers to whether a person is light skinned or dark skinned.

National Origin – This relates to a person's ancestry.

Religion – This deals with a person's religion or faith.

Sex (added to the law in 1974) – This refers to a person's gender, not sexual preference).

Handicap (added in 1988) – This is defined as a person's physical or mental impairment, or history thereof, which substantially limits one or more of a person's major life activities. While this term does include a person diagnosed with HIV/AIDS, it does not include illegal drug use.

Familial Status (added in 1988) – This refers to a pregnant female or a person attempting to obtain legal custody of a child under 18. This term also refers to one or more individuals under the age of 18 living with a parent or another person with the parent's permission.

EQUAL HOUSING OPPORTUNITY

Amendments to the original Fair Housing Act have increased the scope of coverage:

- 1972 added use of the fair housing poster

- 1974 added Sex as a protected category

- 1988 added Handicap and Familial Status as protected categories

2. Protection for Senior Citizens

While there is no protected category for housing discrimination based upon age, Congress has created an exception under the familial status category specifically for older Americans. Under the law, housing may be dedicated to older residents if:

1. The housing is intended for and solely occupied by persons 62 or older, OR
2. The housing is intended for persons 55 or older *and*
   a. At least 80 percent of the occupied units are occupied by at least one person who is 55 or older, and

b. The housing facility has written policies and guidelines showing an intent to follow this law.

3. Applicable Transactions

The Fair Housing Act, as amended, applies to the following types of real estate transactions:

1. Sales
2. Leases/rentals
3. Advertising of real estate
4. Financing of real estate
5. Appraisal

It will also affect the following types of real estate:

1. Single family residences
2. Multi-family residences such as apartments
3. Vacant land intended for housing

4. Fair Housing Poster

In 1972 the regulations of the Department of Housing and Urban Development (HUD), the agency that oversees fair housing issues, required that real estate licensees display a fair housing poster at all of their places of business that participate in residential transactions. This poster is shown in **Figure 7-2**.

The regulations require that the poster be displayed by:

1. multiple listing services (MLS),
2. real estate brokers' organizations (such as local, state, or national boards of REALTORS®), or
3. other services, organizations, or facilities relating to the business of selling or renting dwellings.

The location of displayed posters must be readily apparent to persons seeking to engage in residential real estate-related transactions or brokerage services.

A licensee's failure to display the fair housing poster will be considered as evidence of a discriminatory housing practice in any fair housing complaint.

5. Prohibited Practices

The Fair Housing Act makes it clear that the following acts will be considered to be **illegal discrimination** in housing.

Figure 7-2

U. S. Department of Housing and Urban Development

**EQUAL HOUSING
OPPORTUNITY**

We Do Business in Accordance With the Federal Fair Housing Law

(The Fair Housing Amendments Act of 1988)

It is illegal to Discriminate Against Any Person Because of Race, Color, Religion, Sex, Handicap, Familial Status, or National Origin

---

- ■ In the sale or rental of housing or residential lots

- ■ In advertising the sale or rental of housing

- ■ In the financing of housing

- ■ In the provision of real estate brokerage services

- ■ In the appraisal of housing

- ■ Blockbusting is also illegal

Anyone who feels he or she has been discriminated against may file a complaint of housing discrimination:

    1-800-669-9777 (Toll Free)
    1-800-927-9275 (TTY)

U.S. Department of Housing and Urban Development
Assistant Secretary for Fair Housing and Equal Opportunity
Washington, D.C. 20410

Previous editions are obsolete

form HUD-928.1 (2/2003)

1. To refuse to sell or rent after the making of a bona fide offer, or to refuse to negotiate for the sale or rental of, or otherwise make unavailable or deny, a dwelling to any person because of race, color, religion, sex, familial status, or national origin.

2. To discriminate against any person in the terms, conditions, or privileges of sale or rental of a dwelling, or in the provision of services or facilities in connection therewith, because of race, color, religion, sex, familial status, or national origin.

3. To make, print, or publish, or cause to be made, printed, or published any notice, statement, or advertisement, with respect to the sale or rental of a dwelling that indicates any preference, limitation, or discrimination based on race, color, religion, sex, handicap, familial status, or national origin, or an intention to make any such preference, limitation, or discrimination.

4. To represent to any person because of race, color, religion, sex, handicap, familial status, or national origin that any dwelling is not available for inspection, sale, or rental when such dwelling is in fact so available.

5. For profit, to induce or attempt to induce any person to sell or rent any dwelling by representations regarding the entry or prospective entry into the neighborhood of a person or persons of a particular race, color, religion, sex, handicap, familial status, or national origin (known as **blockbusting** or panic peddling).

6. To discriminate in the sale or rental, or to otherwise make unavailable or deny, a dwelling to any buyer or renter because of a handicap of that buyer or renter, a person residing in or intending to reside in that dwelling after it is so sold, rented, or made available, or any person associated with that buyer or renter.

7. To deny any person access to or membership or participation in any multiple-listing service, real estate brokers' organization or other service, organization, or facility relating to the business of selling or renting dwellings.

Other prohibited practices include **steering** and **redlining**. The law also makes it illegal to coerce, intimidate, threaten, or interfere with any person in the exercise or enjoyment of his/her fair housing rights.

The law directly applies not only to real estate brokers and salespersons, but also to "any person or other entity whose business includes engaging in residential real estate transactions" such as appraisers, lenders, mortgage brokers, surveyors, property inspectors, etc...

a. Forms of Discrimination

Under the Fair Housing Act, illegal discrimination can occur through several methods. First, it can occur through the **commission** of an illegal act or statement. Most notably, this can occur when a minority apartment seeker is falsely told,

Blockbusting – the illegal practice of inducing persons to sell or rent based on representations that members of a protected class will move into the neighborhood.

Steering – an illegal broker practice of channeling prospects of a protected class to or away from a particular neighborhood.

Redlining – an illegal lender practice of excluding loan applicants from particular housing areas perceived to be undesirable in the eyes of the lender.

for example, that the unit he/she was interested in was rented to someone else. Discrimination can also occur by **omission**, for example, by withholding financing information from a minority buyer.

Moreover, it is not legally necessary that a victim of housing discrimination actually prove that there was an intent to discriminate against him/her. The victim need only prove that discrimination did occur regardless of intent.

Consider the following example:

A landlord has just one vacant apartment available. It is located on the third floor of an apartment building. When a pregnant mother of two toddlers applies for the remaining apartment, the landlord refuses to rent because of concern for her safety and the safety of her two small children.

Under the Fair Housing Act, this landlord has committed housing discrimination by refusing to rent to a woman because she was pregnant. It doesn't matter that he did so out of an alleged concern for her safety. The fact remains that his actions constituted illegal discrimination against a member of a protected class. The choice to rent belongs to the prospect, not the landlord.

"Discrimination with a smile is …the landlord who says, 'This apartment is no longer available,' but the apartment is available, the apartment is vacant, it's just not available to you. That's discrimination with a smile. It's just as dangerous, just as destructive, just as divisive as any discrimination we've ever faced."

Former HUD Secretary Mario Cuomo

6. Legal Exemptions (Situations When the Act Does Not Apply)

The Fair Housing Act contains four notable exceptions. These include:

1. The sale or rental of a single-family residence owned by a private individual so long as:

   a. The individual does not own more than 3 such homes,
   b. Such sale occurs no more than once every 2 years,
   c. The services of a broker or salesperson are not used,
   d, No discriminatory advertising is used in the sale.

2. The rental of a room in an owner-occupied 1-4 family dwelling (the so called "Mrs. Murphy" exception).

3. The dwelling unit is owned, controlled, or operated by a religious organization so long as membership in the religious organization is not restricted on the basis of race, color, or national origin.

4. Lodging at a private club for the benefit of its members so long as the lodging is not operated commercially.

7. Advertising Under the Fair Housing Act

The Fair Housing Act also makes it illegal to publish any notice or advertisement which states a *preference* or *limitation* in housing regarding any of the protected categories.

Because the law does not provide any examples of what is permissible, the brokerage industry turned to the Department of Housing and Urban Development (HUD) for guidance. In 1995, the agency released a memorandum which provides some specific examples of permitted and illegal advertising terms. This memorandum is summarized in **Figure 7-3**.

As a side note, while the HUD memorandum is instructive as to which advertising terms will be allowed under the law, it is by no means comprehensive. When faced with evaluating the wording of an advertisement for purposes of complying with the Fair Housing Act, real estate licensees should exercise common sense and simply ask themselves: *Does this advertisement show any sort of preference or limitation regarding any of the protected classes (race, color, religion, etc.)?*

If an advertising term or phrase does not pass the common sense "smell test" then it shouldn't be used.

8. Examples of Illegal Statements Under the Fair Housing Act

Here are some examples of statements which, depending on the circumstances, might be considered to be illegal under the Fair Housing Act:

1. "I'm sorry; we don't rent to families with children."
2. "I don't think you'll like this house. It's not in a mixed race neighborhood. Let me show you another house."
3. "The apartment that was advertised has already been rented."
4. "I'm sorry the agent is too busy to talk to you right now. Why don't you call back later?"
5. "I think you'll like this house. It's located right next to the temple."

Figure 7-3

Fair Housing Guidelines for Real Estate Advertising		
	Unacceptable	**Acceptable**
Race, Color, National Origin	Use of words describing the housing, the current or potential residents, or the neighbors or neighborhood in racial or ethnic terms (i.e., white family home, no Irish) will create liability under this section.	However, advertisements which are facially neutral will not create liability. Thus, complaints over use of phrases such as **master bedroom**, **rare find**, or **desirable neighborhood** should not be filed.
Religion	Advertisements should not contain an explicit preference, limitation or discrimination on account of religion (i.e., no Jews, Christian home). Advertisements which use the legal name of an entity which contains a religious reference (for example, Roselawn Catholic Home), or those which contain a religious symbol, (such as a cross), standing alone, may indicate a religious preference.	However, if such an advertisement includes a disclaimer (such as the statement "This Home does not discriminate on the basis of race, color, religion, national origin, sex, handicap or familial status") it will not violate the Act. Advertisements containing descriptions of properties (apartment complex with chapel), or services (**kosher meals available**) do not on their face state a preference for persons likely to make use of those facilities, and are not violations of the Act. The use of secularized terms or symbols relating to religious holidays such as Santa Claus, Easter Bunny or St. Valentine's Day images, or phrases such as **"Merry Christmas"**, **"Happy Easter"**, or the like does not constitute a violation of the Act.
Sex	Advertisements for single family dwellings or separate units in a multi-family dwelling should contain no explicit preference, limitation discrimination based on sex.	Use of the term master bedroom does not constitute a violation of either the sex discrimination provisions or the race discrimination provisions. Terms such as **"mother-in-law suite"** and **"bachelor apartment"** are commonly used as physical descriptions of housing units and do not violate the Act.
Handicap	Real estate advertisements should not contain explicit exclusions, limitations, or other indications of discrimination based on handicap (i.e., no wheelchairs).	Advertisements containing descriptions of properties (**great view, fourth-floor walk-up, walk-in closets**), services or facilities (**jogging trails**), or neighborhoods (**walk to bus-stop**) do not violate the Act. Advertisements describing the conduct required of residents (**"non-smoking"**, **"sober"**) do not violate the Act. Advertisements containing descriptions of accessibility features are lawful (**wheelchair ramp**).
Familial Status	Advertisements may not state an explicit preference, limitation or discrimination based on familial status. Advertisements may not contain limitations on the number or ages of children, or state a preference for adults, couples or singles.	Advertisements describing the properties (**two bedroom, cozy, family room**), services and facilities (**no bicycles allowed**) or neighborhoods (**quiet streets**) are not facially discriminatory and do not violate the Act.

6. "You'll love this area. It's a great African-American neighborhood."

7. "If we accept an offer to purchase from a minority couple, what will the neighbors think?"

8. "I'm sure your rental references are fine, but we'll have to check those of your roommate."

Even statements intended as innocent remarks could be construed as violations of the fair housing laws.

9. Enforcement Under the Fair Housing Act

The Fair Housing Act may be enforced by any of four different methods:

1. HUD administrative complaint process,
2. Enforcement by the Attorney General,
3. Private litigation,
4. Criminal enforcement

a. Enforcement Through the HUD Administrative Process

The usual means of enforcing the Fair Housing Act is by means of an administrative complaint filed with HUD.

The Complaint. Under the law, a harmed person has one year to file a housing discrimination complaint with HUD. In the absence of a complainant, the law gives HUD the right to serve as the complaining party.

Conciliation Attempt. Early in the proceedings, HUD may urge that the parties enter into a conciliation agreement in an attempt to resolve the dispute. A conciliation agreement is a private settlement that all parties will accept. If the parties enter into a conciliation agreement

> In 2005, HUD received more than 2,200 complaints of housing discrimination. Nearly 40% of the cases processed that year were resolved through conciliation agreements.

the case is closed, otherwise the case moves into the investigative phase.

The Investigation. Once the complaint is filed, the agency has 100 days to conduct an investigation. If the investigation determines that there is no reasonable cause to believe that an act of housing discrimination has occurred, the complaint is dismissed. On the other hand, if the investigation reveals that reasonable cause exists that a discriminatory housing practice has occurred or is about to occur, then formal charges are brought.

The Administrative Hearing. If formal charges are brought, the respondent (the accused) then has 20 days to decide whether to have the case heard by an **administrative law judge** (ALJ) or a judge in a court of law. An ALJ is a hearing official who is empowered to administer oaths, take testimony, rule on questions of evidence and make factual and legal determinations. Upon a hearing before an ALJ, the respondent could be found innocent of housing discrimination and all charges dismissed. On the other hand, if the charges are justified, the respondent could face civil money damages in addition to a government fine of up to $11,000 for a first time offense.

The Court Hearing. If the election is made to proceed to a court of law, instead of an administrative hearing, the government will be represented by the office of the Attorney General who will then bring the case on behalf of the aggrieved party. The court, upon a finding that an act of housing discrimination has occurred, is authorized to impose a number of remedies such as actual damages, punitive damages, injunctive relief (an order to cease doing a particular act), as well as attorney's fees and court costs.

b. Enforcement Through the Attorney General

The office of the United States Attorney General is authorized to enforce the Fair Housing Act in the following situations:

1. Where the housing discrimination matter involves the legality of a state or local zoning or land use law; or
2. Whenever the Attorney General has reasonable cause to believe that any person or group of persons is engaged in a pattern or practice of resistance to the Fair Housing Act or the matter is of general public importance.

The Attorney General's involvement may come as either a new legal proceeding or through intervention of an existing, privately filed lawsuit.

c. Enforcement Through Private Litigation

Regardless of whether a victim of housing discrimination has already filed an administrative complaint with HUD, the complaining party also has the right to file a private lawsuit. This lawsuit must be filed within two years of the alleged wrongful act but may not be brought if the complaining party has entered into a conciliation agreement or if the administrative law judge has already begun to hear the case.

A person who wishes to file a private lawsuit will usually have to hire his/her own lawyer to prosecute the matter, but the law allows the court to appoint an attorney for the complaining party if he/she cannot afford a lawyer.

d. Criminal Enforcement

Finally, the Fair Housing Act may be criminally enforced. Under the law, threats, force, intimidation and attempts to injure someone who is exercising his/her fair housing rights can be criminally prosecuted. Convictions may result in a fine of not more than $1,000, or imprisonment of not more than one year, or both. If bodily injury results a person may be fined up to $10,000, or imprisoned not more than ten years, or both. Finally, if death results from an act of violence involving housing discrimination, a person can receive a life sentence upon conviction.

III. Texas Fair Housing Laws

A. TEXAS FAIR HOUSING ACT

1. Scope of Law

Under the federal Fair Housing Act, housing discrimination complaints may be referred to local or state agencies if the agency has been certified by HUD to follow laws that are **"substantially equivalent"** to the federal Fair Housing Act. As a result, in 1993 Texas passed its own version of the Fair Housing Act, thus becoming the first state to be certified by HUD as providing rights and remedies substantially equivalent to the federal Fair Housing Act.

The Texas Fair Housing Act, located in Title 15 of the Texas Property Code, is very similar to the federal Fair Housing Act. As a result, it prohibits housing discrimination in much the same way as its federal counterpart. The law also exempts certain real estate transactions, much like the federal law.

The agency assigned to enforce the provisions of the Texas Fair Housing Act is the Texas Workforce Commission Civil Rights Division.

2. Enforcement in General

a. Administrative Complaint Process

Enforcement is much like under the federal Fair Housing Act. Under the Texas Fair Housing Act allegations of housing discrimination are administratively enforced by means of a complaint that is to be filed within one year of the date the alleged discriminatory housing practice occurs or terminates, whichever is later. The agency has 100 days to complete its investigation of the complaint during which time it may recommend that the parties enter into a conciliation agreement as a means of resolving their dispute.

In 2005, the Texas Workforce Commission Civil Rights Division received nearly 400 housing discrimination complaints. Nearly half of the complaints filed involved the issue of changing terms and conditions of sale/rental based on one or more of the protected classes.

If a conciliation agreement cannot be reached by the parties, then at the conclusion of the investigative phase, the agency must either dismiss the complaint or bring charges of housing discrimination.

Any party then has 20 days from the date charges are filed to ask a court of law to hear the case or proceed for a hearing before an administrative law judge. The Texas Attorney General will represent the state of Texas and will prosecute the case if the case goes to a court.

b. Private Litigation

It is not necessary to file an administrative complaint in order to enforce the Texas Fair Housing Act. An aggrieved party may file a lawsuit in state district court provided he/she does so within 2 years of the alleged discriminatory housing practice.

B. LOCAL FAIR HOUSING ORDINANCES

In addition to state and federal laws, many communities have enacted their own fair housing laws.

SEC. 20A-2.   DECLARATION OF POLICY.

It is the policy of the city of Dallas, through fair, orderly, and lawful procedures, to promote the opportunity for each person to obtain housing without regard to race, color, sex, religion, handicap, familial status, or national origin. This policy is grounded upon a recognition of the right of every person to have access to adequate housing of the person's own choice, and the denial of this right because of race, color, sex, religion, handicap, familial status, or national origin is detrimental to the health, safety, and welfare of the inhabitants of the city and constitutes an unjust deprivation of rights, which is within the power and proper responsibility of government to prevent.

City of Dallas Ordinance

For example, the city of Dallas, whose ordinance is shown at the left, has enacted its own fair housing law under its local ordinance making powers. Likewise, many other Texas cities have enacted ordinances which make housing discrimination a criminal misdemeanor.

Although violating a city ordinance may appear relatively minor, the consequences of *any form of housing discrimination* case are extremely significant for real estate licensees.

As will be seen later in this chapter, those consequences could include license suspension and/or revocation.

C. THE USE OF TESTERS

Testing is a legal method by which many fair housing organizations check for compliance with anti-housing discrimination laws.

Testing for housing discrimination, sometimes referred to as **auditing**, involves individual testers posing as prospective home buyers or tenants who visit apartments, home sellers and real estate licensees.

> Testers routinely visit real estate licensees on an unannounced basis checking for compliance to the fair housing laws.

Ideally, testers are paired so that they are equally qualified to rent or purchase an apartment or home. They are usually similar in all respects except for one of the protected classes. For example, one apartment seeker may be a white male while another tester is a white female. In both cases, the testers will be financially well qualified to rent an apartment. Each tester will then visit the housing provider separately.

Following the visitation, the testers typically will report their findings in writing and meet with a testing coordinator who will validate the procedure used as well as evaluate the results. If housing discrimination is found, then the results are turned over to a fair housing agency for appropriate action.

D. SPECIAL CONSEQUENCES FOR LICENSEES

As discussed above, a violation of the federal and Texas fair housing laws could result in a judgment for money damages, an injunction, and/or an administrative fine. But a violation of the fair housing laws holds a special consequence for Texas real estate licensees.

Under The Real Estate License Act, real estate licensees could face suspension or revocation of a Texas real estate license by the Texas Real Estate Commission for acts of housing discrimination.

§ 1101.652. GROUNDS FOR SUSPENSION OR REVOCATION OF LICENSE.

(b) The commission may suspend or revoke a license issued under this chapter or take other disciplinary action authorized by this chapter if the license holder, while acting as a broker or salesperson...discriminates against an owner, potential buyer, landlord, or potential tenant on the basis of race, color, religion, sex, national origin, or ancestry, including directing a prospective buyer or tenant interested in equivalent properties to a different area based on the race, color, religion, sex, national origin, or ancestry of the potential owner or tenant....

Even the payment of a small municipal court fine for a violation of a city fair housing ordinance could be considered as an admission of guilt leading to license suspension/revocation by the real estate commission.

Finally, although not covered by any particular law, the violation of a fair housing law could also lead to a termination of the broker-salesperson relationship at the election of the broker. Under The Real Estate License Act, a broker is responsible for the acts of a sponsored salesperson. As a result, any violation of law by the salesperson reflects upon the sponsoring broker and could lead to an immediate termination of the broker-salesperson relationship.

IV. Ethics and Fair Housing Laws

In addition to federal, state, and local laws, real estate licensees are also prohibited from engaging in housing discrimination by professional ethics.

A. TEXAS CANONS OF PROFESSIONAL ETHICS

As was first discussed in the Agency chapter, the first five rules of the Texas Real Estate Commission are considered to be the Canons of Professional Ethics.

Each applicant for licensure pledges that he/she will abide by the provisions of The Real Estate License Act as well as the rules of the Texas Real Estate Commission.

The Canons of Professional Ethics require fidelity, integrity and competency by all licensees, however, it also includes a prohibition against discriminatory housing practices. Specifically, Rule 531.19 prohibits licensees from making any inquiry, response or any sort of disclosure which makes any preference or limitation on housing based upon race, color, religion, sex, national origin, ancestry, familial status, or handicap. The complete rule is shown in **Figure 7-4**.

The rules of the Texas Real Estate Commission apply to all licensees. As a result, the failure to follow these important rules could result in suspension or revocation of a Texas real estate license.

B. NATIONAL ASSOCIATION OF REALTORS® (NAR)

In addition to the rules of the Texas Real Estate Commission, many real estate licensees are also bound by the rules of the National Association of Realtors®. *REALTORS® are voluntary members of the National Association of Realtors®, the Texas Association of Realtors®, or any of the local affiliated real estate boards.*

Figure 7-4

A Side by Side Comparison of the Ethical Provisions Barring Housing Discrimination

NAR Article 10	TREC Rule 531.19 Discriminatory Practices
REALTORS® shall not deny equal professional services to any person for reasons of **race, color, religion, sex, handicap, familial status, or national origin.** REALTORS® shall not be parties to any plan or agreement to discriminate against a person or persons on the basis of **race, color, religion, sex, handicap, familial status, or national origin.** REALTORS®, in their real estate employment practices, shall not discriminate against any person or persons on the basis of **race, color, religion, sex, handicap, familial status, or national origin.**	No real estate licensee shall inquire about, respond to or facilitate inquiries about, or make a disclosure which indicates or is intended to indicate any preference, limitation, or discrimination based on the following: **race, color, religion, sex, national origin, ancestry, familial status, or handicap** of an owner, previous or current occupant, potential purchaser, lessor, or potential lessee of real property. For the purpose of this section, handicap includes a person who had, may have had, has, or may have AIDS, HIV-related illnesses, or HIV infection as defined by the Centers for Disease Control of the United States Public Health Service.
Source: National Association of Realtors® Code of Ethics	*Source: Canons of Professional Ethics, Texas Real Estate Commission*

Like the Texas rules, the NAR Code of Ethics also prohibits housing discrimination. Article 10, as shown in Figure 7-4, requires all Realtors® to avoid housing discrimination practices including any plan to discriminate or deny real estate services on account of race, color, religion, sex, handicap, familial status, or national origin.

V. Other Significant Federal Legislation

In addition to the fair housing laws, real estate licensees are affected by other federal statutes. Among those laws are:

1. The Americans with Disabilities Act,
2. The Community Reinvestment Act,
3. The Equal Credit Opportunity Act, and
4. The Home Mortgage Disclosure Act.

A. AMERICANS WITH DISABILITIES ACT (ADA)

The Americans with Disabilities Act of 1990 is intended to make everyday activities more accessible to people with disabilities.

> **Under the law, an individual with a disability is a person who:**
>
> 1. Has a physical or mental impairment that substantially limits one or more major life activities;
> 2. Has a record of such an impairment; or
> 3. Is regarded as having such an impairment.

In passing this law, Congress determined that some 43,000,000 Americans suffer from one or more physical or mental disabilities. Further, that many disabled persons face discrimination in areas such as employment, housing, public accommodations, education, transportation, communication, recreation, institutionalization, health services, voting, and access to public services.

As a result, the ADA addresses discrimination against disabled individuals in employment, state and local government services, transportation, and telecommunications.

With respect to real property improvements, Title III of the Act requires that all new construction and modifications must be accessible to individuals with disabilities. For existing facilities, barriers to services must be removed if readily achievable.

The ADA generally applies to places of **public accommodations** such as restaurants, hotels, grocery stores, retail stores and the like, as well as privately-owned transportation systems.

B. COMMUNITY REINVESTMENT ACT (CRA)

The Community Reinvestment Act is intended to encourage depository institutions, such as banks and savings and loans, to help meet the credit needs of the low and moderate-income communities they serve in a manner consistent with safe and sound banking practices.

As a result of this federal mandate, federal banking regulators will periodically assess an institution's lending record within the community. Federal regulators will also take those ratings into account the next time the institution makes an application to open a branch or engage in banking mergers and acquisitions.

An amendment to the law in 1990 requires that CRA ratings be made public.

Each bank or thrift must maintain a public file that contains the public section of its most recent CRA performance review, a list of its services and branches, written comments from the public, and certain other information.

Upon completion of a CRA examination, an overall CRA Rating is assigned to an institution using a four-tiered rating system. These ratings are:

1. Outstanding,
2. Satisfactory,
3. Needs to Improve, and
4. Substantial Noncompliance.

C. EQUAL CREDIT OPPORTUNITY ACT (ECOA)

The Equal Credit Opportunity Act is intended to insure that credit providers treat all creditworthy customers equally, fairly and without discrimination.

Under the Equal Credit Opportunity Act, creditors are prohibited from discrimination in credit transactions. These types of credit transactions generally include, but are not limited to business and consumer loans, auto loans, consumer leases, credit cards, and loans to purchase, improve, refinance or construct residential or commercial property.

The protected categories of individuals under the law include:

1. sex,
2. race,
3. color,
4. religion,
5. national origin,
6. marital status,
7. age, or
8. receipt of income from a public assistance program (such as social security income, food stamps, and unemployment compensation).

While the law does prohibit a creditor from considering any of the protected categories in taking, evaluating and acting upon an application for credit, it does not prohibit a creditor from obtaining information necessary to evaluate the creditworthiness of an applicant.

Figure 7-5 lists some of the major elements of this extensive law.

The ECOA can be enforced by means of an administrative proceeding or though a private lawsuit. Liability for punitive damages is restricted to nongovernmental

Figure 7-5

Legal Highlights of the ECOA

When You _Apply_ For Credit, A Creditor _May Not..._
- Discourage you from applying because of your sex, marital status, age, race, national origin, or because you receive public assistance income.
- Ask you to reveal your sex, race, national origin, or religion. Ask if you're widowed or divorced.
- Inquire about your plans for having or raising children.
- Ask if you **receive** alimony, child support, or separate maintenance payments, unless you're first told that you don't have to provide this information if you won't rely on these payments to get credit. However, a creditor may ask if you have to **pay** alimony, child support, or separate maintenance payments.

When _Deciding_ To Give You Credit, A Creditor _May Not..._
- Consider your sex, marital status, race, national origin, or religion.
- Consider whether you have a telephone listing in your name. A creditor may consider whether you have a phone.
- Consider the race of people in the neighborhood where you want to buy, refinance or improve a house with borrowed money.
- Consider your age, unless:
  ✔ you're too young to sign contracts
  ✔ you're 62 or older, and the creditor will favor you because of your age;

When _Evaluating_ Your Income, A Creditor _May Not..._
- Refuse to consider public assistance income the same way as other income.
- Discount income because of your sex or marital status.
- Discount or refuse to consider income because it comes from part-time employment or pension, annuity, or retirement benefits programs.
- Refuse to consider regular alimony, child support, or separate maintenance payments.

You Also Have The Right To...
- Have credit in your birth name (Mary Smith), your first and your spouse's last name (Mary Jones), or your first name and a combined last name (Mary Smith-Jones).
- Get credit without a cosigner, if you meet the creditor's standards.
- Know whether your application was accepted or rejected within **30 days** of filing a complete application.
- Know why your application was rejected. The creditor must give you a notice that tells you either the specific reasons for your rejection or your right to learn the reasons if you ask within 60 days.
- Find out why you were offered less favorable terms than you applied for—unless you accept the terms. Ask for details. Examples of less favorable terms include higher finance charges or less money than you requested.

**Source: The Federal Trade Commission**

entities and is limited to $10,000 in individual actions, and the lesser of $500,000 or one percent of the creditor's net worth in class actions.

D. HOME MORTGAGE DISCLOSURE ACT (HMDA)

The Home Mortgage Disclosure Act requires many financial institutions and certain mortgage lenders to collect and annually disclose data about mortgage applicants in order to prevent mortgage lending discrimination.

The law, first enacted in 1975, was originally designed to help determine whether banks were serving their low to moderate income neighborhoods such as under the Community Reinvestment Act. However, the law soon evolved as a means to determine whether an institution was engaged in discriminatory lending practices (redlining). More recently, the focus of the law has changed again. Under recent amendments, the law is proving useful as a tool to detect against **predatory lending**. *PREDATORY LENDING refers to unfair and abusive lending practices which take an unfair advantage against the borrower.*

At the very heart of the HMDA is its requirement that lenders collect and compile data on applications for new loans, home improvement loans, and home equity loans involving 1-4 unit and multi-family dwellings. Under the law, examples of the type of data to be collected on mortgage loans include:

1. Loan type
2. Property type
3. Loan purpose
4. Race, ethnicity and sex of all applicants
5. Applicant's income
6. Action taken on the loan

Once collected, the law requires the covered lenders to report the data to the government and to the public. Banking regulations additionally require bank branches and loan centers to display an HMDA notice which reads substantially as follows:

HOME MORTGAGE DISCLOSURE ACT NOTICE

The HMDA data about our residential mortgage lending are available for review. The data show geographic distribution of loans and applications; ethnicity, race, sex, and income of applicants and borrowers; and information about loan approvals and denials. Inquire at this office regarding the locations where HMDA data may be inspected. To receive a copy of these data send a written request to _____[address].

www.ffiec.gov/hmdaadwebreport/diswelcome.aspx

HOME

Home Mortgage Disclosure Act

FFIEC

ABOUT CONTENT
REPORT HELP
NOTES

PDF HELP
CONTACT US
PRIVACY POLICY

QUICK LINKS

Aggregate Report
Disclosure Report
National Aggregate

HMDA> Disclosure Report

INSTITUTION SEARCH BY BANK NAME
Or search by HOME OFFICE or LOAN LOCATION

Note: To retrieve a report for an institution, enter search criteria and click "Retrieve Institutions". An Institution Name or Respondent ID field must be entered before performing a search.

* Partial entries allowed.

Year: [   ]

*Institution Name: [   ]

*Respondent ID: [   ]

Agency: [All   ]

Sort by: [Institution Name   ] [Ascending   ]

[Retrieve Institutions]

The Federal Financial Institutions Examination Council ("FFIEC"), an intergovernmental body, is authorized to facilitate public access to information collected under federal law. Using the Council's web page, as shown above, the general public can access a number of on-line reports and disclosures collected under the HMDA as well as the Community Reinvestment Act. The information can be downloaded and often sorted by financial institution.

V. CHAPTER SUMMARY

The term "**fair housing**" refers to a group of federal, state, and local laws that prohibit discrimination in the housing and related fields. In Texas, all real estate applicants are required to have at least three hours of classroom instruction on federal, state, and local laws relating to housing and housing credit discrimination.

There are two key federal fair housing laws. The oldest law is the **Civil Rights Act of 1866** which was enacted immediately after the end of the Civil War. This law prohibits housing discrimination on the basis of race and was enacted mainly to support the **Thirteenth Amendment to the Constitution**, which legally ended slavery in the United States. About 100 years after this important federal legislation was enacted, the Supreme Court of the United States upheld the 1866 Civil Rights Act in the *Jones v. Mayer* decision. As a result, the 1866 Civil Rights Act remains valid law to this very day.

The second key law in the field is the **1968 Fair Housing Act**, which is also known as **Title VIII of the Civil Rights Act of 1968**. This was intended to prohibit discrimination on a much broader basis than the 1866 law. Under the original 1968 law, it is illegal to discriminate on the basis of **race, color, national origin, religion and sex (gender)**. Later amendments made it illegal to discriminate on the basis of **handicap** and **familial status**. Familial status mainly refers to housing for families, including children and pregnant women, as well as persons seeking custody of minor children. But under an exception to the law, housing can be devoted to **senior citizens** if certain conditions are met.

Other allowed exemptions to the Fair Housing Act involve: 1) sales by private owners, 2) the rental of a room in an owner-occupied 1-4 family dwelling, 3) dwelling units owned by religious organizations, and 4) lodging at private clubs. It is important to remember that despite these legal exemptions, racial discrimination is never allowed under any of the fair housing laws.

The Fair Housing Act, as amended, makes certain practices specifically illegal, such as refusing to rent/sell, or changing the terms of conditions of sale/rent on the basis of any of the protected categories. Practices such as **blockbusting** and **steering** are also barred by law.

A third fair housing law is the **Texas Fair Housing Act**. The Texas Fair Housing Act is "substantially equivalent" to the federal Fair Housing Act as it meets the federal requirements for state enforcement of fair housing laws. This means that a housing complaint can be enforced under Texas law rather than under federal law.

Under either law, enforcement is nearly identical. The complaining party may file an administrative complaint with the proper agency. Under the Fair Housing Act, the **Department of Housing and Urban Development (HUD)** will receive the complaint while under the Texas Fair Housing Act, the **Texas Workforce Commission Civil Rights Division** is the proper agency to hear the complaint. Each agency will have 100 days in which to investigate, after which time the agency must dismiss the case or file formal charges. A person formally charged with housing discrimination must then elect whether to have an **administrative law judge** hear the case or have the matter decided by the courts. However, it is not required that a person file an administrative complaint. A victim of housing discrimination may simply file a **private lawsuit** rather than pursue an administrative remedy.

A last category of fair housing laws includes **housing anti-discrimination ordinances** passed on the municipal level. Cities such as Dallas have passed these types of ordinances. While a violation of these laws will not incur a significant penalty, it can serve as a ground for **license suspension** or **revocation** by the Texas Real Estate Commission.

In addition to the fair housing laws, other federal laws play key roles in banning housing and credit discrimination. The **Americans with Disabilities Act** is not a fair housing law, but it does address a wide variety of discrimination faced by handicapped persons. This law mainly deals with employment, transportation, public accommodation and access to government services. A portion of the law requires that all new commercial construction be barrier free and be accessible to persons with disabilities.

The **Community Reinvestment Act (CRA)** affects mainly banks and thrifts and requires these institutions to prove that they are serving their low to moderate income communities. A bank's CRA rating will be publicly disclosed and may affect the bank's ability to seek regulatory approval for other banking activities.

The **Equal Credit Opportunity Act (ECOA)** prohibits discrimination in a person's ability of obtain credit. Much like the Fair Housing Act, the ECOA prevents discrimination on the basis of race, sex, color religion, national origin, but also adds age, marital status and receipt of income from public assistance programs to the protected category list.

Finally, the **Home Mortgage Disclosure Act (HMDA)** requires banks and certain mortgage lenders to collect and annually report to the government data involving race, ethnic group and sex of all mortgage applicants. The reason that this information is frequently asked of mortgage applicants is not so that a lender may use this data as a basis for discrimination, but rather so that patterns or trends of lending discrimination can be revealed.

VI. TERMINOLOGY

A. Administrative Law Judge
B. Americans With Disabilities Act
C. Blockbusting
D. Civil Rights Act of 1866
E. Community Reinvestment Act
F. Conciliation Agreement
G. Equal Credit Opportunity Act

H. Fair Housing Act of 1968
I. Familial Status
J. Handicap
K. Home Mortgage Disclosure Act
L. Jones v. Mayer
M. Omission
N. Predatory Lending
O. Redlining

P. Steering
Q. Testers
R. Texas Fair Housing Act
S. Texas Workforce Commission Civil Rights Division
T. U.S. Department of Housing and Urban Development

1. ___ A 1968 U. S. Supreme Court case resulting in the outlaw of all racial discrimination whether public or private in the sale and rental of housing.

2. ___ Under the Fair Housing Act, this is defined as a physical or mental impairment, or history thereof, which substantially limits one or more of a person's major life activities.

3. ___ A form of housing discrimination by withholding information, action or a benefit from a buyer or seller because he/she is a member of a protected class.

4. ___ Trained individuals who, on a regular basis, visit apartments and real estate offices in teams for the purpose of secretly evaluating compliance with the fair housing laws.

5. ___ A law in Texas prohibiting illegal discrimination in the sale or rental of housing based on the Federal Fair Housing Act of 1968, as amended.

6. ___ A law prohibiting private employers, as well as state and local governments, from discriminating against qualified individuals with disabilities in employment, housing, public accommodations, education, transportation and access to public services.

7. ___ An illegal practice in which real estate licensees encourage homeowners to put their homes on the market by exploiting fears of change in the racial composition of the neighborhood that will, they say, result in declining home values.

8. ___ A judge or hearing examiner specially appointed to hear administrative complaints.

9. ___ Unfair and abusive lending practices which take an unfair advantage against the borrower.

10. ___ A federal law passed shortly after the Civil War intended to enable all Americans to inherit, buy, lease, sell, hold and convey real estate regardless of race.

11. ___ A federal law that prohibits all discrimination in the sale, rental, and financing of dwellings, and in other housing-related transactions, based on race, color, national origin, religion, sex, familial status (including children under the age of 18 living with parents of legal custodians, pregnant women, and people securing custody of children under the ages of 18), and handicap (disability).

12. ___ This law was enacted to encourage depository institutions to help meet the credit needs of the communities in which they operate, including low- and moderate-income neighborhoods.

13. ___ An illegal broker practice of channeling prospective home buyers or renters to or away from a particular area or neighborhood based upon their membership in a protected class.

14. ___ A private agreement by which parties to a fair housing complaint agree to settle their dispute.

15. ___ The Texas agency responsible for enforcing fair housing complaints under the Texas Fair Housing Act.

16. ___ A law that prohibits discrimination in any aspect of a credit transaction on the basis of race, color, religion, national origin, sex, marital status, age, or receipt of income from a public assistance program.

17. ___ One of the protected classes under the 1968 Fair Housing Act, as amended, involving families and pregnant women.

18. ___ An illegal lending practice of denying credit in certain geographical locations based upon a perceived undesirability.
19. ___ A federal law that requires financial institutions to collect and report home mortgage data so as to determine whether the institution is engaged in discriminatory lending practices.
20. ___ The federal agency that enforces provisions of the Fair Housing Act of 1968.

VII. MULTIPLE CHOICE

1. Blockbusting is:
   a. the practice of directing purchasers into or away from a specific neighborhood in order to maintain or change the character of that neighborhood based on one of the protected classes under the Fair Housing Act of 1968.
   b. the practice of inducing homeowners to sell their homes by making representations regarding the entry of persons of a particular race, color, religion or handicap into the neighborhood.
   c. a law created under the Civil Rights Act of 1866.
   d. none of the above.

2. Steering is:
   a. the practice of directing purchasers into or away from a specific neighborhood in order to maintain or change the character of that neighborhood based on one of the protected classes under the Fair Housing Act.
   b. an illegal lender's practice of excluding minority loan applicants from particular housing areas.
   c. a broker's unlawful and abusive lending practice.
   d. none of the above.

3. A law to protect all persons in the United States, regardless of race, in their right to own and enjoy property is:
   a. The Equal Protection Act of 1968.
   b. The Texas Fair Housing Act.
   c. The Civil Rights Act of 1866.
   d. The Fair Housing Act of 1964.

4. The federal Fair Housing Act of 1968 as amended, provides protection in the sale, rental, and financing of housing to the following protected classes:
   a. race, color, national origin, religion, sex, familial status, and handicap status.
   b. race, national origin, religion, sex, familial status, and age.
   c. race, color, religion, sex, martial, and handicap status.
   d. none of the above.

5. Mr. and Mrs. Anderson called a local apartment complex to ask if there were any two bedroom apartments available for rent. The manager said that there were several and would love to take them on a preview of the apartments. That afternoon when they entered the office the manager, seeing they were African-American, said he was sorry but the units had been rented just a few minutes before they had arrived. When a white couple applied for the same apartments ten minutes later, they were available. This is the illegal practice of:

    a. blockbusting.
    b. discrimination based on religion.
    c. discrimination based on race.
    d. discrimination based on familial status.
    e. discrimination based on handicap status.

6. A real estate licensee may face license suspension/revocation for failing to show a house to each of the following, except:

    a. a Hispanic prospect.
    b. an African-American prospect.
    c. a white prospect who is financially unqualified to purchase a house.
    d. none of the above.

7. Which of the following statements might be considered illegal if used in a newspaper advertisement for the sale/rental of a home?

    a. "Merry Christmas"
    b. "Within walking distance to the Catholic Church"
    c. "Comfortable bachelor apartment"
    d. All of the above

8. A Texas real estate licensee may face license suspension/revocation if found guilty of violating the:

    a. 1866 Civil Rights Act.
    b. 1968 Fair Housing Act.
    c. Texas Fair Housing Act.
    d. any of the above.

9. Which of the following are exempt (allowed) practices under the Fair Housing Act?

    a. The sale of property owned by an individual who does not own more than 3 such single family homes at one time, and discriminatory advertising is not used
    b. The rental of dwelling units owned by a religious organization
    c. The rental of a unit in an owner-occupied 1-4 family dwelling
    d. All of the above

10. The Equal Credit Opportunity Act prohibits discrimination in any aspect of a credit transaction on the basis of:

    a. race, color, religion, national origin, sex, and marital status only.

    b. race, color, religion, national origin, sex, marital status, age, or receipt of income from a public assistance program.

    c. race, color, religion, national origin, and sex, but not marital status, age, or receipt of income from a public assistance program.

    d. none of the above.

ANSWERS: 1. b; 2. a; 3. c; 4. a; 5. c; 6. c; 7. b; 8. d; 9. d; 10. b

THE
CHISHOLM
CLUB
RESTAURANT

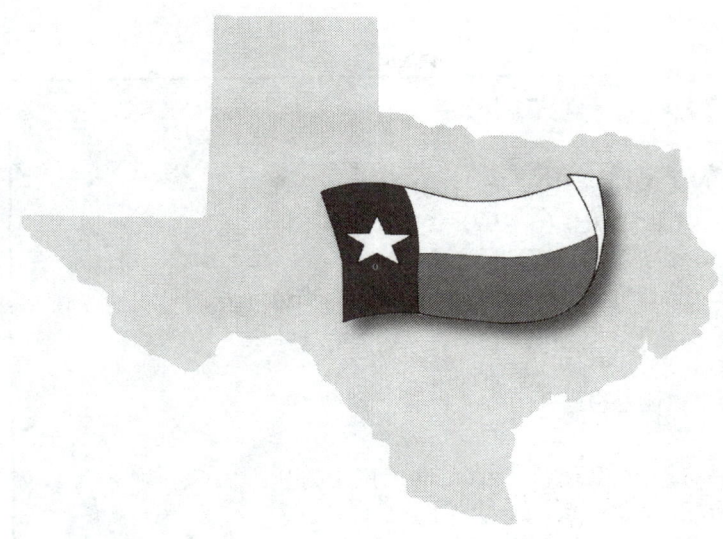

Chapter 8
Landlord and Tenant
(Lessor and Lessee)

I. Landlord and Tenant – An Overview

A landlord and tenant relationship is created when the owner gives the possession and use of his or her property to another for rent or other consideration. The *LANDLORD (LESSOR) is the owner of the property being rented or leased.* The landlord, or his or her agent, may lease only the land, the land and buildings, or only the buildings or parts of the buildings. The *TENANT (LESSEE) is the person or persons renting or leasing the property.*

www.taa.org
Texas Apartment Association

A *LEASE is a contract for a set time, typically one year or longer. A RENTAL AGREEMENT is different in that it is usually made on a monthly basis and is renewable at the end of each period (week-to-week, month-to-month, or any period-to-period up to one year).* Because a rental agreement is a type of lease, the principles are the same as those of the lease, except for the time periods involved.

Chapter 8

CHAPTER 8 OUTLINE

II. Leasehold Estates (No Ownership)

A. TYPES OF LEASEHOLD ESTATES (Tenancies)

A leasehold is a personal property right in real property.

As discussed before, with leasehold estates, there is no direct ownership of real estate. They are chattel real estates. A *CHATTEL REAL is a personal property estate, such as a lease.* We call this type of interest in a property a lease or leasehold estate. A *LEASEHOLD ESTATE is a possessory interest in land where the exclusive right to occupy and use the property is granted on a temporary basis.* There are no ownership rights in real property. The owner has *REVERSIONARY INTEREST, which means that he or she can regain possession at the end of the leasehold period.* **Figure 8-1** shows the four types of leasehold estates.

Figure 8-1

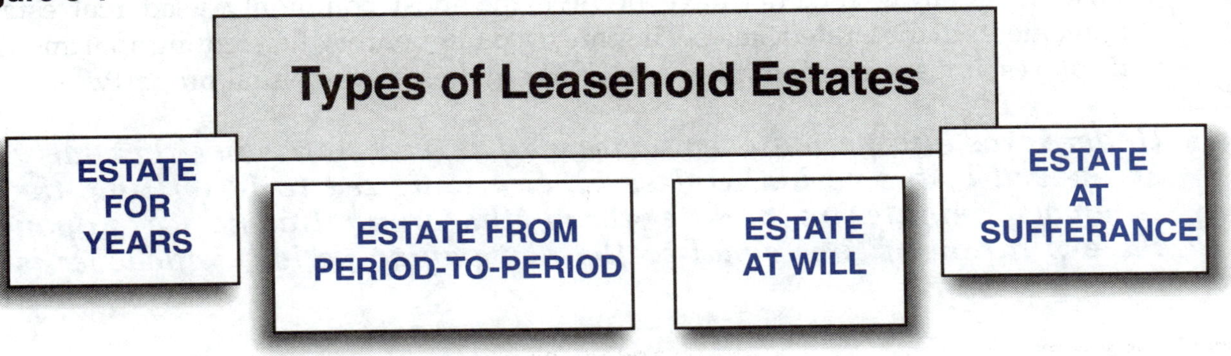

Types of Leasehold Estates: ESTATE FOR YEARS, ESTATE FROM PERIOD-TO-PERIOD, ESTATE AT WILL, ESTATE AT SUFFERANCE

1. Estate For Years (A Lease for a Predetermined Amount of Time)

An estate for years (lease) is usually for a year or more, but can be for any predetermined time, agreed to in advance. The term estate for years is gradually being replaced by the phrase, "tenancy for a fixed term" because it better describes the lease period.

A conveyance of an estate in real property, such as a lease, to someone for a certain length of time is called a **DEMISE**. An **ESTATE FOR YEARS** is an agreement, in advance, between a lessee and a lessor for use of a property for a fixed (predetermined) period of time.

A **LEASE** is a contractual agreement to possess and use a property for an agreed to (predetermined) period of time. If the lease period is longer than one year from the date of the signing, it should be in writing and signed by the parties. The **LESSOR** is the owner, sometimes referred to as the landlord, and the **LESSEE** is the tenant.

At the end of an estate for years lease, the tenant has no right to remain on the property. For the tenant to remain, a new residency agreement of any type must be entered into.

The lessor is the owner of a fee estate or a holder of a life estate who gives up possession to all or part of his or her estate and holds a reversionary interest.

2. Estate From Period-To-Period (Periodic Tenancy – Renewable Each Period)

An **ESTATE FROM PERIOD-TO-PERIOD** is periodic tenancy that continues from year-to-year, month-to-month, week-to-week, or from any other designated period-to-period. As stated above, this period-to-period tenancy, which is automatically renewable, is sometimes referred to as a rental (as distinguished from a lease), which is usually an estate for years. As a general rule, rental agreements do not expire; notice must be given by one of the parties as to their intent to terminate the agreement.

Written rental agreements have become the most commonly used real estate agreements in the United States. They are used frequently when renting apartments, duplexes, houses, condominiums, and other types of residential property.

Under Texas law, periodic tenancies may be terminated by either party at the end of the period. Unless otherwise agreed to in writing, the tenancy terminates on the date given in the termination notice or upon the expiration of time equal to the rent paying period, whichever is later.

A landlord holds a reversionary right to the property. A *REVERSIONARY RIGHT means the landlord grants the tenant the right to occupy (possess) the property, but retains the right to retake possession after the lease or rental term has expired.*

3. Estate At Will (Tenancy At Will)

An *ESTATE AT WILL can be terminated at the will of either the lessor or the lessee, and has no fixed duration period.* The tenant is present "at the will" of the landlord.

4. Estate At Sufferance

An *ESTATE AT SUFFERANCE occurs when a lessee, who has rightfully come into possession of the land, retains possession after the expiration of his/her term.* (In other words, the tenant does not leave after expiration of the lease.) An estate at sufferance does not require a notice of termination because the expiration of the lease is an automatic termination. The occupant has no right to be present, so the landlord will start eviction proceedings if the occupant attempts to stay. If the landlord accepts any payment of rent, the lease reverts to periodic tenancy.

A court action called a "forcible entry and detainer" is used to evict a tenant who stays past the expiration of his or her lease. This is NOT the same as dealing with a trespasser.

B. MINIMUM REQUIREMENTS OF A LEASE (or Rental Agreement)

As long as there is intent to rent property, the creation of a lease requires no particular language and can be either a written or an oral agreement. A lease or rental agreement must, at a minimum, include these four items:

1. **L**ength or duration of the lease.
2. **A**mount of rent.
3. **N**ames of parties.
4. **D**escription of property.

Think of
L.A.N.D. !

The parties to a lease must have the capacity to enter into a contract; they must freely enter into the contract and the use of the property must be for legal purposes.

Leases for one year or less do not need to be in writing, but under the Texas Statute of Frauds any lease lasting longer than one year must be in writing and signed by the party to be charged to be enforceable in a court of law. Under contract law, an unenforceable agreement does not mean it is invalid. Enforceability and validity are two distinct concepts. An oral two-year lease might be perfectly valid but unenforceable in a court of law. Regardless of how long the lease or rental agreement is for, it makes good business sense to "get it in writing."

A lease for more than one year must be in writing and signed by the party to be charged to be enforceable in a court of law.

C. TEXAS LANDLORD-TENANT LAWS

Texas has enacted rather extensive landlord and tenant statutes. While the statute covers both commercial and residential tenancies, the vast majority of the law deals with residential matters.

The law goes into great detail and is essential knowledge for those concerned about landlord-tenant laws. Its length does not permit a full discussion here, but certain statutes are summarized below.

The Texas Property Code
Title 8 Landlord and Tenant

Chapter 91, Provisions Generally Applicable to Landlords and Tenants
Chapter 92, Residential Tenancies
Chapter 93, Commercial Tenancies
Chapter 94, Manufactured Home Tenancies

All Texas statutes can be found at:

www.capitol.state.tx.us/statutes/index.htm

---

1. Provisions Applicable to Any Type of Lease

a. Notice to Terminate

Either a landlord or a tenant may terminate a periodic tenancy by giving notice of termination to the other party. A month-to-month tenancy will terminate on the day the notice is given or one month after the day the notice is given, whichever is later. The exceptions include a clause in a rental contract which calls for a different notice period or a breach of contract.

b. Termination of Lease Due to Public Indecency Conviction

Texas law gives the landlord the right to terminate a lease if the tenant has been finally convicted of a broad category of criminal public indecency offenses as defined in the Texas Penal Code.

c. Remedies Upon Landlord's Unlawful Breach

The law also provides that that a Texas landlord shall be liable to a tenant for damages due to the landlord's unlawful breach so long as the tenant is not in default of the agreement. Additionally, the law gives the tenant a lien on the landlord's non-exempt property in the tenant's possession, as well as on any rents that may be due to the landlord under the subject lease.

d. Subletting Prohibited Without the Landlord's Consent

Although the statute prohibits subleasing, Texas courts have expanded the interpretation of this provision so as to prohibit assignment without the landlord's express consent.

An *ASSIGNMENT of a lease is a transfer of the entire lease by the tenant to another, whereas a SUBLEASE is a transfer of less than the entire time or space of the lease.*

In a sublease, although there may be a new tenant in possession of the property, the original tenant is still obligated for the original lease, whereas in an assignment, all the rights and obligations are transferred (assigned) to a new tenant (the assignee).

e. The Landlord's Duty to Mitigate Damages

Texas law also provides that regardless of whatever the lease may say to the contrary, a Texas landlord always has the obligation to mitigate or lessen any damages he/she may suffer because of the tenant's wrongful abandonment of the property. The landlord must attempt to rent the vacated property and any rent collected from the new tenant will be used to offset the bad tenant's debt.

2. Statutory Provisions for Residential Leases

A number of provisions apply directly to residential leases under Texas law. Here's just a summary.

a. Interruption of Utilities and Tenant Lockout

If a residential tenant is paying for electrical, water or gas service directly to a provider, a Texas landlord may not interrupt the service except for repairs, construction or an emergency. However, if the tenant is paying for electrical service through the landlord, and the tenant is at least seven days late with the rent, the landlord may, under limited circumstances, interrupt service until the back rent is paid.

Under limited circumstances, a Texas residential landlord may also, upon advance written warning, legally lockout a delinquent tenant by changing the door locks. The written notice must state the date the landlord proposes to change the door locks, the amount of the back rent due to prevent the lockout and the name and address of the person to whom the rent may be paid during

normal business hours. However, the landlord will also be required to provide the tenant with new door keys regardless of whether he or she has actually paid the back rent.

b. Repairs

A Texas residential landlord has an affirmative legal duty to make repairs to the subject property if the tenant is current on the rent and the repair involves the habitability of the property. In Texas, *HABITABILITY means a condition that "materially affects the health and safety of an ordinary tenant."*

A Texas landlord is not required by law to repair conditions caused by the tenant, a member of the tenant's family, or a guest. Landlords are also not required to furnish security guards on the rental property.

c. Security Deposits

A *SECURITY DEPOSIT is defined as any advance of money, other than a rental application deposit or advance payment of rent that is intended to secure the tenant's performance under a lease.* The following are highlights of the legal provisions dealing with residential security deposits.

Amount of Deposit. Texas law does not establish a minimum or maximum amount of security deposit that the tenant must pay. Instead, the amount of the security deposit is left up to the parties to negotiate among themselves.

Landlord's Account. The landlord is not required to hold the tenant's deposit in a trust, escrow or even an interest bearing account. If any interest is earned, it belongs to the landlord. But the landlord will be responsible for the timely return of the deposit if a refund is due.

Accounting of Deposit. A landlord is obligated to provide an accounting of the security deposit within 30 days of when a tenant vacates a residence, provided that the tenant has supplied the landlord with his/her forwarding address. If there is a refund, it must be enclosed. However, if the landlord retains all or any part of the deposit, the landlord shall refund the balance, if any, with an itemized list of deductions. A Texas landlord is not required to provide an accounting, however, if the tenant owed back rent and there is no dispute by either party concerning the amount of rent owed.

Landlord's Failure to Comply. A landlord who wrongfully holds a security deposit can be sued by the tenant for $100, plus three times the amount of the deposit wrongfully withheld, along with the tenant's attorney's fees.

It is in the parties' best interests to have an inspection of the premises before the tenant moves in and when the tenant moves out, so as to resolve early any disputes concerning the security deposit.

See **Figure 8-2** for an example of the first page of the Texas Association of Realtors® **Residential Lease Inventory and Condition** form.

d. Security Devices

Most Texas rental homes and apartment units must come equipped, at no charge to the tenant, with the following security devices:

1. a window latch for each exterior window,
2. a doorknob lock or keyed deadbolt for each exterior door,
3. a sliding door pin lock on each exterior sliding glass door,
4. a sliding door handle latch or a sliding door security bar on each exterior sliding glass door, and
5. a keyless bolting device and a door viewer for each exterior door.

Within seven days of tenant moveout, Texas landlords are also required by law to **rekey door locks** as a safety precaution for the benefit of the new tenant. The rekeying must be at the landlord's sole cost and expense. But at any time during a tenant's occupancy, and as often as necessary, a tenant may also legally ask a landlord to rekey door locks. Requests by the tenant, however, will be at the tenant's cost and expense.

e. Smoke Detectors

Landlords are required to provide working smoke detectors in the vicinity of each separate bedroom of a rental home or apartment unit. The smoke detectors may be battery powered or wired directly into the electrical system of the unit and must be designed to detect the visible and invisible products of combustion and designed with an audible alarm. A landlord is required by law to inspect and repair smoke detectors but is not required to provide replacement batteries after a tenant has taken possession of the rental unit.

f. Rental Application Deposits

The Texas residential landlord-tenant laws also require that application deposits be fully refundable if the applicant is rejected. *APPLICATION DEPOSITS are defined as a sum of money given to the landlord in connection with a rental application.* The law requires that the applicant is deemed rejected unless accepted within seven days of the landlord's receipt of an application form or application deposit.

Figure 8-2

TEXAS ASSOCIATION OF REALTORS®
RESIDENTIAL LEASE INVENTORY AND CONDITION FORM
USE OF THIS FORM BY PERSONS WHO ARE NOT MEMBERS OF THE TEXAS ASSOCIATION OF REALTORS® IS NOT AUTHORIZED.
©Texas Association of REALTORS®, Inc. 2005

INVENTORY AND CONDITION FORM CONCERNING THE PROPERTY AT _____

Complete the move-in section of this form and return it to your Landlord within the time required by your lease. <u>All items are presumed to be in good condition unless noted otherwise.</u> Test all locks, window latches, smoke detectors, and equipment. This form is not a repair request. Submit all requests for repairs separately in accordance with your lease. The Landlord may also use this form upon move-out. Keep a copy for your records. *Note any defects in the items listed below.*

A. <u>Exterior Items</u>   Move-In Comments   Landlord's Move-Out Comments
   Mailbox
   Fences & Gates
   Pool/Spa & Equip.
   Lawn, Trees & Shrubs
   Undgrd. Lawn Sprinkler
   Exterior Faucets
   Roof & Gutters
   Siding & Paint
   Driveway
   Front Door
     Door Knob & Lock
     Light/Bulb
     Door Bell
   Back Door
     Door Knob & Lock
     Light/Bulb
   Patio or Deck
   Patio Door
     Door Knob & Lock
     Light/Bulb
   Other
   Water Shut-Off Valve Located? ❑ yes ❑ no   Electrical Breakers Located? ❑ yes ❑ no

B. <u>Garage</u>   Move-In Comments   Landlord's Move-Out Comments
   Ceilings & Walls
   Floor
   Auto Door Opener
     Safety Reversal
     Remotes
   Garage Doors
   Exterior Doors & Stops
   Storage Room
   Other

C. <u>Entry</u>   Move-In Comments   Landlord's Move-Out Comments
   Ceiling & Walls
   Paint & Wallpaper
   Doors & Door Stops

(TAR-2006) 10-5-05   Tenants: ____, ____, ____, ____ & Landlord or Landlord's Representative: ____, ____   Page 1 of 6

304

See **Figure 8-3** for a sample **Residential Lease Application** from the Texas Association of Realtors®.

3. Provisions for Commercial Leases

Due to the complex nature of commercial leases, it is standard practice for both landlord and tenant to have legal representation during the negotiation phase of the lease.

The parties to a commercial lease have certain statutory rights and remedies, many of which will overrule the lease or rental agreement. Here's a sampling.

a. Commercial Tenant's Lockout

A landlord of commercial property has the right, under limited circumstances, to lockout a tenant who is delinquent with all or part of the rent. But, unlike a residential landlord, the commercial landlord is required to readmit a tenant only during regular business hours and only if the tenant pays the delinquent rent.

b. Security Deposit

For a commercial tenant, a security deposit holds the same meaning as for a residential tenant. The commercial landlord will be required to provide an accounting for all deductions, wear and tear excluded, within 60 days of the tenant's surrender of the property. However, the landlord will have no duty to return a security deposit until such time as the landlord receives the tenant's forwarding address.

c. Miscellaneous Lease Charges

Finally, Texas law provides that commercial landlords may not assess a charge to a tenant, other than for rent or for security deposit, unless the charge or the method by which it is calculated is stated in the lease. This provision, however, does not bar any charge that is permitted as a matter of law under another statute or under the common law.

D. LEASE AGREEMENTS FOR TEXAS LICENSEES

The lease form to be used in residential or commercial lease transactions can come from practically any source so long as it is acceptable to the parties and fulfills the requirements of a contract under Texas law. The parties themselves always have the right to develop their own lease forms, or they may ask their lawyers to prepare their lease agreements. Under no circumstances should brokers or salespersons draw up or draft leases unless they are also licensed to practice law in Texas.

Figure 8-3

Received on _____ (date) at _____ (time)

TEXAS ASSOCIATION OF REALTORS®
RESIDENTIAL LEASE APPLICATION
USE OF THIS FORM BY PERSONS WHO ARE NOT MEMBERS OF THE TEXAS ASSOCIATION OF REALTORS® IS NOT AUTHORIZED.
©Texas Association of REALTORS®, Inc. 2005
Each occupant and co-applicant 18 years or older must submit a separate application.

Property Address: _____

      Anticipated: Move-in Date: _____ Monthly Rent: $_____ Security Deposit: $_____

Applicant was referred to Landlord by:

    ❑ Real estate agent _____ *(name)* _____*(phone)*

    ❑ Newspaper ❑ Sign ❑ Internet ❑ Other _____

Applicant's name (first, middle, last) _____

      Is there a co-applicant? ❑ yes ❑ no   *If yes, co-applicant must submit a separate application.*

Applicant's former last name (maiden or married) _____

E-mail _____ Home Phone _____

Work Phone _____ Mobile/Pager _____

Soc. Sec. No. _____ Driver License No. _____ in _____ *(state)*

Date of Birth_____ Height _____ Weight _____ Eye Color _____

Hair Color _____ Marital Status _____ Citizenship _____ *(country)*

Emergency Contact: Name: _____

           Address: _____

           Phone: _____ E-mail: _____

Name all other persons who will occupy the property:

Name:_____ Relationship:_____ Age:_____

Name:_____ Relationship:_____ Age:_____

Name:_____ Relationship:_____ Age:_____

Name:_____ Relationship:_____ Age:_____

Applicant's Current Address: _____ Apt. No._____

                    _____ *(city, state, zip)*

    Landlord's Name: _____

    Phone:*Day:*_____ *Nt:*_____ *Mb:*_____ *Fax:*_____

    Date Moved-In_____ Move-Out Date _____ R____

    Reason for move: _____

Applicant's Previous Address: _____ Apt. No._____

                    _____ *(city, state, zip)*

    Previous Landlord's Name: _____

    Phone:*Day:*_____ *Nt:*_____ *Mb:*_____ *Fax:*_____

    Date Moved-In_____ Date Moved-Out _____ Rent $_____

    Reason for move: _____

Applicant's Current Employer: _____

    Address: _____ *(street, city, state, zip)*

    Supervisor's Name: _____ Phone:_____ Fax_____

    Start Date: _____ Gross Monthly Income: $_____ Position: _____

Applicant's Previous Employer: _____

    Address: _____ *(street, city, state, zip)*

    Supervisor's Name: _____ Phone:_____ Fax:_____

    Employed from _____ to _____ Gross Monthly Income: $_____ Position: _____

(TAR-2003) 10-5-05   Page 1 of 3

Residential Lease Application concerning_____

Describe other income Applicant wants considered: _____

_____

List all vehicles to be parked on the Property:

Type	Year	Make	Model	License/State	Mo.Pymnt.

List all pets to be kept on the Property (dogs, cats, birds, reptiles, fish, and other pets):

Type & Breed	Name	Color	Weight	Age	Gender	Neutered?	Declawed?	Rabies Shots Current?
						❏ yes ❏ no	❏ yes ❏ no	❏ yes ❏ no
						❏ yes ❏ no	❏ yes ❏ no	❏ yes ❏ no

	Yes	No	Explanation
Will any waterbeds or water-filled furniture be on the Property?	❏	❏	_____
Does anyone who will occupy the Property smoke?	❏	❏	_____
Will Applicant maintain renter's insurance?	❏	❏	_____
Is Applicant or Applicant's spouse, even if separated, in military?	❏	❏	_____
If yes, is the military person serving under orders limiting the military person's stay to one year or less?	❏	❏	_____
Has Applicant ever:			
been evicted?	❏	❏	_____
been asked to move out by landlord?	❏	❏	_____
breached a lease or rental agreement?	❏	❏	_____
filed for bankruptcy?	❏	❏	_____
lost property in a foreclosure?	❏	❏	_____
had any credit problems?	❏	❏	_____
been convicted of a crime?	❏	❏	_____
Is any occupant a registered sex offender?		❏	_____
Are there any criminal matters pending against any occupant?	❏	❏	_____
Is there additional information Applicant wants considered?	❏		_____

Authorization & Representation: Applicant authorizes Landlord and Landlord's agent, at any time before, during, or after any tenancy, to: (1) obtain a copy of Applicant's credit report; (2) obtain a criminal background check related to Applicant and any occupant; and (3) verify any rental or employment history or verify any other information related to this application with persons knowledgeable of such information. Applicant represents that the statements in this application are true and complete. Applicant understands that providing false or inaccurate information is grounds for rejection and a breach of any lease.

Notice: Unless agreed otherwise in writing, the Property remains on the market until a lease is signed and Landlord may continue to show the Property to other prospective tenants and accept another offer. Landlord's agent or property manager maintains a privacy policy that is available upon request.

Fees: Applicant submits a non-refundable fee of $_____ for processing and reviewing this application and *(check only one box if applicable)*:

❏ (1) $_____ to be applied to the security deposit upon execution of a lease or returned to Applicant if a lease is not executed.

❏ (2) an Application Deposit of $_____ in accordance with the attached Agreement for Application Deposit and Hold on Property (TAR No. 2009 or similar agreement).

_____   _____
Applicant's Signature   Date

For Landlord's Use: On _____, _____ (name/initials) notified ❏ Applicant ❏ _____
by ❏ phone ❏ mail ❏ e-mail ❏ fax ❏ in person that Applicant was ❏ approved ❏ not approved.

(TAR-2003) 10-5-05   Page 2 of 3

TEXAS ASSOCIATION OF REALTORS®
AUTHORIZATION TO RELEASE INFORMATION
RELATED TO A RESIDENTIAL LEASE APPLICANT
USE OF THIS FORM BY PERSONS WHO ARE NOT MEMBERS OF THE TEXAS ASSOCIATION OF REALTORS® IS NOT AUTHORIZED.
©Texas Association of REALTORS®, Inc. 2005

I, _____ (Applicant), have submitted an application

to lease a property located at _____

_____ (address, city, state, zip).

The landlord, broker, or landlord's representative is:

_____ (name)

_____ (address)

_____ (city, state, zip)

_____ (phone) _____ (fax)

_____ (e-mail)

I give my permission:

(1) to my current and former employers to release any information about my employment history and income history to the above-named person;

(2) to my current and former landlords to release any information about my rental history to the above-named person;

(3) to my current and former mortgage lenders on property that I own or have owned to release any information about my mortgage payment history to the above-named person;

(4) to my bank, savings and loan, or credit union to provide a verification of funds that I have on deposit to the above-named person; and

(5) to the above-named person to obtain a copy of my consumer report (credit report) from any consumer reporting agency and to obtain background information about me.

_____   _____
Applicant's Signature   Date

Note: Any broker gathering information about an applicant acts under specific instructions to verify some or all of the information described in this authorization. The broker maintains a privacy policy which is available upon request.

(TAR-2003) 10-5-05   Page 3 of 3

The Texas Association of Realtors® has developed a **Residential Lease** and a **Commercial Lease** form for use by its members. A sample first page of each lease form is shown in **Figure 8-4**.

III. Termination of a Lease (or Rental Agreement)

A lease or rental agreement can be terminated for a variety of reasons. **Figure 8-5** lists the seven most common reasons for termination. Generally speaking, terminations can be classified into three broad categories: 1) because the law (either statutory or common law) requires it; 2) because of the wrongful acts of the parties; or 3) simply because the agreement has been completed.

A. TERMINATION: COMPLETED TERM OR NON-RENEWAL (Most Common Reason)

A lease or rental agreement may come to an end by "natural" means, namely, when the lease term is completed or the parties no longer wish to renew the agreement. For example, assume that the parties enter into a lease with a primary term of one year (an estate for years). At the end of the primary term, there is no action necessary to terminate the agreement. By the same token, if the parties are in a period-to-period tenancy, the lease will require notice of intent to terminate so as to avoid being automatically renewed.

B. TERMINATION: LACK OF QUIET POSSESSION

A tenant is entitled to the quiet possession and enjoyment of the premises without interference. The lease or rental agreement is made with the assumption that the tenant will have use of the premises and enjoy a peaceable stay. The landlord has the responsibility to to deliver the premises free from any legal disturbances. Failure to do so can give a tenant grounds for terminating a lease.

C. TERMINATION: STATUTORY TERMINATION

The Texas landlord-tenant laws contain a number of situations where failure to follow the law in some significant manner could result in the termination of the lease as a matter of law.

For example, as discussed previously, the law permits a landlord to terminate a lease agreement if:

1. the tenant is under a non-appealable conviction for a public indecency criminal offense; or
2. the landlord is completely closing the rental property.

Figure 8-4

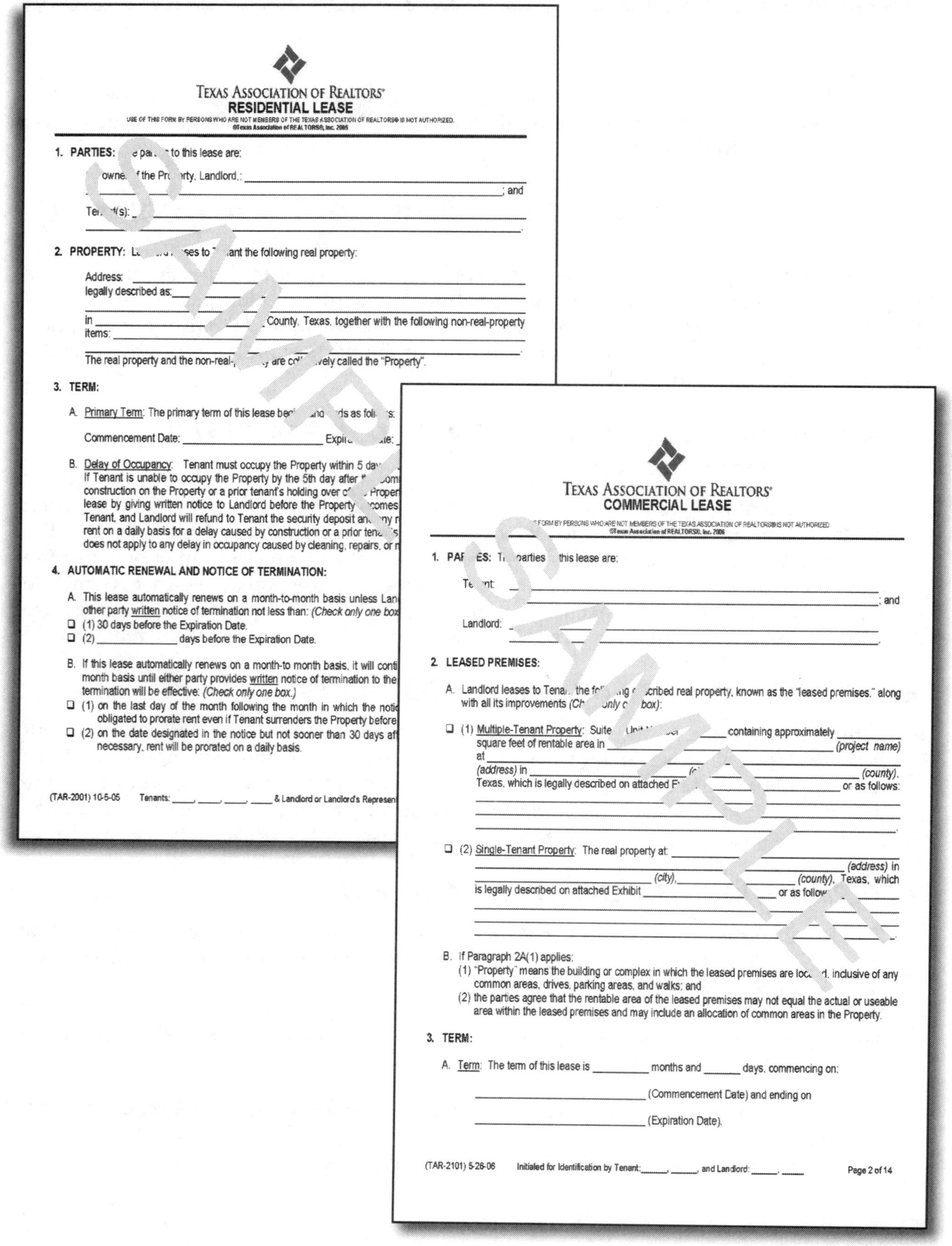

TEXAS ASSOCIATION OF REALTORS®
RESIDENTIAL LEASE
USE OF THIS FORM BY PERSONS WHO ARE NOT MEMBERS OF THE TEXAS ASSOCIATION OF REALTORS® IS NOT AUTHORIZED.
©Texas Association of REALTORS®, Inc. 2005

1. **PARTIES:** The parties to this lease are:

   owner of the Property, Landlord,: _____
   _____; and

   Tenant(s): _____
   _____.

2. **PROPERTY:** Landlord leases to Tenant the following real property:

   Address: _____
   legally described as: _____
   _____
   in _____ County, Texas, together with the following non-real-property
   items: _____
   _____.

   The real property and the non-real-property are collectively called the "Property".

3. **TERM:**

   A. Primary Term: The primary term of this lease begins and ends as follows:

      Commencement Date: _____ Expiration Date: _____

   B. Delay of Occupancy: Tenant must occupy the Property within 5 days...
      If Tenant is unable to occupy the Property by the 5th day after the Comm...
      construction on the Property or a prior tenant's holding over of the Proper...
      lease by giving written notice to Landlord before the Property becomes...
      Tenant, and Landlord will refund to Tenant the security deposit and any r...
      rent on a daily basis for a delay caused by construction or a prior tenant's...
      does not apply to any delay in occupancy caused by cleaning, repairs, or r...

4. **AUTOMATIC RENEWAL AND NOTICE OF TERMINATION:**

   A. This lease automatically renews on a month-to-month basis unless Lan...
      other party written notice of termination not less than: (Check only one box...
      ☐ (1) 30 days before the Expiration Date.
      ☐ (2) _____ days before the Expiration Date.

   B. If this lease automatically renews on a month-to month basis, it will conti...
      month basis until either party provides written notice of termination to the...
      termination will be effective: (Check only one box.)
      ☐ (1) on the last day of the month following the month in which the notic...
      obligated to prorate rent even if Tenant surrenders the Property before...
      ☐ (2) on the date designated in the notice but not sooner than 30 days aft...
      necessary, rent will be prorated on a daily basis.

(TAR-2001) 10-5-05   Tenants: ____, ____, ____, ____ & Landlord or Landlord's Represen...

TEXAS ASSOCIATION OF REALTORS®
COMMERCIAL LEASE
USE OF THIS FORM BY PERSONS WHO ARE NOT MEMBERS OF THE TEXAS ASSOCIATION OF REALTORS® IS NOT AUTHORIZED
©Texas Association of REALTORS®, Inc. 2006

1. **PARTIES:** The parties to this lease are:

   Tenant: _____
   _____; and

   Landlord: _____
   _____.

2. **LEASED PREMISES:**

   A. Landlord leases to Tenant the following described real property, known as the "leased premises," along
      with all its improvements (Check only one box):

      ☐ (1) Multiple-Tenant Property: Suite/Unit Number _____ containing approximately _____
         square feet of rentable area in _____ (project name)
         at _____
         (address) in _____ (city) _____ (county),
         Texas, which is legally described on attached Exhibit _____ or as follows:
         _____
         _____
         _____

      ☐ (2) Single-Tenant Property: The real property at: _____
         _____ (address) in
         _____ (city), _____ (county), Texas, which
         is legally described on attached Exhibit _____ or as follows:
         _____
         _____

   B. If Paragraph 2A(1) applies:
      (1) "Property" means the building or complex in which the leased premises are located, inclusive of any
          common areas, drives, parking areas, and walks; and
      (2) the parties agree that the rentable area of the leased premises may not equal the actual or useable
          area within the leased premises and may include an allocation of common areas in the Property.

3. **TERM:**

   A. Term: The term of this lease is _____ months and _____ days, commencing on:

      _____ (Commencement Date) and ending on

      _____ (Expiration Date).

(TAR-2101) 5-26-06   Initialed for Identification by Tenant: _____, _____, and Landlord: _____, _____   Page 2 of 14

Figure 8-5

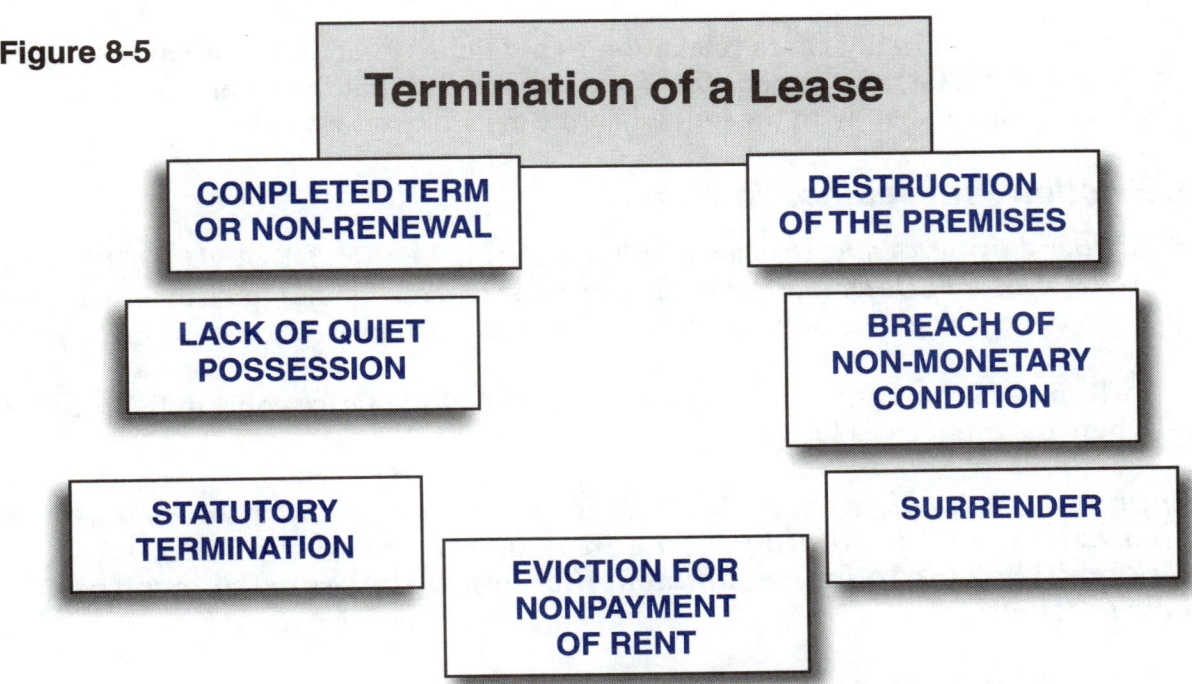

Termination of a Lease

- CONPLETED TERM OR NON-RENEWAL
- DESTRUCTION OF THE PREMISES
- LACK OF QUIET POSSESSION
- BREACH OF NON-MONETARY CONDITION
- STATUTORY TERMINATION
- EVICTION FOR NONPAYMENT OF RENT
- SURRENDER

By the same token, a tenant may terminate a residential lease under Texas law due to the landlord's:

1. wrongful lockout or utility cutoff of a tenant;
2. failure to make repairs affecting the habitability of the premises to a tenant who is current on the rent;
3. failure to install the required security devices; or
4. failure to disclose, upon request by a tenant, the name and address of the true owner of the rental property.

The Texas landlord-tenant statutes are rather exacting as to what conditions must exist, which notices must be filed, and what responses must be made before termination of the lease will be allowed under the law.

D. TERMINATION: EVICTION FOR NONPAYMENT OF RENT

If a tenant does not pay the rent as agreed, the tenant is considered to have wrongfully breached the lease. The legal action available to the landlord is in the form of an eviction. An *EVICTION is the legal process of removing a tenant and regaining possession of the property because there is a breach of the lease or rental agreement such as for nonpayment of rental.*

A *RETALIATORY EVICTION is the process whereby a landlord evicts a tenant in response to a complaint lodged, or a repair deducted from rent, by the tenant.*

A residential tenant may claim retaliation as a defense in an eviction lawsuit, but a landlord will not be held responsible if it is determined that the tenant, for example, was already delinquent with the rent when the eviction suit was filed.

1. Eviction Proceedings in Texas

Evictions in Texas are commonly called **FORCIBLE ENTRY AND DETAINER ACTIONS,** *or* **FEDs** *for short,* even though most tenants did not force their way into the property. These tenants are, however, in wrongful possession of the property.

In Texas, eviction actions are tried in the Justice of the Peace court in the precinct where the property is located.

By phoning a local Justice of the Peace court (or JP court as they are often called) and providing the address of the rental property, most clerks will be able to inform you whether or not the property is within their precinct.

Figure 8-6 summarizes the eviction process in Texas.

E. TERMINATION: SURRENDER

SURRENDER *is the giving up of a lease or other estate, thus terminating any further obligations.* Leases may be surrendered either by mutual agreement of the parties or through operation of law.

If voluntarily surrendering the property to the landlord, it's a good idea for the tenant to seek a release. A **RELEASE** *is a legal document whereby the landlord agrees to give up all right to pursue the tenant for any claims or money owed under the lease.*

If a tenant abandons a property without cause, he or she has, by "operation of law," surrendered the property back to the landlord. Any cost for legal action by the landlord, plus the cost of any rental loss, may be charged to the tenant. The losses will be minimized if the landlord recovers possession and re-leases the premises quickly. A landlord can bring a lawsuit against the tenant for the lost rents, advertising expenses, and repairs or cleaning.

Figure 8-6

The Eviction Process in Texas

1. The Notice to Vacate

If a landlord alleges a tenant is not paying rent, the landlord is required by law to give the tenant **written** notice to vacate the premises. This notice can be delivered to the tenant personally with a witness, by certified mail (return receipt requested) or by any other method allowed by law. As the landlord, your lease specifically states otherwise, the law requires you to deliver the written notice, and then wait three days before filing your suit in Justice Court. This is a legal requirement that must be met and cannot be overlooked.

2. Filing the Suit

You must file an original petition with the Court and pay court costs. These court costs pay for filing your suit, your court hearing, and for the Constable to serve the citation. The citation is the notice to the tenant that you are attempting to evict him/her.

3. Going to Court

You must go to Court and prove your case by a preponderance of the evidence. Simply filing a suit does not necessarily mean you will win your suit. You should bring all documents and other evidence with you to Court in a well organized fashion. At the hearing, you will have to present evidence to show that you are entitled to possession of the premises.

4. Writ of Possession

If you have won your suit in Court, and the mandatory five-day appeal period has passed, and the other party is still in the premises, you can file a Writ of Possession in Court. A Writ of Possession is a Court order to the Constable to place you in possession of the property. The Writ of Possession may be requested at the Justice of the Peace office where the judgment is. The Constable of your particular Precinct can answer your questions about this Writ.

Adapted from Justice of the Peace web page, Collin County, Texas
www.co.collin.tx.us/justices_peace/evictions.jsp

F. TERMINATION: BREACH OF NON-MONETARY CONDITIONS

The violation of any conditions of the lease is a breach of contract and may terminate the agreement. For example, suppose as a condition of the lease a commercial tenant is required to provide evidence of liability insurance. If the tenant fails or refuses to provide written evidence, the tenant may be considered in default of the agreement even though all rent remains current.

Both the lessee and lessor have the responsibility of being informed of all contractual conditions and understand that violation of the conditions may cause termination.

G. TERMINATION: DESTRUCTION OF THE PREMISES

If the rental structure is destroyed in some significant manner, there is usually a clause in most contracts that automatically terminates the lease. After all, if an entire office is destroyed to the ground, what is there to rent? But if the damage is light, the tenant may stay while the landlord makes repairs. A lessee will usually also have the right to terminate the lease if the property is condemned under the process of eminent domain.

Selling an apartment building is "subject to the rights of tenants in possession." It does NOT terminate leases.

IV. Special Purpose Leases

In this section we will cover several unique types of leases designed to meet specific needs.

A. SALE-LEASEBACK

A *SALE-LEASEBACK occurs when an owner sells his or her property to another party and leases it back for a stated period of time; the original owner becomes the lessee.* This is also a financing device, but it is used mostly for commercial buildings where large business concerns are involved. The main reason for this type of lease is that a large company usually builds structures to its specifications. A large amount of money is required, therefore the company sells the building to get back most of its invested capital. By doing this, the company increases its working capital.

Large investors, such as insurance companies and pension funds, will purchase or build such a property, provided they get a well-written, long-term lease. Of course the credit rating and financial position of the lessee must be outstanding. This is one device that nets a high rental income to the investor and allows the business a better cash flow. Chain stores, such as department stores and discount stores, use this device frequently.

Landlord and Tenant (Lessor and Lessee)

The original owner of property in a sale-leaseback becomes the lessee. All lease payments are deductible from taxable income if it is business property (non-residential).

B. LEASE-PURCHASE OPTION

A *LEASE-PURCHASE OPTION exists only when a tenant leases a property with the option to purchase it at some future date.* This gives the lessee the chance to occupy the property and to decide if it suits his or her needs before purchasing it. This is the "try before you buy" idea.

C. GROUND LEASE

A *GROUND LEASE is for the exclusive use and possession of a specific parcel of land.* The ground lease allows a company to build on a parcel of land without investing a large amount of money for the purchase of the land, because the lessor retains ownership of the land. Ground leases can run for as long as 99 years. In other instances, the land may be used for parking spaces, trailer parks, farming, or as recreational land, such as a golf course or motorcycle park.

D. GRADUATED LEASE

A *GRADUATED LEASE provides for a varying rental rate.* Also called a **"stair-step" lease**, it is often based upon future determination, such as periodic appraisals. .

The Consumer Price Index (CPI) might be used to adjust the rent of a graduated lease.

E. GROSS LEASE (Income Property)

A *GROSS LEASE is a lease where the lessee pays only a flat rental fee for the use of the property.* The lessor is responsible for property taxes, insurance, and other property expenses.

F. NET LEASE (Income Property)

A *NET LEASE is one where the lessee pays a proportionate share of property taxes, insurance, and other operating costs in addition to rental payments.* The lessor receives only a net amount and does not pay the other related property expenses. Sometimes the net lease is referred to as a **"triple net lease"** because the lessee generally pays for (1) property taxes, (2) fire and hazard insurance, and (3) assessments or other operating expenses. Since each lease may be different, it's best to read each one carefully to determine exactly which expenses the lessee is required to pay.

315

The lessor benefits from a net lease because it generates a fixed income.

G. PERCENTAGE LEASE (Retail Sales Property)

A *PERCENTAGE LEASE is a commercial (retail sales) lease in which the lessee pays, or may pay, a certain percentage of the monthly gross sales to the lessor.* The idea is that if the lessee has a good or excellent location, the lessor will also benefit. Most percentage leases are written for a base rental amount, paid in advance, with an additional amount due if a predetermined percentage of the gross income receipts exceeds the base rental amount.

Percentage lease payments are based upon monthly gross income receipts (with a fixed minimum rental).

H. CONSUMER PRICE INDEX (CPI)

The *CONSUMER PRICE INDEX (CPI) is a government indicator (also called the "cost of living index") that shows changes in the cost of living from period-to-period.* As one of the largest expenses for consumers, housing expenses are one of the largest denominators used when calculating the CPI. Leases are often tied to the CPI, so that rents will adjust to give the lessor the same relative purchasing power from rents during a period of inflation. Long-term commercial leases generally include an *ESCALATOR CLAUSE, whereby rents increase with inflation.*

The most frequently used standard (index) for making commercial lease adjustments is the Consumer Price Index for Wage Earners and Clerical Workers (CPI-W). Statistics are available for different geographic areas.

I. RELATED TEXAS AGREEMENTS

The final two agreements appear to be leases, but they really are not in the true sense of the word. Under a true lease, the lessee is given permission by the lessor to physical possession of the premises. In these agreements, however, the lessee is being given something a bit different.

1. The Oil and Gas Lease

Although the Texas Railroad Commission regulates the production of oil and gas in Texas, it does not regulate the execution of oil and gas leases.

Under an oil and gas lease, the mineral owner is the lessor and the oil company is the lessee. Remember that in Texas, the owner of the surface estate is not necessarily the owner of the minerals. In any event, the true purpose of this type of lease is to give the oil company the right to explore, drill, and produce oil, gas or other minerals. In exploring for minerals, it is implied under that the law that the lessee may use as much of the surface as is necessary, however, the lessee will be responsible for any damages that may be incurred. This form of lease does provide for lease payments, but it also provides for the payments of royalties to the lessor in the event that minerals are found and produced.

Since this form of leasing is so different from ordinary property leasing, it's best to get an experienced attorney in oil and gas matters to help negotiate the lease.

2. The Texas Hunting Lease

Like its oil and gas counterpart, the Texas hunting lease is not a true lease either. Although it is called a lease, a hunting lease is really a "license" granted by a landowner. A *LICENSE is a personal non-ownership privilege to use personal or real property for an activity that would otherwise not be permitted. In this case, the LICENSOR is the landowner and the permitted activity is usually deer hunting.*

Like in the oil and gas industry, there is no particular "lease" form used, meaning that there is no recognized standard contract. Lease payments, or licensing fees as they should be called, can run anywhere from a modest daily fee to thousands of dollars for the duration of hunting season.

When a landowner grants permission to hunt on his or her property, it is considered a license.

Chapter 8

V. CHAPTER SUMMARY

A **landlord** and **tenant** relationship is created when the owner gives the possession and use of his or her property to another for rent or other consideration. A **lease** is an exclusive right to occupy and use a property typically for a year or longer. A **rental agreement** is typically made on a monthly basis and is renewable at the end of each period. The types of leasehold estates include: 1) an **estate for years**; 2) an **estate from period-to-period**; 3) an **estate at will**; and 4) an **estate at sufferance**.

The minimum requirements of a lease (or rental agreement) can be remembered by the acronym **LAND**, for: 1) **length of time or duration of lease**; 2) **amount of rent**; 3) **names of parties**; and 4) **description of property**.

Texas has enacted landlord-tenant laws for both residential and commercial leases. These laws deal with such topics as the mitigation of damages, tenant lockouts, the interruption of utilities, and the return of security deposits. For residential tenancies, Texas law requires that landlords equip each rental unit with security devices and smoke detectors. Residential landlords are also required to make repairs affecting habitability only if the tenant is current with the rent. The term **"habitability"** is not defined by statute but it refers to a condition which materially affects the health and safety of an ordinary tenant.

A lease or rental agreement can be terminated by: 1) **completion or non-renewal of the term**; 2) **lack of quiet possession**; 3) **statutory termination**; 4) **eviction for nonpayment of rent**; 5) **destruction of the premises**; 6) **breach of non-monetary conditions**; or 7) **surrender**.

In the case of eviction for nonpayment, the landlord must typically mail or deliver a **notice to vacate letter**. The landlord, or his or her agent, can then file a **Forcible Entry and Detainer (FED)** action in the justice of the peace court in the precinct where the property is located. A landlord who prevails at trial will be entitled to both a judgment of possession and a writ of possession. The **writ of possession** is an order of the court directing the sheriff or constable to remove the tenant, with reasonable force if necessary, if the tenant fails to comply with the terms of the order.

Sale-leasebacks, lease purchase options, ground leases, graduated leases, gross leases, net leases, and **percentage leases** are all special purpose leases. In addition, Texas has two agreements which are similar to traditional leases, but are in reality different types of legal documents.

The **oil and gas lease** is not really a lease, in the true sense, but rather an agreement by the mineral owner of the land with an oil producer to search, explore and drill for oil, gas and other minerals. This type agreement does call for the payment of lease payments, but it also provides for royalty payments in the event minerals are discovered on the property. The other type of agreement is called a hunting lease. A **hunting lease** is a really a **license** granted by a landowner so as to allow hunting on his or her property.

VI. TERMINOLOGY

A. Assignment
B. Estate at Sufferance
C. Estate at Will
D. Estate From Period-to-Period
E. Eviction
F. FED
G. Ground Lease
H. Justice of the Peace

I. Lease
J. Leasehold Estate
K. Lease-Purchase Option
L. Lessee
M. Lessor
N. Net Lease
O. Percentage Lease
P. Rental Agreement

Q. Sale-Leaseback
R. Security Deposit
S. Sublease
T. Surrender
U. Tenant
V. Writ of Possession

1. ___ A financial arrangement in which, at the time of sale, the seller retains occupancy by concurrently agreeing to lease the property back from the purchaser.
2. ___ One who pays rent under a lease agreement.
3. ___ A type of lease where the rental payment is determined by a percentage of gross receipts from the business.
4. ___ A possessory interest in land where the exclusive right to occupy and use the property is granted on a temporary basis.
5. ___ The party who leases property to another under a lease agreement.
6. ___ The judge who presides over eviction proceedings.
7. ___ A lease requiring a lessee to pay charges against the property, such as taxes, insurance, and maintenance costs, in addition to rental payments.
8. ___ The party who pays rent to a landlord.
9. ___ A lease agreement for the use of the land only.
10. ___ A tenancy for an indefinite period, terminable by either party.
11. ___ The general name of the process that serves to remove a person from the possession of property due to nonpayment of rent.
12. ___ A lessee's transfer of less than the entire lease to another.
13. ___ An advance payment of money intended to secure performance under a lease.
14. ___ A transfer of a person's entire rights under a contract.
15. ___ A type of tenancy where the tenant's possession continues from period-to-period.
16. ___ A contract between an owner and tenant, setting forth conditions of tenancy for a fixed period of time, usually longer than a year.
17. ___ An estate arising when the tenant wrongfully holds over after the expiration of the term.
18. ___ An agreement for the monthly rental of residential property.
19. ___ The common name of the legal process to initiate the removal of a tenant.
20. ___ Voluntarily returning the leased premises back to the owner.

21. ___ The court order physically expelling a tenant.
22. ___ An option in a lease that includes the right to purchase later.

IX. MULTIPLE CHOICE

1. The lessor is more commonly known as the:

    a. tenant.
    b. landlord.
    c. renter.
    d. agent.

2. Which of the following is an advance of money that is intended primarily to secure performance under a lease?

    a. Security deposit
    b. Application deposit
    c. Escalation fees
    d. License fees

3. A transfer of less than the entire time or space of a lease is called a(n):

    a. assignment.
    b. sublease.
    c. estate from period-to-period.
    d. defeasable transfer.

4. A legal action filed with a court that asserts nonpayment of rent or other illegal acts by the tenant is known as a:

    a. Writ of Possession.
    b. Three-Day Notice.
    c. Notice to Terminate.
    d. Forcible Entry and Detainer.

5. With a sale-leaseback, the original owner assumes the role of:

    a. landlord.
    b. lessee.
    c. lessor.
    d. seller.

6. Percentage lease payments are usually based upon:

    a. gross income receipts.
    b. a predetermined lease amount.
    c. an amount due after taxes and other expenses have been deducted.
    d. an amount due including all taxes and operating expenses.

7. If a unit's furnace quits working in the dead of winter, this condition might be referred to as affecting:

    a. suitability.
    b. habitability.
    c. reliability.
    d. non-homogeneity.

8. Which type of lease is a retail store most likely to use?

    a. Graduated Lease
    b. Ground Lease
    c. Net Lease
    d. Percentage Lease

9. As a general rule, Texas law requires residential landlords to equip a rental property with:

    a. security guards.
    b. security devices.
    c. adequate parking spaces.
    d. wheelchair ramps.

10. If a tenant, during the term of a lease, wishes to surrender rental property to the landlord so that he/she is no longer responsible for the payment of future rentals, he/she should ask for a(n):

    a. eviction.
    b. Writ of Restitution.
    c. reversion.
    d. release.

ANSWERS: 1. b; 2. a; 3. b; 4. d; 5. b; 6. a; 7. b; 8. d; 9. b; 10. d

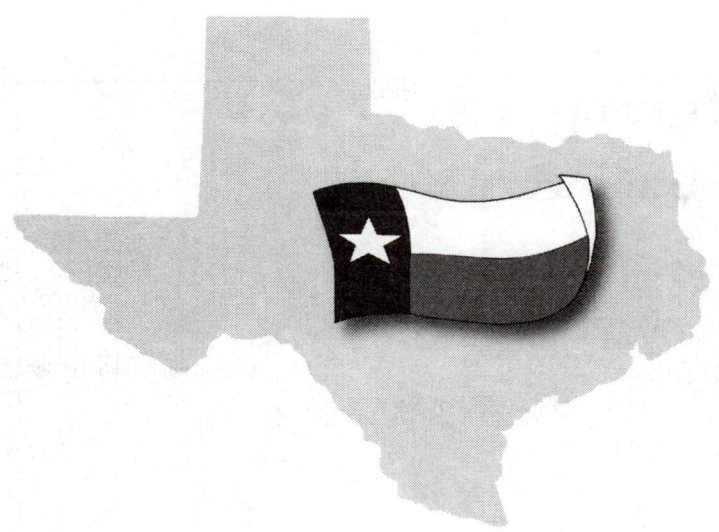

Chapter 9
Property Management

I. The History of Property Management

Property management has been around for several thousand years. The ancient Egyptians had overseers to manage their estates, as did the Greeks and Romans. While they utilized mostly slave labor, their job was to supervise the upkeep of the estates which protected the value and to maximize the income. This isn't much different than the goals of modern day property management.

In the middle ages, property managers in Europe collected rents from the serfs for a lord or vassal. Part of the rent was kept by the lord or vassal and the rest was sent up along the feudal chain to another lord, vassal or king.

Later, in England, estate managers handled the affairs of vast estates including housing for workers, maintenance of improvements as well as agricultural supervision. In pre-revolutionary America, estate managers carried on much these same duties, often for holders of land grants who were absentee owners.

The growth of the cities required housing, which was primarily rental housing, and with this housing the need for management.

CHAPTER 9 OUTLINE

A. THE INDUSTRIAL REVOLUTION

The industrial revolution in England, with the harnessing of first water power and then steam, allowed for factories to mass produce goods that were once produced by hand or otherwise unavailable. The needs of the factories for workers brought laborers in from farm communities leading to a rapid growth of cities and in rental housing. The industrial revolution spread from England to other European countries and the United States. Steam and later electric power allowed for horizontal growth of factories which earlier had power conveyed from water wheels by gears, drive shafts and belts which necessitated vertical factories.

B. CONSTRUCTION ADVANCES

The Otis elevator was the first practical elevator and was powered by electricity. It provided dependable vertical travel, thus allowing tall buildings to be constructed.

This increased the value of land in the central cities as it allowed for greater utilization of ground space. Buildings were still limited as to height by the fact that the lower floors required extremely wide walls to support the masonry construction of the upper floors.

The use of structural steel allowed for modern day skyscrapers. The steel frame allowed relatively light exterior sheathing which made tall buildings possible without the loss of space from massive supporting lower walls.

C. THE GREAT DEPRESSION

The depression that followed the stock market crash of 1929 resulted in thousands of properties being foreclosed and held by lenders who could not find buyers. The great depression was actually a boost for professional management.

II. Career Opportunities in Property Management

There are a number of employment opportunities within the property management field. There is a present need for trained professional property managers in a number of areas. Numerous specialties are available within the property management field to utilize a wide range of talent.

The owner of investment property who requires management has several options as to who will manage the property:

1. **Self Managed** – the owner personally manages the property. This usually occurs when the owner has a small number of properties which do not require much time. An example is the investor who has one or two rental houses.

2. **Employee Manager** – the owner hires an employee who has management duties. The owner is in charge but has hired a staff member to assist.

3. **Independent Property Manager** (also known as **Fee Manager** or **Third Party Manager**) – the owner retains a property management firm owned by someone else and pays them to manage the property. These managers handle property for more than one owner and have agency duties towards each client they represent.

A. THE GOVERNMENT

Federal, state, county, and local governmental units as well as agencies of the government employ property managers. Although titles vary, property managers are responsible for maintenance, repair and protection of real property that is government owned or leased for governmental use. In some cases they actually lease government property to others.

The *GENERAL SERVICES ADMINISTRATION is the real estate management agency for the federal government*. It is the largest single employer of property management personnel in the world.

www.gsa.gov
General Services Administration

B. REAL ESTATE INVESTMENT TRUSTS (REITs)

We are seeing a rapid growth in *REAL ESTATE INVESTMENT TRUSTS (REITs), which buy and manage income properties for the benefit of their stockholders.*

REITs *are publicly traded and, by law, must distribute 95 percent of their funds from operation to the shareholders.*

They have an advantage over corporate structures in that they are not taxed on earnings distributed to shareholders. Therefore, they avoid the double taxation of corporations.

Many large developers, limited partnerships, and other property owners become REITs in order to have liquidity. REIT shares have a ready market. Many are listed on the stock exchange (New York, American, or NASDAQ).

Today, REITs are the primary buyers of large income properties because of their easy access to capital. They can raise capital by selling common stock, preferred stock or bonds. They can also borrow from commercial lenders. Some REITs have open lines of credit approaching the billion dollar mark. While some REITs operate in just a few geographical markets, others operate nationwide.

www.nareit.com

National Association of Real Estate Investment Trusts - NAREITs

Some REITs specialize in types of property. As an example, some REITs buy fast food restaurants of particular franchisees and lease them to the operators. There are a half dozen REITs that only own factory outlet shopping centers. Others own only apartments or shopping centers.

Many REITs operate based on opportunity. They may buy or even develop properties that are residential, office, commercial, and industrial in nature. Some REITs look for distressed properties with serious problems. They then solve the problems. Others only want quality properties.

Because of the significant ownership role of REITs, they are a prominent employer of property managers.

CEOs of REITs tend to have backgrounds in development or finance rather than property management.

A reason for this could be the fact that many REITs were development companies just a few years ago. These companies went public to be able to liquidate assets (stocks) and because of the ability of REITs to both raise equity capital and to borrow funds. Some property managers are now rising to the top as executives retire.

REITs raid other REITs for employees by paying them what they are worth. Many property managers are now making executive salaries from $100,000 to $500,000 per year or more.

The REITs have been one of the best things that ever happened for property management as far as increasing the manager's income is concerned.

Because REITs are publicly traded, management is under tremendous pressure from large institutional stockholders to show significant growth in funds from operations. This is the standard measurement for REIT performance.

Because of this need for growth, there is pressure to show improvements quarter by quarter. This is unfortunate, because in looking at the short-term, long-term goals tend to come secondary. Immediate expenses as to property upgrades might be put back.

Maintenance expenses might also be reduced and staff might suffer layoffs. These short-term fixes to increase *FFO (Funds From Operation)* might in the long-term be detrimental to the shareholders even though they offer instant gratification.

Property managers in some instances know that growth rates of the past cannot be sustained. When growth rates slow or funds from operations actually show a decline, stocks tend to tumble.

Management often has income related to stock performance, so management suffers as well. It is expected that a number of REITs, currently the darlings of Wall Street, will tumble as to stock prices. The REITS themselves are generally healthy. It is just that they cannot show the growth in earnings quarter after quarter that is expected by stock market analysts.

C. FINANCIAL INSTITUTIONS

Many financial institutions such as banks, savings and loans, and credit unions use independent property managers to manage foreclosed real estate. These portfolios, known as *ORE or REO (owned real estate or real estate owned)*, can include anything from foreclosed homes to office buildings and shopping centers. Since financial institutions will rarely want to keep foreclosed property as an investment, they will actively market the property while it is being managed.

D. CORPORATIONS

Many large corporations have over one-half of their assets in real property.

In recent years, they have begun to realize that property management is an executive function and not necessarily a blue-collar function. Property management has been raised to the vice presidential level in many corporations.

Corporate property management might include leasing space and the supervision of leases. The property manager working in a major corporate environment might have responsibilities as to space alterations and maintenance as to both corporate owned and leased space. In many cases, maintenance is separated from corporate property managerial duties and is given to plant superintendents or plant engineers.

Corporate property managers are often responsible for the security of excess property until it is needed or disposed of. However, in many cases, security is under the plant superintendent rather than a property management duty.

Corporate property managers may act as lessors as well as lessees in subleasing or leasing corporate leased or corporate owned property.

E. FRANCHISES

Franchises realize the importance of property management as to leasing and maintenance. Expansion would not be possible without good property management.

F. EMPLOYEES OF PRIVATE OWNERS

Some real estate brokers and non-licensees work as employees of individual owners rather than as agents. They manage one or a group of properties for the owner with employee responsibilities.

G. PRIVATE MANAGEMENT FIRMS

Many real estate brokerage offices operate property management services.

Some just handle a few properties while others are well staffed divisions handling hundreds of properties for dozens if not hundreds of separate owners.

There are many firms which handle property management exclusively. By not competing with general brokerage offices they are able to obtain a significant portion of their business from referrals.

Some property management firms specialize in particular types of property while others only perform a single property management function, such as leasing agents.

H. ON-SITE MANAGEMENT

Most property managers are on-site managers who live and/or work exclusively at a property where they have management duties.

They are generally employees of either the property owners or of a management firm. Most residential managers are employed to manage residential property but on-site managers are found in other areas, such as mini-warehouse management.

III. Why Owners Choose Management

Many owners choose property management for economic and personal reasons.

A. ECONOMIC REASONS

Property managers can simply do a better job of management than most owners because of training and experience.

A professional property manager has a better understanding of the rental market. They are more likely to locate tenants and negotiate leases with more favorable terms than are owners who relegate property management to a part-time business.

Even owners who have the training and ability to do an excellent management job of their own property, nevertheless, will use professional managers. The reason is the value of the owner's time. A surgeon can better use valuable time performing surgery than trying to collect rent from a delinquent tenant or making calls for repairs to a property.

The Main Financial Benefits of Hiring a Property Manager

Increased Rents. The property manager is less eager to give away rent or lower rents when the necessity to do so is not indicated by market conditions.

Reduced Vacancy Factor. By qualifying prospective tenants, the property manager can select tenants who will have a longer tenancy period. This can be aided by lease terms. This results in lower turnover of tenancy which equates to a lower vacancy factor.

Reduce Tenant Damage. Through qualifying tenants and requiring reasonable property damage bonds, the probability of damage to the premises is reduced and when damage does occur, the damage bond is usually sufficient to cover the damage.

Reduced Repair Costs. Good property management will include preventative maintenance programs which will reduce the likelihood of costly emergency repairs for operating systems.

Reduced Expenses. Because of purchasing power in managing a great many units, property managers can obtain services and supplies at significant discounts from the prices offered to an individual owner. In addition, a professional manager is less likely to be taken advantage of by a vendor or service provider.

Management Planning. A professional property manager will plan ahead for changes in tenant mix, changes in uses, changes in lease terms, etc. based on the goals of the owner.

Prolonging Economic Life. Property goes through an "up" period of development and lease. It then goes through what can be a lengthy period of maturity and, finally, it enters a period of decline usually resulting in abandonment or demolition.

Some properties go through these phases rapidly and others very slowly. There are apartment structures in Europe which have been desirable for several hundred years. Physically, nonresidential structures can maintain an economic life span far longer than the 39½ years that the IRS offers for depreciation. Property management cannot only extend a property's life span, it can reverse the clock through remodeling or restoration.

B. PERSONAL REASONS

Many property owners realize that they don't have the temperament to deal with tenants or problems. Some let problems bother their peace of mind. Others are too nice and end up being taken advantage of by tenants. These property owners hesitate to get tough as to rule violations, rent collections and evictions. There are thousands of owners who give their tenants below-market rent. They're afraid to raise rents or just don't want to appear to be a bad person. In many cases, owners have run their properties as charitable institutions rather than in a businesslike manner.

Those owners who recognize their short comings choose professional management.

IV. The Management Plan

Your *PROPERTY MANAGEMENT PLAN is an analysis of the present state of the property as to physical condition, nature of tenants, rents, lease provisions, etc., as well as what you expect to achieve and how you will achieve it*. The management plan should seek to fill the owner's goals.

The property management plan might be prepared prior to obtaining management. The prepared plan would be used as a tool to persuade owners that, as the property manager, you understand their property and their goals and will be able to meet those goals.

What owners want must be an integral part of the management plan.

If you regard your management plan as an important document, owners will treat it in a similar manner. Therefore, many property managers place their management plans in a finished binder and indicate on the cover that it was prepared for a particular property and owner.

It's a good idea for the management plan to be formally presented to the owner at a time and place where it can be explained in detail without interruption.

A. PROPERTY ANALYSIS

Your analysis of the property should include the following:

1. Location of the Property

The strengths and weaknesses of the location should be considered. Location is one factor that cannot be changed.

2. The Physical Structure

This would include construction type and quality, age and general conditions of the property including deferred maintenance.

3. Grounds and Parking

The condition of the grounds and adequacy of parking should be considered.

4. Current Tenants

Who the current tenants are, rent levels, and current vacancies should be covered. This should include strengths and weaknesses of current tenants and the relationship of current rent to market rent.

5. Area Analysis

The analysis should include the demographics and changes in the area, as well as the vacancy factor for similar property in the area. New construction in the area and changes in property use should be covered as to how it will affect the subject property.

Chamber of Commerce information can be valuable in that it will probably have supporting data. The larger banks have economists who prepare a variety of reports as to regions and particular cities. This information can be invaluable in supporting your management plan.

6. Other Possible Uses

Different uses of the property should be considered if applicable.

7. Photos

Include photos to emphasize points being made such as deferred maintenance, competing properties, etc.

B. GOALS

The "management plan" might include one-year goals as well as longer term five-year goals.

The goals should be measurable and meaningful. The intermediate steps proposed in the management plan should lead naturally toward those goals.

Goals might include control as to growth of expenses or to actually reducing expenses. Goals might be to increase rents, obtain longer-term leases as well as to reduce the vacancy factor.

Showing a desired rent schedule is NOT enough. Your management plan must show how you will arrive at this goal.

Your plan might actually call for increasing expenses to upgrade the physical plant. This would in turn result in an immediate reduction in cash flow in order to insure later benefits of greater cash flow and property value.

Your management plan might include prioritizing corrective action as to the condition of the property. It would include a time table for corrective action. Your plan might even include financing arrangements to cover corrective action and/or property improvements.

Suggested improvements should include estimated costs for the work. You have to realize that your plan must sell the owner on the benefits of making the improvements and any change in operations.

You must keep in mind that your management plan involves much more than planning. It is a tool for action. The plan is worthless if not implemented.

C. PRO-FORMA STATEMENT

*Your property management plan should include a budget for the first year based on anticipated expenses and anticipated revenue, which is your **PRO-FORMA STATEMENT**.* Assumptions made in your pro-forma statement should be clearly explained. The owner must realize that your anticipated income will be directly related to the anticipated expenses, and that a change in net income might not be possible without a change in the budget. In some cases, a pro-forma statement can be based on a change in use.

Your desired rent schedule should be included and your figures should consider current lease restraints on rent adjustments.

Zero based budgeting can be used effectively to show owners what can be done. *ZERO BASED BUDGETING requires every expense to be justified as well as every staffing position.* It starts from scratch rather than with the prior year's budget. All too often, managers simply add on inflationary adjustments to prior years of expenses to estimate the next year's expenses. This common approach does not consider if the last year's budget was excessive or too lean and, if so, where the fat or inadequacies are located in the budget.

D. STAFFING

Your management plan should include present staffing and any recommended changes in staffing. Any changes should be supported.

E. COST SAVINGS

If savings are possible through your purchasing power, use of contract work, etc., your management plan should spell out just what these savings will be.

F. RESERVE REQUIREMENTS

Your management plan should justify the amount of funds to be held as a reserve against unbudgeted expenses.

G. ECONOMIC CHANGES

Property is NOT managed in a vacuum. National and local economic conditions will affect your plan. They affect rents, vacancy factors, and costs.

Any assumption that you make should be clearly covered in your management plan. You must be as realistic as possible. Owners know if the neighborhood where the property is located is declining. They want the truth.

H. MARKETING PLAN

The management plan should cover how you intend to market the vacant space. This could include:

1. Signs;
2. Press releases;
3. Preparation of property briefs and brochures;
4. Advertising preparation;
5. Advertising budget and media selections;
6. Open houses (residential);
7. Providing information to cooperating brokers;

8. Phone contacts;
9. Personal contacts;
10. Using present tenants as a source of leads.

I. MANAGEMENT PLAN PRIOR TO CONSTRUCTION

Property management can actually begin prior to construction.

Persons having extensive experience in leasing will have a good feel for which amenities will have little, if any, effect on rents for the unit being planned and which amenities will have significant economic effects.

As an example, a trash compactor might add little, if any, as to rent, but it could add additional maintenance costs to a particular rental range and area. A convertible den might be more important than a formal dining area where there is a kitchen dining nook. Tennis courts might not be economical amenities in some areas, but in other areas they would be economically very viable additions.

Besides amenities, at least one developer of high-rise office structures has the initial blueprints reviewed for maintenance purposes. Some of the suggestions the developer adopted were wall-hung stools and partitions to reduce cleaning time, washbasins accessible for the handicapped, redesigned janitorial closets to permit cleaning carts and electrical hall outlets for vacuums and floor polishers. Small details of operation and use can be easily provided for in the planning stages but, if not solved, can create problems in operation.

For large projects, the leasing start-up and applicable maintenance contracts and staffing decisions should be made prior to completion.

Some large apartment developments spend almost a year for stabilization (a reasonable occupant level). Shortening the time frame can mean significant savings to the owners.

V. Refusing Management

Just as a sales listing should be refused when the agent feels he or she cannot adequately represent the owner or where the problems associated with listing outweigh the reward, property managers must evaluate whether they want to manage a property for an owner.

A. SPECIALIZATION

A property management firm may refuse to manage a property because of its geographical location. A property outside of the area where the firm is operating might require more effort to manage the property than the rewards justify.

A firm that specializes in residential management might turn down the opportunity to manage a small industrial complex knowing that they lack the expertise to handle industrial leases.

B. UNREALISTIC FEES

A property manager is NOT going to remain in business if he or she is NOT adequately compensated.

Don't try to buy a management contract by cutting fee schedules or agreeing to accept what an owner offers if you do not feel the compensation is adequate. Accepting bargain-basement fees will affect your efforts. It will also affect your reputation if you perform at less than maximum effectiveness.

When you allow one owner a significant break on fees, that owner may brag about how he or she beat you down. When other property owners discover your two-tier fee schedule, they're going to be unhappy even though you are doing an excellent job for them. The owners will feel you have taken advantage of them.

In competitive situations where you have shown what you can do, always compete on a professional basis and NOT because of lower prices.

You must be fair to yourself as well as others. If you stick to your fee schedule, you'll find that when an owner asks you to cut your fee, they generally have already decided that you will handle their property. They're just trying to see if they can save at your expense.

C. SLUMLORDING

Don't accept a management position where an owner wants to milk a property for rents without regard to tenant services.

Property owners with large numbers of poor, minority tenants often take advantage of them as the owner knows that many tenants won't complain about uninhabitable conditions. These owners will want you to act in their place and carry on as they would. By taking the management position, you open yourself to liability under the law and lose your own self respect in the process. You're damaging your professional

reputation in the community and it will negatively affect your economic status because other owners will be unwilling to entrust their properties to you.

There could be other reasons for the owner to milk a property and not do reasonable repairs and maintenance. An owner may intend to demolish the structure to use the site for a more productive purpose. The owner could be facing foreclosure and simply wants to grab the last few months' rent before the property is lost to the lender. The effect is the same for whatever reason. You don't want to be a party to an attempt by the owner to maximize income at the expense of reasonable treatment of tenants.

D. NEGATIVE CASH FLOWS

Management of rental property that can be expected to result in a negative cash flow for an owner should be avoided unless the owner fully understands the financial picture and has the resources and willingness to support the property. *NEGATIVE CASH FLOW exists when cash disbursements exceed cash (rental) income, requiring the owner to continue to put more money in the property.*

Some owners of negative cash flow properties are reluctant to approve necessary repairs, are slow to make payments to the management company and can create a nightmare for the property manager.

E. CODE VIOLATIONS

You should avoid getting involved in property that is currently in violation of codes or zoning ordinances unless the owner has shown the ability and willingness to correct any problems.

Some owners offer management so that the manager appears as a buffer between the owner and public authorities. You don't want to be the one who has to answer to a judge regarding any violations of the property. The problems of such properties can far outweigh the benefits of what otherwise appears to be a very lucrative management contract.

F. PLAYING SCROOGE

Owners who otherwise manage their own property might offer you the management because they don't want to get involved in particularly unpleasant tasks. As an example, several management firms declined an offer to manage an apartment building that had received approval for condominium conversion. The owner wanted the manager to collect rents for one month and give 30-day notices to all the tenants. Management was to cease when the tenants left. A management contract of this sort makes the manager the "bad guy" and provides no real benefits.

In this case, had the owners been willing to provide adequate funding to assist the tenants in relocating, and managerial duties included tenant relocation, then handling this client would not reflect negatively on the management firm.

G. OWNERS WHO WANT TO CONTROL

Management can be a disaster when owners refuse to give up control. Sometimes it can be a lack of complete trust in you and other times it is just the personalities of the owners. Owners may want you to react more as an employee than as their agent. You're asking for trouble if you accept the management contract with untenable conditions placed on your actions that allow the owner to become a co-manager.

To give back a management contract is better than trying to share management duties.

Owners who constantly visit their property and give orders to maintenance personnel and on-site managers tend to interfere with proper management. Orders from owners tend to prioritize what they want rather than what good management would dictate. Confusion sets in and this becomes a bad situation for the resident manager and staff.

Some owners want approval of very minor expenses or want you to deal only with particular service providers. In one case, an owner required a particular service provider who gave exorbitant billings. The owner then received cash rebates from that service provider.

You don't want to get involved in tax fraud.

Even where there is no fraud involved, when you are dictated as to which contractors or service providers you must use, you lose control over these people and end up with no say in requiring quality and the timeliness of job completion. Some owners want you to do their repairs or contract for them. This affects the manager's ability to properly deal with tenants.

A property manager should avoid involvement with an owner unless an atmosphere of trust and respect exists between them.

You can readily see that changes are required if 10 percent of your management income is derived from property that takes 50 percent of your management time.

VI. The Property Management Contract

The *PROPERTY MANAGEMENT CONTRACT is the agency agreement between an owner and a property manager.* It spells out what is expected from the property manager by delineating the manager's level of authority as well as the manager's duties and obligations. The contract will also set forth the obligations and responsibilities of the property owner. In short, it is the primary operating agreement between the parties.

A. SAMPLE AGREEMENT

A property management agreement will be appropriate to the type of property being managed, i.e., commercial, industrial, etc. A commonly used commercial management agreement used in Texas is the TAR property management agreement. As with any TAR form, this agreement is intended for use only by members of the Texas Association of REALTORS® or with the express written consent of TAR.

An example of the first page of the TAR Commercial Property Management Agreement is shown in **Figure 9-1**.

Another commonly used form is the **Building Owner's and Manager's Association (BOMA) International Standard Agency Management Agreement**. In addition, many Texas property owners use contract forms which are self prepared or drafted by their lawyers. As a result, there is no one single property management form in use throughout the state.

B. KEY CONTRACT PROVISIONS

Regardless of the form used, a well drafted contract should include, at the very least the following key elements.

1. Identity of Parties

Correctly naming the parties to the contract can eliminate many legal problems which might arise because of confusion. Suppose for example, that Peter Martin agrees to manage the Happy Gardens Apartments, which is owned by Oscar Owner. Is Peter's contract between himself and Oscar or is it with the Happy Gardens Apartments?

Since Oscar is the owner of the complex, the contract would be between Peter Martin and Oscar Owner, doing business as the Happy Gardens Apartments.

As with any legal document, it's always important that the parties be correctly named.

Figure 9-1

TEXAS ASSOCIATION OF REALTORS®

COMMERCIAL PROPERTY MANAGEMENT AGREEMENT

USE OF THIS FORM BY PERSONS WHO ARE NOT MEMBERS OF THE TEXAS ASSOCIATION OF REALTORS® IS NOT AUTHORIZED.
©Texas Association of REALTORS®, Inc. 2005

1. PARTIES:

A. The parties to this agreement are:

Owner: _____

Address: _____
City, State, Zip: _____
Phone: _____ Mobile: _____
E-Mail: _____ Fax: _____

Broker: _____
Address: _____
City, State, Zip: _____
Phone: _____ Mobile: _____
E-Mail: _____ Fax: _____

B. If Owner is not an individual, Owner is an: ❑ estate ❑ corporation ❑ limited liability company (LLC) ❑ trust ❑ partnership ❑ limited liability partnership (LLP), which entity was charted or created in _____ (State). The individual signing this agreement for the owner represents to Broker that he or she has the authority to bind Owner to this agreement, to act for Owner, and is acting under his capacity as _____ (title) for the Owner.

C. Owner appoints Broker as Owner's sole and exclusive agent of the real property described in Paragraph 2 to:
   ❑ (1) manage the Property, but not lease the Property.
   ❑ (2) manage and lease the Property.

2. PROPERTY: "Property" means:

Address: _____
_____
legally described as: _____
_____
_____
in _____ County, Texas, together with the following non-real-property items: _____
_____

"Property" also includes any other Property described in any attached Multiple Property Addendum.

3. TERM:

A. <u>Primary Term</u>: The primary term of this agreement begins and ends as follows:

Commencement Date: _____ Expiration Date: _____

B. <u>Automatic Extension</u>: Unless either party provides written notice of termination to the other party at least 30 days before the Expiration Date, this agreement will automatically extend on a monthly basis until either party terminates by providing at least 30 days written notice to the other party.

(TAR-2202) 5-5-05   Initialed for Identification by Broker/Associate _____ and Owner _____, _____   Page 1 of 9

2. Relationship of Parties

The parties will want it understood that the property manager is an independent contractor of the owner in the performance of this contract. Recall from Chapter 4 that a contractor is hired for results and requires no direct supervision. Additionally, independent contractors are generally responsible for the payment of their owner income taxes. As a result, both parties will want absolutely no misunderstanding as to their relationship to each other. The manager will only be an independent contractor and nothing more. They are not business partners.

3. Contract Term

A management contract's length should be related to the services provided and the owner reimbursement.

Many contracts contain a primary term consisting of a negotiated number of months or years, for example, a one year contract or a six month contract. In this case, it is appropriate to specify an automatic renewal period unless any of the parties objects in writing before the end of the term.

It is also possible that the contract can be established on a periodic basis, for example on a month to month basis. Much like the self renewing one year contract, a month to month contract will also self renew unless one or both of the parties objects in writing.

If a Texas real estate licensee agrees to perform services for which a real estate license is required, the contract must contain a termination date, otherwise the licensee could face license suspension proceedings.

4. Manager's Duties

The contract should not only clearly set out what the manager is expected to do, but also give him/her the authority to do so. For example, many contracts require the manager to manage, supervise, control, and coordinate all business matters relating to the operation of a named property.

Although these duties appear to be overly broad, from a legal viewpoint the manager should not assume these duties include property leasing unless the contract authorizes the manager to do so. For example, if the management contract requires the manager to maintain the property, but not to lease units, the contract should state so.

The contract should specify exactly what is expected of the property manager. If the manager exceeds the limits of what the contract requires, he/she could be considered to be a breach of contract.

While it is advantageous for the owner to specify exactly what is expected of the manager, the manager should insist that the owner grant him/her with the authority to perform the required duties. This grant should also state if there are any limits, dollar or otherwise, to this authority. After all, the property manager is the agent of the owner.

5. Collection of Funds

The management contract should also address the collection and accounting of funds such as rents and security deposits. For example, is the property manager required to maintain a separate account for the purpose of depositing rents and security deposits? Or may the manager deposit these funds in the general operating account?

Similarly, the manager should be required to use some identifiable standard in the collection and enforcement of lease payments. For example, will the manager be required to use "reasonable efforts" to collect lease payments or is the manager given wide discretion in all tenant collections? Additionally, is the manager empowered to commence suit in eviction cases only, or will this authority extend to any situation where money is owed in connection with the property?

A property manager may be held legally responsible for the mishandling of funds.

6. Manager's Compensation

From the manager's perspective, among the most important provisions of this agreement will be how he/she will be compensated. A manager's compensation may be based on any the following:

1. A flat fee amount;
2. A percentage of rental income;
3. A commission or bonus for new leases and/or renewals;
4. A base fee plus lease commissions;
5. A base fee plus rent percentage;
6. An hourly, daily or weekly rate; or
7. Any combination of the above.

Obviously there are a number of ways that a property manager can be compensated. But regardless of the method negotiated, as stated above, it's best there be some relationship between the term of the contract and the manager's compensation.

As an example, it might not be a good idea for a manager to enter into a short term management contract based upon a straight percentage of the rents received if

there were a significant number of vacancies. In such a contract, the owner could take advantage of you and let you stabilize the property. You would do the hard work and the owner would take over when the property was fully leased. On the other hand, the owner takes most of the risk in flat fee management agreement if the rents decrease.

If the manner of compensation includes commissions or bonuses based on rental, the contract should specify such things as the commission rate, when such commissions are earned and payable, whether commissions are based upon lease renewals, and whether the manager will be entitled to a commission if the owner leases his/her own property. Furthermore, the contract should also consider whether the manager will be entitled to commissions based upon his/her leasing efforts, but received by the owner following the expiration of the manager's contract.

7. Record Keeping and Property Reports

A management agreement should also include a requirement that the manager is to provide the owner with a periodic report of the property. Such a report may be conduced on a monthly basis or as often as the owner requires.

Moreover, the contract should specify what topics are to be covered by the report. For example, will the report include finances as well as operations? In other words, will the report include receipts, disbursements, service contracts, security incidents, or tenant complaints? It's up to the parties to determine what and how often reports are made.

An owner is legally entitled to be kept informed regarding the management of his/her property.

8. Audits

Closely related to the record keeping requirement is the auditing provision. A property management agreement should allow the owner to audit the manager's books and records at any reasonable time or upon reasonable notice to the manager. The management agreement should clearly state who will bear the cost of all audits.

9. Preparation and Approval of Budgets

Many good management agreements will hold the manager to a budget. In these situations, the relevant questions become: 1) when will a proposed budget actually approved by the owner, and 2) is there a provision for modifying the budget once it has been approved?

As discussed earlier in this chapter, a pro forma statement is a critical part of a good management plan, but at what point is the owner obligated to approve the budget? For example, is there a stated time limit in which the owner must approve the budget?

Once the budget is formally approved by the owner, the manager should then be authorized to make expenditures in accordance with the approved budget. If exceptions are to be made to budgeted expenditures, the contract should specify how those matters are handled. For example, suppose a manager is authorized to spend a stated amount for repairs. May the manager exceed that authority in emergency situations? If so, what is the dollar limit for emergency repairs and when should the manager advise the owner?

The budget process should not only plan for the normal day to day expenses, but for the emergency expenses as well. In this way both parties understand the limit of the manager's spending authority.

10. Execution of Contracts

If the manager is authorized to sign contracts on behalf of the owner, the contract should so state. For example, is the manager authorized to enter into book keeping, lawn maintenance, janitorial, or construction contracts? May the term of those contracts exceed the term of the manager's contract? How may those contracts be terminated? Also may the owner terminate those contracts?

11. Owner's Responsibilities

The owner should be legally required to make representations regarding the ownership and condition of the property and to cooperate with the manager in the performance of the manager's duties.

For example, an owner should be able to represent to the manager that he/she owns the subject property in fee simple. The owner should also represent that the person signing the management agreement is authorized to sign the contract on behalf of the owner. Finally, the owner should represent that he/she is not in default of any loan agreement on the property or that the property is facing any type of legal proceedings in connection with the condition or use of the property. In other words, is the property facing any health, building, or fire code violations? Or worse yet, is the owner facing any zoning problems, eminent domain proceedings, or foreclosure hearings involving the property?

The contract should also require the owner to work with, and not against, the property manager so as to enable the manager to perform his/her duties. For example, at the commencement of the management contract will there be sufficient

funds in the operating account for the manager to run the property? Or what if, for example, the operating account falls below a designated balance? Will the owner be required to replenish funds? If the manager expends his/her own personal funds to operate the property, how will the manager be reimbursed?

Finally, if the owner owns other properties in the geographic area, the owner should represent that he/she will not compete against the property manager or undermine the manager's efforts in the performance of his/her duties.

12. Insurance Coverage

A property management agreement should require the owner to carry and keep in force adequate policies of insurance during the term of the property management agreement. Generally, these policies of insurance include the following:

1. Fire and extended coverage (including vandalism)
2. Commercial liability
3. Plate glass coverage
4. Worker's compensation (for employees)
5. Rental interruption insurance

Liability insurance covers third parties, for both injury and property damage, due to the condition or operation of a property.

Although an owner may require a property manager to carry liability insurance, normally the owner's policy will provide the primary coverage in the event of claims resulting from the operation of the property. Accordingly, the manager should be named as an additional insured under the owner's policy.

Finally, to the extent that the manager hires employees, the manager should also be required to hold worker's compensation insurance as well to obtain fidelity bonds for all employees who handle money or other valuables. This would obviously protect the interests of the owner.

13. Indemnification

An indemnification is a promise to protect someone from financial loss. Most property managers will want to be indemnified and held harmless from any claims or damages arising from anything the owner might have done before the commencement of the property management agreement. Likewise, the owner wants to be indemnified from anything the property manager might do. And in both cases, the parties will not want to be responsible to each other for anything that might be committed by third parties.

Because indemnification involves potentially complex issues of law, it's best to consult with a knowledgeable attorney before drafting broad indemnification provisions.

14. Miscellaneous Provisions

Finally, the well drafted property management agreement should contain a number of other standard provisions, such as the following:

Notice Provisions – A provision detailing exactly where and how the parties may send notices to each other.

Attorney's Fees – A provision that states that if a lawsuit is instigated concerning the performance of this contract, the winning party shall be entitled to costs plus reasonable attorney fees. (This provision will reduce the likelihood of a frivolous lawsuit.)

Mediation/Arbitration – Some management contracts provide for dispute resolution by means of arbitration. This means that the parties agree to have a third party neutral resolve their dispute instead of going to court. Other agreements provide that a third party mediator may be used to help facilitate a settlement. Regardless of whether arbitration or mediation is used, these are affordable alternatives to costly court litigation in the event of a dispute.

Assignment – A paragraph that states that the terms of this agreement are binding on the successor and assigns of the parties.

Modification and Amendments – A provision that states that any modification or amendment to the contract must be in writing and signed by both parties to be effective.

Obviously the parties may wish to negotiate and draft other provisions as part of a property management agreement, but the provisions listed above are the ones considered essential for a well drafted agreement.

VII. Agency Termination

Recall from Chapter 4 that an agency, which includes management contracts, can be terminated in a number of ways.

A. TERMINATION BY ACT OF THE PARTIES

1. Accomplishment of Purpose

2. Expiration of Term
3. Mutual Agreement
4. Renunciation by the Agent
4. Revocation by the Principal
6. Abandonment by the Agent

B. TERMINATION BY OPERATION OF LAW

1. Death or Incapacity
2. Destruction of the Property
3. Illegality
4. Bankruptcy of the Owner

Either the principal or the agent can cancel a management contract since courts will not force an agency relationship on anyone.

If either party cancels without just cause, they can be held liable for damages resulting from the wrongful cancellation.

VIII. The Rental Process

A. PREPARING TO LEASE

When a unit becomes vacant, any delay in preparing for a rental is costly because every day delayed is a day's rent which can never be recovered.

Waiting two weeks for a crew to remove junk left in an apartment, touch up the paint, and clean the carpet could exceed the cost of preparing the unit for rental. It might be better to pay a premium to people who will get in immediately when a unit becomes vacant and finish the work in a few days.

You want the unit sparkling to rent it. That means a shine on tile, clean carpets, walls that look freshly painted, clean light fixtures and spotless windows as well as appliances that sparkle. Some property managers use car wax on appliances and fixtures. There can be no unpleasant odors in the apartment.

All light fixtures should have enough wattage to flood the apartment with light. Window shades, blinds and curtains should be pulled back to have natural light. You want the unit to appear bright and cheerful. Keep in mind that people are not entirely economic when renting. Emotion can trigger desire and you want your properties to evoke positive emotions.

When there are a number of identical unit vacancies, you can prepare one as a sample unit. It might even be decorator furnished. This is an excellent rental tool when units have recently been completed. You must be certain that all units will be prepared for rental in an identical manner or you will end up with some unhappy short-term tenants.

B. PRE-QUALIFYING YOUR PROSPECTIVE TENANTS

Before you take prospects into a unit, you should determine if the unit is within their budget and if the size of the unit meets their needs. You should have also gone over with them all deposit requirements and the policy about pets.

If they can't afford the unit or it is too small, you are just wasting your time and theirs. In the end, you could lose a tenant for a unit which better suits their needs.

Be certain that you obtain names and telephone numbers before showing prospective tenants units.

C. SHOWING TO PROSPECTIVE TENANTS

Resident managers and leasing agents should turn on all the lights when showing a property.

They should be showing property to prospective renters who are satisfied with location and size requirements of the property and can meet the financial requirements.

A straight-forward approach is best even if the rental agent is not receiving any feedback from the prospective renters as to their satisfaction with the unit. Resident managers and leasing agents should be trained to present a closing script similar to the following:

"This apartment is available [now/on July 1st] for [$610] per month [which includes one garage space and one parking space]. It requires a property damage bond of [$500 plus a $15 key deposit]. If you like this apartment, I can take your application for rent with a [refundable] deposit of [$50]. I will be able to notify you within [24 hours] if your rental application is accepted. Is this satisfactory with you?"

Their answer will be either yes or no. If the answer is yes, begin filling out the rental application which the prospects will then sign. A residential lease application form is shown in Chapter 8.

Ask to see a photo ID. You want to be certain that your renters are who they say they are.

Finally, make sure you collect their check.

D. THE QUALIFICATION PROCESS

As covered in Chapter 8, you should check the applicant's credit as well as check the accuracy of the current employment data. You also want to check with past landlords.

A screening fee may be charged for out-of-pocket costs for information about a rental application (credit reports and reference checks).

Don't take short cuts or assume because a person drives a fancy car and dresses well that they will be good tenants.

Be leery of tenants who need immediate occupancy.

If your check of a prospective tenant's employment and/or prior landlords cannot be verified, you should go further and check with references. Ask the references to give you the names of two other people who know the applicants. These are more likely to provide you with honest information about the applicants.

The qualification process should be regarded as a priority. Process your inquiries quickly.

E. THE LEASE SIGNING

Notify the applicants as soon as they have been approved. Set up an appointment for them to pay the balance of the first month's rent and any deposits due. The applicants should understand the total financial obligation at the time they sign any lease.

Carefully go over every provision of the lease with the tenant as well as any applicable occupancy rules. Tenants need to understand that the rules are important. The better the tenants understand the rules, the fewer problems management will encounter. The tenants then sign the lease and accompanying rules. They should know where they will obtain the key to the unit.

You should consider giving your tenants a check list with telephone numbers for utilities, post office, school registration, etc.

You might want to sign the lease on the premises where furnished rentals are involved. The tenants should also sign an inventory list of items furnished in the units. A residential lease inventory and condition form is shown in Chapter 8.

It's also a good idea to take instant photos of the furnished units prior to renting and have the tenants sign and date each photo. This will help you should there be a dispute later as to damage to the units.

F. LESSOR DISCLOSURES

A number of lessor disclosures are required. These include the following.

1. Disclosure of Ownership

Texas law requires that tenants of residential dwellings must be provided with the name and address of the property owner as well as the name and address of the property manager if the manager is located off-site. The law says that this disclosure can be one of three ways:

1. By providing this information to the tenant in writing within 7 days of a tenant's request;
2. By posting this information in the manager's office; or
3. By including this information in the tenant's lease or any written rules given to each tenant.

The failure to provide this information could subject the owner and/or manager to a legal penalty.

2. Lead-Based Paint Disclosure

As will be discussed further in Chapter 15, owners of units designated as "target" housing (single-family homes and HUD related apartments) must make certain disclosures concerning the use of lead-based paint. For the property manager this means providing the tenant of a residential unit built before 1978 with a TREC disclosure form OP-L together with a booklet entitled *Protect your Family from Lead in your Home.*

Federal laws state that the following housing is excluded from the disclosure requirements:

1. Housing built after 1977;
2. Zero-bedroom units, for example efficiencies, lofts, and dormitories;
3. Housing with leases for less than 100 days;
4. Housing exclusive for elderly or handicapped residents (unless children live here also);
5. Rental housing that has been inspected by a certified inspector and found to be free of lead-based paint; and
6. Houses sold as a result of foreclosure.

IX. Professional Associations

A. INSTITUTE OF REAL ESTATE MANAGEMENT® (IREM)

The Institute of Real Estate Management® (IREM) was created by the National Association of Realtors® as a professional society for real property managers. To bolster professionalism within the industry, they offer the designation Certified Property Manager® (CPM) to qualified candidates who can demonstrate a high standard of competence, ethics, and experience. Property management companies may apply for the Accredited Management Organization® (AMO) designation, while residential on-site managers, who live up to the education and experience guidelines, are bestowed with the Accredited Resident Managers® (ARM) designation.

www.irem.org
Institute of Real Estate Management

B. BUILDING OWNERS AND MANAGERS ASSOCIATION INTERNATIONAL (BOMA)

Founded in 1907, BOMA is a federation of 94 local associations with over 16,000 members representing more than six billion square feet of commercial property in North America. BOMA has local chapters in all major cities. BOMA holds an annual convention which is a major event as well as an important office building show.

BOMA has an educational institute (BOMI) which promotes the interests of the real estate industry through programs of personal development and by collecting, analyzing and disseminating information.

www.boma.org
Building Owners and Managers Association International - BOMA

BOMI offers several important designations: the Real Property Administrator (RPA), the Facilities Management Administrator (FMA), a Systems Maintenance Technician (SMT) and Systems Maintenance Administrator (SMA) designation upon completion of required courses.

BOMA courses prepare individuals NOT only for top management positions but also for hands-on operating positions working in the trenches.

C. NATIONAL PROPERTY MANAGEMENT ASSOCIATION (NPMA)

This professional group consists primarily of property managers in the Washington, D.C. area. There are monthly meetings and special seminars. They do have members in other areas of the country.

www.npma.org
National Property Management Association - NPMA

NPMA has a number of excellent publications, such as:

1. Lighting for Safety and Security.
2. Roofing: A Guide to Specifying and Obtaining Services by Contract.
3. Safety and Security: A Guide to Obtaining Services by Contract.
4. Swimming Pool Management: A Guide to Specifying and Obtaining Services by Contract.
5. Pest Control: A Guide to Specifying and Obtaining Services by Contract.
6. Risk Management and Insurance: A Guide to Specifying and Obtaining Services by Contract.
7. Elevator Maintenance: A Guide to Specifying and Obtaining Services by Contract.
8. Grounds Care: A Guide to Specifying and Obtaining Services by Contract.
9. Painting: A Guide to Specifying and Obtaining Services by Contract.

From the above partial list of publications (which are also available to non-members) you can see that the NPMA is a "hands on" type of organization. They also have a monthly bulletin with informative articles about upcoming seminars. "How To Collect Rent" is an example of one of the NPMA's more practical seminars.

D. INTERNATIONAL REAL ESTATE INSTITUTE (IREI)

Membership in the association includes the professional designation RPM (Registered Property Manager). There are no educational requirements for this designation, but the institute does offer educational programs and numerous publications including the Global Real Estate News.

www.iami.org/irei.html
International Real Estate Institute

E. URBAN LAND INSTITUTE (ULI)

The Urban Land Institute was founded in 1926 as a nonprofit education and research institute. Its 13,000 members cover the entire spectrum of land use and development. The ULI sells over 50,000 books annually offering professional information. They also conduct seminars. While primary emphasis is on development, the ULI also researches and publishes excellent material on the leasing and management of both residential and commercial properties.

www.uli.org
Urban Land Institute

F. AIR COMMERCIAL REAL ESTATE ASSOCIATION (AIREA)

The association has available excellent lease and contract forms for both industrial and commercial property.

www.airea.com
Air Commercial Real Estate Association

Another organization that offers a complete set of property management forms is Professional Publishing.

www.formulator.com
Professional Publishing - Property Management Forms

G. INTERNATIONAL COUNCIL OF SHOPPING CENTERS (ICSC)

This is a specialty organization which offers a number of excellent educational programs as well as professional designations and marketing awards. They also publish an extensive array of books covering all aspects of shopping center management.

www.icsc.org
International Council of Shopping Centers - ICSC

This organization offers the following designations: Certified Leasing Specialist (CLS), Certified Shopping Center Manager (CSM), Accredited Shopping Center Manager (ASM), and Accredited Marketing Director (AMD). Senior level designation is also available for Certified Shopping Center Managers (SCSM) and Certified Marketing Directors (SCMD).

Over 2,400 professionals from all over the world have achieved the designation of Certified Shopping Center Manager. Requirements include experience, education substitution, and passing a comprehensive examination.

H. COMMUNITY ASSOCIATIONS INSTITUTE (CAI)

www.caionline.org
Community Association Institute

The Community Associations Institute (CAI) acts as a clearinghouse for ideas and practices for successful operations and management of all types of residential common-interest housing. Membership includes homeowner associations, property management firms and service providers.

CAI offers workshops, conferences, educational programs, as well as books, periodicals, and newsletters. They also have a website for subjects relating to common interest developments. There are currently 59 local chapters.

CAI offers a number of professional designations such as the Certified Manager of Community Associations (CMCA), the Association Management Specialist (AMS), and the Professional Community Association Manager (PCAM) which is the highest professional designation available from this organization. To achieve this designation, candidates are required to have at least three years of experience in common interest development management plus having graduated from an extensive educational program set forth by CAI. The designation must be renewed every three years through work experience, service activities and continuing education.

I. INTERNATIONAL FACILITY MANAGEMENT ASSOCIATION (IFMA)

IFMA is an international organization of management involved in coordinating the physical workplace with the people and work of the firm. They primarily deal with managing industrial and commercial facilities. Membership is available to professionals and educators involved in at least two of the following activities:

1. Long-range facility planning;
2. Annual facility planning;
3. Facility financial forecasting and budgeting;
4. Real estate acquisition and/or disposal;
5. Interior space planning;
6. Architectural and engineering planning and design;
7. Environmental health and safety;
8. New construction and/or renovation work;
9. Maintenance and operations management of the physical plant;
10. Facility business functions.

www.ifma.org
International Facility Management Association - IFMA

IFMA has programs and conventions around the world and offers specialized councils for specialized management that include health care facilities, academic facilities, museums/cultural institutions, religious facilities, research and development facilities, sports and recreational facilities, etc. Members can earn the Certified Facility Manager (CFM) designation through education and testing.

X. CHAPTER SUMMARY

Property management has been around for thousands of years. From the ancient Greeks and Romans to medieval times, there has always been a need for persons to care for the property of others. In modern times, the field of property management was spurred on by the development of the elevator which made tall buildings possible, thus allowing for greater use of ground space.

An owner of real property has essentially three choices when it comes to property management. First, the owner can manage the property himself/herself. Next, the owner can hire an employee to manage the property. The owner can also hire the services of an outside property management firm.

Aside from working for private management firms, persons who wish to work in the property management field can work in the **public sector (government)**, for **financial institutions** (such as **banks, savings banks,** and **credit unions**), and other **private corporations**. Most property managers are **on-site managers**. That means they live and/or work at the property where they have management duties.

From the owner's perspective, the main economic reasons to hiring a property manager include: **increased rents, reduced vacancy factors, reduced tenant damage, reduced repair costs, reduced expenses, management planning,** and **prolonging economic life of the property**. Another reason for hiring an outside property manager may be simply because the property owner cannot or does not want to deal with the problems associated with managing a property.

A **property management plan** is a tool to be used to analyze a property that is to be managed. The plan consists of a physical analysis of the property such as the location, physical condition of the property, and tenant makeup. The plan should also contain a **pro-forma statement** which is a budget forecast based on projected expenses and revenue. The plan should additionally identify potential cost savings, if any, as well as future staffing recommendations. There should also be a **marketing plan** designed to attract new tenants. In order to implement the plan, a series of concrete and attainable goals should be set out for the property owner's consideration. A property management plan can be an extremely valuable tool for property managers; however, it will be totally worthless unless it can be implemented.

Although property managers often seek out property owners, there may be times when it's best to walk away from a management opportunity. These times may include when the management opportunity involves a type of property that the manager is unfamiliar with. It might also be best to walk away from a management opportunity if the property produces a consistent negative cash flow, or the property is in below par condition and the owner appears unwilling to correct any deficiencies.

It's also never a good idea to underbid yourself. Property managers deserve fair compensation.

When working for an owner, it's best to be working from a written agreement. Having a well **written management agreement** not only specifies the type of agency relationship, and hence the authority delegated to the property manager, but it also sets out the duties and responsibilities of each of the parties, as well as the compensation of the manager. If a property owner requires periodic operations reports, the management agreement can specify the format, frequency, and content of the reports.

One property management agreement is prepared by the **Texas Association of REALTORS®** for the use of its members. Property management agreements are also available from many other sources. However, regardless of the actual contract used, the management agreement should clearly represent the agreement of the parties so that there is no room for misunderstandings.

With a management agreement in place, the manager can tend to business at hand such as the active **leasing** of units to prospective tenants. This process includes the steps necessary to make the units ready for occupancy, the prequalification of tenants, the showing of the units, the formal tenant qualification, and finally the signing of the leases. The **pre-qualification process** involves determining what unit is appropriate for a particular tenant, while the qualification process is a determination whether a particular tenant can afford a particular unit. The qualification process should be a top priority for the manager.

XI. TERMINOLOGY

A. Arbitration
B. BOMA
C. Commingling
D. Employee Manager
E. General Services Administration
F. Hold Harmless Clause
G. Independent Contractor
H. Independent Property Manager

I. IREM
J. Lead-Based Paint Disclosure
K. Lessee
L. Lessor
M. Management Plan
N. Marketing Plan
O. Negative Cash Flow
P. Pro-Forma Statement
Q. Property Management Contract

R. Qualifying Tenants
S. Real Estate Investment Trust
T. Real Estate Owned (REO)
U. Self Managed Property
V. Zero Based Budgeting

1. ___ The real estate management agency for the federal government.

2. ___ An outside property management firm that is hired by a property owner to manage the owner's property.

3. ___ An employee of the owner who is hired to manage the owner's property.

4. ___ A property that is managed by the owner himself/herself.

5. ___ A large publicly traded firm which buys and manages income properties for the benefit of its stockholders.

6. ___ The portfolio of foreclosed real estate properties held by a financial institution. This portfolio of assets must be managed while it is being listed for sale by the institution.

7. ___ A written analysis of the present state of a particular property with respect to, for example, physical condition, nature of tenants, lease provisions, etc...

8. ___ A forecast budget based on projected expenses and revenue.

9. ___ A budget that requires each expense and or position be justified each year.

10. ___ An economic situation which results when more money goes out than comes into a business.

11. ___ The Building Owners and Managers Association International.

12. ___ A plan by which a property manager intends to seek prospective tenants.

13. ___ An agency agreement between a property owner and a property manager which sets out, among other things, the duties, authority and compensation of the manager.

14. ___ Mixing the property manager's funds with the funds of another person, such as the property owner.

15. ___ A disclosure required by federal law for housing designated as "target housing," such as residential units built before 1978.

16. ___ The process of determining whether a prospective tenant has the income, credit and character to be a good tenant.

17. ___ A resolution technique where a neutral third party, instead of a court, hears and rules on a dispute.

18. ___ Institute of Real Estate Management.

19. ___ A contract provision in a property management agreement whereby the property owner agrees to hold the manager harmless for damages or injuries to persons or property when the manager is carrying out provisions of the contract.

20. ___ A person or firm, not associated with the principal, that is hired on the basis of results and requires no supervision.

21. ___ A landlord or his/her agent.

22. ___ A tenant.

XII. MULTIPLE CHOICE

1. A technological advancement which made tall buildings a reality was:

    a. the elevator.
    b. reinforced concrete.
    c. structural steel.
    d. a and c.

2. If a property owner wishes to utilize the services of an property management firm, the owner would use a(n):

    a. employee manager.
    b. self managed property manager.
    c. independent property manager.
    d. personal property investment manager.

3. Property managers are often used by:

    a. the federal government.
    b. banks and financial institutions.
    c. real estate investment trusts.
    d. all of the above.

4. The main financial benefits of hiring a property manager include all of the following, except:

    a. increased rents.
    b. increased expenses.
    c. management planning.
    d. prolonging economic life.

5. A complete analysis of the owner's property is known as a:

    a. pro forma statement.
    b. budget analysis.
    c. property management plan.
    d. statement of income and expenses.

6. Which of the following is a valid reason for a property manager to refuse to manage a particular property?

    a. The property continually suffers from a negative cash flow
    b. The property is constantly facing city code violations
    c. The property manager will not be adequately compensated
    d. All of the above

7. The property manager should form an agency relationship with the property owner by means of a:

    a. handshake.
    b. complete oral understanding as to the job required.
    c. written agreement.
    d. none of the above.

8. It's a good idea to pre-qualify prospective tenants:

    a. to determine if the tenant can afford the rent.
    b. to determine how much rent to charge the tenant.
    c. in order to rent a unit quickly.
    d. none of the above.

9. The reason that a Texas residential landlord must disclose the identity of the owner is because:

    a. it is courteous to do so.
    b. it is required by law.
    c. property owners require it.
    d. property managers require it.

10. A good property manager must:

    a. place his/her interests above that of the owner.
    b. place the owner's interest above that of his/her own.
    c. place the tenant's interest above that of the owner's.
    d. all of the above.

ANSWERS: 1. d; 2. c; 3. d; 4. b; 5. c; 6. d; 7. c; 8. a; 9. b; 10. b

SUITE **10**

TEXAS AMERICAN TITLE COMPANY

NORMA J. PASCHALL
MANAGER/ESCROW OFFICER

West Island Professional Center
6511 Stewart

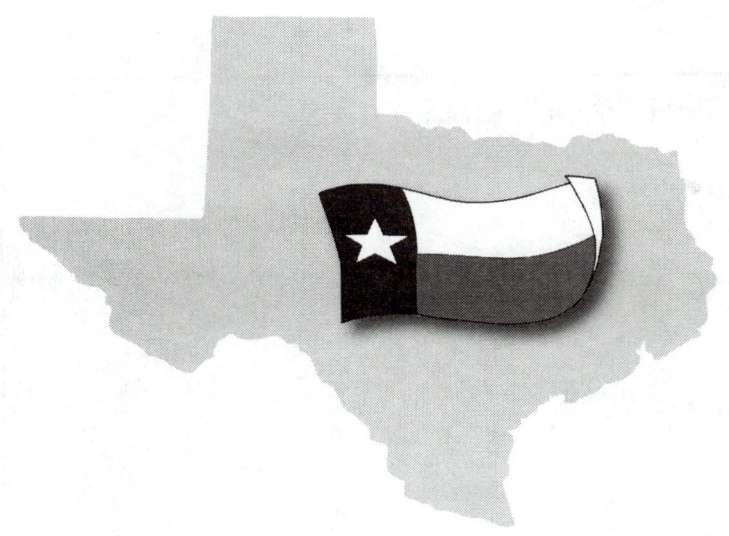

Chapter 10
Escrow, Title Insurance, and Settlement

I. The Real Estate Closing

A. THE CLOSING IN GENERAL

A real estate closing is a transaction that finalizes the real estate sales contract. It is the event which formalizes the buyer's delivery of funds to the seller and the seller's delivery of good title to the buyer. In Texas, a closing is typically held at a title insurance company.

For the parties, a real estate closing can appear to be a confusing process. From their perspective the process looks like this: the parties are asked to meet at a local title company. At the appointed place and time, the parties are then ushered into a conference room where they meet with a closing officer. The closer then pushes a mountain of paperwork before each party to review and sign. When completed, the closer smiles and hands over the keys to the buyer's new house.

Closings are not simple, but they are not as mysterious as they may appear to the parties.

CHAPTER 10 OUTLINE

What may not be obvious to the parties is that in the days or weeks since the real estate sales contract was initially forwarded to the title company, a small army of professionals has been hard at work behind the scenes to make certain that the transition of ownership goes smoothly. Typically, this means at a minimum:

1. Researching the seller's ownership and title;
2. Preparing a preliminary report of the status of title;
3. Researching property tax and insurance information;
4. Ordering tax certificates and other legal documents;
5. Requesting loan documents , if a new loan is involved;
6. Prorating expenses of sale among the parties;
7. Collecting additional funds from the buyer, if necessary;
8. Paying off the seller's existing loan;
9. Paying other expenses of sale, including broker's commissions;
10. Disbursing net proceeds to the seller;
11. Recording of legal documents;
12. Filing of federal tax forms;
13. Preparing a settlement statement;
14. Issuing a title insurance policy; and
15. Supervising the execution of all documents.

Far from being chaotic, a real estate closing is a methodical transaction that involves sufficient lead time and requires significant "behind the scenes" work.

B. REASONS FOR THE CLOSING

There are three basic reasons for holding the closing:

1. A real estate closing serves to "complete" the mutual promises made by the parties in the sales contract. That is to say, the closing serves to organize and facilitate the transfer of the title from seller to buyer, and the payment of funds from buyer to seller.

2. The closing serves to complete the lender's requirements for funding the buyer's loan.

3. The closing provides an accounting and settlement of the transaction for the benefit of both parties.

Although a closing is NOT required by Texas law, most lenders will require that the transaction be completed by means of a closing.

C. PARTIES TO THE CLOSING

1. The Seller's Role

At the closing, the seller's main role is to sign any and all documents necessary to deliver good title to the buyer. The seller will also be required to physically deliver any transferred insurance policies, appliance or home warranties, and door keys to the buyer. Finally, the seller will be required to review and approve all expenditures of sale made on his/her behalf as reflected in the settlement statement. Of course, the seller will also want to be present to receive a check for his or her net sales proceeds.

2. The Buyer's Role

The buyer's role at closing is more complex. First, if any part of the purchase price is being financed, the buyer will be required to sign all documents necessary to complete the buyer's loan. Typically, this will include, at the very least, executing a promissory note which formally evidences the debt owed to the lender and signing a Deed of Trust which grants to the lender a lien on the property.

Next, the buyer will be required at the closing to pay the unpaid balance of the purchase price and any related unpaid expenses of the sale, while receiving full credit for any earnest money previously paid and the amount financed by his/her lender. Under rules set forth by the Texas Department of Insurance, which regulates title insurance companies, title insurance companies are required to collect monies under the "good funds" rule. This is so that the title insurance company will have sufficient funds available to disburse at closing since they will not have to worry about a check bouncing. Each title company will advise its customers as to the exact type of funds required .

GOOD FUNDS generally means payment with:

1. *Cash or wire transfers,*
2. *Cashier's checks,*
3. *Certified checks,*
4. *Teller's checks,*
5. *US Treasury checks,*
6. *State of Texas warrants, and*
7. *Personal checks, traveler's checks, and money orders, provided that the combined amount of these instruments does not exceed $1,500.*

If buyers are required to pay any additional sums at closing, they should pay using "Good Funds."

Lastly, like the seller, the buyer will also be required at the closing to review the settlement statement and approve of all expenses of sale.

3. The Role of the Parties' Agents

Although the agents for the parties have no direct role in the closing, it's always a good idea for them to be present. After all, under most listing and representation agreements, a broker's commission is not earned until the property closes. As a result, the agent should be present to, at the very least, observe the proceedings, and to answer any general questions that might arise. However, the agent actually has a more important and interactive role.

First, the agent should adequately prepare his/her client before the closing to demystify the proceedings. Remember, for many people, a home purchase will be the largest single expense of their lives. Add to this the stress of having to sign dozens of forms and documents in a relatively short period to time and you may now have a frustrated and anxious client. Verbally "walking" the client through the process before the closing may relieve some of the anxiety as you prepare him/her for what is to come.

During the closing process, an agent should be on hand to very generally explain the proceedings while being very careful not to give legal advice.

Under Texas law, a broker/salesperson may face license suspension for drafting a legal document other than a sales contract, or giving advice concerning the validity of a legal document or of title to real estate.

Since these types of questions may arise during the closing, the agent should clearly advise the client to seek the advice of an attorney in order to answer any legal questions that he/she may have.

The agent's third role during the closing will be to give reassuring support to the client. This support may take the form of making last minute phone calls to repairmen on behalf of the client, arranging for the delivery of documents, helping to mediate disputes between the parties, or simply just getting a nervous client a drink of water. Remember, while a real estate closing may be old hat to you, it's new, different, and even scary for your client.

4. Attorneys

The job of giving legal advice to a party is a role left to that person's attorney. As a result, attorneys can be key participants in real estate closings. Unfortunately,

some parties do not understand the need for legal representation until a problem arises. Worse yet, some feel that their real estate agents are able to answer their legal questions.

It's never a good idea for an agent to ask his/her own lawyer to answer legal questions for a client. Nor is it a good idea to recommend a particular lawyer to them. Instead, the best practice is to urge the party to seek independent and qualified counsel early in the proceedings so that the client can determine how the attorney can best represent him/her.

5. The Closer

As a conductor leads the symphony, a **CLOSER** *directs the real estate closing*. More importantly, the closer usually handles dozens of details and coordinates all activities so that the transaction goes as smoothly as possible.

In Texas, closers or closing agents as they are sometimes called, may order and/or review title reports, surveys, property tax certificates or any number of other documents prior to closing. The closing agent will typically review and confirm the unpaid balance on all liens existing on the property so that their release can be secured. The closer will arrange for the transfer of title, and if the transaction involves financing of any sort, the closer will also work with the lender to determine the lender's requirements for funding the loan. Since only lawyers can draft legal documents such as deeds, deeds of trust, and promissory notes, closers will make arrangements with staff attorneys or outside law firms to prepare and deliver these documents to the closing office.

A closing agent will also coordinate the final settlement of sale by determining which expenses of sale have been paid, which expenses remain to be paid, and, if it's a shared expense, how the expense will be allocated, or prorated among the parties. Finally, a closer will prepare all closing documents and coordinate the closing "ceremony".

In busy Texas markets, it's not unusual for a single closing office to handle 30-40 closings in a single day in order to accommodate parties who wish to close on the last day of the month!

D. FUNDING ISSUES

It's possible that a buyer, having endured what may seem like a marathon document signing session, may not receive the keys to his/her new home upon the conclusion of the closing.

A real estate closing does not necessarily mean that the buyer is entitled to immediate possession of the property.

This is because the promulgated real estate contracts that Texas brokers and salespersons are generally required to use allow the buyer possession only after closing *and* funding.

So while the closing may have occurred, unless the buyer's loan has actually funded or other provisions have been made, such as the execution of a temporary lease, the buyer is not entitled to the keys to the property.

Suppose, for example, a third party lender requires the buyer to execute a promissory note and deed of trust at the closing. After the buyer does so, the lender may also insist upon receiving a copy of the documents before funding the loan. If the closing occurs early in the day, this may not present a problem. However, if the closing is to occur late on a Friday afternoon and the lender is located in a different time zone, funding (and thus, possession) may not occur until Monday! By the same token, the seller's net proceeds check may be held up for the same reason.

Careful agents should remind their clients that closing alone does not guarantee possession. Texas real estate contracts usually allow the buyer to possess the property only after closing and funding. The parties, once reminded of this contractual obligation, can hopefully plan accordingly.

II. Escrow Closings

A. ESCROW BASICS

An escrow is basically the process by which the seller gives his/her deed to a *neutral third party, known as an ESCROW AGENT,* to hold until such time as the buyer complies with the financing and other conditions of the contract. When those conditions have been satisfied, the escrow agent releases the deed to the buyer and pays the funds to the seller.

In Texas, most real estate closings are conducted through the escrow process.

By using a neutral third party, the seller can rest assured that that the escrow agent will not release the deed until all the conditions of the contract have been met by the buyer, and the buyer is comforted that title will not pass until such time as the seller's liens have been fully paid and released.

By closing in escrow, both parties additionally benefit because they do not have to be present at the same time for the closing to occur.

Suppose a seller cannot attend a Friday morning closing because of an upcoming business trip. On the Tuesday before the trip, the seller signs the deed and submits it to the escrow agent. By closing in escrow, the seller can go on that business trip because the closing is literally in the hands of the escrow agent.

Now, suppose further, that due to funding issues, the closing is delayed until Friday afternoon. Because deed delivery is a critical element of passage of title, when is the deed legally considered to be transferred to the buyer?

Under the "Doctrine of Relation Back," the deed is considered to have been delivered to the buyer when it was first placed into escrow.

Thus, it does not actually matter when the closing occurs. Assuming that all the requirements of the contract are met and all escrow provisions are met, the buyer's deed is considered to have been delivered when it was deposited with the escrow agent. On the other hand, should the contract provisions not be met, there will be no delivery of deed to the buyer.

B. CREATION AND OPERATION OF THE ESCROW

Escrows are opened or created when the parties agree to deposit the earnest money and/or the contract itself with the escrow agent.

In Texas, there is no written agreement between the parties which outlines exactly what the escrow agent is to do. But, under common law rules, the escrow agent, while representing neither party, owes duties of honesty and fairness to both parties.

The basic promulgated residential real estate sales contract does offer some guidance on this relationship, however. The contract states that:

1. The escrow agent is not a party to the sales contract and as such has no liability for the parties' performance or non-performance under the contract.

2. The escrow agent is not liable for the payment of any interest on earnest money paid under the contract; and

3. The escrow agent is not liable for any loss of earnest money due to the failure of a financial institution, unless the financial institution is acting as the escrow agent.

In Texas, few, if any, explicit instructions are given to escrow agents. One instruction is found, however, in the basic real estate sales contract. There, escrow agents are to instructed to apply earnest money in the following order:

1. First, to the cash down payment;
2. Next, to the buyer's expenses; and
3. Last, any surplus is to be refunded to the buyer.

Escrow agents quite frequently follow the express instructions of third party lenders who are often very specific about loan and funding requirements, hazard insurance requirements, and the payment of mortgage costs and fees, just to name a few.

In Texas, escrow agents frequently operate in the absence of a written agreement and instructions. Nevertheless, they are held to a high level of care and responsibility.

Escrow Company Reports Information to the I.R.S.

All real estate transactions must be reported to the Internal Revenue Service. This is done by the escrow company or whoever handles the the closing. A 1099 Form is required for any sale or exchange.

Escrow agents report real estate transactions to the I.R.S. using the seller's social security number.

C. TERMINATING ESCROW

The escrow is complete when: 1) all conditions of the escrow have been met; 2) all conditions of the parties have been met; and 3) the parties have received an accounting of the procedure.

During the escrow period, should the parties wish to make a change in, for example, the allocation of the purchase price or expenses of sale, the change can be put into effect at any time, provided, however, both parties are given notice of the change and both sides agree by amending the sales contract. However, if a dispute should arise, the escrow agent will not proceed until both parties come to terms. If the parties cannot agree to terms, an escrow agent will bring an interpleader action (court action) to determine where the money or consideration goes. **Figure 10-1** illustrates the three ways in which an escrow can be terminated.

D. WHO MAY SERVE AS ESCROW AGENT

In Texas, it is the principals to a real estate transaction who may decide who shall act as escrow agent. But any of the following may serve as escrow agent, if selected by the parties:

Figure 10-1

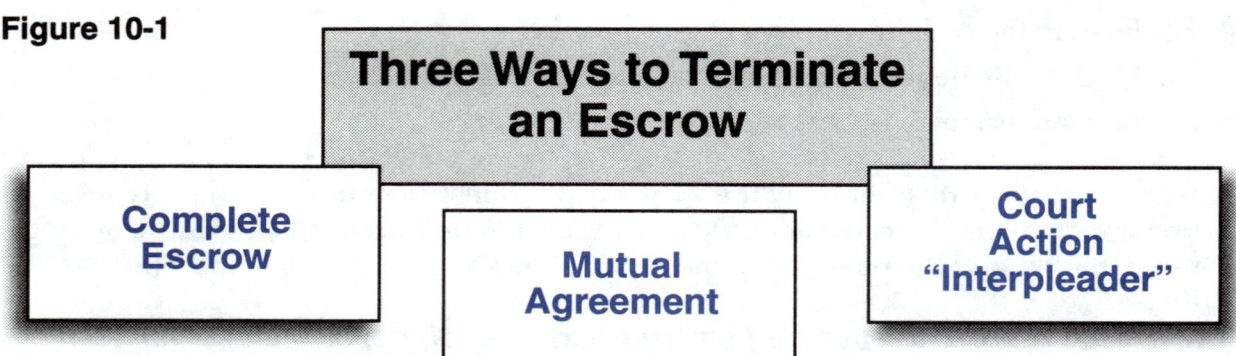

1. Corporations, such as financial institutions and bonded escrow companies may provide escrow services.

2. A Texas licensed attorney may also provide escrow services.

3. A Texas real estate broker may act as an escrow agent, provided, however, that the parties freely select the broker to serve as their escrow agent. In other words, a broker may not require his/her own selection as escrow agent as a requirement of the real estate transaction. However, insofar as an escrow agent owes duties of fair dealings and impartiality to both sides, it might not be wise for one of the brokers to serve as escrow agent. Under no circumstances may a Texas licensed salesperson serve as escrow agent.

4. Licensed Texas title insurance companies may also provide escrow services in connection with the issuance of title insurance. Under Texas law, *escrow agents, known as **ESCROW OFFICERS**,* must be licensed by the Texas Department of Insurance and are required to post a bond.

In Texas, nearly all residential closings are conducted at title insurance companies.

III. Evidence of Title

As part of the closing process, a purchaser wants assurance that:
  1) he/she is acquiring TITLE to the subject property, and
  2) the title is of sufficient quality so as to avoid legal problems of ownership in the future.

Since anyone can prepare a deed, a deed is NOT considered evidence of title. Instead, in Texas, the primary methods of providing evidence of title are:
  1) an attorney's title opinion, and/or
  2) title insurance.

A. REQUIRED BROKER'S DISCLOSURES

Texas law requires license holders to advise potential purchasers to have the title investigated prior to purchase.

Under The Real Estate License Act, when an offer to purchase is signed, brokers and salespersons must advise each buyer in writing that the buyer should either have the abstract of title examined by an attorney or obtain a title insurance policy.

The law does not require purchasers to choose between a lawyer's opinion or a title insurance policy. Instead, that decision is left up to the lender, who will most likely require title examination as a condition to making the loan. But, if brokers and salespersons do not make this written disclosure to the purchaser, then it is a ground of license suspension.

Texas purchasers are well advised to follow their broker's advice and have the title "researched and reviewed" prior to closing.

B. ABSTRACT OF TITLE AND ATTORNEY'S OPINION

Abstract of title: a written summary of a property's documents that evidences title.

When one person sells a property to another person, *a recorded public history of a specific property, called the* **CHAIN OF TITLE**, is compiled. By reviewing the chain of title, an analyst can trace the ownership of a particular tract of land from the earliest of times to the present day owner. Ideally, an examination of the abstract should result in one continuous succession of ownership. But it is equally important to determine if there exists, for example, any "broken" links to the chain of title, known as gaps in title, or any unexpected additional links.

An attorney's legal opinion of title based on a review of the abstract of title can be a powerful tool in determining the nature and quality of ownership being passed to the purchaser. It can also be used to determine what corrective action, if any, should be taken so that the purchaser does receive good title.

Although legal title opinions are still used regularly in rural parts of the state, **they are not considered to be the preferred manner of providing evidence of title**. Even the most careful and comprehensive opinion of title offers the purchaser limited financial protection in the event of title problems. **That's why a title insurance policy offers the consumer more protection**. With title insurance the same careful title research is conducted, however, now the research is backed up with an indemnifying insurance policy.

C. TITLE INSURANCE

Unlike an attorney's title opinion, a "title insurance policy" protects the property owner against financial loss due to hidden liens, encumbrances or other defects in title. It also serves to protect third party lenders by insuring against the impairment of their liens.

Title insurance policies are widely available throughout Texas. Because they offer broader protection compared to just an attorney's title opinion, title insurance policies are a popular method of providing evidence of title.

1. Title Insurance Basics

Title insurers, working though **underwriters**, examine the record documenting the chain of title so as to correct any defects, and insure title to the property. **Figure 10-2** emphasizes the four most important functions of title insurance.

Figure 10-2

Title Insurance

| A SEARCH OF RECORDS | EXAMINES "OFF" RECORD RISKS | INTERPRETS LEGALITY OF RECORDS | INSURES AGAINST ECONOMIC LOSS |

But, unlike other types of insurance policies which protect against occurrences in the future, a title policy protects against events which have happened in the past. Furthermore, such protection is based upon the payment of a one time insurance premium payable at closing.

A title insurance policy will NOT guarantee that the purchaser will be able to later sell the property for a profit nor will it even guarantee continued ownership in the event of a claim. It will, however, provide coverage as provided in the policy, but only up to the "original purchase price" of the property.

Title insurance companies are regulated by the Texas Department of Insurance and, as such, policies are issued on standardized forms and subject to regulated premiums. Fee schedules for title insurance are based upon a sliding scale and are generally available to the public upon request. To guarantee solvency, each title insurance company must set aside reserves. **Figure 10-3** shows the closing process at a title company.

Figure 10-3   ## The Closing Process

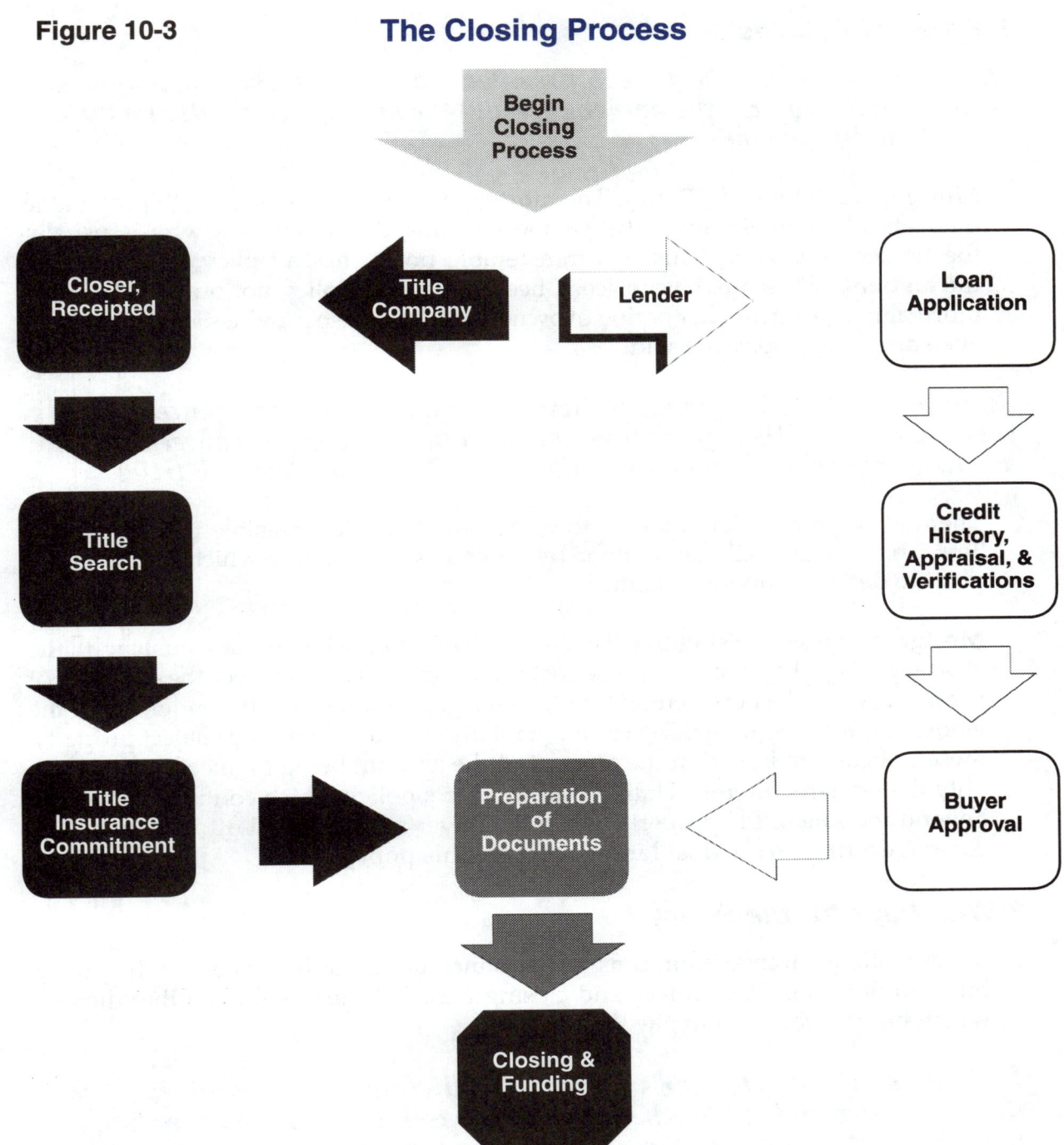

2. Types of Policies

There are generally two types of residential policies: the mortgagor's policy which protects the homebuyer and the mortgagee's policy which protects only the lender.

Mortgagor's (Owner's) Policy. The mortgagor's policy is designed to protect the interests of the mortgagor (the person granting the mortgage), who is usually the homeowner-to-be. This non-transferable policy has a policy limit equal to the amount of the purchase price. Once issued, this policy not only protects the mortgagor during his/her period of ownership, but it also provides legal protection even after the property is sold!

By issuing a title insurance policy, the insurer is not guaranteeing to the owner that title is perfect—no title company can guarantee that— but rather that the owner has GOOD AND INDEFEASIBLE title.

There is no precise definition as to what "good and indefeasible title" means in Texas, but it's generally understood by the courts to mean title which is sufficiently good to defeat competing claims.

Mortgagee's (Lender's) Policy. This policy is often issued simultaneously with the mortgagor's policy for a nominal cost and is intended to protect the interests of the mortgagee (the person receiving the mortgage), known as the lender. Since the lender is interested in making certain it retains a valid lien on the subject property, these policies are issued in the amount of the amount being financed and protect only the lender's interest. Unlike a mortgagor's policy which continues coverage beyond the sale of the property, when the buyer's loan is paid off, this insurance coverage terminates. (**Most lenders require this policy.**)

3. Who Pays for the Policy?

By law, title insurance premiums in Texas include not only the cost of the policy, but also title examination fees and closing fees. But there is no law that dictates which party is required to pay this cost.

The cost of the mortgagor's (owner's) policy is a negotiable expense item to be determined by the parties, themselves. On the other hand, the real estate contract specifies that the mortgagee's (lender's) policy is an expense that the purchaser will have to pay.

4. The Title Commitment

The first step towards the issuance of a title insurance policy is the delivery of the title commitment.

A *TITLE COMMITMENT* is not the title policy. Instead, it is a commitment by the title insurance company, valid for 90 days, to issue a policy of title insurance based upon certain exclusions, conditions, and stipulations, which are carefully laid out for the buyer to read.

The biggest mistake a buyer can make is to ignore the information contained in the commitment.

Under the promulgated residential sales contracts, the commitment must be delivered to the buyer within 20 days of when the title company receives the contract into escrow. A blank title commitment is shown in **Figure 10-4**.

The standard Texas title commitment contains the following sections.

a. Schedule A

This schedule contains some basic information about the transaction. For example, this schedule identifies:

1. The name of the proposed insured;
2. The proposed policy amount;
3. The interest in land to be sold (typically, "Fee Simple");
4. The name of the property owner (hopefully, this is the same as the person selling the property);
5. A legal description of the property to be sold; and
6. The "GF" number of the transaction. In this case, GF stands for Guaranty File and it's the reference number assigned to this transaction by the title company. Use this number when communicating with the title company about this particular transaction.

b. Schedule B

The purpose of Schedule B in the title commitment (as well as the eventual title policy) is to reveal to the purchaser proposed exceptions to coverage.

"Exceptions" to coverage are NOT the same as "exclusions" to coverage.

EXCLUSIONS are items or conditions that insurance companies simply will never cover, for example, a loss of title due to eminent domain. EXCEPTIONS will also not be insured, but since they are items unique to this property, it is possible they may be removed completely.

Figure 10-4

THE FOLLOWING COMMITMENT FOR TITLE INSURANCE IS NOT VALID UNLESS YOUR NAME AND THE POLICY AMOUNT ARE SHOWN IN SCHEDULE A, AND OUR AUTHORIZED REPRESENTATIVE HAS COUNTERSIGNED BELOW.

COMMITMENT FOR TITLE INSURANCE

Issued by

We (_____) will issue our title insurance policy or policies (the Policy) to You (the proposed insured) upon payment of the premium and other charges due, and compliance with the requirements in Schedule B and Schedule C. Our policy will be in the form approved by the Texas Department of Insurance at the date of issuance, and will insure your interest in the land described in Schedule A. The estimated premium for our Policy and applicable endorsements is shown on Schedule D. There may be additional charges such as recording fees, and expedited delivery expenses.

This Commitment ends ninety (90) days from the effective date, unless the Policy is issued sooner, or failure to issue the Policy is our fault. Our liability and obligations to you are under the express terms of this Commitment and end when this Commitment expires.

_____

By:_____
ATTEST:

_____
                Secretary

_____
                                    Authorized Signatory

CONDITIONS AND STIPULATIONS

1. If you have actual knowledge of any matter which may affect the title or mortgage covered by this Commitment, that is not shown in Schedule B, you must notify us in writing. If you do not notify us in writing, our liability to you is ended or reduced to the extent that your failure to notify us affects our liability. If you do notify us, or we learn of such matter, we may amend Schedule B, but we will not be relieved of liability already incurred.

2. Our liability is only to you, and others who are included in the definition of Insured in the Policy to be issued. Our liability is only for actual loss incurred in your reliance on this Commitment to comply with its requirements, or to acquire the interest in the land. Our liability is limited to the amount shown in Schedule A of this Commitment and will be subject to the following terms of the Policy: Insuring Provisions, Conditions and Stipulations, and Exclusions.

(continued)

SCHEDULE A

Effective Date:_____   GF

No._____

Commitment No._____, issued _____, 20 ___,

_____m.

1. The policy or polices to be issued are:

   (a) OWNER POLICY OF TITLE INSURANCE (Form T-1)
      (Not applicable for improved one-to-four family residential real estate)

      Policy Amount: $
      PROPOSED INSURED:

   (b) TEXAS RESIDENTIAL OWNER POLICY OF TITLE INSURANCE
      ----ONE-TO-FOUR FAMILY RESIDENCES (Form T-1R)
      Policy Amount: $
      PROPOSED INSURED:

   (c) MORTGAGEE POLICY OF TITLE INSURANCE (Form T-2)
      Policy Amount: $
      PROPOSED INSURED:
      Proposed Borrower:

   (d) TEXAS SHORT FORM RESIDENTIAL MORTGAGEE POLICY OF TITLE
      INSURANCE (Form T-2R)
      Policy Amount: $
      PROPOSED INSURED:
      Proposed Borrower:

   (e) MORTGAGEE TITLE POLICY BINDER ON INTERIM CONSTRUCTION LOAN
      (Form T-13)
      Binder Amount: $
      PROPOSED INSURED:
      Proposed Borrower:

   (f) OTHER
      Policy Amount: $
      PROPOSED INSURED:

2. The interest in the land covered by this Commitment is:
3. Record title to the land on the Effective Date appears to be vested in:
4. Legal description of the land:

                                                    (continued)

SCHEDULE B
EXCEPTIONS FROM COVERAGE

In addition to the Exclusions and Conditions and Stipulations, your Policy will not cover loss, costs, attorney's fees, and expenses resulting from:

1. The following restrictive covenants of record itemized below (We must either insert specific recording data or delete this exception):
2. Any discrepancies, conflicts, or shortages in area or boundary lines, or any encroachments or protrusions, or any overlapping of improvements.
3. Homestead or community property or survivorship rights, if any of any spouse of any insured. (Applies to the Owner Policy only.)
4. Any titles or rights asserted by anyone, including, but not limited to, persons, the public, corporations, governments or other entites,
   a. to tidelands, or lands comprising the shores or beds of navigable or perennial rivers and streams, lakes, bays, gulfs or oceans, or
   b. to lands beyond the line of the harbor or bulkhead lines as established or changed by any government, or
   c. to filled-in lands, or artificial islands, or
   d. to statutory water rights, including riparian rights, or
   e. to the area extending from the line of mean low tide to the line of vegetation, or the rights of access to that area or easement along and across that area.
5. Standby fees, taxes and assessments by any taxing authority for the year ____, and subsequent years; and subsequent taxes and assessments by any taxing authority for prior years due to change in land usage or ownership, but not those taxes or assessments for prior years because of an exemption granted to a previous owner of the property under Section 11.13, Texas Tax Code, or because of improvements not assessed for a previous tax year. (If Texas Short Form Residential Mortgagee Policy of Title Insurance (T-2R) is issued, that policy will substitute "which become due and payable subsequent to Date of Policy" in lieu of "for the year ____ and subsequent years.")
6. The terms and conditions of the documents creating your interest in the land.
7. Materials furnished or labor performed in connection with planned construction before signing and delivering the lien document described in Schedule A, if the land is part of the homestead of the owner. (Applies to the Mortgagee Title Policy binder on Interim Construction Loan only, and may be deleted if satisfactory evidence is furnished to us before a binder is issued.)
8. Liens and leases that affect the title to the land, but that ere subordinate to the lien of the insured mortgage. (Applies to Mortgagee Policy (T-2) only.)
9. The Exceptions from Coverage and Express Insurance in Schedule B of the Texas Short Form Residential Mortgagee Policy of Title Insurance (T-2R). (Applies to Texas Short Form Residential Mortgagee Policy of Title Insurance (T-2R) only. Separate exceptions 1 through 8 of this Schedule B do not apply to the Texas Short Form Residential Mortgagee Policy of Title Insurance (T-2R).
10. The following matters and all terms of the documents creating or offering evidence of the matters (We must insert matters or delete this exception.):

(continued)

SCHEDULE C

Your Policy will not cover loss, costs, attorneys fees, and expenses resulting from the following requirements that will appear as Exceptions in Schedule B of the Policy, unless you dispose of these matters to our satisfaction, before the date the Policy is issued:

1. Documents creating your title or interest must be approved by us and must be signed, notarized and filed for record.

2. Satisfactory evidence must be provided that:

   ---no person occupying the land claims any interest in that land against the persons named in paragraph 3 of Schedule A,

   ---all standby fees, taxes, assessments and charges against the property have been paid,

   ---all improvements or repairs to the property are completed and accepted by the owner, and that all contractors, sub-contractors, laborers and suppliers have been fully paid, and that no mechanic's, laborer's or materialmen's liens have attached to the property,

   ---there is legal right of access to and from the land,

   ---(on a Mortgagee Policy only) restrictions have not been and will not be violated that affect the validity and priority of the insured mortgage.

3. You must pay the seller or borrower the agreed amount for your property or interest.

4. Any defect, lien or other mater that may affect title to the land or interest insured, that arises or is filed after the effective date of this Commitment.

(Form T-7: Commitment for Title Insurance)

Here is a summary of the standard **exceptions** typically listed in Schedule B:

1. Restrictive covenants, if any, on the property;

2. Problems with shortages in area or boundary lines, or encroachments/ protrusions on the subject property. However, by providing a property survey to the title company and paying an additional premium, this exclusion can be removed from the title policy thus affording the homeowner additional protection;

3. Any homestead or community property rights held by the spouse of the buyer;

4. Any water rights held by third parties, including governments;

5. Property taxes and assessments;

6. Any liens created as a result of the purchase of this property; and

7. Any junior liens or leases that affect the property, if any.

Just because something is listed as an exception to coverage does NOT necessarily mean it will be a problem for the new owner. It's possible something listed here will never be a problem for the new property owner; just the same, it will not be covered.

c. Schedule C

This schedule contains a listing of all currently existing mortgage liens, property tax and IRS liens, state and federal judgment liens, and other significant title issues. For example, if the seller has granted a lien in favor of his/her lender, it will be listed here. The title company will also require that it be paid off completely before this title policy is issued.

It is essential that the buyer carefully read the commitment "prior to closing" so that he/she may understand any title issues that may exist on the subject property. A buyer who does not understand the title commitment would be very wise to hire an attorney at this time.

IV. Real Estate Settlement Procedures Act (RESPA)

RESPA allows borrowers to shop for settlement services. The law covers first loans on one-to-four unit residential dwellings.

The **REAL ESTATE SETTLEMENT PROCEDURES ACT (RESPA)** *is a federal law for the sale or transfer of one-to-four residential units requiring: 1) specific procedures and 2) forms for settlements (closing costs) involving most home loans from financial institutions with federally insured deposits, including FHA and VA loans.*

This law, although amended several times, states that the closing settlement cost of a real estate transaction must be made known to the borrower, on or before the settlement date, although, at the buyer's request, it must be provided one business day before escrow closes.

Before this law was passed, buyers were unaware of the exact amount needed until the actual escrow closing day. Sometimes the buyers were surprised to find that more money than expected was needed to complete the procedure. The current law alleviates this problem.

RESPA disclosure requirements are for federally related lenders. This means almost all lenders.

Other provisions required by the Real Estate Settlement Procedures Act include the following:

1. At the time of loan application, or within three business days, the lender must give a good faith estimate of the total closing charges to the borrower.
2. At the same time, the lender must furnish the buyer with an information booklet.
3. The escrow agent must give a uniform settlement statement to the borrower, the seller, and the lender. It must be furnished by the time of settlement, except when the borrower waives it, or in areas where the HUD (Department of Housing and Urban Development) permits a later date for supplying it.

The settlement statement must be delivered on or before the date of settlement, at no charge. The buyer can request it one business day before closing.

4. Individuals are prohibited from receiving kickbacks and unearned fees. Payments to cooperating brokerages and referral agreements between brokers are exempt.
5. No seller may require a buyer to purchase title insurance from any particular company as a condition of sale. However, because many new home builders, for example, have an ownership interest in or a close working relationship with a particular title insurance company, the seller may sometimes "strongly urge" that a particular company be used.

There are penalties for "kickbacks" and unearned fees. The seller may request a particular title insurer, but only the buyer can require a specific insurance company.

V. Settlement

"Settlement" is the final accounting of all charges, credits and other expenses between a seller and buyer of real estate.

The real estate closing serves not only to pass title from seller to buyer, but also to settle all accounts between the parties.

Obviously, the seller is interested in receiving at closing a check for his/her net proceeds from the sale, after the proper deduction for all expenses and costs that the seller is responsible for paying. On the other hand, the buyer wants assurance that he/she is receiving the full credit for earnest money previously paid and all sums to be financed, as well as the proper allocation of the buyer's expenses. Since the buyer cannot normally finance 100% of the sales price and closing costs, he/she will want to know how much

more money is needed at the closing table. **Figure 10-5** illustrates the HUD-1 settlement form in a hypothetical real estate transaction where all the accounting is done.

A. DOUBLE ENTRY BOOKKEEPING

The HUD-1 statement is an example of **DOUBLE ENTRY BOOKKEEPING**, *which is a type of accounting system used to balance and complete the buyer's and seller's part of the form.* For both the buyer's and seller's portion of the balance sheet, each party is entitled to debits and credits.

A **DEBIT** *is money that is owed or taken away.* As an example, think of a debit card. A debit entry for a buyer is anything charged against or subtracted from his or her account. The purchase price of the property is an example of something debited to the buyer. A debit entry for the seller means the same thing. A good example might be unpaid property taxes.

A **CREDIT** *is money that is received.* A credit entry for a buyer is anything received or added to his or her account. The earnest money paid by the buyer is a good example of a buyer's credit. A good example of a credit entry for the seller would be prepaid property taxes.

See Chapter 17 for a more detailed explanation on how to manually compute debits and credits.

B. THE SETTLEMENT STATEMENT

1. Basic Organization

Although it may look complicated, the HUD-1 settlement statement is fairly straightforward. At the top of the first page in boxes B through I are some basic information regarding this transaction, such as the type of loan and the identity of the parties. Note, that while the seller is identified, there is no buyer. Instead, the buyer is referred to as the "borrower."

Sections J and K are merely summaries of both the borrower's and seller's transaction and will be further explained below. Page 2 of the settlement statement contains an itemization of the expenses of sale and allocates the expense to one or both of the parties. The basic question of "who pays for what" shouldn't come as a surprise to anyone. The answer should have been set out in the basic sales contract.

2. Who Pays for What?

The sales contract contains the blueprint of the entire transaction and specifies the expenses that the parties will be responsible for paying at the closing.

Figure 10-5

OMB No. 2502-0265

A. Settlement Statement

U.S. Department of Housing
and Urban Development

B. Type of Loan

			6. File Number	7. Loan Number	8. Mortgage Ins Case Number
1. ☐ FHA	2. ☐ FmHA	3. ☐ Conv Unins	TR05-314145	12345	
4. ☐ VA	5. ☒ Conv Ins.	6. ☐ Seller Finance			

C. Note: This form is furnished to give you a statement of actual settlement costs. Amounts paid to and by the settlement agent are shown. Items marked "(p.o.c.)" were paid outside the closing; they are shown here for informational purposes and are not included in the totals.

D. Name & Address of Borrower	E. Name & Address of Seller	F. Name & Address of Lender
Bob B. Buyer 1234 Oak Street Dallas, TX 75000	Sam S. Seller and Sandra Seller 5432 W. Pine Street Dallas, TX 75000	Acme Lending, Inc. 444 Main Street Dallas, TX 75000

G. Property Location	H. Settlement Agent Name Title, Inc.	
Woodland Village, Block A, Lot 99, Dallas County 5432 W. Pine Street Smithtown, TX 75000	Place of Settlement Title, Inc. 987 W. Main Street Anytown, TX 75000	I. Settlement Date 8/15/2005 Fund:

J. Summary of Borrower's Transaction		K. Summary of Seller's Transaction	
100. Gross Amount Due from Borrower		**400. Gross Amount Due to Seller**	
101. Contract Sales Price	$450,000.00	401. Contract Sales Price	$450,000.00
102. Personal Property		402. Personal Property	
103. Settlement Charges to borrower	$12,723.29	403.	
104. HOA dues / transfer		404.	
105.		405.	
Adjustments for items paid by seller in advance		**Adjustments for items paid by seller in advance**	
106. City property taxes		406. City property taxes	
107. County property taxes		407. County property taxes	
108. Annual assessments		408. Annual assessments	
109. School property taxes		409. School property taxes	
110. MUD taxes		410. MUD taxes	
111. All Taxes		411. All Taxes	
112.		412.	
113.		413.	
114.		414.	
115.		415.	
116.		416.	
120. Gross Amount Due From Borrower	$462,723.29	**420. Gross Amount Due to Seller**	$450,000.00
200. Amounts Paid By Or in Behalf Of Borrower		**500. Reductions in Amount Due to Seller**	
201. Deposit or earnest money	$1,000.00	501. Excess Deposit	
202. Principal amount of new loan(s)	$450,000.00	502. Settlement Charges to Seller (line 1400)	$30,370.00
203. Existing loan(s) taken subject to		503. Existing Loan(s) Taken Subject to	
204. Commitment fee		504. Payoff of first mortgage loan	$103,800.00
205.		505. Payoff of second mortgage loan	
206.		506.	
207.		507.	
208.		508.	
209.		509.	
Adjustments for items unpaid by seller		**Adjustments for items unpaid by seller**	
210. City property taxes 01/01/05 thru 08/15/05	$932.88	510. City property taxes 01/01/05 thru 08/15/05	$932.88
211. County property taxes 01/01/05 thru 08/15/05	$1,243.84	511. County property taxes 01/01/05 thru 08/15/05	$1,243.84
212. Annual assessments		512. Annual assessments	
213. School property taxes 01/01/05 thru 08/15/05	$1,865.75	513. School property taxes 01/01/05 thru 08/15/05	$1,865.75
214. MUD taxes		514. MUD taxes	
215. All Taxes		515. All Taxes	
216.		516.	
217.		517.	
218.		518.	
219.		519.	
220. Total Paid By/For Borrower	$455,042.47	**520. Total Reduction Amount Due Seller**	$138,212.47
300. Cash At Settlement From/To Borrower		**600. Cash At Settlement To/From Seller**	
301. Gross Amount due from borrower (line 120)	$462,723.29	601. Gross Amount due to seller (line 420)	$450,000.00
302. Less amounts paid by/for borrower (line 220)	$455,042.47	602. Less reductions in amt. due seller (line 520)	$138,212.47
303. Cash From Borrower	$7,680.82	603. Cash To Seller	$311,787.53

Previous Editions are Obsolete   Page 1   form HUD-1 (3/86)
Handbook 4305.2

File No. TR05-314145

L. Settlement Charges

700. Total Sales/Broker's Commission based on price $450,000.00 @6 % = $27,000.00		Paid From Borrower's Funds at Settlement	Paid From Seller's Funds at Settlement
Division of Commission (line 700) as follows:			
701. $13,500.00	to **Residential Brokerage**		
702. $13,500.00	to **ABC Realty**		
703. Commission Paid at Settlement		$0.00	$27,000.00
704. The following persons, firms or corp.	to		
705. received a portion of the real estate	to		
706. commission amount shown above:	to		
800. Items Payable in Connection with Loan			
801. Loan Origination Fee 1%	to **Acme Lending, Inc.**	$4,500.00	
802. Loan Discount %	to		
803. Appraisal Fee	to **Acme Lending, Inc.**	$500.00	
804. Credit Report	to **Acme Lending, Inc.**	$50.00	
805. Lender's Inspection Fee	to		
806. Mortgage Insurance Application	to		
807. Processing Fee	to **Acme Lending, Inc.**	$300.00	
808. Underwriting Fee	to **Acme Lending, Inc.**	$500.00	
900. Items Required by Lender To Be Paid in Advance			
901. Interest from 8/4/2005 to 9/1/2005 @ $20.03/day		$560.84	
902. Mortgage Insurance Premium for months to			
903. Hazard Insurance Premium for 1 years	to **Anystate Insurance**	$1,111.00	
1000. Reserves Deposited With Lender			
1001. Hazard insurance	2 months @ $99.00 per month	$198.00	
1002. Mortgage insurance	months @ per month		
1003. City property taxes	6 months @ $100.00 per month	$600.00	
1004. County property taxes	6 months @ $200.00 per month	$1,200.00	
1005. Annual assessments	months @ per month		
1006. School property taxes	6 months @ $300.00 per month	$1,800.00	
1007. MUD taxes	months @ per month		
1008. All Taxes	months @ per month		
1011. Aggregate Adjustment			
1100. Title Charges			
1101. Settlement or closing fee	to		
1102. Abstract or title search	to		
1103. Title examination	to		
1104. Title insurance binder	to		
1105. Document preparation	to		
1106. Notary fees	to		
1107. Attorney's fees	to		
(includes above items numbers:)			
1108. Title insurance	to **Title, Inc.**	$595.45	$2,803.00
(includes above items numbers:)			
1109. Lender's coverage	$450,000.00/$595.45		
1110. Owner's coverage	$450,000.00/$2,803.00		
1111. Escrow fee	to **Title, Inc.**	$200.00	$200.00
1112. Courier fees	to **Title, Inc.**	$50.00	$50.00
1113. State of Texas Policy Guaranty Fees	to **Title, Inc.**	$1.00	$1.00
1114. Restrictions/Copies	to **Title, Inc.**	$23.00	
1200. Government Recording and Transfer Charges			
1201. Recording fees Deed $31.00 ; Mortgage $48.00 ; Rel $16.00	to **Title, Inc.**	$79.00	$16.00
1202. City/county tax/stamps Deed ; Mortgage	to		
1203. State tax/stamps Deed ; Mortgage	to		
1204. Tax Certificates (prepared by:	to		
1205. Certified Tax Services	to **Title, Inc.**	$60.00	
1206. Additional Recording Fees	to		
1207. Electronic Recording Fees	to **Title, Inc.**		
1300. Additional Settlement Charges			
1301. Survey	to **ABC Survey Co.**	$350.00	
1302. Pest inspection	to		
1303. Home Warranty	to **Home Warranty Company**	$45.00	$300.00
1400. Total Settlement Charges (enter on lines 103, Section J and 502, Section K)		$12,723.29	$30,370.00

I have carefully reviewed the HUD-1 Settlement Statement and to the best of my knowledge and belief, it is a true and accurate statement of all receipts and disbursements made on my account or by me in this transaction. I further certify that I have received a completed copy of pages 1, 2 and 3 of this HUD-1 Settlement Statement.

Bob B. Buyer   Sam S. Seller

SETTLEMENT AGENT CERTIFICATION
The HUD-1 Settlement Statement which I have prepared is a true and accurate account of this transaction. I have caused the funds to be disbursed in accordance with this statement.   Sandra Seller

Settlement Agent _____ _____ Date

Warning: It is a crime to knowingly make false statements to the United States on this or any other similar form. Penalties upon conviction can include a fine and imprisonment. For details see: Title 18 U.S. Code Section 1001 and Section 1010.

Previous Editions are Obsolete

form **HUD-1** (3/86)
Handbook 4305.2

Using the promulgated TREC residential contract, here are some examples of seller's expenses:

a. Releases of existing liens (including pre-payment penalties and recording fees);

b. Expenses related to releasing seller's loan liability;

c. Tax statements or certificates;

d. Preparation of deed;

e. 50% of the escrow fee; and

f. Any other expense the seller has agreed to pay.

Here are some examples of buyer's expenses as used in the TREC residential contract:

a. Loan fees (loan origination, discount, buy-down and loan commitment fees);

b. Appraisal fees, loan application fees, credit reports, the cost of all loan documents, recording fees and generally any other expense relating to obtaining the loan;

c. Mortgagee's title insurance policy;

d. 50% of the escrow fee; and

e. Any other expense the buyer has agreed to pay.

It's always a good idea to double check the expenses set out in the contract against those contained on page 2 of the settlement statement.

3. The Borrower's Transaction

The borrower's transaction as contained in section J of the settlement statement can be summed up in the following manner:

	Action	Statement Line
Step 1:	Pay contract sales price + borrower's share of expenses = Total sum borrower must pay	(Line 120)
Step 2:	Earnest money already paid + sum of all financing for this purchase = Total sum of borrower's funds thus far	(Line 220)

Step 3:   Total sum borrower must pay (from step 1)
           <u>(less) Total sum paid thus far (from step 2)</u>
           Amount borrower needs to pay (or refund)   (Line 303)

The buyer wants to determine: 1) how much he/she is obligated to pay; 2) if he/she is getting full credit for sums already paid; and 3) how much more, if anything, does he/she need to bring to the closing table.

4. The Seller's Transaction

The seller's transaction is summarized in section K. Here's a breakdown of this side of the balance sheet.

	Action	Statement Line
Step 1:	Receive full contract sales price <u>+ any adjustments to sales price</u> = Total sum seller will receive	(Line 420)
Step 2:	Seller's share of expenses <u>+ pay off of all existing liens</u> = Total amount of deductions	(Line 520)
Step 3:	Total sum seller should receive (from step 1) <u>(less) Total sum of deductions (from step 2)</u> Net proceeds payable to seller	(Line 603)

The seller's net proceeds are calculated by determining how much the seller is entitled to receive under the contract, less expenses of sale and the payoff of any existing liens.

C. PRORATION FUNDAMENTALS

PRORATION is the process of proportionately dividing expenses or income to the precise date that the sale closes, or any other date previously agreed upon.

In preparing the settlement statement, it is often necessary to prorate certain expenses which relate solely to the property. Since the payment dates for these types of expenses fall at various times throughout the year, it is only fair that if the seller has paid the expense, he/she be reimbursed at closing by the buyer. And if the expense is to be paid by the buyer sometime after closing, it's only fair that the buyer collect money from the seller. What follows then are some basic rules involving prorations. See Chapter 17 for some math problems involving prorations.

1. Not All Expenses are Prorated

As was discussed earlier in this chapter, not all expenses are subject to proration. As stated above, the real estate sales contract allocates certain expenses to buyer or seller. However, there are yet other agreements which may require payment from just one of the parties. For example, the obligation to pay a broker's commission is usually contained in a listing or buyer's representation agreement. By the same token, there may be other contracts which require just one of the parties to pay. Often these expenses are included in the settlement statement as a line item on page 2 but sometimes they are simply shown as *"POC," which means, "paid outside of closing."*

If the sales or other contract stipulates that just one party pay an expense of sale, it's not a prorated expense.

2. Prorated Expenses

Expense items that are commonly prorated include the following:

   a. property taxes,
   b. homeowner association dues,
   c. interest on assumed loans, and
   d. rental payments from the subject property.

If the buyer is obtaining a new mortgage loan, the interest on the new loan would not be prorated because it is an expense required of the buyer under the buyer's new loan documents. But, if the seller's loan is being assumed by the buyer, the expense is prorated because the obligation to pay interest is being passed from the seller to the buyer.

Rental payments are also prorated. But what if the property being sold is a rented duplex where each of the tenants has paid a $1,000 security deposit. How are security deposits prorated? The answer is, they are not.

Security deposits are passed intact from the seller who received the deposits to the buyer.

3. Manner and Frequency of Expense Payment

The third step regarding prorations is to understand the normal manner and frequency of the prorated expense item. This involves knowing two things about each type of proratable expense: 1) whether the expense is typically paid on a monthly or yearly basis, and 2) within that time frame, if the expense is typically paid up-front or at the end of the typical accounting period.

Rents and mortgage interest are paid on a monthly basis, while property taxes are paid yearly. This is a key fact to know because the accounting period will determine if the person making the calculations will have to take into account a single month or a full year.

It is also necessary to know if the expense is typically paid at the beginning of the accounting period or at the end. For example, suppose a person is employed at a factory and is a paid monthly. *That person will receive his/her first paycheck after having worked an entire month. The worker has received his money in ARREARS.* Although it is also possible that the employee could have been *paid up-front, or on an ACCRUED basis,* that's not very likely because that's not the way wages are paid. By the same token, for every expense item to be prorated, it's necessary to know whether the expense was paid on an accrued or arrears basis.

Homeowners' association dues and rental payments received from tenants are examples of expenses that are typically paid up-front (accrued), or in advance, at the beginning of the accounting term. On the other hand, mortgage interest on assumed loans and property taxes are paid in arrears.

4. The Date of Closing

The information necessary to calculate the proration is nearly complete. We now understand from this section:

  a. The expenses normally subject to proration are taxes, insurance, mortgage interest on assumed loans, and rental payments received;

  b. Depending on the expense, it is paid either monthly or annually;

  c. Some expenses are paid in arrears while others are accrued expenses.

Who owns the property on the day of closing?

If the contract states that prorations are to be made **"to the day of closing,"** the **buyer** is the owner for that day.

But if the contract states **"through the date of closing,"** then the **seller** is the owner for that day.

All that is needed to conduct the actual calculation is to know the amount of the expense and the date of closing. The actual calculation is explained further in Chapter 17 of this book, but it's rather straightforward. Based on the date of closing, count the number of days that "belong" to the subject party and do a simple calculation to determine how much of this expense fairly belongs to the subject party.

The last question, then, involves the actual date of closing. For proration purposes, who owns the property on the closing date? The answer again is found in the TREC promulgated sales contract which provides that expenses are to be prorated "through the date of closing."

According to the contract, prorations are made "through the closing date," meaning that on (and through) the day of closing, the property belongs to the seller.

As a result, if a closing occurs on the 10th day of the month, for proration purposes, the house belongs to the seller on that day, even though the buyer will be the new owner at the conclusion of the closing meeting.

VI. CHAPTER SUMMARY

The **closing** is the transaction that finalizes the real estate sales contract. It formalizes the buyer's delivery of funds and the seller's delivery of good title. In Texas, closings are usually held at **title companies**.

Although it may appear to be confusing to the parties, a real estate closing is quite methodical and is the result of a lot of hard work. The **closer** orders tax certificates, determines loan pay-offs, delivers the title report to the buyer, requests new loan documents, prepares the settlement statement and provides a number of valuable functions to the parties.

The three main reasons for a closing are: 1) the closing serves to "complete" the contractual obligations of the parties to deliver funds in exchange for the title; 2) the closing additionally completes the lender's requirements for the buyer's new loan; and 3) the closing provides an accounting or settlement of the transaction.

Escrow is basically the process by which a seller gives his/her deed to a **neutral third party**, the **escrow agent**, to hold until such time as the buyer complies with the financing and other conditions of the contract. By using an escrow agent, the seller can rest assured that title will not be delivered until the loan has been funded, and the buyer knows that the funds will not be paid until the seller's liens have been paid and released.

By closing in escrow, the parties do not have to be present at the same time for the closing to occur. They may close separately. Under the **doctrine of relation back**, the seller's deed will be considered to have been delivered to the buyer when the deed was first placed with the escrow agent.

In Texas, no written agreement is necessary to create an escrow. The escrow is created when the contract and earnest money, if any, are deposited with the escrow agent. Despite the lack of a written agreement, escrow agents are held to a very high level of care and responsibility. Escrows will be considered complete when: 1) all the conditions of the escrow have been met; 2) the conditions of the parties have been met; and 3) a settlement has been made.

If a dispute arises that cannot be easily resolved, the escrow agent may **interplead** disputed funds with a court so that the parties may legally fight it out there.

In Texas, corporations, attorneys, and even brokers can serve as escrow agents. However, a broker cannot require the parties to select him/her as the escrow agent within the same transaction. **In no event may a salesperson ever serve as escrow agent**. If a title company provides escrow services, escrow agents must be licensed by the **Texas Department of Insurance** and bonded.

In Texas, the two major means of providing evidence of title are through an **attorney's title opinion** and a **title policy of insurance**. Both methods involve an examination and analysis of the written history of ownership, which is known as an **abstract of title**.

While a highly qualified attorney provides an opinion of title under one method, an insurance company issues a policy of title insurance in the other method. In either case, Texas brokers are first required to advise the parties in writing to have their title investigated whenever an offer to purchase property is made. **Failure to advise the parties may result in license suspension against the broker**.

Unlike most forms of insurance, a title insurance policy protects the new owner and/or lender for claims against title based on events which have occurred in the past. Under a **mortgagor's (owner's) policy of insurance**, the insurance company is guaranteeing that the new owner will have **good and indefeasible title** and will protect the new owner up to the amount of the purchase price of the property. While under a **mortgagee's (lender's) policy**, the company is guaranteeing that the lender holds a valid first lien.

A mortgagee's policy will normally expire when the lien securing the property is paid off, but a mortgagor's policy will protect the owner long after he/she has sold the property. In Texas, the cost of a mortgagor's policy premium is an expense normally negotiated by and between the parties, while the cost of a mortgagee's policy premium is usually paid by the owner.

The first step towards issuing a title policy is to deliver to the buyer the title commitment. The **title commitment** is a commitment by the insurance company, which is open for 90 days, to issue a policy of insurance subject to certain exclusions, conditions, and stipulations. Various conditions and exceptions to coverage are spelled out in the schedules which make up the commitment. Insofar as the commitment eventually becomes the title policy, a buyer should be very careful to read the conditions and exclusions contained in the commitment.

The **Real Estate Settlement Procedures Act (RESPA)** involves most federally insured home loans. It is a federal law relating to the sale or transfer of one-to-four residential units requiring specific procedures and forms for settlement closing costs. All settlement closing costs must be disclosed to the borrower one business day before escrow closes.

Lastly, the settlement is the final accounting of all charges, credits and other expenses between the buyer and seller. The **HUD-1 statement** uses **double entry bookkeeping** in order to determine the credits and debits each party is entitled to receive. **Proration** is the process of dividing expenses or income proportionately between buyer and seller to the precise date that escrow closes, or an agreed date.

Not all expenses are prorated, but items commonly prorated include: property taxes, insurance, interest on assumed loans, and rental income.

In order to calculate prorations, it is necessary to determine which expenses are payable on a monthly or yearly basis and which expenses are payable at the beginning (**accrued**) or end (**arrears**) of the accounting period. When calculating prorations, it's important to know that in Texas the date of closing usually belongs to the seller.

VII. TERMINOLOGY

A. Abstract of Title
B. Attorney's Title Opinion
C. Chain of Title
D. Date of Closing
E. Escrow

F. Escrow Officer
G. Good and Indefeasable Title
H. Mortgagee's Policy
I. Mortgagor's Policy
J. Proration

K. Doctrine of Relation Back
L. RESPA
M. Settlement
N. Title Commitment
O. Title Insurance

1. ____ Insurance to protect a real property owner or lender up to a specified amount against problems of title.

2. ____ The process of depositing documents and funds with a third neutral party who finalizes the transaction.

3. ____ A recorded public history of transactions involving a specific property.

4. ____ The fair division of expenses such as interest, taxes, insurance, etc., as of the closing or agreed upon date.

5. ____ The licensed and bonded person at a title company who handles the closing.

6. ____ The final accounting of all charges, credits and other expenses between a buyer and seller.

7. ____ A title policy which is designed to protect only the proposed purchaser of real property.

8. ____ The title policy which is intended to insure only the lender.

9. ____ A legal doctrine that holds that a deed is deemed to be delivered when it is first placed into escrow.

10. ____ A written summary of a property's documents that evidences title.

11. ____ The date a title insurance policy is issued.

12. ____ A federal statute requiring disclosure of certain costs in the sale of residential property.

13. ____ An offer by a title company to issue a title policy based on certain conditions and stipulations.

14. ____ A method of providing evidence of title that only involves an attorney's examination and analysis of title.

15. ____ The standard by which a title insurance company will insure title.

VIII. MULTIPLE CHOICE

1. When a property is sold, the parties often use an escrow (agent) in order to:
    a. obey the civil code.
    b. serve as a witness.
    c. assure conditions are met.
    d. provide a legal service.

2. Which of the following is NOT a requirement of a valid escrow?
    a. Escrow officer must be a licensed attorney
    b. Obligation of fairness and honesty
    c. Neutral third party
    d. Conditional delivery

3. Of the following, which would be the last function in an escrow sequence of events?
    a. Issuing the title policy
    b. Research property tax information
    c. Request new loan documents
    d. Delivering the title commitment to buyer

4. A type of title insurance policy intended to benefit only the lender is the:
    a. mortgagor's policy.
    b. mortgagee's policy.
    c. homeowner's policy.
    d. none of the above.

5. Once an escrow is in place and underway, the only way that changes may be made is by:
    a. the escrow officer.
    b. mutual consent of the parties.
    c. the listing broker.
    d. operation of law.

6. A mortgagor's policy of insurance would never insure your property against:
    a. protrusions onto your property.
    b. loss of title due to eminent domain.
    c. problems with encroachments.
    d. none of the above.

7. All the following factors are important when calculating prorations, except:
    a. if the expense is paid in arrears.
    b. if the expense is paid using good funds.
    c. if the expense is paid monthly.
    d. the date of closing.

8. Who selects which party will pay for a mortgagor's title policy?
    a. The parties
    b. The lender
    c. The broker
    d. The mortgagee

9. Who selects the escrow agent?
    a. Agent only
    b. Buyer only
    c. Seller only
    d. Buyer and seller

10. Which of the following would probably NOT be a prorated expense of closing?
    a. Broker's commission
    b. Property taxes
    c. Homeowners' association dues
    d. Interest on an assumed mortgage

ANSWERS: 1. c; 2. a; 3. a; 4. b; 5. b; 6. b; 7. b; 8. a; 9. d; 10. a

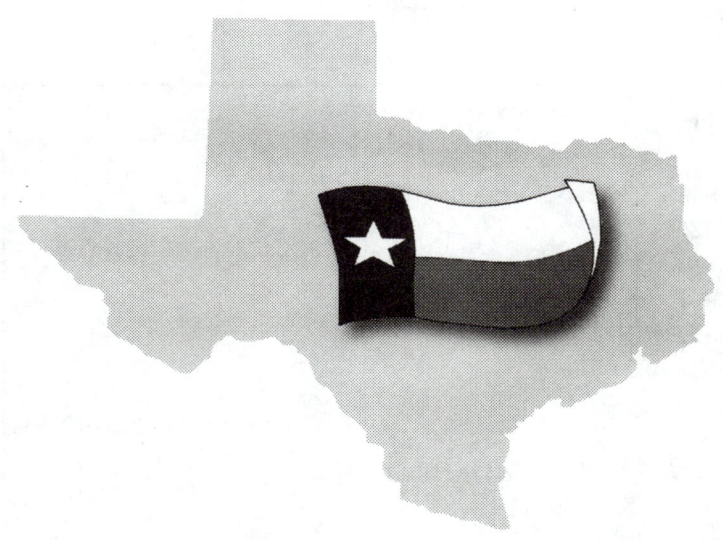

Chapter 11
Real Estate Finance

Real estate is expensive compared to most other possessions. A person or business seldom has enough cash to buy the real estate outright, and therefore must borrow the necessary money to help finance the transaction. If a buyer makes a cash down payment of 20% for example, he or she must then obtain a loan for the remaining 80% of the purchase price. Most buyers must finance at least part of the purchase, so a good rule to remember is, "If you can't finance a property, you probably can't sell it later." If a property can't be easily financed, don't waste time with it: find another, more easily financed property.

To utilize the "principle of leverage," an investor uses the maximum amount of borrowed money.

Even buyers with large amounts of cash rarely purchase real estate outright. An investment principle known as "leverage" favors buying real estate using borrowed funds. *LEVERAGE is the practice of purchasing real estate using a small amount of your own money and a larger proportion of borrowed funds.* The more money borrowed to buy a property, the greater the leverage.

Example: If you buy a $300,000 house with 20% down, the down payment is $60,000. If inflation increases the value by 30% over 10 years, you have increased the market value by $90,000 on a $60,000 initial investment.

CHAPTER 11 OUTLINE

Employing leverage makes it possible for real estate investors to reap the same profits as those buying entirely with their own funds without having to tie up as much cash. This chapter explores the different ways in which real estate can be financed. Each type of financing instrument will be discussed, including the many clauses in the note and deed of trust.

I. Hypothecation (Property as Collateral)

Real estate finance is based on the principle of hypothecation. To **HYPOTHECATE** *is to provide title to a property as security for a loan without giving up possession.* Although one can hypothecate or "pledge" stocks as security for a bank loan, most real property buyers hypothecate their property as security for a real estate loan. In neither case does the person surrender the use or possession of the property. The hypothecation principle is fundamental to the major instruments of real estate finance: the deed of trust and the less common mortgage. Each of these instruments creates a lien on the property and uses the promissory note as the primary evidence of debt.

II. The Promissory Note

A ***PROMISSORY NOTE*** *is the basic instrument used to evidence the obligation or debt. It is an unconditional promise, in writing, by one person to another, promising to pay on demand, or over a fixed determinable time, a certain sum of money.* Borrowers hypothecate real property as security for payment of the promissory note. The deed of trust or mortgage is used with the promissory note to hypothecate the property as security for the note.

> ***Co-borrowers responsible for each other's debts sign the promissory note as "jointly and severally obligated."***

A loan payment on a note is made up of principal and interest. ***PRINCIPAL*** *is the dollar amount of the loan.* Commonly, it is called the amount of money remaining to be paid off on a promissory note (the loan balance). ***INTEREST*** *is the rent charged for the use of money.*

> ***Interest on most real estate loans is "simple interest." Simple interest is interest paid only on the principal amount owed.***

Figure 11-1 illustrates the three basic kinds of promissory notes that affect real estate financing.

Figure 11-1

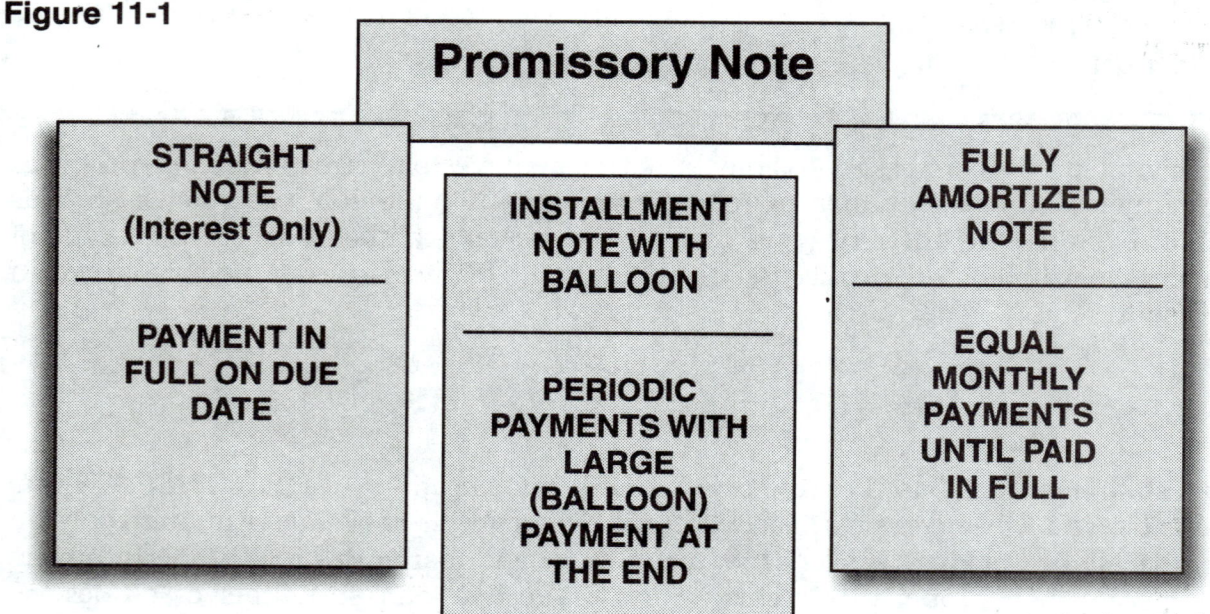

A. STRAIGHT NOTE (Interest Only)

A *STRAIGHT NOTE is a promissory note in which a borrower repays the principal in one lump sum, at maturity, while interest is paid in installments or at maturity.* The parties could agree that interest be paid monthly, quarterly, annually, or any agreed-to term, but the principal is a lump sum payment. In real estate, this type of note is usually for relatively small amounts of money being borrowed for a short time.

B. INSTALLMENT NOTE WITH A BALLOON PAYMENT

An *INSTALLMENT NOTE WITH A BALLOON PAYMENT (PARTIALLY AMORTIZED NOTE) is a promissory note with periodic payments of principal and interest and a large payment at the end (maturity date or due date).* This type of note and the straight note are usually reserved for second lien financing.

C. FULLY AMORTIZED INSTALLMENT NOTE

A *FULLY AMORTIZED INSTALLMENT NOTE is a promissory note for which both the principal and interest are paid in equal installments until the debt is paid in full.* Installments make it easy to pay off a note, and there is no balloon payment at the end of the loan period.

For real estate financing in Texas, the fully amortized installment note is the most commonly used type of note. Loan payments are either fixed or adjustable (see **Figure 11-2**).

To "amortize" is to slowly reduce the principal owed.

A fully amortized loan has equal monthly payments except for the last payment, which is slightly higher or lower. With *EQUAL MONTHLY PAYMENTS, the monthly payment amount, including principal and interest, is constant, but as the loan is paid off, the amount of the payment attributed to interest decreases and the amount attributed to principal increases.*

III. Negotiable Instruments

A. PROMISSORY NOTES, CHECKS, OTHERS

Negotiable instruments are easily transferable from one person to another. Promissory notes are negotiable. The most common example is a personal check.

A *NEGOTIABLE INSTRUMENT is any financial document (promissory note, check, or other type of similar instrument) that can be passed easily from one person to another, if it*

Figure 11-2

REAL ESTATE LIEN NOTE

Date: March 1, 20xx

Maker: Henry and Henrietta Homebuyer

Maker's Mailing Address (including county):

> 1702 Elm
> Big City, TX 77777
> Cowboy County

Payee: Big Bank of Texas, National Association

Place for Payment (including county):

> Cowboy County, Texas, or such other place as Payee shall specify in writing

Principal Amount: TWO HUNDRED FIFTY THOUSAND AND NO/100 DOLLARS ($250,000.00)

Annual Interest Rate on Unpaid Principal Balance from Date of Funding: 7% Per Annum

Maker may prepay all or any part of the principal of this note before maturity without penalty, and interest shall immediately cease to accrue on any amount so prepaid. Prepayments shall be applied to installments on the last maturing principal, and interest on that prepaid principal shall immediately cease to accrue.

Annual Interest Rate on Matured Unpaid Amounts: The maximum lawful rate of interest per annum provided for under the laws of the State of Texas.

Terms of Payment (principal and interest): For value received, the Maker promises to pay to the order of the Payee the Principal Amount plus interest in monthly installments each in the amount of $1,663.26, commencing on the 1st day of April, and on the first day of each month thereafter until the 1st day of March, 20xx, at which time any remaining unpaid principal and accrued interest shall be due and payable in full without further notice.

Security for Payment: This note is secured a deed of trust of even date from Maker to Terry Trustee, Trustee, covering the following described real property:

> **Lot 10, Block 15 of Happy Homeowners Addition, an addition to the City of Big Homes, Cowboy County, Texas, according to the Plat thereof recorded in Volume 18, page 109, Map Records, Cowboy County, Texas**

Borrower's initials _____ _____

If any installment becomes overdue for more than fifteen days, at Payee's option, a sum equal to 5% of the payment may be charged in order to defray the expense of handling the delinquent payment.

Maker promises to pay to the order of Payee at the place for payment and according to the terms of payment the principal amount plus interest at the rates stated above. All unpaid amounts shall be due by the final scheduled payment date.

If Maker defaults in the payment of this note or in the performance of any obligation in any instrument securing or collateral to it, and the default continues after Payee gives Maker notice of the default and the time within which it must be cured, as may be required by law or by written agreement, then Payee may declare the unpaid principal balance and earned interest on this note immediately due. Upon default, Maker and each surety, endorser, and guarantor waive all demands for payment, presentations for payment, notices of intention to accelerate maturity, notices of acceleration of maturity, protests, and notices of protest, to the extent permitted by law.

If this note or any instrument securing or collateral to it is given to an attorney for collection or enforcement, or if suit is brought for collection or enforcement, or if it is collected or enforced through probate, bankruptcy, or other judicial proceeding, then Maker shall pay Payee all costs of collection and enforcement, including reasonable attorney's fees and court costs, in addition to other amounts due. Reasonable attorney's fees shall be 10% of all amounts due unless either party pleads otherwise. Notwithstanding the foregoing, the Maker, his successors and assigns shall have no personal liability for the payment of the unpaid principal balance of this note upon default, and Payee agrees to look to the Property only for recover, but said Maker, successors and assigns shall remain liable for accrued and unpaid interest and for real estate taxes which may have accrued prior to the time when the Payee shall retake title to the Property.

Interest on the debt evidenced by this note shall not exceed the maximum amount of nonusurious interest that may be contracted for, taken, reserved, charged, or received under law; any interest in excess of that maximum amount shall be credited on the principal of the debt or, if that has been paid, refunded. On any acceleration or required or permitted prepayment, any such excess shall be canceled automatically as of the acceleration or prepayment or, if already paid, credited on the principal of the debt or, if the principal of the debt has been paid, refunded. This provision overrides other provisions in this and all other instruments concerning the debt.

Each Maker is responsible for all obligations represented by this note.

When the context requires, singular nouns and pronouns include the plural.

Executed on the date first set forth above.

_____	_____
Henry Homebuyer	Henrietta Homebuyer

meets certain legal requirements. Any promissory note may be a negotiable instrument that is freely transferable. A negotiable instrument must be:

1. an unconditional promise,
2. in writing,
3. made by one person to another,
4. signed by the maker,
5. payable on demand or on a set date,
6. for a set amount of money.

In a typical real estate transaction, the "promissory note" is considered to be a negotiable instrument, while the mortgage or deed of trust is not.

B. TRANSFER AND ENDORSEMENTS

Because promissory notes are negotiable instruments they are easily bought and sold among financial institutions and investors. A promissory note can be sold when a buyer purchases the instrument from the holder. A *HOLDER refers to the person who presently owns the negotiable instrument. The seller of the instrument then signs his/her name on the instrument (the ENDORSEMENT)*, thus transferring it to the new holder. By endorsing the instrument to the new holder, the endorser is making himself/herself responsible for the full payment of the promissory note in the event the original maker does not pay.

Not only are makers fully responsible for the full payment of the promissory note, but so are any endorsers.

IV. Important Clauses in Financial Instruments

The following financial instrument clauses are the most commonly used terms, and they have definite meanings that affect the financial obligations of both a lender and borrower.

A. ACCELERATION CLAUSE (Entire Amount Due)

In an *ACCELERATION CLAUSE, upon the occurrence of a specific event, the lender has the right to demand immediate payment of the entire note.* An acceleration clause is used to demand immediate payment in full because of a default in loan payments, property taxes, fire insurance, or upon the transfer of property. The main purpose of an acceleration clause is to make the entire balance of the loan due and payable at once. A *LATE PAYMENT, on the other hand, is a payment that is paid after a due date.* A late payment does not normally trigger an acceleration of the entire amount due under a note.

An acceleration clause "speeds up" the balance due based on the occurrence of a specific event.

B. ALIENATION CLAUSE (Due on Sale)

An *ALIENATION CLAUSE is a form of the acceleration clause, stating that the entire loan becomes due and payable when the property is sold, assigned, transferred, or otherwise alienated.* The lender, whether a financial institution or a private party, is given the right to full payment when the original borrower transfers the property. This is also commonly referred to as a "due on sale" clause.

With an alienation clause, the lender demands that the entire balance of the loan is due when the owner is alienating, transferring (selling), or "conveying" the property.

C. ASSUMPTION

In order to assume an existing loan, the promissory note cannot include an automatic alienation clause.

If a buyer *ASSUMES a loan on a property that is already encumbered, he or she accepts responsibility, with the lender's consent, for the full payment of the loan.* The name on the loan is changed to that of the buyer. With a true assumption, the seller has secondary responsibility. Today, assumable loans are very rare in Texas.

A seller is protected from liability for payments on an existing loan when the buyer "assumes" the note liability.

When a buyer purchases a property "subject to," he or she has no responsibility in the event of a default; the seller retains responsibility. "Subject to" benefits the buyer.

Taking title *SUBJECT TO a prior loan constitutes an agreement to take over and make the payments or lose the property.* However, the current seller (the buyer to whom the loan was originally made) remains legally responsible for the note, but the new buyer makes the payments.

D. SUBORDINATION CLAUSE
(Current Loan Stands Still; New Loan Moves Ahead)

A *SUBORDINATION CLAUSE is part of a deed of trust or mortgage that allows for a future change in the priority of financial liens.* It is used when the buyer wants future financial liens to have priority over a lien he or she is now acquiring. The seller of vacant land will sometimes lend money to the buyer as part of the transaction and will allow the subordination of that loan to any new construction loans.

The subordination clause is used to change the priority on one or more lien holders, but the terms of a subordination clause must be clear and definite. Subordination clauses are not used that often, but a salesperson must know and understand them.

E. PREPAYMENT PENALTIES (Fee for Early Payment)

A *PREPAYMENT PENALTY is a charge to the borrower for paying off all or part of a loan balance before the due date.*

Some financial institutions use a prepayment penalty clause on loans. Penalties do vary among lenders and a lender may sometimes waive the prepayment penalty if the borrower obtains a new loan from that institution, or if the money market is tight and the lender needs to use the money to lend out at a higher interest rate. In Texas, home lenders may not impose a prepayment penalty if the interest rate exceeds 12%. Furthermore, nearly all new FHA and VA loans prohibit prepayment penalties as well.

To find out if a particular loan contains a prepayment penalty provision, simply ask the lender or just read the loan documents.

F. IMPOUND ACCOUNTS (Reserves)

IMPOUND ACCOUNTS (RESERVES) are moneys collected in advance from borrowers to assure the payment of recurring costs, such as property taxes and fire insurance. Most lenders require impound accounts. Impound accounts are especially appropriate when there is a relatively low down payment.

Impounds are reserves (money) on hand for recurring costs, such as property taxes and fire insurance. Impounds CANNOT be used to pay interest.

G. ASSIGNMENT OF RENTS (Take Possession of Rents)

An *ASSIGNMENT OF RENTS clause allows a lender, upon default of the borrower, to take possession of the property, collect rents, and pay expenses.* For example, assume that the promissory note relates to the purchase of an apartment complex. If the borrower defaults on the payment of the loan, the lender, under an assignment of rents clause, can direct all tenants to pay the lender directly, rather than the property owner.

V. Interest and Types of Loans

A. INTEREST (Simple Interest)

INTEREST is the charge for borrowing money. In real estate we use simple interest, not compound interest. Interest can be thought of as a rental charge for the use of money.

The "Nominal Interest Rate" is the rate stated in the note. The "Effective Interest Rate" is the rate the borrower is actually paying (including interest, points, and loan fees).

The formula for calculating interest is:

$$I = P \times R \times T \text{ or Interest} = \text{Principal} \times \text{Rate} \times \text{Time}$$

To find the interest on an $240,000 loan at 12 percent interest for 3 years, we would make the following calculation:

$$I = P \times R \times T \ \$86,400 = \$240,000 \times .12 \times 3 \text{ years}$$

(See Chapter 17 for a more detailed discussion of interest calculations.)

B. FIXED INTEREST RATES (Fixed Rate)

A *FIXED INTEREST RATE LOAN is a loan for which the payments are the same each month for the life of the loan.* The equal monthly payment includes both the principal and the interest. A loan with this kind of fixed rate of interest is said to be a "fully amortized fixed rate loan."

C. AMORTIZATION PAYMENTS

AMORTIZATION is the repaying of a loan (principal and interest), in regular payments, over the term of the loan. This repayment is usually in monthly payments but can be paid quarterly or semi-annually. Amortization comes from the term, "to kill off" and refers to the gradual total repayment of the loan principal and interest.

NEGATIVE AMORTIZATION means the interest rate charges are higher than the monthly payment. Negative amortization means that the loan payment does not cover the interest charges, and the amount of unpaid interest is added to the unpaid loan balance.

Real estate salespeople should always have amortization books handy so that they can figure out the monthly payment on any loan. The *AMORTIZATION (SCHEDULE) BOOK shows the monthly payments necessary to amortize a loan over a given number of years at different interest rates and for different loan amounts.* This amortization table book is usually given free, upon request, to salespeople by title insurance companies or financial institutions. Salespeople can also use specially programmed, hand-held loan calculators to instantly determine the monthly payment amount.

Figure 11-3 is an example of an amortization table at 7% interest per annum for 20, 25, 30, and 40 years at different loan amounts. The loan amounts range from $100 to $100,000, but any loan amount can be obtained by adding the necessary increments.

Figure 11-3

Monthly Payments Necessary to Amortize a Loan

7%

TERM AMOUNT	20 YEARS	25 YEARS	30 YEARS	40 YEARS
$100	0.78	0.71	0.67	0.62
200	1.55	1.41	1.33	1.24
300	2.33	2.12	2.00	1.86
400	3.10	2.83	2.66	2.49
500	3.88	3.53	3.33	3.11
600	4.65	4.24	3.99	3.73
700	5.43	4.95	4.66	4.35
800	6.20	5.65	5.32	4.97
900	6.98	6.36	5.99	5.59
1,000	7.75	7.07	6.65	6.21
2,000	15.51	14.14	13.31	12.43
3,000	23.26	21.20	19.96	18.64
4,000	31.01	28.27	26.61	24.86
5,000	38.76	35.34	33.27	31.07
6,000	46.52	42.41	39.92	37.29
7,000	54.27	49.47	46.57	43.50
8,000	62.02	56.54	53.22	49.71
9,000	69.78	63.61	59.88	55.93
10,000	77.53	70.68	66.53	62.14
20,000	155.06	141.36	133.06	124.29
30,000	232.59	212.03	199.59	186.43
40,000	310.12	282.71	266.12	248.57
50,000	387.65	353.39	332.65	310.72
100,000	775.30	706.78	665.30	621.43

If, for example, we want to determine the monthly payments for a $155,000 loan at 7% interest for 30 years, this is what we would do:

1. Check the 30 years' column for the monthly payment on $100,000.
2. Next, determine the monthly payment for $50,000 and $5,000 using the same method.
3. Lastly, add the monthly payment amounts together.

Amount	Payment
$100,000.00	$665.30
50,000.00	$332.65
5,000.00	$33.27
TOTAL LOAN $155,000.00	**$1,031.22 Monthly Payment**

Lenders determine monthly payments by using amortization tables.

www.bankrate.com/gookeyword/mortgage-calculator.asp
Bankrate.com Mortgage calculator
www.interest.com/hugh/calc/
Hugh's Mortgage and Financial Calculators

D. ADJUSTABLE RATE MORTGAGE (ARM)

Many lenders will allow the borrower a choice of either: 1) a fixed interest rate loan, or 2) an adjustable rate mortgage (ARM) loan. An ARM allows the interest rate to fluctuate (go up or down) depending on money market conditions. Rather than making equal monthly payments as with a fixed rate loan, the ARM payments will vary over the term of the loan.

An *ADJUSTABLE RATE MORTGAGE (ARM) is a loan in which the interest rate fluctuates periodically, based on a specific index, which makes the payment amount also change.* Each lending institution has its own ARM terms and provisions.

Figure 11-4 illustrates how an adjustable rate mortgage (ARM) works. The interest rate, and therefore the payments, will change often over the term of the loan. ARM lenders attempt to make this type of loan more attractive to a potential borrower by offering the loan at a much lower starting interest rate than with a fixed interest rate loan.

www.loanpage.com
The LoanPage

E. SOME SPECIAL PURPOSE TYPES OF LOANS

1. Graduated Payment Mortgage (For First-Time Buyers)

A *GRADUATED PAYMENT MORTGAGE is a type of fixed interest rate loan for which the monthly payments start out lower and then gradually increase (for example, after five years the payments will be higher for the remainder of the loan payment).* Although the final level of payments is higher than the payments would have been had the loan been fully amortized, the initial payments are much lower than the fully amortized rate.

Figure 11-4

How ARMs Work

THE INDEX

The **INDEX** *is the starting interest rate used as the indicator so that changes from it can be calculated.* If the index rises 1%, the ARM interest rate you pay goes up 1%. The index must be: 1) beyond the control of the lender, and 2) available and verifiable by the public. Examples of indexes used are the Cost of Living Index, the 11th District Cost of Funds Index, the One Year T-Bill, and the London Interbank Offered Rate (LIBOR).

THE ADJUSTABLE INTERVAL

The **ADJUSTABLE INTERVAL** *is the frequency with which interest rates are reset.* This period can be monthly, quarterly, every six months, or even once a year. If the index has risen .3% by the end of the interval period, the interest rate you pay goes up .3%.

THE CAP

The **CAP** *is a percentage rate ceiling or restriction on both the 1) periodic (adjustable) interval; and 2) lifetime change in interest rates or payments.* An adjustable interval cap limits the percentage of change upward or downward to, for example, 1/2% every quarter. The lifetime cap is often around a maximum of 5% above or below the initial agreed-to contract rate.

THE MARGIN

The **MARGIN** *is the spread between the index rate and the initial contract rate from which the lender will make a profit and cover its costs.* It is the agreed to (in advance) amount of profit for the lender. If the index rate is 4% and the margin is 3%, then the current interest rate paid by the borrower is 7%. Even if the index rate moves up to 5%, the margin will always remain at 3% and the new interest rate will be 8%. Some adjustables have **teaser rates** that are even below the starting rate to entice the borrower into the transaction. The borrower is qualified based on the teaser rate, which only lasts for a short period of time and then goes up to the agreed upon rate.

ADVANTAGES OF ARMs

The main advantage of an ARM is a lower interest rate than can be found with a fixed rate loan because the lender is protected if interest rates rise over the loan period. This makes an ARM more affordable, thus more people can qualify for it. Generally there are no prepayment penalties, and an assumption is usually permitted if the new buyer meets credit standards. ARMs benefit first-time buyers and short-term investors who just want a lower interest rate, because interest rates are initially lower.

2. Biweekly Mortgage (26 Payments)

A *BIWEEKLY MORTGAGE is a fixed interest rate loan for which the payments are made every two weeks, but each payment is one-half the amount of a regular monthly payment.* Since there are 52 weeks in a year, the borrower pays a total of 26 payments.

3. 15-Year Fixed and Adjustable Rate Loans

Fifteen-year fixed rate loans are gaining in popularity because, for a slight increase in the monthly payment, the loan can be paid off in only 15 years, usually at a lower interest rate than 30-year loans.

4. Reverse Annuity Mortgages (Seniors Who Need Income)

REVERSE ANNUITY MORTGAGES are loans in which the lender pays the borrower a fixed monthly payment based on the value of the property. The loan is not repaid until the last owner dies or the property is sold, at which time it is paid back through probate. In Texas, this type of loan is available for senior citizens, age 62 and over, who need a monthly income and have a large amount of equity in their homes. The senior citizens can pay off the loans earlier if they so desire.

VI. Points, Loan Fees, and Usury

A. POINTS (1 POINT = 1% OF THE LOAN AMOUNT)

A point is one percent of the loan amount. Five points on a $300,000 loan is $15,000.

A *POINT is an amount equivalent to 1% of the amount borrowed, charged by the lender.* Most financial institutions charge the borrower an origination fee expressed in points when he or she obtains a new loan. Points vary, but generally range from 1% to 7% of the loan amount. They are usually paid by the buyer but, if so negotiated, the seller may also pay.

If you purchase a home for $300,000 and obtain a loan for $240,000 plus two points, the loan points will cost you $4,800 ($240,000 x .02). These points are an additional cost

and are added to the down payment and other closing costs required to complete the transaction at the time of purchase.

Points paid are usually adjustments to the interest rate. If the interest rate quoted is lower than what is currently being charged, more points are charged to make up the difference, which is paid to the lender. If a savings bank wants to quote a lower interest rate, the borrower can expect a larger point charge.

B. LOAN FEES

There is usually a loan fee in addition to points. A *LOAN FEE is the fee charged by the lender in order to apply for a loan*. This charge runs about $250 to $400. Other charges may include the appraisal and credit report.

C. USURY

USURY is charging more than the legally allowed percentage of interest. In Texas, the maximum interest rate charged for various loans is set by law. Anyone charging more than the designated rate is committing usury and is breaking the law. In determining whether an interest charge is usurious or not, all loan fees and points are added to the interest rate. Prepayment penalties are not included in the usury law test.

To determine the usury rate in Texas is not an easy task. As a starting point, Texas law provides that the maximum rate of interest to be charged is 10 percent, "except as otherwise allowed by law." However, the law also allows a number of complicated rate ceilings which apply in different types of loan transactions. Texas law also provides that state rate ceilings are subject to federal law. As with most other areas, it's best to check with an attorney to fully understand your rights and obligations under the law.

Texas law provides civil and even criminal penalties for lenders who engage in usurious lending practices.

VII. Security Devices

SECURITY DEVICES (FINANCIAL INSTRUMENTS) are written documents that pledge real property as security for a promissory note.

The three financial instruments (security devices to collateralize real property) used in Texas are: mortgages, deeds of trust, and land contracts.

In Texas, we have three types of security devices (financing instruments) (see **Figure 11-5**). Any of the three previously mentioned promissory notes may be used in conjunction with these financial instruments.

Figure 11-5

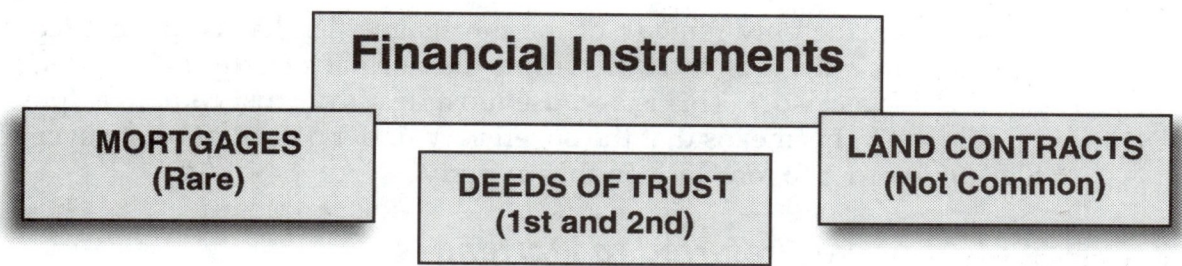

A. MORTGAGES

A *MORTGAGE is a financial instrument, in the form of a lien, that secures a property for payment of a promissory note.* It is not common in Texas for residential financing. The *MORTGAGOR is the buyer/owner who is borrowing,* and the *MORTGAGEE is the lender.* If the mortgagor defaults in his or her payments, foreclosure may be commenced.

Mortgagee = Lender
Mortgagor = Buyer/Owner who is borrowing

1. Power of Sale Clause

Most mortgages have a power of sale clause. A *POWER OF SALE CLAUSE allows the mortgagee to sell the property without a court proceeding (much like a trustee's sale) if the mortgagor is in default.* But it still requires a lengthy proceeding. If there is no power of sale clause, court (judicial) action is required for a foreclosure.

Mortgage: A General Term

Although mortgages are rarely used in Texas, the term 'mortgage" is so ingrained in the tradition of lending that often deeds of trust and other loans are referred to as "mortgages." Adjustable Rate Mortgages and Fixed Rate Mortgages, for example, are deeds of trust. Often these terms are used interchangeably, but mortgagee or mortgagor, as used in this chapter, technically refers to mortgages and the terms trustee, trustor, and beneficiary refer only to deeds of trust.

---

2. Mortgages Compared to Deeds of Trust

a. Parties

In the mortgage there are two parties: 1) the mortgagor (borrower) and 2) the mortgagee (lender). The deed of trust has three: 1) grantor/trustor (borrower), 2) trustee (third party), and 3) beneficiary (lender).

b. Remedy for Default

In a mortgage, the only remedy of the mortgagee (lender) is judicial (court) foreclosure. In a deed of trust, however, the normal remedy is by means of non-judicial foreclosure. This is because most deeds of trust contain a "power of sale clause." This means that the beneficiary under a deed of trust never has to file suit in order to foreclose on the property.

3. Deeds of Trust are Preferred to Mortgages

In Texas, the deed of trust is preferred to the mortgage as the usual financing device for residential real estate. For the lender, the primary advantage is the ease and convenience, without having to resort to court action, with which the property may be sold to satisfy the debt if the borrower defaults. Texas laws favor lenders who use the deed of trust, which allows them more freedom in granting loans to deserving buyers.

B. DEEDS OF TRUST

1. Deeds of Trust are Used in Texas

Deeds of trust are held by mortgage lenders as personal property.

In Texas, the deed of trust is the usual financing instrument for residential real estate. The **DEED OF TRUST** *is a security device that makes the real property collateral for the promissory note.* **Figure 11-6** shows the first page of the Fannie Mae Deed of Trust form.

A deed of trust needs a note to create the financial obligation, but a note does NOT need a deed of trust. A deed of trust is not a negotiable instrument; the note is. If the conditions of a note and the deed of trust are in conflict, the note prevails.

2. Parties to a Deed of Trust

In a deed of trust there are three parties. The **GRANTOR/TRUSTOR** *is usually the party who is borrowing the money.* This is often the buyer, but may also be the owner if the property is being refinanced. The **BENEFICIARY** *is the lender who is lending money for the purchase of real property.* The **TRUSTEE** *is the third, disinterested party (usually an attorney or corporation) who holds the deed in trust for the benefit of the beneficiary.* **Figure 11-7** illustrates this three-party relationship.

A trustor usually signs the promissory note and deed of trust at closing. The promissory note is evidence of the amount owed and the deed of trust makes the real estate security for the loan.

Figure 11-6

After Recording Return To:

_____

_____

_____

_____

_____ [Space Above This Line For Recording Data] _____

DEED OF TRUST

DEFINITIONS

Words used in multiple sections of this document are defined below and other words are defined in Sections 3, 11, 13, 18, 20 and 21. Certain rules regarding the usage of words used in this document are also provided in Section 16.

(A) **"Security Instrument"** means this document, which is dated _____, _____, together with all Riders to this document.

(B) **"Borrower"** is _____. Borrower is the grantor under this Security Instrument.

(C) **"Lender"** is _____. Lender is a _____ organized and existing under the laws of _____ _____. Lender's address is _____. Lender is the beneficiary under this Security Instrument.

(D) **"Trustee"** is _____. Trustee's address is _____.

(E) **"Note"** means the promissory note signed by Borrower and dated _____, _____. The Note states that Borrower owes Lender _____ Dollars (U.S. $_____) plus interest. Borrower has promised to pay this debt in regular Periodic Payments and to pay the debt in full not later than _____.

(F) **"Property"** means the property that is described below under the heading "Transfer of Rights in the Property."

(G) **"Loan"** means the debt evidenced by the Note, plus interest, any prepayment charges and late charges due under the Note, and all sums due under this Security Instrument, plus interest.

TEXAS--Single Family--**Fannie Mae/Freddie Mac** UNIFORM INSTRUMENT   Form 3044   1/01 *(page 1 of 17 pages)*

Figure 11-7

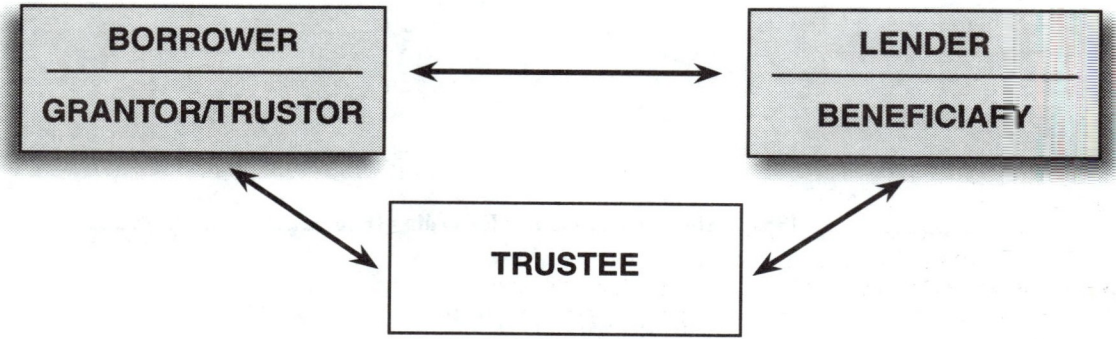

A deed of trust must have all three parties: grantor/trustor, trustee, and beneficiary. The deed of trust forms the lien on the property until such time as the promissory note is paid in full, at which time the lien is released by means of a release of lien. If the trustor defaults in payments, the grantor/trustor will be in default. If the default is not cured, it could ultimately lead to foreclosure.

The lender of the money is called the "beneficiary" who holds the lien and promissory note.

Texas is considered a lien theory state. In *LIEN THEORY STATES, the grantor/trustor, or borrower/owner, owns full title to the property even while the owner is making payments on the promissory note. The beneficiary holds only a lien interest. When the note is paid in full, the beneficiary need only issue a release of lien in order to terminate the lender's interest.*

In *TITLE THEORY STATES, on the other hand, the owner holds "equitable title" in the real property, but conveys to the trustee "legal title." This makes the trustee essentially a part-owner of the property. At the point that the promissory note is paid completely, the trustee must convey, by means of a reconveyance deed, full title to the property.*

Texas is considered a Lien Theory state, which means that the beneficiary only holds a lien on the property. In Title Theory states, the trustee actually holds the legal title.

3. Release of Lien (Proof of Payment in Full)

Since Texas is a lien theory state, a *RELEASE OF LIEN serves to release the lien created by the deed of trust upon full payment of all sums owed under the deed of trust.* Typically, the deed of trust will require the beneficiary to prepare the release of lien and mail it to the owner. It is then the owner's responsibility to file it of record in the county clerk's office. As with any other recorded document, unless the release of lien is filed, no one other than the trustor and the beneficiary will know of its existence. A sample release of lien is shown in **Figure 11-8**.

Figure 11-8   **RELEASE OF LIEN**

THE STATE OF TEXAS §
  § KNOW ALL MEN BY THESE PRESENTS:
COUNTY OF COWBOY §

WHEREAS, on June 1, 19xx A.D., Henry Homebuyer and Henrietta Homebuyer, (hereinafter called "Maker", whether one or more, masculine, feminine or neuter) did execute, acknowledge and deliver to Terry Trustee, Trustee, for the use and benefit of Big Bank of Texas, National Association (hereinafter called "Payee", whether one or more, masculine, feminine or neuter) a Deed of Trust recorded on June 2, 19xx, in Cowboy County under Volume 20, Page 15 of the Real Property Records of Cowboy County, Texas, and covering the following described real estate located in Cowboy County, Texas:

Lot 10, Block 15 of Happy Homeowners Addition, an addition to the City of Big Homes, Cowboy County, Texas, according to the Plat thereof recorded in Volume 18, page 109, Map Records, Cowboy County, Texas,

to secure the prompt payment of one promissory note executed by the said Maker and payable to the order of the Payee upon the terms therein provided; and,

WHEREAS, said promissory note with accrued interest thereon has been paid in full or otherwise fully settled and compromised to the undersigned, being the legal and equitable owner and holder of said note; and,

NOW, THEREFORE, the undersigned, as the lawful owner and holder of the aforementioned promissory note, in consideration of the premises and of the full payment of said note, the receipt of which is hereby acknowledged, has this day, and does by these presents **RELEASE, DISCHARGE AND QUITCLAIM** in full unto the Maker, his, her or its successors, heirs or assigns, as the case may be, all the right, title, interest and estate in and to only the property above described which the undersigned has or may be entitled to by virtue of said deed of trust, any renewals and extensions thereof, and any contemporaneous vendor's lien, and does hereby declare the all the same fully released and discharged therefrom, and from any and all other liens and security interests securing said indebtedness held by the undersigned, whatsoever.

In Witness Whereof I have hereunto set my hand this _____ day of _____ , 20xx.

_____
John Smith, Vice President, Lending

ACKNOWLEDGMENT

This instrument was acknowledged before me on the _____ day of _____, 20xx by John Smith, the Vice President of Lending of Big Bank of Texas, National Association, a national banking association on behalf of said association.

_____
Notary Public

After recording return to:

Henry and Henrietta Homebuyer
105 Hobo Drive
Cowboy, Texas 78777

A homeowner who inadvertently forgets to record a release of lien will be in for a rude awakening when he/she attempts to sell the property and is told by the title company that a lien still appears in the property records office.

VIII. Default and Foreclosure of a Deed of Trust

A. DEFAULT UNDER A DEED OF TRUST

In Texas, the procedure and remedy for nonpayment of a promissory note secured by a deed of trust is well established by law. Insofar as the deed of trust creates a lien on the property involved, the lender has the legal right to foreclose on the property. Moreover, since deeds of trust typically contain power of sale clauses, the foreclosure occurs non-judicially.

The foreclosure process is triggered when the trustor is in default of either the promissory note of the deed of trust. *DEFAULT is a breach of a specified duty under the promissory note and deed of trust.* Defaults can be classified into monetary and non-monetary defaults. An example of a monetary default is the trustor's (homeowner) failure to make his or her monthly note payment. A non-monetary default would be the owner's failure to pay property taxes so that the taxing entity takes a lien against the property.

The foreclosure process is triggered by a default of a monetary or non-monetary nature that remains uncured.

Although a promissory note requires homeowners to make their payment on time, late payments will generally not automatically trigger a default. Even though the note may contain language stating that "the maker will be in default if payment is not timely made," the law implies a modest grace period for making payments. Under the terms of many promissory notes and deeds of trust, the lender is entitled to a late charge if payment is not received on a specified date.

A *GRACE PERIOD is typically a number of days in which a lender will allow a payment to be late without penalty other than perhaps a late charge.* The lender, at any time after the grace period, however, may start foreclosure action against the trustor or homeowner.

Figure 11-9 shows the general sequence of events that will follow if the trustor does not make the loan payments.

When a borrower defaults under the terms of the deed of trust or promissory note, the beneficiary's remedy is to begin foreclosure proceedings. Assuming the default consists of failure to make monthly loan payments, the beneficiary notifies the trustee

Figure 11-9

PAYMENT PAST DUE	NOTICE TO CURE DEFAULT	NOTICE OF SALE	FORECLOSURE SALE
If the promissory note and/or deed of trust so allow, the lender may be entitled to a late charge for late payments. But if the default continues past the implied grace period, the lender may declare a default.	By law, the loan servicer or whoever actually collects the loan payments must give a residential borrower **20 days** written notice to cure any default before the Notice of Sale can be given.	The Notice of Sale is given by the loan servicer or trustee **21 days** before the foreclosure sale occurs. The sale must actually occur at or within 3 hours of the time stated in the notice.	The trustee's sale of foreclosure occurs in a public area of the courthouse on the first Tuesday of each month between the hours of **10:00 AM and 4:00 PM**.

and the trustee begins the process of sending notices as required by law. However, Texas law now allows mortgage servicers to administer a foreclosure (become the trustee) of property on behalf of a lender provided that the lender and the servicer agree to this administration and that this fact is disclosed to the borrower/trustor in the notices.

Assuming that the trustor refuses or fails to respond to the notice to cure default within the time allowed, the Notice of Sale, commonly known as the "21-day notice" is mailed. By law, the 21-day notice must be:

1. Posted at the courthouse door, or any other place at the courthouse that has been designated as the area where the foreclosures are to take place;
2. Filed with the county clerk's office; and
3. Mailed by certified mail to each person legally obligated for paying the mortgage loan.

State law dictates exactly how notices should be given.

B. FORECLOSURE PROCEEDINGS

1. The Homeowner's Rights Prior to Foreclosure

Prior to the foreclosure sale, the trustor has certain rights and limited options.

In some cases, these options and alternatives may serve as a legal basis for countering the foreclosure sale, or they may be simply to gain additional time in which to borrow money or refinance the debt.

For example, by law, the homeowner has a legal right to receive a copy of all notices prior to foreclosure. Armed with this information, the homeowner knows how much money is required of him/her, and more importantly, knows how quickly he/she must act. By law, the lender or the person conducting the foreclosure proceedings must mail the notices to the debtor's last known address. It is no defense if a homeowner argues a failure to receive these notices. The law states that the mailing of the notices is sufficient regardless of whether the homeowner actually receives them. Besides, the law requires the homeowner to update his/her address with the mortgage servicer.

At any time prior to the foreclosure the debtor-homeowner may exercise his/her **EQUITABLE RIGHT OF REDEMPTION** *by paying any and all amounts necessary to redeem the property and stop the foreclosure process.*

A Texas homeowner has no **STATUTORY RIGHT OF REDEMPTION** (*some state statutes allow owners who were foreclosed on for nonpayment of taxes to redeem property even up to two years following the sale*) for a foreclosure resulting from nonpayment of the loan.

A homeowner may also enter into a forebearance agreement or workout plan with a willing lender prior to the foreclosure sale. A **FORBEARANCE AGREEMENT** *is a contract with the lender where the lender, for the right amount of consideration, agrees not to exercise its legal right to foreclose, at least temporarily.* Under a **WORKOUT PLAN**, *the lender agrees to restructure or refinance the loan so as to make it possible for the homeowner to continue residing in the property without the threat of foreclosure.* Contrary to popular belief, lenders quite often wish to avoid foreclosure as much as the homeowner, and thus, may be willing to work towards a satisfactory resolution. However, the homeowner must also prove his/her worthiness of a second chance.

Forbearance agreements and workout plans are two means by which a homeowner can avoid or delay a foreclosure if the lender is willing to take a risk on the homeowner.

A homeowner may also wish to consider filing for protection under the federal bankruptcy laws. A bankruptcy filing will immediately stop any and all action against a debtor include pending foreclosure proceedings. Under a Chapter 13 bankruptcy, the homeowner may be able to force the lender to accept payments for the arrearage owed. However, the debtor will be required to maintain current loan payments thereafter as a condition to the plan. This can slow down a foreclosure, but it does not necessarily mean that the debt is forgiven.

New bankruptcy rules now in effect will make it harder for homeowners to file for federal bankruptcy protection. Homeowners should consult with a legal specialist to determine if bankruptcy is an option.

2. The Trustee's Sale (Foreclosure Sale)

A trustee's sale is only for the real property backing up the deed of trust.

The trustee's sale is held at the time and place stated in the notice of sale. By law it must occur on the first Tuesday of each month, following a 21-day notice to the trustor. They are generally held on the steps of the courthouse or wherever county officials designate the sales should occur. At the public sale, the trustee publicly announces the purpose of the sale and describes the property to be sold. All bids must be in the form of cash or cashier's checks.

The first lien holder may bid up to the total amount of the debt without cash. Because it costs the first lien holder nothing more than what he or she is already owed, that person will usually make the first bid. The highest bidder obtains the property and will be issued a trustee's deed. Any money in excess of the amount owed, together with expenses of the sale, is reimbursed to the trustor. The new owner is entitled to immediate possession. By law, the purchase of the property is "as is" without any expressed or implied warranties and at the purchaser's own risk.

A trustee's sale is an out-of-court procedure under the "power of sale" clause in the deed of trust and promissory note. It is the quickest and easiest way for a beneficiary to foreclose on a default of a deed of trust.

3. Judicial Court Foreclosure for a Deed of Trust (Rare)

Despite the fact that a non-judicial foreclosure represents a relatively quick method of foreclosure, there may be times when it is necessary or desirable to resort to the courts. If either party wishes to have the court determine some relevant issue related to the foreclosure, then it is appropriate to have the courts hear the matter. By law, home equity loans in Texas must be foreclosed judicially.

Judicial foreclosures will obviously take longer to resolve and will be costlier to manage than a non-judicial proceeding, but it will allow both sides to "have their day in court."

4. Deed in Lieu of Foreclosure

A DEED IN LIEU OF FORECLOSURE is a deed given by an owner (borrower) to a lender to prevent the lender from bringing foreclosure proceedings. The lender (beneficiary)

becomes the new owner of the property bypassing completely the foreclosure process. It is up to the lender to accept or reject such an offer.

Texas law allows the lender to cancel a deed received in lieu of foreclosure within four years if it is discovered that the borrower failed to disclose, and the lender had no knowledge of the existence of any other lien or encumbrance on the property.

A deed in lieu of foreclosure may save the borrower's credit in some circumstances by avoiding a foreclosure.

C. LIENS NOT ELIMINATED BY FORECLOSURE SALE

Most junior liens are eliminated by a foreclosure sale. The following liens are not necessarily eliminated:

1. Federal tax liens
2. State, county, and city taxes or assessments
3. Mechanic's liens for work begun before the deed of trust was recorded

D. DEFICIENCY JUDGMENTS

In Texas, a **DEFICIENCY JUDGMENT** *can be obtained against the borrower when the property sold at foreclosure is insufficient to satisfy the debt owed to the lender.* By law, deficiency lawsuits must be brought within two years of the foreclosure. A lender will not be entitled to a deficiency judgment, however, when the loan is made on a non-recourse basis. In a **NON-RECOURSE LOAN**, *the lender agrees to look only to the collateral in satisfaction of the debt.*

For example, if a home was sold at a foreclosure sale for $217,000 and $240,000 was owed on the property at the time of the sale, a lender would normally be entitled to a $23,000 deficiency judgment against the borrower. However, if the loan was a non-recourse loan, no deficiency judgment may be obtained against the borrower. In Texas, reverse annuity mortgages which are intended for homeowners aged 62 and over are non-recourse loans.

In Texas, any party who may be obligated in a deficiency lawsuit may ask the court to determine the fair market value of the property as of the date of foreclosure. If the court determines that the value of the property was higher than the foreclosure sale amount, the debtors will be entitled to a reduction in the deficiency owed. Moreover, the debtor(s) must be given credit for any payments that the lender has received from private mortgage insurance.

IX. Junior Liens

When the current financial market is tight, a seller may be willing to take back a second lien (trust deed) as part of his or her equity in order to make the sale.

Even if a buyer qualifies for a loan to cover 80% of the cost of a home, he or she may still have a difficult time scraping together the 20% needed for the down payment. When a buyer does not have enough cash to cover the gap between the sales price and the loan amount, another loan, or "second" deed of trust loan, is sometimes obtained (often from the seller).

A. JUNIOR LIENS

Besides seconds, it is also possible for borrowers who qualify to obtain "third" or "fourth" liens, but they are all commonly referred to as second or junior liens. They all may be called second liens but their priority is determined by the order in which they were recorded. *Any loan on real property obtained after the first deed of trust and secured by a second, third, or subsequent lien, is known as a JUNIOR LIEN.* The most senior lien, on the other hand, is the first deed of trust.

When a buyer wants to make a smaller cash down payment or an owner wants to convert equity into cash, the best source for a junior loan is a private lender.

Example: Jane Smith is buying a house with a sale's price of $250,000. She assumes the seller's loan on the property of $200,000. She applies to her company credit union and obtains a second lien loan of $30,000, so all she needs is a cash down payment of $20,000, plus closing costs, to complete the transaction.

B. HOME EQUITY LOANS

Second lien loans are not only obtainable as part of the financing package when a property is first being purchased. Seconds and other junior liens may be arranged any time a qualified borrower wants to borrow money, for whatever reason, as long as there is sufficient equity and enough ready income to support the payments.

EQUITY is the fair market value of a property, minus the amount of money owed to lenders and all other lien holders. HOME EQUITY LOANS are loans based on the homeowner's increase in equity caused by inflation, rising property values, and the reduction, by payments, of the existing loan balance.

Let's suppose Jane Smith, who purchased that new home for $250,000, finds herself in need of money after a few years. Fortunately, her property has increased in market

value and is now worth more than $300,000. Even though Smith is already mortgaged up to her ears, she can borrow against her equity.

Home equity loans were first introduced to Texas in 1997 when voters approved amending the Texas Constitution. By law, home equity loans are non-recourse loans that must be judicially foreclosed in the event of default. These loans require a 12-day waiting period to fund, and the loan amount, when combined with the other existing liens, cannot exceed 80% of the fair market value of the home.

Figure 11-10 contains a legally required notice that outlines the key elements of home equity loans.

A Texas home equity loan is a highly regulated loan program, which when successfully used, enables Texas homeowners to borrow against a portion of the equity in their homes.

C. HOLDER OF A SECOND DEED OF TRUST LOAN

Sometimes, when purchasing a property, additional funds will be required beyond the cash down payment and the first lien deed of trust. As a result, the seller may loan the buyer more money through the use of a loan secured by a second deed of trust. Usually, the second trust deed has a higher rate of interest and a shorter payoff period because of the higher risk involved.

Second lien deeds of trust often require a balloon payment at the end of the term because they are not always fully amortized.

The holder of a second lien or any junior lien has the same legal rights as does the holder of the first lien.

Junior lien holders are entitled to payment each month, as the first lien holder. If the trustor defaults on the loan secured by a second lien, that lien holder, just like the first lien holder, can commence foreclosure proceedings. Likewise, if the trustor defaults on the first lien promissory note, the second lien holder can reinstate the note by catching up all past due amounts and commence foreclosure action against the trustor. Obviously, if the property holds significant equity, it is a wise move for the second lien holder to start his or her own foreclosure action.

D. WRAP-AROUND LOANS

A *WRAP-AROUND LOAN is a second lien loan with a face value of both the new amount it secures and the balance due under the first trust deed.* The wrap-around is seldom used except when a property is difficult to sell or credit is tight (high interest rates). This form of security may be used to increase the lender's (seller's) yield upon the sale

NOTICE CONCERNING EXTENSIONS OF CREDIT
DEFINED BY SECTION 50(a)(6), ARTICLE XVI, TEXAS CONSTITUTION

SECTION 50(A)(6), ARTICLE XVI, OF THE TEXAS CONSTITUTION ALLOWS CERTAIN LOANS TO BE SECURED AGAINST THE EQUITY IN YOUR HOME. SUCH LOANS ARE COMMONLY KNOWN AS EQUITY LOANS. IF YOU DO NOT REPAY THE LOAN OR IF YOU FAIL TO MEET THE TERMS OF THE LOAN, THE LENDER MAY FORECLOSE AND SELL YOUR HOME. THE CONSTITUTION PROVIDES THAT:

(A) THE LOAN MUST BE VOLUNTARILY CREATED WITH THE CONSENT OF EACH OWNER OF YOUR HOME AND EACH OWNER'S SPOUSE;

(B) THE PRINCIPAL LOAN AMOUNT AT THE TIME THE LOAN IS MADE MUST NOT EXCEED AN AMOUNT THAT, WHEN ADDED TO THE PRINCIPAL BALANCES OF ALL OTHER LIENS AGAINST YOUR HOME, IS MORE THAN 80% OF THE FAIR MARKET VALUE OF YOUR HOME;

(C) THE LOAN MUST BE WITHOUT RECOURSE FOR PERSONAL LIABILITY AGAINST YOU AND YOUR SPOUSE UNLESS YOU OR YOUR SPOUSE OBTAINED THIS EXTENSION OF CREDIT BY ACTUAL FRAUD;

(D) THE LIEN SECURING THE LOAN MAY BE FORECLOSED UPON ONLY WITH A COURT ORDER;

(E) FEES AND CHARGES TO MAKE THE LOAN MAY NOT EXCEED 3% OF THE LOAN AMOUNT;

(F) THE LOAN MAY NOT BE AN OPEN-END ACCOUNT THAT MAY BE DEBITED FROM TIME TO TIME OR UNDER WHICH CREDIT MAY BE EXTENDED FROM TIME TO TIME UNLESS IT IS A HOME EQUITY LINE OF CREDIT;

(G) YOU MAY PREPAY THE LOAN WITHOUT PENALTY OR CHARGE;

(H) NO ADDITIONAL COLLATERAL MAY BE SECURITY FOR THE LOAN;

(I) THE LOAN MAY NOT BE SECURED BY AGRICULTURAL HOMESTEAD PROPERTY, UNLESS THE AGRICULTURAL HOMESTEAD PROPERTY IS USED PRIMARILY FOR THE PRODUCTION OF MILK;

(J) YOU ARE NOT REQUIRED TO REPAY THE LOAN EARLIER THAN AGREED SOLELY BECAUSE THE FAIR MARKET VALUE OF YOUR HOME DECREASES OR BECAUSE YOU DEFAULT ON ANOTHER LOAN THAT IS NOT SECURED BY YOUR HOME;

(K) ONLY ONE LOAN DESCRIBED BY SECTION 50(a)(6), ARTICLE XVI, OF THE TEXAS CONSTITUTION MAY BE SECURED WITH YOUR HOME AT ANY GIVEN TIME;

(L) THE LOAN MUST BE SCHEDULED TO BE REPAID IN PAYMENTS THAT EQUAL OR EXCEED THE AMOUNT OF ACCRUED INTEREST FOR EACH PAYMENT PERIOD;

(M) THE LOAN MAY NOT CLOSE BEFORE 12 DAYS AFTER YOU SUBMIT A WRITTEN APPLICATION TO THE LENDER OR BEFORE 12 DAYS AFTER YOU RECEIVE THIS NOTICE, WHICHEVER DATE IS LATER; AND IF YOUR HOME WAS SECURITY FOR THE SAME TYPE OF LOAN WITHIN THE PAST YEAR, A NEW LOAN SECURED BY THE SAME PROPERTY MAY NOT CLOSE BEFORE ONE YEAR HAS PASSED FROM THE CLOSING DATE OF THE OTHER LOAN;

(N) THE LOAN MAY CLOSE ONLY AT THE OFFICE OF THE LENDER, TITLE COMPANY, OR AN ATTORNEY AT LAW;

(O) THE LENDER MAY CHARGE ANY FIXED OR VARIABLE RATE OF INTEREST AUTHORIZED BY STATUTE;

(P) ONLY A LAWFULLY AUTHORIZED LENDER MAY MAKE LOANS DESCRIBED BY SECTION 50(a)(6), ARTICLE XVI, OF THE TEXAS CONSTITUTION; AND

(Q) LOANS DESCRIBED BY SECTION 50(a)(6), ARTICLE XVI, OF THE TEXAS CONSTITUTION MUST:
  (1) NOT REQUIRE YOU TO APPLY THE PROCEEDS TO ANOTHER DEBT EXCEPT A DEBT THAT IS SECURED BY YOUR HOME OR OWED TO ANOTHER LENDER;
  (2) NOT REQUIRE THAT YOU ASSIGN WAGES AS SECURITY;

(continued)

(3)   NOT REQUIRE THAT YOU EXECUTE INSTRUMENTS WHICH HAVE BLANKS LEFT TO BE FILLED IN;

(4)   NOT REQUIRE THAT YOU SIGN A CONFESSION OF JUDGMENT OR POWER OF ATTORNEY TO ANOTHER PERSON TO CONFESS JUDGMENT OR APPEAR IN A LEGAL PROCEEDING ON YOUR BEHALF;

(5)   PROVIDE THAT YOU RECEIVE A COPY OF ALL DOCUMENTS YOU SIGN AT CLOSING;

(6)   PROVIDE THAT THE SECURITY INSTRUMENTS CONTAIN A DISCLOSURE THAT THIS LOAN IS A LOAN DEFINED BY SECTION 50(a)(6), ARTICLE XVI, OF THE TEXAS CONSTITUTION;

(7)   PROVIDE THAT WHEN THE LOAN IS PAID IN FULL, THE LENDER WILL SIGN AND GIVE YOU A RELEASE OF LIEN OR AN ASSIGNMENT OF THE LIEN, WHICHEVER IS APPROPRIATE;

(8)   PROVIDE THAT YOU MAY, WITHIN 3 DAYS AFTER CLOSING, RESCIND THE LOAN WITHOUT PENALTY OR CHARGE;

(9)   PROVIDE THAT YOU AND THE LENDER ACKNOWLEDGE THE FAIR MARKET VALUE OF YOUR HOME ON THE DATE THE LOAN CLOSES; AND

(10)   PROVIDE THAT THE LENDER WILL FORFEIT ALL PRINCIPAL AND INTEREST IF THE LENDER FAILS TO COMPLY WITH THE LENDER'S OBLIGATIONS UNLESS THE LENDER CURES THE FAILURE TO COMPLY AS PROVIDED BY SECTION 50 (a)(6)(Q)(x), ARTICLE XVI, OF THE TEXAS CONSTITUTION; AND

(R)   IF THE LOAN IS A HOME EQUITY LINE OF CREDIT:

(1)   YOU MAY REQUEST ADVANCES, REPAY MONEY, AND REBORROW MONEY UNDER THE LINE OF CREDIT;

(2)   EACH ADVANCE UNDER THE LINE OF CREDIT MUST BE IN AN AMOUNT OF AT LEAST $4,000;

(3)   YOU MAY NOT USE A CREDIT CARD, DEBIT CARD, SOLICITATION CHECK, OR SIMILAR DEVICE TO OBTAIN ADVANCES UNDER THE LINE OF CREDIT;

(4)   ANY FEES THE LENDER CHARGES MAY BE CHARGED AND COLLECTED ONLY AT THE TIME THE LINE OF CREDIT IS ESTABLISHED AND THE LENDER MAY NOT CHARGE A FEE IN CONNECTION WITH ANY ADVANCE;

(5)   THE MAXIMUM PRINCIPAL AMOUNT THAT MAY BE EXTENDED, WHEN ADDED TO ALL OTHER DEBTS SECURED BY YOUR HOME, MAY NOT EXCEED 80 PERCENT OF THE FAIR MARKET VALUE OF YOUR HOME ON THE DATE THE LINE OF CREDIT IS ESTABLISHED;

(6)   IF THE PRINCIPAL BALANCE UNDER THE LINE OF CREDIT AT ANY TIME EXCEEDS 50 PERCENT OF THE FAIR MARKET VALUE OF YOUR HOME, AS DETERMINED ON THE DATE THE LINE OF CREDIT IS ESTABLISHED, YOU MAY NOT CONTINUE TO REQUEST ADVANCES UNDER THE LINE OF CREDIT UNTIL THE BALANCE IS LESS THAN 50 PERCENT OF THE FAIR MARKET VALUE; AND

(7)   THE LENDER MAY NOT UNILATERALLY AMEND THE TERMS OF THE LINE OF CREDIT.

THIS NOTICE IS ONLY A SUMMARY OF YOUR RIGHTS UNDER THE TEXAS CONSTITUTION. YOUR RIGHTS ARE GOVERNED BY SECTION 50, ARTICLE XVI, OF THE TEXAS CONSTITUTION, AND NOT BY THIS NOTICE.

_____

The undersigned owner/borrower(s) and spouse(s) acknowledge receipt of this Notice on

_____ , _____ .

_____   _____

_____   _____

of property and to provide easy financing for the buyer. Rather than having a new buyer assume an existing loan, the seller carries back a wrap-around note at a higher rate of interest (if the loan is assumable). The seller continues to pay off the first deed of trust out of the payment received from the buyer. Since these payments are larger, the seller gets a margin of profit. The buyer, in turn, gets easy financing and avoids the new loan fees charged by institutional lenders. As always, an attorney should be consulted because wrap-around contracts may require special handling and will not be available with all loans.

If a deed of trust contains a "due on sale" clause, meaning that the promissory note must be paid in full if the property is sold, wrap-around financing may not be possible.

Example: Sam Seller has a $300,000 property with an existing 6% interest loan of $150,000. He makes a $900 loan payment every month. Bill Buyer wants to buy the property and gives Sam $30,000 in cash down, while Sam carries a wrap-around note for the remaining $270,000 owed. He charges Bill 7% interest payable in monthly installments of $1,132. When Sam receives his $1,132 each month, he uses $900 of it to pay off his 6% loan while pocketing the remaining $232.

X. Land Contract
(Conditional Installment Sales Contract
Also Known as a Contract for Deed)

Deeds of trust, mortgages, and land contracts are all methods of financing; they are financing instruments referred to as "security devices."

The **LAND CONTRACT** *is an instrument of finance in which the seller retains legal ownership of the property until the buyer has made the last payment.* It is usually called a land contract in Texas, but may also be referred to as a "contract of sale," "contract for deed," "conditional sales contract," or an "installment sales contract." Since this is a contract between the buyer and seller, the requirements as to the down payment and other conditions of the land contract are negotiable.

When financing is hard to obtain, this can be an alternative to the usual financing methods. Although it is not widely used, it is a valid financing device and most often utilized by the Texas Veterans Land Board for the sale of real estate.

An owner selling under a land contract is known as a **VENDOR.** *A* **VENDEE** *is a buyer using a land contract.*

With a conditional sales contract (land contract), the seller (vendor) gives the buyer (vendee) equitable title and possession but keeps legal title. The vendor is the lender and the vendee is the borrower.

With a land contract the buyer holds **equitable title**, like a borrower purchasing under a trust deed. He/she is entitled, though, to the full use and enjoyment of the property. **Legal title** is held by the seller until the land contract terms have been completely fulfilled.

A deed to the property is given only when the land contract is paid off in full.

In Texas, land contracts, other than those used by the Texas Veterans Land Board, are mainly governed by state law. The law requires that if negotiations take place in a language other English, then the seller must provide copies of all required documents in that language. Furthermore, before a sale takes place, the seller must provide the buyer with a recent survey, copies of any document which may affect title and a property disclosure form as shown in **Figure 11-11**. The failure to provide these documents will entitle the purchaser to rescind the contract as well as expose the seller to the harsh provisions of the Texas Deceptive Trade Practices Act.

But since the greatest risk a purchaser under an installment sales contract faces is that he/she will fall behind by one payment and literally lose the farm, the law concentrates on this area.

If a purchaser under an installment contract defaults, which is defined as the failure to make a timely payment or perform some other contract term, then the seller is required to mail the buyer a notice specifying the exact nature of the default and giving the purchaser 30 days to cure. Should the purchaser fail to cure the default within that time, the seller is entitled to rescind the contract, effectively leaving the purchaser with nothing.

However, if the purchaser defaults after having paid the seller 40 percent or more of the sales price or the equivalent of 48 monthly payments, then the seller's remedy is different.

Under the law, the seller here will be required to post the property for foreclosure, much like that of an ordinary Texas deed of trust with power of sale provisions. And like a deed of trust, the purchaser will be entitled to any surplus funds that may result from the trustee's sale or he/she will be liable for any deficiency.

Finally, to ensure that the seller holds up his/her part of the bargain, state law mandates sellers to transfer title to the purchaser within 30 days after the seller receives the purchaser's final payment. Should the seller fail or refuse to do so, purchaser may legally impose liquidated damages of $250 per day beginning on day 31. Beginning on day 91

Figure 11-11

WARNING

IF ANY OF THE ITEMS BELOW HAVE NOT BEEN CHECKED, YOU MAY NOT BE ABLE TO LIVE ON THE PROPERTY.

SELLER'S DISCLOSURE NOTICE

CONCERNING THE PROPERTY AT (street address or legal description and city)

THIS DOCUMENT STATES CERTAIN APPLICABLE FACTS ABOUT THE PROPERTY YOU ARE CONSIDERING PURCHASING.

CHECK ALL THE ITEMS THAT ARE APPLICABLE OR TRUE:

_____ The property is in a recorded subdivision.

_____ The property has water service that provides potable water.

_____ The property has sewer service.

_____ The property has been approved by the appropriate municipal, county, or state agency for installation of a septic system.

_____ The property has electric service.

_____ The property is not in a floodplain.

_____ The roads to the boundaries of the property are paved and maintained by:
 _____ the seller;
 _____ the owner of the property on which the road exists;
 _____ the municipality;
 _____ the county; or
 _____ the state.

_____ No individual or entity other than the seller:
 _____ (1) owns the property;
 _____ (2) has a claim of ownership to the property; or
 _____ (3) has an interest in the property.

_____ No individual or entity has a lien filed against the property.

_____ There are no restrictive covenants, easements, or other title exceptions or encumbrances that prohibit construction of a house on the property.

NOTICE: SELLER ADVISES PURCHASER TO:

(1) OBTAIN A TITLE ABSTRACT OR TITLE COMMITMENT COVERING THE PROPERTY AND HAVE THE ABSTRACT OR COMMITMENT REVIEWED BY AN ATTORNEY BEFORE SIGNING A CONTRACT OF THIS TYPE; AND

(2) PURCHASE AN OWNER'S POLICY OF TITLE INSURANCE COVERING THE PROPERTY.

_____   _____
(Date)   (Signature of Seller)

_____   _____
(Date)   (Signature of Purchaser)

431

Chapter 11

after the seller has received the final payment the damage amount jumps to $500 per day.

Parties contemplating using a land contract to finance the purchase and sale of real estate in Texas should consult with an attorney before entering this highly risky form of purchasing real estate.

XI. Truth in Lending Act (Regulation "Z") and Other Acts

The purpose of the Federal Truth in Lending Act is for the lender to disclose the cost of credit terms to the buyer.

This disclosure must be presented to the borrower within 3 business days of receiving the borrower's loan application.

Regulation Z, which implements the provisions of the federal Truth in Lending Act, applies to dwellings with only one-to-four residential units. Agricultural loans are exempt from the truth in lending law as are business and commercial loans.

A. TRUTH IN LENDING

The Truth in Lending Act, sometimes called "Regulation Z" even though the regulation implements the law, was enacted to protect the consumer by requiring that the lender (creditor) tell the borrower how much he or she is paying for credit. This enables the consumer to make comparisons between various credit sources. Regulation Z also states that the lender (creditor) must express all related financing costs as a percentage, known as the annual percentage rate (APR).

Regulation Z requires a creditor to make important financial disclosures. These required disclosures include:

1. Annual Percentage Rate (APR)*
2. Finance charges
3. Amount financed*
4. Total number of payments
5. Total sales price (credit sales)

The two most important items, according to Regulation Z, are the APR and the amount financed.

The provisions of Regulation Z can be enforced by means of a private lawsuit, but the law is publicly enforced by the Federal Trade Commission (FTC).

A low down payment and a long-term loan will increase the total financing cost.

1. Annual Percentage Rate (APR)

The APR is the measure or "relative cost of credit" expressed as a yearly rate. It is a percentage rate, NOT an interest rate. If the APR appears in an advertisement, NO other disclosure of terms need be stated because it includes all credit costs.

The *ANNUAL PERCENTAGE RATE (APR) represents the relationship between the total of the finance charges (interest rate, points, and the loan fee) and the total amount financed, expressed as a percentage*. It must be computed to the nearest one-quarter of one percent and must be printed on the loan form more conspicuously than the rest of the printed material.

Interest rates can be calculated by many different methods that can be very confusing to the borrower. The APR standardizes these figures, calculating all rates by the same formula. Borrowers should look for the APR figure (usually in a box) to compare and find the best APR available.

The APR includes all "finance charges," including assumption charges, but it does NOT include: 1) the cost of a credit report; and 2) appraisal fees, which are exempt.

2. Advertising Terms May Require Additional Disclosures

Anyone placing an advertisement for consumer credit must comply with the advertising requirements of the Truth in Lending Act. Disclosures must be made "clearly and conspicuously." If only the annual percentage (APR) rate is disclosed, additional disclosures are not required. If, however, an advertisement contains any one of the following terms, then the ad must also disclose other credit terms:

1. The amount or percentage of any down payment
2. The number of payments or period of repayment
3. The amount of any payment
4. The amount of any finance charge

When advertising a graduated payment loan, differences in monthly payments must be disclosed.

B. RIGHT TO CANCEL (Federal Notice of Right to Cancel)

Loans subsequent (future loans) have a 3-day right of rescission by the borrower (not original deeds of trust).

The **RIGHT TO CANCEL** *is the federal law that gives a borrower the right to rescind (cancel) any loan transaction only if it is a business loan or a second deed of trust secured by the borrower's home.* The borrower has until midnight of the third business day following the signing to cancel.

A promissory note secured by a first lien deed of trust which is used to finance the purchase of the borrower's home carries no right of rescission. However, a first loan secured on the borrower's home for any other purpose, including refinancing, or a second loan on the same home, may be canceled within 3 business days .

The borrower has the right to rescind when a loan is secured by a second lien deed of trust on an owner-occupied single-family residence already owned by the borrower.

C. EQUAL CREDIT OPPORTUNITY ACT

The **EQUAL CREDIT OPPORTUNITY ACT** *is a federal law prohibiting those who lend money from discriminating against borrowers based on their race, sex, color, religion, national origin, age, or marital status.*

It can also require lenders to consider individuals on the merits of their personal credit, as distinct from the bad credit history of a joint account. It also insists that lenders respond quickly to loan applications and be prepared to explain any loan refusal.

A more detailed discussion of this federal law is contained in Chapter 7.

D. SOLDIERS AND SAILORS CIVIL RELIEF ACT

The **SOLDIERS AND SAILORS CIVIL RELIEF ACT** *is a law passed by Congress to protect persons serving in the military, and their dependents, from loss of real property through foreclosure.*

In general, the law prohibits the sale or foreclosure of real estate owned by a military person without his or her expressed approval or a court order. It also extends foreclosure proceedings and the mortgage redemption period. Career soldiers are exempt.

XII. CHAPTER SUMMARY

Leverage is the practice of purchasing real estate using a small amount of your own money and a larger proportion of borrowed funds. Buyers generally **hypothecate** their property as security for a real estate loan, meaning they provide title as security for the loan, without giving up possession.

A **promissory note** is the basic instrument used to evidence the obligation or debt and can be a **straight note**, an **installment note** with a **balloon payment** or the most commonly used in Texas, a **fully amortized installment note**.

If it meets all the legal requirements, a promissory note can be a **fully negotiable instrument**, like a check, meaning that it is easily transferred to an innocent third party, known as a **holder in due course**.

An **acceleration clause** speeds up the balance due based on the occurrence of a specific event. A buyer can **assume** a loan on a property by accepting responsibility (with the lender's consent) for the full payment of the loan, but cannot assume an existing loan that contains an **alienation clause** (where the entire balance becomes due when the property is sold, assigned, or transferred). A **subordination clause** allows a borrower to obtain additional loans on the property that have a higher priority. A **prepayment penalty** may not be charged on new FHA and VA loans.

Real estate loans involve **simple interest**. The **nominal interest rate** is stated in the note, whereas the **effective interest rate** includes **interest, points,** and **loan fees**. The formula for finding interest is:

$$\text{Interest} = \text{Principal} \times \text{Rate} \times \text{Time}$$

With a **fixed interest rate loan**, the payments are the same for the life of the loan.

Amortization is the repaying of a loan (principal and interest) in regular payments over the term of the loan. If the interest rate charges are higher than the monthly payment, it's called **negative amortization**. An **adjusted rate mortgage (ARM)** has a fluctuating interest rate based on a specific index, meaning the payment amounts may also change.

A **point** equals 1% of the loan amount. **Usury** is charging more than the legally allowed percentage of interest.

The three financial instruments (security devices) used in Texas are: 1) **mortgages** (rare), 2) **deeds of trust** (1st and 2nd liens are common), and 3) **land contracts** (uncommon).

In Texas, the terms mortgage and trust deed are often used interchangeably, but in reality, we are usually referring to deeds of trust.

A **deed of trust** is personal property, and needs a **promissory note** for security. It is not a **negotiable instrument**, but the promissory note is. The **trustor** borrows the money from the **beneficiary**, who is the lender. A **trustee** is the third, disinterested party (usually an attorney or corporation) who holds an interest in the property on the condition it may have to be sold for the beneficiary if the trustor defaults. Since Texas is a **lien theory state**, full title is held by the trustor, while the beneficiary or lender holds a lien interest in the property. But in **title theory states**, the trustee holds legal title until such time as the note is paid in full. In Texas, when the loan is completely paid, the trustor or homeowner is entitled to a **release of lien** as proof that a promissory note as secured by the deed of trust has been paid in full.

If a borrower defaults on the repayment of a promissory note, the remedy is to commence **foreclosure** proceedings. **Default** is a breach of a specified duty under a promissory note and deed of trust. The foreclosure process consists of a default, followed by a **20-day Notice to Cure** default, a **21-day Notice of Sale**, and the foreclosure sale. By law, foreclosures must occur between the hours of **10:00 AM and 4:00 PM on the first Tuesday of the month** following the 21-day Notice of Sale. The foreclosure sale occurs on the steps of the courthouse or wherever county officials designate such sales should occur.

A homeowner facing foreclosure proceedings has the right to receive all notices concerning the pending foreclosure and may additionally enter into a **Forbearance Agreement** or **Workout Plan** with a willing lender. A forbearance agreement is a contract whereby the lender agrees not to exercise its legal right to foreclose. Otherwise, a debtor facing foreclosure proceedings also has an equitable right of redemption. But once the foreclosure sale occurs, the right of redemption terminates. Finally, if the foreclosure sale results in the sale of the property for amount less than what is owed to the lender, the debtor-homeowner may face a deficiency judgment for the balance. A lender will usually be entitled to a deficiency judgment against the note maker unless it is a **non-recourse**, loan in which case the lender will agree to limit its recovery to only the value of the collateral.

Any loan on real property secured by a second, third, or subsequent deed of trust is known as a **junior lien**. The best sources for junior liens are **private lenders**.

Home equity loans are based on the increase in equity caused by inflation, rising property values, and the reduction, by payments, of the existing loan balance. They are generally secured by second (junior) liens and subject to strict requirements under Texas law.

A **land contract** is also called a **real property sales contract**, an **agreement of sale**, a **contract for deed**, or an **installment sales contract**. It is an instrument of finance in which the **vendor** (seller) retains legal ownership of property until the **vendee** (buyer) has made the last payment. A **wrap-around loan** is a second lien financing device with a face value of both the new amount it secures and the balance due under the first deed of trust. Wrap-around financing may not be available if the loan has a due on sale clause.

The **Truth in Lending Act** as implemented by **Regulation Z** requires lenders to disclose the costs of credit terms to borrowers within three business days of receiving a loan application. The two most important terms are the **Annual Percentage Rate (APR)** and amount financed. APR is the "cost of credit" expressed in percentage terms.

A borrower has the right to rescind within three days when a loan is secured by a second lien and on an owner-occupied single-family residence already owned by the borrower.

The **Equal Credit Opportunity Act** is a federal law prohibiting money lenders from discriminating against borrowers based on race, sex, color, religion, national origin, age, or marital status. The **Soldiers and Sailors Civil Relief Act** protects military personnel and their dependents from foreclosure.

XIII. TERMINOLOGY

A. Acceleration Clause
B. Adjustable Rate Mortgage
C. Alienation Clause Mortgage
D. Amortization
E. Amortization Table
F. Annual Percentage Rate
G. Assumption
H. Beneficiary
I. Default
J. Deficiency Judgment
K. Equal Credit Opportunity
L. Equitable Right of Redemption
M. Equitable Title
N. Equity
O. Forebearance Agreement

P. Grace Period
Q. Graduated Payment
R. Holder in Due Course
S. Hypothecation
T. Interest
U. Junior Lien or Second Deed of Trust Deed
V. Land Contract
W. Legal Title
X. Leverage
Y. Non-Recourse Loan
Z. Point
AA. Prepayment Penalty
BB. Promissory Note

CC. Release of Lien
DD. Right to Cancel
EE. Straight Note
FF. Subordination Clause
GG. Deed of Trust
HH. Trustee
II. Trustee's Sale
JJ. Trustor
KK. Truth in Lending Act
LL. Usury
MM. Vendee
NN. Vendor
OO. Wrap-Around Loan

1. ____ An instrument used to release a lien against real property obtained under a deed of trust.

2. ____ A second lien loan for which the monthly payment includes the amount of monthly payment on the existing first lien loan.

3. ____ Federal law granting women financial independence and preventing lenders from considering such negative credit aspects as the possibility of a woman having children and dropping out of the labor market.

4. ____ A mortgage or deed of trust for which the payments increase over the term of the loan. The payments may increase as the buyer's earnings increase.

5. ____ The amount for which the borrower is personally liable on a note and mortgage if the foreclosure sale does not bring enough to cover the debt.

6. ____ A penalty under a note, mortgage, or deed of trust imposed when the loan is paid before it is due.

7. ____ The total cost of financing expressed as one simple annual percentage rate. This rate must be clearly expressed on any loan agreement.

8. ____ A promise in writing to pay a specified amount during a limited time, or on demand, to a named person.

9. ____ Clause used in a deed of trust that gives the lender the right to demand payment in full upon the happening of a certain event.

10. ____ Ownership by one who does not have legal title, such as a vendee under a land contract.

11. ____ A sale at auction by a trustee under a deed of trust, pursuant to foreclosure proceedings.

12. ____ A type of lien that is subordinate to a prior lien.

13. ____ An instrument commonly used in Texas and used in place of a mortgage whereby a lien is given to a lender in order to secure payment under a promissory note.

14. ____ A type of acceleration clause, calling for a debt under a mortgage or deed of trust, to be due in its entirety upon transfer of ownership.

15. ____ The use of financing to allow a small amount of cash to purchase and control a large property investment.

16. ____ A period of time past the due date for a payment (mortgage, insurance, etc.) during which a payment may be made and not considered delinquent.

17. ____ A purchaser or buyer, especially on a land contract.

18. ____ A non-amortized note for which the principal is due in a lump sum upon maturity.
19. ____ Charging an illegal rate or amount of interest on a loan.
20. ____ Payment of debt in regular, periodic installments of principal and interest, as opposed to interest only payments.
21. ____ The seller of property under a land contract.
22. ____ The kind of title held by the vendor under a land contract who is still owed money by the buyer.
23. ____ An installment contract for the sale of land. The seller (vendor) has legal title until paid in full. The buyer (vendee) has equitable title during the contract term.
24. ____ A financing charge equal to one percent of the amount of the loan.
25. ____ Money charged for the use of money.
26. ____ A failure to perform a specified duty under a promissory note and deed of trust.
27. ____ A holder of a check or note who takes the note in good faith, on the assumption it is valid.
28. ____ The borrower under a deed of trust.
29. ____ In a deed of trust, the person who will normally conduct the foreclosure sale as requested by the beneficiary.
30. ____ A lender for whose benefit a deed of trust is created.
31. ____ The ownership interest in real property; it is the market value minus any unpaid loan amount.
32. ____ Agreement by the buyer to take over the financial responsibility for real property under the existing note and deed of trust.
33. ____ An agreement by which a lender substitutes a junior loan position for a senior loan position.
34. ____ A table of monthly loan payments that varies according to interest rates and number of monthly payments.
35. ____ Mortgage loans on which the interest rate is periodically adjusted to more closely coincide with current rates.
36. ____ A federal law that requires a credit purchaser be advised, in writing, of all costs connected with the credit portion of his/her purchase.
37. ____ The principle of using real property as security for a debt while the borrower retains possession.
38. ____ A trustor's right to redeem real property prior to the foreclosure sale.
39. ____ A loan which, if the trustor defaults, will not result in a deficiency judgment because the lender has agreed to look only to the collateral in satisfaction of debt.
40. ____ A part of the Truth In Lending Act that allows a borrower to rescind a loan transaction until midnight of the third business day on business loans and second lien loans secured by a borrower's residence.
41. ____ An agreement, supported by consideration, where a lender agrees not to exercise a legal right to do something it is entitled to do such as continue with a foreclosure action.

XIV. MULTIPLE CHOICE

1. Which of the following elements is not required for a promissory note to be considered a negotiable instrument?

    a. Signed by the maker
    b. The amount of interest to be charged
    c. Payable on demand or set date
    d. The exact amount of money to be loaned

2. Before a trustee can issue a Notice of Sale, a residential borrower facing foreclosure is entitled by law to receive a:

    a. Notice of Equitable Redemption.
    b. Notice to Cure Default.
    c. Forbearance Agreement.
    d. none of the above.

3. In Texas, non-judicial foreclosure sales must occur:

    a. on the first day following the expiration of 21 days from the Notice of Sale.
    b. between the hours of 9:00AM and 3:00 PM.
    c. on the first Tuesday of the month.
    d. as ordered by a judge.

4. A lender that has been completely paid should provide to a trustor a(n):

    a. Notice of Satisfaction.
    b. Forbearance Agreement.
    c. Release of Lien.
    d. All Bills Paid Affidavit.

5. In real estate terms, "hypothecation" means to:

    a. sell real estate.
    b. pledge real estate as collateral.
    c. amortize real estate.
    d. none of the above.

6. A minimum of how many days must elapse between the Notice of Sale and the actual date of the trustee's foreclosure sale?

    a. 90
    b. 111
    c. 21
    d. None of the above

7. The figure that represents the relationship of the total finance charges to the total amount financed is known as the:

    a. lender's percentage rate.
    b. borrower's percentage rate.
    c. annual percentage rate.
    d. finance percentage rate.

8. What kind of instrument refers to real property that is sold on credit where the seller retains legal title until the debt is paid off?

    a. VA loan
    b. Pledge agreement
    c. Mortgage
    d. Land contract

9. One month's interest payment on a straight note amounts to $180. At 9% per annum interest rate, what is the face amount of the note?

    a. $26,000
    b. $24,000
    c. $20,000
    d. $27,000

10. The practice of charging more interest than legally allowed is known as:

    a. hypothecation.
    b. domination.
    c. usuary.
    d. dation of payment.

ANSWERS: 1. b; 2. b; 3. c; 4. c; 5. b; 6. c; 7. c; 8. d; 9. b; 10. c

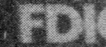

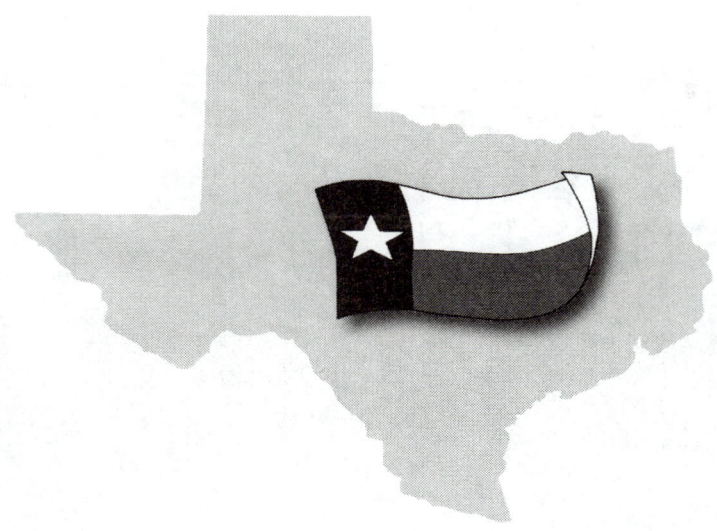

Chapter 12
Financial Institutions

www.countrywide.com
Countrywide Financial - Large Home Lender

The real estate money market, like any other commodity market, changes constantly. Money for financing real estate may be plentiful in one month or quarter, then scarce and expensive in the next. The money market is no longer national, it has become a global market. A broker must be able to finance real estate transactions every month if he or she expects to remain in business. Because of this, a broker must be able to use all the standard financing methods and any unconventional methods that may fit the time and situation.

Before you advertise a property or present it to a prospect, try to visualize all the ways the property may be financed. The more alternatives available, the more likely you are to negotiate a sale. Real estate finance continues to become more variable and more complex as time goes on. This chapter will explain the sources of funds available from financial institutions, the government's role, and other creative prospects and information that will assist you when offering financing.

CHAPTER 12 OUTLINE

I. Our Ever Changing Economy (Economic Cycles)

With regard to inflation, market value increases and sales price increases. When the general level of prices decreases, the value of money increases.

Because our government's spending and taxing policies shift with every new election, our economy is in a constant state of transition. From month-to-month, it is difficult to predict what amount of financing money will be available and what rate of interest will be charged. These influences, multiplied over a period of years, make it nearly impossible to accurately project long-term trends in the money supply.

INFLATION is the result of too much money chasing too few goods. When the economy is going very well, most people are making more money and spending it too freely, thereby driving up the price of real estate and other goods. The Fed, sensing that inflation is out of control, starts applying the brakes and starts restricting the amount of money available.

This and higher interest rates decrease borrowing. If the Fed is forced to apply the brakes hard, deflation will occur. **DEFLATION** *is when prices of real estate, goods, and services go down.*

> *A "seller's market" is when prices rise due to shortages of available properties, and a "buyer's market" is when prices fall.*

It is a **BUYER'S MARKET** *when the prices of real estate are down; terms are easy and there is usually a great deal of real estate listed for sale or rent.* Buyers have a choice; there is more to pick and choose from, at lower prices. In a **SELLER'S MARKET**, *the prices of real estate are up and there is less real estate listed for sale or rent. This is due to increased demand and lagging supplies.*

A. THE FEDERAL RESERVE BANKING SYSTEM ("Fed")

The Federal Reserve Banking System is the single greatest influence on the cost and supply of money for real estate loans. It is the link between America's private financial institutions and the taxing and spending policies of the federal government. The **FEDERAL RESERVE BANKING SYSTEM (The "Fed")** *is the nation's central banking authority.* If the Fed makes money tight, thus restricting the amount of available loan funds, demand for the available funds increases, pushing interest rates higher. Conversely, if the Fed increases the amount of money in circulation, interest rates go down. In this way they keep centralized control over the interest rates for not only banks, but for all lending institutions.

> *When the Federal Reserve wants to obtain a tight money market, it raises the discount rate and sells government bonds. When the federal reserve wants a "loose" money market, it buys back bonds and lowers reserve requirements of banks.*

These operations and the other important functions of the Federal Reserve System are supervised by the Federal Reserve Board. The **FEDERAL RESERVE BOARD** *is a committee appointed by the President, but is politically independent.* In regulating the amount and flow of loan money available to banks, the board has indirect but far-reaching influence over all lending institutions and the economy as a whole.

The Federal Reserve's monetary policies influence the supply of money by:

1. buying and selling government T-bonds and T-securities;
2. raising and lowering the reserve requirement;
3. raising and lowering the discount rate to member banks; and
4. margin requirements (percentage loaned on stocks and bonds).

www.federalreserve.gov/sitemap.htm (Federal Reserve Board)
www.ustreas.gov (U.S. Treasury)
www.occ.treas.gov (Office of the Comptroller of the Currency)
www.frbsf.org (Federal Reserve Bank of San Francisco - 12th District)

B. GROSS DOMESTIC PRODUCT (Measures Economic Activity)

We can monitor growth in our economy and the influence of the Fed by watching closely any changes in the gross domestic product. The *GROSS DOMESTIC PRODUCT (GDP) is the total value of all goods and services produced by an economy during a specific period of time.* It serves as a kind of monetary barometer that shows us the rate and areas of greatest growth.

Depression, recession, expansion, and prosperity represent four phases of the business cycle.

C. CHANGING INTEREST RATES (Affect Real Estate)

The economy goes in cycles. Interest rates go up and down. When interest rates go down, people will buy more homes. When interest rates go up, people will buy fewer homes, and have a harder time selling their homes. When interest rates go down, homes become more affordable.

If a homeowner has a high interest rate and the rate goes down, he or she may choose to refinance. *REFINANCING is the process of obtaining a new loan to pay off the old loan.* If interest rates fall dramatically, it is wise to consider refinancing.

In a tight money market, lenders may waive prepayment penalty clauses in order to lend out that money at a higher rate than old loans.

II. Shopping for a Loan

All the variables of our changing economy come home in a very personal way when a borrower goes out to look for a loan. For the average person, borrowing the money necessary to buy a house is the largest financial obligation he or she is likely to assume in his or her lifetime. It's an extremely important decision, second only to the selection of the property itself. The salesperson should advise caution and careful consideration before a promissory note is signed. Shopping around for a loan from several different loan sources is an excellent idea. Even if the borrower has found financing that he or she feels is acceptable, talking to other lenders should never be discouraged. **Figure 12-1** provides a detailed discussion of the steps in obtaining a loan.

Figure 12-1

Steps in Obtaining a Loan

1. Application

After deciding that a real estate loan is necessary, the first step in obtaining the loan is filling out a loan application. It would be a good idea to shop around and check for the best rate and terms at various institutions or with a mortgage broker before applying because, despite what many people suspect, every lender is different. Finding the right loan is as important as finding the right piece of real estate. The application will request detailed information regarding both the property and the borrower.

2. Analysis

The application generally receives a preliminary screening to determine if there are any obvious and glaring reasons why either the prospective borrower or the property could not qualify for a loan. This process is accomplished by credit scoring. This analysis is followed by a professional appraisal of the property and an in-depth investigation into the credit background of the applicant (in addition to credit scoring). The lender wants to know how likely the borrower is to meet monthly payments and pay back the loan. This is analyzed with reference to the borrower's "capacity" and "desire" to pay.

CAPACITY is determined based upon a borrower's savings, valuable property, and income, and is evaluated in terms of the reliability of these assets. Excellent evidence of capacity would be good collateral. COLLATERAL is valuable property pledged as a guarantee for payment of a loan. DESIRE (to pay) is demonstrated by a good credit history reflecting the discipline to make monthly payments on time. A background of late payments and loan defaults would make it difficult to get loan approval.

3. Processing

If loan analysis proves favorable and financing terms are acceptable to all parties, it is then time to get the terms of the agreement down on paper. Processing involves typing up the loan documents, preparing necessary disclosure statements, and issuing instructions to the escrow holder.

4. Escrow

All the paperwork of the loan transaction ends up in escrow along with all the other contracts involved in the purchase of real property. The deed and promissory note are signed and passed along to the escrow company where the deal is closed. In Texas, a title insurance company usually prepares the documents, acts as escrow agent, and provides title insurance.

5. Servicing

Loan servicing involves mailing monthly loan statements, collecting payments, and seeing to it that all records are kept up to date. Some lenders service their own loans while others hire independent mortgage companies to handle the paperwork for them. Loan servicing also involves all correspondence for late and delinquent payments.

Qualifying for a Loan

All lenders set their own standards for evaluating who qualifies and who does not qualify for loan money. These standards are reflected in the interest rates charged. Some lenders have very strict requirements, while others will take a greater risk but charge a higher rate of interest—especially on second lien notes. Real estate agents can obtain more specific guidelines simply by contacting local lenders.

Previously, lending institutions decided whether or not a borrower was qualified based upon a simple formula: the property should not cost more than two-and-a-half times the borrower's annual income. Today, however, many lenders recognize that this method can be very inadequate. It fails to take into account other debts that the borrower might be paying off and doesn't give the middle income property buyer, or those entering the housing market for the first time, much of a chance with today's high-cost real estate.

New rules of thumb relate to qualifying ratios which take into consideration the ratio of debt to income in two major ways:

1. The ratio of the total monthly house payment (PITI – principal, interest, taxes, insurance) to all total gross monthly income. The generally accepted standard is that the total monthly payment should be about 28% of all total gross monthly income.
2. The ratio of all long term monthly debt, including PITI, to all total gross monthly income. The generally accepted standard is that the total debt should be about 36% of all total gross monthly income.

Appraisal of the Property

Just as the borrower is evaluated during the loan process, lenders evaluate the property being purchased. They want to be certain that the price being paid reflects a fair market value. If a property is overpriced and the borrower defaults, it might be difficult for the lender to recoup the amount of the loan. This process of determining a property's fair market value is known as appraisal and is discussed in detail in Chapters 13 and 14.

Institutional lenders will lend the entire amount needed for the purchase of a property to a qualified buyer but prefer to lend less than the entire amount. Most often they will determine the fair market value and lend a set percentage of that amount. The L-T-V is generally 80-100%. Collateral is required but most often the property itself (include any structures) is used as security for the loan.

The lower the L-T-V, the greater the down payment required.

A. LOAN TO VALUE (Percent of Appraised Value Lender Will Loan)

LOAN TO VALUE is the percentage of appraised value the lender will loan to the borrower to purchase the property. It is abbreviated as L-T-V or L to V. The lower the L-T-V, the higher the down payment has to be. The lower the L-T-V, the more equity is required.

B. ESTIMATE OF SETTLEMENT COSTS (RESPA)

The lender must give the applicant the HUD booklet that explains closing costs and has until three business days after receipt of a loan application to provide a good faith estimate of the actual settlement costs to the borrower.

The Real Estate Settlement Procedures Act (RESPA) disclosure must include:

1. the rate of interest;
2. points to be charged;
3. any additional loan fees and charges; and
4. escrow, title, and other allowable costs, which could add up to $1,000 or more above lender's estimates.

The idea is to alert the borrower, at the beginning of the loan process, to how much cash besides the down payment will be needed to close escrow. Usually the lender will provide the complete estimated settlement cost form along with the loan application.

C. CREDIT SCORING (Access to Credit Profile)

CREDIT SCORING gives lenders a fast, objective measurement of your ability to repay a loan or make timely credit payments. It is based solely on information in consumer credit reports maintained at one of the credit reporting agencies. Factors comprising a credit score include:

1. **Payment History** – What is your track record?
2. **Amounts Owed** – How much is too much?
3. **Length of Credit History** – How established is yours?
4. **New Credit** – Are you taking on more debt?
5. **Types of Credit Use** – Is it a "healthy" mix?

The most widely used credit bureau scores are developed by Fair, Isaac and Company. These are known as **FICO SCORES**. See **Figure 12-2** for a fuller description of credit scoring.

If a credit agency refuses to provide a copy of a credit report to an applicant who is denied credit, the applicant can:

Figure 12-2

Credit Scoring

Over the past several years, lenders have increased their use of "credit scores," derived from information in a consumer's credit report, using a mathematical model to develop a three-digit score and determine whether or not to make a loan, and at what interest rate.

WHAT IS CREDIT SCORING?

Credit scores are assigned numbers used by lenders to determine whether a consumer will get a loan and at what interest rate. Individual lenders often contract with a credit reporting agency such as Trans Union, Experian, or Equifax who compile consumer credit information. These companies then contract with a credit scoring company, more often than not, Fair, Isaac and Company (www.fairisaac.com), who own the mathematical model used to create the score. They provide the lender with a list of "reason codes" that the lender can choose from when receiving scores for consumers applying for mortgages. The reason codes can include things like, "too few bank card accounts," "too many sub-prime accounts," etc. The credit scoring company uses information from a consumer's credit report, together with these reason codes and the mathematical formula to create an individual's credit score.

What factors are considered in a FICO credit score?

Weight	Factor
35%	Payment history
30%	Amounts owed and relationship with credit limit.
15%	Length of credit history
10%	New credit and credit inquiries
10%	Types of credit lines

www.transunion.com
TransUnion
www.experian.com/consumer/index.html
Experian
Equifax- www.equifax.com
Equifax

1. file civil action against the credit agency;
2. negotiate a settlement; or
3. require the credit agency to pay all legal fees.

D. THE LOAN APPLICATION

The lender needs a loan application from the borrower so that the borrower's financial condition can be analyzed. **Figure 12-3** shows two pages of the FHLMC/FNMA application form that is used by most financial institutions. The application provides the lender with the following:

1. Information about property being financed
2. Information about borrower (and co-borrower, if any)
3. Sources of income and analysis
4. Monthly housing expenses (present and proposed)
5. Balance sheet
6. Other information relevant to the borrower's financial status

If a loan application section requests information regarding marital status or race, the applicant can refuse to complete this section.

E. EQUITY (Market Value Less Debt)

When shopping for a loan, the lender wants to determine your worth, or equity, so they will require you to fill out an accounting balance sheet as part of the application.

EQUITY is your net worth; it is the amount that is left after subtracting all that you owe (DEBT) from what you own (ASSETS). Lenders want to see your equity on paper. Equity shows them your ability to make the down payment and meet other expenses. It is common practice to ask buyers what the equity is in their current home in order to determine if they financially qualify for the price of a new home.

F. LIQUIDITY (Convert Assets into Cash)

LIQUIDITY is the ease and rate with which an asset can be converted into a medium of exchange (like cash). It is not enough to make money; there also must be the ability to pay bills on time. Real estate has very little liquidity. Depending on market conditions, it could take a very long time to sell a piece of real estate. On the other hand, income property may bring in more cash monthly than goes out for expenditures.

G. OPPORTUNITY COST (Cost of Non-Liquidity)

OPPORTUNITY COST is the lost profit one could have made by the alternative investment action not taken. It is the cost of non-liquidity. If you own a home, the lost return on that equity is referred to as opportunity cost.

Figure 12-3

Uniform Residential Loan Application

This application is designed to be completed by the applicant(s) with the lender's assistance. Applicants should complete this form as "Borrower" or "Co-Borrower", as applicable. Co-Borrower information must also be provided (and the appropriate box checked) when ☐ the income or assets of a person other than the "Borrower" (including the Borrower's spouse) will be used as a basis for loan qualification or ☐ the income or assets of the Borrower's spouse will not be used as a basis for loan qualification, but his or her liabilities must be considered because the Borrower resides in a community property state, the security property is located in a community property state, or the Borrower is relying on other property located in a community property state as a basis for repayment of the loan.

I. TYPE OF MORTGAGE AND TERMS OF LOAN

Mortgage Applied for:	☐ VA ☐ FHA	☐ Conventional ☐ FmHA	☐ Other:	Agency Case Number		Lender Case No.
Amount $	Interest Rate %	No. of Months	Amortization Type:	☐ Fixed Rate ☐ GPM	☐ Other (explain): ☐ ARM (type):	

II. PROPERTY INFORMATION AND PURPOSE OF LOAN

Subject Property Address (street, city, state, & ZIP)　　　　　　　　　　No. of Units

Legal Description of Subject Property (attach description if necessary)　　　　Year Built

Purpose of Loan	☐ Purchase ☐ Refinance	☐ Construction ☐ Construction-Permanent	☐ Other (explain):	Property will be: ☐ Primary Residence ☐ Secondary Residence ☐ Investment

Complete this line if construction or construction-permanent loan.

Year Lot Acquired	Original Cost $	Amount Existing Liens $	(a) Present Value of Lot $	(b) Cost of Improvements $	Total (a + b) $

Complete this line if this is a refinance loan.

Year Acquired	Original Cost $	Amount Existing Liens $	Purpose of Refinance	Describe Improvements ☐ made ☐ to be made Cost: $

Title will be held in what Name(s)　　　　　Manner in which Title will be held　　　Estate will be held in: ☐ Fee Simple ☐ Leasehold (show expiration date)

Source of Down Payment, Settlement Charges and/or Subordinate Financing (explain)

III. BORROWER INFORMATION

Borrower	Co-Borrower
Borrower's Name (include Jr. or Sr. if applicable)	Co-Borrower's Name (include Jr. or Sr. if applicable)

Social Security Number	Home Phone (incl. area code)	Age	Yrs. School	Social Security Number	Home Phone (incl. area code)	Age	Yrs. School
☐ Married ☐ Separated ☐ Unmarried (include single, divorced, widowed)	Dependents (not listed by Co-Borrower) no.　ages			☐ Married ☐ Separated ☐ Unmarried (include single, divorced, widowed)	Dependents (not listed by Borrower) no.　ages		

Present Address (street, city, state, ZIP) ☐ Own ☐ Rent ___ No. Yrs.	Present Address (street, city, state, ZIP) ☐ Own ☐ Rent ___ No. Yrs.

If residing at present address for less than two years, complete the following:

Former Address (street, city, state, ZIP) ☐ Own ☐ Rent ___ No. Yrs.	Former Address (street, city, state, ZIP) ☐ Own ☐ Rent ___ No. Yrs.

Former Address (street, city, state, ZIP) ☐ Own ☐ Rent ___ No. Yrs.	Former Address (street, city, state, ZIP) ☐ Own ☐ Rent ___ No. Yrs.

IV. EMPLOYMENT INFORMATION

Borrower	Co-Borrower

Name & Address of Employer ☐ Self Employed	Yrs. on this job	Name & Address of Employer ☐ Self Employed	Yrs. on this job
	Yrs. employed in this line of work/profession		Yrs. employed in this line of work/profession
Position/Title/Type of Business	Business Phone (incl. area code)	Position/Title/Type of Business	Business Phone (incl. area code)

If employed in current position for less than two years or if currently employed in more than one position, complete the following:

Name & Address of Employer ☐ Self Employed	Dates (from - to)	Name & Address of Employer ☐ Self Employed	Dates (from - to)
	Monthly Income $		Monthly Income $
Position/Title/Type of Business	Business Phone (incl. area code)	Position/Title/Type of Business	Business Phone (incl. area code)

Name & Address of Employer ☐ Self Employed	Dates (from - to)	Name & Address of Employer ☐ Self Employed	Dates (from - to)
	Monthly Income $		Monthly Income $
Position/Title/Type of Business	Business Phone (incl. area code)	Position/Title/Type of Business	Business Phone (incl. area code)

Freddie Mac Form 65　　　　　　　　　　　　　　　　　　　Fannie Mae Form 1003

453

Gross Monthly Income	Borrower	Co-Borrower	Total	Combined Monthly Housing Expense	Present	Proposed
Base Empl. Income *	$	$	$	Rent	$	
Overtime				First Mortgage (P&I)		$
Bonuses				Other Financing (P&I)		
Commissions				Hazard Insurance		
Dividends/Interest				Real Estate Taxes		
Net Rental Income				Mortgage Insurance		
Other (before completing, see the notice in "describe other income," below)				Homeowner Assn. Dues		
				Other:		
Total	$	$	$	Total	$	$

* Self Employed Borrower(s) may be required to provide additional documentation such as tax returns and financial statements.

Describe Other Income *Notice:* Alimony, child support, or separate maintenance income need not be revealed if the Borrower (B) or Co-Borrower (C) does not choose to have it considered for repaying this loan.

B/C		Monthly Amount
		$

This Statement and any applicable supporting schedules may be completed jointly by both married and unmarried Co-Borrowers if their assets and liabilities are sufficiently joined so that the Statement can be meaningfully and fairly presented on a combined basis; otherwise separate Statements and Schedules are required. If the Co-Borrower section was completed about a spouse, this Statement and supporting schedules must be completed about that spouse also.

Completed [ ] Jointly [ ] Not Jointly

ASSETS Description	Cash or Market Value	Liabilities and Pledged Assets. List the creditor's name, address and account number for all outstanding debts, including automobile loans, revolving charge accounts, real estate loans, alimony, child support, stock pledges, etc. Use continuation sheet, if necessary. Indicate by (*) those liabilities which will be satisfied upon sale of real estate owned or upon refinancing of the subject property.	Monthly Payt. & Mos. Left to Pay	Unpaid Balance
Cash deposit toward purchase held by:	$	**LIABILITIES**		
		Name and address of Company	$ Payt./Mos.	$
List checking and savings accounts below				
Name and address of Bank, S&L, or Credit Union				
		Acct. no.		
		Name and address of Company	$ Payt./Mos.	$
Acct. no.	$			
Name and address of Bank, S&L, or Credit Union				
		Acct. no.		
		Name and address of Company	$ Payt./Mos.	$
Acct. no.	$			
Name and address of Bank, S&L, or Credit Union				
		Acct. no.		
		Name and address of Company	$ Payt./Mos.	$
Acct. no.	$			
Name and address of Bank, S&L, or Credit Union				
		Acct. no.		
		Name and address of Company	$ Payt./Mos.	$
Acct. no.	$			
Stocks & Bonds (Company name/number & description)	$			
		Acct. no.		
		Name and address of Company	$ Payt./Mos.	$
Life insurance net cash value	$			
Face amount: $				
Subtotal Liquid Assets	$			
Real estate owned (enter market value from schedule of real estate owned)	$	Acct. no.		
Vested interest in retirement fund	$	Name and address of Company	$ Payt./Mos.	$
Net worth of business(es) owned (attach financial statement)	$			
Automobiles owned (make and year)	$			
		Acct. no.		
Other Assets (itemize)	$	Alimony/Child Support/Separate Maintenance Payments Owed to:	$	
		Job Related Expense (child care, union dues, etc.)	$	
		Total Monthly Payments	$	
Total Assets a.	$	Net Worth	$	**Total Liabilities b.**	$

III. Demand For Real Estate Funds

The remainder of this chapter will deal with the different institutions that lend money to finance the purchase of real property. Details concerning the types of lenders and how they make loans will be explained and different kinds of government loan participation are compared and discussed.

The three areas of demand for borrowing money are:

1. Construction funds to build
2. Financing a purchase
3. Refinancing

IV. Institutional Lenders

INSTITUTIONAL LENDERS are very large corporations that lend the money of their depositors to finance real estate transactions. Their principal function is to act as financial intermediaries; to transfer money from those who have funds to those who wish to borrow. **Figure 12-4** illustrates which groups are institutional and which are noninstitutional lenders.

Figure 12-4

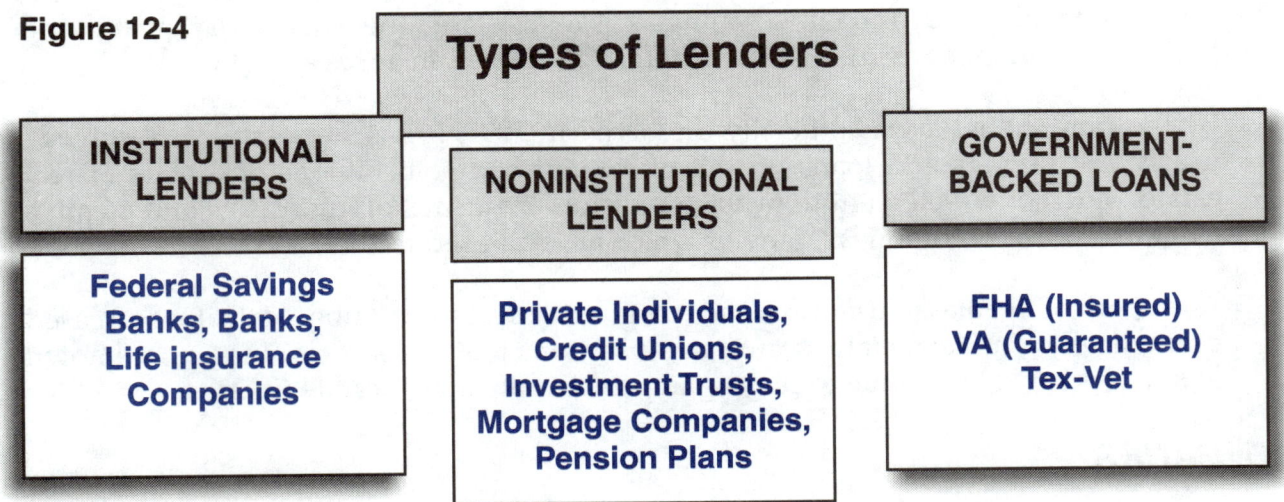

Types of Lenders

INSTITUTIONAL LENDERS	NONINSTITUTIONAL LENDERS	GOVERNMENT-BACKED LOANS
Federal Savings Banks, Banks, Life insurance Companies	Private Individuals, Credit Unions, Investment Trusts, Mortgage Companies, Pension Plans	FHA (Insured) VA (Guaranteed) Tex-Vet

A. SAVINGS BANKS

Historically, savings banks (thrifts – formerly known as savings and loans) have been the oldest and largest source of funds for financing residential property.

Over the years, savings banks carried out their historic function of investing on average 75% of their funds in the single-family residential market. They were able to dominate local mortgage markets despite the fact that commercial banks had more assets. Since they were able to offer higher interest rates than the commercial banks, they had no trouble attracting deposits during the period of prosperity from World War II until the 1970s.

As interest rates surged in the late 1970s and early 1980s, thrifts saw their deposit base erode in favor of competing investments such as money market funds and government bonds that offered much higher rates of return. To counter these losses, thrifts turned to high yield, but risky investments. These risky investments, combined with other factors, such as industry deregulation, lax federal regulation, inept management, criminal activity, and falling real estate prices led to what is now known as the **Savings and Loan Crisis**.

In response to the Savings and Loan Crisis of the late 1980s, Congress responded by enacting the **Financial Institutions Reform, Recovery, and Enforcement Act of 1989 (FIRREA)**. This sweeping set of laws created, among other things, a new, but temporary federal agency known as the Resolution Trust Corporation (RTC), that was given the job of reorganizing and liquidating, where necessary, the assets of the failed thrifts.

It's been estimated that on the day the RTC was created, it inherited $40 billion worth of foreclosed real estate from failed savings and loans across the nation. Of that amount, half, or $20 billion of distressed real estate, was located in Texas alone!

By the time the RTC was officially dissolved in 1995, it has successfully "resolved" nearly 750 savings and loans. In the process, it had sold billions of dollars of real estate, much of which went to private investors by means of innovative and creative asset marketing techniques, many of which are still used to this day.

As a result of the massive failures and reorganizations, the number of thrifts decreased dramatically. The financially secure organizations that did survive (and now known as savings banks) continue to play an important role in real estate finance.

B. BANKS

Banks are *GENERAL PURPOSE LENDERS, which means they lend money for anything from real estate to sailboats.* All national banks are required to be members of the Federal Reserve System, while a state bank may be a member by choice. Moreover, many banks are members of the Federal Deposit Insurance Corporation (FDIC).

There is no great difference between real estate loans that a state bank makes and loans that the federal banks make. Interest rates and other loan terms are comparable to those offered by mutual savings banks.

Priorities of Institutional Lenders

Federal Savings Banks (Residential Lenders)	Banks (General Purpose Lenders)	Life Insurance Companies (Big Money Lenders)
1. Single-family homes and condos	1. Business and auto loans	1. Large shopping centers and office buildings
2. Apartment buildings	2. Conventional home loans	2. Hotels and industrial properties
3. Home improvement loans	3. Government-backed FHA and VA home loans	3. FHA and VA home loans through mortgage companies (Government-backed loans)
4. Manufactured homes	4. Credit cards	
	5. Construction loans	

Any commercial bank may lend money on real property if it is a first lien loan on that property. In general, there are four types of real estate financing:

1. **First Lien Loans** – The bank finances long-term loans for existing land and the buildings.

2. **Construction Loans (or Interim Loans)** – Money is provided for the construction of a building, to be repaid when the construction is complete.

Construction loan and interim loan are synonymous.

3. **Take-Out Loans (Repayment of Interim Loan)** – Permanent long-term loans are made to pay off the interim lender upon completion of construction of commercial or apartment projects and are called "takeout loans" because they take out the interim lender.

4. **Home Improvement Loans** – This type of loan is for repairing and modernizing existing buildings.

C. LIFE INSURANCE COMPANIES

Life insurance companies have more money to lend than either a bank or a savings bank. They are more conservative lenders and specialize in large loans for commercial

How Financial Institutions Determine Interest Rates

Financial institutions obtain funds from their depositors and pay a modest return in the form of interest or dividends to keep their depositors money invested with them. In order to make money, the spread that a financial institution must make between the interest rate it charges on loans and the interest rate paid to its depositors must be at least 2%. So if a bank pays 7% to depositors, it must make loans at 9% or higher in order to stay in business.

---

projects, but they also make conventional loans on residential property. These companies supply most of the loan funds for properties where a great deal of capital is required (such as high-rise office buildings, shopping centers, industrial properties, and hotels).

Life insurance companies also invest large amounts of money in mortgages and/or deeds of trust that are either insured by the FHA or guaranteed by the VA. Mortgage companies make such loans for insurance companies. Quite often, these mortgage companies, in return for a servicing fee, collect the loan payments for the insurance company.

An insurance company is the least likely source to refinance an existing home loan.

Truth in Savings Act

"Annual Percentage Yield" defined as APY

The Truth in Savings Act requires depository institutions to furnish "clear, complete, and uniform disclosures" of the terms of their savings and checking deposit accounts. It also requires institutions to pay interest on the consumer's daily balance. Certain practices are no longer permitted, such as advertising "Free Accounts" and then charging maintenance or per-check fees, or requiring minimum balances.

This Act introduces a standard method of expressing interest paid to depositors called "Annual Percentage Yield" or APY. This new method takes into account the interest rate and also the compounding. So if the APY is 4.46 percent, a hundred dollars will earn $4.46 in one year. The higher the APY, the more interest is paid.

The Many Roles of the FDIC

When most people think of the **Federal Deposit Insurance Corporation**, they typically think of the sign in the bank that says that the account of each depositor is insured up to $100,000. While the FDIC does not insure all the products or investments that a bank may offer its customers, **Deposit Insurance** is an integral part of the American banking system. But the FDIC does more than just serve as the insurer of deposit accounts.

As the **manager of the Deposit Insurance Fund (DIF)**, the FDIC oversees a multi-billion dollar reserve account which is primarily used to protect depositors in the event of bank failure or other loss. The source of these funds is not from federal tax dollars, but rather from risk-based assessments charged to member banks.

As a **primary bank regulator**, the FDIC is charged with the responsibility of maintaining confidence within the banking system by examining and supervising nearly half of the banking institutions in the United States.

And as a **receiver**, the FDIC stands ready to take over, reorganize, and liquidate, if necessary, the assets of troubled and failing financial institutions.

The FDIC was created in 1933 as a result of the banking failures created by the Great Depression.

www.fdic.gov
Federal Deposit Insurance Corp.

Life insurance companies are governed by the laws of the state in which they are incorporated, as well as the laws of the states in which they do business. There is no state restriction concerning the number of years for which a loan can be made. However, company policy usually restricts the term to no more than 30 years and requires a loan to be amortized.

V. Non-Institutional Lenders

Non-institutional lenders are smaller lenders, including: credit unions, investment trusts, pension plans, and mortgage companies.

NON-INSTITUTIONAL LENDERS *are individuals and organizations that lend on a private or individual basis.* Both institutional and noninstitutional lenders make loans that may be or may not be backed by one of the government loan programs.

CONVENTIONAL LOANS *are loans that are not insured or guaranteed by the United States government.*

A. PRIVATE INDIVIDUALS

Any real estate loan by an individual is considered a private individual loan. Most individuals who lend money on real estate are sellers who take back a second lien as part of the real estate transaction. The seller will be a likely lender when the buyer needs a little more money to purchase a property. Most second lien loans are of this type.

When the current money market is tight, it often means that a seller will have to take back a second lien as part of the equity in his/her home. Many second loans on real estate, called junior loans (second lien loans), are obtained from private parties.

Common second lien loan terms are:

1. The loan amount is usually relatively small (under $50,000).
2. There is a relatively high interest rate (8% to 15%).
3. The loan term is usually from 3 to 7 years, with payments on a monthly basis.
4. Loan payments are usually 1% of the original loan, and there is usually a balloon payment at the end of the term (if more than six years).
5. There is usually an acceleration clause that makes the entire loan due if any payment is missed or the property is transferred.

B. CREDIT UNIONS

A ***CREDIT UNION*** *is a co-operative association organized to promote thrift among its members and provide them with a source of credit.*

Under the Federal Credit Union Act of 1934, a credit union charter may be given to any group having a common bond of association or occupation—a factory, store, office, church, trade group, club, or fraternal organization.

Although there are thousands of credit unions across the country, they play a much smaller role than banks, savings banks, and insurance companies in financing real estate. The typical credit union is smaller than the average commercial bank or savings bank.

Most credit unions are incorporated and accumulate funds by selling shares to members. From this pool of funds, loans are made at an interest rate equal to or below the current market rate. Low interest rate loans to members are a big plus for credit unions.

The modern credit union offers savings plans, credit cards, ATM cards, travelers' checks, vehicle loans, signature loans, and real estate loans. All deposit accounts have FDIC insurance up to $100,000.

Recent changes in the law have enabled credit unions to make not only second lien loans, but also primary mortgage loans. This source of real estate funding is expected to grow and expand in coming years.

C. REAL ESTATE INVESTMENT TRUSTS (REITs)

A *REAL ESTATE INVESTMENT TRUST (REIT) is a type of company that sells securities to invest in real estate properties.* If the company distributes 95 percent or more of its income to its shareholders, it does not pay federal income taxes on that distribution. Because of these formalities, a real estate investment trust is taxed like any other real estate investment.

An *EQUITY TRUST is a company that invests in real estate itself or several real estate projects.* The *MORTGAGE TRUST is a company that invests in mortgages and other types of real estate loans or obligations.* Now there are even combination trusts that invest in real estate and lend money in the form of real estate mortgages.

D. PENSION PLANS

A *PENSION PLAN is an investment organization that obtains funds from people before they retire and invests this money for their clients' retirement.* Company pension plans have become a popular source of real estate funds and are expected to grow even larger in the future. Enormous amounts of money, gathered through deductions from each pay period, are held by these plans. Those who administer pension money are becoming more and more inclined to invest it directly in large real estate projects rather than investing in the stock market or simply investing in savings institutions and insurance companies.

E. MORTGAGE BANKERS (COMPANIES)

MORTGAGE BANKERS (COMPANIES) usually lend their own money or roll it over so they can originate, finance, and close first lien mortgages secured by real estate. They then sell the loans to institutional investors and service the loans through a contractual relationship with the investors.

Do not confuse a mortgage banker with a mortgage broker. A "mortgage broker" is a middleman who, for a fee, shops the application with various lenders. "Mortgage bankers," on the other hand, lend their own money.

VI. Conventional and Government-Backed Loans

A. CONVENTIONAL LOANS

A *CONVENTIONAL LOAN is a loan where the lender is solely at risk in making the loan.* Ordinarily the value of the property and the creditworthiness of the borrower serve to protect the lender from losses. However, many lenders of conventional loans will require private mortgage insurance if the borrower is financing more than 80% of the loan.

PRIVATE MORTGAGE INSURANCE (PMI) is a guarantee to lenders that the upper portion of a conventional loan will be repaid if a borrower defaults and a deficiency occurs at the foreclosure sale.

> **Example:** Smith is buying a property for $300,000 but he has only $15,000 for a down payment. He approaches lender Jones for financing. Lender Jones is eager to see this sale go through but he does not feel entirely comfortable putting up $285,000 when normally he would limit the loan to 80%, or $240,000. He is uncomfortable lending Smith the extra $45,000. He agrees to make the loan if Smith will pay for private mortgage insurance to cover the upper portion ($45,000) of the $285,000 loan.

Private mortgage insurance is obtainable on properties with one-to-four units and generally covers the top 20% of the loan amount. The borrower generally pays an initial premium or an annual fee of one-half of one percent on the remaining principal balance.

B. GOVERNMENT-BACKED LOANS

In a government-backed loan, private lenders loan their own funds and receive assurances against losses because of their participation in government programs. Under these federal programs, the government does not lend any actual money. Instead the government approved loans are made by private lenders (see **Figure 12-6**).

Figure 12-6

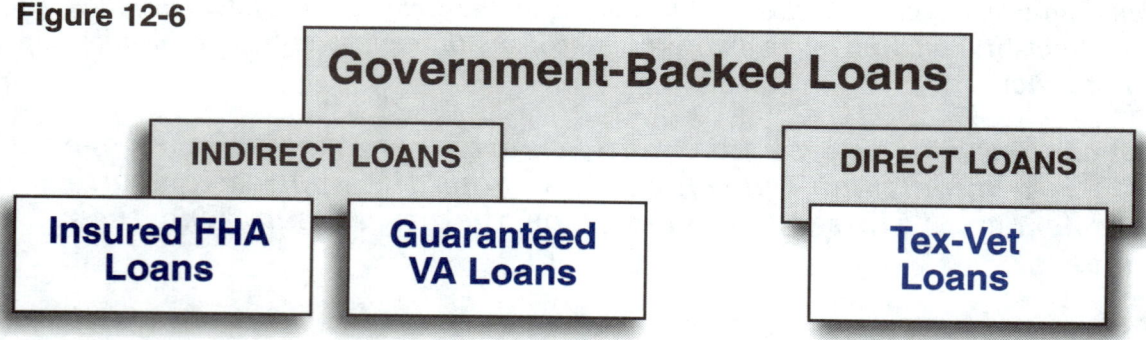

Two of the most popular government-backed loans are FHA insured loans (managed by the Department of Housing and Urban Development), and VA loans which are guaranteed by the Department of Veteran's Affairs.

In addition, the State of Texas has a direct loan program using money raised from bond sales to finance limited land and home purchases by eligible and qualified Texas veterans.

1. FHA Insured Loans (Managed by HUD)

Unlike conventional lenders, the Federal Housing Administration (FHA) does not make loans, but insures them.

The FHA has two main programs that affect Texas homeowners and buyers: 1) Title I home improvement loans, and 2) Title II (Section 203b) purchase and construction loans. There are other types of FHA financing available. For information, contact a lender who specializes in FHA loans.

www.hud.gov
Housing and Urban Development

a. FHA Title I: Home Improvement Loans

The FHA can make home improvement loans to a maximum of $25,000. The funds can be used only for home improvement purposes.

Minimum Property Requirements (MPRs)

All of these government-backed finance programs have increased the number of houses and condominiums that people in Texas can afford to buy. They also have an indirect influence on the quality of homes constructed because they require that the home involved meet minimum property requirements as a prerequisite to financing. Minimum Property Requirements (MPR) are set standards of materials and construction required for FHA and VA loans. These requirements are often more restrictive than the building codes. As a real estate licensee, you should be familiar with the basic financing programs and qualification requirements. In addition, most mortgage companies will help you qualify the buyer and complete the necessary forms for FHA and VA loans.

Minimum Property Requirements (or MPR) are minimum quality standards established by the FHA and VA.

b. FHA Title II: Home Purchase or Build Loans

The maximum FHA loan amount varies from area-to-area in Texas and could change each year if median home prices change or Federal National Mortgage Association (FNMA) loan amounts change.

The maximum loan amount is determined as follows:

1. 98.75% for homes $50,000 or less
2. 97.75% for homes over $50,000

Obviously, different geographical areas warrant different maximum loans based on the median home values. Accessing the HUD's website will give the agent the latest quotes for the various counties.

All FHA home buyers must obtain loans at an approved lender's office. The approved local lender (such as banks, insurance companies, and mortgage companies) will make the loan if the FHA qualifies the buyer. The FHA has many requirements for its different loan programs. Both the borrower and the property must meet these criteria. If either the borrower or the property does not meet the minimum standards, it would probably be better to look for a lender who deals in conventional rather than FHA loans.

The FHA does not lend the money. It only insures the approved lender against foreclosure loss. The FHA collects a percentage of the loan for this insurance called the mortgage insurance premium. The ***MORTGAGE INSURANCE PREMIUM (MIP)*** *is the protection for the FHA that insures the lender for any loss if there is a foreclosure.* It is an up-front fee (paid by the borrower) in cash, or through insurance as part of the loan. If there is a foreclosure, FHA will take over the property and reimburse the lender for the cost of default.

An ***FHA MORTGAGE LOAN CORRESPONDENT*** *is a mortgagee approved by the Secretary of the Department Housing and Urban Development.* The loan correspondent has as his/her principal activity either: 1) the origination of mortgages for sale or transfer to a sponsor or sponsors; or 2) satisfies the definition of a supervised mortgagee contained in the regulations of the Secretary of the Department of Housing and Urban Development.

c. Advantages FHA Financing

1. Low down payment compared to conventional loans.
2. Loans are assumable. Loans require approval of the FHA and non-owner-occupied are prohibited.
3. No prepayment penalty is allowed by the FHA.

4. Minimum property requirements (MPRs) give the buyer a quality home.

5. 5. A seller receives all cash because of the high loan-to-value ratio.

There are NO prepayment penalties on FHA loans.

d. Disadvantages of FHA Financing

1. Lots of processing time and red tape.

2. Existing properties may require repairs necessary to meet minimum property requirements.

C. DEPARTMENT OF VETERANS AFFAIRS (VA)

1. VA Loans (Loan Guarantees to Approved Lenders)

Congress has passed legislation to assist veterans in obtaining housing. A *VA LOAN is not a loan, but rather a guarantee to an approved institutional lender.*

a. Veteran's Eligibility

Veterans are eligible for a Department of Veterans Affairs (VA) loan guarantee if they served on active duty for 90 days or more (181 days during certain peacetime periods) and were honorably discharged.

American citizens who served in the armed forces of our Allies in World War II may also apply. Widows or widowers of service people or veterans who were eligible at the time of death, but did not use their benefits, may apply to use their husbands' or wives' benefits. Also, the VA Adjudication Board, at its discretion, may give eligibility to any veteran who received other than an honorable discharge.

b. Veterans May be Entitled to More Than One Loan

A veteran may restore his/her eligibility and apply for an additional loan if the previous home was sold and its loan paid in full. Other veterans who are eligible for a new VA loan program may apply even if they have a prior VA loan, if the prior loan is not in default and if the veteran no longer owns the property. The previous VA loan need not be paid off. The veteran who purchased a home under a previous program may be eligible again under a new program.

2. Certificate of Reasonable Value (CRV)

A *CERTIFICATE OF REASONABLE VALUE (CRV) is an appraisal of the property to be purchased by the veteran.* The property is appraised by an independent fee appraiser who is appointed by the Department of Veterans Affairs. Although the

appraisal may be paid for by the veteran, it may also be paid for by the seller. The CRV appraisal expires after six months.

3. VA Loan Provisions

VA loans require NO down payment (100% financing), and NO prepayment penalties.

The veteran has the choice of several types of VA loans. They include fixed-rate mortgages, graduated payment mortgages, growing equity mortgages, and buy-down loans. The duration of a VA loan is generally 30 years. Discount points charged sellers and interest rates vary according to the current economic conditions. **The main advantage to the veteran is that no down payment is needed**, unless the property's price exceeds the VA's appraisal. This "no money down" feature is unique among government programs. Loans can be above the $240,000 guaranteed maximum loan amount, but require that the difference between the $240,000 maximum and the actual loan be in the form of a cash down payment.

4. Advantages of VA Financing

1. No down payment, but a funding fee paid is by the veteran
2. Low interest rate because of the VA loan guarantee
3. No prepayment penalty is allowed by the VA

5. Disadvantages of VA Financing

1. Buyer's creditworthiness is a requirement for assumption; VA must approve credit and a fee of up to $500 is required; assumption only after one year if owner-occupied or after two years if investor owned
2. Buyer or seller can pay discount points
3. Lengthy processing time and red tape

D. TEXAS VETERANS LAND BOARD (Tex-Vet)

Since the earliest days of the Texas Republic, there has been a strong connection between land and its soldiers. During Sam Houston's tenure, soldiers were often paid for their service to the Republic by means of land grants. Today, Texas soldiers are no longer paid for their services with land, but there are several land programs available for Texas vets.

In 1946 the Texas Legislature created the ***TEXAS VETERANS LAND BOARD (VLB)*** *to administer the first of several land programs exclusively for Texas veterans.* Today these programs consist of:

1. The Texas Veterans Land Program
2. The Veterans Housing Assistance Program
3. The Home Improvement Program

Eligible Texas vets can use all three loan programs at one time and since they are not associated with the federal VA program, they can be used to supplement VA loans.

1. Texas Veterans Land Program

Under this program, the Texas Veterans Land Board (VLB) provides financing for up to $60,000 to qualified veterans for the purchase of land. This state sponsored land program is fairly straightforward. The qualified veteran selects the land he/she wishes to purchase. The Texas Veterans Land Board will then purchase the desired tract of land from the original seller. The VLB, in turn, will resell the land to the veteran under a 30-year contract for sale. When the terms of the contract for sale are fulfilled, the VLP will then transfer the property to the purchaser.

www.glo.state.tx.us/vlb

Texas Veterans Land Board
Jerry Patterson, Chairman

General Information
Board Meetings and Members
Housing Assistance
Home Improvement
Land
Forfeited Land Tracts
Interest Rates
Forms
Texas Veterans Homes

In Texas, call us Toll Free: 1-800-252-VETS (8387) Outside Texas?
Call 1-512-463-5060 (long distance charges apply)

News

Message from Chairman Patterson

Chairman Jerry Patterson Speaks to Veterans About the Veterans Land Board. (run time: 10:15)

Play Video High | Low

Under a land contract, the Texas Veterans Land Board retains legal title to the land until the loan is paid in full.

Since its inception, more than 120,000 Texas vets have taken advantage of this self-supporting program at no cost to the taxpayers. This program is funded by issuing bonds as authorized by the voters. The bonds, as well as all administrative costs of the program, are paid by the veterans who utilize this program.

2. Texas Housing Assistance Program (THAP)

The Texas Housing Assistance Program (THAP) can be used by eligible veterans to acquire a new residence. This program consists of two elements.

a. Direct Loan Program

Under the Direct Loan Program, qualified veterans can obtain a loan directly from the Texas Veterans Land Board for up to $45,000. All VLP originated loans are subject to an 85% L-T-V ratio. This means that the VLP will lend only 85% of the home's appraised value up to $45,000. The term for direct loans may be for 15, 20, 25, or 30 years.

b. Lender Originated Loans

Loans in excess of $45,000, up to a maximum of $240,000, are arranged through participating lenders and in conjunction with FHA, VA, or conventional financing. Under this program, there is no dollar limit to the residence being purchased, but the program will finance only up to $240,000. The term of this loan will be for 15, 20, 25, or 30 years and an escrow account for taxes and insurance will be required.

3. Veterans Home Improvement Program

Under this program, the VLB will lend eligible and qualified veterans a maximum of $25,000 for up to a 20 year term for repairs to an existing residence. For loans of less than $10,000 the longest loan term will be 10 years. Under program guidelines, all loans are FHA insured and require the VLB to be in a first or second lien position. The veteran is not permitted to advance any funds to the contractor or purchase material prior to receipt of the loan proceeds from the VLB.

4. Eligibility

To be eligible for a loan from the Texas Veterans Land Board, the applicant must be a veteran in much the same manner as for a VA loan. Additionally, the veteran must be a Texas veteran which means he/she:

1. listed Texas as the home of record at the time of entry into the military; OR

2. must have been a legal resident of Texas for at least twelve consecutive months immediately prior to filing an application; OR

3. be on active military duty, stationed in Texas, and have changed his/her state of legal residency to Texas.

The applicant must also be a bona fide resident of Texas at the time the application is made. This may include a Texas resident currently serving on active military duty outside of Texas. Under agency rules, presence in Texas due solely to military service may not establish bona fide residency.

E. TEXAS DEPARTMENT OF HOUSING AND COMMUNITY AFFAIRS

The Texas Department of Housing and Community Affairs administers a number of programs designed to assist low- to moderate-income homebuyers. These programs are funded from both public and private sources and include the following.

1. Down Payment Assistance Program (DPAP)

The Down Payment Assistance Program (DPAP) helps very low- and low-income families purchase a home by providing an interest-free loan ranging from $5,000 to $10,000, depending on the county in which the property is located. This assistance is for down payment and eligible closing costs, and the borrower pays the loan when the home is either sold or refinanced, or at the maturity of the original mortgage.

2. Texas "Bootstrap" Loan Program

The Texas Bootstrap Loan Program makes available $3 million for mortgage loans to very low-income families (60% Area Median Family Income) not to exceed $30,000 per unit. This program is a self-help construction program, which is designed to provide very low-income families an opportunity to help themselves through the form of sweat equity. All participants under this program are required to provide at least 60 percent of labor that is necessary to construct or rehabilitate the home.

3. Texas First-Time Homebuyer Program

The Texas First-Time Homebuyer Program channels below-market interest rate mortgage money through participating Texas lending institutions to eligible families who are purchasing their first home, or to those who have not owned a home in the past three years.

For additional information, contact the Texas Department of Housing and Community Affairs at (800) 525-0657.

VI. Lending Corporations and the Secondary Mortgage Market

A. PRIVATE AND QUASI-GOVERNMENTAL CORPORATIONS

There were once three federal corporations that used cash to buy and sell loans and mortgages between financial institutions. These corporations are now either private or quasi-governmental and provide stability and flexibility for real estate financing in the United States. Each has different programs and areas of focus, but all work together to keep sufficient financing money available at lending institutions so they can make home loans.

B. SECONDARY MORTGAGE MARKET

Lenders in the secondary market are concerned with the "liquidity and marketability" of loans.

The **SECONDARY MORTGAGE MARKET** *provides an opportunity for financial institutions to buy from, and sell first mortgages (trust deeds) to, other financial institutions. The secondary mortgage market enables lenders to keep an adequate supply of money for new loans.*

1. Fannie Mae (Formerly Known as the Federal National Mortgage Association) – Private

Fannie Mae (which was formerly known as the Federal National Mortgage Association or FNMA), dominates the secondary mortgage market. Originally it bought and sold only FHA and VA loans deeds. In 1968 it became a private corporation and now sells securities over the stock exchange to get money so that it can buy and sell conventional loans in addition to government-backed notes. It is not a demand source.

Fannie Mae is the largest investor in the secondary market.

www.fanniemaefoundation.org
Fannie Mae

2. Government National Mortgage Association (Ginnie Mae)

The Government National Mortgage Association (GNMA) is a government corporation referred to as Ginnie Mae. It sells secondary mortgages to the public and provides the federal government with cash. These loans are grouped together in pools, and shares are sold on the stock market exchange. All shares are federally guaranteed, making this one of the safest investments available.

www.ginniemae.gov
Ginnie Mae

3. *Federal Home Loan Mortgage Corporation (Freddie Mac)*

The Federal Home Loan Mortgage Corporation (FHLMC), commonly known as Freddie Mac, is a government corporation that issues preferred stock to the public. It is supervised by the Federal Home Loan Bank Board. It helps savings banks maintain a stable and adequate money supply by purchasing their home loan mortgages and repackaging them for sale to investors. The savings banks use the money obtained to make new loans available for home buyers.

The Federal Home Loan Mortgage Corporation, commonly called "Freddie Mac," increases the availability of funds through its involvement in the maintenance of the secondary mortgage market.

www.freddiemac.com
Freddie Mac

"Equity Sharing"

A Different Financing and Ownership Idea

EQUITY SHARING (SHARED EQUITY FINANCING) is a contractual arrangement whereby an investor shares any equity gain with a homeowner. The concept is that an investor puts up most of the down payment, and receives no interest deductions but shares in any equity gain when the property is sold. The homeowner gets his or her home quickly with a minimum down payment, with relaxed credit, and with full income tax write-offs. Consult an attorney or CPA before investing.

VIII. CHAPTER SUMMARY

Inflation (when prices appreciate) protects both lender and trustor because there will be more equity protecting the lender in the case of a default. When prices decrease, the value of money increases and vice versa. In a **seller's market**, prices rise due to a shortage of properties available, whereas in a **buyer's market**, prices fall, terms are easy and properties plentiful.

The **Federal Reserve (Fed)** is the nation's central banking authority and controls the availability of loan funds, but has nothing to do with raising or lowering interest rates. The Fed's influence on the economy is evidenced by changes in the **Gross Domestic Product (GDP)**.

The three areas of demand for borrowing money are: construction funds, financing a purchase, and refinancing. Most lenders request a **L-T-V (loan to value) ratio** between 80% and 100%. The lower the L-T-V, the greater the down payment.

The primary purpose of **RESPA** is to require lenders to make special disclosures, without cost to the borrower, for loans involving the sale or transfer of one-to-four residential dwellings.

Large **institutional lenders** who pool funds to lend to individual borrowers, include: **insurance companies, savings banks,** and **banks**. Depositor's accounts in savings banks and banks are insured up to $100,000 by the **Federal Deposit Insurance Corporation (FDIC)**. Savings banks have the highest percentage of funds invested in real estate loans, followed by banks, which are **general purpose lenders**.

Smaller, **noninstitutional lenders** include: private lenders, mortgage companies, investment trusts, pension plans and credit unions. Private investors make many of the **second (junior) loans** on real estate. **Real estate investment trusts (REITs)** sell securities specializing in real estate ventures, and are of two types, 1) **equity trust** and 2) **mortgage trust**.

Mortgage bankers (companies) like to make loans that can be sold easily on the **secondary mortgage market**, which is a resale marketplace for smaller lenders, to sell their loans to larger lenders. Lenders may be required to obtain **private mortgage insurance (PMI)** to protect the lender in case of default.

The **Federal Housing Administration (FHA)** is a division of **HUD** that **insures loans** but does not make them. **FHA Title 1** involves home improvement loans and **FHA Title II** insures home loan purchase or building loans. The **Mortgage Insurance Premium (MIP)** is the FHA insurance protection against owner default (also called mutual mortgage insurance).

Veterans may qualify for a **Department of Veterans Affairs (VA) Loan**, which is not really a loan, but a **loan guarantee** to approved institutional lenders. The amount of down payment on a VA loan is determined by the **Certificate of Reasonable Value (CRV)**. Vets may be required to pay origination fees and discount points. On the state level, the **Texas Veterans Land board (VLB)** will make loans to Texas veterans for purchasing land, housing, and home improvements. For the land program, the VLB will purchase the land for the veteran and retain title until the veteran pays off the loan in full.

The **secondary mortgage (deed of trust) market** is the market where lenders buy and sell mortgages. **Fannie Mae** buys and sells conventional loans. It helps set loan standards and maintain the secondary market, but is not a demand source to borrow money. **Freddie Mac (FHLMC)** purchases home loan mortgages and repackages them for sale to, investors, freeing up savings banks to make new loans. Conventional loans are riskier than FHA loans; the higher the risk the higher the interest rates.

Ginnie Mae (GNMA) sells secondary mortgages to the public and provides the federal government cash.

IX. TERMINOLOGY

A. Buyer's Market
B. Certificate of Reasonable Value (CRV)
C. Collateral
D. Conventional Loan
E. Credit Score
F. Equity Investment Trust
G. Fannie Mae
H. FDIC
I. Federal Reserve Board
J. Federal Reserve System
K. FHA Loans
L. FICO

M. Ginnie Mae
N. Gross Domestic Product (GDP)
O. Insurance Company
P. Loan to Value (L-T-V)
Q. Minimum Property Requirements (MPRs)
R. Mortgage Company Financing
S. Mortgage Investment Trust
T. Private Mortgage Insurance (PMI)
U. Seller's Market

V. Texas Department of Housing and Community Affairs
W. Texas First Time Homebuyer Program
X. Texas Housing Assistance Program
Y. Texas Veterans Land Board
Z. VA Loans

1. ___ A company providing mortgage financing with its own funds rather than simply bringing together lender and borrower, as does a mortgage broker. The mortgages are sold to investors within a short time.

2. ___ The largest purchaser of loans on the secondary market.

3. ___ A private company (Fair, Isaac and Company) that pioneered the use of credit scoring for use by lenders.

4. ___ The federal agency that insures bank deposits against loss up to a maximum of $100,000 per depositor.

5. ___ Insurance issued by a private insurance company against a loss by a lender in the event of default by a borrower (mortgagor). The premium is paid by the borrower and is included in the mortgage payment.

6. ___ A state agency which administers loan program for qualified Texas veterans.

7. ___ A mortgage loan that does not involve a government insured or guaranteed program.

8. ___ The money value of all goods and services produced by a nation's economy for a given period of time.

9. ___ A government corporation, managed by HUD, which buys loans on the secondary market.

10. ___ A program administered by the Texas Department of Housing and Community Affairs for eligible families who are purchasing their first home, or to those who have not owned a home in the past three years.

11. ___ Housing loans to qualified veterans by banks, savings banks, or other lenders that are guaranteed by the Department of Veteran's Affairs, enabling veterans to buy a residence with little or no down payment.

12. ___ Mortgage loans which are originated through private lenders, but insured by the federal government.

13. ___ The central banking system that controls the amount of money and the rate of interest in the United States.

14. ___ The powerful nine-member banking panel which controls the destiny of the United State's monetary system. Along with the President of the United States, the Chairman is one of the most powerful positions in the country.

15. ___ The percentage of appraised value that a lender will loan to the borrower to purchase the property.

16. ___ A state agency which administers a number of loan programs for low to moderate income homebuyers.

17. ___ The real estate pledged to back up a loan. The value of the real estate should be worth substantially more than the loan amount.

18. ___ A major real estate lender whose primary business is selling insurance policies to consumers.

19. ___ An appraisal document stating the fair market value of real estate under a VA loan.

20. ___ The minimal property standards for a property to qualify for an FHA loan.

21. ___ A loan program administered by the Texas Veterans Land Board that enables qualified Texas veterans to obtain a loan in order to purchase home.

22. ___ A market condition favoring the seller, when fewer homes are for sale than there are interested buyers.

23. ___ A trust company specializing in making mortgages as an investment.

24. ___ A trust company that specializes in taking an ownership position in other projects.

25. ___ A market condition favoring the buyer, when more homes are for sale than there are interested buyers.

26. ___ An assigned number used by lenders to determine whether a consumer will get a loan and what interest rate.

X. MULTIPLE CHOICE

1. With regard to inflation:
   a. market value increases and sales price increases.
   b. sales price increases and market value decreases.
   c. market value decreases and sale price decreases.
   d. sale price decreases and market value increases.

2. When the general level of prices decreases:
   a. the value of money decreases.
   b. the value of money increases.
   c. inflation increases.
   d. the GNP increases/market value increases.

3. When the federal reserve wants a "loose" money market:
   a. the fed buys back bonds and lowers reserve requirements of banks.
   b. the fed sells bonds and increases the reserve requirements of banks.
   c. the fed sells bonds and keeps the reserve requirements the same.
   d. none of the above.

4. A credit score is likely to be comprised of which of the following:
   a. payment history.
   b. amounts owed.
   c. types of credit use.
   d. all of the above.

5. Which of the following is a likely source for a home loan?

    a. The Federal Reserve

    b. Fannie Mae

    c. A credit union

    d. A large insurance company

6. For financing the purchase of residential properties, the principal lender of money is:

    a. Fannie Mae.

    b. federal savings banks.

    c. insurance companies.

    d. Ginnie Mac.

7. Institutions that specialize in making home loans most commonly get their funds from:

    a. mortgage bankers.

    b. mortgage brokers.

    c. individual savings.

    d. Federal Reserve.

8. Which of the following are synonymous?

    a. Interim loan/take out loan

    b. Take out loan/construction loan

    c. Construction loan/interim loan

    d. None of the above

9. For which of the following purposes may a Texas veteran obtain a Tex-Vet loan?

    a. A loan to purchase a home

    b. A loan to purchase raw land

    c. A loan to remodel an existing home

    d. All of the above

10. Many lenders consider the liquidity and marketability of loans to be very important when they make a loan secured by a mortgage. The importance of liquidity and marketability relates to:

    a. activities of the secondary mortgage markets.

    b. desirability of fixed rate loans over adjustable rate loans.

    c. ability to resell homes.

    d. the mix of loans made by banks only.

ANSWERS: 1. *a;* 2. *b;* 3. *a;* 4. *d;* 5. *d;* 6. *c;* 7. *c;* 8. *c;* 9. *d;* 10. *a*

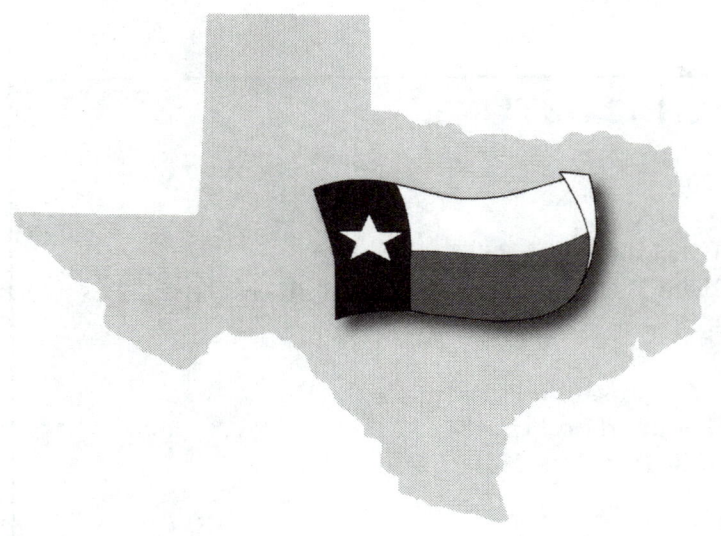

Chapter 13
Appraisal Basics

I. What is an Appraisal?

An ***APPRAISAL*** is an opinion as to the monetary value of a particular property at a given date. One of the most important factors for you to consider in deciding whether to sell or buy a home or any specific piece of real estate is its selling price. Each parcel of land (and the buildings on it) is unique. No two are exactly alike, so prices vary. The ***MARKET PRICE (SELLING PRICE)*** is the total price, including down payment and financing, that a property actually brought when sold. Market price is what it sold for, whereas market value is what it should have sold for in a competitive market.

The market value is what the property is actually worth. ***MARKET VALUE*** is the price that a willing buyer will pay and a willing seller accept, both being fully informed and with the sale property exposed for a reasonable period. The courtroom definition is even more technical:

> *"The highest price, estimated in terms of money, that a property will bring if it is exposed for sale in the open market, allowing a reasonable length of time to find a buyer who buys with full knowledge of all the uses to which it is adapted and for which the property is capable of being used."*

Real estate economically has value because it is the maximum utility of available resources.

CHAPTER 13 OUTLINE

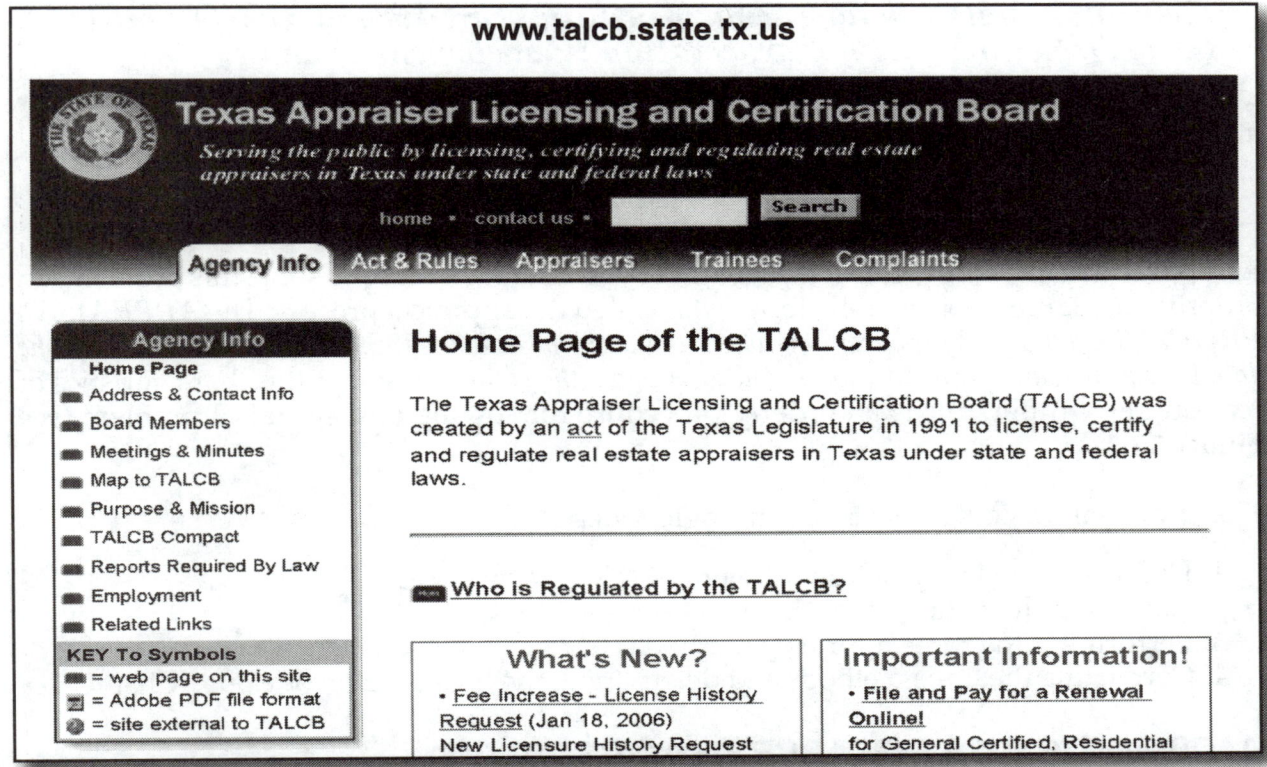

IMPROVED VALUE OF LAND *is the market value of the land and any improvements.*

> *In comparing real property price to value, a change in financing terms will affect price, but NOT value.*

Current market value is not affected in any way by the original cost of the property. The market value of a particular property is an opinion of value, by an appraiser, based on analysis of actual and relevant data, as of a given date. Appraisers must have the required experience, education, and have passed the exams required by the Texas Appraiser Licensing and Certification Board. The end of Chapter 14 details these requirements.

> *Market value is primarily based upon the "willing buyer and willing seller" concept.*

A. FOUR ESSENTIAL ELEMENTS OF VALUE

VALUE *is a relationship between the thing desired and a potential purchaser.* Four elements must be present to create and maintain value. The four essential elements of value are:

    D   **1. Demand** – the desire, need, and ability to purchase
    U   **2. Utility** – usefulness; ability to instill a desire for possession
    S   **3. Scarcity** – in short supply, usually more expensive
    T   **4. Transferability** – can change ownership, as with a deed.

Elements of value include demand, utility, scarcity, and transferability (DUST). Neither cost nor expectation is an element of value.

II. The Appraisal Process (Four Logical Steps)

An appraisal is the solution to the problem of determining value. To solve this problem, an orderly procedure has been developed; it is called the appraisal process. The *APPRAISAL PROCESS is an orderly program by which the problem is defined, the work is planned, and the data is gathered, analyzed, and correlated to estimate the value*. Although the characteristics of real property differ, this is an orderly procedure for solving any appraisal problem (see **Figure 13-1**).

The appraisal process consists of four logical steps:

1. Defining and clarifying the problem
2. Gathering the data
3. Performing the three appraisal methods (Chapter 14)
4. Correlating the three methods and determining the final opinion of value. (Chapter 14)

A. DEFINITION OF THE APPRAISAL PROBLEM (1st Step in the Appraisal Process)

The first step in the appraisal process must include a definition of what questions are to be answered during the appraisal. To begin with, the precise location of the property must be established. Next, the extent of ownership (fee simple or partial) to be appraised must be identified. The date and purpose of the appraisal (usually to establish market value) is then determined. Any limiting conditions (facts unknown to the appraiser) must be clarified. Finally, the appraiser will determine the fee for his or her services.

1. Purpose of an Appraisal

An appraisal can serve several purposes. Here is a partial list of the kinds of appraisals that you, as an owner or a potential owner, may need:

1. Market Value
2. Insurance Value
3. Loan Value
4. Tax Assessment Value
5. Rental Value
6. Value for certain Internal Revenue Service Purposes
7. Settlements
8. Salvage Value
9. Other

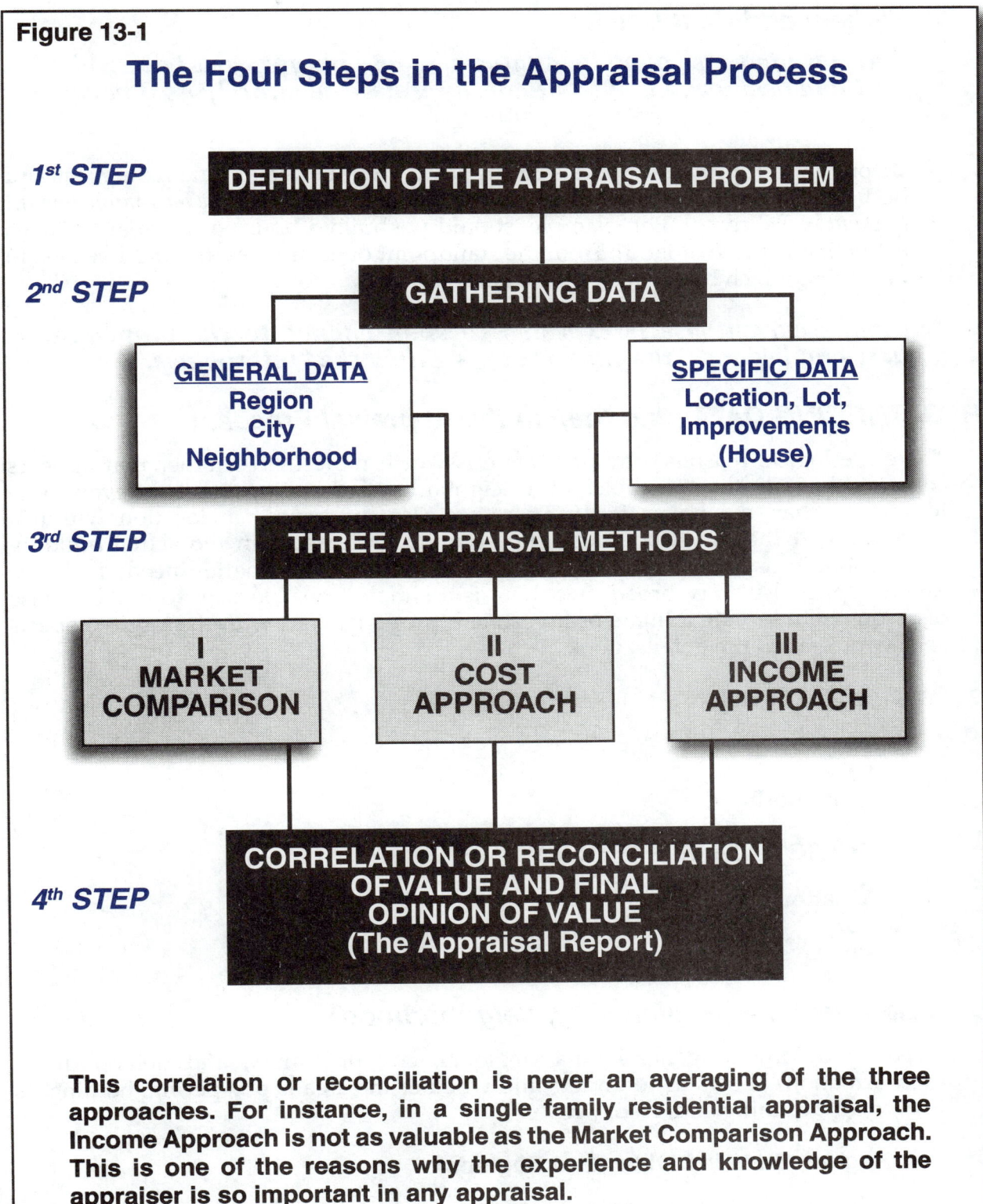

Figure 13-1

The Four Steps in the Appraisal Process

1st STEP — DEFINITION OF THE APPRAISAL PROBLEM

2nd STEP — GATHERING DATA

GENERAL DATA
Region
City
Neighborhood

SPECIFIC DATA
Location, Lot,
Improvements
(House)

3rd STEP — THREE APPRAISAL METHODS

**I
MARKET
COMPARISON**

**II
COST
APPROACH**

**III
INCOME
APPROACH**

4th STEP — CORRELATION OR RECONCILIATION OF VALUE AND FINAL OPINION OF VALUE (The Appraisal Report)

This correlation or reconciliation is never an averaging of the three approaches. For instance, in a single family residential appraisal, the Income Approach is not as valuable as the Market Comparison Approach. This is one of the reasons why the experience and knowledge of the appraiser is so important in any appraisal.

2. Highest and Best Use

The primary purpose of a site analysis by an appraiser is to determine highest and best use. Land is always appraised separately as if vacant and available for highest and best use.

Before we can properly appraise a property, we must determine its highest and best use. *HIGHEST AND BEST USE is the use that will produce the maximum amount of profit or net return.* For example, should we build a house or an apartment on an available piece of land? From the standpoint of economics, it would be best to build that which brings the highest net return.

When the current use is expected to soon change to the property's highest and best use, the current use is called the "interim use."

B. GATHERING DATA (2nd Step in the Appraisal Process)

There are logical reasons why one home is worth more than another that appears comparable and why the choice of a neighborhood is as important, or even more important, than the house itself. There are also differences in location within a neighborhood that must be taken into account. Differences in the actual building construction must also be considered. The background information needed for real estate appraisal is very broad, but there is a simple, sensible way to make a wise decision about buying a home or investment property. Start with the largest aspects and work toward the details. Look at:

1. GENERAL DATA

   a. Region
   b. City
   c. Neighborhood

2. SPECIFIC DATA (Site Analysis)

   a. Location
   b. Lot
   c. Improvements (House)

1. General Data (Region, City, Neighborhood)

The gathering of general data (regional, city or county, and neighborhood information) allows us to understand whether the area is prospering, holding its own, or declining and, if so, why.

a. Region (State is Divided into Regions)

The condition of the nation's economy can be reflected in the Texas real estate market and can affect the ease with which financing is available. But real estate markets are essentially regional and local. If the regional or local economy is expanding, people are working and can afford to buy homes because lending institutions are eager to grant loans. In a recession, jobs are less secure, confidence is low, and financing may not be as easy to obtain. So, the economic mood of the nation as a whole can indirectly affect the economic mood in Texas, but it is the local and regional economy that directly affects the mood in a particular real estate market.

A regional economy is affected by upturns and also downtrends. Not only do large areas reflect the national picture, but they also respond to more localized forces, such as the rapid growth of large cities and industrial complexes and the down-sizing of defense-related industries or even the weather in agricultural areas. Texas is divided into north, south, east, west, and central regions, and many sub-regions and cities.

Texas, like most large states, is a very geographically diverse state. Geographical considerations can easily affect an entire region. For example, if an area has rain for many months of the year, the value of the property may be increased when compared to regions that have significantly less rain. Or compare the moderate temperatures of a winter in South Texas with the cold winters of the panhandle.

b. City (or County)

A desirable city or county is a growing area where people can get good jobs and where people want to live. If the city is undesirable or even unsafe, people want to leave. Features to look for in cities, besides the availability of work and safety, are good public facilities, parks, good school systems, and active citizens who care and take part in the city's affairs.

c. Neighborhood

A residential *NEIGHBORHOOD is normally a limited area where the homes are physically similar and where the occupants have a certain degree of social and economic background in common.* It may cover a few square miles or it may be only one block square. Boundaries may be defined by physical, social, or economic differences. The important thing is that your neighborhood is the environment in which you live day in and day out. **The neighborhood in which you live is usually a more important factor than the house itself!** This is because the surroundings of a house influence the property value even more than the house itself.

Neighborhoods influence homeowners' more than renters' location decisions. The reason is that many people rent apartments in neighborhoods in which they would never think of buying, because they plan to stay there for only a short time. Renters may rent in a less desirable area, but when they buy they will select a neighborhood they like.

Owner-occupied homes lend economic stability to a neighborhood, as owners tend to take better care of property than renters.

The selection or acceptance of a neighborhood should come before the actual decision of whether to buy a particular house or not. The four primary forces that affect value of a neighborhood are shown in **Figure 13-2**.

Neighborhoods are always changing, sometimes at a fast pace, but usually at a slow, steady pace. The four considerations discussed in Figure 13-2 can change a prestigious area to a shabby neighborhood or vice versa. Each consideration can change the outlook for any neighborhood.

Social forces, economic influences, and political influences are all forces affecting value. Private deed restrictions are NOT a force affecting value.

2. Specific Data (Property Itself)

There is plenty of land in the world, but the exact location of each parcel makes it unlike any other on earth. Its location is the major factor that determines its value.

a. Location

A **SITE** *is a particular parcel within a neighborhood.* Since each parcel is unique, the individual site that one selects for a home should be chosen with care. There are several site selection factors that affect the value of the home, but the personal needs and objectives of the buyer should be of the utmost concern.

Site: the location of a plot of ground for a building.

b. Lot (Types)

There are six major types of lots (see **Figure 13-3**):

1. Cul-de-sac (**Lot A**)
2. Corner (**Lot B**)
3. Key (**Lot C**)
4. T-Intersection (**Lot D**)
5. Interior (**Lot E**)
6. Flag (**Lot F**)

1. Cul-De-Sac Lot

The **CUL-DE-SAC LOT** *is a lot facing the turnaround portion of a dead-end street.* Figure 13-3 shows that Lot A is a cul-de-sac. The main advantage of

Figure 13-2

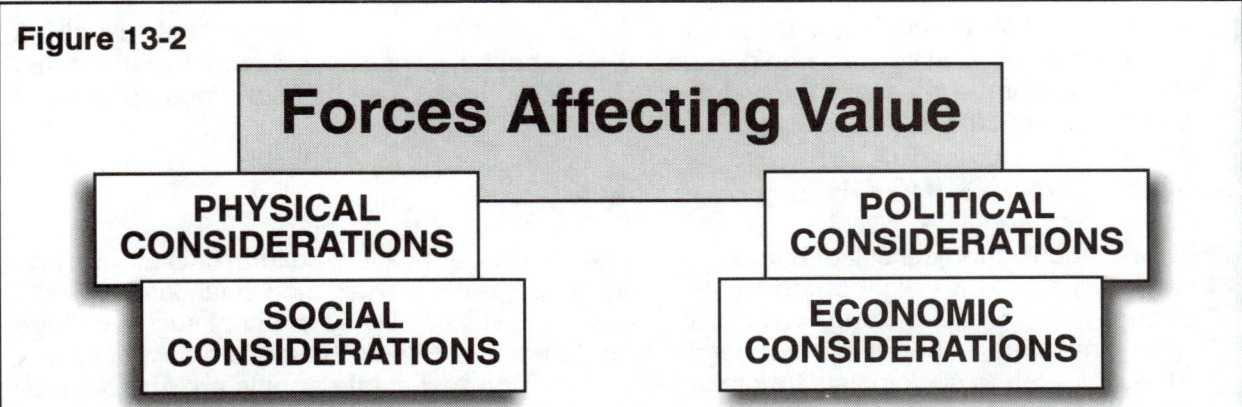

Forces Affecting Value

PHYSICAL CONSIDERATIONS

SOCIAL CONSIDERATIONS

POLITICAL CONSIDERATIONS

ECONOMIC CONSIDERATIONS

PHYSICAL CONSIDERATIONS

A neighborhood that is close to a commercial area is generally highly desirable. Being close to downtown areas, employment centers, and major shopping areas only adds to this desirability, as long as an owner is not located right next to such a facility. If the street patterns are curved and there are wide boulevards, the neighborhood also looks more attractive.

Access to transportation is necessary. The availability of freeways, transit systems, and convenient parking is an important consideration in making comparisons between various areas. However, this factor is less important in high-value suburban areas where estate living is desirable.

Balanced Land Use

The best efficiency and highest value come when there is a balance between different types of use. A city is a naturally attractive environment when it has a proper balance between residential, commercial, industrial, and recreational space.

Families are attracted to a neighborhood with good schools. Certain private or parochial schools may create a demand for homes in that area. Churches are also a definite benefit. Other institutions such as libraries, colleges, and universities may also enhance a community.

The first trip into a neighborhood may be impressive, or, on the other hand, it may be depressing. First impressions are important; the landscaping, architectural style, and the streets can create either impression. Well-maintained buildings create enhanced marketability.

Physical conditions such as lakes, beaches, rivers, or hilly areas may be either advantageous or disadvantageous depending on where they are. A feature such as a wooded hillside or lake front property would probably enhance a neighborhood, but a river that frequently floods the surrounding area is a disadvantage. **(continued)**

Invasion of a residential area by commercial or industrial usage around it is usually a disadvantage, especially if the neighborhood is exposed to noise or odors. A bar located across from a home is usually a devaluing factor. Some areas may be hazardous because of heavy truck and auto traffic.

SOCIAL CONSIDERATIONS

Neighborhoods often consist of persons of similar income, education, cultural background and lifestyle. As such, the neighborhood may or may not appeal to certain individual buyers. Could a change in the social makeup of a neighborhood affect values? Whether or not such a change has any influence, either positive or negative, and the effect of any change is a field of inquiry that must be left to sociologists. Appraisers, lenders, and real estate agents are forbidden by both federal and state law to consider race, religion, sex, ethnicity, or lifestyle as factors of value. Only economic factors may be considered by real estate professionals.

BLIGHT occurs as a result of a lack of property maintenance in a neighborhood. This is generally due to an economic inability to provide maintenance on the part of the owners. The result is lowered property values.

GENTRIFICATION is the rehabilitation of a blighted neighborhood. It is generally a result of low property values attracting buyers who are economically able to upgrade and maintain the properties in the neighborhood.

ECONOMIC CONSIDERATIONS

Population growth is an indication of the economic health of a neighborhood. If more people want to live in an area, then it must be desirable; an economically alive neighborhood has well-maintained lawns and buildings, whereas in a deteriorating neighborhood, the lack of maintenance is obvious and so is the lowered value of the homes.

The rents charged and income levels of the people indicate a community's prestige (or lack of it). **The larger the percentage of home ownership versus those renting, the more economically stable the area is**. If many rentals are vacant, you can surmise that renters are not interested in the area. New construction, on the other hand, indicates that the area is growing and its value is increasing.

POLITICAL CONSIDERATIONS

Property tax rates vary from area to area. Wealthy, more stable economic areas usually have a slightly higher tax rate because the residents are willing and have the ability to pay for more public services. In areas where the taxes are very high, potential buyers are often scared off. Special assessments for lighting, sewers, and street improvements may temporarily turn some people away, but they generally add to the property's total value.

Some cities use **zoning** and **building codes** as devices to ensure the continued stability of a neighborhood. If the desirability of the neighborhood warrants such regulation, then the city will continue to be a growing one. In the end, most city leaders politically control changes in their cities by enacting zoning and building codes.

a cul-de-sac lot is privacy and lack of traffic one gets by living on a "not a through" street. Due to its pie-shaped design, it has the disadvantage of a small front yard, but this is offset by generally having a large backyard. The design makes it more secluded and limits through traffic from both autos and pedestrians. Limited parking and front yard space does not stop it from rivaling the corner lot as one of the most desirable types of lots. A cul-de-sac lot's desirability may vary due to view, size, area, and family characteristics. **Figure 13-3, Lot A, Cul-de-sac**.

Figure 13-3

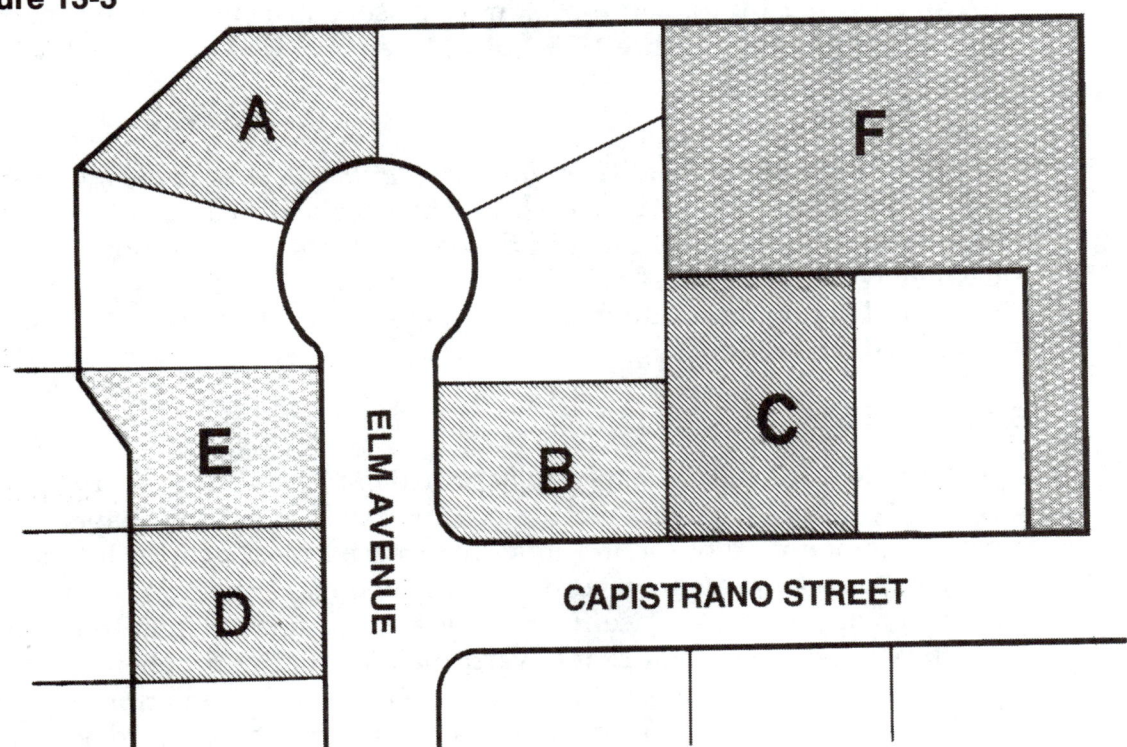

2. Corner Lot

The **CORNER LOT** *is a lot that is located at the intersection of two streets.* A corner site frequently has a higher value than a lot fronting only on one street. The appraiser must be careful to look at the local market in determining the actual effects of a corner influence on the surrounding lots. *CORNER INFLUENCE is the theory that a variety of forces affect corner lots (and also lots located near a corner) to a greater degree than most other lots.* A corner lot is generally more desirable if there is access to the backyard for items such as a trailer or camper. Other people like it because there are fewer homes nearby, which allows for more light, fresh air, and also more lot area for gardens and other types of landscaping.

The main disadvantage of a corner lot is the loss of privacy and higher cost, since both sides of the lot require off-site improvements, such as streets, curbs, gutters, and sidewalks. Also, zoning setbacks may reduce the buildable lot space. Usually commercial corner lots benefit because of easy access and added traffic exposure. **Figure 13-3, Lot B, Corner.**

3. Key Lot

KEY LOT is a lot that is bordered on the side by the back of other lots that front on another street. Key lots are the least desirable lots because of the lack of privacy caused by the close proximity of several neighbors abutting the side of the property. **Figure 13-3, Lot C, Key.**

4. T-Intersection Lot

The *T-INTERSECTION LOT is an interior lot that is faced head-on by a street; it is the lot at the end of a dead-end street.* The streets form a "T" shape. It is an interior lot with one advantage and two disadvantages. The advantage is a clear view down the street, which gives a more spacious feeling. Intersection noise and annoying headlights at night are its disadvantages. **Figure 13-3, Lot D, T-Intersection.**

5. Interior Lot

An *INTERIOR LOT is a lot generally surrounded by other lots on three sides.* It is usually in the shape of a rectangle, but can be almost any shape. It is the most common type of lot and it is preferred by most people. Interior lots have larger backyards than corner lots, which make them much better for recreational purposes. Since the front yards are smaller than those found on corner lots, they require less yard maintenance and benefit from less intersection noise. Because of typical long block design, interior lots are by far the most numerous. The disadvantages are limited backyard access and three or more adjoining neighbors. **Figure 13-3, Lot E, Interior.**

6. Flag Lot

A *FLAG LOT is a rear lot, in back of other lots, with a long, narrow access driveway.* This type of lot takes on the shape a flag. The flag lot's shape allows for a maximum of privacy and can be easily gated. In hilly areas, flag lots have some of the better views, while others can be pushed up against a steep mountain side. The value of a flag lot verses other types of lots depends on the circumstances. The same can be said about all other types of lots: their value depends on the specifics of each lot and the local market conditions. It is up to the salesperson to gain a working knowledge of lot shapes and the pluses and minuses attributed to each type of lot. **Figure 13-3, Lot F, Flag.**

c. Physical Aspects of a Lot

The major physical aspects of the actual site are:

1. Size and shape
2. Slope, drainage, and soil (lot design layouts)
3. View, exposure to sun, and weather
4. Improvements (on-site and off-site)

1. Size and Shape of Lot

Lots or parcels can be subdivided into almost any shape imaginable, but most lots are rectangular and front onto a street. Any lot is valuable if it offers enough area to build a house that is compatible with the surroundings. In general, the more land or frontage on the street, the higher the value of the land. An example of a depth table will explain this concept. A *DEPTH TABLE is a percentage table that illustrates how the highest value is located in the front part of a lot*. **Figure 13-4** is an example of the "4-3-2-1" depth table. The "4-3-2-1 rule" is best used by appraisers to determine the value of commercial properties on which the lots vary in depth.

Figure 13-4

The "4-3-2-1" Depth Table

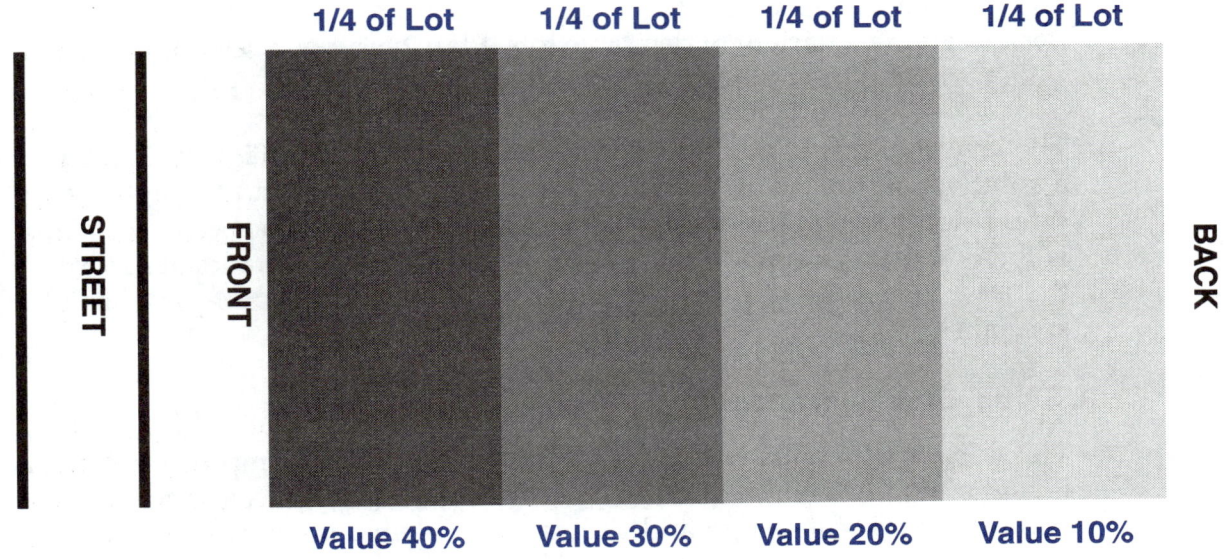

The percentage of value for each ¼ or 25% section of the lot varies: 40%, 30%, 20%, to 10% in value for each quarter back from the front.

In Figure 13-4, the highest value is in the front portion of the lot. For example, a small backyard will not affect the value of the property as much as a small front yard. This is especially true with commercial property such as shopping centers where there is plenty of parking in the back, but most people prefer to park in the front. Remember, though, that the percentage and values of a depth table vary from property to property.

Since the front portion of the lot has the most value, the more frontage there is, the better. *FRONT FOOTAGE is the width of the property in the front, along the street.* Generally speaking we can say that a house with a large front yard is worth more than the same house with a large backyard. But people do have different preferences, such as large backyards for swimming pools, tennis courts, or other recreational activities.

When two or more properties are joined to make one property (assemblage), and become more valuable than the sum of the properties separately, it is called an increase in "plottage value." The process of assemblage results in an increase of "plottage value."

2. Lot Design Layouts

There are several ways to lay out lots in a parcel of land being subdivided. Zoning regulations usually state the minimum amount of square feet a lot can have, but a developer can get better prices if he or she divides the land wisely. **Figure 13-5** shows the same parcel of land twice. **Plan 1** is a good design, giving a variety of desirable lots. **Plan 2** is a poor design, giving too little variation, too little front area and too much depth.

The layout of lots in a large subdivision is illustrated in **Figure 13-6**. Often a subdivision tract with fewer, well-planned lots will bring a higher total sales price than a poorly designed tract with more lots. The best tract layout is the one that considers all the costs involved and the marketability of all the lots. This kind of planning is not easy and requires the services of a specialist.

3. Slope, Drainage, and Soil

The slope of a lot will lower its value if it will be costly to improve. A lot that is higher or lower in relation to the street level may be costly to improve because of possible slope and drainage problems. Erosion may also be a part of slope or drainage problems. These problems, however, can be easily offset by an excellent view or location.

The soil composition of a lot may or may not be of any great concern. There are certain types of soil, however, that may create a problem depending

Figure 13-5

PLAN 1   GOOD LAYOUT – LOTS ARE WELL DESIGNED

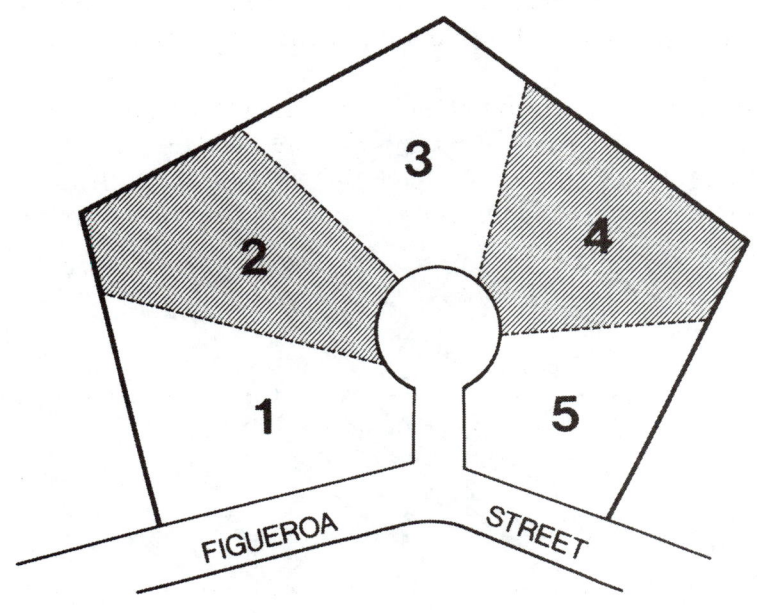

PLAN 2   POOR LAYOUT – LOTS ARE TOO DEEP

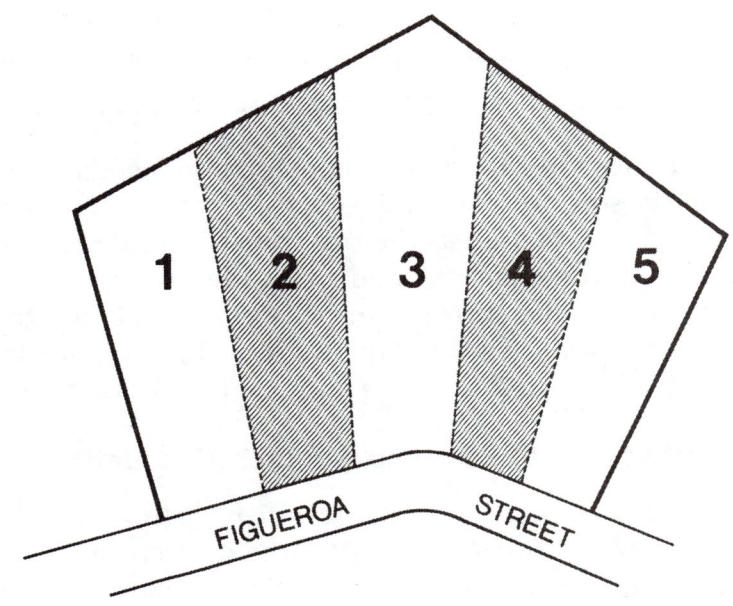

Figure 13-6

TENTATIVE SUBDIVISION MAP

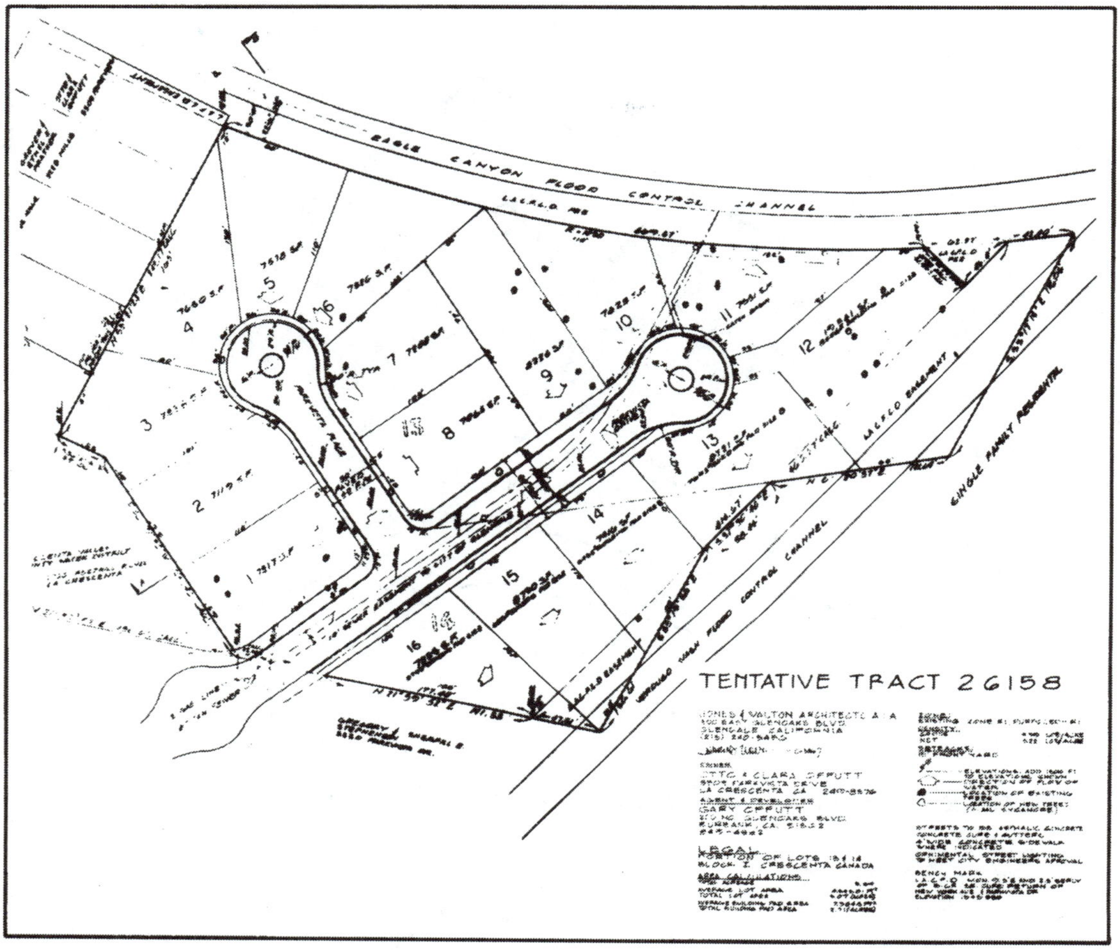

on your lifestyle or possible construction needs. In some regions there are certain soil problems that must be corrected before a foundation can be poured. In other areas the soil content can destroy a pipeline within 10 years. If you like gardens and plant life, it is wise to see how the plants are growing in the surrounding lots. Some hill country tracts are built on bedrock covered by a thin layer of topsoil; to dig a swimming pool might even require blasting with dynamite, which is very costly.

4. View, Exposure to Sun, and Weather (Orientation)

The south and west sides of streets are preferred by merchants: pedestrians seek the shady side and displayed merchandise is not damaged by the sun. The northeast corner is the least desirable.

Most people appreciate a good view from their homes; it is pleasant to sit back and enjoy the beautiful surroundings. In a new tract of homes, the lots with the best views usually sell first and apartments with views rent for more. Places like Canyon Lake near San Antonio, Lake Travis near Austin, and The Woodlands near Houston are examples of areas that are expensive because of their beautiful views.

ORIENTATION is planning the most advantageous place on a parcel of land for an improvement to be located. The exposure of a house to the sun and weather elements may influence a person's decision to buy a house. If the wind usually blows from the northwest, it is best for the house to face the northwest. In this case the house can be a shield for backyard entertaining. The exposure to the sun is a different matter. Most people prefer the sun to shine on their backyard, so the backyard should face the south or the west. In this way the backyard receives the best exposure throughout the day. In windy areas on the coast, sheltered patios away from cold sea breezes are desirable.

A map showing the house and its location relating to other plants, buildings, and streets is an example of "orientation."

AMENITIES are those improvements or views that increase the desirability or enjoyment rather than the necessities of the residents. For example, a view of a lake, hills, or city lights at night increase the value of a home. Amenity improvements would include jacuzzis, swimming pools, and tennis courts.

Amenity properties are usually single-family residences.

III. Improvements

Real estate is logically divided into land (site) and improvements. *IMPROVEMENTS are any buildings, walkways, pools, and other structures. CAPITAL IMPROVEMENTS are permanent improvements made to increase the useful life of the property or increase the property's value. They stay with the property.* These include off-site improvements (streets and utilities) and on-site improvements (buildings). *OFF-SITE IMPROVEMENTS are the improvements made to areas adjoining the parcel that add to the parcel's usefulness and sometimes its value.* Examples of off-site improvements are: streets, street lights, sewers, sidewalks, curbs, and gutters. These items generally add value to urban property but may be of little value in rural areas. Off-site improvements are usually paid for by the homeowners through the levying of special assessments. On the other hand, *ON-SITE IMPROVEMENTS are structures erected permanently for use on a site, such as buildings and fences.*

The three steps or phases in construction of a home are land acquisition, development, and construction.

A. HOUSE STRUCTURE ILLUSTRATED

This section identifies different parts of a house. Figure **13-7** shows roof types. **Figure 13-8** is a diagram of a house that illustrates the 20 most used construction terms. Each part is labeled and defined so that it can be identified. **Figure 13-9** lists construction and other terms.

B. HOME WARRANTY PLANS

A *WARRANTY PLAN is an insurance plan that provides financial protection against defects in any major home construction.* There are a growing number of such warranty plans in Texas. These warranty plans, also known as **residential service contracts**, insure the new owner of an existing home against such things as malfunction of built-in appliances and defects in major systems such as structure, roof, heating, plumbing, and electrical wiring. For this protection, the previous owner or the buyer pays a fee that varies according to the type of coverage received. Some companies inspect the property (thereby giving notice of any existing defects). The standard TREC promulgated residential contract informs the parties that residential service contracts are available. But this item, along with who pays for the warranty plan, is negotiable.

IV. Basic Appraisal Principles

There are several "principles of appraisal." These principles are valid economic concepts that are applied to the appraisal of real estate. A few of the basic principles are explained so that you can understand the logic and reasons why a particular home is worth more than another. **Figure 13-10** shows you seven of the basic appraisal principles.

A. PRINCIPLE OF SUPPLY AND DEMAND

The principle of supply and demand shows why "location" is important. The *PRINCIPLE OF SUPPLY AND DEMAND states that as the supply of land decreases, the value of land increases because more people are competing for the desirable land.* Living next to a lake is expensive because the land is scarce. Even small lots bring very high selling prices in these areas. To water lovers, these are the most desirable neighborhoods because there are only so many lake view lots. In areas where there are many lots available, the supply is large and the price of a lot can be very low. Downtown high-rise commercial locations in cities like Dallas, Houston, and Austin are scarce and therefore expensive.

Figure 13-7

ROOF TYPES

Before purchasing a house, a potential buyer should carefully evaluate the structure, checking to see that its style of architecture is compatible with that of the surrounding neighborhood. This should also be an element of consideration when building a new house or remodeling.

The material used in covering the roof is very important. If the material is not flammable and is durable, such as tile or slate, it adds to the value of the home. However, if it is flammable and wears out/cracks/splits easily, such as wood shingles, the value is diminished.

Examining the type of roof, the way it is framed and finished, is one of the simplest ways to assess the architectural compatibility of a given house.

Pictured below are several of the most common roof types. One is likely to see examples of flat, gable, hip, gambrel, mansard, and pyramid roofs throughout Texas.

A roof sloping on all four sides is called a "hip roof."

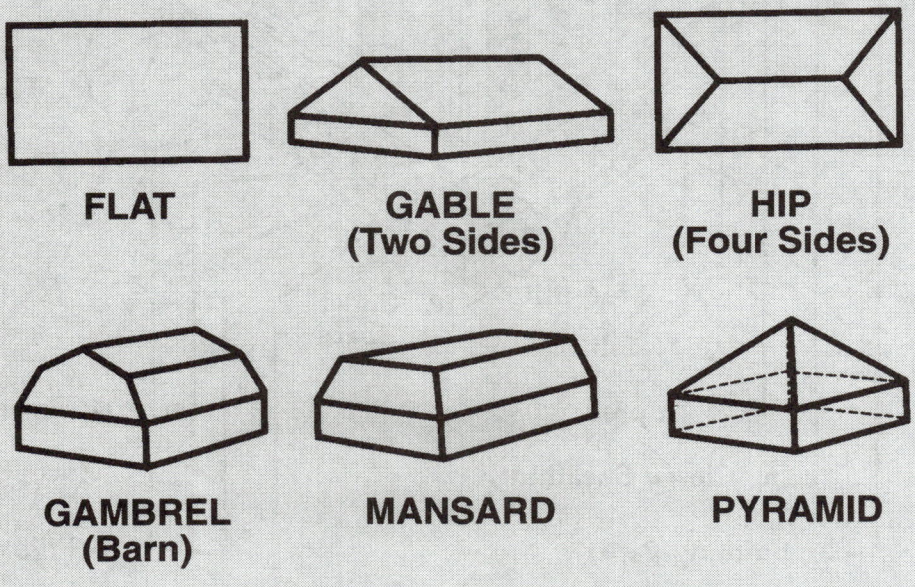

| FLAT | GABLE (Two Sides) | HIP (Four Sides) |

| GAMBREL (Barn) | MANSARD | PYRAMID |

Figure 13-8

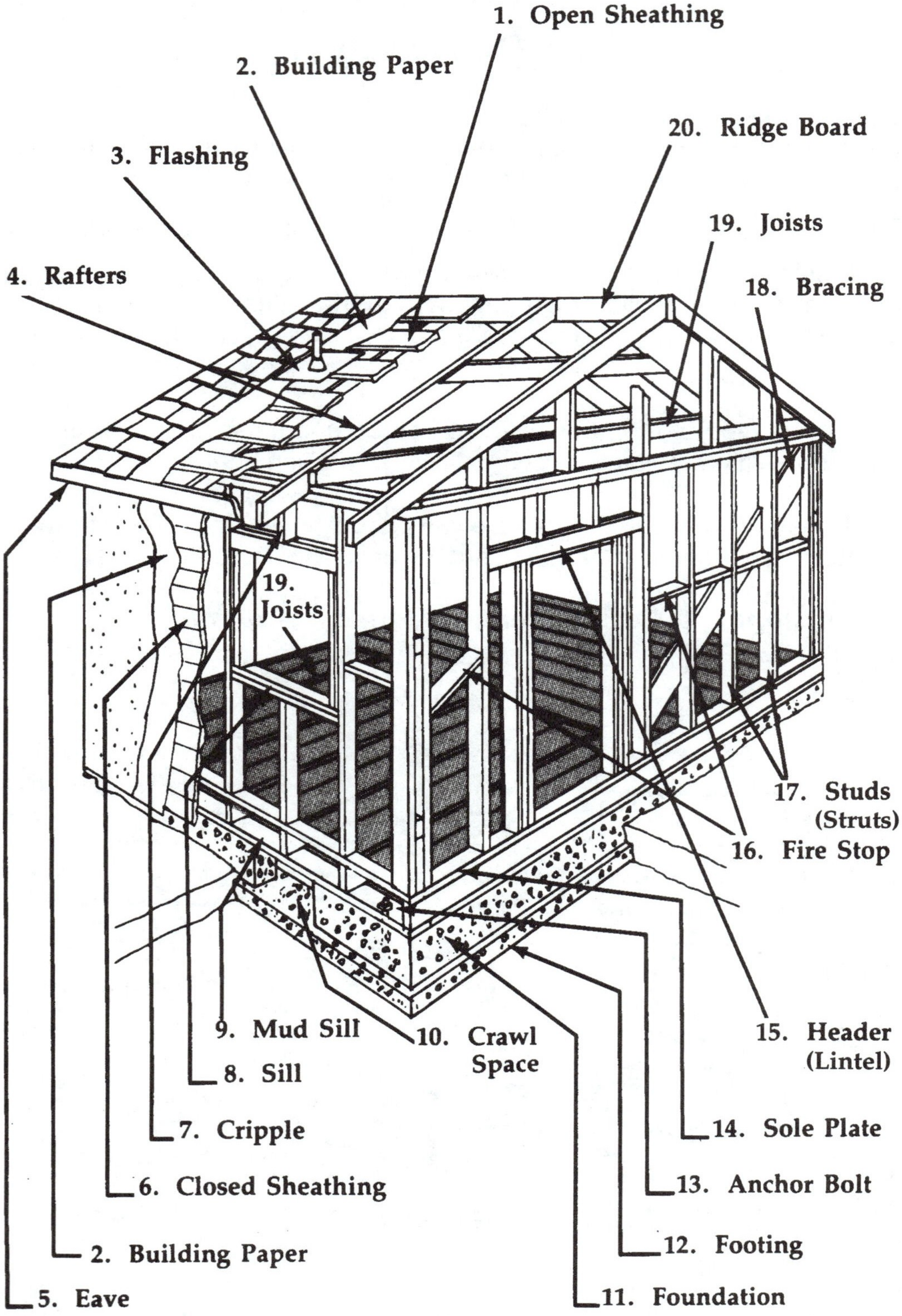

1. Open Sheathing

2. Building Paper

20. Ridge Board

3. Flashing

19. Joists

4. Rafters

18. Bracing

19. Joists

17. Studs (Struts)

16. Fire Stop

9. Mud Sill

10. Crawl Space

8. Sill

7. Cripple

6. Closed Sheathing

2. Building Paper

5. Eave

15. Header (Lintel)

14. Sole Plate

13. Anchor Bolt

12. Footing

11. Foundation

EXPLANATION OF DIAGRAM DETAILS

1. Open Sheathing — Boards nailed to rafters as foundation for the roof covering. Open sheathing is used with wood shingles.

2. Building Paper — Heavy waterproof paper used between sheathing and roof covering or siding.

3. Flashing — Sheet metal used to protect a roof from seepage.

4. Rafters — Sloping members of a roof used to support the roof boards and shingles (Maximum 24" apart).

5. Eave — Protruding underpart of roof overhanging exterior walls.

6. Closed Sheathing — Boards nailed to studding as foundation for exterior siding. "Closed" means butted together.

7. Cripple — Stud above or below a window opening or above a doorway.

8. Sill — Bottom portion lining doorway or window.

9. Mud Sill — Treated lumber (or redwood) bolted to the foundation.

10. Crawl Space — Unexcavated area under the house (**Minimum 18˝**).

11. Foundation — Concrete base of house.

12. Footing — The spreading element that supports a pier, column, wall, or foundation. (**Can be located in the interior of a house**.)

13. Anchor Bolt — Large bolt used for fastening mud sill to foundation. Bolt is anchored into concrete foundation.

14. Sole Plate — Support on which the studs rest.

15. Header (Lintel) — The beam over a doorway or window.

16. Fire Stop — Blocking used to restrict flames from spreading to attic. May be placed horizontally or diagonally.

17. Studs (Struts) — Vertical 2˝ x 4˝ framework in the walls **spaced 16˝ on center**.

18. Bracing — Board running diagonally across the wall framing to prevent sway.

19. Joists — Structural parts supporting floor or ceiling loads. A beam which supports them would be called a girder.

20. Ridge Board — Highest point of construction in a frame building.

> **Figure 13-9**

Construction and Other Terms

Backfill – The replacement of excavated earth against a structure (wall). If a property is backfilled, it will fill in around foundation slabs, piers, columns, and footings.

A contractor/builder who buys a large quantity of backfill is probably using it to fill in space around the foundation, retaining wall, or other excavations.

Bearing Wall – A strong wall supporting any vertical load in addition to its own weight, usually a roof or floor above.

Boardfoot – 1 board foot = 6 inches x 12 inches x 2 inches.

BTU (British Thermal Unit) – A unit of measurement used to calculate heat - the quantity of heat required to raise one pound of water one degree Fahrenheit.

Capital Assets – Expenditures of a permanent nature that increase property values. Examples: buildings and street improvements.

Cash Flow – In investment property, the actual cash the investor will receive after deduction of operating expenses and debt servicing (loan payment) from his or her gross income.

Conduit – A flexible metal pipe used to protect the electrical wiring inside.

Dry Wall – Plaster walls that are installed in dry sheets.

EER (Energy Efficiency Ratio) – A measure of energy efficiency; when an air conditioning unit has a higher energy efficiency ratio, the unit is more efficient.

Elevation Sheet – A rendering that shows the front and side views of a building; it shows the exterior views.

Foundation Plan – **A plan that refers to slabs, piers, columns, and footings.**

H_2O Pressure – Testing water pressure by turning on all faucets and flushing all toilets.

HVAC – **Heating, ventilation, and air conditioning systems in commercial buildings.**

Hoskold Tables – Concept of a "sinking fund" as a compound interest-bearing account, into which the portion of the investment returned each year is reinvested immediately.

(continued)

Construction and Other Terms

Inwood Tables – Concept of using present value of income in a perpetuity table to help appraisers.

Joists – Parallel wooden members used to support floor and ceiling loads.

Kiosk – An information booth.

Local Building Inspector – Person who enforces construction standards.

Over-Improvement – An expenditure to a property that doesn't improve its value.

Percolation Test – A test to determine how well water is absorbed by the soil. (Used when installing a sewage system.)

Plot Plan – The placement of improvements (buildings) on a lot.

Potable Water – Drinkable water.

Property Residual, Building Residual, and Land Residual – All are methods of working backwards to find the unknown variable when appraising property.

R-Value – A measure used to calculate the heat resistance of insulation (the higher the better). Insulation is considered adequate if the temperature on the inside of an exterior wall is the same as the temperature on an interior wall.

Rehabilitation – The restoration of a property to a satisfactory condition without changing the interior or exterior design.

Soil Pipe – A pipe used to carry waste and sewage from a property.

Toxic Waste Report – A report evaluating how harmful the dangerous material is on a property.

Turnkey Property – A single-family home ready to move into.

Unearned Increment – An increase in value of real estate due to no effort on the part of the owner; often caused by population increase.

Wainscoting – The wood lining of the lower portion of an interior wall with the upper portion wallpapered or covered with another material different from the lower portion.

Figure 13-10

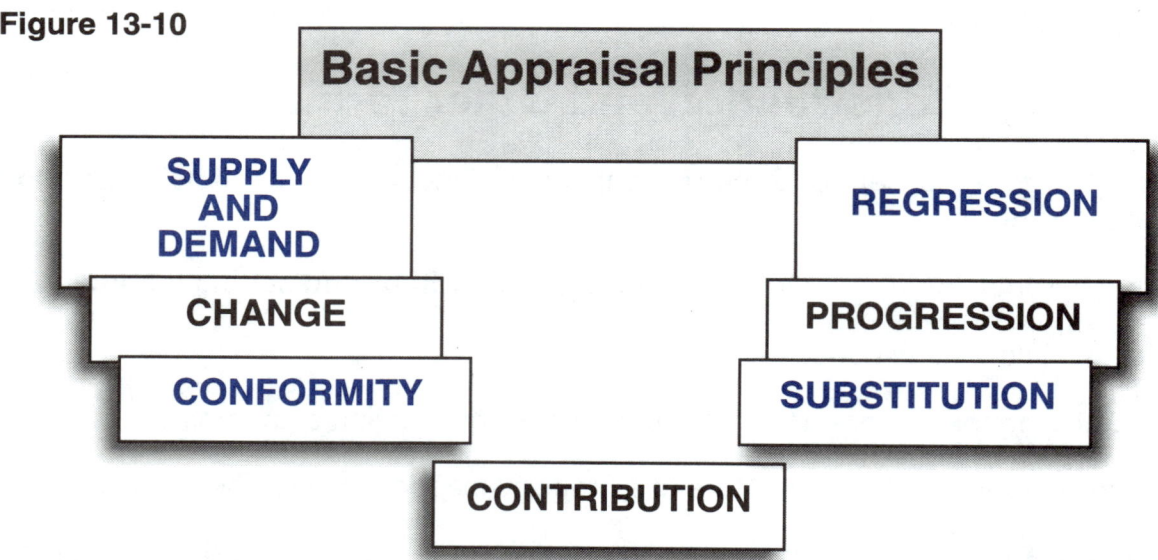

Basic Appraisal Principles

SUPPLY AND DEMAND

CHANGE

CONFORMITY

REGRESSION

PROGRESSION

SUBSTITUTION

CONTRIBUTION

B. PRINCIPLE OF CHANGE

The **PRINCIPLE OF CHANGE** *is that real property is constantly changing.* Value is influenced by changes in such things as: population size, shopping centers, schools and colleges, freeways, economic and social trends. It is hard to see change on a day-to-day basis, but if you go back to the area where you grew up, the change is apparent.

The real property life cycle goes through three stages: development, maturity, and decline, which are illustrated in **Figure 13-11**.

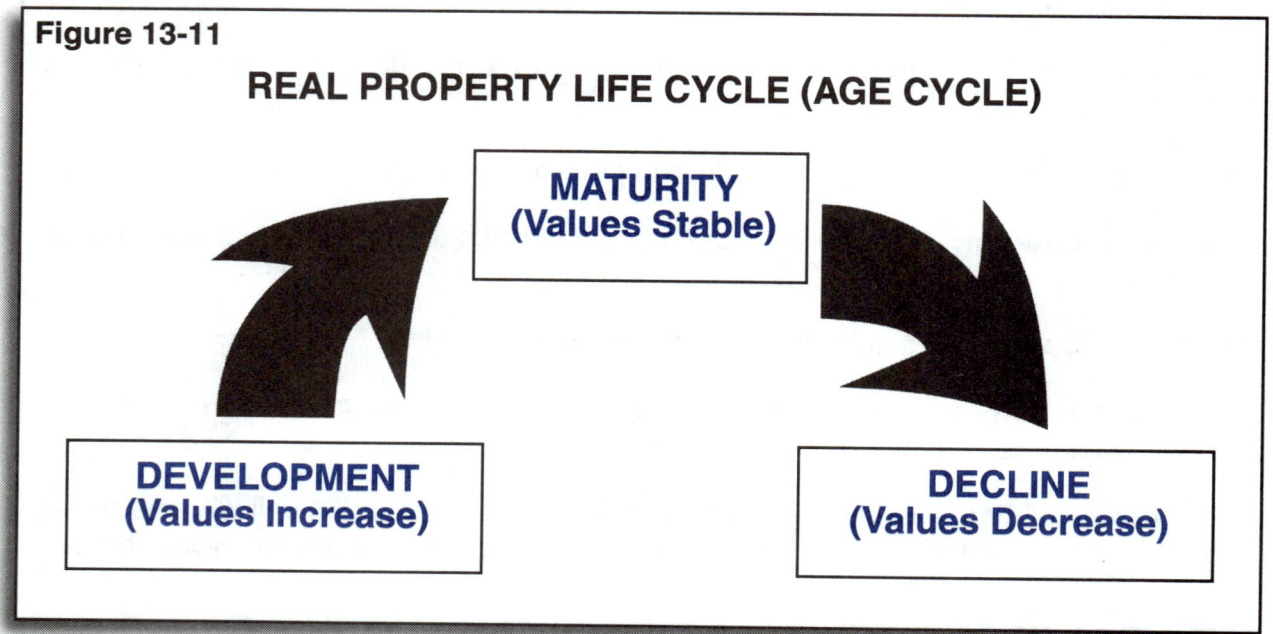

Figure 13-11

REAL PROPERTY LIFE CYCLE (AGE CYCLE)

MATURITY
(Values Stable)

DEVELOPMENT
(Values Increase)

DECLINE
(Values Decrease)

1. Development (Integration)

This is the stage when the land is subdivided into lots, the streets are paved, and street lights are installed. Soon, homes are built and the community starts. As new people move in, landscaping and fences improve the homes.

The three steps in construction of a home are land acquistion, development, and construction.

2. Maturity (Equilibrium)

The maturity stage starts when the homes become older and the children grow up and move away. Most of the residents are long-time homeowners and the community has a solid, well-established look.

3. Decline (Disintegration)

In this stage, the buildings show some wear and tear and the oldest buildings are starting to deteriorate. As the useful life of the property declines, lower social or economic groups move into the area. Large homes may be converted into multiple family use.

The life cycle of real property may take a few years, such as that of a mining town going "bust," or may span a century, such as that of a community that constantly revitalizes itself.

C. PRINCIPLE OF CONFORMITY

The **PRINCIPLE OF CONFORMITY** *states that the maximum value is obtained when a reasonable degree of building similarity is maintained in the neighborhood.* So, if all the homes in an area are similar (not identical), the maximum value of real property is created. The word "similar" is the key. If all the tract homes are identical, as if they were all made with the same cookie cutter, the maximum value is not present.

When a residential neighborhood is composed mostly of owner-occupied residential properties, it tends to stabilize values.

The principle of conformity is one of the primary reasons for zoning regulations (discussed in Chapter 15) or deed restrictions (discussed in Chapter 3). They protect the

neighborhood from other nonconforming uses and from infiltration of incompatible structures. An attractive neighborhood would quickly decline in value if zoning or deed restrictions did not help protect its conformity.

D. PRINCIPLE OF CONTRIBUTION

The **PRINCIPLE OF CONTRIBUTION** *states that the value of a particular component is measured in terms of its contribution to the value of the whole property.* Consequently, cost does not necessarily equal value. It either adds more or less to the value of real property.

> **Example:** If an apartment building produces a 10% return to investors, a $50,000 investment in a swimming pool, without an equal ($50,000 x 10%) $5,000 or higher increase in rents, would not be a good idea.

Thus, in some cases, a property's market value may not increase even if it has had additions, alterations, or has been rehabilitated. If a skateboard park was added to a senior citizen apartment community, the property would be considered "over-built." The principle of contribution is also referred to as increasing and (decreasing) "diminishing returns" in economic textbooks.

E. PRINCIPLE OF SUBSTITUTION

Under the **PRINCIPLE OF SUBSTITUTION**, *a buyer will not pay more for a particular property if it costs less to buy a similar property of equal utility and desirability.* People prefer the less expensive price if all other things are considered equal. When appraisers use the principle of substitution, they compare properties to adjust for differences. The maximum value of a property tends to be set by the cost of acquiring an equally desirable substitute property.

F. PRINCIPLE OF REGRESSION (Value Goes Down)

When a house of greater value is adversely affected by houses of comparably lesser value, it is called the **PRINCIPLE OF REGRESSION**. For example, if a house that would easily be worth $790,000 in a neighborhood of similar homes was to be built in a neighborhood of $210,000 homes, it would not sell for $790,000. Anyone in the market for a $790,000 house would not want to live in a tract where the average price of a house was $210,000. Because of its superior quality or size, the house would undoubtedly sell for more than the average house in the tract, but it would not approach $790,000.

The same principle applies to the over-improved home. When owners invest very large sums in major additions, lavish landscaping, and swimming pools, and the other residents do not improve their homes, the house is no longer similar to the others. The owners of the over-built house will not receive the full value for the cost of improvements they have made.

When the best property in the neighborhood is adversely affected by the presence of a substandard property, it is called regression.

G. PRINCIPLE OF PROGRESSION (Value Goes Up)

In the **PRINCIPLE OF PROGRESSION**, *the value of a lesser residence is increased in value by its location in a neighborhood of better homes.* This is the opposite of the principle of regression. A smaller, unattractive, and poorly maintained home in an exclusive area will sell for much more than if it were located in a comparable neighborhood. People who wish to live in an exclusive area would think of the smaller home as a bargain.

V. CHAPTER SUMMARY

An **appraisal** is an opinion of value based on judgment and professional experience for a **specific property as of a certain date**. Appraisers, who must be licensed in Texas, want "open market results," not prudent values or prices. The **value** of a property is determined by the elements of **demand**, **utility**, **scarcity**, and **transferability**. Cost and/or expectation are never one of these elements.

The **appraisal process** consists of four steps: 1) **defining the problem**, 2) **gathering the data**, 3) **performing the three appraisal methods**, and 4) **determining the final opinion of value**. Whether the reason for the appraisal is transfer of ownership, obtaining a loan, condemnation, or insurance, the first step is to do a **site analysis** to determine **highest and best use**.

The second step involves gathering data, including **general data** (region, city, and neighborhood) and **specific data** (location, lot, and improvements). The **neighborhood** is the most important general data. The **four forces** affecting value are: **physical, social, economic**, and **political considerations**. The most important economic characteristic is area preference (**location**).

Front footage is a pricing tool used to sell commercial property and a **4-3-2-1 depth table** is used when the lots vary in depth. **Plottage** (assemblage) refers to separately owned, contiguous lots brought under single ownership. The **shady south and west sides of streets** are preferred by merchants with the northeast corner being the least desirable.

There are several principles of appraisal, including **supply and demand**, and the **principle of change**, which is evident in the **real estate life cycle of development, maturity**, and **decline**. The **principle of conformity** states that the maximum value is obtained when building similarity is maintained in the neighborhood, and is one of the major reasons for **zoning regulations**.

The **principle of contribution** (or diminishing returns) states that the value of a particular component is measured in terms of its contribution to the value of the whole property. The **principle of substitution** states that a buyer will not pay more for a particular property if it costs less to buy a similar property of equal utility and desirability.

The **principle of regression** states that between properties in the same neighborhood, the value of the best property will be negatively affected by the value of the other properties. The opposite of regression is the **principle of progression**, where a lesser residence increases in value by its location in a neighborhood of better homes.

VI. TERMINOLOGY

A. Appraisal
B. Appraisal Process
C. Change
D. Conformity
E. Corner Lot
F. Cul-de-Sac
G. Depth Table
H. Flag Lot

I. Frontage
J. Highest and Best Use
K. Interior Lot
L. Key Lot
M. Market Price
N. Market Value
O. Neighborhood
P. Off-Site Improvements

Q. Progression Principle
R. Regression Principle
S. Site
T. Supply and Demand
U. T-Intersection Lot
V. Warranty Plan

1.____ The appraisal principle that maintains the maximum value of a property is realized when a reasonable degree of similarity is present in the area where the property is located.

2.____ The least desirable type of lot because the back ends of other lots face one of its sides.

3.____ A general term describing people living or working together in an area of similar properties with similar social, economic, and political backgrounds.

4.____ The highest price a willing buyer would pay and a willing seller accept, both being fully informed, and the property exposed for a reasonable period of time. This value may be different from the price a property can actually be sold for at a given time.

5.____ Not a corner lot, but an inside lot; the most common type of lot.

6.____ Development of large parcels into smaller lots suitable for construction. This includes sidewalks, curbs, streets, sewers, streetlights, etc.

7.____ A lot at the U-shaped end of a street. Even though they are narrower in the front and wider in the back, these lots are popular because the street itself makes the area exclusive.

8.____ An opinion of real property value based upon a factual analysis by a qualified (licensed) person with education and experience.

9.____ The use of land that will bring the greatest economic return over a given time.

10.____ The price a property sells for, which may be higher or lower than its actual market value.

11.____ The orderly process of determining the fair market value of real property by: 1) defining the problem, 2) gathering the data, 3) applying the three methods of appraisal (cost approach, market comparison approach, income approach), and 4) correlating the information for a final estimate of value.

12.____ A general term for a lot or plot of land.

13.____A lot with both the front and side facing different streets. Such a residential lot is generally more desirable because of its increased exposure to light and fresh air. A commercial lot benefits from better street access and exposure to traffic patterns.

14.____An interior lot facing down a street into traffic. Such a lot benefits from the view down the open street, but suffers from additional traffic noise and oncoming headlights at night.

15.____A lot with a long, narrow entrance, forming the shape of a flag. While it has limited frontage, such a lot can be very desirable if the odd shape is accompanied by a spectacular view in the back.

16.____A chart illustrating the principle that the greatest value exists in the front portion of the lot, and the value of the land decreases the further back from the street you go.

17.____The linear measure of the front portion of a parcel facing a major street, walkway, or lake.

18.____An insurance plan covering the major systems of a home such as electrical, heating, plumbing, and major appliances.

19.____A principle of real estate appraisal suggesting that the value of property increases when there is more demand and a short supply in an area. Conversely, the value decreases when there is an abundant supply and less demand.

20.____The concept that although changes may be imperceptible, neighborhoods are constantly changing. Population shifts and economic changes, along with many other variables, will constantly work to alter the value of property.

21.____The real estate principle that a smaller, low-quality home will gain value if larger, nicer homes are being built in the neighborhood.

22.____The real estate principle that a larger, nicer home will not enjoy its full value if it is located in a neighborhood of smaller, low-quality homes.

VII. MULTIPLE CHOICE

1. In comparing real property price to value, a change in financing terms will affect:
   a. price, but not value.
   b. value, but not price.
   c. price and value.
   d. neither price nor value.

2. The primary purpose of a site analysis by an appraiser is to determine the:
   a. applicable zoning laws.
   b. highest and best use.
   c. soil conditions.
   d. available amenities.

3. When the highest and best use of a property is expected to change, the current use is called:
   a. the interim use.
   b. the temporary use.
   c. the transitional use.
   d. the possible use.

4. When two properties are joined to make one property, and becomes more valuable than the sum of the properties separately, it is called:
   a. leverage.
   b. inflation.
   c. plottage.
   d. subdividing.

5. A map shows the house and its location relating to other plants, buildings, and streets. This is an example of:
   a. plottage.
   b. orientation.
   c. elevation.
   d. topography.

6. Which of the following is one board foot?
   a. Six inches x twelve inches x one foot
   b. Six inches x twelve inches x two inches
   c. Six inches x six inches x two inches
   d. Six inches x twelve inches x one inch

7. When an air conditioning unit has a higher energy efficiency ratio (EER), the:

    a. unit needs more watts of electricity.
    b. unit is more efficient.
    c. unit is less efficient.
    d. BTUs are larger.

8. "HVAC" refers to:

    a. heating, ventilation, and air conditioning systems in commercial buildings.
    b. Home Value After Correlation.
    c. Highest Value Appraising Consideration.
    d. House Vitality Area Consultants.

9. When a residential neighborhood is composed mostly of owner-occupied residential properties it tends to:

    a. attract commercial shopping centers to the neighborhood.
    b. stabilize values.
    c. deteriorate faster than areas with many rental properties.
    d. lower property values.

10. When a house of greater value is adversely affected by houses of comparably lesser value, it is called:

    a. anticipation.
    b. regression.
    c. contribution.
    d. balance.

ANSWERS: 1. a; 2. b; 3. a; 4. c; 5. b; 6. b; 7. b; 8. a; 9. b; 10. b

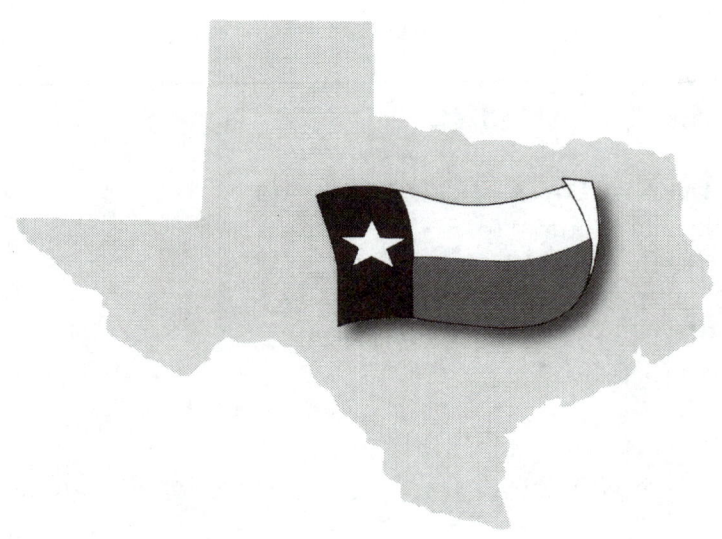

Chapter 14
Appraisal Methods

Real estate salespeople need to know enough about appraisal techniques and practices so that they can determine, in advance, the approximate selling price of a property. Salespeople have the advantage of determining the "probable" sales price of a property quickly because they see what similar properties in their area sell for each day. They can be on top of the market because of their multiple listing service and close contact with other knowledgeable agents. They are constantly being updated as to the current listing and selling prices.

A **Competitive Market Analysis (CMA)** form, or "comp," is filled out and presented to sellers so they can see at a glance the selling prices of other houses or condos in their neighborhood. This enables the sellers to "price their listings" close to a realistic selling price.

A MLS (Multiple Listing Service) member agent can download comparable sales information (comps) in a variety of forms by accessing an MLS website. The local association of REALTORS® will maintain the MLS website for members.

CHAPTER 14 OUTLINE

www.appraisalfoundation.org
Appraisal Foundation
www.asfmra.org/
American Society of Farm Managers and Rural Appraisers (ASFMRA)
http://aicanada.org
The Appraisal Institute of Canada

A salesperson or broker may establish a "sales price" for a property without an appraisal license, but a professional appraisal must be completed by a licensed or certified appraiser.

A state licensed (expert) appraiser will use all three of the valuation approaches to determine the value of a property, but will emphasize only one to establish the final value.

These approaches are:

    I. COMPARATIVE APPROACH (MARKET DATA METHOD)
    II. COST (REPLACEMENT) APPROACH
    III. CAPITALIZATION (INCOME) APPROACH

The appraisal is also an opinion of a value "range." Let us assume that a range of $450,000 to $500,000 is established from the three appraisal approaches mentioned above. By correlating the economic information from the three approaches, an experienced appraiser can estimate a more precise value. The results of the three approaches can be weighed and it can then be determined which method has provided the best information about the property. In this case, let's say that the appraiser felt he or she should emphasize the market comparison approach that was $490,000. The appraiser would state that, in his or her opinion, the property was worth $490,000; but the value "ranged" from $450,000 to $500,000.

I. Comparative Approach (Market Data Method)

Of the three approaches previously mentioned, the market comparison method is the one most frequently used. It is easy for an alert student to master this technique within a short time, and it is the most logical way to appraise a house. The market data method uses the "principle of substitution" to compare similar properties. **A person will not pay more for a property if he/she can buy something similar for less.**

The market data method uses the "principle of substitution" to compare similar properties.

The **MARKET DATA METHOD** *is a method of appraising real property by comparing the current selling prices of recently sold similar properties and adjusting those prices for any differences.* The comparative (market data method) approach uses the principle of substitution; a person will not pay more for a property if he or she can buy something similar for less.

Simply adjust the value of the comparable sales price. If a house is comparable except that it has a pool, sells for $640,000 and the value of the $40,000 pool is subtracted, the house we are appraising is valued at $600,000.

A. HOW TO ADJUST FOR A COMPARABLE SALE (Comps)

The term "Comps" is used to mean (similar) comparable properties.

The market data method is basically common sense. If your neighbor has a similar house to yours that he just sold for $400,000, then yours is worth about $400,000. The only problem is that adjustments must be made for any differences between the houses. For example, if a similar $400,000 house had a fireplace worth $8,000 and yours did not, then your house would be worth $392,000 ($400,000 - $8,000). Adjustments should be made to the selling price of the comparable house for any differences between the properties. **The usual adjustments are made for differences in location, age, lot size, building size, condition of the property, and any time difference between the sales.**

Subtract or add from or to the selling price of the comparable property to adjust for differences.

If the comparable property has an item not present in the subject property, the appraiser subtracts the value of the item from the comparable property's selling price. Likewise, if the subject property has an item not present in the comparable property, the appraiser adds the value of the item to the comparable property's selling price. After all these adjustments are made to the comparable selling price, the resulting figure gives the appraiser the subject property's value.

By comparing recent selling prices of properties in the same area, it is easy to see the trends in selling prices and why certain properties sell for more than others. The more comparable sales you gather, the more reliable the results. Real estate salespeople often refer to comparable sales as "comps."

An appraiser using the market data approach would be most interested in the date that the price was agreed upon.

Unsold properties are important when using the market data method. If a property has been listed "for sale" for a long time, it is usually overpriced. Such comparable "unsold properties" suggest an upper limit of value. Unsold listings can therefore help establish the highest comparable price. An experienced appraiser can easily estimate the amount of an adjustment. The adjustment is an estimate or opinion determined solely by the appraiser, and reflects his or her broad experience and education.

Comparable sales information can be obtained from many different sources. Brokers and salespeople are familiar with property sales prices in their area, so naturally they are a good source for appraisal data. In addition, most brokers are members of the local multiple listing service and have access to past sales information. Other people in the real estate field, such as loan officers, title insurance agents, and escrow officers can also supply comparable sales information.

It is essential that: 1) the information is from a reliable source; 2) there is an adequate number of comparable sales; and 3) the comparable sales are truly comparable.

The market data method is the most common approach for houses and condominiums. It is also the best method for appraising lots and vacant land (unimproved property). The market comparison approach is best for single-family residences (houses or condos) and vacant land (lots).

Figures 14-1 shows the Uniform Residential Appraisal Report (URAR) that is accepted by Fannie Mae and Freddie Mac.

B. ADVANTAGES OF THE MARKET DATA METHOD

This method is excellent for appraising single-family homes. Here are the reasons why:

1. The market data method is easy to learn, and with a little experience it is easy to apply.
2. Since there are usually many recent comparable sales, the required information is readily available.
3. This method is used mostly for houses or condos, which makes this method the most relevant to us as homeowners, salespeople, or investors.

The most difficult part of the market data method is to adjust similar properties for differences. The market data method is limited when market conditions are rapidly changing.

Marketability and desirability of a property are the primary concerns when appraising a residential property. Marketability is the ultimate test of functional utility.

Figure 14-1

Uniform Residential Appraisal Report   File

The purpose of this summary appraisal report is to provide the lender/client with an accurate, and adequately supported, opinion of the market value of the subject property.

SUBJECT

Property Address		City		State	Zip Code

Borrower _____ Owner of Public Record _____ County _____

Legal Description _____

Assessor's Parcel # _____ Tax Year _____ R.E. Taxes $ _____

Neighborhood Name _____ Map Reference _____ Census Tract _____

Occupant ☐ Owner ☐ Tenant ☐ Vacant   Special Assessments $ _____   ☐ PUD   HOA $ _____ ☐ per year ☐ per month

Property Rights Appraised ☐ Fee Simple ☐ Leasehold ☐ Other (describe) _____

Assignment Type ☐ Purchase Transaction ☐ Refinance Transaction ☐ Other (describe) _____

Lender/Client _____ Address _____

Is the subject property currently offered for sale or has it been offered for sale in the twelve months prior to the effective date of this appraisal? ☐ Yes ☐ No

Report data source(s) used, offering price(s), and date(s). _____

CONTRACT

I ☐ did ☐ did not analyze the contract for sale for the subject purchase transaction. Explain the results of the analysis of the contract for sale or why the analysis was not performed. _____

Contract Price $ _____ Date of Contract _____ Is the property seller the owner of public record? ☐ Yes ☐ No Data Source(s) _____

Is there any financial assistance (loan charges, sale concessions, gift or downpayment assistance, etc.) to be paid by any party on behalf of the borrower? ☐ Yes ☐ No
If Yes, report the total dollar amount and describe the items to be paid. _____

NEIGHBORHOOD

Note: Race and the racial composition of the neighborhood are not appraisal factors.

Neighborhood Characteristics	One-Unit Housing Trends	One-Unit Housing	Present Land Use %
Location ☐ Urban ☐ Suburban ☐ Rural	Property Values ☐ Increasing ☐ Stable ☐ Declining	PRICE $ (000) AGE (yrs)	One-Unit ____ %
Built-Up ☐ Over 75% ☐ 25–75% ☐ Under 25%	Demand/Supply ☐ Shortage ☐ In Balance ☐ Over Supply		2-4 Unit ____ %
Growth ☐ Rapid ☐ Stable ☐ Slow	Marketing Time ☐ Under 3 mths ☐ 3–6 mths ☐ Over 6 mths	Low	Multi-Family ____ %
Neighborhood Boundaries		High	Commercial ____ %
		Pred.	Other ____ %

Neighborhood Description _____

Market Conditions (including support for the above conclusions) _____

SITE

Dimensions _____ Area _____ Shape _____ View _____

Specific Zoning Classification _____ Zoning Description _____

Zoning Compliance ☐ Legal ☐ Legal Nonconforming (Grandfathered Use) ☐ No Zoning ☐ Illegal (describe) _____

Is the highest and best use of the subject property as improved (or as proposed per plans and specifications) the present use? ☐ Yes ☐ No If No, describe _____

Utilities	Public	Other (describe)		Public	Other (describe)	Off-site Improvements—Type	Public	Private
Electricity	☐		Water	☐		Street	☐	☐
Gas	☐		Sanitary Sewer	☐		Alley	☐	☐

FEMA Special Flood Hazard Area ☐ Yes ☐ No FEMA Flood Zone ____ FEMA Map # ____ FEMA Map Date ____

Are the utilities and off-site improvements typical for the market area? ☐ Yes ☐ No If No, describe _____

Are there any adverse site conditions or external factors (easements, encroachments, environmental conditions, land uses, etc.)? ☐ Yes ☐ No If Yes, describe _____

IMPROVEMENTS

General Description	Foundation	Exterior Description materials/condition	Interior materials/condition
Units ☐ One ☐ One with Accessory Unit	☐ Concrete Slab ☐ Crawl Space	Foundation Walls	Floors
# of Stories	☐ Full Basement ☐ Partial Basement	Exterior Walls	Walls
Type ☐ Det. ☐ Att. ☐ S-Det./End Unit	Basement Area ____ sq. ft.	Roof Surface	Trim/Finish
☐ Existing ☐ Proposed ☐ Under Const.	Basement Finish ____ %	Gutters & Downspouts	Bath Floor
Design (Style)	☐ Outside Entry/Exit ☐ Sump Pump	Window Type	Bath Wainscot
Year Built	Evidence of ☐ Infestation	Storm Sash/Insulated	Car Storage ☐ None
Effective Age (Yrs)	☐ Dampness ☐ Settlement	Screens	☐ Driveway # of Cars
Attic ☐ None	Heating ☐ FWA ☐ HWBB ☐ Radiant	Amenities ☐ Woodstove(s) #	Driveway Surface
☐ Drop Stair ☐ Stairs	☐ Other ____ Fuel ____	☐ Fireplace(s) # ____ ☐ Fence	☐ Garage # of Cars
☐ Floor ☐ Scuttle	Cooling ☐ Central Air Conditioning	☐ Patio/Deck ☐ Porch	☐ Carport # of Cars
☐ Finished ☐ Heated	☐ Individual ☐ Other	☐ Pool ☐ Other	☐ Att. ☐ Det. ☐ Built-in

Appliances ☐ Refrigerator ☐ Range/Oven ☐ Dishwasher ☐ Disposal ☐ Microwave ☐ Washer/Dryer ☐ Other (describe) _____

Finished area above grade contains: ____ Rooms ____ Bedrooms ____ Bath(s) ____ Square Feet of Gross Living Area Above Grade

Additional features (special energy efficient items, etc.) _____

Describe the condition of the property (including needed repairs, deterioration, renovations, remodeling, etc.). _____

Are there any physical deficiencies or adverse conditions that affect the livability, soundness, or structural integrity of the property? ☐ Yes ☐ No If Yes, describe _____

Does the property generally conform to the neighborhood (functional utility, style, condition, use, construction, etc.)? ☐ Yes ☐ No If No, describe _____

Uniform Residential Appraisal Report

File #

There are	comparable properties currently offered for sale in the subject neighborhood ranging in price from $		to $
There are	comparable sales in the subject neighborhood within the past twelve months ranging in sale price from $		to $

FEATURE	SUBJECT	COMPARABLE SALE # 1		COMPARABLE SALE # 2		COMPARABLE SALE # 3	
Address							
Proximity to Subject							
Sale Price	$		$		$		$
Sale Price/Gross Liv. Area	$ sq. ft.	$ sq. ft.		$ sq. ft.		$ sq. ft.	
Data Source(s)							
Verification Source(s)							
VALUE ADJUSTMENTS	DESCRIPTION	DESCRIPTION	+(-) $ Adjustment	DESCRIPTION	+(-) $ Adjustment	DESCRIPTION	+(-) $ Adjustment
Sale or Financing Concessions							
Date of Sale/Time							
Location							
Leasehold/Fee Simple							
Site							
View							
Design (Style)							
Quality of Construction							
Actual Age							
Condition							
Above Grade	Total	Bdrms.	Baths	Total	Bdrms.	Baths	Total	Bdrms.	Baths	Total	Bdrms.	Baths
Room Count							
Gross Living Area	sq. ft.	sq. ft.		sq. ft.		sq. ft.	
Basement & Finished Rooms Below Grade							
Functional Utility							
Heating/Cooling							
Energy Efficient Items							
Garage/Carport							
Porch/Patio/Deck							
Net Adjustment (Total)		☐ + ☐ -	$	☐ + ☐ -	$	☐ + ☐ -	$
Adjusted Sale Price of Comparables		Net Adj. % Gross Adj. %	$	Net Adj. % Gross Adj. %	$	Net Adj. % Gross Adj. %	$

I ☐ did ☐ did not research the sale or transfer history of the subject property and comparable sales. If not, explain

My research ☐ did ☐ did not reveal any prior sales or transfers of the subject property for the three years prior to the effective date of this appraisal.

Data source(s)

My research ☐ did ☐ did not reveal any prior sales or transfers of the comparable sales for the year prior to the date of sale of the comparable sale.

Data source(s)

Report the results of the research and analysis of the prior sale or transfer history of the subject property and comparable sales (report additional prior sales on page 3).

ITEM	SUBJECT	COMPARABLE SALE # 1	COMPARABLE SALE # 2	COMPARABLE SALE # 3
Date of Prior Sale/Transfer				
Price of Prior Sale/Transfer				
Data Source(s)				
Effective Date of Data Source(s)				

Analysis of prior sale or transfer history of the subject property and comparable sales

Summary of Sales Comparison Approach

Indicated Value by Sales Comparison Approach $

Indicated Value by: Sales Comparison Approach $ Cost Approach (if developed) $ Income Approach (if developed) $

This appraisal is made ☐ "as is", ☐ subject to completion per plans and specifications on the basis of a hypothetical condition that the improvements have been completed, ☐ subject to the following repairs or alterations on the basis of a hypothetical condition that the repairs or alterations have been completed, or ☐ subject to the following required inspection based on the extraordinary assumption that the condition or deficiency does not require alteration or repair:

Based on a complete visual inspection of the interior and exterior areas of the subject property, defined scope of work, statement of assumptions and limiting conditions, and appraiser's certification, my (our) opinion of the market value, as defined, of the real property that is the subject of this report is $, as of   , which is the date of inspection and the effective date of this appraisal.

Uniform Residential Appraisal Report

File #

COST APPROACH TO VALUE (not required by Fannie Mae)

Provide adequate information for the lender/client to replicate the below cost figures and calculations.

Support for the opinion of site value (summary of comparable land sales or other methods for estimating site value)

ESTIMATED ☐ REPRODUCTION OR ☐ REPLACEMENT COST NEW	OPINION OF SITE VALUE .... = $
Source of cost data	Dwelling Sq. Ft. @ $ .... =$
Quality rating from cost service Effective date of cost data	Sq. Ft. @ $ .... =$
Comments on Cost Approach (gross living area calculations, depreciation, etc.)	Garage/Carport Sq. Ft. @ $ .... =$
	Total Estimate of Cost-New .... = $
	Less Physical Functional External
	Depreciation =$( )
	Depreciated Cost of Improvements...................... =$
	"As-is" Value of Site Improvements.................... =$
Estimated Remaining Economic Life (HUD and VA only) Years	Indicated Value By Cost Approach .... =$

INCOME APPROACH TO VALUE (not required by Fannie Mae)

Estimated Monthly Market Rent $ X Gross Rent Multiplier   = $ Indicated Value by Income Approach

Summary of Income Approach (including support for market rent and GRM)

PROJECT INFORMATION FOR PUDs (if applicable)

Is the developer/builder in control of the Homeowners' Association (HOA)? ☐ Yes ☐ No   Unit type(s) ☐ Detached ☐ Attached

Provide the following information for PUDs ONLY if the developer/builder is in control of the HOA and the subject property is an attached dwelling unit.

Legal name of project

Total number of phases   Total number of units   Total number of units sold

Total number of units rented   Total number of units for sale   Data source(s)

Was the project created by the conversion of an existing building(s) into a PUD? ☐ Yes ☐ No   If Yes, date of conversion

Does the project contain any multi-dwelling units? ☐ Yes ☐ No   Data source(s)

Are the units, common elements, and recreation facilities complete? ☐ Yes ☐ No   If No, describe the status of completion.

Are the common elements leased to or by the Homeowners' Association? ☐ Yes ☐ No   If Yes, describe the rental terms and options.

Describe common elements and recreational facilities

Uniform Residential Appraisal Report

This report form is designed to report an appraisal of a one-unit property or a one-unit property with an accessory unit; including a unit in a planned unit development (PUD). This report form is not designed to report an appraisal of a manufactured home or a unit in a condominium or cooperative project.

This appraisal report is subject to the following scope of work, intended use, intended user, definition of market value, statement of assumptions and limiting conditions, and certifications. Modifications, additions, or deletions to the intended use, intended user, definition of market value, or assumptions and limiting conditions are not permitted. The appraiser may expand the scope of work to include any additional research or analysis necessary based on the complexity of this appraisal assignment. Modifications or deletions to the certifications are also not permitted. However, additional certifications that do not constitute material alterations to this appraisal report, such as those required by law or those related to the appraiser's continuing education or membership in an appraisal organization, are permitted.

SCOPE OF WORK: The scope of work for this appraisal is defined by the complexity of this appraisal assignment and the reporting requirements of this appraisal report form, including the following definition of market value, statement of assumptions and limiting conditions, and certifications. The appraiser must, at a minimum: (1) perform a complete visual inspection of the interior and exterior areas of the subject property, (2) inspect the neighborhood, (3) inspect each of the comparable sales from at least the street, (4) research, verify, and analyze data from reliable public and/or private sources, and (5) report his or her analysis, opinions, and conclusions in this appraisal report.

INTENDED USE: The intended use of this appraisal report is for the lender/client to evaluate the property that is the subject of this appraisal for a mortgage finance transaction.

INTENDED USER: The intended user of this appraisal report is the lender/client.

DEFINITION OF MARKET VALUE: The most probable price which a property should bring in a competitive and open market under all conditions requisite to a fair sale, the buyer and seller, each acting prudently, knowledgeably and assuming the price is not affected by undue stimulus. Implicit in this definition is the consummation of a sale as of a specified date and the passing of title from seller to buyer under conditions whereby: (1) buyer and seller are typically motivated; (2) both parties are well informed or well advised, and each acting in what he or she considers his or her own best interest; (3) a reasonable time is allowed for exposure in the open market; (4) payment is made in terms of cash in U. S. dollars or in terms of financial arrangements comparable thereto; and (5) the price represents the normal consideration for the property sold unaffected by special or creative financing or sales concessions* granted by anyone associated with the sale.

*Adjustments to the comparables must be made for special or creative financing or sales concessions. No adjustments are necessary for those costs which are normally paid by sellers as a result of tradition or law in a market area; these costs are readily identifiable since the seller pays these costs in virtually all sales transactions. Special or creative financing adjustments can be made to the comparable property by comparisons to financing terms offered by a third party institutional lender that is not already involved in the property or transaction. Any adjustment should not be calculated on a mechanical dollar for dollar cost of the financing or concession but the dollar amount of any adjustment should approximate the market's reaction to the financing or concessions based on the appraiser's judgment.

STATEMENT OF ASSUMPTIONS AND LIMITING CONDITIONS: The appraiser's certification in this report is subject to the following assumptions and limiting conditions:

1. The appraiser will not be responsible for matters of a legal nature that affect either the property being appraised or the title to it, except for information that he or she became aware of during the research involved in performing this appraisal. The appraiser assumes that the title is good and marketable and will not render any opinions about the title.

2. The appraiser has provided a sketch in this appraisal report to show the approximate dimensions of the improvements. The sketch is included only to assist the reader in visualizing the property and understanding the appraiser's determination of its size.

3. The appraiser has examined the available flood maps that are provided by the Federal Emergency Management Agency (or other data sources) and has noted in this appraisal report whether any portion of the subject site is located in an identified Special Flood Hazard Area. Because the appraiser is not a surveyor, he or she makes no guarantees, express or implied, regarding this determination.

4. The appraiser will not give testimony or appear in court because he or she made an appraisal of the property in question, unless specific arrangements to do so have been made beforehand, or as otherwise required by law.

5. The appraiser has noted in this appraisal report any adverse conditions (such as needed repairs, deterioration, the presence of hazardous wastes, toxic substances, etc.) observed during the inspection of the subject property or that he or she became aware of during the research involved in performing this appraisal. Unless otherwise stated in this appraisal report, the appraiser has no knowledge of any hidden or unapparent physical deficiencies or adverse conditions of the property (such as, but not limited to, needed repairs, deterioration, the presence of hazardous wastes, toxic substances, adverse environmental conditions, etc.) that would make the property less valuable, and has assumed that there are no such conditions and makes no guarantees or warranties, express or implied. The appraiser will not be responsible for any such conditions that do exist or for any engineering or testing that might be required to discover whether such conditions exist. Because the appraiser is not an expert in the field of environmental hazards, this appraisal report must not be considered as an environmental assessment of the property.

6. The appraiser has based his or her appraisal report and valuation conclusion for an appraisal that is subject to satisfactory completion, repairs, or alterations on the assumption that the completion, repairs, or alterations of the subject property will be performed in a professional manner.

Uniform Residential Appraisal Report

File #

APPRAISER'S CERTIFICATION: The Appraiser certifies and agrees that:

1. I have, at a minimum, developed and reported this appraisal in accordance with the scope of work requirements stated in this appraisal report.

2. I performed a complete visual inspection of the interior and exterior areas of the subject property. I reported the condition of the improvements in factual, specific terms. I identified and reported the physical deficiencies that could affect the livability, soundness, or structural integrity of the property.

3. I performed this appraisal in accordance with the requirements of the Uniform Standards of Professional Appraisal Practice that were adopted and promulgated by the Appraisal Standards Board of The Appraisal Foundation and that were in place at the time this appraisal report was prepared.

4. I developed my opinion of the market value of the real property that is the subject of this report based on the sales comparison approach to value. I have adequate comparable market data to develop a reliable sales comparison approach for this appraisal assignment. I further certify that I considered the cost and income approaches to value but did not develop them, unless otherwise indicated in this report.

5. I researched, verified, analyzed, and reported on any current agreement for sale for the subject property, any offering for sale of the subject property in the twelve months prior to the effective date of this appraisal, and the prior sales of the subject property for a minimum of three years prior to the effective date of this appraisal, unless otherwise indicated in this report.

6. I researched, verified, analyzed, and reported on the prior sales of the comparable sales for a minimum of one year prior to the date of sale of the comparable sale, unless otherwise indicated in this report.

7. I selected and used comparable sales that are locationally, physically, and functionally the most similar to the subject property.

8. I have not used comparable sales that were the result of combining a land sale with the contract purchase price of a home that has been built or will be built on the land.

9. I have reported adjustments to the comparable sales that reflect the market's reaction to the differences between the subject property and the comparable sales.

10. I verified, from a disinterested source, all information in this report that was provided by parties who have a financial interest in the sale or financing of the subject property.

11. I have knowledge and experience in appraising this type of property in this market area.

12. I am aware of, and have access to, the necessary and appropriate public and private data sources, such as multiple listing services, tax assessment records, public land records and other such data sources for the area in which the property is located.

13. I obtained the information, estimates, and opinions furnished by other parties and expressed in this appraisal report from reliable sources that I believe to be true and correct.

14. I have taken into consideration the factors that have an impact on value with respect to the subject neighborhood, subject property, and the proximity of the subject property to adverse influences in the development of my opinion of market value. I have noted in this appraisal report any adverse conditions (such as, but not limited to, needed repairs, deterioration, the presence of hazardous wastes, toxic substances, adverse environmental conditions, etc.) observed during the inspection of the subject property or that I became aware of during the research involved in performing this appraisal. I have considered these adverse conditions in my analysis of the property value, and have reported on the effect of the conditions on the value and marketability of the subject property.

15. I have not knowingly withheld any significant information from this appraisal report and, to the best of my knowledge, all statements and information in this appraisal report are true and correct.

16. I stated in this appraisal report my own personal, unbiased, and professional analysis, opinions, and conclusions, which are subject only to the assumptions and limiting conditions in this appraisal report.

17. I have no present or prospective interest in the property that is the subject of this report, and I have no present or prospective personal interest or bias with respect to the participants in the transaction. I did not base, either partially or completely, my analysis and/or opinion of market value in this appraisal report on the race, color, religion, sex, age, marital status, handicap, familial status, or national origin of either the prospective owners or occupants of the subject property or of the present owners or occupants of the properties in the vicinity of the subject property or on any other basis prohibited by law.

18. My employment and/or compensation for performing this appraisal or any future or anticipated appraisals was not conditioned on any agreement or understanding, written or otherwise, that I would report (or present analysis supporting) a predetermined specific value, a predetermined minimum value, a range or direction in value, a value that favors the cause of any party, or the attainment of a specific result or occurrence of a specific subsequent event (such as approval of a pending mortgage loan application).

19. I personally prepared all conclusions and opinions about the real estate that were set forth in this appraisal report. If I relied on significant real property appraisal assistance from any individual or individuals in the performance of this appraisal or the preparation of this appraisal report, I have named such individual(s) and disclosed the specific tasks performed in this appraisal report. I certify that any individual so named is qualified to perform the tasks. I have not authorized anyone to make a change to any item in this appraisal report; therefore, any change made to this appraisal is unauthorized and I will take no responsibility for it.

20. I identified the lender/client in this appraisal report who is the individual, organization, or agent for the organization that ordered and will receive this appraisal report.

Freddie Mac Form 70 March 2005 — Page 5 of 6 — Fannie Mae Form 1004 March 2005

520

Uniform Residential Appraisal Report

21. The lender/client may disclose or distribute this appraisal report to: the borrower; another lender at the request of the borrower; the mortgagee or its successors and assigns; mortgage insurers; government sponsored enterprises; other secondary market participants; data collection or reporting services; professional appraisal organizations; any department, agency, or instrumentality of the United States; and any state, the District of Columbia, or other jurisdictions; without having to obtain the appraiser's or supervisory appraiser's (if applicable) consent. Such consent must be obtained before this appraisal report may be disclosed or distributed to any other party (including, but not limited to, the public through advertising, public relations, news, sales, or other media).

22. I am aware that any disclosure or distribution of this appraisal report by me or the lender/client may be subject to certain laws and regulations. Further, I am also subject to the provisions of the Uniform Standards of Professional Appraisal Practice that pertain to disclosure or distribution by me.

23. The borrower, another lender at the request of the borrower, the mortgagee or its successors and assigns, mortgage insurers, government sponsored enterprises, and other secondary market participants may rely on this appraisal report as part of any mortgage finance transaction that involves any one or more of these parties.

24. If this appraisal report was transmitted as an "electronic record" containing my "electronic signature," as those terms are defined in applicable federal and/or state laws (excluding audio and video recordings), or a facsimile transmission of this appraisal report containing a copy or representation of my signature, the appraisal report shall be as effective, enforceable and valid as if a paper version of this appraisal report were delivered containing my original hand written signature.

25. Any intentional or negligent misrepresentation(s) contained in this appraisal report may result in civil liability and/or criminal penalties including, but not limited to, fine or imprisonment or both under the provisions of Title 18, United States Code, Section 1001, et seq., or similar state laws.

SUPERVISORY APPRAISER'S CERTIFICATION: The Supervisory Appraiser certifies and agrees that:

1. I directly supervised the appraiser for this appraisal assignment, have read the appraisal report, and agree with the appraiser's analysis, opinions, statements, conclusions, and the appraiser's certification.

2. I accept full responsibility for the contents of this appraisal report including, but not limited to, the appraiser's analysis, opinions, statements, conclusions, and the appraiser's certification.

3. The appraiser identified in this appraisal report is either a sub-contractor or an employee of the supervisory appraiser (or the appraisal firm), is qualified to perform this appraisal, and is acceptable to perform this appraisal under the applicable state law.

4. This appraisal report complies with the Uniform Standards of Professional Appraisal Practice that were adopted and promulgated by the Appraisal Standards Board of The Appraisal Foundation and that were in place at the time this appraisal report was prepared.

5. If this appraisal report was transmitted as an "electronic record" containing my "electronic signature," as those terms are defined in applicable federal and/or state laws (excluding audio and video recordings), or a facsimile transmission of this appraisal report containing a copy or representation of my signature, the appraisal report shall be as effective, enforceable and valid as if a paper version of this appraisal report were delivered containing my original hand written signature.

APPRAISER	SUPERVISORY APPRAISER (ONLY IF REQUIRED)
Signature_____	Signature_____
Name _____	Name_____
Company Name _____	Company Name _____
Company Address_____	Company Address_____
_____	_____
Telephone Number _____	Telephone Number _____
Email Address_____	Email Address_____
Date of Signature and Report_____	Date of Signature _____
Effective Date of Appraisal _____	State Certification # _____
State Certification #_____	or State License # _____
or State License #_____	State _____
or Other (describe) _____ State # _____	Expiration Date of Certification or License _____
State _____	
Expiration Date of Certification or License _____	SUBJECT PROPERTY
	☐ Did not inspect subject property
ADDRESS OF PROPERTY APPRAISED	☐ Did inspect exterior of subject property from street
_____	Date of Inspection _____
_____	☐ Did inspect interior and exterior of subject property
APPRAISED VALUE OF SUBJECT PROPERTY $ _____	Date of Inspection _____
LENDER/CLIENT	
Name _____	COMPARABLE SALES
Company Name _____	☐ Did not inspect exterior of comparable sales from street
Company Address_____	☐ Did inspect exterior of comparable sales from street
_____	Date of Inspection _____
Email Address_____	

C. DISADVANTAGES OF THE MARKET DATA METHOD

The disadvantages of using the market data method are concentrated into several areas listed below:

1. This method requires many recent comparable sales of similar properties.
2. This method is least reliable when there are rapid economic changes. If market prices are increasing rapidly, the comparables, which are based on past sales prices, lag behind. If prices are decreasing rapidly, the comparables, which are based on past sales prices, still remain high.
3. The market data method is less valid with certain income properties because a separate analysis of the income is required.

The effectiveness of the market data approach is limited by economic conditions that change rapidly.

II. Cost Approach (Replacement Cost Method)

The **COST APPROACH** *is the process of calculating the cost of the land and buildings (as if they were new today) and then subtracting the accrued depreciation to arrive at the current value of the property.* To use the cost approach, the appraiser must be able to determine the new construction cost of replacing the building today, using current construction methods. Depreciation is estimated by the appraiser and is then subtracted from the estimated cost of the new building. The value of the lot and depreciated building is then added to find the market value.

The cost approach objective is to determine the land value plus the cost to replace the improvements new (minus depreciation) while maintaining the same utility value.

Of the three approaches, the cost approach tends to set what the appraisers call an "upper limit of value." Most home buyers or investors prefer a newer building over an older one if the price is about the same. The cost approach therefore tends to set the highest price that a knowledgeable person will pay for a property. Why not build if the construction cost of a newer building is close to the sales price of an older building?

In relation to the other appraisal methods, the cost approach tends to set the "upper limit of value" (highest price someone will pay).

The cost approach is most useful when appraising: 1) new buildings and 2) special purpose or unique structures. Estimating depreciation is critical in this approach. As a building gets older, the depreciation becomes more difficult to estimate, eventually making the cost approach impractical. Since newer structures have little depreciation, the cost approach is the most suitable. The cost approach may also be preferred for special purpose or unique structures as they have few, if any, market comparable sales. Special purpose structures, such as an airplane factory, a city hall, or a church, are best appraised by the cost approach.

The cost approach is more appropriate for new buildings because there is almost no depreciation. It's also ideally suited for special use buildings since they tend to be "one of a kind" with few, if any, sales comparables.

It is limited in its effectiveness for appraising old buildings because determining depreciation is the most difficult part of the cost approach for the appraiser.

Some properties **require** the use of the cost approach. If, for example, there have been no recent sales in an area, the market comparison approach cannot be used effectively. Furthermore, if there is no income (as for example, from government-owned properties), the appraiser must rely solely on the cost approach.

A. COSTS ARE BOTH DIRECT AND INDIRECT

Any method used for estimating cost requires the calculation of direct (hard) or indirect (soft) costs. Both types of costs are equally necessary for construction and must be measured accurately.

DIRECT COSTS are expenditures for labor and materials used in the construction of the improvement(s). A contractor's overhead and profit are generally treated as direct costs.

INDIRECT COSTS are expenditures other than material and labor costs. Examples are administrative costs, professional fees, financing costs, insurance, and taxes. Indirect costs are usually calculated separately from direct costs.

B. STEPS IN THE COST APPROACH

The steps used in the cost approach are easy to follow, but studying **Figure 14-2** will help to explain each step.

1. Estimate the value of the land (use the market comparison approach).
2. Estimate the replacement cost of the building as if it were new.
3. Deduct estimated depreciation from the replacement cost of the building.
4. Add the value of the lot (Step 1) and the replacement cost of a new building and subtract estimated depreciation (Steps 2 and 3) to find the total value (Step 4).

Value of the land plus (+) new cost of buildings today minus (-) depreciation equals (=) current market value of the property.

Figure 14-2

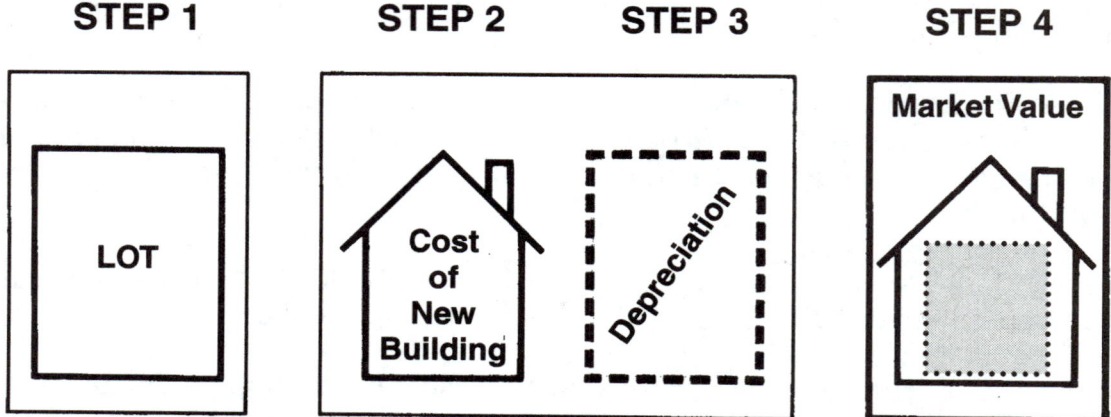

1. Step 1 – Appraise the Land (Lot) Separately

Appraise the land (lot) separately. The value of the vacant land is determined by comparing the lot of the property to be appraised with similar lots that have just been sold. The market comparison approach is used by the appraiser to estimate the lot value of the appraised property.

The cost approach requires the appraiser to identify land values separately by the use of the market data approach.

2. Step 2 – Estimate Replacement Cost

Estimate the replacement cost of the improvements to the land. This includes all the buildings and the landscaping improvements.

"Replacement cost" is the present cost to build a building having the same amount of utility.

a. Replacement Cost

REPLACEMENT COST is the cost of building a similar (having utility equivalent) new structure today using modern construction methods. These methods may differ from the original building techniques, but are becoming an important factor due to the ever-increasing costs of new construction. As construction costs increase for new homes, the replacement cost of existing homes also increases. Therefore, well-located older homes will keep rising in value year after year, no matter how old they are, because the newer substitutes are so costly. This is not necessarily because of excellent upkeep, but because it is becoming impossible to find a newer home with the same features at a reasonable price.

REPRODUCTION or REPLICATION COST is the cost of reproducing a structure (usually destroyed) at current prices using similar (older) style materials and methods as used in the original structure. This method is rarely used, but it is the type, for example, used by Disneyland to recreate its historical Main Street.

The rarely used reproduction (replication) method is an exact replica— it is the most expensive. New construction methods (replacement costs vs. replication costs) are almost always cheaper.

b. Three Replacement Methods

1. The *COMPARATIVE-UNIT METHOD is used to derive a cost estimate in terms of dollars per square foot or per cubic foot, based on known costs of similar structures and adjusted for time and physical differences.* The comparative-unit method represents a relatively uncomplicated, practical approach to a cost estimate and is widely used.

2. The *UNIT-IN-PLACE METHOD employs unit costs for the various building components such as foundations, floors, walls, windows, and roofs as installed, and uses square foot, linear foot, or other appropriate units of measurement to estimate each component part.* These estimates include labor and overhead. To use this method, the appraiser must have specialized construction knowledge.

3. The *QUANTITY SURVEY METHOD involves detailed estimates of the quantities of raw materials used, such as brick, lumber, cement, the price of such materials, and the labor costs.* It is the most comprehensive and accurate method of cost estimating, but too complicated to fully explain here.

The Comparative-Unit Method (estimating dollars per square foot) is the most commonly used replacement cost method.

Although there are several ways to determine replacement cost, the simplest way is to *measure the outside of the building to determine SQUARE FOOTAGE.* After you determine the square footage, multiply it by the current cost of construction, per square foot, to get the value (as if it were new) of the building.

To determine square feet, use the formula: **LENGTH X WIDTH**

Square-foot cost for a smaller house is higher than the square-foot cost for a larger house. If other factors are equal, including square footage, the cost of building a two-story house is up to 50% cheaper than a one-story house.

The cubic foot method is used to appraise warehouses. To determine cubic feet, use the formula: **LENGTH X WIDTH X HEIGHT**

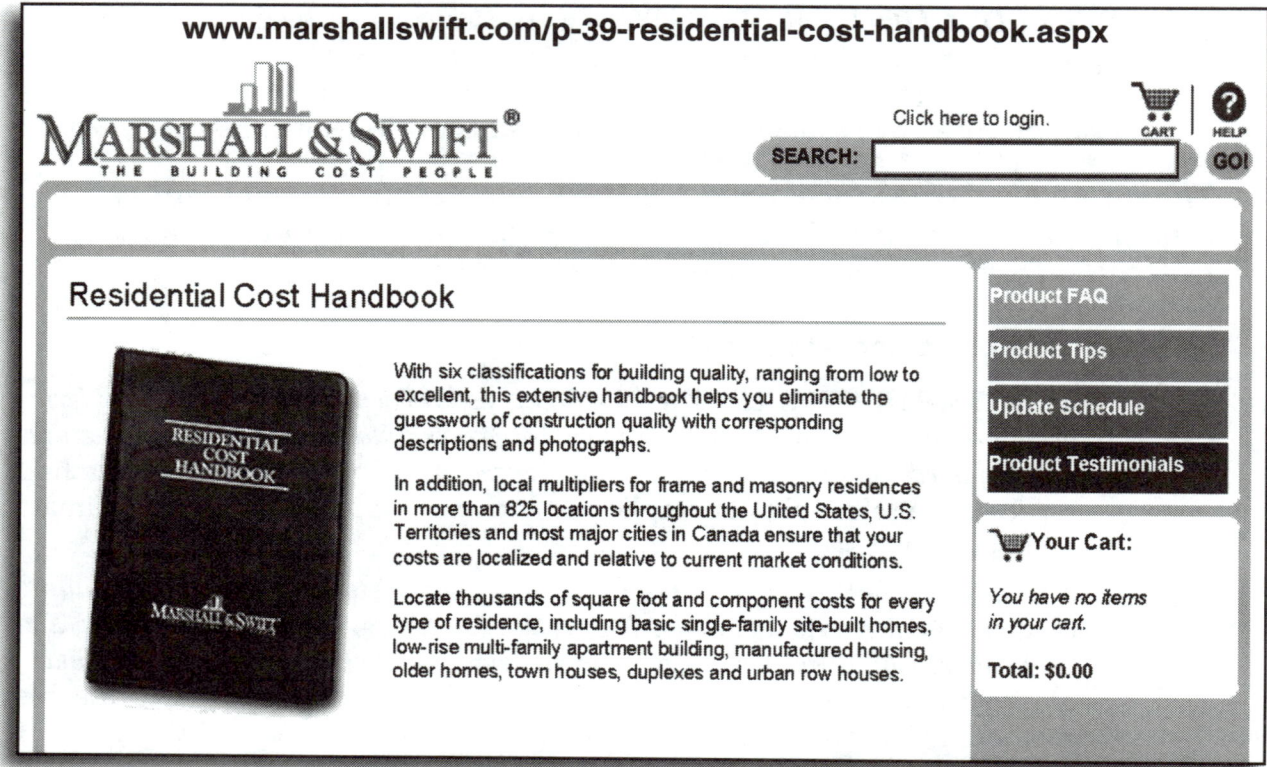

MARSHALL & SWIFT®
THE BUILDING COST PEOPLE

Click here to login.
CART | HELP
SEARCH: [   ] GO!

Residential Cost Handbook

Product FAQ

Product Tips

Update Schedule

Product Testimonials

With six classifications for building quality, ranging from low to excellent, this extensive handbook helps you eliminate the guesswork of construction quality with corresponding descriptions and photographs.

In addition, local multipliers for frame and masonry residences in more than 825 locations throughout the United States, U.S. Territories and most major cities in Canada ensure that your costs are localized and relative to current market conditions.

Locate thousands of square foot and component costs for every type of residence, including basic single-family site-built homes, low-rise multi-family apartment building, manufactured housing, older homes, town houses, duplexes and urban row houses.

Your Cart:

You have no items in your cart.

Total: $0.00

A warehouse building is appraised by the cubic foot but is usually rented by the square foot. Caution: the industrial land the warehouse is on is appraised by the square foot.

As construction costs vary from city to city and from builder to builder, many appraisers use cost engineers to help them determine the square foot cost of different types of construction. One of the most popular building cost information services is Marshall and Swift. They annually compile a residential cost handbook that details the current cost of most types of residential construction in Texas.

3. Step 3 – Estimate and Deduct Depreciation

DEPRECIATION is a reduction in the value of a property due to any cause. The difference between replacement cost of a property and its market value is depreciation.

Depreciation is a loss in value from any cause. Depreciation is either curable (profitable to repair) or incurable (unprofitable to repair).

Estimate and deduct the depreciation from the replacement cost of the building being appraised. This accumulated depreciation is sometimes called accrued depreciation. *ACCRUED DEPRECIATION (OBSERVED) is the loss in value of improvements from any cause at the date of the appraisal.* Accrued depreciation is what has happened in the past, whereas the accrual for depreciation is the amount of future depreciation. There are five methods of estimating accrued depreciation:

1. Capitalized Income
2. Market
3. Straight-line (most common and explained below)
4. Engineering
5. Breakdown

The straight-line method is explained here. For information on the other methods, please see Educational Textbook Company's *Real Estate Appraisal, Principles and Procedures,* by Walt Huber, Levin P. Messick, IFAC, and William Pivar (see order form at back of this book).

The **STRAIGHT-LINE METHOD (AGE LIFE)** *assumes the value declines in equal amounts of depreciation each year, until it reaches zero.* A building with an economic life of 50 years would depreciate 2 percent (100 percent ÷ 50 years = 2 percent) in value each year. Actual age is the current (real) age of the building. When using the age life method, an appraiser will use an age other than the actual age of the building. This is known as the effective age. **EFFECTIVE AGE** *is determined by the condition of the building rather than the actual age.* If a building has been maintained, its effective age may be less than the actual age; if there has been inadequate maintenance, it may be greater. **ECONOMIC LIFE** *is the estimated number of years of anticipated usefulness of the improvements.*

"Effective age" is determined by the condition and usefulness of the property, NOT the actual age. The economic life of an improvement is usually shorter than its estimated physical life.

ACCRUAL FOR DEPRECIATION *is the concept of estimating the amount of depreciation there will be in the future.* The accrual for depreciation is used in the income approach, discussed in the next section.

To accurately estimate accrued depreciation, the appraiser must have experience, skill, and good judgment. He or she must not only estimate the physical wear and tear on the building, but also the losses in value due to outmoded styles, poor design, and neighborhood changes that tend to reduce the value of the improvements. A property can lose value through three different types of depreciation.

The three types of depreciation causes are: 1) physical, 2) functional, and 3) economic.

Curable – Repairs that add more to the value of a property than they cost.
Incurable – Repairs that cost more than the value they add.

a. Physical Deterioration (Curable or Incurable)

PHYSICAL DETERIORATION is the loss in value due to wear and tear. As a building gets older, its age will start to show visibly. Since most types of physical deterioration (like a deteriorated driveway) can be repaired, we usually think of it as curable depreciation. On the other hand, severe structural deterioration may not be curable. Physical deterioration can be either curable or incurable. *CURABLE DEPRECIATION includes repairs that add more to a building's value than they cost. INCURABLE DEPRECIATION refers to repairs that would be so expensive they are not economically feasible.*

Examples of physical deterioration (curable or incurable) are:

1. all forms of wear and tear;
2. damage from dry rot and termites;
3. negligent care (deferred maintenance); and
4. depreciation that has already occurred.

Obsolescence is NOT a method of calculating depreciation, but is a term meaning a "major cause" of depreciation.

b. Functional Obsolescence (Curable or Incurable)

FUNCTIONAL OBSOLESCENCE is the loss in value due to outmoded style or non-usable space. Examples of functional obsolescence would be a bedroom that can be reached only by walking through another bedroom. By modern standards this is very inconvenient and reduces the value of the second bedroom. Another devaluing factor is a home with a single-car garage. Functional depreciation is hard to cure. If the cost of curing the defect adds at least the same amount to the property's value, then it is worth the investment.

Types of functional obsolescence (curable or incurable) are:

1. an outdated kitchen;
2. antique fixtures;
3. a four-bedroom, one-bath home;
4. a one-car garage; and
5. massive cornices.

The cost approach would be the least useful for appraising older structures with many functional deficiencies.

c. Economic Obsolescence (Incurable)

If neighborhood commercial tenants are doing poorly, it is a sign of economic obsolescence.

> *ECONOMIC OBSOLESCENCE (also referred to as SOCIAL OBSOLESCENCE) is the loss in value due to changes in the neighborhood and is external to the property itself.* It is always incurable. If a freeway is built next to your property, your home will decrease in value because of the noise and nuisance factor. On the other hand, if the freeway is three blocks away, your house will increase in value because of improved freeway access. If social or economic factors (such as loss of jobs) cause a neighborhood to become shabby and run-down, the value of your property will decrease accordingly.

Since economic obsolescence results from "off the property" causes, it is always incurable. Economic (profitable) life remaining is the main concern when purchasing an older property.

Types of economic obsolescence (incurable) are:

1. an oversupply of similar or competitive units;
2. aircraft noise;
3. adverse zoning and legislative acts;
4. economic recession;
5. departure of major industries from the area; and
6. increase in number of rental units increases.

> **Example:** Average-priced homes coming into an area of high-priced homes would cause real estate values to become unstable.

> **Example:** An airport flight pattern is changed and causes the affected homes to decrease in value due to economic obsolescence.

4. Step 4 – Value of the Property

The last step in the cost approach is to add the depreciated value of any improvements to the value of the land. This figure is the market value of the property using the cost approach.

C. ADVANTAGES OF THE COST APPROACH

The cost approach is best for new, unique architecture and public buildings.

The main advantage of the cost approach is that it can be used on: 1) newly constructed buildings; 2) unique structures; and 3) public buildings. Since there is little depreciation, if any, to calculate on newer buildings and there is available construction cost data, the value can be easily determined using the cost approach. Unique structures, public buildings, and one-of-a-kind structures have no comparables, so the cost approach may be the only logical way to appraise them.

D. DISADVANTAGES OF THE COST APPROACH

The disadvantages of using the cost approach are listed below:

1. There must be an accurate value of the site (land).
2. Since determining depreciation is more difficult as buildings age, the reliability of the depreciation estimate may be questioned.
3. This approach may be difficult to apply to condos or planned unit developments because the land, improvements and marketing costs are not always easy to determine just for appraising one unit.

Economic obsolescence is the hardest or most difficult to change.

III. Capitalization Approach (Income Approach)

The income approach determines the "present worth of future net income." Capitalization is the process of converting income into value.

The **INCOME APPROACH** *is the process of analyzing the future net income from a property to determine its current market value.* Another word for this process is capitalization. The appraiser, when using the income approach, is determining the present property value based upon the information he or she has on future income and expenses of that given property.

The actual process of capitalization is simple. Divide a capitalization rate into the yearly net income; the answer you obtain is the value of the property.

$$\frac{\text{NET INCOME}}{\text{CAPITALIZATION RATE}} = \text{VALUE OF PROPERTY}$$

$$\frac{\$110,000}{10\%} = \$1,100,000$$

Rent-producing (income) properties such as apartments, offices, warehouses, and manufacturing concerns can best be appraised by the income approach. This is because the people who invest in such projects are primarily interested in the income that they will receive. It is only natural that an investor would choose the property producing the highest return. The income approach allows a comparison of different types of income-producing real estate and, at the same time, analyzes each as to the return of income to be received from that investment in the future.

The basis for the income approach is that investors purchase the income-producing property because of its revenue; the higher the revenue, the higher the value, and likewise, the lower the income, the lower the value.

A. STEPS IN THE INCOME APPROACH

There are five basic steps to establish value using the income approach:

1. Calculate the annual effective gross income.
2. Complete an operating expense statement.
3. Deduct related operating expenses from gross income to get net income.
4. Divide net income by the appropriate capitalization rate.
5. Result of dividing net income by capitalization rate.

Figure 14-3 illustrates the five steps.

Figure 14-3

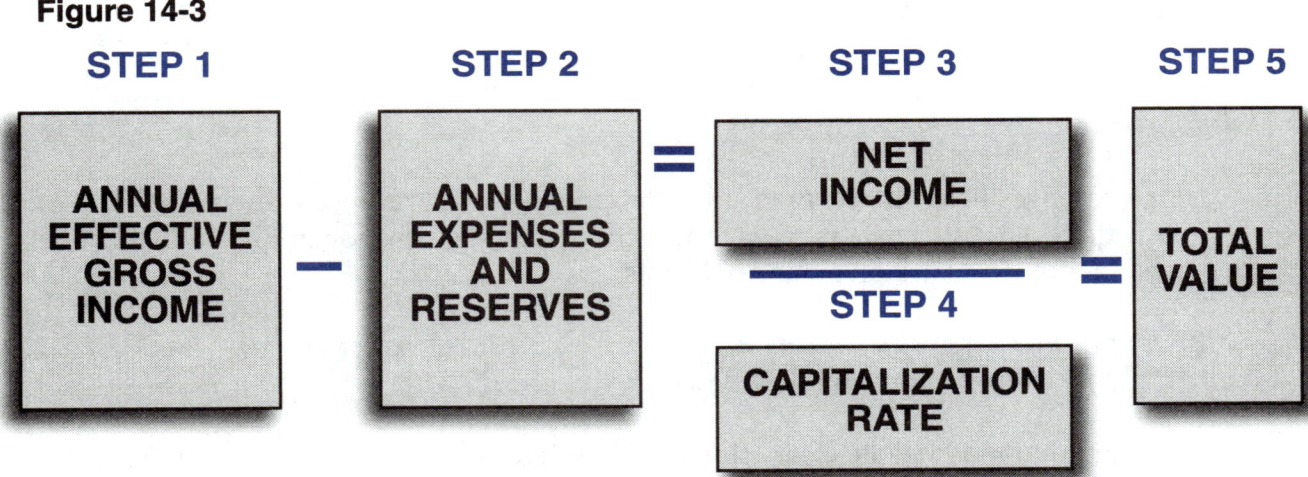

1. Step 1 – Calculate the Annual Effective Gross Income

Rental income schedules for various units are best established by the market approach.

Calculate the annual effective gross income from the investment property. *EFFECTIVE GROSS INCOME is the gross income minus any vacancies or rental losses.*

In the case of rental properties, the annual gross rental income will be the annual rent that an owner receives if he or she charges the going rental rates with no vacancies.

Sometimes managers charge rents that are below the market level, resulting in a very low number of vacancies. On the other hand, rents that are set too high usually yield a higher vacancy rate. The *VACANCY FACTOR is the loss in rents due to any cause.* This is commonly expressed as a percentage. The vacancy factor increases while trying to find a new tenant or because of cleaning, repairs, or non-paying renters.

Subtract deductions from the gross rental income for vacancies or any rental losses to arrive at the "effective gross income."

2. Step 2 – Complete an Operating Expense Statement

Complete an operating expense statement. The six basic operating expense categories for this type of statement are listed below:

1. Property taxes
2. Insurance and licenses
3. Manager fees
4. Utilities
5. Maintenance, repairs, and services (i.e., gardeners)
6. Replacement reserves

Management fees and replacement reserves must always be included in the basic operating expenses.

The expenses listed in the operating statement should represent the actual cost of each item. Though costs may vary, it is the appraiser's responsibility to determine what actual costs are on an annual basis.

Never deduct mortgage payments of principal or interest (cost of capital) from the operating expense statement.

An item that may need explanation is the replacement reserve. A *REPLACEMENT RESERVE consists of funds set aside for the purpose of replacing items in the future.* An example of a replacement reserve cost would be a $2,000 water heater with a life expectancy of five years. The replacement reserve for this item would be $400 per year ($2,000 ÷ 5).

"Variable costs" are operating expenses that can vary (utilities and repairs). "Fixed costs" remain constant, such as property taxes and fire insurance.

3. Step 3 – Deduct Related Operating Expenses From Gross Income to Get Net Income

To determine net income, simply deduct the related operating expenses (Step 2) from the annual effective gross income (Step 1).

To arrive at net income, deduct the operating expenses from effective gross income.

4. Step 4 – Divide Net Income by the Appropriate Capitalization Rate

Divide the net income by the appropriate capitalization rate.

Rule: Always convert a monthly or quarterly net income into an annual net income before dividing by the capitalization rate.

Selection of a capitalization rate can be a delicate task. A one percent change in the capitalization rate, for example, can alter the estimated value of a property by up to ten percent or more. The capitalization rate is comprised of a return to the investor "on" his or her original investment and "of" the amount to replace the building later.

For example, an investor may want an annual return of eight percent "on" his or her original investment, but two percent a year is needed to replace the building when its economic life is over. Determination of the appropriate capitalization rate takes skill and training.

The greater the risk, the greater the cap rate. Leasing to a flower shop, for example, poses a greater risk of vacancy than a post office, therefore the cap rate would be higher.

There are several ways to select the proper capitalization rate. One way of selecting the appropriate capitalization rate is to sample similar recent apartment sales. Simply divide the net income by the sales price to obtain the capitalization rate used in that particular area.

Establishing the capitalization rate is the most difficult step for appraisers using the income approach.

The capitalization rate is comprised of two parts: (1) a rate of return "on" the money invested and (2) a return "of" the asset that may be decreasing in value, but is rising in replacement cost. This is commonly referred to as the recapture rate, or depreciation (see **Figure 14-4**).

Figure 14-4

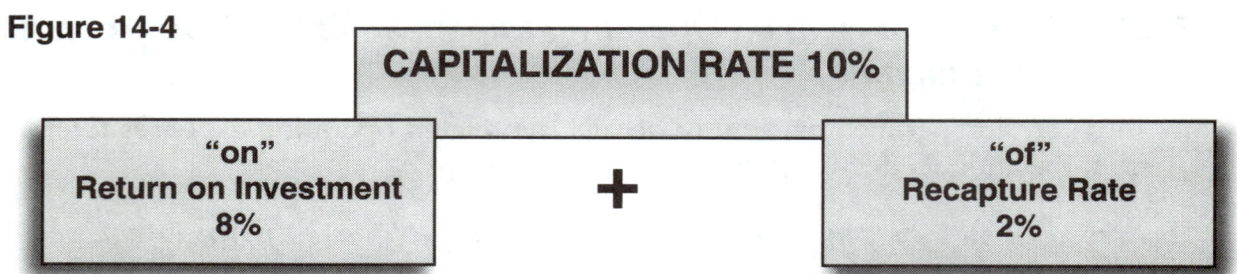

The capitalization rate is comprised of two parts: the rate "on" the money invested (expected investor's return) and the annual rate "of" depreciation (recapture) on the improvements.

Capitalization rates are part of the "language" of an appraiser and can be determined by these advanced methods (not discussed here):

1. Comparison
2. Summation
3. Bands of Investment

5. Step 5 – Result of Dividing Net Income by Capitalization Rate

This is the easiest and final step in the income approach. It is simply the result of dividing net income by the capitalization rate.

Net Income divided by Capitalization Rate = Market Value

$$\frac{\text{Net income } \$65,000}{\text{Capitalization Rate 10\% (.10)}} = \$650,000 \text{ Estimated Market Value}$$

THE MARKET VALUE, WHEN USING THE INCOME APPROACH, IS $650,000

As the "capitalization rate" increases, the appraisal value decreases.

B. GROSS RENT MULTIPLIER – GRM (RULE OF THUMB)

A quick way to convert gross income into the approximate value is to use the gross rent multiplier.

GROSS RENT MULTIPLIER (GRM) is both a figure and a multiplication rule of thumb used to convert the rental income into market value. If we use a gross rent multiplier of 125 times the monthly rent of $1,000, the property is worth approximately $125,000 (125 x $1,000). See **Figure 14-5** for more details. This is definitely not an accurate way to appraise a property, but it does give a quick estimate of value. Many professional investors

Figure 14-5

Gross Rent Multiplier

The **GROSS RENT MULTIPLIER (GRM)** *is a rough, quick way of converting gross monthly rent into market value.* To obtain the gross rent multiplier, divide the monthly rent into the "sales" price. It is not a very accurate method, but it is a good estimator because it is so easy. The gross rent multiplier is best used for single or small multi-family residential properties.

$$\frac{\text{SALES PRICE}}{\text{RENT}} \quad = \quad \text{GROSS RENT MULTIPLIER}$$

TYPICAL PROBLEMS:

If a house that rented for $600 a month sold for $78,000, what is the gross rent multiplier?

$$\frac{\$78,000 \text{ Sales price}}{\text{Monthly Rent }\$600} \quad = \quad 130 \text{ (Gross Rent Multiplier)}$$

If a similar house down the street is renting for $690, what would the selling price be?

Monthly Rent $690 x 130 (Gross Rent Multiplier) = $89,700

CAN ANNUAL RENTS BE USED?

The gross rent multiplier is not a percentage, so it can be expressed as either a monthly or annual figure. If the above problem were expressed as an annual rent figure, the gross rent multiplier would have to be divided by 12. The annual gross rent multiplier is 10.83 (130 ÷ 12).

If a house that rents for $72,000 a year sold for $780,000, what is the annual gross multiplier?

$$\frac{\$780,000 \text{ Sales Price}}{\text{Annual Rent }\$72,000} \quad = \quad 10.83 \text{ Annual Gross Rent Multiplier}$$

NOTE: Sometimes a different multiplier is used, the Gross Income Multiplier (GIM), when the revenues being considered are not just from rental income (like coin-operated washers and dryers). The GIM is preferred for commercial and income properties.

use it as a screening device to eliminate undesirable investment opportunities. This monthly gross multiplier is often used for single-family homes and small apartment buildings.

The **GROSS RENT** *is the money received from a property before any expenses are deducted*. It can be expressed as monthly or annual income, as long as it is applied consistently.

The Gross Rent Multiplier (GRM) is based on "monthly rent only" and is used for residential properties. The "Gross Income Multiplier (GIM)" is used for commercial and industrial properties when part of the gross income comes from non-rental sources.

> **Example:** A desert cabin that rents for $600 per month just sold for $96,000. A similar property rents for $660 per month, so the market value is most likely to be near $105,600.
>
> Remember the rule! Confirmed sales price ($96,000) divided by gross monthly rent ($600) equals gross rent multiplier of 160; then it follows that the gross rent multiplier of 160 times the rent ($660) of a similar property equals a $105,600 market value.

In the real estate investment field (commercial and industrial), it is common knowledge that the annual gross income multiplier of "x 6.2" is a good "rule of thumb" for an investment. For example, if the annual gross income from an apartment project is $40,000, its value should be approximately $248,000 ($40,000 x 6.2). The annual gross income multiplier varies from "x 5" to "x 12," depending upon the location of the property and the condition of the individual buildings. Remember: this is an approximation device and should be used only as a quick estimate—not in place of an actual appraisal.

C. ADVANTAGES OF THE INCOME APPROACH

The advantage of the income approach method is that no other method focuses solely on determining the present value of the future income stream from the subject property. It is a little different than the other two methods of determining value in that "if the purpose of the property is to generate income, use the income approach." For example, a house that is zoned for commercial use may be valued at a much higher amount when used as an insurance office rather than as a house. The location may bring in a great deal of income; as a house, the market value is low, but as an income-producing property, the market value may be very high.

The "present worth of future benefits" is what the income approach is all about.

It is most often used for multi-family residential income property, but could be used on any type of property that generates income.

D. DISADVANTAGES OF THE INCOME APPROACH

The disadvantage of the income approach is that it may be difficult to determine the proper capitalization rate. For example, it may be impossible to ascertain the cap-rate for a theme park or alligator farm. These other items used in the income approach may also be difficult to estimate: vacancy rate, economic rent, operation expenses, and reserve requirements.

IV. Correlation of Value (Bracketing)

The last and most important part of the appraisal process is the correlation (sometimes referred to as reconciliation) of the three approaches to value. *CORRELATION is the process of selecting the most appropriate approach for the particular appraisal job and giving it the most consideration in pinpointing the final value.* Although all three methods are used in appraisal, one is usually most appropriate for a specific appraisal problem.

As a general rule:

- *the "market comparison approach" is best for single-family homes or lots.*
- *the "cost approach" is best for new, unique or unusual structures.*
- *the "income approach" is best for properties that can be used to generate income.*

V. Final Estimate of Value (Appraisal Report)

The *APPRAISAL REPORT is the documentation of the appraiser's findings.* It can be a prepared fill-in form. However, if it is complicated or subject to close interpretation, the report should be written in a narrative form with supporting data contained in supplemental exhibits. In practice, most appraisal reports are written.

Chapter 14

There are two main types of written appraisal reports:

1. Short form (a form with checks and explanations, often used by lenders)

A short form appraisal report is called a short form, form report, or summary report.

2. Narrative report (most complete and extensive)

A narrative report is the most comprehensive and complete appraisal report, and contains such headings as "Introduction," "Site and Improvements Analysis," and "Supporting Data."

Whether the report is a simple one-page report or an extensive volume, the following information should be presented:

1. An adequate description for the property that is being appraised.
2. A statement as to the purpose and scope of the appraisal.
3. An adequate description of the neighborhood.
4. The date on which the value is estimated.
5. The qualifying conditions and assumptions.
6. The factual data, maps, and photos with their analysis and interpretations.
7. The processing of the data by one or more of the three approaches to value (correlation).
8. The estimate of value.
9. The name, address, type of license (and any certifications), and signature of the appraiser.

An appraiser's **DATE OF VALUE** *is the date of the inspection of the property.*

An appraiser's **DATE OF APPRAISAL** *is the date of the final writing or delivery of the appraisal report.*

An appraisal is effective on the date the appraiser delivers his/her report.

There is NO information about the buyer's or seller's financial condition on an appraisal report.

Many community colleges and universities offer courses in appraisal or investment properties to acquaint you with the techniques involved in the income approach.

A. COST OF AN APPRAISAL

Appraisal costs can vary from relatively small amounts to thousands of dollars. The cost of an appraisal may be affected by its purpose, the qualifications of the appraiser, and how detailed the appraisal. An appraisal used to document a court case could cost several thousand dollars.

It would be impractical to spend thousands of dollars for a home appraisal just to determine a selling price. If you are thinking about selling your home, your local real estate broker will probably do this at no cost. Local brokers are familiar with your area and are knowledgeable about current sales prices of similar homes in your neighborhood. On the other hand, appraisal of large parcels, commercial buildings, and apartment houses, or appraisals to be used in court, may require the services of a highly skilled appraiser. Although the fees are higher, they reflect the experience and ability of the appraiser. The appraisal fee and an outline of what is to be accomplished in the appraisal should be set in advance. It is unethical to set an appraisal fee as a percentage of the determined value. This may influence the appraiser to increase the value.

Appraisal Report Copies

A lender must provide a notice to a loan applicant stating that the applicant is entitled to a copy of the appraisal report if the applicant requests and pays for the report.

The notice must be provided on any loan secured by residential property and on purchase money financing (or refinancing of purchase money debt) on non-residential property.

VI. Licensing, Fee Appraisers, and Appraisal Organizations

A. THE SAVINGS AND LOAN CRISIS

In the late 1980s, due to a number of financial, regulatory, and ethical problems (including numerous criminal activities), the nation faced a major economic crisis in connection with the savings and loan industry. This financial crisis hit Texas especially hard as law and policymakers faced the issue of what do to with staggering losses faced by thrift institutions as well as an ever-increasing portfolio of foreclosed real estate. In response to what would later be known as the Savings and Loan Crisis, Congress passed the Financial Institutions Reform, Recovery, and Enforcement Act of 1989 (FIRREA) to deal with the issue. Under this legislation Congress created the Resolution Trust Corporation (RTC) to manage and ultimately "resolve" hundreds

of ailing thrifts. As part of this strategy, Congress determined that the agency should place as much distressed real estate back into the private sector as possible.

Fortunately, FIRREA, for the first time ever, mandated uniform guidelines and procedures for the appraisal of real estate. In this way, real estate assets could be accurately appraised in a uniform and systematic fashion without regard to unusual and seemingly arbitrary local practices and traditions. Thus, in response to a national financial crisis, uniform appraisal practices and procedures were created.

B. APPRAISAL LICENSE AND CERTIFICATION

In order to license, certify and regulate appraisers, the Texas Legislature, in 1991, created the Texas Appraiser Licensing and Certification Board (TALCB) as an independent subdivision of the Texas Real Estate Commission. Today, the TALCB recognizes five categories of appraisers in Texas. These categories include:

1. **APPRAISER TRAINEE**
2. **PROVISIONAL LICENSED REAL ESTATE APPRAISER**
3. **STATE LICENSED REAL ESTATE APPRAISER**
4. **STATE CERTIFIED RESIDENTIAL REAL ESTATE APPRAISER**
5. **STATE CERTIFIED GENERAL REAL ESTATE APPRAISER**

Figure 14-6 shows a summary of the licensing, certification, and/or approval permitted for each category of appraiser in Texas. For a detailed list of requirements, see the Texas Appraiser Licensing and Certification Board at **www.talcb.state.tx.us**.

Effective in 2008. there is a dramatic increase in these requirements by the Appraisal Foundation!

C. FEE APPRAISERS

While the USPAP Appraisal Standards permit an appraiser to appraise a property in which he or she has an interest, as long as the fact is disclosed to the lender/client in writing, it would be highly unusual for it to be accepted by any lender/client.

A *FEE APPRAISER is an independent, self-employed appraiser; he or she appraises for a fee or charge.* In Texas, a license or certification is required to appraise real estate as a profession. Other appraisers are dependent on large corporations or organizations for their employment. Gas, electric, telephone, and other utility companies have appraisal departments. Banks, savings banks, mortgage companies, and other lenders often have in-house appraisal staffs. Most cities and counties have large appraisal staffs in their assessors' offices. There are also various state agencies that maintain appraisal staffs.

A fee appraiser is self-employed; he or she appraises for a fee or charge.

Figure 14-6

TEXAS APPRAISER AND CERTIFICATION BOARD REQUIREMENTS

APPRAISER TRAINEE

Education: None
Experience: None
Exam: None
Scope: May appraise only those properties, under the active, personal, and diligent supervision of their sponsoring certified appraiser, which the supervising certified appraiser sponsor is permitted to appraise.

PROVISIONAL LICENSED REAL ESTATE APPRAISER

Education: A minimum of 90 hours of appraisal related education covering the specific topics required by the Appraiser Qualifications Board (AQB), including the 15-hour National Uniform Standards of Professional Appraisal Practice (USPAP) course.
Experience: None, however, the licensee has 60 months to obtain 2,000 hours of experience, otherwise the license will be revoked.
Exam: AQB approved exam for this level of license.
Scope: May appraise non-complex 1-to-4 unit residential property valued at less than $1 million and complex 1-4 family residential units valued at less than $250,000. May also appraise vacant land for which the highest and best use is 1-4 family purposes.

STATE LICENSED REAL ESTATE APPRAISER

Education: A minimum of 90 hours of appraisal related education covering the specific topics required by AQB, including the 15-hour National USPAP course.
Experience: A minimum of 2,000 hours of acceptable appraisal experience.
Exam: AQB approved exam for this level of license.
Scope: May appraise non-complex 1-4 family residential units valued at less than $1 million and complex 1-4 family residential units valued at less than $250,000. May also appraise vacant land for which the highest and best use is 1-4 family purposes.

STATE CERTIFIED RESIDENTIAL REAL ESTATE APPRAISER

Education: A minimum of 120 hours of appraisal related education covering the specific topics required by AQB, including the 15-hour National USPAP course.
Experience: A minimum of 2,500 hours and two years of acceptable appraisal experience.
Exam: AQB approved exam for this level of license.
Scope: May appraise 1-4 family residential units (no limit to value) and vacant land for which the highest and best use is 1-4 family purposes.

STATE CERTIFIED GENERAL REAL ESTATE APPRAISER

Education: A minimum of 180 hours of appraisal related education covering the specific topics required by AQB, including the 15-hour National USPAP course.
Experience: A minimum of 3,000 hours and two and one-half years of acceptable appraisal experience. At least 1,500 hours of the experience must be non-residential properties.
Exam: AQB approved exam for this level of license.
Scope: May appraise all types of real property without regard to transaction value or complexity.

D. PROFESSIONAL APPRAISAL ASSOCIATIONS

American Society of Appraisers (ASA)
P.O. Box 17265
Washington, D.C. 20041-0265
www.appraisers.org

American Society of Farm Managers and Rural Appraisers (ASFMRA)
9505 Cherry Street, Suite 508
Denver, CO 80222
www.asfmra.org

Appraisal Institute (AI)
875 North Michigan Avenue, Suite 2400
Chicago, IL 60611-1980
www.appraisalinstitute.org

Appraisal Institute of Canada
1111 Portage Avenue
Winnipeg, MB, Canada R3GO58
www.aicanada.org

International Association of Assessing Officers (IAAO)
1313 East 60th Street
Chicago, IL 60637
www.iaao.org

International Right of Way Association (IRWA)
13650 Gramercy Place
Gardena, CA 90249
www.irwaonline.org

National Association of Independent Fee Appraisers (NAIFA)
7501 Murdoch Avenue
St. Louis, MO 63119
www.naifa.com

National Association of Master Appraisers (NAMA)
303 West Cypress Street
P.O. Box 12617 San Antonio, TX 78212-0617
www.masterappraisers.com

VII. CHAPTER SUMMARY

A licensed appraiser will use three different approaches to establish final value. These include the: 1) comparative (market data) approach; 2) cost (replacement) approach; and 3) capitalization (income) approach.

The **market data method (or sales comparison approach)** takes the current selling prices of similar or comparable properties **(comps)** and adjusts for any differences. The **principle of substitution** is applied, assuming a person will not pay more for a property when something similar is available for less.

The **cost approach or (replacement cost method)** determines the **current market value** of a property by adding the value of the land plus (+) replacement or reproduction cost of buildings today, minus (-) depreciation, maintaining the same amount of utility.

The cost approach consists of four steps as follows:

1. The appraiser finds the **value of the land** using the market data approach.
2. The **reproduction** or **replacement cost** is calculated as if the building was new.
3. **Depreciation** is determined and deducted from the reproduction/replacement cost of the building.
4. The depreciated value of the building is added to the value of the land to find the **market value of the property**.

The three replacement methods include: 1) the **comparative-unit method** (most commonly used), 2) the **unit-in-place method**, and 3) the **quantity survey method**.

The three types of depreciation are: 1) **physical**, 2) **functional**, and 3) **economic**, and each can be **curable** (profitable to repair) or **incurable** (unprofitable to repair).

The **capitalization (or income) approach** is concerned with the present worth of future benefits. The basic formula to determine total value is: **Annual effective gross income minus (-) annual expenses and reserves equals (=) net income**. Then divide the net income by the capitalization rate to find (=) market value. The **cap rate** is the percentage rate that an investor expects to earn "on" a real estate investment. A quick **rule of thumb** to convert gross income into approximate value is to use the **gross rent multiplier**, which is based on monthly rent and is used for residential properties. The **gross income multiplier** is based on annual rents and is used for commercial properties.

Correlation (or reconciliation) is the process of selecting the most appropriate approach for the appraisal job. Generally, the market comparison approach is best for single-family homes or lots; the cost approach is best for new, unique or unusual structures; and the income approach is best for properties that can be used to generate income.

The **final estimate of value (or appraisal report)** is then generated, the **narrative report** being the most comprehensive and complete.

The cost of an appraisal can be effected by its purpose, how detailed it is, and the experience of the appraiser. All appraisers in Texas must be licensed, certified, or otherwise approved by the **Texas Appraiser Licensing and Certification Board**. These categories include **Trainee, Provisional Licensed Appraiser, State Licensed Appraiser, Certified Residential Appraiser**, and **Certified General Appraiser**. A **fee appraiser** is self-employed, and charges a fee for his/her services. Although highly unusual, it is technically permissible for a fee appraiser to appraise a property in which he or she owns an interest as long as it is disclosed in writing. **It is the marketability of real property that concerns appraisers and real estate agents.**

VIII. TERMINOLOGY

A. Accrual for Depreciation
B. Accrued Depreciation
C. Actual Age
D. Correlation
E. Cost Approach
F. Curable Depreciation
G. Depreciation
H. Direct Cost

I. Economic Life
J. Economic Obsolescence
K. Effective Age
L. Effective Gross Income
M. Functional Obsolescence
N. Gross Rent Multiplier
O. Income Approach
P. Incurable Depreciation

Q. Indirect Costs
R. Market Comparison
S. Physical Deterioration
T. Replacement
U. Replacement Reserve
V. Reproduction Cost
W. Square Footage
X. Vacancy Factor

1. ____ The estimated percentage of vacancies in a rental property, such as in an apartment building.

2. ____ The use of different appraisal methods to reach an estimate of the value of a property. The methods must be weighed as to which is most appropriate for the type of property being appraised.

3. ____ The theoretical cost of replacing a building with one of equivalent usefulness.

4. ____ A simple method of using gross monthly or yearly rents to obtain an approximate value of an income property.

5. ____ The need to replace part of a structure because new improvements have come along that make the older structure inefficient by comparison. For example, a one-bathroom, eight-bedroom house.

6. ____ An appraisal method, estimating the replacement cost of a structure, less depreciation, plus land value.

7. ____ Loss of desirability and useful life of a property through economic forces, such as zoning changes, traffic pattern changes, etc., rather than wear and tear.

8. ____ A decrease in the value of real property improvements for any reason.

9. ____ An appraisal method to determine the present value today of rental property by estimating the income it will generate over the life of the structure.

10. ____ A way of measuring real property in 1 ft. by 1 ft. segments.

11. ____ The method of estimating the value of real property by adjusting the sales price of comparable properties for differences.

12. ____ Gradual physical wear and tear on a structure that decreases its value.

13. ____ Periodically setting money aside to replace systems and appliances in a building. For example, a landlord putting aside a portion of monthly rents toward a new roof or water heater.
14. ____ The chronological age of a structure as opposed to its effective or economic life.
15. ____ Accumulation of depreciation.
16. ____ Construction costs (material and labor).
17. ____ The cost of reproducing a property (usually one that has been destroyed) at current prices using the same materials.
18. ____ Repairs that would be so expensive they are not economically feasible.
19. ____ Age of a structure as estimated by its condition rather than its actual age.
20. ____ Repairs that are economically logical to do.
21. ____ Costs other than labor and materials.
22. ____ Amount of depreciation in the future, not past.
23. ____ The "profitable" life of an improvement. Generally shorter than the physical life.
24. ____ Gross income of a building if fully rented, less an allowance for estimated vacancies.

IX. MULTIPLE CHOICE

1. An army base moved out of an area, which caused unemployment and housing values to drop. This is referred to as:
    a. economic obsolescence.
    b. functional obsolescence.
    c. physical obsolescence.
    d. none of the above.

2. In the appraisal of residential property, the cost approach is most useful in the case of:
    a. single-family dwellings.
    b. older, greatly depreciated properties.
    c. middle-aged properties.
    d. a very extreme modernistic home.

3. Which is the best method for appraising single-family homes?
    a. Market approach
    b. Income approach
    c. Cost approach
    d. Correlation approach

4. The appraiser must determine the construction expense of replacing a building today, using current construction methods, with the:
    a. market approach.
    b. cost approach.
    c. income approach.
    d. expense approach.

5. Wear and tear on the roof of an urban office building would constitute:

    a. physical deterioration.
    b. functional obsolescence.
    c. economic depreciation.
    d. commercial damages.

6. If an appraiser lowered the value of a house due to functional obsolescence, he/she would be referring to:

    a. termites.
    b. economic decline in the neighborhood.
    c. single-car garage.
    d. damage to the foundation.

7. Loss of value due to changes in the neighborhood and external to the property is called:

    a. economic obsolescence.
    b. physical deterioration.
    c. functional obsolescence.
    d. income obsolescence.

8. A mathematical rule of thumb used to convert the rental value into market value is known as the:

    a. correlation multiplier.
    b. net multiplier.
    c. gross rent multiplier.
    d. evaluation process.

9. A water heater costs $1,000 and is expected to last five years. The $200 a year that would be put aside for this expense is called the:

    a. maintenance cost.
    b. plumbing reserve.
    c. replacement reserve.
    d. operating expense.

10. Which of the following would NOT normally be appraised by the income method?

    a. Apartments
    b. Government land
    c. Warehouses
    d. Offices

ANSWERS: 1. *a*; 2. *d*; 3. *a*; 4. *b*; 5. *a*; 6. *c*; 7. *a*; 8. *c*; 9. *c*; 10. *b*

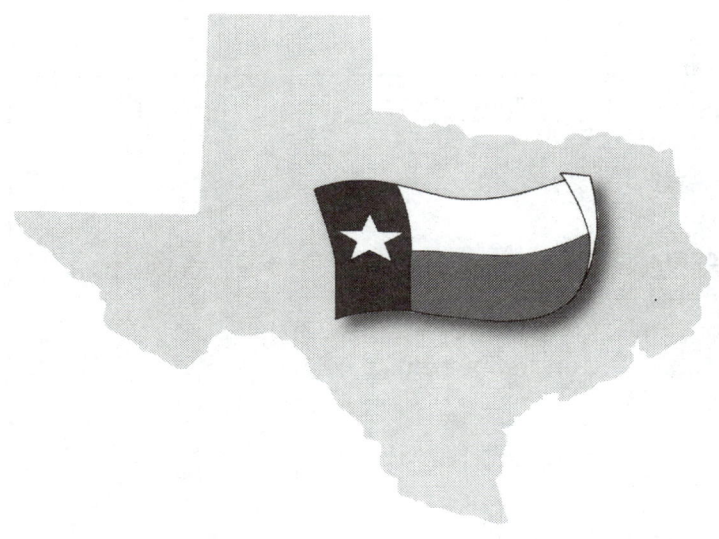

Chapter 15
Government Control of Real Estate

I. Governmental Powers

The "bundle of legal rights" that characterizes a person's ownership of real property does not exist in an isolated environment. A person's legal rights are subject to ongoing government control.

With a population of more than 23 million people, Texas is the second most populous state. Between 2000 and 2003, Texas added nearly 1.3 million new residents including more than 350,000 children under the age of 18. This age group represents the largest gain of any state in the nation. With such a growing population and the projected increase in housing, the challenges facing real estate ownership can be significant.

The state and local governments have the responsibility (under the doctrine of police power) to enact and enforce legislative acts to protect the general public.

This public protection in the real estate area prevents fraud, misrepresentation, and deceit. **Figure 15-1** shows seven basic areas of government control at either the state or local level.

CHAPTER 15 OUTLINE

The powers of government include: the police powers, the power of eminent domain, the power of taxation, and escheat.

A. POLICE POWER

Police power is the right of public officials to enact laws for the health, safety, and general welfare of the public.

POLICE POWER *is a broad term that refers to the power of the government to make rulings to control private property for the protection of the public's health, safety, and welfare.* Police power allows the state, county, or city to protect its citizens by controlling how land is being used.

While government control involves nearly every aspect of real property, the police powers that most people think of first are the ones that they are most likely to directly come in contact with.

1. Building, Fire, and Design Ordinances

By means of building codes, local municipalities extend the reach of the police power into a person's home. *BUILDING CODES are city ordinances that dictate how structures and other types of improvements can be built by specifying the quality of materials, the design, and the construction standards to be used.*

Figure 15-1

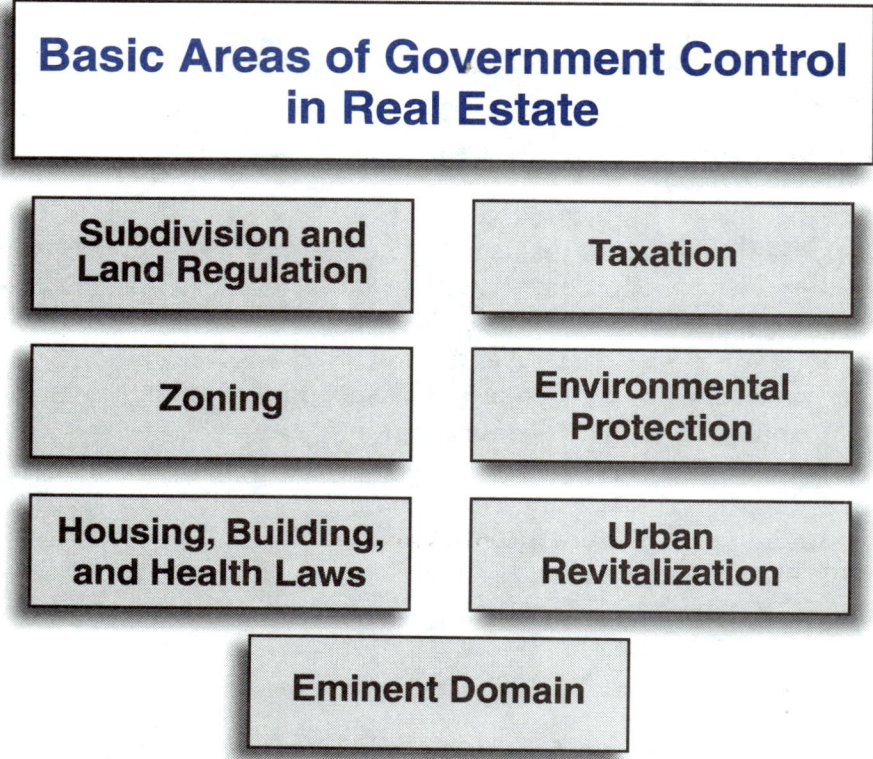

Basic Areas of Government Control in Real Estate

Subdivision and Land Regulation	Taxation
Zoning	Environmental Protection
Housing, Building, and Health Laws	Urban Revitalization
Eminent Domain	

Local building codes will affect nearly all aspects of construction including heating, air conditioning, plumbing, electrical, ventilation and overall safety.

New construction or major building alterations require a building permit. A **BUILDING PERMIT** *is an approved building application that includes plans, specifications, and a plot plan.* After an examination of the application, plans and any revisions of the plans, the building permit is issued. No construction or alteration can be started until the building permit has been issued. Thereafter, during and upon completion of the construction, inspections will be required before final approval can be given. Final approval is usually signified by means of the issuance of a **CERTIFICATE OF OCCUPANCY**, *which signifies that the structure has met all building requirements and may now be occupied.*

Related ordinances may regulate the care and upkeep of private property such as prohibiting overgrown weeds in a yard, regulating the manner in which trash is placed for pickup, limiting the number and type of pets allowed, and requiring homeowners to make certain repairs such as broken water pipes and leaky roofs.

Municipal ordinances are a prime example of the government's police power. Local ordinances establish uniform standards of building materials and construction techniques, but also require ongoing compliance with health and safety issues.

2. Licensing and Regulation Statutes

Another exercise of the government's police power is in the field of real estate licensing and regulation. The Texas Real Estate Commission regulates real estate salespersons, brokers, right-of-way agents, property inspectors, real estate education providers, as well as time-share properties and residential service companies. Other real estate related professions regulated by other agencies include attorneys, accountants, appraisers, surveyors, auctioneers, mortgage brokers, insurance agents, and homeowner's and title insurance companies.

Texas does not license real estate developers, homebuilders, or building contractors. Homebuilders and repair contractors are required to be registered with the newly created Texas Residential Construction Commission (TRCC). The TRCC not only governs the registration process, but it also has oversight of a state sponsored inspection and dispute resolution process (SIRP) for construction defects.

The government's police power extends to the licensing and regulation of real estate professions as well as to real estate related industries.

3. Federal Housing, Construction, and Occupancy Laws

The government's power will also extend deeply to the residential housing area. For example, the Federal Housing Administration (FHA) and the Department of Veterans Affairs (VA) will not insure or guarantee private loans unless the residence to be purchased is first inspected to determine if it meets minimum housing standards. These Minimum Property Requirements (MPRs) are usually more restrictive than state housing or local building codes.

Under the fair housing laws as discussed in Chapter 7, stiff penalties exist for housing discrimination in connection with the sale, purchase, rental or lease of private property. Furthermore, many private landlords who participate in federal subsidized housing programs will be required to meet property condition standards, rent guidelines and even occupancy limits as established by the department of Housing and Urban Development (HUD).

Many federal laws and regulations affect housing, even private residential property, by governing housing discrimination, mortgage lending, housing standards, property condition and occupancy limits of federally assisted housing.

B. EMINENT DOMAIN (Involuntary Taking – Condemnation)

INVOLUNTARY CONVERSION is the legal conversion of real property to personal property (money) without the voluntary act of the owner. This occurs when property is taken through the power of eminent domain. Under the United States Constitution as well as the Texas Constitution, no private property may be taken for public use without just compensation. As a result, two key questions involve whether the goal of an eminent domain action is a "public use" and secondly whether the compensation proposed is "just."

1. Public Use

Historically, local communities have been given wide leeway in determining exactly what constitutes public use. Traditionally, cities have used the power of eminent domain to build public works projects such as roads, highways, airports, libraries, wharves, and parks. But may a city use eminent domain to build an office-retail complex simply in the name of economic development? In a recent U.S. Supreme Court decision, the high court said "yes," so long as the private land was being taken pursuant to a well thought out economic development plan intended to revitalize blighted portions of a city. The court ruled that so long as the plan was intended to benefit the entire community and not a few individuals, a mixed-use office-retail project could fit the definition of "public use."

As a result of the Supreme Court's decision, the definition of "public use" has been broadened so as to include projects that are intended to promote the economic development of a city.

2. "Just" Compensation

In Texas, the power of eminent domain is frequently accomplished by means of a **condemnation suit** filed in a state district court.

In the vast majority of the condemnation cases, the issue is NOT whether the condemning authority may take the property, rather the issue is how much will be paid for the property.

Before a suit is filed, however, state law requires that the parties attempt to negotiate a settlement. If a settlement cannot be reached, then it's off to court where the judge will appoint three disinterested local residents to serve as special commissioners. These commissioners will hear testimony and evidence as presented by the parties and make an award based on the evidence presented. If an entire tract is condemned, then the commissioner's award will be based on the local market value of the property. However, if only a portion is being condemned, then the commissioners may award damages after estimating the extent of the injury and the benefit to the property owner.

If the landowner is dissatisfied with the commissioner's award, he or she may appeal the case to the court where a judge will hear the matter.

3. Eminent Domain Income Tax Issues

For tax purposes, eminent domain is considered to be an involuntary conversion for which special tax rules apply.

Under federal income tax laws, the landowner may be allowed to convert back to real property (buy another property) without paying tax on the gain from the condemnation. This must be done within a three-year period and the prices of the old and new property are considered to form a new tax base.

Tax laws are complicated and subject to change, so professional tax advice is always wise.

C. TAXATION

AD VALOREM TAXATION (according to value) is a power held by state and local government that permits taxation of real property according to the value of the property. It is the primary but not the exclusive means of providing for the financial needs of cities, counties, school districts, community colleges and other districts. Ad valorem taxation is more fully discussed in Chapter 16.

However, just as taxation is an important power of government, the power not to tax is equally as important. When taxing districts choose not to tax, it is known as "tax abatement."

1. Tax Abatements and Reinvestment Zones

Local governments often use the power of tax abatements in order to attract new business and industries in a particular area or to keep existing businesses from leaving. To accomplish this, Texas cities and counties are authorized by law to grant property tax abatements within specially designated reinvestment zones.

A reinvestment zone can be a blighted area or it can be an area likely to attract major businesses.

A reinvestment zone may consist of a single parcel of land or the zone may consist of an area containing several parcels.

Many cities and counties are assisted by local economic development foundations. These private organizations seek out new businesses

that may be willing to relocate to a given community for the right incentive.

2. Tax Increment Financing (TIF)

Tax Increment Financing (TIF) provides a mechanism for financing public improvements such as streets, sidewalks, and sewer systems without requiring voter approval. This manner of financing is usually spearheaded by a city (although it may be requested by the taxpayers themselves) and basically involves devoting a portion of the tax revenues that are attributable to the increase in property values within a reinvestment zone (the tax increment) to finance specified city improvements (see **Figure 15-2**).

Figure 15-2

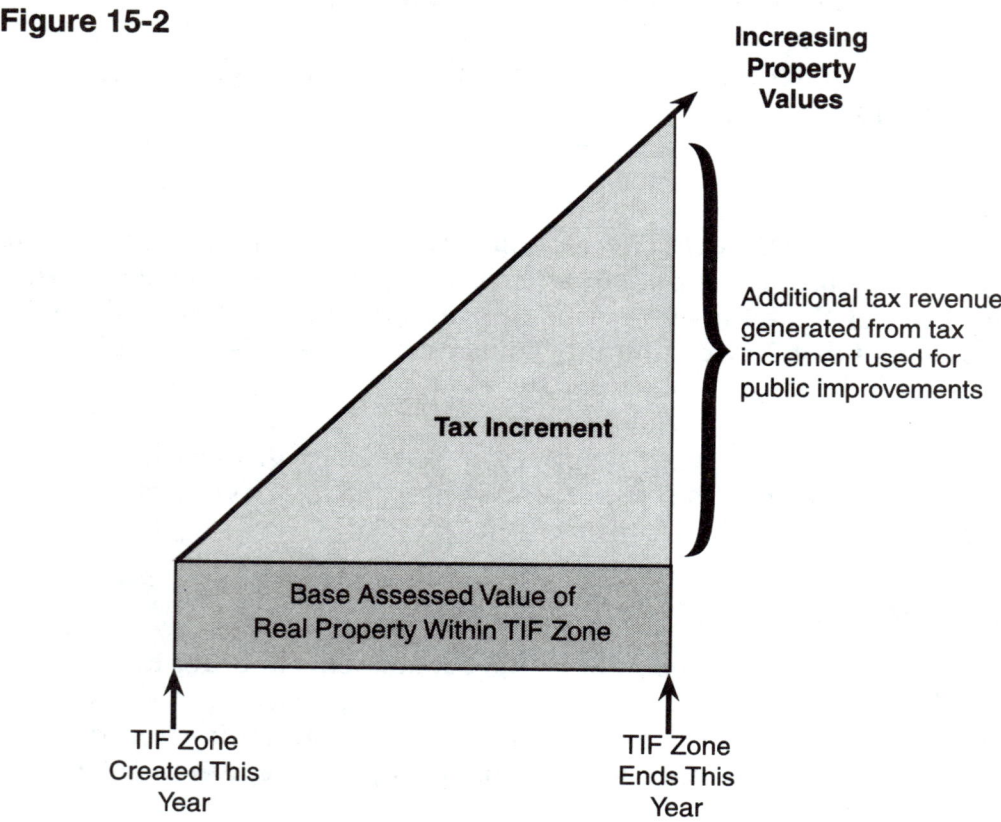

"Tax Increment Financing (TIF)" does NOT mean that the property tax rate will be increased. Instead, it means that if property values go up, resulting in an increase in tax revenue, the increased portion will be devoted to paying for certain city improvements.

Tax abatements seek to attract new business to a given area by reducing or eliminating property taxes. Tax increment financing, however, pays for certain city improvements by devoting a portion of the projected tax revenues due to increased property values within a TIF district.

3. Enterprise Zones

An **ENTERPRISE ZONE** *helps to attract new businesses to a particular area through incentives.* By partnering with the state of Texas, local communities can attract new business by offering a variety of financial incentives, not just tax abatements. These incentives can, of course, include tax abatements, but they can also mean a refund of local sales and use taxes, low interest business development loans, or a variety of other financial benefits.

Enterprise zones are intended to help severely distressed areas of the state by granting a variety of state and local financial incentives with the aim of increasing employment and local development.

4. Impact Fees

Impact fees are NOT considered taxes. They are a form of assessing charges against property owners, but usually developers, in order to finance the capital expenditures of a city resulting from new development.

Impact fees are legally defined as ..."*a charge or assessment imposed by a political subdivision against new development in order to generate revenue for funding or recouping the costs of capital improvements or facility expansions necessitated by and attributable to the new development.*"

State law requires that impact fees be generally used only for water supply, waste water treatment, drainage, and roadway purposes. Thus, for example, a city might impose an impact fee in order to help recover the cost of installing a waste water treatment plant because of a new subdivision.

While the city could rely on ad valorem taxes and/or bonds to pay for the improvement, "impact fees" represent a method to recover a capital improvement expense they imposed on the group most affected by the improvement (for example, new condo construction) without having to financially burden the unaffected citizens.

D. ESCHEAT

ESCHEAT is a legal term used to describe the process of unclaimed property reverting or returning to the state. This would occur when a person dies without a will, leaving

no heirs to take his or her real and personal property. The practice is based on the English principle that unclaimed property must be returned to the sovereign. Under English law and tradition, since all property originally came from the king, unclaimed property should be returned to the king.

In Texas, a legal proceeding must be held to determine if unclaimed property should escheat to the state of Texas. Should the court determine that the property is unclaimed, then a judgment will be entered passing title of the property to the state of Texas. Escheated real property becomes part of the lands of the Texas Permanent School Fund, a large fund first created in 1854 for the benefit of public education in Texas.

To check for unclaimed property, check online with the state comptroller's office (**see next page**).

II. Subdivision, Condos, and Timeshare Interests (State and Local Regulation)

State and local governments hold limited regulatory powers over how private developments and property interests may actually be created.

In Texas, many communities strictly regulate how new housing subdivisions are created while the state, on the other hand, governs the creation of condominiums and timeshare units.

A. SUBDIVISION PLAT (MAP) APPROVAL

Texas law gives cities the right to adopt rules governing the filing of plats and subdivisions of land within each city in order to promote the health, safety, morals or general welfare of the municipality. As a result, many municipalities have enacted subdivision ordinances in order to provide for orderly and organized development.

A plat is a "map" of a proposed development on a piece of land that will have more than one tract on it. To "subdivide" property means to legally divide a tract of land into two or more parcels of land.

While anyone can seek to subdivide property, in Texas the term is closely associated with developers who subdivide large tracts of land in order to build homes.

Although each municipality's subdivision ordinance may be different, as a general rule, cities will allow a plat (map) of subdivided property to be officially recorded when the subdivider or developer has met certain requirements.

www.window.state.tx.us/up

WINDOW ON STATE GOVERNMENT-   CAROLE KEETON STRAYHORN   Texas Comptroller of Public Accounts

Search

Texas Finances

Unclaimed Property

Search Online for
Your Property

General
Information

Reclaiming Your
Property

Special Notices

Proving
Ownership

Check Your Claim
Status

Holder
Information

Voluntary
Disclosure
Agreement

Unclaimed
Property Auction

**A Message from Texas Comptroller
Carole Keeton Strayhorn**

Dear Fellow Texan:

From a long-dormant bank account to a forgotten utility
deposit or family heirloom in an abandoned safe deposit
box, the state may be holding valuable property that
belongs to you. If so, I want to return your property to you.

In today's mobile society, Texans can easily lose track of
uncashed stock dividend checks, insurance proceeds, utility
and rent deposits, and other assets that may escape
attention.

As Texas Comptroller, I am responsible for collecting these
abandoned assets. I am committed to returning them to
their rightful owners.

Click Here to find out if unclaimed property is being held
for you.

Sincerely,

Carole Keeton Strayhorn

Carole Keeton Strayhorn
Texas Comptroller

For example, a city might require a developer to submit a preliminary plan of the development so that it is reviewed by city planners and engineers. If the developer is relatively unknown, the city might want legal assurances that the property development will actually be completed as promised. And, like a new home being constructed, a city will probably want to conduct a final inspection of the subdivision before formally approving a final plat. Final plat approval is important because houses cannot be sold until the plat is recorded. And, after investing possibly millions of dollars worth of streets, curbs, and below-ground improvements, a developer is eager to sell lots to individual purchasers.

A city's subdivision ordinance will govern how new subdivisions are created.

State law also allows cities and even certain counties to approve subdivisions that are outside the limits of a city. Cities generally also have the power to approve subdivisions within their **EXTRATERRITORIAL JURISDICTION (ETJ)**, *which means land lying outside and immediately adjacent to the city border.*

A city's ETJ will depend on the size of the city, but it generally cannot extend beyond five miles from the city limit.

B. CONDOMINIUMS

A "condominium" is legally defined as a form of real property with portions of the real property designated for separate ownership or occupancy, and the remainder of the real property designated for "common area ownership" solely by the owners of those portions.

Condominiums are generally governed by the **Texas Condominium Act**. Under the Act, condominiums are created by means of the filing of a declaration which must be filed in the country clerk's office. The declaration must contain information such as a legal description of the property, a description of each unit's boundaries, a plat of the complex, and any restrictions on the use of the units.

Although each unit is individually and privately owned, management of the condominium is by an owners' association.

Such associations must be organized as either a for-profit or a nonprofit Texas corporation. Owners' associations are given by statute a broad range of power such as to adopt bylaws and budgets, hire and fire managers, enter into contracts, and assess charges to the individual unit owners.

By law, a purchaser of a condominium unit has a limited right to cancel the sales contract if he or she has not timely received certain condominium information. The law requires a seller to provide the purchaser with a copy of the declaration, the bylaws, association rules, and a resale certificate before the purchaser executes the contract. Failure to provide these documents may entitle the purchaser to cancel the contract without penalty.

By carefully reviewing the condominium declaration, bylaws, association rules, and the resale certificate (if a resale), the purchaser can learn of all relevant facts concerning his/her condominium ownership.

C. TIMESHARES

Timeshare interests are strictly controlled by the Texas Timeshare Act. *TIMESHARING is a form of ownership where each investor holds a share in a specific unit or home and possesses the right to occupy that home for a specified period each year.* See **Figure 15-3**.

A **timeshare regime**, as it is called, is created by recording a master deed, master lease, or timeshare declaration in the county clerk's office. By law, the declaration must contain a legal description, a ground plan, a list of amenities furnished, a description of each unit including a floor plan, and a statement of the percentage that each unit bears to the whole.

Timeshare properties must be registered with the Texas Real Estate Commission and sellers of timeshare interests, other than the owner, must hold a valid Texas real estate license.

Texas law has provided two important safeguards for the prospective purchaser of a timeshare interest. First, prior to contract execution, timeshare developers are required to give purchasers a comprehensive 19-point disclosure statement regarding the property. This statement covers such items as an annual operating budget as well as disclosure of any pending lawsuits that may materially affect a timeshare interest.

Secondly, a purchaser has, by law, a six day cancellation option as evidenced by the required contract language shown in **Figure 15-4**. Regardless of what a contract may say, under state law, a purchaser may not waive this right to cancel.

III. Zoning (Local Regulation)

Zoning allows cities to categorize land into districts or zones so that its use can be regulated for the protection of the public's health, safety, and welfare as allowed by the U.S. Constitution. Zoning is probably the strongest use of the "police power" by cities.

Figure 15-3

TIMESHARING:

Pro or Con? — You Decide! A chalet at Aspen...a condo at South Padre...a bungalow in the Caribbean...

TIMESHARING is a form of ownership where each investor holds a share in a specific unit or home and possesses the right to occupy that home for a specified period each year. For instance, fifty-two owners may each own a one-week share in the property. Each is given a grant deed and each has the right to sell his or her share, rent out the week, or stay there for one seven-day period every year. The ownership week is fixed, but it is possible to trade with other owners. Similarly, there are timesharing groups across the country and around the world, which allow investors to exchange time with owners of comparable properties in other desirable locations.

Advantages

The advantages to this kind of ownership are obvious. The buyer has a vacation home without the expense of purchasing the complete home outright. This kind of plan provides access to some of the most unique and scenic property in the world. Once these very special locations are sold, they are gone; they cannot be replaced in the marketplace.

Disadvantages

On the negative side, these properties tend to be disproportionately high priced. For instance, if you multiplied the cost of one share in a week-based timeshare by an even 50, it would total much more than the market value of the property purchased. Those selling timeshares are burdened with tremendous marketing expenses. Rather than selling once, each property must be sold many times, complete with financing and paperwork.

Restrictions

A brokerage license is required to sell a timeshare package. Under state law, a purchaser of a timeshare interest will have up to six days to cancel a timeshare contract.

Figure 15-4

PURCHASER'S RIGHT TO CANCEL

(1) BY SIGNING THIS CONTRACT YOU ARE INCURRING AN OBLIGATION TO PURCHASE A TIMESHARE INTEREST. YOU MAY, HOWEVER, CANCEL THIS CONTRACT WITHOUT PENALTY OR OBLIGATION BEFORE THE SIXTH DAY AFTER THE DATE YOU SIGN AND RECEIVE A COPY OF THE PURCHASE CONTRACT, OR RECEIVE THE REQUIRED TIMESHARE DISCLOSURE STATEMENT, WHICHEVER IS LATER.

(2) IF YOU DECIDE TO CANCEL THIS CONTRACT, YOU MAY DO SO BY EITHER HAND-DELIVERING NOTICE OF CANCELLATION TO THE DEVELOPER, BY MAILING NOTICE BY PREPAID UNITED STATES MAIL TO THE DEVELOPER OR THE DEVELOPER'S AGENT FOR SERVICE OF PROCESS, OR BY PROVIDING NOTICE BY OVERNIGHT COMMON CARRIER DELIVERY SERVICE TO THE DEVELOPER OR THE DEVELOPER'S AGENT FOR SERVICE OF PROCESS. YOUR NOTICE OF CANCELLATION IS EFFECTIVE ON THE DATE SENT OR DELIVERED TO (INSERT NAME OF DEVELOPER) AT (INSERT ADDRESS OF DEVELOPER). FOR YOUR PROTECTION, SHOULD YOU DECIDE TO CANCEL YOU SHOULD EITHER SEND YOUR NOTICE OF CANCELLATION BY CERTIFIED MAIL WITH A RETURN RECEIPT REQUESTED OR OBTAIN A SIGNED AND DATED RECEIPT IF DELIVERING IT IN PERSON OR BY OVERNIGHT COMMON CARRIER.

(3) A PURCHASER SHOULD NOT RELY ON STATEMENTS OTHER THAN THOSE INCLUDED IN THIS CONTRACT AND THE DISCLOSURE STATEMENT.

Source: Texas Property Code §221.043

A. GENERAL ZONING REGULATIONS

Zoning regulations must be uniform for each type of building within a zoning district, but regulations may vary from district to district.

This means that as a general rule, the zoning regulations must be the same within a zoning district. This ensures the compatibility of land uses.

1. Purposes

State law allows cities to regulate the use of land and buildings by imposing restrictions and development standards in the following respects:

1. the height, number of stories, and size of buildings;
2. the percentage of a lot that may be occupied;
3. size of the yards and other open spaces;
4. population density;

5. the location and use of buildings; and
6. the pumping of groundwater for health and safety reasons.

Texas cities may also regulate areas of historical, cultural, or architectural importance by regulating construction, reconstruction, alteration or razing of structures.

2. Distinguished from Deed Restrictions

Although zoning and private deed restrictions may appear to serve a similar purpose, they are two entirely different things. Deed restrictions, as discussed in Chapter 3, are private development restrictions placed upon the land. Zoning, on the other hand, is a use restriction created by a city ordinance. It is a public restriction placed on private property.

While most Texas cities have enacted zoning ordinances, Houston, interestingly, has not. As a result, residents of Houston must rely on private deed restrictions to control land use.

Due to a special state law, the city of Houston and certain County Attorneys are allowed in special circumstances to enforce private deed restrictions. In those cases where enforcement is permitted, they may intervene in an existing lawsuit, or file their own suit to enjoin (stop) the offending land use activity. In no case may restrictive covenants dealing with race, color, religion, or national origin be enforced.

3. The Comprehensive City Plan

By law, all zoning regulations must be adopted in furtherance of a city's Comprehensive or Master Plan so as to:

1. lessen traffic congestion;
2. promote public safety;
3. promote health and the general welfare of the city;
4. provide adequate light and air;
5. prevent the overcrowding of land;
6. avoid undue concentration of population; or
7. facilitate the adequate provision of transportation, water, sewers, schools, parks, or other public requirements.

The ***MASTER PLAN*** *is a comprehensive guide through which zoning establishes an ideal plan for the city's development in the future.* ***DIRECTIONAL GROWTH*** *is the actual growth path of urban development.* Properties in the direction of growth tend to increase in value, especially if the growth is steady and rapid.

The primary purpose of a Master Plan is to set forth existing and future matters concerning land use, transportation and public facilities.

B. KEY PARTICIPANTS IN THE ZONING PROCESS

There are four key players in the zoning process: the landowner, the planning and zoning commission, the zoning board of adjustment, and the city council. Each has a unique role to play in the overall process.

1. The Property Owner

Many zoning issues are usually initiated by an affected property owner. This may be a resident who is concerned about a nearby "big box" retail giant disrupting neighborhood traffic patterns. Or a zoning issue can be raised by a business owner who wants to expand or change his property into a use that is not currently permitted. A large developer may request that a tract of land be rezoned so as to be able to build a 900-home residential subdivision. Or perhaps a zoning issue might be raised by a single homeowner who wants to remodel so as to have a side-entry garage in a neighborhood where all the other garages are front-entry. Zoning issues may be raised by local citizens, interested parties, and even government agencies.

Property and business owners, developers and subdividers, interested parties, and even government agencies can raise zoning issues.

2. Planning and Zoning Commission

The primary responsibility of a *CITY PLANNING AND ZONING COMMISSION (sometimes called a CITY ZONING COMMISSION) is to make recommendations for zoning district boundaries for the city council's formal approval.*

Usually, planning and zoning commissions will hold their own public hearings, gather information, cite other examples, and come up with their own innovations in an attempt to make some order out of the chaos into which a city may have fallen. Commissions have discovered that preplanning exactly which types of buildings can go where, before they are constructed, saves more time and money than all the zoning laws made after the building is done. As a result, planning commissions make growth and development predictions so as to ensure that today's residential, commercial, and industrial areas will not collide in the future due to expansion of both areas.

3. Zoning Board of Adjustment (ZBA)

Another participant in the zoning process is the *ZONING BOARD OF ADJUSTMENT (ZBA), which is charged with the responsibility of interpreting zoning ordinances as they apply to particular landowners.*

The ZBA plays no role in creating or changing zoning. Instead, it focuses on how existing zoning affects individual landowners.

The ZBA is legally authorized to grant special exceptions or variances from the effects of zoning. As a result, if a person is complaining about personal hardship from the effects of rezoning several large tracts of land, he/she would probably complain to the planning and zoning commission. However, if the same landowner wants to challenge the current fence height requirements around his/her own property, the property owner would go to the zoning board of adjustment.

While the planning and zoning commission may examine the effects of zoning with respect to an entire city, the zoning board of adjustment looks at the effects of zoning with respect to one particular landowner.

4. City Council

As the city's main legislative body, the **CITY COUNCIL** *is legally responsible for enacting and enforcing the city's zoning ordinance.* Although zoning regulations and district boundaries may be recommended by other city departments or agencies, it is the city council that must formally approve them.

Although each city's zoning classifications may be different, here's an example of how these classifications might look in a typical Texas city:

A – This symbol might indicate an agricultural area such as farm or ranch land. In some cases, a symbol beginning with "A" stands for an airport.

C – The "C" symbol might represent commercial areas. In these areas anything from an office building to a community shopping center may exist. There may be other, more specific, "C" symbols regulating the construction of such commercial properties.

M – This classification may stand for manufacturing. Under this classification, a city might allow industrial complexes to be built only in this area.

P – Although there could be many different interpretations of the "P" symbol, this category might include parking lots and/or park areas.

R – A city might designate the "R" symbol to stand for Residential and is probably the most important symbol to the real estate licensee. This symbol (and its derivations) designates those areas in which homes, condominiums, or apartments may be built or maintained.

Each of these symbols is usually followed by a number. For example, "R" may be followed by 1, 2, 3, or 4. The number indicates a higher density or use for that particular zone. The following examples will help explain each use:

R1 – In many jurisdictions, this may stand for a single-family residential dwelling. Sometimes this may be abbreviated as an SFR classification.

R2 – This is for two dwelling units. Depending on the city, this might also be shown as a MFR (multi-family residential) classification.

R3 – This category might be reserved for multiple dwellings, depending on square footage and height of apartment buildings, condominiums, etc.

R4 – This might be reserved for higher density multiple dwellings with certain square footage.

R5 – This may, depending on the city, refer to requirements and maximum height allowable concerning motels, hotels, and high-rise apartments or condominiums.

No matter how the individual zoning categories are actually labeled, the city council is ultimately legally responsible for the implementation and enforcement of the zoning ordinance.

C. CHANGES TO ZONING

Zoning is a control that attempts to ensure uniform land use while also meeting the occasional needs of the community. When community needs change, there are several devices that can be utilized.

1. Nonconforming Use

As conditions in the area change, the zoning of existing parcels may also change. The change may cause some of the existing structures to become nonconforming.

NONCONFORMING USE is a property use that does not conform to the current zoning, but existed legally before zoning changes were enacted. An example of nonconforming use is an apartment building with one parking space per unit where zoning changes require two parking spaces per unit. It is a general policy to let nonconforming uses continue for a time if conformity creates unnecessary hardships. However, the growing trend is for cities to attach other restrictions or conditions on the property in order for the property owner to qualify for a nonconforming use.

A "grandfather clause" allows an owner to continue using his or her property in a way prohibited by the new zoning (nonconforming use).

2. Variance (For Private Hardship)

One way to provide reasonable conformity is to allow zoning variances. A *VARIANCE is an exception to the existing zoning regulations in cases of special need for circumstances that might create serious hardship for property owners.* Zoning restrictions, such as setbacks, may be removed by petitioning the zoning board of adjustment for a variance.

Variance is for one lot; rezoning is for many lots.

For example, if an individual wants to construct a building that does not comply with the local zoning rule, he or she may petition for a variance. When filing this petition, the individual must prove that the changed use will not be detrimental to the public interest and that a literal enforcement of the zoning ordinance would result in unnecessary hardship to the property owner and, furthermore, that the hardship is not self-created. Variances are often granted with special conditions such that both plans and construction be approved and initiated within a specified time.

3. Conditional Use Permit (For Public Benefit)

A *CONDITIONAL USE PERMIT is an exception to the current zoning for the public welfare or benefit.* Variances, on the other hand, are based on a personal benefit. Conditional use permits allow a property to be used in a manner that is inconsistent with current zoning regulations subject to specifically named conditions. If the stated conditions are not met, then the permission is withdrawn. Since conditional use permits affect the "big picture," they are often the domain of the planning and zoning commission rather than the zoning board of adjustment.

4. Other Zoning Terms

Buffer Zone. A *BUFFER ZONE is a generic term for a strip of land that separates two types of land use.* The buffer could be a vacant tract or perhaps even a greenbelt (strip of intentionally undeveloped land or natural area) between residential subdivisions, for example.

Down Zoning. *DOWN ZONING refers to a change from a high-density use to a lower density use.* Down zoning may occur, for example, when an area's zoning is changed from commercial to residential. It can also occur when a residential area is changed from R4 to R1.

Inclusionary Zoning. *INCLUSIONARY ZONING requires builders of new residential housing to provide a certain number of low- and moderate-income units (known as* *"affordable housing")* in a given area in exchange for other zoning incentives. Unless the developer/builder agrees to these conditions, the project will not be allowed to continue.

Spot Zoning. *SPOT ZONING is a small area that is zoned differently from the surrounding area.* For example, the value and utility of a residential area might be enhanced if a nearby area is spot zoned for light retail-commercial use.

D. THE ZONING PROCESS

The zoning process is typically initiated by a written request or application for a zoning change. The request is first analyzed and forwarded to the city's planning and zoning commission where a public hearing is scheduled. During the public hearing, members of the public, including affected neighboring landowners, will be allowed to voice their opinions concerning the proposed zoning change. Following the hearing, the planning commission will issue its recommendation to the city council who will formally act on the recommendation. Although every city's zoning ordinance is different, **Figure 15-5** shows how the zoning process works in one Texas city.

IV. Interstate Real Estate Transactions

In addition to local and state governments, the federal government is directly involved in real estate regulation.

A. INTERSTATE LAND SALES FULL DISCLOSURE ACT

The **Federal Interstate Land Sales Act** was passed by Congress in 1968 due in large part to several well-publicized real estate schemes that took advantage of purchasers. The law requires that land promoters who offer 100 or more acres of undeveloped land through the U.S. mail or by any means of interstate commerce, to register the development with HUD and provide a property disclosure to potential buyers. Under the law, all potential purchasers must receive a comprehensive **property report** at least 48 hours before signing a contract of sale. Purchasers who receive the property report will have a seven-day "cooling off" period in which to rescind the contract. However, if the property report is never delivered, the consumer may cancel the contract for up to two years following contract execution.

Under this federal law:

1. All potential purchasers must receive a comprehensive property report at least 48 hours before signing a contract of sale.

2. Purchasers who receive the property report will have a seven-day "cooling off" period in which to rescind the contract.

Figure 15-5   **Zoning Process Flowchart**

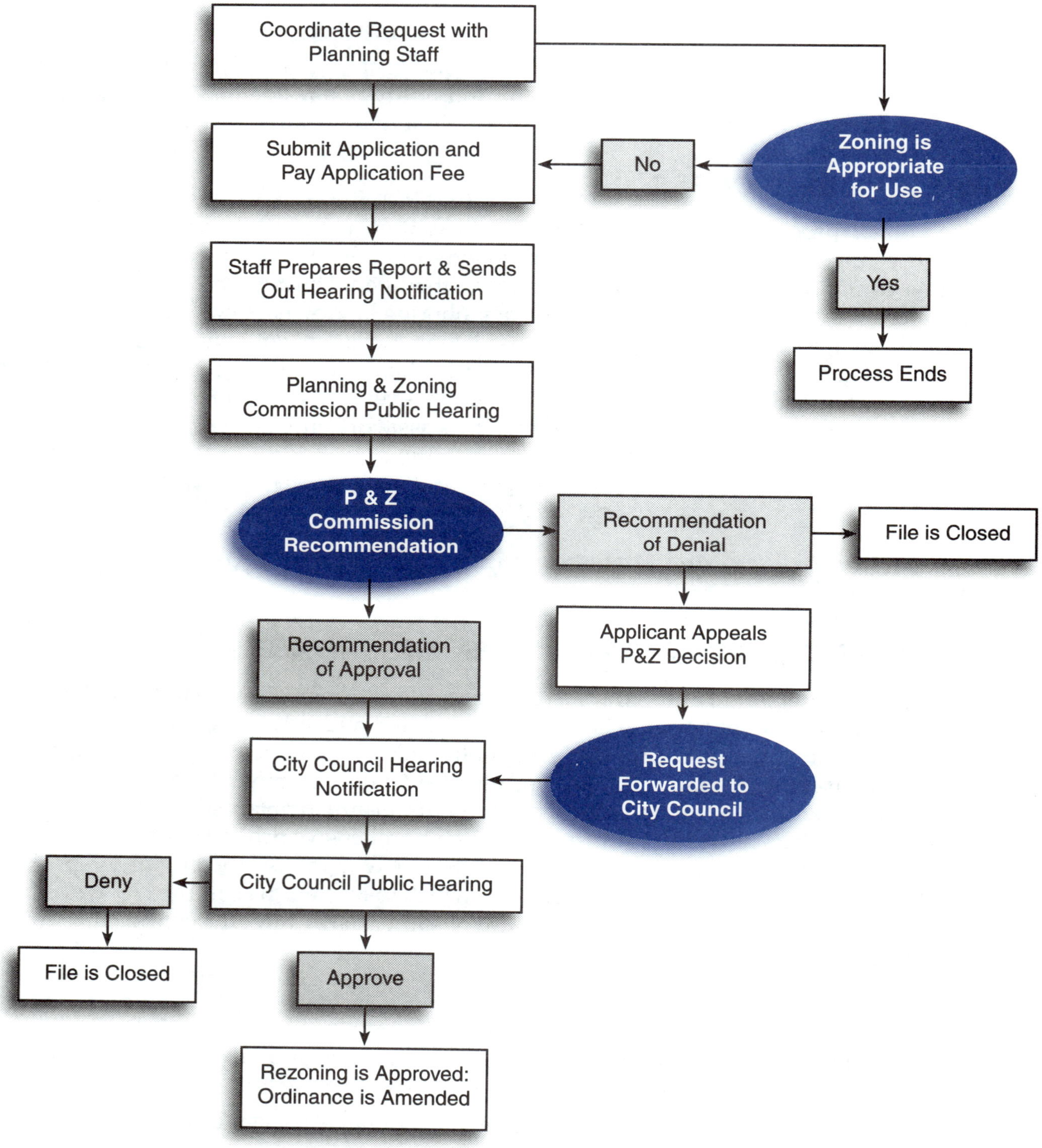

Coordinate Request with
Planning Staff

Submit Application and
Pay Application Fee

No

Zoning is
Appropriate
for Use

Staff Prepares Report & Sends
Out Hearing Notification

Yes

Planning & Zoning
Commission Public Hearing

Process Ends

P & Z
Commission
Recommendation

Recommendation
of Denial

File is Closed

Recommendation
of Approval

Applicant Appeals
P&Z Decision

City Council Hearing
Notification

Request
Forwarded to
City Council

Deny

City Council Public Hearing

File is Closed

Approve

Rezoning is Approved:
Ordinance is Amended

3. If the property report is never delivered, the consumer may cancel the contract within two years following contract execution.

Although the registration of the property is made with HUD, allegations of fraud and misrepresentation are prosecuted by the Department of Justice.

B. SECURITIES REGULATION

The sale of certain types of real estate interests that involve securities is also subject to registration and disclosure requirements under the Securities Act of 1933 and the Securities Exchange Act of 1934. The registration will be with the Securities and Exchange Commission, and the disclosure to prospective purchasers will be by means of a **PROSPECTUS**, *which is essentially an abbreviated version of the registration statement.* Just like under the Interstate Land Sales Disclosure Act, the failure to provide a prospectus can result in contract rescission by the purchaser.

At first glance, it does not seem likely that the sale of real estate would include traditional securities, such as stocks and bonds. However, the term also includes "investment contracts." As a result, investment contracts may very well include interests in Real Estate Investment Trusts (REITs), as well as interests in certain limited partnerships.

Like most federal statutes, this law is rather technical and contains a number of exemptions. It's best to consult with a securities lawyer for a full understanding of a party's legal rights and responsibilities under the law.

C. OTHER FEDERAL LEGISLATION

There are a number of other federal laws regulating real estate, many of which have already been mentioned but in a different context. By way of example:

1. The Real Estate Settlement and Procedures Act (RESPA), discussed in Chapter 9, requires the disclosure of certain information in connection with the settlement and closing of real estate transactions.

2. The Civil Rights Act of 1866 and the Federal Fair Housing Act of 1968, as discussed in Chapter 7, bar housing discrimination.

3. The Equal Credit Opportunity Act and The Federal Truth in Lending Act both require financial disclosures regarding the obtaining of credit and the costs of credit.

4. In addition, there exists an entire alphabet soup of federal agencies and programs involved in real estate such as HUD, IRS, VA, FHA, and, as discussed in the previous section, the SEC.

The next section of this chapter will briefly discuss the role of the Environmental Protection Agency (EPA).

V. Environmental Laws

In recent years, there has been increasing attention focused on the problems of our environment. These problems include energy, water pollution, air contamination, population growth, preservation of wild life, waste disposal and the quality of life issues in general. In response, the federal and state governments have passed laws and regulations to help protect us and our environment.

A. LEAD HAZARDS (Federal Government)

Lead is a toxic metal that can cause a number of serious health problems, especially in children, 6 years old and younger.

Problems from lead poisoning can include learning disabilities, behavioral problems, brain disorders, and seizures, and may even result in death.

Perhaps the greatest source of lead poisoning is from deteriorating lead-based paint. Even though the risk of lead exposure has reduced greatly since the 1970s when the manufacture of lead-based paint was discontinued, federal law still requires that purchasers of single-family homes built before 1978 be advised of the dangers of lead poisoning.

1. Lead-Based Paint Addendum for Texas Contracts

Under federal law and regulations, sellers and landlords of "target" housing must comply with certain disclosure duties that indicate their knowledge of any lead-based paint or hazard within the property. Target housing generally includes most private housing, public housing, federally owned housing, and housing receiving federal assistance. **Figure 15-6** shows a list of property that is excluded from disclosure.

Although the seller/landlord is required to make disclosure for lead-based hazards, the buyer, on the other hand, is not obligated to perform an inspection.

In order to comply with federal lead-based paint disclosures with respect to target housing, real estate brokers are required to do the following:

Figure 15-6

Housing Excluded From Lead-Based Paint Disclosures

- Housing built after 1977;
- Zero-bedroom units, for example efficiencies, lofts and dormitories;
- Housing with leases for less than 100 days;
- Housing exclusive for elderly or handicapped residents (unless children live here also);
- Rental housing that has been inspected by a certified inspector and found to be free of lead-based paint; and
- Houses sold as a result of foreclosure.

1. The broker must provide the buyer with the EPA pamphlet, *Protect Your Family From Lead in Your Home*. This booklet is also available in Spanish.

2. The broker must use TREC Lead-based Paint addendum to the residential contract for the sale or lease of all housing built before 1978. A copy of this addendum is shown in **Figure 15-7**. This addendum meets the federal disclosure requirements by containing:

   a. Lead Warning Statement;
   b. Requires the seller to disclose all existing lead-based paint hazards;
   c. Requires the seller to produce all lead hazard inspection reports; and
   d. Gives the buyer 10 days to conduct his or her own lead-based paint inspection.

Note that this addendum also contains a space for the brokers to sign.

3. Lastly, the broker is required to retain a copy of the lead-based paint addendum for three years following the sale of the property in order to prove that appropriate disclosures were made.

Under federal law, any person who violates this law, regardless of whether a party or a broker, could be subject to civil money penalties of up to $10,000, as well as treble (triple) money damages!

2. Other Sources of Lead Poisoning

Previous home renovations may have resulted in contaminated soils from lead-based paint particles and shavings. In addition, some neighborhoods may be at risk of high lead levels in soil because of airborne contamination from long closed, nearby industrial and manufacturing facilities.

Figure 15-7

APPROVED BY THE TEXAS REAL ESTATE COMMISSION

02-09-2004

ADDENDUM FOR SELLER'S DISCLOSURE OF INFORMATION ON LEAD-BASED PAINT AND LEAD-BASED PAINT HAZARDS AS REQUIRED BY FEDERAL LAW

CONCERNING THE PROPERTY AT _____

(Street Address and City)

A. **LEAD WARNING STATEMENT:** "Every purchaser of any interest in residential real property on which a residential dwelling was built prior to 1978 is notified that such property may present exposure to lead from lead-based paint that may place young children at risk of developing lead poisoning. Lead poisoning in young children may produce permanent neurological damage, including learning disabilities, reduced intelligence quotient, behavioral problems, and impaired memory. Lead poisoning also poses a particular risk to pregnant women. The seller of any interest in residential real property is required to provide the buyer with any information on lead-based paint hazards from risk assessments or inspections in the seller's possession and notify the buyer of any known lead-based paint hazards. A risk assessment or inspection for possible lead-paint hazards is recommended prior to purchase."

NOTICE: Inspector must be properly certified as required by federal law.

B. **SELLER'S DISCLOSURE:**

1. PRESENCE OF LEAD-BASED PAINT AND/OR LEAD-BASED PAINT HAZARDS (check on box only):

☐ (a) Known lead-based paint and/or lead-based paint hazards are present in the Property (explain): _____
_____

☐ (b) Seller has no actual knowledge of lead-based paint and/or lead-based paint hazards in the Property.

2. RECORDS AND REPORTS AVAILABLE TO SELLER (check one box only):

☐ (a) Seller has provided the purchaser with all available records and reports pertaining to lead-based paint and/or lead-based paint hazards in the Property (list documents):_____
_____ .

☐ (b) Seller has no reports or records pertaining to lead-based paint and/or lead-based paint hazards in the Property.

C. **BUYER'S RIGHTS** (check one box only):

☐ 1. Buyer waives the opportunity to conduct a risk assessment or inspection of the Property for the presence of lead-based paint or lead-based paint hazards.

☐ 2. Within ten days after the effective date of this contract, Buyer may have the Property inspected by inspectors selected by Buyer. If lead-based paint or lead-based paint hazards are present, Buyer may terminate this contract by giving Seller written notice within 14 days after the effective date of this contract, and the earnest money will be refunded to Buyer.

D. **BUYER'S ACKNOWLEDGMENT** (check applicable boxes):

☐ 1. Buyer has received copies of all information listed above.

☐ 2. Buyer has received the pamphlet *Protect Your Family from Lead in Your Home.*

E. **BROKERS' ACKNOWLEDGMENT:** Brokers have informed Seller of Seller's obligations under 42 U.S.C. 4852d to: (a) provide Buyer with the federally approved pamphlet on lead poisoning prevention; (b) complete this addendum; (c) disclose any known lead-based paint and/or lead-based paint hazards in the Property; (d) deliver all records and reports to Buyer pertaining to lead-based paint and/or lead-based paint hazards in the Property; (e) provide Buyer a period of up to 10 days to have the Property inspected; and (f) retain a completed copy of this addendum for at least 3 years following the sale. Brokers are aware of their responsibility to ensure compliance.

F. **CERTIFICATION OF ACCURACY:** The following persons have reviewed the information above and certify, to the best of their knowledge, that the information they have provided is true and accurate.

_____   _____   _____   _____
Buyer   Date   Seller   Date

_____   _____   _____   _____
Buyer   Date   Seller   Date

_____   _____   _____   _____
Other Broker   Date   Listing Broker   Date

The form of this addendum has been approved by the Texas Real Estate Commission for use only with similarly approved or promulgated forms of contracts. Such approval relates to this contract form only. TREC forms are intended for use only by trained real estate licensees. No representation is made as to the legal validity or adequacy of any provision in any specific transactions. It is not suitable for complex transactions. Texas Real Estate Commission, P.O. Box 12188, Austin, TX 78711-2188, 1-800-250-8732 or (512) 459-6544 (http://www.trec.state.tx.us)

Form OP-L   01A

On the bright side, the EPA has been successful in curtailing other sources of lead, such as eliminating lead-based gasoline and reducing lead in drinking water supplies. Even better news is that there is strong evidence to support that the anti-lead campaign is making a difference.

The EPA reports that in 1979 there were nearly four million children with elevated blood levels. By 2002, the level had declined to only 310,000, and the level continues to decline.

B. MOLD (State Regulation)

In recent years, the issue of mold has caused a near panic in Texas in both the healthcare and homeowner's insurance fields.

1. The Issue

Essentially, molds are simple microscopic organisms that thrive in areas of high humidity, especially in homes along and near the Texas gulf coast. Molds require both a food source and moisture to survive. As a result, they can be found in areas of high humidity on many household surfaces such as walls, furniture and even clothes.

Left unchecked, molds can result in damage to a home and its furnishings, but the greater danger is probably to the health of the occupants living inside the home.

Molds have been linked to a variety of health problems such as allergic reactions and irritation, and even infections. Health symptoms include eye irritation, sneezing, coughing, headaches, fatigue and a number of respiratory problems.

2. Insurance Coverage

In the late 1990s, as news was beginning to spread about the health effects of mold, homeowners were discovering that most Texas homeowner's policies carried limited coverage for mold remediation. As a result, mold-related insurance claims exploded.

One major Texas insurance carrier noted that mold related claims grew from just 12 in 1999 to 8,000 by 2001. Industry wide, Texas mold claims by 2001 skyrocketed to nearly $800 million or approximately $25,000 per claim.

In order to stem the huge losses faced by insurance carriers, the standard Texas homeowner's policy was amended in 2001 to drop most forms of mold coverage

unless due to the sudden and accidental damage as a result of, for example, a burst pipe. Today, homeowners who desire additional protection for mold damage can still purchase such coverage by paying an additional premium.

3. Responsibilities

Having discovered a mold problem, a homeowner needs to take steps to stop the problem and, if necessary, repair any damage. See **Figure 15-8** for some helpful hints at eliminating the moisture problem. However, for a homeowner selling his/her home, several legal duties may arise.

Figure 15-8

Guard Yourself Against Mold Problems

Experts say the only way to eliminate mold problems is to remove the moisture source. If the water source isn't found and stopped, the mold problem will not go away. This can be done in several ways:

- Reduce moisture to below 60% by venting bathrooms or other areas that create and trap moisture. Use air conditioners, de-humidifiers and exhaust fans.

- Locate and stop all forms of water leaks such as from broken water hoses, drain lines, and leaking windows, tubs, sinks, or toilets. In addition, routinely inspect places that are prone to leaks like attics, under sinks and window seals so that leaks don't develop in the first place.

- Homeowners can take other precautionary measures such as making certain that downspouts carry water away from the house and that the yard has a proper slope. Also, don't block weep holes in the brickwork; they're intended to release moisture.

In high humidity areas of Texas, following these steps won't necessarily eliminate molds in the outdoor environment, but they'll go a long way to reducing the mold problem in the home.

A seller's real estate agent is under no legal duty or obligation to inspect a home for mold, or any other type of damage for that matter.

Since an agent is under no legal obligation to inspect, the licensee should not even attempt to look for problems. That is the job of a qualified home inspector. However, if the seller's agent does discover damage, he/she will be under a duty to see that all facts are disclosed to a prospective purchaser.

The situation for a homeowner is different. Under Texas law, all sellers of residential property have a duty to disclose known facts concerning the condition of the property, unless legally exempt from the disclosure requirements.

See **Figure 15-9** for a copy of the state required **Seller's Disclosure of Property Condition** form.

The failure to disclose such known conditions could expose the seller to liability after the sale. A seller's agent can face the same liability if it can be proven that the agent knew about the problem and failed to disclose it.

4. Mold Assessment and Remediation

As a result of legislation passed in 2003, all persons and businesses that conduct mold assessments and mold remediation in Texas will be required to be licensed. *MOLD ASSESSMENT means conducting an investigation or survey of a dwelling to provide the owner or occupant with information regarding the presence of mold.* **MOLD REMEDIATION** *generally means the removal, cleanup and treatment of mold or mold contaminated material.* Under the new law, no later than 10 days after the completion of a mold remediation program, a property owner is entitled to receive a Certificate of Mold Remediation.

By law, homeowners who have undergone a mold remediation program are required to provide a copy of a Certificate of Mold Remediation to any buyer.

A copy of a **Consumer Mold Information Sheet** is shown in **Figure 15-10**.

C. ASBESTOS (Federal Government)

Once considered to be a miracle substance for its durability and insulation characteristics, asbestos has become a legal nightmare for many property owners.

Asbestos is a known cause of lung cancer and a rare cancer known as mesothelioma. To make matters worse, it is still found in many homes, office buildings and factories.

Even though it is rare today to use asbestos in new building and construction materials, **Figure 15-11** shows a list of products where asbestos may still be found.

However, it's important to note that NOT all asbestos is dangerous. Asbestos is only considered dangerous when it is in a "friable" state, meaning that it releases airborne fibers that can be inhaled.

Figure 15-9

APPROVED BY THE TEXAS REAL ESTATE COMMISSION (TREC)   10-25-93

SELLER'S DISCLOSURE OF PROPERTY CONDITION

(SECTION 5.008, TEXAS PROPERTY CODE)

CONCERNING THE PROPERTY AT_____
(Street Address and City)

THIS NOTICE IS A DISCLOSURE OF SELLER'S KNOWLEDGE OF THE CONDITION OF THE PROPERTY AS OF THE DATE SIGNED BY SELLER AND IS NOT A SUBSTITUTE FOR ANY INSPECTIONS OR WARRANTIES THE PURCHASER MAY WISH TO OBTAIN. IT IS NOT A WARRANTY OF ANY KIND BY SELLER OR SELLER'S AGENTS.

Seller ☐ is ☐ is not occupying the Property. If unoccupied, how long since Seller has occupied the Property? _____

1. The Property has the items checked below [Write Yes (Y), No (N), or Unknown (U)]:

___Range	___Oven	___Microwave
___Dishwasher	___Trash Compactor	___Disposal
___Washer/Dryer Hookups	___Window Screens	___Rain Gutters
___Security System	___Fire Detection Equipment	___Intercom System
___TV Antenna	___Cable TV Wiring	___Satellite Dish
___Ceiling Fan(s)	___Attic Fan(s)	___Exhaust Fan(s)
___Central A/C	___Central Heating	___Wall/Window Air Conditioning
___Plumbing System	___Septic System	___Public Sewer System
___Patio/Decking	___Outdoor Grill	___Fences
___Pool	___Sauna	___Spa___Hot Tub
___Pool Equipment	___Pool Heater	___Automatic Lawn Sprinkler System

___Fireplace(s) & Chimney(Woodburning)	___Fireplace(s) & Chimney (Mock)	___Gas Lines (Nat./LP)
___Gas Fixtures	Garage:___Attached ___Not Attached	___Carport
Garage Door Opener(s):	___Electronic	___Control(s)
Water Heater:	___Gas	___Electric

Water Supply: ___City   ___Well   ___MUD   ___Co-op

Roof Type:_____   Age:_____(approx)

Are you (Seller) aware of any of the above items that are not in working condition, that have known defects, or that are in need of repair? ☐ Yes ☐ No ☐ Unknown. If yes, then describe. (Attach additional sheets if necessary): _____
_____
_____

2. Are you (Seller) aware of any known defects/malfunctions in any of the following? Write Yes (Y) if you are aware, write No (N) if you are not aware.

___Interior Walls	___Ceilings	___Floors
___Exterior Walls	___Doors	___Windows
___Roof	___Foundation/Slab(s)	___Basement
___Walls/Fences	___Driveways	___Sidewalks
___Plumbing/Sewers/Septics	___Electrical Systems	___Lighting Fixtures
___Other Structural Components (Describe)		

_____
_____
_____

01A   TREC No. OP-H

If the answer to any of the above is yes, explain. (Attach additional sheets if necessary): _____
_____
_____

3. Are you (Seller) aware of any of the following conditions? Write Yes (Y) if you are aware, write No (N) if you are not aware.

___Active Termites (includes wood-destroying insects)   ___Termite or Wood Rot Damage Needing Repair   ___Previous Termite Damage

___Previous Termite Treatment   ___Previous Flooding   ___Improper Drainage

___Water Penetration   ___Located in 100-Year Floodplain   ___Present Flood Insurance Coverage

___Previous Structural or Roof Repair   ___Hazardous or Toxic Waste   ___Asbestos Components

___Urea-formaldehyde Insulation   ___Radon Gas   ___Lead Based Paint
___Aluminum Wiring   ___Previous Fires   ___Unplatted Easements
___Landfill, Settling, Soil Movement, Fault Lines   ___Subsurface Structure or Pits

If the answer to any of the above is yes, explain. (Attach additional sheets if necessary): _____
_____
_____

4. Are you (Seller) aware of any item, equipment, or system in or on the Property that is in need of repair? ☐ Yes (if you are aware) ☐ No (if you are not aware). If yes, explain (attach additional sheets as necessary). _____
_____

5. Are you (Seller) aware of any of the following? Write Yes (Y) if you are aware, write No (N) if you are not aware.

___ Room additions, structural modifications, or other alterations or repairs made without necessary permits or not in compliance with building codes in effect at that time.

___ Homeowners' Association or maintenance fees or assessments.

___ Any "common area" (facilities such as pools, tennis courts, walkways, or other areas) co-owned in undivided interest with others.

___ Any notices of violations of deed restrictions or governmental ordinances affecting the condition or use of the Property.

___ Any lawsuits directly or indirectly affecting the Property.

___ Any condition on the Property which materially affects the physical health or safety of an individual.

If the answer to any of the above is yes, explain. (Attach additional sheets if necessary): _____
_____
_____

_____   _____   _____   _____
Date   Signature of Seller   Date   Signature of Seller

The undersigned purchaser hereby acknowledges receipt of the foregoing notice.

_____   _____   _____   _____
Date   Signature of Purchaser   Date   Signature of Purchaser

01A   TREC No. OP-H

Chapter 15

Figure 15-10

CONSUMER MOLD INFORMATION SHEET*
Regulation of Mold Assessment and Remediation in Texas

How are businesses that do testing for mold or mold cleanup regulated?

Such businesses are now regulated by the Department of State Health Services (DSHS), based on legislation passed in 2003 (Texas Occupations Code, Chapter 1958). Under the **Texas Mold Assessment and Remediation Rules (Rules)** (25 TAC §§295.301-295.338), all companies and individuals who perform mold-related activities will have to obtain appropriate licensing from the department by January 1, 2005. Applicants must meet certain qualifications, have required training and pass a state exam in order to receive their licenses. Mold remediation workers must have training and be registered with the department. Laboratories that analyze mold samples must also be licensed and meet certain qualifications. The rules set minimum work standards that licensees must follow and require them to follow a code of ethics. To prevent conflicts of interest, the rules also prohibit a licensee from conducting both mold assessment and mold remediation on the same project.

How can I know if someone is licensed?

A licensed individual is required to carry a photo ID issued by the department with a license number on it. The names of currently licensed companies and individuals are available on the Mold Licensing Program website at: www.tdh.state.tx.us/beh/mold.

What is "mold assessment?"

Mold assessment involves an inspection of a building to evaluate whether mold growth is present, and to what extent. Samples may be taken to determine the amount and types of mold that are present; however, sampling is not necessary in many cases. A mold assessment consultant is responsible for developing a **mold remediation protocol**, that specifies the estimated quantities and locations of materials to be remediated, the proposed methods to use and clearance criteria that must be met.

What is meant by "clearance criteria?"

Clearance criteria refer to the level of "cleanliness" that is to be achieved by the persons conducting the mold clean up. It is very important that you understand and agree with the assessor prior to starting the project what an acceptable clearance level will be, including what will be acceptable results for any air sampling or surface sampling for mold. There are no national or state standards identifying a "safe" level of mold. Mold spores are a natural part of the environment that are always present at some level in the air and on surfaces all around us. See below for more information about **post-remediation assessments**.

What is "mold remediation?"

Mold remediation is the clean up and removal of mold growth from surfaces and/or contents in a building. It also refers to actions taken to prevent mold from growing. **Mold remediators** must follow the **mold remediation protocol** described above and their own **mold remediation work plan** that provides specific instructions and/or standard operating procedures for how the project will be done.

Before a remediation project can be deemed successful, a **post-remediation assessment** must be conducted by a **mold assessment consultant**. This is an inspection to ensure that the work area is free from all visible mold and wood rot, the project was completed in compliance with the remediation protocol and remediation work plan, and meets all clearance criteria that were specified in the protocol. The assessment consultant must give you a **passed clearance report** documenting the results of this inspection. If the project fails clearance, further remediation as prescribed by a consultant will be necessary.

What is a Certificate of Mold Remediation?

No later than 10 days after a mold remediation job has passed a clearance inspection, the remediation contractor is required to give you a **Certificate of**

(continued)

Mold Remediation. This certificate must also be signed by the licensed **mold assessment consultant** who conducted the post-remediation assessment. The consultant is required to state on the certificate that the mold contamination identified for the project has been remediated and whether or not the underlying cause of the mold has been corrected. (That work may involve other types of professional services that are not regulated by these rules, such as plumbers or carpenters.) Receiving a **Certificate of Mold Remediation** documenting that the underlying cause of the mold was remediated is an advantage for a homeowner. This certificate prevents an insurer from make an underwriting decision on the residential property based on previous mold damage or a claim for mold damage. If you later sell your property, the law requires that you provide the buyer a copy of all **Certificates of Mold Remediation** you have received for that property.

How is a property owner protected if a mold assessor or remediator does a poor job or actually damages the property?

The rules require licensees to have commercial general liability insurance in the amount of $1 million, or be self-insured, to cover any damage to your property. Before hiring anyone, you should ask for proof of such insurance coverage. You may wish to inquire if the company carries additional insurance, such as professional liability/errors and omissions (for consultants) or pollution insurance (for contractors), that would provide additional recourse to you, the consumer, should the company fail to perform properly.

How is my confidentiality protected if I share personal information about myself with a company?

The code of ethics in the rules states that licensees are required to the extent required by law, to keep confidential any personal information about a client (including medical conditions) obtained during the course of a mold-related activity. If you desire more privacy, you may be able to negotiate a contract to include language that other personal information be kept confidential unless disclosure "is required by law." However, licensees are required to identify dates and addresses of projects and other details that can become public information.

How do I file a complaint about a company?

Anyone who believes a company or individual has violated the rules can file a complaint with the Department of State Health Services. For more information on this process and to obtain a complaint form, call (800) 293-0753, or download the complaint form at www.tdh.state.tx.us/beh/mold.

Can property owners do mold assessment or remediation on their own property without being licensed?

Yes. A homeowner can take samples for mold or clean up mold in his own home without a license. An owner, or a managing agent or employee of an owner of a residential property owned by that person is not required to be licensed, **unless** the property has 10 or more residential dwelling units. For non-residential properties, an owner or tenant, or a managing agent or employee of an owner or tenant, is not required to be licensed to do mold assessment or remediation on property owned or leased by the owner or tenant, **unless** the mold contamination affects a total surface area of 25 contiguous square feet or more. Please refer to 25 TAC 295.303 for further details on exceptions and exemptions to licensing requirements.

Where can I get more information?

For more information about mold and the Texas Mold Assessment and Remediation Rules, please visit the Mold Licensing Program website at www.tdh.state.tx.us/beh/mold, or contact program staff at 512-834-4509 or 800-293-0753.

****

*State law [25 TAC 295.306(c)] requires a licensee, except for a mold analysis laboratory, who is overseeing mold-related activities, to give each client a copy of this **Consumer Mold Information Sheet** before starting any mold-related activity.

Mold Licensing Program

Publication # 18-12049   Rev. 7/04

Figure 15-11

Building Products and Materials in Which Asbestos May Possibly Still Be Found

Cement Pipes
Cement Wallboard
Cement Siding
Asphalt Floor Tile
Vinyl Floor Tile
Vinyl Sheet Flooring
Flooring Backing
Construction Mastics
Acoustical Plaster
Decorative Plaster
Textured Paints/Coatings
Ceiling Tiles and Lay-in Panels
Spray-Applied Insulation
Blown-in Insulation
Fireproofing Materials
Taping Compounds (Thermal)
Packing Materials (for Wall Penetrations)
High Temperature Gaskets
Laboratory Hoods/Table Tops
Laboratory Gloves
Fire Blankets
Fire Curtains
Elevator Equipment Panels

Elevator Brake Shoes
HVAC Duct Insulation
Boiler Insulation
Breaching Insulation
Flexible Fabric Connections
Cooling Towers
Pipe Insulation
Heating and Electrical Ducts
Electrical Panel Partitions
Electrical Cloth
Electric Wiring Insulation
Chalkboards
Roofing Shingles
Roofing Felt
Base Flashing
Thermal Paper Products
Fire Doors
Caulking/Putties
Adhesives
Wallboard
Joint Compounds
Vinyl Wall Coverings
Spackling Compounds

Source: Environmental Protection Agency

In older homes, asbestos may be found in some roofing, siding, and floor tiles. Unfortunately, there's no way to tell if a product contains asbestos based on physical examination alone. It will probably have to be tested at a special lab.

If a homeowner suspects that there may be asbestos products in the home, the best practice is to simply LEAVE IT ALONE if it is intact.

There are two ways of dealing with hazardous asbestos: removal and/or encapsulation. *REMOVAL simply means removing the hazardous material using very stringent (and expensive) safety precautions. ENCAPSULATION involves leaving the asbestos in place, but treating the material with a sealant so that fibers are not released.*

Either way, the work should be done by highly qualified contractors. In Texas, asbestos remediation professionals are required to be licensed by the Texas Department of Health.

D. HAZARDOUS WASTE SITES (Federal and State)

There are a myriad of federal and state laws regarding the cleanup of toxic waste sites. Here's a very small sampling.

1. Comprehensive Environmental Response, Compensation, and Liability Act (CERCLA) (Superfund)

In response to the massive chemical contamination found at Love Canal in New York, Congress passed the **Comprehensive Environmental Response, Compensation, and Liability Act (CERCLA)** in 1980. The purpose of the law was to gather information on chemical dump sites, authorize the federal government to clean up the sites, *establish a large trust fund known as a SUPERFUND to pay for the cleanup costs,* and to make persons responsible for cleanup so that costs could be recovered. The Environmental Protection Agency is in charge of the national Superfund program and decides which contaminated properties should be placed on the National Priorities List.

Under CERCLA, not only is the party who created the contamination considered a "responsible party" for cleanup purposes, but so is the current owner or operator of a hazardous waste facility!

2. The Innocent Purchaser Defense

Of major concern to purchasers of commercial and industrial property is the possibility of being held legally responsible for cleanup costs as the result of a prior owner's contamination. Although early CERCLA law gave protection from cleanup costs to innocent property owners, a 2002 federal statute further defined and clarified the property owner's legal responsibility.

Under the *SMALL BUSINESS LIABILITY RELIEF AND BROWNFIELDS REVITALIZATION ACT, a property owner will not be liable under CERCLA for the cleanup costs associated with contaminated property provided that he/she can prove certain facts.*

These facts can be summarized as follows:

1. That the property owner did not cause the contamination;
2. That the property owner is not related, contractually or otherwise, with the party who caused the contamination; and
3. The property owner exercised "appropriate care" with respect to hazardous materials found on the property by taking steps to:

a. Stop any continuing release of hazardous waste;
b. Prevent future release; and
c. Limit toxic exposure.

The innocent purchaser must cooperate with cleanup officials, and, more significantly, the purchaser must also prove that an "appropriate inquiry" was made when the property was initially acquired.

With environmental concerns taking a greater role in property acquisitions, prospective purchasers of commercial and industrial properties are well advised to seek advice from qualified environmental contractors and lawyers before completing the purchase.

3. Texas Environmental Cleanup

The **TEXAS COMMISSION ON ENVIRONMENTAL QUALITY (TCEQ)**, *formerly the Texas Natural Resource Conservation Commission, is the state's primary environmental agency for purposes of water, soil, and air quality.* Among other duties, the TCEQ administers the state's Superfund program and maintains the State Superfund Registry of contaminated Texas properties for cleanup purposes.

By participating in the state's Voluntary Cleanup Program (BCP), a non-responsible landowner can be protected from future environmental enforcement liability by entering into an agreement with the state to clean up a contaminated site.

If successful, the program participant will receive a Certificate of Completion, which protects the landowner and all future lenders and owners from future environmental enforcement from the state of Texas resulting from the cleanup.

E. OTHER ENVIRONMENTAL ISSUES

Prospective purchasers can face a number of other environmental concerns that threaten to affect their property ownership. These concerns can range from air and water quality issues to restrictions on construction due to endangered species.

A prospective purchaser who has environmental concerns should attach to the sales contract the addendum promulgated by the Texas Real Estate Commission shown in **Figure 15-12**. Under this

Figure 15-12

10-25-93

ENVIRONMENTAL ASSESSMENT, THREATENED OR ENDANGERED SPECIES, AND WETLANDS ADDENDUM

PROMULGATED BY THE TEXAS REAL ESTATE COMMISSION (TREC)

ADDENDUM TO EARNEST MONEY CONTRACT BETWEEN THE UNDERSIGNED PARTIES CONCERNING THE PROPERTY AT _____
(Address)

☐   A.   ENVIRONMENTAL ASSESSMENT: Buyer, at Buyer's expense, may obtain an Environmental Assessment Report prepared by an environmental specialist.

☐   B.   THREATENED OR ENDANGERED SPECIES: Buyer, at Buyer's expense, may obtain a report from a natural resources professional to determine if there are any threatened or endangered species or their habitats as defined by the Texas Parks and wildlife Department or the U.S. Fish and Wildlife Service.

☐   C.   WETLANDS: Buyer, at Buyer's expense, may obtain a report from an environmental specialist to determine if there are wetlands, as defined by federal or state law or regulation.

Within _____ days after the Effective Date of the contract, Buyer may terminate the contract by furnishing Seller a copy of any report noted above that adversely affects the use of the Property and the Earnest Money shall be refunded to Buyer. If Buyer does not furnish Seller a copy of the unacceptable report within the prescribed time and give Seller notice that Buyer has terminated the contract, Buyer shall be deemed to have accepted the Property.

_____   _____
Buyer   Seller

_____   _____
Buyer   Seller

The form of this addendum has been approved by the Texas Real Estate Commission for use only with similarly approved or promulgated forms of contracts. No representation is made as to the legal validity or adequacy of any provision in any specific transactions. It is not suitable for complex transactions. (10-93) TREC No. 28-0.

01A   TREC No. 28-0

addendum, if the buyer has any concerns about endangered species, protected wetlands or any other environmental issue, he/she should conduct an investigation at the buyer's expense before purchasing the property.

VI. CHAPTER SUMMARY

Federal, local, and state governments are very much involved in the private ownership of real estate. The government holds broad police powers over private real estate ownership, as it directly regulates different types of real estate. It can control the use of property by means of **zoning**, it regulates interstate real estate transactions, and it protects property and the general public by means of environmental legislation.

The powers of government generally include: the police power, the power of eminent domain, the power of taxation, and escheat power. Under the **police power**, the government enacts laws that are designed to protect the public from fraud, misrepresentation, and deceit. The state's real estate licensing laws and local building codes are good examples of the police power. **Eminent domain**, which is usually accomplished in Texas by means of a **condemnation suit**, is the right of the government to take private property from a landowner in exchange for just compensation for the "public good."

In most condemnation lawsuits, the issue is not necessarily whether the government can take private property, but what the owner will be paid. However, there is growing concern over whether private property can be taken by cities for economic purposes.

The government also holds the broad power to **tax real estate**. Closely associated with this power is the government's right not to tax certain businesses or offer other incentives in the name of attracting businesses to poorly developed areas. Under **tax increment financing** and **impact fees**, governments can creatively finance public improvement projects without having to increase the tax rate. Finally, under **escheat** power, the government has the power to take ownership of unclaimed property.

State and local governments also have limited regulatory powers in connection with certain types of property interests. For example, Texas cities have the right to make rules and enact ordinances for creating **residential subdivisions**. This power not only affects new subdivisions within the city, but also land in a city's extraterritorial jurisdiction. Timeshare interests and condominiums are regulated under state law. **Condominiums** are defined as a form of real property ownership where a portion of the property is earmarked for private ownership and the remainder designated for common ownership. Texas law dictates how condominiums are created and in what form they should be managed. **Timeshare** interests are defined as ownership in a share of real property with the right to physically occupy the premises for a specified time each year. Under state law, prospective purchasers have the right to a comprehensive disclosure statement prior to contract execution and will have a **six-day right of rescission** even after contract signing.

Zoning is an exercise of the police power that is granted to the cities by the state.

Zoning is the right to regulate the use of land and buildings by imposing restrictions and development standards. While **deed restrictions** are an exercise of private land use restrictions, zoning is a public land use restriction. Zoning regulations should be exercised in the context of a comprehensive city plan. A comprehensive or **master plan** is a guide through which zoning establishes an ideal plan for the city's development in the future.

The zoning process works with the interaction of four groups: the affected landowner, the planning and zoning commission, the zoning board of adjustment, and the city council. Zoning issues are often initially raised by the affected landowners who have the most to gain and lose from zoning actions. The **planning and zoning commission** proposes district zoning boundaries, while the **zoning board of adjustment** rules on the zoning issues facing a particular property owner. The **city council** is the official legislative body of the city. By the same token, **conditional use permits** allow a zoning change for the good of the city, while **variances** allow a change of zoning for the benefit of an individual property owner.

The federal government regulates interstate real estate land sales in several ways. First, under the **Interstate Land Sales Full Disclosure Act**, prospective purchasers must be given a federally required property report before purchasing, and will even have a "cooling off" period after the contract is signed. Second, the sale of certain types of real estate securities, as that term has been legally interpreted, requires the seller to provide purchasers with a **written prospectus** before purchasing the real property investments. If the prospectus is not given to consumers, it forms the basis of potential contract cancellation by the purchaser.

The federal government has also taken a front-row seat with environmental legislation. Federal law requires sellers of homes built before 1978 to provide a warning statement concerning the hazards of **lead-based paint**. Lead is an extremely toxic substance for young children. In Texas, this warning is accomplished by means of a **lead-based paint addendum** that is attached to a residential sales contract. The **addendum must be used for any home built before 1978**, regardless of whether the home actually contains lead-based paint. Other common environmental issues involve **mold** and **asbestos**. Both are harmful substances, and remediation experts for both substances must be licensed by the state of Texas.

The **Environmental Protection Agency** is in charge of the national **Superfund** program created by Congress in 1980 as a result of massive contamination at **Love Canal**. Under the law, not only is the person or business that created the contamination responsible for cleanup costs, but so is any subsequent owner. Fortunately, recent legislation has further defined the **Innocent Purchaser Defense**.

The new law, however, will require subsequent purchasers to prove that they made an "appropriate inquiry" into the property prior to purchase.

In Texas, the **Texas Commission on Environmental Quality** is in charge of the state's Superfund program. Innocent landowners can avoid cleanup enforcement if they participate in the state's **Voluntary Cleanup Program**. By the same token, if purchasers of residential property have concerns regarding environmental issues, they should attach an **environmental addendum** to the sales contract so as to have adequate time to have the property tested or checked out prior to purchase.

VII. TERMINOLOGY

A. Building Code
B. Building Permit
C. Encapsulation
D. Owners' Association
E. Zoning Board of Adjustment
F. Conditional Use Permit
G. Condominium
H. Eminent Domain
I. Timeshare Interest
J. Texas Commission on Environmental Quality

K. Down Zoning
L. Tax Increment
M. Mold
N. Master Plan
O. Asbestos
P. Nonconforming Use
Q. Escheat
R. Planning Commission
S. Prospectus
T. Lead-Based Paint Addendum
U. Superfund

V. Extraterritorial Jurisdiction
W. Taxation
X. Spot Zoning
Y. Buffer Zone
Z. EPA
AA. Certificate of Occupancy
BB. Variance
CC. Zoning Laws

1. _____ A comprehensive plan to help a city grow in an orderly and sound manner.
2. _____ An insulating material now known to cause lung cancer.
3. _____ A permit given by a local government to construct a building or make improvements.
4. _____ A disclosure report given prior to the purchase of real estate related securities.
5. _____ Zoning on a parcel-by-parcel basis, rather than under a comprehensive or master plan.
6. _____ A large fund created by Congress in 1980 for purposes of hazard waste cleanup.
7. _____ The local government board that must recommend zoning districts for approval by the city council.
8. _____ The power of government to take ownership of unclaimed property.
9. _____ A form of ownership by which each investor owns a share in a specific unit along with the right to physical possession for a specified period each year.
10. _____ Tax revenue from a particular area derived solely as a result of increasing property values.
11. _____ A change of zoning requirements for a particular property owner, based upon personal hardship.
12. _____ The power of government to charge real property in order to provide for the financial needs of cities, counties, school districts, community colleges, and other districts.
13. _____ A panel of individuals who are charged with the responsibility of determining whether a particular landowner should be entitled to a variance from local zoning laws.
14. _____ An organization of unit owners formed for the purpose of managing a condominium building.

15. ____ A property that does not conform to the current zoning of the area. Typically, a property built in conformity to existing requirements before the zoning was changed.

16. ____ A form of real property ownership where units are individually owned and the balance of the property is owned in common by all the owners.

17. ____ A comprehensive set of city ordinances that control the construction and repair of buildings, including design, materials used, and construction standards.

18. ____ A Texas real estate sales contract "addendum" required to be used for the sale of residential property constructed before 1978.

19. ____ A governmental right to acquire, by condemnation, private property for public use in exchange for the payment of just compensation.

20. ____ Microscopic organisms that thrive in areas of high humidity that have been linked to a variety of health problems.

21. ____ Ordinances that allow cities to specify the uses allowable for real property in different districts or zones.

22. ____ The federal agency responsible for environmental matters such as lead remediation and the Superfund.

23. ____ A specific exception to zoning laws, granted for the general good of the community.

24. ____ A strip of land that typically separates different zoning types or intensities of use.

25. ____ A method of treating asbestos so that hazardous fibers are sealed.

26. ____ A term used to describe a zoning change from a high-density use to a lower-density use.

27. ____ The Texas agency in charge of environmental matters such as the state's Superfund program.

28. ____ The area immediately outside the city limits over which many municipalities may approve the creation of new subdivisions.

29. ____ A certificate granted by a city that indicates that a building or structure has met all building requirements and may now be occupied.

VIII. MULTIPLE CHOICE

1. The ordinance that allows a city to regulate how structures and other types of improvements may be built is generally called the:
    a. Improvements Code.
    b. Building Code.
    c. Subdivision Act.
    d. none of the above.

2. The Lead-Based Paint Addendum must be attached to each Texas real estate sales contract in connection with the sale of a home:
    a. that contains asbestos.
    b. that requires remediation from lead-based paint.
    c. built before 1978.
    d. built in 1978.

3. In Texas, timeshare properties must be registered with the:
    a. Texas Real Estate Commission.
    b. Texas Commission on Environmental Quality.
    c. Texas Department of Health.
    d. Texas Commission on Timeshare Registration.

4. The organization that determines whether a special exception to zoning may be allowed based upon "personal hardship" to the landowner is the:
    a. Variance Review Board.
    b. Zoning Board of Adjustment.
    c. Planning Commission.
    d. Special Exceptions Committee.

5. The written disclosure report that must be given in advance to prospective purchasers of real estate interests involving "securities" is called the:
    a. Property Condition Report.
    b. Prospectus.
    c. Property Report.
    d. Investment Analysis Report.

6. If a property owner is unhappy about restrictions on the legal use of his/her property, the owner will be complaining about the effects of:
    a. zoning.
    b. taxation.
    c. eminent domain.
    d. none of the above.

7. Eminent domain is accomplished by means of:
   a. Contamination proceeding.
   b. Condemnation lawsuit.
   c. Res Ipsa Loquitor action.
   d. Conditional Use Permit.

8. Using that portion of tax revenue resulting from rising property values in a particular zone to fund city improvements is called:
   a. Enterprise Zone Financing.
   b. Tax Increment Financing.
   c. Tax Abatement Financing.
   d. Impact Fee Financing.

9. The federal law that created the Superfund is:
   a. Interstate Land Disposal Act.
   b. National Priorities Act.
   c. CERCLA.
   d. TCEQ.

10. Which of the following is an improper exercise of the power of eminent domain?
   a. To build a public school
   b. To benefit private individuals
   c. To build a public stadium
   d. To build a public road

ANSWERS: 1. b; 2. c; 3. a; 4. b; 5. b; 6. a; 7. b; 8. b; 9. c; 10. b

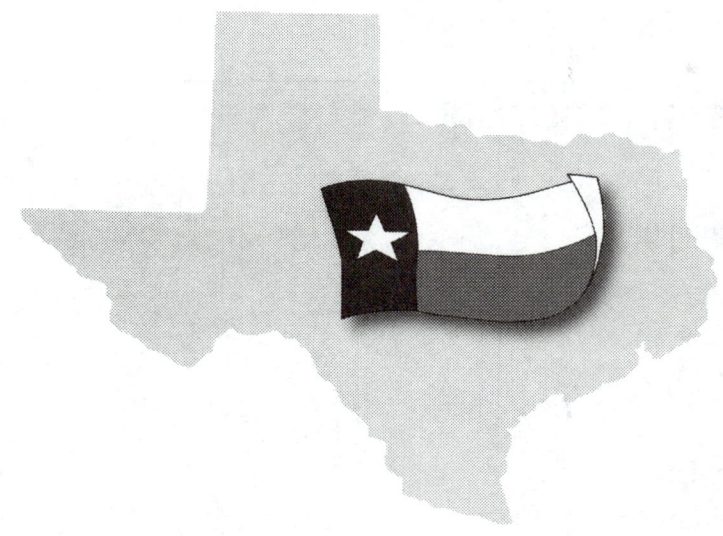

Chapter 16
Taxation of Real Estate

Taxes are an important aspect of all real estate transactions. Property owners are taxed annually on the property they own. In addition, there are other taxes that must be paid related to buying, selling or giving away real property. The amount of tax and who must pay the tax are often major factors to consider in the transfer of real estate.

I. Property Taxes

In Texas, cities, counties, and school districts, to name a few, receive most of their operating revenue from the assessment and collection of real property taxes. *REAL PROPERTY TAXES are taxes determined according to the value of the real property, and are generally paid annually.* These taxes are called ad valorem taxes. An *AD VALOREM TAX is a tax that is charged in proportion to the value of the property.* Property taxes are based on the concept that taxes should be assessed in accordance with a person's ability to pay. In the case of real estate, the higher the value of the property, the higher the property taxes.

"Ad valorem" means that property is taxed "according to value."

The Texas Constitution provides the legal framework for ad valorem taxation.

CHAPTER 16 OUTLINE

First, taxation must be equal and uniform, meaning that taxation must be fair for each type of property. Next, all real property must be taxed in proportion to its value. Each tract of land must be taxed based upon a single value. There must be a procedure to equalize or adjust value for taxpayers when appropriate. And for those who qualify, exemptions may relieve the taxpayer from payment of all or part of the tax.

In order to implement ad valorem taxation, there are various key players.

A. KEY ROLES IN AD VALOREM TAXATION

1. Appraisal Districts

By law, an appraisal district must be created within each of the state's 254 counties. The *APPRAISAL DISTRICT, sometimes referred to as CAD for COUNTY APPRAISAL DISTRICT, is responsible for appraising property located within the district for each applicable taxing unit.* Its primary function is to carry out the "one tract-one value" mandate as required by the Texas Constitution and establish **appraised value** for each tract of land as of January 1 for tax purposes. It also has secondary job of administering exemptions from taxation. The most common exemptions will be listed further below. The *CHIEF APPRAISER is the administrator of each appraisal district and oversees the day-to-day operations of the CAD.*

In addition, each appraisal district must have, by law, an Appraisal Review Board (ARB), comprised of at least three local residents. The Appraisal Review Board is an entity separate and apart from the appraisal district and serves a very important function. The *APPRAISAL REVIEW BOARD is the primary body that hears and rules on protests and challenges dealing with appraised value from both taxpayers and the taxing entities.* It may also hear arguments whether a particular exemption applies.

By May 15 of each year, the CADs are responsible for mailing a **Notice of Appraised Value** to each taxpayer. See **Figure 16-1** for a list of key dates in property taxation.

Figure 16-1

Texas Property Tax Calendar	
January 1	Values established as of January 1 for most properties. Also tax liens are imposed upon property for any taxes that may become due over the next year.
January 31	Last day to pay the previous years property taxes without penalty.
February 1	Penalties and interest begin to accrue on unpaid property taxes.
May 15	**Notice of Appraised Value** must be mailed to each taxpayer no later than this date.
May 31	Deadline for taxpayers to file valuation protests (or 30 days after Notice of Appraised Value, whichever occurs later).
May – July	**Appraisal Review Board** conducts protest hearings.
July 25	**Chief Appraiser** certifies the appraisal roll to each taxing unit.
Aug – Sept	**Taxing units** set their official tax rates.
Aug – April	CAD appraisers inspect properties and gather appraisal data.
October 1	Tax bills mailed out by Tax **Assessor-Collector**.
December 31	Last day to pay property taxes in order to claim a deduction on this year's federal income tax.

Taxpayers who choose to protest their appraised value must do so within 30 days of receiving the Notice of Appraised Value or by May 31, whichever is later. At the hearing before the ARB, the taxpayer is entitled to present evidence and cross examine witnesses. If a taxpayer is dissatisfied with the ruling of the ARB, the taxpayer may pursue the challenge into the court system.

The main job of each appraisal district is to establish a single appraised value for each tract of land located within the district and to administer tax exemptions.

2. Taxing Jurisdictions

For ad valorem tax purposes, the role of the taxing jurisdictions is to establish the official tax rate. By law, this process must begin after the ARB has heard all of its appeals and the Chief Appraiser has certified the appraisal roll which must occur no later than July 25. The tax rate is the result of a deliberative process that takes into account the budgetary and financial needs of the taxing authority combined with the size of the appraisal roll and the availability of funds from other sources, such as, for example, state sales tax revenues for cities. Once the tax rate has been decided upon, it must be officially adopted by means of an ordinance, resolution or order, depending on how the taxing authority normally passes legislative matters.

Taxing jurisdictions will vary from county to county, but they generally include the following:

1. Cities,
2. Counties,
3. School Districts,
4. Junior and Community Colleges,
5. Municipal Utility Districts,
6. Hospital Districts,
7. Road Districts,
8. Mosquito Control Districts, and
9. Emergency Services Districts.

When officially set, tax rates are usually expressed in dollars and cents, along with the phrase "per $100 valuation."

As will be seen below, this phrase is critical element when computing property taxes.

3. Tax Assessor-Collector

With the tax rate officially set, it is now the job of the local tax assessor–collector to formally assess and collect the property tax for the respective taxing jurisdictions. Tax bills must be mailed to the taxpayer by October 1 and are due upon receipt. By law, the taxpayer's failure to receive a tax bill will not affect the validity of the tax, any penalty or interest that may become due, the due date, or any tax collection procedure. Taxing authorities may allow for the payment of taxes in two equal installments, otherwise, taxes must generally be paid in one payment. Tax payments may be paid using cash, checks, money orders, and even electronic fund transfers. But if paid with a credit card, the tax assessor-collector is entitled to collect a credit card fee.

Although some taxing jurisdictions may offer a discount of up to 3% if taxes are paid right away, the taxes will be considered delinquent if not paid by February 1 of the following year.

With respect to taxes, Texas follows the "Mailbox Rule," which means that taxes will be considered timely paid so long as they are postmarked by January 31, even if they are received after the delinquency deadline.

B. TAX COLLECTIONS AND LIENS

Beginning on February 1, unpaid property taxes begin to accrue significant penalties and interest. The penalty begins at 6% of the tax due and increases to 12% by July 1. In addition to the penalty, interest is added at the rate of 1% per month, as long as the tax remains unpaid. Each taxing authority may also decide to assess an additional collection fee if the matter has to be referred to an attorney for a collection suit.

In addition, state law provides for an automatic tax lien to attach to property as of January 1 of each year in order to secure the payment of all unpaid taxes, penalties, and interest that may be incurred for the year. Tax liens take priority over most other liens, including that of a mortgage lender and can result in foreclosure proceedings against the homestead.

Significant tax penalties and interest will begin to accrue beginning February 1 on unpaid taxes. In addition, an automatic tax lien attaches against real property as of January 1 in order to secure payment of any tax, penalty or interest that may become due that year.

C. TAX SALES AND REDEMPTIONS

A property tax delinquency can result in a foreclosure of the tax lien. Under the law, a taxing unit owed taxes may apply to the state district courts for a tax warrant which directs the sheriff or constable to seize the subject property. Then following written notice to the taxpayer, the officer may sell the property in order to recover the unpaid taxes, interest, penalties and the costs of sale. Upon sale, title to the foreclosed property passes by means of a tax deed which transfers "good and perfect title" to the purchaser. The purchaser's ownership is subject only to pre-existing restrictive property covenants, easements, and the taxpayer's right of redemption.

Under the taxpayer's **STATUTORY RIGHT OF REDEMPTION**, *a taxpayer is legally permitted to purchase back property sold at tax foreclosure, so long as it is done within two years of the sale*. In order to exercise this right, the taxpayer must pay the purchaser:

1. The amount the purchaser bid for the property,

2. The amount of the deed recording fee,

3. The amount the purchaser paid for taxes, penalties, interest and costs on the property, and

4. A state required redemption premium of 25% of the entire amount owed if the property is redeemed during the first year of sale or 50% if paid during the second year.

In addition to a tax collection lawsuit, a taxpayer may face foreclosure proceedings due to unpaid taxes. However, if property is sold at a court ordered foreclosure sale, the property has up to 2 years to redeem the subject property by reimbursing the purchaser for all sums paid and paying a redemption premium of up to 50% of all sums owed.

D. PROPERTY TAX EXEMPTIONS

An **EXEMPTION** *is a legally allowed allowance that reduces appraised value so that the taxpayer pays reduced taxes or no taxes at all, depending on the type of exemption.*

Generally speaking, property of a charitable organization created for religious, charitable, scientific, literary, or educational purposes is totally exempt from the payment of property taxes.

A hallmark of these types of "total" exemptions is that they are normally granted only to organizations rather than to individuals. Individuals, on the other hand, may qualify for a number of exemptions which may result in a tax discount.

Unlike charitable organizations which can be totally exempt from the payment of property taxes, many individuals may qualify for exemptions on homestead property which result in the payment of reduced taxes.

It is important to remember that the homestead exemptions discussed below are not the same as the homestead protection discussed in Chapter 2. These are two distinct and separate issues.

Homestead exemptions, where they are allowed, result in reduced taxes against the homestead, while the homestead protection afforded under the Texas Constitution protects the family homestead from the forced sale by general creditors.

1. The Qualifying Residence

To qualify under a residential homestead exemption, the property must generally consist of a structure (including a mobile home) and land, not to exceed 20 acres, which is:

a. Designed or adapted as a human residence;

b. Used as a residence; and

c. Occupied by an owner as his/her principal residence as of January 1.

The fact that a portion of the residence is rented to another person will not cause the entire property to lose its homestead exemption status. In such cases, the owner will qualify for a partial exemption based upon his/her occupancy and use.

If a homeowner temporarily moves out of his/her residence, the owner may still qualify for the entire exemption so long as the owner's absence is for less than 2 years and the owner intends to return to the residence. However, once the owner establishes a different principal residence, he/she may no longer claim the original residence for homestead exemptions purposes. In no event may a person claim two homestead residences at the same time.

2. The General Homestead Exemption

By law, school districts must grant homeowners a $15,000 general homestead exemption. This exemption applies only for school district taxes. However, see **Figure 16-2** for a special note on Texas school district financing.

But any taxing unit, assuming the taxing unit votes to offer it, may grant a general exemption of no less than $5,000 nor more than 20% of the property's value. For example, assuming that a city votes to offer the general exemption at the full 20% limit, if a property is appraised at $100,000 for tax purposes, the homeowner would be able to deduct 20% or $20,000 from the appraised value before computing the tax.

Don't assume that every taxing unit offers this general exemption. Check your own taxing jurisdiction to see if it is offered and, if so, the extent of the exemption.

3. The "65 and Over" Exemption

In addition to the $15,000 general homestead exemption offered by school districts, persons age 65 and over can qualify for an additional exemption of $10,000. As a result, a homeowner aged 65 or older, living in his/her own home may deduct $25,000 from appraised value before calculating school district taxes.

And like the optional general exemption described above, any taxing unit may vote to grant a 65 and over exemption. If allowed, the amount of the exemption must be at least $3,000.

But Texas seniors are also entitled to other tax advantages, as described below.

Figure 16-2

A Special Note About School District Financing in Texas

After several failed attempts, the Texas Legislature in 2006 finally tackled the thorny problem of providing for fair public school financing. The problem is due in large part to the fact that school districts depend a great deal on local property taxes. As a result, the school districts in the wealthier parts of the state tend to raise more tax dollars than districts in the not-so-wealthy parts of the state. This results in an inherent imbalance in the way that school districts are funded.

One attempt to address this funding imbalance, the so-called **Robin Hood Plan**, was declared unconstitutional by the Texas Supreme Court in 2005 and the state was ordered to come up with a new plan. Following heated political battles which resulted in several failed legislative sessions, state lawmakers finally came up with a compromise solution in May, 2006. This legislative "fix" consists of the following major elements:

Taxpayer relief in the form of a 30% reduction in local school district property taxes to be phased in over 2 years (other property taxes remain unaffected);

- A $2,000 across the board pay raise for teachers;

- Increased business taxes;

- Increased cigarette taxes; and

- Increased taxes on the sale of used cars.

a. Tax Ceiling

When Texas residents turn 65, they are entitled by law to a cap on school district taxes for so long as they live in their home. **This means that school district taxes will never exceed the ceiling set in the year the taxpayer turns 65, no matter how much the taxes increase**.

The ceiling can be adjusted for improvements added to a house. For example, suppose a 70-year-old homeowner decides to add a swimming pool to his/her home. In such a case, the tax ceiling will be adjusted the following year by the value of the improvements added.

b. "Portability" of Ceiling

Suppose that the same 70-year-old homeowner decides to sell his Houston residence and move to Dallas. Is the school district tax ceiling lost? Fortunately, Texas law states no.

State law allows the homeowner to take the tax savings he enjoys to another homestead residence in the same proportion as is enjoyed in the original home. So if the homeowner enjoyed a 30% tax savings in the Houston home because of the tax freeze, the homeowner can enjoy the same 30% savings in the Dallas home. In order to "prove" the tax savings to the new appraisal district, the homeowner need only request a certificate from the Chief Appraiser of the old appraisal district showing the tax savings.

c. Surviving Spouse

Upon death, the school district tax freeze enjoyed by a Texas senior can pass to that that person's surviving spouse so long as the surviving spouse is 55 years of age or older and the spouse continues living in the homestead residence. The tax freeze will continue until such time as the surviving spouse dies or moves out of the residence.

In 2003, the Texas voters approved expanding the 65 and over tax ceiling to taxes imposed by counties, municipalities, and junior colleges, provided, however, that the individual taxing units vote to do so. Since that time, many, but not all, of the affected taxing units, have voted to expand the freeze.

d. Deferral

Texans 65 and over have another tax advantage not available to the general public. They may be able to legally defer tax collection proceedings, including tax foreclosures of the homestead property, due to unpaid property taxes. In order to claim the deferral, the taxpayer need only file an affidavit with the Chief Appraiser, setting forth the relevant age facts. Thereafter, the affected taxing units may not institute collection or foreclosure procedures until 6 months after the person no longer owns the residence.

It's important to remember that the taxes are not eliminated. The tax due, penalties, interest, and even the tax lien will continue during the deferral period.

e. Installment Payments

As mentioned briefly above, certain taxing authorities may allow any taxpayer to pay in two equal installments. However, if the taxpayer is 65 and over and taxes are not delinquent, the taxpayer must be allowed to pay homestead taxes in four installments. Under the law, the installments must be made according to the following schedule:

Payment 1 before February 1,
Payment 2 before April 1,
Payment 3 before June 1, and
Payment 4 before August 1.

If the taxpayer misses an installment, the taxes are considered delinquent and additional penalties and interest will accrue.

f. Work for Taxes

Lastly, a person 65 years of age or older may pay off property taxes in an unusual way. He or she may work off the taxes by providing a service to the taxing unit in lieu of payment. In order to utilize this seldom used law, the taxing unit must execute a contract with the senior before the taxes become delinquent specifying, among other things, the exact nature of the work to be performed, when and where the work will be performed, and the hours of work. Homeowners will then receive credit at the federal minimum hourly wage rate.

So long as the resident is performing satisfactorily, his/her taxes will not become delinquent. But the resident should understand that by working for the taxing unit, the taxpayer does not become an employee of the unit, nor does the resident enjoy any of the normal benefits of employment.

4. Exemptions for Disabled Persons

Disabled residents of any age may qualify for generally any exemption offered to persons age 65 or older with one very important exception: **a person may not qualify for both 65 and over AND a disabled person's exemption**. It must be one or the other.

To be considered disabled, a person must present proof that he/she is receiving disability insurance benefits under Federal Old Age, Survivors and Disability Insurance.

Although many believe that persons 65 and over who are disabled should enjoy the benefits of dual tax exemptions, Texas law is quite clear. The taxpayer either enjoys 65 and over exemption or disabled exemption, but not both.

5. Veterans with Disabilities

A disabled armed forces veteran, or the surviving spouse (along with each unmarried child under the age of 18) of a veteran who dies while on active duty, is also entitled to a special property tax exemption. The exemption can be as high as $12,000, depending on a disability rating of at least 10% as determined by the VA.

But unlike most homestead exemptions which apply only to the taxpayer's residence, disabled veteran's exemptions may apply to any property the taxpayer owns, so long as the veteran designates the property to which the exemption applies.

In order to receive any of the above described exemptions, a taxpayer must apply through the appraisal district office and complete the required application form. By law, the Chief Appraiser must rule on each application.

E. SPECIAL AGRICULTURAL VALUATION ISSUES

For tax purposes, agricultural property in Texas is appraised in a different manner than most other types of real estate. This difference in valuation method is not by accident. Instead, this difference is the result of a deliberate political and economic process memorialized in the Texas Constitution and designed to benefit farm and ranch production. As a result, this method of valuation (often erroneously referred to as an "Ag Exemption"), which is based upon the lands productivity, will result in considerably lower property taxes than, for example, a comparably sized tract of residential property.

Failing to understand the full effects of agricultural valuation methods can have a significant impact on the purchaser of farm and ranch property in Texas.

There are two types of farm and ranch property valuation: **Ag-Use Appraisal** and **Open Space Appraisal**. Both types will use an agriculturally based method of property valuation for tax purposes, but the real difference lies in who may qualify for this special valuation. **Figure 16-3** summarizes the differences between the two methods of valuation.

Interestingly, the tax savings generated by these two methods of valuation are not limited to the remote portions of the state.

Suppose for example, that a major Texas corporation owns a large tract of land adjacent to its corporate headquarters. The company could save a substantial sum on annual

Figure 16-3

Ag-Use Appraisal	Open Space Appraisal
To qualify for this type of property appraisal, the owner's occupation and primary source of income must be from agriculture, for example, as a farmer. The land must actually be used to produce plant or animal products (including fish or poultry products).	Under this method of appraisal, the owner's occupation is not important, rather, the property must qualify. Here, the land must have been devoted to one of several categories of agricultural use (such as crops, livestock, floriculture, horticulture) or production of timber or forest products for 5 of the past 7 years.

taxes by bringing onto its property a herd of grazing longhorn cattle exactly as a large company has done in suburban Dallas. In this case, since this Fortune 500 company is not involved in farming or ranching as its primary source of income, it can only qualify under Open Space Appraisal provided the property meets the agricultural use requirements under the law.

But agriculturally valued property holds a serious drawback for purchasers of farm and ranch property.

Under the law, if the purchaser of such property changes the use of the property a new and instant tax ("rollback tax") is imposed to recapture the difference for what has been paid and what should have been paid for up to the previous five years. For the purchaser, this unexpected cost can be substantial.

This rollback tax is secured by a tax lien, which is immediately imposed against the property in order to assure the payment of the tax.

Under the promulgated contract forms, rollback taxes are typically the responsibility of the party whose actions caused the rollback to take effect in the first place. Thus, if a developer purchases a large tract of land for purposes of building a housing subdivision from a farmer who held the property under an agricultural valuation, the developer had better be prepared to also pay the rollback tax associated with the changed use. On the positive side, however, the developer can recover the tax paid when he/she sells the lots to new homebuyers.

A buyer, knowledgeable of potential rollback consequences, can hopefully better prepare for this expense by taking this tax into account when negotiating for the property. As the old saying goes, "a well informed buyer is also a happy buyer."

F. COMPUTING THE PROPERTY TAX

Solve the following property tax problem.

Problem:

A property owner owns a house subject to city taxes. The property is currently appraised by the appraisal district for $280,000 and the homeowner qualifies for a homestead exemption based on 15% of the appraised value.

Assuming that the city passes a tax rate of 0.925 per hundred dollar valuation, how much will the homeowner pay in city taxes this year?

Solution:

The first step is to determine the amount of the exemption. Here, the exemption is 15% of $280,000 or $42,000. That means that the house will be taxed only on $238,000 of value. This is known as the taxable value.

Next, before we compute the tax, it's necessary to do a minor calculation. Since the tax is assessed on a "per $100 valuation" basis, it is necessary to **divide** the taxable value by 100. The answer is $2,380. By the same token, if the tax rate had been expressed in "per $1,000 valuation," we would have divided by 1,000.

The last step is to multiply $2,380 by the tax rate of 0.925 which yields a tax due of $2,201.50.

Bonus Question:

Assuming the local tax assessor-collector mailed out the tax bill on October 15 of this year, on what day will the unpaid taxes become delinquent?

Answer:

February 1 of the following year.

For practice problems dealing with tax prorations, please see Chapter 17.

II. Gift and Estate Taxes

For federal purposes, the transfer of property by a gift or inheritance is taxed. Exemptions may reduce the taxes and sometimes eliminate them. **Figure 16-4** illustrates the federal taxes encountered by transferring property as a gift or by inheritance.

Figure 16-4

Property Given Away

✔ **WHILE LIVING**   ✔ **AFTER DEATH**

Federal Gift Tax   **Federal Estate Taxes**

A gift of real estate may avoid federal estate taxes. So if a person wants to give a property away, it will most likely escape (the future) federal estate taxes. But, if you are to avoid federal gift taxes, usually only a fractional interest worth up to $11,000 in the property should be given away each year. For example, you could give a son and daughter each a 1/30 interest in your home every year for 15 years to give the house to your children.

A. FEDERAL GIFT TAXES

Estate taxes and income taxes on appreciated property may be avoided by giving it away or by donating it to a non-profit organization. See a CPA or tax expert for advice.

Frequently, as an individual family matures, the value of the real property owned by the family increases, and the owning family may consider bestowing it as a gift. When a family gives property, whether real or personal, to another individual, there may be federal gift taxes that must be paid. If the value of the property is higher than an exempt amount, the donor must pay a gift tax. A *DONOR is the person or persons giving the property as a gift.* Generally, people give their property away to relatives on a systematic basis so that taxes are avoided. The *DONEE is the person or persons who receive the property as a gift.* The federal gift tax law also provides for a $11,000 annual exemption per donee.

B. FEDERAL ESTATE TAX

A federal estate tax return must be filed for the estate of every resident of the United States whose gross estate exceeds $1,000,000 ($1,500,000 in 2004, $2,000,000 in 2006) in value at the date of death. Estate tax exemptions will gradually increase the size of

estates that are exempt from $1,000,000 to being repealed in 2010. However, the estate tax can be restored in 2011.

C. TEXAS INHERITANCE TAX

Texas law requires that a state inheritance tax return be filed for the estate of every Texas decedent (the deceased person) whose date of death was on or after September 1, 1983, if:

1. a Federal Estate Tax return (IRS Form 706) must be filed; and
2. the decedent was at the time of death a Texas resident, a non-resident with property taxable in Texas, or an alien with property taxable in Texas.

Generally speaking, the Texas inheritance tax due on property transfers at death is computed based on a percentage of the federal tax credit. This tax is collected by the State Comptroller of Public Accounts. See your tax professional for additional advice.

III. Federal Income Taxes

The annual Federal Income Tax Form 1040 (see **Figure 16-5**) is a bookkeeping or accounting summary of the prior year's financial facts. These facts are a history and cannot be altered at the time of filing the income tax return.

www.irs.ustreas.gov
Internal Revenue Service (IRS)

Tax matters should be considered prior to buying and continued during ownership until the estate's ultimate disposition.

We will discuss only the most basic concepts of reducing the income tax bite for the average citizen. A basic knowledge of the requirements necessary to take advantage of federal income tax incentives is helpful. Arranging the purchase of real estate in a manner that reduces your personal income taxes is the purpose of tax planning. This may allow you to reduce the income taxes you pay, or at least postpone such taxes.

Tax shelters are the reduction in income taxes. Now is the time to start tax planning for your future income tax return.

Figure 16-6 shows the five main areas of the federal income tax laws that are incentives to owning real estate. Each area will be explained only to give the general concepts or ideas behind the laws. To obtain the exact meaning and clauses of the law, an owner or investor

Figure 16-5

Form **1040** Department of the Treasury—Internal Revenue Service
U.S. Individual Income Tax Return 20XX (99) IRS Use Only—Do not write or staple in this space.

For the year Jan. 1–Dec. 31, 20XX, or other tax year beginning , 20XX, ending , 20XX | OMB No. 1545-0074

Label
(See instructions on page 16.)
Use the IRS label. Otherwise, please print or type.

L A B E L H E R E

Your first name and initial | Last name | Your social security number

If a joint return, spouse's first name and initial | Last name | Spouse's social security number

Home address (number and street). If you have a P.O. box, see page 16. | Apt. no. | ▲ You must enter your SSN(s) above. ▲

City, town or post office, state, and ZIP code. If you have a foreign address, see page 16. | Checking a box below will not change your tax or refund.

Presidential Election Campaign ► Check here if you, or your spouse if filing jointly, want $3 to go to this fund (see page 16) ► ☐ You ☐ Spouse

Filing Status
Check only one box.

1 ☐ Single
2 ☐ Married filing jointly (even if only one had income)
3 ☐ Married filing separately. Enter spouse's SSN above and full name here. ►
4 ☐ Head of household (with qualifying person). (See page 17.) If the qualifying person is a child but not your dependent, enter this child's name here. ►
5 ☐ Qualifying widow(er) with dependent child (see page 17)

Exemptions

6a ☐ **Yourself.** If someone can claim you as a dependent, do not check box 6a . . . . ✓
b ☐ **Spouse** . . . .
c **Dependents:**

(1) First name Last name	(2) Dependent's social security number	(3) Dependent's relationship to you	(4) ✓ if qualifying child for child tax credit (see page 19)
			☐
			☐
			☐
			☐

If more than four dependents, see page 19.

d Total number of exemptions claimed . . . .

Boxes checked on 6a and 6b
No. of children on 6c who:
• lived with you
• did not live with you due to divorce or separation (see page 20)
Dependents on 6c not entered above
Add numbers on lines above ► ☐

Income

Attach Form(s) W-2 here. Also attach Forms W-2G and 1099-R if tax was withheld.

If you did not get a W-2, see page 22.

Enclose, but do not attach, any payment. Also, please use Form 1040-V.

7 Wages, salaries, tips, etc. Attach Form(s) W-2 . . . . | 7 |
8a **Taxable interest.** Attach Schedule B if required . . . . | 8a |
b Tax-exempt interest. **Do not** include on line 8a . . . | 8b |
9a Ordinary dividends. Attach Schedule B if required . . . . | 9a |
b Qualified dividends (see page 23) . . . . . | 9b |
10 Taxable refunds, credits, or offsets of state and local income taxes (see page 23) . . | 10 |
11 Alimony received . . . . | 11 |
12 Business income or (loss). Attach Schedule C or C-EZ . . . . . . | 12 |
13 Capital gain or (loss). Attach Schedule D if required. If not required, check here ► ☐ | 13 |
14 Other gains or (losses). Attach Form 4797 . . . . | 14 |
15a IRA distributions . | 15a | b Taxable amount (see page 25) | 15b |
16a Pensions and annuities | 16a | b Taxable amount (see page 25) | 16b |
17 Rental real estate, royalties, partnerships, S corporations, trusts, etc. Attach Schedule E | 17 |
18 Farm income or (loss). Attach Schedule F . . . . | 18 |
19 Unemployment compensation . . . . | 19 |
20a Social security benefits . | 20a | b Taxable amount (see page 27) | 20b |
21 Other income. List type and amount (see page 29) . . . . | 21 |
22 Add the amounts in the far right column for lines 7 through 21. This is your **total income** ► | 22 |

Adjusted Gross Income

23 Educator expenses (see page 29) . . . . . . | 23 |
24 Certain business expenses of reservists, performing artists, and fee-basis government officials. Attach Form 2106 or 2106-EZ | 24 |
25 Health savings account deduction. Attach Form 8889 . . | 25 |
26 Moving expenses. Attach Form 3903 . . . . . . | 26 |
27 One-half of self-employment tax. Attach Schedule SE . . | 27 |
28 Self-employed SEP, SIMPLE, and qualified plans . . | 28 |
29 Self-employed health insurance deduction (see page 30) . | 29 |
30 Penalty on early withdrawal of savings . . . . . . | 30 |
31a Alimony paid b Recipient's SSN ► | 31a |
32 IRA deduction (see page 31) . . . . | 32 |
33 Student loan interest deduction (see page 33) . . . . | 33 |
34 Tuition and fees deduction (see page 34) . . . . | 34 |
35 Domestic production activities deduction. Attach Form 8903 | 35 |
36 Add lines 23 through 31a and 32 through 35 . . . . | 36 |
37 Subtract line 36 from line 22. This is your **adjusted gross income** . . . . . ► | 37 |

For Disclosure, Privacy Act, and Paperwork Reduction Act Notice, see page 78. | Cat. No. 11320B | Form **1040** (2005)

Figure 16-6

Basic Income Tax Incentives
For Real Estate Owners

✔ **INTEREST DEDUCTION**   ✔ **EXCHANGES**

✔ **SALE OF YOUR RESIDENCE**   ✔ **INSTALLMENT SALES**

✔ **DEPRECIATION**

should seek the help of a Certified Public Accountant for advice on the accounting, or an attorney who is familiar with tax problems. Remember, these are only generalizations, and our income tax laws are more complex than the basic concepts presented here.

IV. Taxes on Personal Residence

Homeowners can annually deduct these three items from their income taxes based on their personal residence:

1. Mortgage Interest on Loans
2. Property Taxes
3. Prepayment Penalties

By the way, you cannot deduct the cost of personal residence repairs from your federal taxes, except for **uninsured casualty losses**. For example, if your roof blows off and you have no insurance to cover it, the replacement cost can be deducted from your federal income taxes.

A. DEDUCTION OF INTEREST

Deduction of interest on your home loan from your income taxes is one of the major tax advantages of owning real estate. Buying a first and second home provides the average family with the biggest buffer against income taxes that it is likely to enjoy. Despite recent income tax reforms, the federal tax laws still provide incentives to those who purchase a first and even a second home. When buying these homes you may finance up to $1 million ($1,000,000) with all the interest paid out during the year fully tax deductible. An additional deduction is available on the interest from home equity loans, taken for any purpose, even buying a second home, of up to $100,000 in principal. The $1,000,000 and $100,000 debit limit is a total applied against both first and second homes together or one owner-occupied home taken separately.

B. DEDUCTION OF PROPERTY TAXES

Property taxes on your 1st and 2nd homes are deductible from your income taxes. This makes us feel better about paying local property taxes.

C. DEDUCTION OF PREPAYMENT PENALTIES

Prepayment penalties are also deductible from your income taxes. If you pay off or drastically reduce your home loan balance, there may be a prepayment penalty.

Interest, property taxes, and prepayment penalties paid on your personal residence can be deducted from your income taxes.

D. SALE OF YOUR RESIDENCE

When selling a personal residence, the seller can deduct up to $250,000 ($500,000 if married) of any capital gain. This could be used only once every two years.

Federal income tax laws allow a taxpayer to exclude up to $250,000 of gain for each individual ($500,000 if married and on the title). This benefit may only be used once every two years for a residence.

While the law allows this deduction once every two years, you must reside in the home for two out of the last five years to qualify. In other words, if you live in the home for a year, then rent it out for three years, you would have to move back in for another year in order to take advantage of this tax break.

You can deduct a loss on sale of a personal residence if you have turned it into income producing property by renting it.

The only way to deduct a loss on a personal residence is to turn that property into income-producing property first by renting it. Then any loss based on its sale is deductible because it is income-producing property, not a personal residence.

V. Taxes for Income Producing Properties

Investors of income-producing properties can annually deduct these items from their income taxes:

1. Mortgage Interest on Loans (no maximum)
2. Property Taxes
3. Prepayment Penalties

In addition they can deduct:

4. Operating Expenses
5. Depreciation of Improvements

In addition to deducting mortgage interest (no maximum), property taxes, and prepayment penalties, income property owners can deduct operating expenses and depreciation. Owners CANNOT deduct losses due to vacancies.

A. DEPRECIATION OF BUSINESS PROPERTY

DEPRECIATION FOR TAX PURPOSES is a yearly tax deduction for wear and tear on investment property that is deducted from the taxpayer's income on his or her income tax form. This deduction applies only to investment property or property used in a business, not on a taxpayer's personal residence. Apartment buildings, commercial buildings, and any building improvements to investment property can be depreciated. The land itself cannot be depreciated.

Only the buildings and other improvements on income, trade, or business property can be depreciated, NOT the land.

One can only depreciate property that is improved. Since land cannot be depreciated, only the improvements can be depreciated. Currently, the straight-line method is the accepted way to depreciate buildings and other improvements.

Residential (homes and apartments) property depreciation schedule: Minimum 27.5 years (Straight-line)

Commercial improvements depreciation schedule: Minimum 39 years (Straight-line).

The amount of depreciation must be spread uniformly over the useful life of the property, with the same amount deducted each year (straight-line depreciation). Since most buildings in these inflationary times actually increase in value, depreciation is usually just a technique for postponing income taxes until the property is sold.

Example: If you own a cabin in the desert that you rent to vacationers and the cabin cost $100,000 and the land value is $25,000, this leaves improvements of $75,000. Divide this $75,000 by 30 years, giving you a depreciation of $2,500 for each year of the 30 years. If we had used a 27.5 year formula, the yearly depreciation amount would be slightly higher.

Remember: A property owner can deduct depreciation on income, trade, or business real property, NOT on a residence.

B. ADVANTAGES OF "SALE-LEASEBACK" (Buyer Gets to Depreciate New Building Cost)

If the owner of a business sells his/her building for cash, and then leases it back, the seller becomes a lessee and the buyer the lessor.

The advantage to the seller: all lease payments can be deducted from income taxes and he or she receives cash for the building.

The advantage to the buyer: he or she can use the purchase price as the new basis for depreciation and establish a new depreciation schedule.

The seller (now the renter) deducts 100% of future rents paid. The buyer can depreciate the new cost of buildings (even if they have been depreciated previously).

VI. Sale of Real Property

A. CAPITAL ASSETS (Gains and Losses)

In real estate a capital asset includes your personal residence (including your second home) and any other real estate because they are long-term investments. When you sell your home or other real estate, there is usually a capital gain or loss. *CAPITAL GAINS are taxed at a lower rate than is ordinary income*, but *CAPITAL LOSSES can be deducted from capital gains*. A capital gain is taxed at a lower rate than is ordinary income. It is in the public interest to foster investment in land and buildings and other long-term assets so that businesses are encouraged to expand. This, in turn, creates more job opportunities for everyone.

The four capital gains tax rates as follows:

   20% maximum capital gains tax rate if held for more than 18 months
   15% maximum capital gains tax rate if held for more than 7 years
   10% capital gains tax rate if net income is less than $50,000
   5% capital gains tax rate (over 7 years) if net income is less than $50,000

Gains are taxed at the lower capital gains tax rates (lower than ordinary income tax rates).

There should be a tax benefit to encourage entrepreneurs to risk investing long-term in things such as equipment, stocks, bonds, and real estate in order to obtain capital gains or losses. Other countries, like Japan and Germany, have very low capital gain tax rates which encourage investment in companies so that more career opportunities are generated for their employees. The size of the nation's "economic pie," which everyone enjoys, increases.

B. FEDERAL INCOME TAX RATES

As the old saying goes, "Nothing in life is certain, except death and taxes." One other certainty is the constant change in federal tax rates. Income tax rates are progressive.

PROGRESSIVE TAXES are taxes where the rates (percentage paid) increase as the amount to be taxed increases. So as you make more money, not only does the amount increase, but the rate at which income is taxed also increases. The end effect is that higher income families (the exact ones who usually own businesses and can expand job opportunities) pay most of the income taxes.

MARGINAL TAX RATE is the rate that the next dollar earned puts you into.

REGRESSIVE TAXES use the same rate no matter how much is spent or earned. Sales tax is an example of a regressive tax. The rate is the same, so in effect, the poor pay a higher percent of their income.

Income tax rates are progressive. Sales taxes are regressive.

C. ACCOUNTING FOR THE SALE OF REAL ESTATE

The method of determining a profit or loss on the sale of real property is spelled out by the Internal Revenue Service. Steps 1 and 2 must be completed before determining the profit or loss on a sale (Step 3).

Step (1) Cost Basis (Purchase price)	$500,000
+ Improvements	200,000
= Subtotal	$700,000
- Depreciation (tax records)	$30,200
= Adjusted Cost Basis	$669,800
Step (2) Sale price	$1,000,000
- Sale Expenses	32,500
= Adjusted Sale Price	$967,500
Step (3) Adjusted Sale Price	$967,500
- Adjusted Cost Basis	$669,800
= Gain	**$297,700**

"Adjusted cost basis" is the base cost, plus capital improvements, minus depreciation and sale expenses. A broker's commission is an expense of the sale.

VII. Installment Sales and Exchanges

A. INSTALLMENT SALES OF REAL ESTATE

An *INSTALLMENT SALE is the sale of real estate in which the payments for the property extend over more than one calendar year*. Installment sales are used to spread a gain over two or more calendar years so that the entire gain is not taxed all in the first year. Our income tax system has progressive rates, which means that the higher the income, the higher the income tax rate for that year. If a person can spread a gain over more than one calendar year, the same income may be taxed at a lower rate.

By doing this the seller avoids the disadvantages of paying for his or her entire gain in one year and thereby has a substantial savings on his or her income taxes. This method is usually used when selling large tracts of land held for a period of time or large buildings owned by one individual.

Installment sales are used because a gain is only taxed in the year that it is received. Spreading the gain over several years may drop you into a lower tax bracket (marginal tax rate).

A sale of a large lot for $100,000 all at once might force you into a higher tax bracket. So, by having an installment sale of $25,000 for each of the next four years, you may substantially reduce the total income taxes paid. An installment sale may be a good way to defer income taxes if your income varies from year to year; just arrange to get larger installment payments in years when your ordinary income is low.

B. EXCHANGES TAX-DEFERRED (Federal and State) (Section 1031 of the I.R.S. Code)

In an exchange, the adjusted cost basis of the old property becomes the basis of the new property.

An *EXCHANGE is a transfer of real estate where one party trades property for another's property*. The property must be of "like kind" in nature or character, not in use, quality, or grade. The exchange may be a straight trade (tax-free) or one party may receive cash in addition to the property (partially tax-free). An exchange can be income tax free, partially taxed, or fully taxed, depending on the cost factors in each particular exchange. Exchanges are too detailed to explain here, but it is a way of deferring or possibly eliminating income taxes on the transfer of real estate.

To defer all current taxes, a party in an exchange would need to receive a more valuable building with a larger loan on it than the current property and pay compensation to the other party for any difference in the equities. *Any net cash or net mortgage relief that a participant in an exchange might receive in addition to the actual property is known as BOOT.* All boot is taxable to the extent of the gain in this partially tax-free exchange (see **Figure 16-7**).

Figure 16-7

Tax-Deferred Exchanges

In a "tax-deferred" exchange, boot is defined as cash or mortgage relief given in addition to the property. Boot is the amount received to balance the equities in the exchange. Brokers often encounter the term "boot" when talking with a client about income taxes.

The person receiving boot has a net gain and has to pay taxes on it. When no boot is given or received, then the basis remains the same.

In a tax free exchange, properties must be of a "like kind" in nature or character, not in use, quality or grade. "Tax free" merely means to DEFER the payment of taxes until a later time. Since you can move your equity to another property, it is almost like buying and selling without paying income taxes.

The actual techniques used to understand exchanging are too complex to be explained here, but many six-hour seminars and exchange clubs are available to interested people.

Exchanges are based on "equity value." Equity is market value minus liens.

"Boot" is cash or debt relief. The receiver has recognized gain. If there is NO boot in an exchange, the old basis is the new basis.

Exchanges are popular among apartment owners and commercial property investors. This is because these owners are usually in a high-income tax bracket, and exchanging enables them to move up to a more valuable property without paying taxes on the gain. People in higher income tax brackets usually keep their money invested in real estate, and they find exchanges to be a way of selling and buying simultaneously.

VIII. We Are Now Tax Collectors (Federal Income Tax Laws— Escrow Usually Takes Care of This)

A. FEDERAL TAX COLLECTION REQUIREMENTS AND EXEMPTIONS (If a Foreigner)

Persons buying property from foreign investors (sellers) are required to set aside 10% of the purchase price for the Internal Revenue Service. This 10% withholding is kept by the IRS to ensure that property capital gains taxes are paid on the transaction. Both the buyer and broker share liability. If this amount is not withheld, the broker may be liable for the full amount of the tax not paid.

In effect, this law holds brokers responsible to check the citizenship of all sellers and see to it that the buyer retains either a 10% deposit, an affidavit from the seller stating that he or she is not a foreigner, or a waiver from the IRS. Residential property purchased for under $300,000 to be used as the buyer's residence is exempted from this withholding. The key points for licensees to remember are these:

1. **Inquire** into the citizenship of all sellers of residential or commercial properties priced at $300,000 or more, even if a foreigner holds only partial or syndicate interest.

2. **Require** a statement of citizenship as part of the listing agreement and then follow up in escrow by having the seller or sellers sign a sworn affidavit.

3. **Do not discriminate.** Require this information of all sellers in transactions of $300,000 or more. Even if someone does not appear to be an alien, they might hold foreign citizenship.

This law puts the burden on the buyer, NOT the seller. In Texas escrow officers will help with this withholding requirement. In any event, buyer and broker must retain the documentation for 5 years.

IX. CHAPTER SUMMARY

Real property taxes are determined by the value of the real property (**ad valorem**) and represent the primary way that that cities, counties, and school districts receive their revenue. The Texas Constitution provides some safeguards for assessing property taxes: they must be equal and uniform, real property must be taxed in proportion to its value, there must be a way to adjust values for taxpayers when appropriate, and exemptions may be possible for those who qualify.

There are three key roles in ad valorem taxation. The **Appraisal District** establishes the value of each tract of land located with the district as of January 1 of each year. The district is headed by a **Chief Appraiser** who oversees the day-to-day operations of the district or CAD as it is sometimes called. The Chief Appraiser also rules on exemption applications that are submitted to the district. In addition, an **Appraisal Review Board (ARB)**, comprised of at least three district citizens is established to hear valuation protests from residents as well as challenges from the various taxing units. If a resident is unhappy with a ruling received from the ARB, he/she may appeal the decision to the courts.

For property tax purposes, the various taxing units, such as cities, counties, school districts, and junior and community colleges, have the responsibility of setting the **official tax rate**. This process begins shortly after the Chief Appraiser has certified the tax roll and takes into account the budgetary requirements of each taxing unit, the size of the tax base as well as other sources of income. Tax rates in Texas are expressed in dollars and cents and are usually assessed **"per hundred dollar valuation."**

The Tax **Assessor-Collector** has the job of formally assessing and collecting the tax from residents. In Texas, tax bills are typically mailed out by October 1 and are due upon receipt. Some, but not all tax collectors, offer discounts for early payment, otherwise all taxes will be due no later than January 31 of the following year.

Taxes unpaid as of February 1 are considered to be **delinquent** and begin to accrue penalties and interest until paid. Property is also subject to a **tax lien**, which takes priority over most mortgage liens. A taxpayer with unpaid taxes may face a collection lawsuit or even a foreclosure sale. If the property is sold at a foreclosure sale, the taxpayer may still redeem the subject property under a **statutory right of redemption** for up to **two years after the sale**. To redeem the property, the purchaser will be required to reimburse the purchaser for the bid price paid and all taxes, penalties, and interest paid, as well as to pay a redemption premium of up to 50%.

Texas law allows exemptions from tax for qualified organizations such as charitable, religious and educational groups. However, only individuals may claim an exemption based upon **homestead** property.

In order to qualify as homestead property, the subject property must used, owned and occupied as a residence. However, Texas law does allow the owner temporary absences from the property for up to two years.

By law, school districts in Texas must grant a general homestead exemption, but any taxing unit is permitted to allow one as well. Many taxing units also grant an **"age 65 and over"** exemption as well. Many Texas seniors also have the added benefit of a **tax ceiling**, which can be applied to a new residence even if the resident buys a new home, the deferral of tax collection actions, the ability to pay taxes in installments, and the possibility of working off their taxes. A homeowner age 65 and over who is **disabled** generally has a choice of choosing the exemption for being 65 and over or disabled, but not both. Finally, Texas does allow an exemption for Texans and/or their families who become disabled or die while serving on active duty. To request an exemption, a person needs to submit the proper application form to the **Chief Appraiser of the Appraisal District**.

Special valuation rules apply to Texas farm and ranch property. If the property and/or the owner qualify, these rules permit the property to be appraised much lower than for comparable residential property. However, it is important to know that a purchaser of property under an **agricultural valuation** faces substantial **rollback taxes** for changing the use of the property. Rollback taxes are computed as the difference between the tax paid and what should have been paid under a non-agricultural valuation for up to five years prior to the sale. These taxes are immediately due and a tax lien is attached to the property to secure payment of the taxes.

In addition to local property taxes, a variety of federal tax laws can apply. For example, interest, property taxes, and prepayment penalties paid on a personal residence can be deducted from income taxes. Federal income tax allows a taxpayer to exclude up to $250,000 of gain for each individual ($500,000 if married and on title). When you sell your home (**capital asset**), a **capital gain or loss** results. Capital gains are taxed at a lower rate than ordinary income tax rates.

A loss on a sale of a personal residence can also be deducted if it is turned into income-producing property by renting it. Income property owners can deduct mortgage interest, property taxes, and prepayment penalties, as well as operating expenses and depreciation, but not losses due to vacancies. If a business owner sells a building for cash, then leases it back (a **sale-leaseback**), the seller becomes the lessee and the buyer the lessor, and the seller can deduct 100% of future rents paid.

Federal taxes are **progressive**, meaning the percentage paid increases as the amount to be taxed increases, which is the opposite of sales taxes, which are **regressive**.

In addition to depreciation, two major tax benefits of owning income-producing property are **installment sales** (gain is only taxed in the year it is received) and **1031 tax-deferred exchanges** (a means of deferring or eliminating income taxes on property transfers). Cash or debt relief gained in a tax deferred exchange is known as **boot**.

Persons buying property from foreign investors are required to set aside 10% of the purchase price for the IRS, to insure the property capital gains taxes are paid on the transaction. In this case, the burden is on the buyer and broker, not the seller.

X. TERMINOLOGY

A. Ad Valorem
B. Appraised Value
C. Boot
D. Appraisal District
E. Tax Assessor-Collector
F. Depreciation for Tax Purposes
G. Appraisal Review Board

H. Donee
I. Donor
J. Exchange
K. Federal Income Tax
L. Federal Estate Tax
M. Federal Gift Tax
N. Tax Ceiling
O. Installment Sale

P. Statutory Right of Redemption
Q. Real Property Taxes
R. Homestead Exemption
S. Rollback Taxes
T. Two Out of the Last 5 Years
U. $250,000

1. ____ Value placed upon property, for property tax purposes, by the appraisal district.
2. ____ The sale of property in installments that spreads tax on profit from a sale of property over a number of years.
3. ____ A tax charged according to the value of the property.
4. ____ One who gives a gift.
5. ____ A tax against the property of a deceased, based on the value of the estate.
6. ____ One who receives a gift.
7. ____ In a tax-deferred exchange, any cash or other property included in the transaction to make the exchange an even proposition.
8. ____ The trading of parcels of real property to obtain tax benefits that might not be available in a normal sale. Generally considered tax-deferred, not tax-exempt.
9. ____ An annual tax that applies to real estate that is based on the appraised value of the property.
10. ____ The official who is responsible for assessing and collecting property taxes.
11. ____ The entity responsible for placing a value on property for tax purposes.
12. ____ An reduction in property taxes due to a person's ownership and occupancy of a primary residence.
13. ____ A loss in value of improvements as an accounting procedure: used as a deduction on income taxes.
14. ____ Taxes imposed due to a change in use of property under a special agricultural valuation.
15. ____ A panel of local residents who hear and rule on property value protests.
16. ____ Federal taxes paid on the giving of real property as a gift, if over an exempted amount.
17. ____ A right granted by statute that allows taxpayers to redeem property up to two years following a tax foreclosure sale.
18. ____ Personal taxes paid annually on your taxable income.
19. ____ A limitation on school district taxes (and perhaps other taxes as well) due to the taxpayer turning age 65.
20. ____ The length of time a couple must live in their house to qualify for a $500,000 exclusion.
21. ____ The amount of gain that is exempt if a single person sells his or her house.

XI. MULTIPLE CHOICE

1. The primary job of the various appraisal districts is to:
    a. establish the tax rate.
    b. set property value.
    c. collect taxes.
    d. impose tax liens.

2. Appraisal districts are responsible for annually mailing to each taxpayer:
    a. Notice of Statutory Redemption.
    b. Notice of Rollback Tax.
    c. Notice of Assessment Ratio.
    d. Notice of Appraised Value.

3. Of the following, which one would best describe income taxes?
    a. Regressive
    b. Progressive
    c. Marginal
    d. Repressive

4. A tax that is charged in proportion to the value of the property is referred to as a(n):
    a. ad valorem tax.
    b. progression tax.
    c. progressive tax.
    d. excise tax.

5. If not paid, property taxes are considered delinquent on:
    a. February 1.
    b. January 31.
    c. October 1.
    d. April 15.

6. A person can exclude $250,000 of gain from federal income taxes if he/she lives in the house for:
    a. one year.
    b. two out of the last five years.
    c. five years.
    d. ten years.

7. On what date does a tax lien attach for unpaid property taxes?

    a. February 1

    b. January 31

    c. January 1

    d. April 15

8. Assuming no exemptions apply, what is the amount of tax due for a $250,000 home if the tax rate is $2.25 per $100 valuation?

    a. $2,500

    b. $2,250

    c. $5,625

    d. None of the above

9. A tax imposed as a result of a change of use for agriculturally valued property is called a(n):

    a. rollback tax.

    b. rollup tax.

    c. change of use tax.

    d. agricultural development tax.

10. The person who gives a gift is called a:

    a. trustor.

    b. donee.

    c. donor.

    d. none of the above.

ANSWERS: 1. b; 2. d; 3. b; 4. a; 5. a; 6. b; 7. c; 8. c; 9. a; 10. c

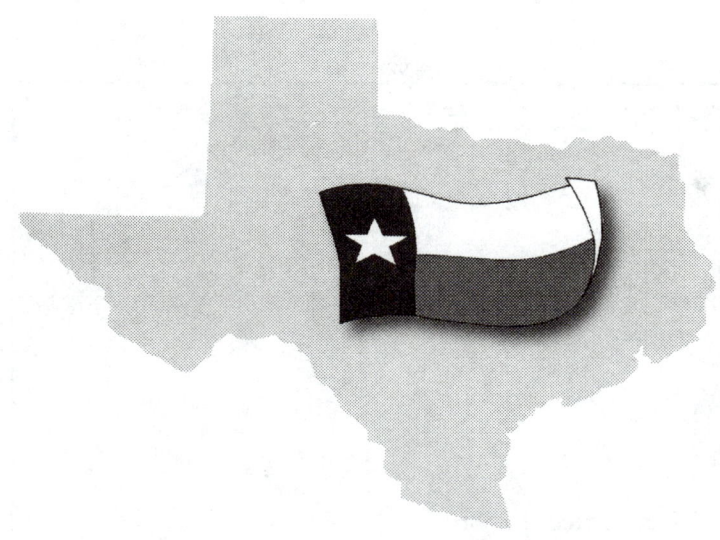

Chapter 17
Real Estate Math

Real estate, as you have learned, can be an extremely profitable profession. The licensee who is able to compute quickly and accurately the mathematics underlying most transactions will be in a better position to capitalize on opportunities as they arise.

This chapter will illustrate and explain some basic mathematical skills useful to a career in real estate. Familiarity with fundamental arithmetic and a few simple formulas along with plain common sense will provide the necessary background. Such knowledge will not only assist in the practice of real estate, but should also prove advantageous in passing the licensing exam. **Figure 17-1** is a table of common measurements.

It might also prove to your advantage to bring a calculator with you when taking the salesperson's examination. The state permits license applicants to use keyboardless electronic calculators as long as they are battery operated, non-programmable, silent, and without printout capability. Such a device will free you from tedious and time-consuming arithmetic work in order to concentrate on the reasoning behind the problems you will encounter.

CHAPTER 17 OUTLINE

Figure 17-1

Measurements

(A Salesperson Should Be Familiar With These)

LINEAR

1 foot (ft.) = 12 inches (in.)
1 yard (yd.) = 3 feet (ft.)
1 rod = 16.5 ft. = 5.5 yd.
1 mile = 5,280 ft. = 1,760 yd. = 320 rods

SQUARE

1 sq. ft. = 144 sq. in. (12 in. x 12 in.)
1 sq. yd. = 9 sq. ft. (3 ft. x 3 ft.)
1 acre = 43,560 sq. ft. = 4,840 sq. yd. = 160 sq. rods
1 sq. mile = 5,280 ft. x 5,280 ft.

CUBIC

1 cu. ft. = 1,728 cu. in. (12 in. x 12 in. x 12 in.)
1 cu. yd. = 27 cu. ft. (3 ft. x 3 ft. x 3 ft.)

LAND DESCRIPTION

1 link = 7.92 inches
1 rod = 25 links
1 chain = 100 links = 66 ft. = 4 rods
1 mile = 80 chains
1 acre = 43,560 sq. ft.
1 township = 36 sections = 36 square miles = 23,040 acres
1 section = 1 mile square = 640 acres = 1/36 of a township
1 circle = 360 degrees (°)
1 quadrant = 90 degrees (°)
1 degree (°) = 60 minutes (′)
1 minute (′) = 60 seconds (′′)

I. Area Measurement

LAND AREA is the surface space between lot lines measured in square feet.

A. AREA OF A RECTANGULAR LOT

A RECTANGULAR LOT is a four-sided parcel whose opposite sides are equal in length and right angles are formed by the intersection of the sides. The dimensions of a rectangle are equal on two sides. Most lots encountered will be rectangular in shape.

1. How Do We Get "Square" Measurement?

The area of a rectangular or square lot is determined by multiplying the length by the width. The result is expressed in square feet, square yards, or some similar expression. The formula is:

$$A = L \times W$$
$$AREA = LENGTH \times WIDTH$$

EXAMPLE: How many square feet would there be in a rectangular parcel 100 feet long and 50 feet wide?

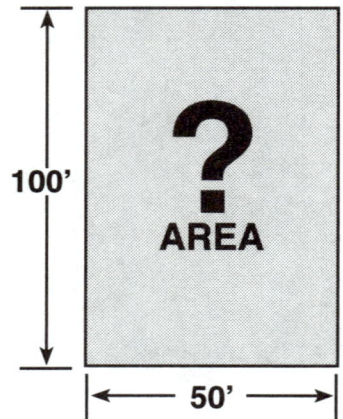

A = L x W

AREA = LENGTH x WIDTH

AREA = 100 FEET x 50 FEET

A = 100 x 50

A = 5,000 SQUARE FEET

ANSWER: The area of this lot is calculated to be 5,000 square feet.

B. AREA OF A TRIANGULAR LOT

A TRIANGULAR LOT is a three-sided parcel.

In order to determine the area of a triangular parcel, we must know the measurements of its base and height.

The *BASE OF A TRIANGULAR LOT is the side that is horizontal.* The *HEIGHT OF A TRIANGULAR LOT is the perpendicular distance from the base to the highest point.*

The area of a triangular parcel is determined by multiplying the base by the height, and then dividing by two. This is normally expressed by the formula:

$$A = \frac{B \times H}{2}$$

$$AREA = \frac{BASE \times HEIGHT}{2}$$

Here is a sample exercise for you to try:

EXAMPLE: How many square feet would there be in a triangular lot with a 150 foot base and a height of 100 feet?

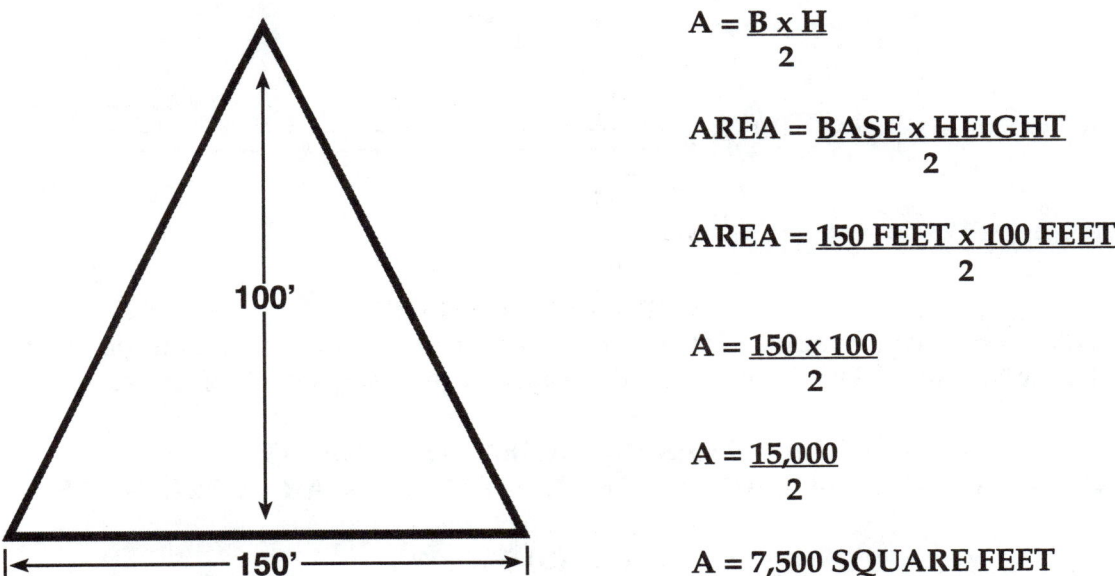

$$A = \frac{B \times H}{2}$$

$$AREA = \frac{BASE \times HEIGHT}{2}$$

$$AREA = \frac{150 \text{ FEET} \times 100 \text{ FEET}}{2}$$

$$A = \frac{150 \times 100}{2}$$

$$A = \frac{15,000}{2}$$

$$A = 7,500 \text{ SQUARE FEET}$$

ANSWER: The area of this lot is 7,500 square feet.

C. AREA OF AN IRREGULAR LOT

An *IRREGULAR LOT is a parcel that does not consist of a single known shape.* Often the area of an irregular or circular parcel cannot be measured accurately without the help of a land measurement expert, such as a surveyor. Many times, though, an irregular lot is simply made up of a series of rectangles and triangles, the combined measures of which make up the measure of the whole. In these cases the square footage of the parcel can be determined through the use of techniques already described in this chapter.

The area of an irregular parcel is determined by breaking the lot up into the various rectangles and triangles which comprise it, and totaling their areas.

1. An Irregular Lot Problem

EXAMPLE: What would be the total area of the irregular lot shown below? Use the dimensions given to calculate your answer.

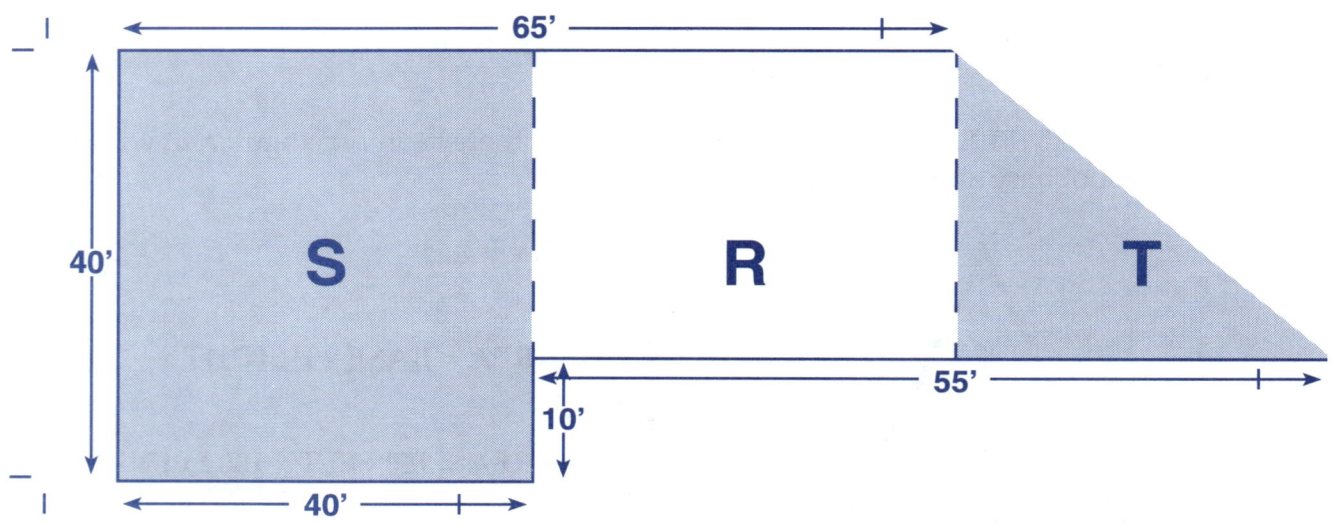

ANSWER: The irregular lot is broken up into a square, a rectangle, and a triangle. The area of the parcel is the total of the areas of each of these.

TOTAL AREA = AREA (S) + AREA (R) + AREA (T)
TOTAL AREA = AREA SQUARE + AREA RECTANGLE + AREA TRIANGLE

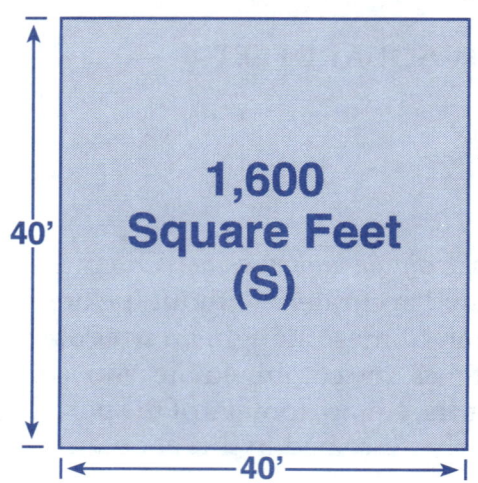

AREA (S) = L x W

AREA (S) = LENGTH x WIDTH

AREA (S) = 40 FEET x 40 FEET

AREA (S) = 40 x 40

AREA (S) = 1,600 SQUARE FEET

The area of the square (S) is 1,600 square feet.

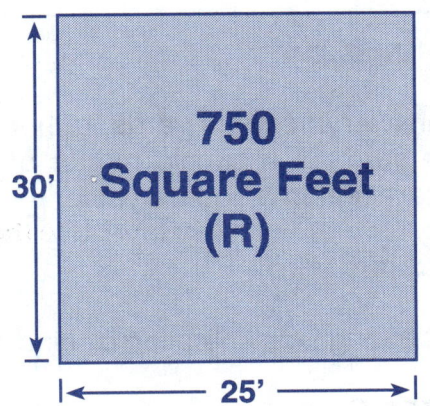

AREA (R) = L x W

AREA (R) = LENGTH x WIDTH

AREA (R) = 30 FEET x 25 FEET

AREA (R) = 30 x 25

AREA (R) = 750 SQUARE FEET

The area of the rectangle lot (R) is 750 square feet.

AREA (T) = $\frac{B \times H}{2}$

AREA (T) = $\frac{BASE \times HEIGHT}{2}$

AREA (T) = $\frac{30\ FEET \times 30\ FEET}{2}$

AREA (T) = $\frac{30 \times 30}{2}$

AREA (T) = $\frac{900}{2}$

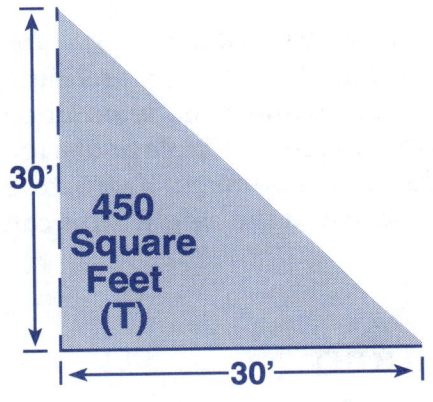

AREA (T) = 450 SQUARE FEET

The area of the triangle (T) is 450 square feet.

Irregular Problem Solution

AREA (S) = 1,600 SQUARE FEET

AREA (R) = 750 SQUARE FEET

AREA (T) = 450 SQUARE FEET

TOTAL AREA = AREA (S) + AREA (R) + AREA (T)

TOTAL AREA = 1,600 + 750 + 450

TOTAL AREA = 2,800 SQUARE FEET

ANSWER: The total area of this irregular lot is 2,800 square feet.

Conversion: Square Feet to SquareYards

Many questions on area will ask that you present the answer in square yards, rather than square feet. Conversion of square feet to square yards is a simple matter of dividing the answer by nine, because there are nine square feet in a square yard.

(3 feet x 3 feet = 9 square feet or 1 square yard)

Square yards, likewise, may be converted into square feet through multiplication by nine.

SQUARE YARDS = SQUARE FEET
9
SQUARE FEET = SQUARE YARDS x 9

D. VOLUME OF A STRUCTURE

STRUCTURAL VOLUME is the square or cubic measure of the space within a structure. Structural volume measurement is generally used when renting space in a warehouse type structure. Square measure is the area of the floor space, and it is determined through the use of the same techniques that apply to finding the square footage of a lot. *CUBIC MEASURE is the area volume or total air space.* The cubic volume of a structure is determined by multiplying the interior length by the width and the height. This can be expressed by the formula:

$$V = L \times W \times H$$
$$\text{VOLUME} = \text{LENGTH} \times \text{WIDTH} \times \text{HEIGHT}$$

EXAMPLE: How many cubic feet would there be in a room that is 15 feet long, 10 feet wide, and 10 feet high?

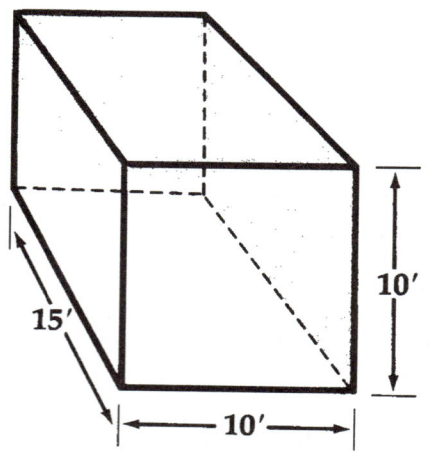

$V = L \times W \times H$
VOLUME = LENGTH x WIDTH x HEIGHT
VOLUME = 15 FEET x 10 FEET x 10 FEET
VOLUME = 15 x 10 x 10
VOLUME = 150 x 10
VOLUME = 1,500 CUBIC FEET

ANSWER: The cubic volume of this room would be 1,500 cubic feet.

II. Percentage Problems

The majority of math problems that you will encounter in real estate involve the use of percent. It is important, therefore, for you to understand certain general rules about percentage problems before dealing with any of the particular types.

There are three factors in any percentage problem:

1. The amount *PAID (P) is the amount invested.*
2. The *RATE (%) is the percentage.*
3. The amount *MADE (M) is the amount earned.*

In percentage problems, **one** of the three factors is missing. There are three rules for finding the missing factor:

1. To find the amount **PAID (P)**, divide **MADE (M)** by the **RATE (%)**.
2. To find the amount **MADE (M)**, multiply **PAID (P)** by **RATE (%)**.
3. To find the **RATE (%)**, divide **MADE (M)** by (**PAID (P)**.

A. OTHER FACTOR TERMS

MADE	PAID%	RATE
Return	Investment	Rate of return
Profit	Cost	Rate of profit
Commission	Price	Rate of commission
Net income	Value	Rate of capitalization
Interest	Principal	Rate of interest

Whenever you are working a percent problem, you will be dealing with one of these equations or a modification of one of them. The typical percent problem will supply you with two of the variables. You may easily determine the third through the use of the proper equation.

B. TEXAS TRIANGLE

If you feel that you might have trouble committing the percent equations to memory, you might want to make use of the Texas percent problem "triangle" instead. Shown in **Figure 17-2**, this diagram points out what operation is required to find each of the variables.

To use the Texas Triangle, simply cover the chamber you are trying to find and then perform the required math:

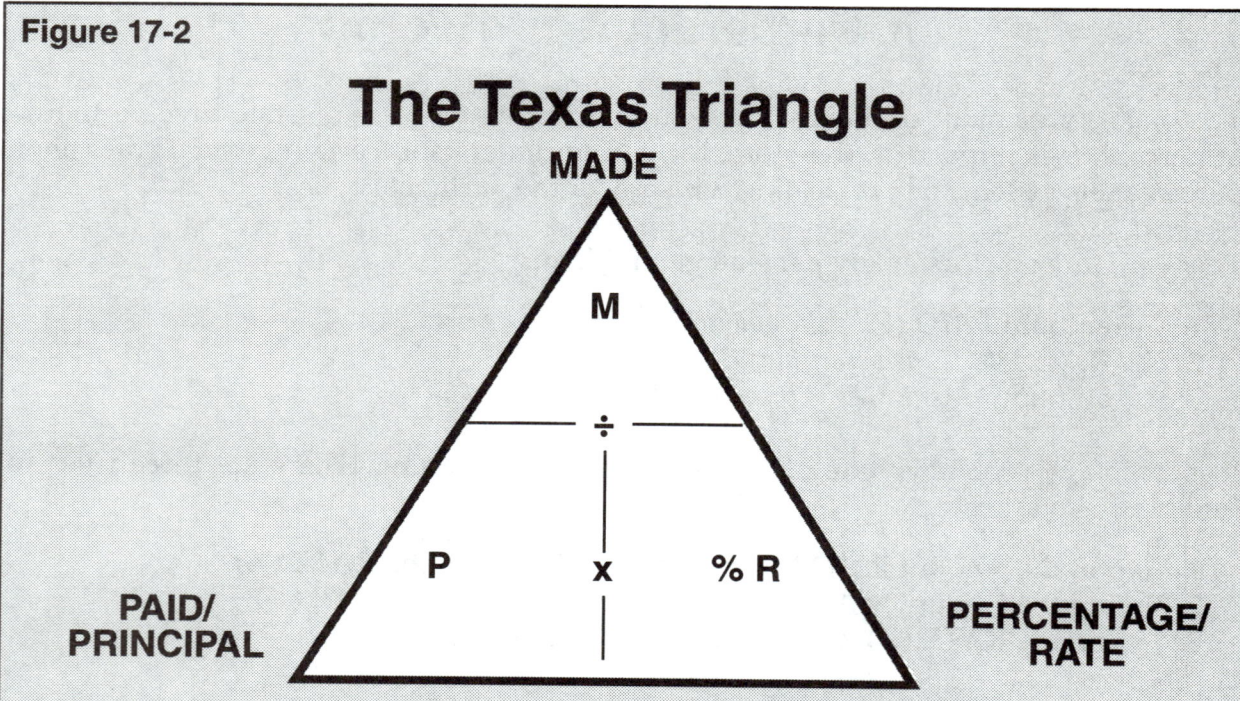

Figure 17-2

The Texas Triangle
MADE

M

÷

P   x   % R

PAID/
PRINCIPAL

PERCENTAGE/
RATE

The Texas Triangle consists of three sections, or chambers (which can be modified to four chambers for certain problems). The top chamber is the **MADE (M)** chamber. It is separated from the other two chambers by a **division sign**. The bottom left chamber is the **PAID** or **PRINCIPAL (P)** chamber. The bottom right chamber is the **RATE (%)** chamber. It is separated from the PAID chamber by a **multiplication sign**.

1. To find M, cover M and multiply P x %
2. To find P, cover P and divide M by %
3. To find %, cover % and divide M by P

When doing a math problem involving three or more variables, first draw the Texas Triangle and plug in the available figures, then perform the required action.

Your success in solving percentage problems will depend largely on your ability to spot and identify the three variables as they are presented. In most problems the **PAID** and the **MADE** will both be labeled as money. But the **PAID** (generally the larger amount) will usually be given as a base amount such as a price, investment, or loan balance. The **MADE**, on the other hand (generally the smaller amount), will be a sum made or lost from the **PAID**. Returns, profits, net income, taxes, interest, and commissions are all common labels identifying the **MADE**. The rate is easy to identify because it will always be given as some form of a percentage (%).

Here is a sample percent exercise for you to try:

EXAMPLE: Your agency purchases a lot for $9,000. In selling it later, you made a profit of $3,000. What was your percentage of profit?

ANSWER: The first step is to identify the variables. The principal (paid) is the purchase price of $9,000. The result (made) is the $3,000 margin of profit that resulted from the transaction. The rate is the percentage that we are asked to determine. To find it we use the rate equation:

$$\% = \frac{M}{P}$$

RATE = MADE ÷ PAID

RATE = $3,000 ÷ $9,000

RATE = 3,000 ÷ 9,000

RATE = .3333 = 33.33%

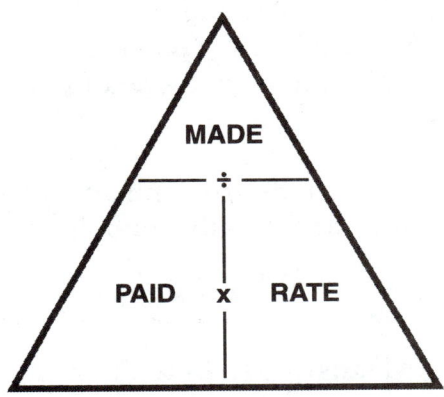

So, your agency made a 33.33% profit on the transaction.

Figure 17-3

DECIMAL TO PERCENT

.095 = 9.5%

1.2 = 120%

.009 = .9%

The above problem was looking for the rate (a percentage). The decimal number .3333 is not a percentage and so it had to be converted into a percentage in the final step of the sample exercise.

To convert a decimal number into a percentage, you simply move the decimal point two spaces to the right, adding zeros if needed. **Figure 17-3** gives some examples of this type of conversion.

In problems where you are asked to compute the results (paid) and the principal (made) it will be necessary for you to multiply or divide by the rate. In these cases you will have to convert the percentage into a decimal before completing the operation. This is done by reversing the process above: Move the decimal point two spaces to the left, and drop the percent sign. This changes a percent into its equivalent decimal form. **Figure 17-4** demonstrates this process.

Figure 17-4

PERCENT TO DECIMAL

8.5% = .085

50.% = .5

110% = 1.1

Another simple way to remember percents is to relate them to dollars and cents.

10 cents	=	.10	10% =	.10
50 cents	=	.50	50% =	.50
$1.50	=	1.50	150% =	1.50

C. DETERMINING COMMISSIONS AND SELLING PRICE

A *COMMISSION RATE is a percentage of the selling price that is used to calculate the commission. The* **COMMISSION** *is the dollar amount received by a real estate agent for completing the sale.* A real estate agent wants to know how much he or she will be paid for doing his or her job. Most real estate salespeople are paid on a commission basis. As a licensed real estate agent, one of your most pleasant duties will be determining your commission.

When dealing with math problems in real estate, it is important to translate "words" into "math words" and "math symbols."

WORD	MATH WORD	MATH SYMBOL
OF (Means)	MULTIPLY	x
IS (Means)	EQUALS	=

In commission problems you are supplied with the **PRINCIPAL (PAID)**, which is the property selling price, and the **RATE (%)**, which is the rate of commission, and asked to find the **RESULT (MADE)**, the agent's commission. Such problems use the result equation: **M = P x %**.

> **EXAMPLE:** You have completed the sale of a $100,000 home. The rate of commission is 6%. How much money have you made?

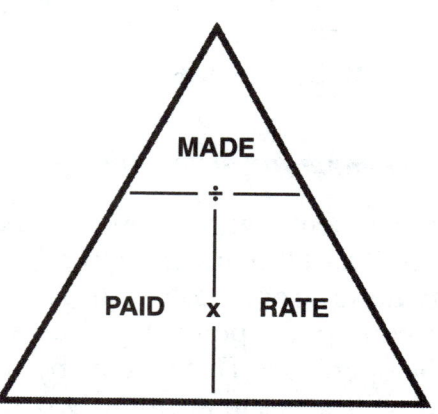

$$M = P \times \%$$

$$\text{MADE} = \text{PAID} \times \text{RATE}$$

$$\text{MADE} = \$100,000 \times 6\% \ (.06)$$

$$\text{MADE} = \$6,000$$

ANSWER: Your commission is $6,000.

1. Splitting Commissions

Most often when you have completed a sale, your brokerage firm will not be entitled to the entire commission. A second firm might be involved. If you were representing the seller, for example, you might very likely split your commission with a broker and salesperson for the buyer. You will have earned a percentage of the amount earned by your broker, depending on the percentage both of you have agreed to in advance. The rates here are negotiable and usually vary with your experience and success.

When determining the splits of a commission, you use the result **(MADE)** equation. The total commission represents the principal **(PAID)** and the percentage **(RATE)** is whatever rate of commission was agreed to between the parties. **Figure 17-5** illustrates how a commission might be split.

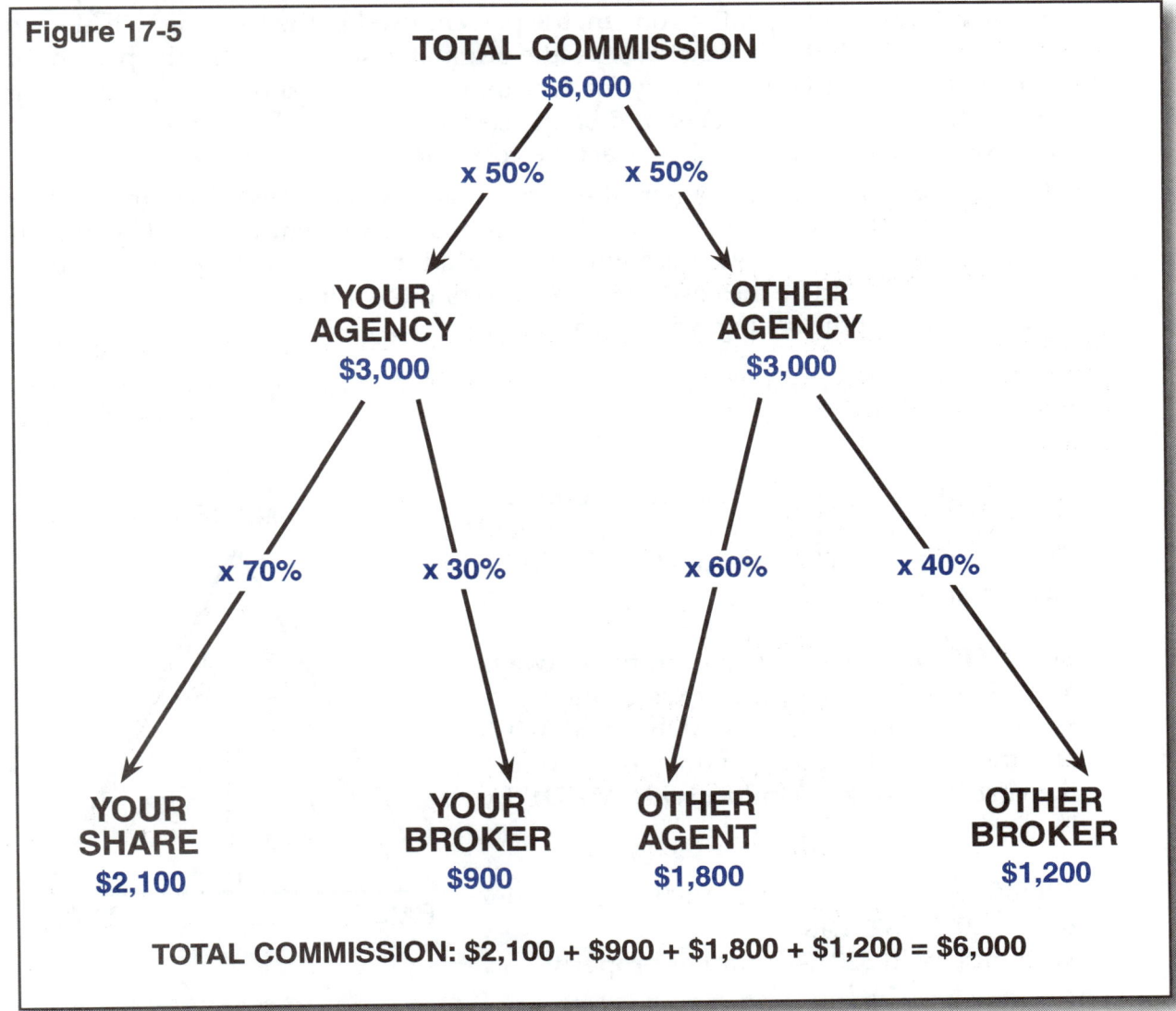

Figure 17-5

TOTAL COMMISSION
$6,000

x 50%   x 50%

YOUR AGENCY $3,000   OTHER AGENCY $3,000

x 70%   x 30%   x 60%   x 40%

YOUR SHARE $2,100   YOUR BROKER $900   OTHER AGENT $1,800   OTHER BROKER $1,200

TOTAL COMMISSION: $2,100 + $900 + $1,800 + $1,200 = $6,000

D. PROFIT AND LOSS

When dealing with profit and loss problems, you must establish the value, or cost, before profit (+), or loss (-).

The terms "value" and "cost" are interchangeable in real estate math problems; **it is what you paid for the property**.

Key terms when working profit and loss problems:

1. **SELLING PRICE** – the dollar value after the profit or loss has been added or subtracted from the original cost.

2. **COST** – the dollar value before the profit or loss has been added or subtracted. Cost is often stated as purchase price or original price.

3. **1 + % PROFIT** – in a profit problem, the percent used in the formula will always be greater than 100%; in other words, the original cost (100%) plus the percent of profit. If you sold your property for 40% more than you paid for it, your selling price (100% + 40% = 140%) would be the cost x 140 % (1.40). To find the amount of profit (+40%), you would subtract the cost from the selling price.

4. **1 - % LOSS** – for a loss problem, the percent used will always be less than 100%; in other words, the original cost (100%) minus the percent of loss. If you sold your property for 25% less than what you paid for it, your selling price (100% - 25% = 75%) would be the cost x 75% (.75). To find the amount of loss (- 25%), you would subtract the selling price from the cost.

The key to working these types of problems is to determine what percent to use.

EXAMPLE: Ms. Smith sold her home for $250,000, which was 8% more than she paid for the property. How much did Ms. Smith pay for the property?

SOLUTION: Remember that profit is **always a % of cost**. If we use the Texas triangle, we know the Selling price (MADE) is $250,000 and the rate (%) is 108% (100% + 8%). To find the cost (PAID), we would **divide MADE by %**.

ANSWER: (rounded) $250,000 divided by 108% (1.08) = **$231,481**
Ms. Smith paid $231,481 for her property.

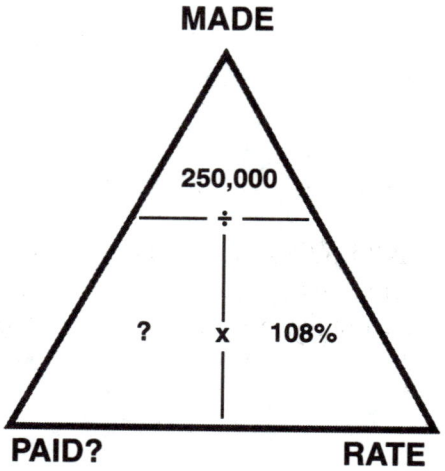

Let's try another problem:

> **EXAMPLE:** Mr. Bush bought a new home on January 14 for $280,000. On July 6, he was transferred to a new city and sold his home for $270,000. What was his percent of loss?
>
> **REMEMBER:** the percent of loss is based on what the home cost, not what it sold for.
>
> **SOLUTION:** First we determine the amount of loss: $280,000 - $270,000 = $10,000.
>
> Now we plug in the figures: MADE ($10,000) divided by PAID ($280,000) = percent (%) of loss.
>
> **ANSWER:** Mr. Bush's percent of loss was 4% (.03572, or .04).

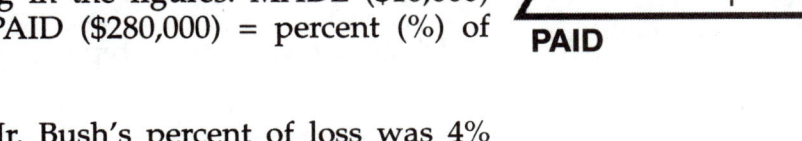

Remember: In profit problems, percent will always be greater than 100%. In loss problems, percent will always be less than 100%.

E. PRINCIPAL AND INTEREST CALCULATIONS

Use a 30-day month (banker's month) in calculating interest payments; thus 1 year = 360 days (statutory or banker's year). A calendar year of 365 days, or a leap year of 366 days, can be utilized, but is usually not used.

Great amounts of capital are necessary to complete most real estate transactions. As a licensed real estate agent, financing will often be one of the major concerns of your clients. It will be advantageous, therefore, for you to be able to provide loan counseling as a part of your services. Essential to this service will be your ability to readily calculate principal and interest payments.

INTEREST is a fee paid for the use of other people's money, stated in dollars and cents. When one leases an apartment, he or she pays rent to the landlord for the use of the property. Similarly, when one borrows money he or she pays "rent" to the lender for the use of the money. This "rent" is called interest. *SIMPLE INTEREST is the term used to describe interest on the unpaid balance.*

Most interest problems will supply you with the principal **(PAID)**, which is the amount borrowed, and the rate **(%)**, which is the percentage being charged. You are asked to determine the interest **(MADE)**. We learned this formula earlier:

$$M = P \times R \ (\%)$$

There is an extra variable that is a factor in all interest problems: time. The duration of the loan determines how much interest is owed at the annual rate. One year equals one, one month equals 1/12, and one day equals 1/360. In order to take this factor into consideration, we modify the MADE equation slightly, with **MADE (M)** becoming **INTEREST (I)**:

$$I = P \times R \times T$$

INTEREST (MADE) = PRINCIPAL (PAID) x RATE (%) x TIME

When doing principal and interest problems, you are trying to find one of four unknowns: **INTEREST (I), PRINCIPAL (P), INTEREST RATE (R),** or **TIME (T).**

We will use this modified Texas Triangle to work these types of problems:

Remember: To use the Texas Triangle, simply cover the chamber you are trying to find and then perform the required math.

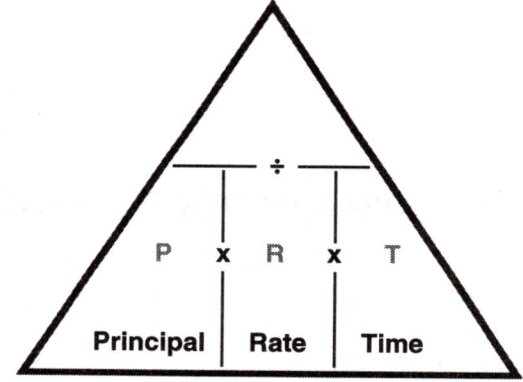

1. Interest Problem

Interest is the payment made for using other people's money. The formula for finding interest is:

$$I = P \times R \times T$$

Here is a sample exercise for you to try:

EXAMPLE: What would be the interest due on a loan of $10,000, borrowed at 9%, for a period of 2 years?

I = P x R x T

INTEREST = PRINCIPAL x RATE x TIME

INTEREST = $10,000 x 9% x 2 YEARS

INTEREST = $10,000 x .09 x 2

INTEREST = $900 x 2

INTEREST = $1,800

ANSWER: The interest would be $1,800.

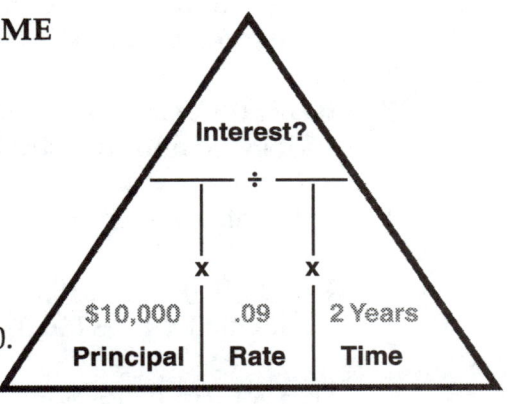

2. Principal Problem

As used in real estate finance problems, *PRINCIPAL is the amount borrowed in dollars.* To find the principal (amount borrowed), we would use the following formula:

$$P = \frac{I}{R \times T}$$

EXAMPLE: Mr. Johnson has a loan with annual interest payments of $5,200. If the rate of interest is 10%, how much did he borrow?

SOLUTION: We know that the interest (I) is $5,200, the rate (%) is 10% (.10) and the time (T) is 1 year. Using the above formula:

$$P = \frac{\$5,200}{.10 \times 1} = \frac{\$5,200}{.10} = \$52,000$$

ANSWER: Mr. Johnson borrowed $52,000.

3. Interest Rate Problem

The *INTEREST RATE is the percent of interest charged.* The purpose of principal and interest problems is to determine what we are paying **(INTEREST)** for the use of the amount borrowed **(PRINCIPAL)** and expressing that amount as a percentage **(INTEREST RATE)**. We use the following formula to find the interest rate:

$$R = \frac{I}{P \times T}$$

EXAMPLE: Ms. Bishop borrows $150,000 from 1ST Bank to purchase a condominium. If, after the first year, she owes the lender $15,000 interest, what is the rate of interest?

SOLUTION: We know that the **INTEREST (I)** is $15,000, the **PRINCIPAL (P)** is $150,000 and the **TIME (T)** is one year.

Using the above formula:

$$R = \frac{\$15,000}{\$150,000 \times 1} = \frac{\$15,000}{\$150,000} = (.10) \text{ or } 10\%$$

ANSWER: Ms. Bishop's rate of interest is 10%.

Unless stated otherwise, the interest rate is assumed to be in annual terms.

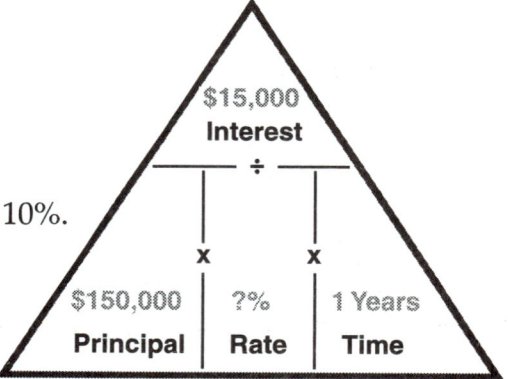

Figure 17-6 explains some useful terms in calculating interest rate problems.

Figure 17-6

In Calculating Interest Rate Problems:

Annual = once a year
Semiannual = twice a year at 6 month intervals
Biannual = twice a year
Bimonthly = 6 times a year (every 2 months)
Monthly = 12 times a year
Semimonthly = twice a month
Biennial = once every 2 years
1 Year = 12 months = 52 weeks = 360 days
1 Month = 30 days

---

4. Time Problem

TIME is used for periods less than or greater than one year. Time is expressed as a fraction or percent of a year (1/12th or .0833) if a payment is to be made monthly. As stated earlier, **interest rates** are assumed to be annual unless otherwise stated. However the payment of **principal and interest** is usually done on a monthly basis. The previous problems used a one year time period. If the time period is more or less than a year, then **TIME (T)** takes on a different value:

Monthly payment: T = 1/12 or .0833

Semiannual payment: T = 1/2 or .5

EXAMPLE: Mr. Philips borrows $200,000 at 9.5 % interest. What is the monthly interest payment?

SOLUTION: PRINCIPAL (P) is $200,000, **RATE (R)** is 9.5% and **TIME (T)** is 1/12 or .0833.

$$I = P \times R \times T$$

I = $200,000 x .095 x .0833 = $1,583

ANSWER: Mr. Philips makes a monthly interest payment of $1,583.

F. DISCOUNT POINTS ("Points")

1 discount point = 1% of the loan amount

DISCOUNT POINTS *are charges made by a lender to increase the yield on a loan: one point equals 1% of the loan.*

EXAMPLE: Mr. and Mrs. Majors are purchasing a house for $155,000. They will put $30,000 down and borrow the rest, which will include a 4 point charge by the savings bank. How much will the points cost them?

SOLUTION: First we must determine the amount being borrowed:

$155,000 - $30,000 = $125,000

Next we compute the discount rate:

1 point = 1% of the loan amount = .01 x $125,000 = $1,250

Finally, we calculate the amount of discount:

4 x $1,250 = $5,000

ANSWER: The Majors will pay $5,000 for the discount points from the borrowed $125,000.

III. Determining Prorations

PRORATION is the process of proportionately dividing (prorating) expenses or income to the precise date that escrow closes, or any other date previously agreed upon. Its purpose is to apportion income and expense items correctly between the parties of a sale. These are divided (or **prorated**) in proportion to the time that each owned or will own the property.

In analyzing proration problems, you will first need to determine **who** will be credited with a dollar amount at closing. It is obvious that a seller has owned the property for the period *before* the day of closing and that the buyer will own the property *after* the day of closing. But who owns the property on the day of the closing itself? The real estate contract will usually answer this question.

If the contract determines prorations "to the day of closing," the buyer is considered the owner for that day. But if the contract reads "through the day of closing," the seller is considered the owner for that day for the purpose of determining proration calculations.

> *In Texas, the TREC promulgated contracts call for prorations <u>through</u> the day of closing.*

The contract will also specify the type year to be used for prorations (a calendar-- 365 day year or a banker's statutory year—360 days).

The next thing that you need to consider is **how much** will be credited. Items that are normally prorated include mortgage interest, taxes, homeowners' association dues, rent, and assessments. In some areas, prorations are also known as **adjustments** or **apportionments**.

For computations of prorations

Calendar Year – Each month uses the actual number of days in that month. This is the method used in Texas unless the contract calls for banker's year.

Banker's Year – Each month uses 30 days.

Proration involves dividing the dollar amount associated with the time an expense or income occurred between two parties (the buyer and seller). Rent and interest are usually paid in one month intervals, while property taxes are paid once a year. An important question that must be answered is who gets credit for an item. The rules are simple.

> *On an escrow statement a CREDIT is something that is received and a DEBIT is something that is owed.*

A. Rents (Income)

In determining the proration of rents, it is important to know what type year is being used (banker's year or calendar year). The calendar year is generally used.

Buyer's and Seller's Settlement Statements

DOUBLE ENTRY BOOKKEEPING *is the balancing procedure used to complete a settlement statement.* (Accountants will find this the opposite of true accounting.) The statement consists of two parts: a **buyer's statement** and a **seller's statement**. Each of these is divided into a **debit column** and a **credit column**.

A ***DEBIT*** *is something that is owed.* A debit entry for a buyer is anything charged against or subtracted from his or her account. The purchase price of the property is an example of something debited to the buyer. A debit entry for a seller means the same thing. Unpaid property taxes are a good example.

A ***CREDIT*** *is something that is received.* A credit entry for a buyer is anything received or added to his or her account. The deposit made on the property is a good example of something credited to the buyer. A good example of a credit entry for the seller would be prepaid property taxes.

If an item was **paid** before closing, the buyer's closing statement will be debited and the seller's statement will be credited. If **income** was received before closing, the buyer's statement will be credited and the seller's statement will be debited. Though items on closing statements follow no set order of entry, **the purchase price is usually the first entry and the amount due from/to buyer to close, and the amount due to/from seller to close are the last entries**.

The portion of income that is granted to each party can be represented as a fraction. The denominator will be the number of days in the month, while the numerator will vary depending upon what day in the month escrow closes.

EXAMPLE: If the escrow closes on the 20th day of 30-day month, how would you divide a prepaid rent of $1,500 between the seller and the buyer?

ANSWER: The seller's share would be 20/30 of the whole, because he holds ownership through the 20th day. The share of the other 10 days (10/30) would go to the buyer.

SELLER'S SHARE	BUYER'S SHARE
$\dfrac{20}{30} \times 1,500 = \$1,000$	$\dfrac{10}{30} \times 1,500 = \$500$

So, the seller would receive $1,000 of the rent money, while the buyer would be prorated $500.

If the seller has collected a security deposit, it's important to remember that security deposits are not prorated. They are usually paid directly from the seller to the buyer.

B. PROPERTY TAXES (EXPENSES) – BUYER'S AND SELLER'S

Property taxes are assessed in the fall of a year and are paid in arrears, which means they are paid after the period has ended. For example, taxes for 2006 will be paid in 2007. But what if the property closes at the end of June, 2006, is not assessed until October, 2006, and not payable until February, 2007? The person calculating the prorations must make a good faith estimate of tax prorations. The TREC promulgated residential sales contract provides "if taxes vary from the amount prorated at closing, the parties shall adjust the prorations when tax statements for the current year are available."

> **EXAMPLE:** A property will close on September 14. Remember that in Texas prorations are made through the day of closing using a calendar year. What amount will the seller pay the buyer for taxes for the year if the estimated tax bill is $3650? Also, who gets the credit and who gets the debit?

ANSWER:

Figure daily prorated amount: $3650/365 days = $100/day

Figure the number of days in ownership:

Seller owns property		
	Jan	31 days
	Feb	28 days
	Mar	31 days
	Apr	30 days
	May	31 days
	Jun	30 days
	Jul	31 days
	Aug	31 days
	Sep	14 days
Seller's total days		257 days

Multiply # of days by daily amount: 257 days x $100/day = $2,570

Who gets credited/debited?

> The $2570 is a debit (TAKE AWAY) for the seller and a credit (GIVE TO) for the buyer. *Remember, we will always reimburse (credit) the party who paid the*

expense. In this case, since the entire tax bill is to be paid by the buyer long after the closing has occurred, it's only fair to make the seller pay for his/her fair share of the taxes at closing.

IV. Amortization

When the payments on a loan consist of principal (P) and interest (I) and are made in equal installments until the loan is paid off, the process of **AMORTIZATION** *has occurred.* In fact, the term "amortize" literally means "to kill off." As a result, the loan is being killed off, a little at a time.

The interest is paid to the lender and the principal portion of the loan payment is applied to the loan balance. This occurs until the loan balance becomes zero and then the loan has been paid in full.

While financial calculators will quickly perform amortization computations, the following steps will illustrate the process.

> **EXAMPLE:** If the original loan is for $100,000 and monthly loan payments are $665.30 on a 7% loan for 30 years, what is the loan balance after the second payment?

ANSWER:

Multiply the beginning balance by the interest rate in order to determine the amount of interest paid for the entire year.

$100,000 x 7% = $7,000 (interest paid for the entire year)

Next, divide the annual interest by 12 to determine the interest paid for the first month.

$7,000/12 months = $583.33 (interest paid for the first month)

Subtract the interest from the first monthly payment in order to determine the amount of principal to be applied to the loan balance.

$665.30 - $583.33 = $81.97 (principal applied to loan balance)

Next determine the new loan balance following the first month's payment.

$100,000 - $81.97 = $99,918.03 (new loan balance for month two)

Again, multiply the loan balance by the interest rate in order to determine the amount of interest for the entire year.

$99,918.03 x 7% = $6,994.26 (interest paid for the entire year)

Again, divide the annual interest by 12 to determine the interest paid for the next month.

$6,994.26/12 months = $582.86

Subtract the interest from the second monthly payment in order to determine the amount of principal to be applied to the loan balance.

$665.30 - $582.86 = $82.44 (principal applied to loan balance)

Finally, determine the new loan balance following the second month's payment and here's our answer.

$99,918.03 (prev. loan bal.) - $82.44 = **$99,835.59** (bal. after 2nd month)

V. Depreciation (For Tax Purposes)

DEPRECIATION *(for income taxes)* *is a diminishing (loss) in the value of buildings and other improvements.* All new depreciation schedules for normal income tax purposes involving real property must be straight-line.

A. STRAIGHT-LINE DEPRECIATION

STRAIGHT-LINE DEPRECIATION *is a method of computing depreciation on assets other than land for income tax purposes in which the difference between the original cost and salvage value is deducted in installments evenly over the life of the asset.* It is based upon the assumption that depreciation is dependent solely on the passage of time. Depreciation is spread uniformly over the useful life of a property (building).

When doing depreciation problems, it is important to remember that land does NOT depreciate.

To find depreciation using the straight-line method use:

ANNUAL DEPRECIATION (A) = $\dfrac{\text{VALUE (COST) OF IMPROVEMENTS (V)}}{\text{ECONOMIC LIFE (E)}}$

or simplified:

$$A = \frac{V}{E}$$

Let's try a problem using straight-line depreciation:

EXAMPLE: Mr. and Mrs. Roberts purchased some income property for $475,000. The land was valued at $200,000. The improvements had an estimated economic life of 27.5 years. What would be the depreciated value of the property after 17 years?

ANSWER: We must first determine the value of the depreciable asset (improvements) because land is not depreciated.

$475,000 **(land and improvements)**
- 200,000 (land)
$275,000 **(COST of improvements)**

$\underline{A} = V = A = \underline{\$275,000} = $ **$10,000 depreciation per year**
E   27.5

$10,000 x 17 years = $170,000 **accumulated depreciation**
$275,000 - $170,000 = $105,000 **depreciated value of the improvements only**
$105,000 + $200,000 **(value of land)** = $305,000

$305,000 is the depreciated value of the property.

The IRS allows a minimum of 27.5 years straight-line depreciation on residential properties and 39 years on commercial properties.

VI. How to Find the Value of a Parcel

SECTION 7

NW 160 Acres	NE
40 Acres ▮	SE

SECTION 4

NW	▮ 80 Acres
SW	SE

PROBLEM: The NW¼ of the SW¼ of Section 7 is valued at $800 per acre. The N½ of the NE¼ of Section 4 is valued at $500 per acre. What is the difference in value between the two parcels?

SOLUTION:

1 section = 640 acres
¼ section = 160 acres
¼ of ½ section = 40 acres
40 acres x $800 per acre = $32,000
½ of ¼ section = 80 acres
80 acres x $500 per acre = $40,000
$40,000 - $32,000 = $8000

ANSWER: $8,000

VII. CHAPTER SUMMARY

This chapter illustrates some of the basic mathematical skills useful for a career in real estate. Familiarity with fundamental arithmetic and a few simple formulas, along with plain common sense, will provide the necessary background. Such knowledge will not only assist in the practice of real estate, but should also prove advantageous in passing the licensing exam. You should know the following common measurements:

LINEAR

1 foot (ft.) = 12 inches (in.)
1 yard (yd.) = 3 feet (ft.)
1 rod = 16.5 ft. = 5.5 yd.
1 mile = 5,280 ft. = 1,760 yd. = 320 rods

SQUARE

1 sq. ft. = 144 sq. in. (12 in. x 12 in.)
1 sq. yd. = 9 sq. ft. (3 ft. x 3 ft.)
1 acre = 43,560 sq. ft. = 4,840 sq. yd. = 160 sq. rods
1 sq. mile = 5,280 ft. x 5,280 ft.

CUBIC

1 cu. ft. = 1,728 cu. in. (12 in. x 12 in. x 12 in.)
1 cu. yd. = 27 cu. ft. (3 ft. x 3 ft. x 3 ft.)

LAND DESCRIPTION

1 link = 7.92 inches
1 rod = 25 links
1 chain = 100 links = 66 ft. = 4 rods
1 mile = 80 chains
1 acre = 43,560 sq. ft.
1 township = 36 sections = 36 square miles = 23,040 acres
1 section = 1 mile square = 640 acres = 1/36 of a township
1 circle = 360 degrees (°)
1 quadrant = 90 degrees (°)
1 degree (°) = 60 minutes (´)
1 minute (´) = 60 seconds (´´)

The agent needs to know measurements. The buyer wants to know how much land and building space he or she is buying. **Area measurements (length times width)** in square feet gives him or her that information.

Land area is the surface space between lot lines measured in square feet. **Building area** is the space enclosed by the exterior walls, measured in square feet.

Rectangular Lot: 4-sided parcels. Opposite sides are equal in length and right angles are formed by the intersection of the sides. Area equals Length times Width: **A = L x W.**

Triangular Lot: 3-sided parcel. Area equals Base (horizontal side) times Height (perpendicular distance from base to highest point) divided by 2: **A = B x H ÷ 2.**

Irregular Lot: Parcel that does not consist of a single known shape. Area is determined by breaking lot into rectangles and triangles and totalling the areas: **Total Area = Area (S) + Area (R) + Area (T).**

Structural Volume is the cubic measure of the space within a structure. Structural volume measurement is generally used when renting space in a warehouse type structure. **Cubic Measure** is determined by multiplying the interior length by the width and the height: **V = L x W x H.**

The majority of math problems that you will encounter in real estate involve the use of **percentages**. It is important, therefore, for you to understand certain general rules about percentage problems before dealing with any of the particular types.

Percentage problems: Factors are: (1) Amount invested is the amount **Paid (P)**; (2) The rate is the **Percentage (%)**; and (3) The amount **Made (M)** is the amount earned. One of the three factors is usually missing. To compute the missing factor:

Amount Paid (P)   =   Amount Made (M) ÷ Percentage Rate (%)
Amount Made (M)   =   Amount Paid (P) x Percentage (%)
Percentage Rate (%) =   Amount Made (M) ÷ Amount Paid (P)

The **commission** is the dollar amount received by a real estate agent for completing the sale.

Determining Commissions and Selling Price: The **Commission Rate** is a percentage of selling price. The **Commission** is the dollar amount received for completing the sale:

Commission = Principal Paid x Percentage Rate

Profit and Loss: Profit is the excess of revenues over expenses. **Loss** is the excess of expenses over revenues. **Profits = Revenues minus Expenses**.

Large amounts of capital are necessary to complete most real estate transactions. As a licensed real estate agent, financing will often be one of the major concerns of your clients. It will be advantageous for you to be able to provide loan counseling as a part of your services. Your ability to readily calculate **principal and interest payments** will be essential to this service.

Principal and Interest Calculations: Interest is the fee paid for the use of other people's money. **Interest (Amount Made) = Principal (Amount Paid) x Percentage Rate (%) x Time (T)**.

Determining Prorations: Dividing expenses (property taxes) or income (rents) to a specified date, close of escrow or other agreed upon date, in proportion to the time each party owned or will own the property, is called proration. In determining the proration of rents, it's important to remember that all escrow companies use a 365-day calendar year unless the contract specified otherwise. It is important to remember that under the TREC contracts prorations are made through the day of closing which gives the seller any prorated amounts for that day.

Amortizations: To amortize a loan means to make payment installments of principal and interest so that the loan is completely paid off at the end of the term. In fact the word amortize means to "kill off." As a result, an amortized loan will be killed off a little at a time. Performing amortizations is easily done on a financial calculator, but it is also fairly straightforward using simple arithmetic.

To determine the interest portion of a loan payment, multiply the remaining loan balance by the annual interest rate, then divide the result by 12. Then, in order to determine the amount of principal to be paid in the same monthly loan payment, simply subtract the interest amount from the monthly loan payment. The remaining amount is the principal paid for that month. Subtracting the principal amount from our previous loan balance will give us the new loan balance.

Straight-line depreciation is the difference between original cost of improvements and salvage value that is deducted in even installments over the life of the asset. When doing depreciation problems, it is important to remember that land does not depreciate, just the cost of improvements depreciate. The IRS allows straight-line depreciation of 27.5 years on residential properties and 39 years on commercial properties.

Annual Depreciation (A) = Cost of Improvements - salvage value (V) ÷ Economic Life (E)

VIII. TERMINOLOGY

A. Area
B. Commission
C. Credit
D. Cubic Area
E. Debit
F. Depreciation

G. Discount Points (Points)
H. Interest
I. Interest Rate
J. Irregular Lot
K. Principal (Amount Paid)
L. Proration

M. Rectangular Lot
N. Result (Amount Made)
O. Straight-Line Depreciation
P. Triangular Lot

1.____ The amount of money borrowed.
2.____ Money owed, as it is shown on the settlement statement.
3.____ The up-front charge by a lender to obtain and to increase the yield on a loan.
4.____ The amount paid to a real estate broker usually expressed as a percentage of the sale price.
5.____ To divide property taxes, insurance premiums, rental income, etc. between buyer and seller proportionately to time of use or the date of closing.
6.____ Decrease in value to real property improvements by any cause.
7.____ The rent or charge for the use of money.
8.____ The surface of land or building. Length (in feet) times width (in feet).
9.____ The area of this shaped lot is obtained by multiplying base times height and dividing by 2.
10.____ Money received, as it is shown on the settlement statement.
11.____ Principal (paid) times rate (%) equals?
12.____ The percentage paid for the use of borrowed money. Usually expressed as an annual percentage.
13.____ Equal amount of depreciation each year. A loss in the value of improvements, used as an accounting (income tax) procedure.
14.____ A lot with an unusual shape.
15.____ The result of multiplying length times width times height.
16.____ Four-sided figure with opposite sides equal in length and intersecting corners forming right angles.

IX. MULTIPLE CHOICE

1. Mrs. Donaldson owns a duplex and rents each unit for $900 a month. She sells the property with an April 22 closing. Having collected the April rent on April 1, which of the following is true?

    a. Debit seller $1320 and credit buyer $1320

    b. Debit seller $480 and credit buyer $480

    c. Credit seller $480 and debit buyer $480

    d. Credit seller $1320 and debit buyer $480

2. Carol borrowed $5,200 and signed a straight note with an interest rate of 7% per annum. If she paid $1,125 in interest during the term of the note, what was the term of the note?

    a. 22 months

    b. 27 months

    c. 32 months

    d. 37 months

3. A woman owns a rental unit that nets her $450 per month. She realizes a 10% return on her investment each year. What is her investment in the property?

    a. $45,000

    b. $48,500

    c. $54,000

    d. None of the above

4. The assessed value of a piece of property is $48,700. The tax is $1.02 per $100 of assessed valuation. The tax is:

    a. $496.74.

    b. $489.60.

    c. $584.40.

    d. $594.14.

5. How much would have to be invested at 7% in order to provide an investor with $640 monthly income?

    a. $9,143

    b. $91,429

    c. $109,714

    d. $53,760

6. The second quarter interest on a $7,600 term loan at 8% interest is:

    a. $76.

    b. $152.

    c. $608.

    d. none of the above.

7. An apartment complex cost $450,000. It brings in a net income of $3,000 per month. The owner is making what percentage of return on her investment?

    a. 7%
    b. 8%
    c. 11%
    d. 12%

8. Broker Jones negotiates a lease for 3,000 square feet of warehouse storage space at a monthly rental of $0.50 per square foot. Jones' commission is 8% of the first year's gross. Jones will receive:

    a. $1,180.
    b. $1,340.
    c. $1,440.
    d. none of the above.

9. Frank holds a five-year trust deed and note that was paid off at 7.2% interest per annum. If the total interest he received from the borrower was $4,140, what, approximately, was the original amount of the loan?

    a. $11,500
    b. $29,700
    c. $33,650
    d. $57,500

10. A builder constructed a home for $350,000 and sold it for a 20% profit. What is the amount of profit?

    a. $17,500
    b. $20,000
    c. $35,000
    d. $70,000

ANSWERS: 1. b; 2. d; 3. c; 4. a; 5. a; 6. b; 7. b; 8. c; 9. a; 10. d

The definitions given here explain how the listed terms are used in the real estate field. Some of the terms have additional meanings, which can be found in a standard dictionary.

A

Abandonment: Failure to occupy and use property; may result in a loss of rights.

Abstract of Judgment: A summary of the provisions of a court judgment; when recorded, it creates a lien on all the real property of the debtor in the county where recorded.

Abstract of Title: A brief, chronological summary of the recorded documents affecting the title to a particular parcel of real property. COMPARE: Title Commitment.

Acceleration Clause: 1. A provision in a loan agreement allowing the lender to declare the entire debt due immediately if the borrower defaults. Also known as a call provision. 2. A due-on-sale clause.

Acceptance: 1. Agreeing to the terms of an offer to enter into a contract, thereby creating a binding contract. 2. Taking delivery of a deed.

Accession: The acquisition of title to additional property by its annexation to real estate already owned. This can be the result of human actions or natural processes. SEE: Annexation; Accretion.

Accord and Satisfaction: An agreement to accept something different than (and usually less than) what the original contract called for.

Accretion: A gradual addition to dry land by the forces of nature, as when the tide deposits waterborne sediment on shoreline property. SEE: Accession; Alluvion.

Accusation: A written statement of rules violated, used in a property right hearing.

Acknowledgment: When a person who has signed a document formally declares to an authorized official (usually a notary public) that he or she signed voluntarily. The official attests that the signature is voluntary and genuine.

Act: A statute.

Actual Notice: SEE: Notice, Actual.

ADA: Americans with Disabilities Act.

Adjustable-Rate Mortgage (ARM): A mortgage or deed of trust with a variable interest rate (an interest rate that changes periodically).

Adjudicative Methods: The resolution of a dispute by mirroring the judicial process in that a third party decides the controversy much as a judge does in court.

Administrative Agency: A government agency (federal, state, or local) that administers a complex area of law, adopting and enforcing detailed regulations that have the force of law.

Administrative Law Judge: A law judge that conducts administrative hearings enforcing the detailed regulations that have the force of law, by a government agency. An administrative law judge is not the same as a judge of a court of law.

Ad Valorem: A Latin phrase meaning "according to value"; used to refer to taxes assessed on the value of property.

Adverse Possession: Acquiring title to someone else's real property by possession of it. The possession must be actual, open, notorious, hostile, exclusive, continuous, and uninterrupted for a period of years. COMPARE: Prescription.

Affiant: One who swears to an affidavit.

Affidavit: A sworn statement that has been written down and acknowledged; may be submitted as evidence in a trial.

Affidavit of Commencement: An affidavit filed by a contractor used to establish the priority of a mechanic's lien in Texas. The affidavit is filed with the county clerk of the county in which the work is to be performed.

Affirm: In an appeal, to rule that the lower court's decision was correct, rejecting the appellant's arguments.

After-Acquired Title: SEE: Title, After-Acquired.

Agency: A relationship of trust created when one person (the principal) gives another (the agent) the right to represent the principal in dealings with third parties.

Agency, Apparent: SEE: Agency, Ostensible.

Agency, Exclusive: SEE: Listing, Exclusive Agency.

Agency, Ostensible: 1. When someone who has not been authorized to represent another acts as if he or she is that person's agent. 2. When an agent acts beyond the scope of his or her authority, giving a third party the impression that the acts are authorized. Also called apparent agency.

Agent: A person authorized to represent another (the principal) in dealings with third parties.

Agent, General: An agent authorized to handle all of the principal's affairs in one area or in specified areas.

Agent, Special: An agent with limited authority to do a specific thing or conduct a specific transaction.

Agent, Universal: An agent authorized to do everything that can be lawfully delegated to a representative.

Agreement: SEE: Contract.

Ag-Use Appriasal: SEE: Rollback Taxes.

Air Lot: A parcel of property above the surface of the earth, not containing any land; for example, a condominium unit on the third floor.

Air Rights: The right to undisturbed use and control of the airspace over a parcel of land; may be transferred separately from the land.

Alienation: The transfer of ownership or an interest in property from one person to another, by any means.

Alienation, Involuntary: Transfer of an interest in property against the will of the owner, or without action by the owner, occurring through operation of law, natural processes, or adverse possession.

Alienation, Voluntary: When an owner voluntarily transfers an interest to someone else.

Alienation Clause: SEE: Due-on-sale Clause.

Alternative Dispute Resolution (ADR): The resolution of disputes by nonjudicial means, such as negotiation, mediation, and arbitration.

Alluvion: The solid material deposited along a shore by accretion. Also called alluvium.

Alluvium: SEE: Alluvion.

Ambiguous: Capable of being understood in more than one sense; having a double meaning.

Amortization Book: A book containing tables and charts by which loan payments may be easily calculated.

Amortized: SEE: Note, Installment.

Amount in Controversy: The amount of money at issue in a lawsuit; used as a limitation on the jurisdiction of some courts.

Annexation: Attaching personal property to land so that the law views it as part of the real property (a fixture). Annexation can be actual or constructive.

Annexation, Actual: A physical attachment of personal property to land. SEE: Fixture.

Annexation, Constructive: When personal property is associated with real property in such a way that the law treats it as a fixture, even though it is not physically attached to the real property.

Annual Percentage Rate (APR): the charges a borrower pays a lender for a loan (interest, discount points, loan fees, etc.), expressed as an annual percentage.

Antitrust: A term referring to federal laws designed to combat anticompetitive, unfair and monopolistic practices by large business interests.

Appeal: The process in which a higher court reviews the decision of a lower court or an administrative tribunal.

Appellant: The party who files an appeal because he or she is dissatisfied with the lower court's decision. Also known as the petitioner.

Appellee: In an appeal, the party who did not file the appeal. Also known as the respondent.

Appraisal: An estimate or opinion of the value of a piece of property as of a certain date. Also called valuation.

Appraisal District: A district established in each Texas county which is responsible for the appraisal of all property within the district for ad valorem tax purposes; also known as a county appraisal district.

Appraisal Review Board: A body of citizens who hear and resolve protests over appraisal matters.

Appraiser: One who appraises property, especially an expert qualified to do so by education and experience.

Appurtenance: A right that goes along with ownership of a piece of real property; usually transferred with the property, but may be sold separately.

Appurtenance, Intangible: An appurtenant right that does not involve ownership of physical objects; for example, an easement (as opposed to mineral rights).

Appurtenant Easement: SEE: Easement, Appurtenant.

APR: Annual percentage rate.

Arbitration: The act of a neutral third party who listens to each party's position and makes a final binding decision.

Arbitrator: A neutral third party who receives evidence and resolves the dispute. COMPARE: Mediator.

ARM: Adjustable rate mortgage.

Artificial Person: A person created by law, as distinguished from a natural person, a human being; usually refers to a corporation.

Asbestos: A mineral fiber formerly commonly used for fireproofing and insulation; now known to cause a number of serious diseases including cancer and asbestosis if inhaled.

"As Is" Clause: A provision in a deposit receipt stating that the buyer accepts the property in its present condition.

Assessment: 1. A government's valuation of property for tax purposes. 2. A special assessment.

Assessor: An official who determines the value of property for taxation.

Assign: To transfer a right or an interest in property to another.

Assignee: One to whom a right or interest has been assigned.

Assignor: One who assigns a right or interest to another.

Assumption: When a buyer takes on personal responsibility for paying off a mortgage or deed of trust that was originally taken out by the seller.

Assumption Fee: A sum paid to the lender, usually by the buyer, when a mortgage or deed of trust is assumed.

Attachment: Court-ordered seizure of property belonging to a defendant in a lawsuit, so that it will be available to satisfy a judgment. In the case of real property, attachment creates a lien.

Attachments, Man-Made: SEE: Fixture.

Attachments, Natural: Things growing on a piece of land, such as trees, shrubs, or crops. SEE: Emblements, Doctrine of; Fructus Industriales; Fructus Naturales. COMPARE: Fixture.

Attestation: The act of witnessing the execution of an instrument (such as a deed or will).

Attorney in Fact: Any person authorized to act for another by a power of attorney; not necessarily a lawyer (an attorney at law).

Authority, Actual: Authority actually given to an agent by the principal, either expressly or by implication.

Authority, Apparent: SEE: Agency, Apparent.

Authority, Implied: An agent's authority to do everything reasonably necessary to carry out the principal's express orders.

Avulsion: 1. When land is suddenly (not gradually) torn away by the action of water, potentially causing a transfer of title. 2. A sudden shift in a watercourse, which doesn't cause a transfer of title.

Award: The decision of the arbitrator.

B

Balloon Payment: A final payment on a loan that is significantly larger than the earlier installment payments. SEE: Note. Installment.

Base Line: In the government survey system, a main east-west line from which township lines are established. Each principal meridian has one base line associated with it.

Basis: A figure used in calculating gain on the sale of real estate for income tax purposes. Initially, the basis is the amount the owner originally paid for the property, but the figure is adjusted to reflect improvements, cost recovery deductions, and other factors.

Bench Mark: A metal disk set in a stable position at a known elevation, used as a reference point in calculating the elevation of land and other objects in a surveyed area.

Beneficiary: 1. One for whom a trust is created and on whose behalf the trustee administers the trust. 2. The lender in a deed of trust transaction. 3. One entitled to receive real or personal property under a will; a legatee or devisee.

Bequeath: To transfer personal property to another by a will.

Bequest: Personal property transferred by a will. Also called a legacy.

Bill: A proposed law formally submitted to a legislature for consideration.

Bill of Sale: A document used to transfer title to personal property from one person to another.

Binding Arbitration: The decision of the arbitrator that is final and not reviewable by the courts.

Block: In reference to platted property, a group of lots surrounded by streets or unimproved land.

Blockbusting: The illegal practice of inducing owners to sell their homes (often at a deflated price) by suggesting that the ethnic or racial composition of the neighborhood is changing, with the implication that property values will decline as a result. Also called panic peddling.

Bona Fide: In good faith; genuine.

Boot: In an exchange, any property that isn't treated as like-kind for income tax purposes; for example, if a building is traded for vacant land and a yacht, the yacht is boot.

Boundary: The perimeter or border of a parcel of land; the dividing line between one piece of property and another.

Bounds: Boundaries. SEE: Metes and Bounds Description.

Breach: Violation of an obligation, duty, or law.

Breach, Material: A breach of contract important enough so that it excuses the nonbreaching party from performing his or her contractual obligations.

Breach of Contract: An unexcused failure to perform according to the terms of a contract.

Broker: 1. A person who is licensed for compensation to represent one or more of the parties in a real estate transaction, for compensation. 2. An advanced Texas real estate license.

Brokerage: A broker's business of buying, selling, leasing, listing, exchanging property.

Building Code: A set of rules establishing minimum standards for construction methods and materials.

Buffer Zone: An area of land designed to separate one zoning use from another.

Burden of Proof: SEE: Proof, Burden of.

Business Compulsion: SEE: Duress, Economic.

C

Cancellation: Termination of a contract without undoing acts that have already been performed under the contract. COMPARE: Rescission.

Canons of Professional Ethics: The first five rules of the Texas Real Estate Commission that all Texas real estate licensees have pledged to obey.

Capacity: Legal ability to perform some act, such as enter into a contract or execute a deed or will. SEE: Competent; Minor.

Capital Expenditure: Money expended on improvements and repair to prolong property life; not deductible. COMPARE: Deduction, Repair.

Carryback Loan: SEE: Loan, Carryback.

Case Law: Rules of law developed in court decisions, as opposed to constitutional law, statutory law, or administrative regulations. Also called decisional law.

Caucus: Occurs when the mediator meets with each party individually.

Caveat Emptor: A Latin phrase meaning "let the buyer beware." It expresses the common law rule that a buyer is expected to examine the property carefully instead of relying on the seller to disclose problems. The rule has lost most of its strength, particularly in residential transactions.

CC&Rs: A declaration of covenants, conditions, and restrictions; usually recorded by a developer to create a common plan of private restrictions for a subdivision.

CERCLA: Comprehensive Environmental Response, Compensation, and Liability Act.

Certificate Holder: A person registered under TREC to buy, sell, lease or transfer easements or rights of way for utilities, railroads, pipelines or telecommunication firms. COMPARE: Broker; Residential Rental Locator; Salesperson.

Certificate of Occupancy: A statement issued by a local government verifying that a newly constructed building is in compliance with all codes and may be occupied.

Chain of Title: SEE: Title, Chain of.

Chattel: A piece of personal property.

Chattel Real: Personal property that is closely associated with real property, such as a lease.

Civil Law: The body of law concerned with the rights and liabilities of one individual in relation to another; includes contract, tort, and property law. COMPARE: Criminal Law.

Civil Rights: Fundamental rights guaranteed to all persons by the law. The term is primarily used in reference to constitutional and statutory protections against discrimination based on race, religion, sex, or national origin.

Civil Wrong: SEE: Tort.

Client: One who employs a broker, lawyer, or other professional. A real estate broker's client can be the seller, the buyer, the landlord, or tenant. As an Intermediary, a broker may represent more than one client at a time. SEE: Intermediary; Principal; COMPARE: Customer.

Closing: The final stage in a real estate transaction, when the seller receives the purchase money and the buyer receives the deed.

Closing Costs: Expenses incurred in the transfer of real estate in addition to the purchase price; for example, the appraisal fee, title insurance premiums, and broker's commission.

Closing Statement: SEE: Settlement Statement.

Cloud on the Title: A claim, encumbrance, or apparent defect that makes the title to real property unmarketable.

Codicil: An addition to or revision of a will. It must be executed with the same formalities as a will.

Codification: Collection and organization of piecemeal laws into a comprehensive code.

Collateral: Anything of value used as security for a debt or obligation.

Collusion: An agreement between two or more persons to defraud someone.

Color of Title: A title that appears to be a good title, but which in fact is not.

Commercial Property: Property zoned and used for business purposes, such as a store, restaurant or office building; as distinguished from residential, industrial, or agricultural property.

Commingling: Illegally mixing personal funds with money held in trust on behalf of a client. SEE: Conversion.

Commission: The compensation paid a broker for services in a real estate transaction; usually a percentage of the sales price rather than a flat fee.

Common Areas: The land and improvements in a condominium, planned development, or cooperative that are owned and used collectively by all the residents, such as the parking lot, hallways, and recreational facilities; does not include the individual apartment units or homes.

Common Grantor: A person who owned two or more adjacent properties and then sold them to different buyers.

Common Law: 1. Early English law. 2. Long-established rules based on English law, followed in many states including Texas. 3. Case law.

Common Law Remedy: Money awarded to the plaintiff in a civil lawsuit; damages. COMPARE: Equitable Remedy.

Community Property: Property owned jointly by a married couple in Texas; any property acquired through the labor or skill of either spouse during marriage. COMPARE: Separate Property.

Competent: 1. Of sound mind, for the purposes of entering a contract or executing a will; not suffering from mental illness, retardation, or senility. 2. Of sound mind and having reached the age of majority.

Complaint: 1. The document a plaintiff files with the court to start a lawsuit. 2. The document upon which an administrative proceeding is based.

Conciliation Agreement: A settlement agreement reached among the parties to a fair housing administrative complaint.

Concurrent Ownership: Any form of ownership in which two or more people share title to a piece of property, holding undivided interests. Also called co-tenancy. SEE: Community Property; Tenancy, Joint; Tenancy in Common.

Condemnation: 1. Taking private property or public use through the government's power of eminent domain. 2. A declaration that a structure is unfit for occupancy and must be closed or demolished.

Condition: A provision in an agreement or deed that makes the parties' rights and obligations depend on the occurrence (or nonoccurrence) of a particular event. Also called a contingency clause.

Conditional Use Permit: A permit issued by a zoning authority that allows property to be used in a manner not ordinarily allowed in the zone where it's located; primarily for uses that benefit the public, such as hospitals, schools, and cemeteries. Also called a special exception permit.

Condominium: Property developed for concurrent ownership, where each co-owner has a separate interest in an individual unit, combined with an undivided interest in the common areas of the property. COMPARE: Cooperative.

Condominium Association: The organization that manages the operation of a condominium, imposing assessments and arranging for the maintenance of the common areas. The association's members are the unit owners, and they usually elect a board of directors.

Condominium Declaration: The document that must be filed for record when property is developed as or converted to a condominium.

Consideration: Anything of value given to induce another to enter into a contract, such as money, services, goods, or a promise. Sometimes called valuable consideration.

Consideration, Adequate: Consideration that is comparable in value to the consideration the other party to the contract is giving. A contract is enforceable even if the consideration is inadequate, but a court can't order specific performance in that case.

Constitution: A fundamental document that establishes a government's structure and sets limits on its power.

Constitutional: 1. Pertaining to or based on a constitution. 2. Not in violation of the U.S. Constitution or a state constitution.

Constructive Eviction: SEE: Eviction, Constructive.

Constructive Notice: SEE: Notice, Constructive.

Consummate: To complete.

Contingency Clause: SEE: Condition.

Contract: An agreement between two or more persons to do or not do a certain thing. The requirements for an enforceable contract are capacity, mutual consent, a lawful purpose, and consideration. In addition, many contracts, especially real estate contracts, must be in writing to be enforceable.

Contract, Bilateral: A contract in which each party promises to do something. COMPARE: Contract, Unilateral.

Contract, Executed: A contract in which both parties have completely performed their contractual obligations.

Contract, Executory: A contract in which one or both parties have not yet completed performance of their obligations.

Contract, Express: A contract that has been put into words, either spoken or written.

Contract, Implied: An agreement that has not been put into words, but is implied by the actions of the parties.

Contract, Installment Land: SEE: Contract, Land.

Contract, Land: A contract for the sale of property in which the buyer pays in installments, taking possession of the property immediately, but not taking title until the purchase price has been paid in full. Also called an installment land contract, installment sales contract, land sales contract, real estate contract, and other names.

Contract, Oral: A spoken agreement, as opposed to a written one.

Contract, Unenforceable: An agreement that a court would refuse to enforce; for example, it may be unenforceable because its contents cannot be proven, or because it is not in writing, or because the statute of limitations has run out.

Contract, Unilateral: When one party promises to do something if the other party performs a certain act, but the other party does not promise to perform it; the contract is formed only if the other party does perform the requested act. COMPARE: Contract, Bilateral.

Contract, Valid: A binding, legally enforceable contract.

Contract, Void: An agreement that is not an enforceable contract because it lacks a required element or is defensive in some other respect.

Contract, Voidable: A contract that one of the parties can disaffirm without liability because of lack of capacity or a negative factor, such as fraud or duress.

Conversion: 1. Misappropriating property or funds belonging to another. 2. Changing an existing rental apartment building into a condominium.

Conveyance: The transfer of title to real property from one person to another by means of a written document, such as a deed.

Cooperative: A building owned by a corporation, where the residents are shareholders in the corporation; each shareholder receives a proprietary lease on an individual unit and the right to use the common areas. COMPARE: Condominium.

Corporation: An association organized according to strict regulations, in which individuals purchase ownership shares; regarded by the law as an artificial person, separate from the individual shareholders. COMPARE: Partnership.

Corporation, Domestic: A corporation doing business in the state where it was created (incorporated).

Corporation, Foreign: A corporation doing business in one state, but created (incorporated) in another state.

Correction Lines: Adjustment lines used in the government survey system to compensate for the curvature of the earth. They occur at 24-mile intervals (every fourth township line), where the distance between range lines is corrected to 6 miles.

Co-Tenancy: SEE: Concurrent Ownership.

Co-Tenant: Anyone who shares ownership of a piece of property with another; may be a joint tenant, a tenant in common, a tenant in partnership, or a spouse owning community property.

Counter Offer: A response to an offer to enter into a contract, changing some of the terms of the original offer. A counter offer is a rejection of the offer (not a form of acceptance), and does not create a binding contract unless accepted by the original offeror.

County Appraisal District: See Appraisal District.

Course: A direction, stated in terms of a compass bearing, in a metes and bounds description of property.

Covenant: 1. A contract. 2. A promise. 3. A guarantee (express or implied) in a document such as a deed or lease. 4. A restrictive covenant.

Covenant, Restrictive: SEE: Restrictive Covenant.

Covenant of Quiet Enjoyment: A promise that a buyer or tenant's possession will not be disturbed by the previous owner, the lessor, or anyone else claiming an interest in the property.

Covenants, Conditions, and Restrictions: SEE: CC&Rs.

CRA: Community Reinvestment Act.

Credit: A payment receivable (owed to someone), as opposed to a debit, which is a payment due (owed by someone).

Creditor: One who is owed a debt.

Creditor, Secured: A creditor with a lien on specific property, which enables him or her to foreclose and collect the debt from the sale proceeds if it is not otherwise paid.

Criminal Law: The body of law concerned with crimes or an individual's actions against society. COMPARE: Civil Law.

Cure: To remedy a default by paying money that is overdue or by fulfilling other obligations.

Customer: A person involved in a real estate transaction (buyer, seller, landlord, tenant) whom the broker does not represent. COMPARE: Client.

D

Damages: An amount of money a defendant is ordered to pay to a plaintiff.

Damages, Actual: Compensatory damages.

Damages, Compensatory: Damages intended to compensate the plaintiff for harm caused by the defendant's act or failure to act, including personal injuries (physical and mental), property damage, and financial losses.

Damages, Consequential: Damages compensating for losses that were not the direct result of the defendant's wrongful act, but which were a foreseeable consequence of it.

Damages, Exemplary: Punitive damages.

Damages, Liquidated: A sum that the parties to a contract agree to in advance (at the time of entering into the contract) that will serve as compensation in the event of a breach.

Damages, Punitive: An award added to compensatory damages, to punish the defendant for malicious or outrageous conduct and discourage others from similar acts.

Datum: An artificial horizontal plane of elevation, established in reference to sea level, used by surveyors as a reference point in determining elevation.

Dealer Property: Property held for sale to customers rather than as a long-term investment; a developer's inventory of subdivision lots, for example.

Debit: A charge or a debt owed to another.

Debtor: One who owes money to another.

Decedent: A person who has died.

Decisional Law: SEE: Case Law.

Designation of Homestead: The signed document that establishes a person's homestead.

Declaration of Restrictions: SEE: CC&Rs.

Dedication: An appropriation or gift of private property for public use; may transfer ownership or simply create a public easement.

Dedication, Implied: Involuntary dedication, resulting from an owner's acquiescence to public use of his or her property for at least five years. Also called common law dedication. COMPARE: Prescription.

Dedication, Statutory: A dedication required by law; for example, dedication of property for streets and sidewalks as a prerequisite to subdivision approval.

Deduction: An amount a taxpayer is allowed to subtract from his or her income before calculating the tax on the income.

Deduction, Cost Recovery: An income tax deduction that allows the taxpayer to recover the cost of depreciable property used for the production of income or used in a trade or business. Formerly called a depreciation deduction.

Deduction, Depreciation: SEE: Deduction, Cost Recovery.

Deduction, Repair: An income tax deduction allowed for expenditure made to keep property in ordinary, efficient operating condition; not allowed for a principal residence or personal use property. COMPARE: Capital Expenditure.

Deed: An instrument that conveys ownership of real property from the grantor to the grantee.

Deed, Correction: A deed used to correct minor mistakes in an earlier deed, such as misspelled names or errors in the legal description.

Deed, General Warranty: A deed in which the grantor warrants the title against defects that might have arisen before or during his or her period of ownership. In Texas the grantor typically warrants that he/she has not previously conveyed the property to anyone else and that the grantor will convey the property free and clear of all liens. COMPARE: Deed, Special Warranty.

Deed, Gift: A deed that isn't supported by valuable consideration; often lists "love and affection" as the consideration.

Deed, Quitclaim: A deed that conveys any interest in a piece of real property the grantor has at the time the deed is executed. Often used to clear up a cloud on the title. It contains no warranties of any kind, and does not convey after-acquired title.

Deed, Sheriff's: A deed delivered by the sheriff, on court order, to the holder of the certificate of sale when the redemption period after a mortgage foreclosure has expired.

Deed, Special Warranty: A deed in which the grantor warrants title only against defects that arose during the time he or she owned the property, and not against defects that arose before that time; often used by new homebuilders and sellers of previously foreclosed property. COMPARE: Deed, General Warranty.

Deed, Trustee's: A deed given to a purchaser of property at a trustee's sale.

Deed in Lieu of Foreclosure: A deed given by a borrower to the lender to satisfy the debt and avoid foreclosure.

Deed of Trust: An instrument that creates a voluntary lien on real property to secure the repayment of a debt. The parties to a deed of trust are the grantor or trustor (borrower), beneficiary (lender), and trustee (neutral third party). Unlike a mortgage, a deed of trust includes a power of sale, allowing the trustee to foreclose nonjudicially.

Deed of Trust, Blanket: 1. A deed of trust that covers more than one parcel of real estate. 2. A deed of trust that covers an entire building or development, rather than an individual unit or lot.

Deed of Trust, First: The deed of trust that has higher priority than any other on a property. This is usually the one that was recorded first, unless there is a subordination agreement. SEE: Subordination Agreement.

Deed of Trust, Junior: A second (or third, etc.) deed of trust, with lower lien priority than the first trust deed.

Deed of Trust, Senior: A deed of trust with higher priority than another deed of trust on a property.

Deed Restriction: A restrictive covenant in a deed.

Default: Failure to fulfill an obligation, duty, or promise, as when a borrower fails to make payments, or a tenant fails to pay rent. COMPARE: Grace Period.

Defeasible Fee: SEE: Fee Simple Defeasible.

Defendant: 1. The person being sued in a civil lawsuit. 2. The accused person in a criminal lawsuit.

Deferment: A right to delay fulfillment of an obligation (such as paying a tax) until a later date.

Deficiency Judgment: A personal judgment entered against a debtor if the proceeds from a foreclosure sale of security property are not enough to pay off the debt.

Delivery: The legal transfer of a deed (or other instrument). A valid deed doesn't convey title until it has been delivered (annually or constructively) to the grantee. SEE: Donative Intent.

Deposition: The formal, out-of-court testimony of a witness in a lawsuit, taken before the trial; used as part of the discovery process to determine the facts of the case, or if the witness won't be able to attend the trial. A transcript of a deposition can be introduced as evidence in the trial.

Depreciable Property: Property that is eligible for depreciation (cost recovery) deduction, because it will wear out and have to be replaced. SEE: Deduction, Cost Recovery.

Depreciate: To decline in value.

Devise: 1. (noun) Real property transferred in a will. 2. (verb) To transfer real property by will. COMPARE: Bequeath; Bequest; Legacy.

Devisee: A recipient of real property under a will. COMPARE: Beneficiary; Legatee.

Disaffirm: To ask a court to terminate a voidable contract.

Discount Point: One percent of the principal amount of a loan, paid to the lender at the time the loan is made, to give the lender an additional yield above the interest rate. Because of the points paid at the outset, the lender is willing to make the loan at a lower interest rate.

Discrimination: Arbitrarily treating people unequally because of their race, religion, sex, national origin, age, or some other characteristic.

Domicile: The state where a person has his or her permanent home.

Dominant Tenement: SEE: Tenement, Dominant.

Donative Intent: An intent to transfer title immediately and unconditionally.

Due-on-Sale Clause: A clause in a loan agreement giving the lender the right to declare the entire amount of the loan due immediately if the security property is sold. Also called an alienation clause.

Due Process: A fair hearing before an impartial judge. Under the U.S. Constitution, no one may be deprived of life, liberty, or property without due process of law.

Duress: Unlawfully confining someone to force him or her to sign a document, or confining the signer's spouse, child, or other close relative. COMPARE: Menace.

Duress, Economic: Threatening to take some action that will be financially harmful to a person, to force him or her to sign a document; for example, threatening to breach a contract. Also called business compulsion.

E

Earnest Money: A cash deposit that gives evidence of a buyer's intent to carry out the terms of a real estate contract.

Easement: A right to use some part of another person's real property for a particular purpose; unlike a license, an easement is irrevocable and creates an interest in the property.

Easement, Appurtenant: An easement that benefits a particular piece of property, the dominant tenement. COMPARE: Easement in Gross.

Easement, Implied: SEE: Easement by Implication.

Easement, Negative: An easement that prevents the servient tenant from using his or her own land in a certain way (instead of allowing the dominant tenant to use it). Essentially the same thing as a restrictive covenant.

Easement, Prescriptive: An easement acquired by prescription.

Easement by Express Grant: An easement granted to another in a deed or other document.

Easement by Express Reservation: An easement created in a deed when a landowner is dividing the property, transferring the servient tenement but retaining the dominant tenement.

Easement by Implication: An easement created by law (not by express grant) when a parcel of land is divided, if there is a long-standing, apparent use that is reasonably necessary for the enjoyment of the dominant tenement. Also called an implied easement. COMPARE: Easement by Necessity.

Easement by Necessity: A special type of implied easement; when the dominant tenement would be completely useless without an easement, an easement exists even if it is not a long-standing, apparent use.

Easement in Gross: An easement that benefits a person instead of a piece of land; there is a dominant tenant, but no dominant tenement. COMPARE: Easement, Appurtenant.

ECOA: Equal Credit Opportunity Act.

Emblements, Doctrine of: The rule that an agricultural tenant has the right to enter the land to harvest crops after the lease ends.

Eminent Domain: The government's constitutional power to take (condemn) private property for public use, as long as the owner is paid just compensation.

Employee: Someone who works under the direction and control of another. COMPARE: Independent Contractor.

Encroachment: A physical intrusion onto neighboring property, usually due to a mistake regarding the boundary.

Encumbrance: A nonpossessory interest in property; a lien, easement, or restrictive covenant burdening the property owner's title.

Endorsement: When the payee on a negotiable instrument (such as a check or promissory note) assigns the right to payment to another by signing the back of the instrument.

Enjoin: To prohibit an act, or command performance of an act, by court order; to issue an injunction.

Enterprise Zone: A distressed area within a Texas city or county that has been targeted for special financial incentives in order to promote economic development and to create jobs.

Equal Protection Requirement: Under the U.S. Constitution, all citizens are entitled to equal protection of the laws; no law may arbitrarily discriminate between different groups, or be applied to different groups in a discriminatory manner.

Equitable Remedy: A judgment granted to a plaintiff that is something other than an award of money (damages); an injunction, quiet title, rescission, and specific performance are examples. COMPARE: Common Law Remedy.

Equitable Title: SEE: Title, Equitable.

Equity: 1. An owner's unencumbered interest in his or her property; the difference between the value of the property and the liens against it. 2. A judge's power to soften or set aside strict legal rules, to bring about a fair and just result in a particular case.

Erosion: A gradual loss of soil due to the action of water or wind.

Escheat: When unclaimed property reverts to the state after a person dies.

Escrow: The system in which things of value (such as money or documents) are held on behalf of the parties to a transition by a disinterested third party (an escrow agent), until specified conditions have been complied with.

Escrow Agent: A neutral third party, acting as a fiduciary, who holds money or documents pursuant to the instructions of both buyer and seller. In Texas, title company escrow agents are required to be licensed and bonded.

Estate: 1. A possessory interest in real property; either a freehold or a leasehold. 2. The property left by someone who has died.

Estate for Life: SEE: Life Estate.

Estate for Years: A leasehold estate set to last for a definite period (one week, three years, etc.), after which it terminates automatically. Also called a term tenancy.

Estate in Fee Simple: SEE: Fee Simple.

Estate in Remainder: SEE: Remainder.

Estate in Reversion: SEE: Reversion.

Estoppel: A legal doctrine that prevents a person from asserting rights or facts that are inconsistent with his or her earlier actions or statements.

Ethics: A system of accepted principles or standards of moral conduct.

Eviction: Dispossessing or expelling someone from real property. SEE: Forcible Entry and Detainer.

Eviction, Actual: Physically forcing someone off of property (or preventing them from reentering), or using the legal process to make someone leave. COMPARE: Eviction, Constructive.

Eviction, Constructive: When a landlord's act (or failure to act) interferes with the tenant's quiet enjoyment of the property, or makes the property unfit for its intended use to such an extent that the tenant is forced to move out.

Eviction, Retaliatory: When a landlord evicts a tenant in retaliation for requesting repairs, filing a complaint against the landlord, or organizing or participating in a tenants' rights group.

Eviction, Self-Help: When a landlord uses physical force, a lockout, or a utility shutoff to get rid of a tenant, instead of using the legal process.

Eviction, Wrongful: When a landlord evicts a tenant in violation of the tenant's rights.

Exceptions: Items or conditions listed within a title insurance policy that are unique to the subject property and may possibly be covered, such as issues involving encroachments. COMPARE: Exclusions.

Exclusions: Items or conditions listed within a title insurance policy that the policy will never cover such as losses due to future changes in zoning. COMPARE: Exceptions.

Exclusive Agency: SEE: Listing, Exclusive Agency.

Exclusive Right to Sell: SEE: Listing, Exclusive Right to Sell.

Execute: 1. To sign. 2. To perform or complete. SEE: Contract, Executed.

Execution: The legal process in which a court orders an official (such as a sheriff) to seize and sell the property of a judgment debtor to satisfy a judgment lien.

Executive: The head of a government, such as president, governor, or mayor.

Executor/Executrix: A person named in a will to carry out its provisions. A man is referred to as an executor; a woman is an executrix.

Exemption: 1. A provision holding that a law or rule doesn't apply to a particular person or group. 2. In ad valorem taxation, a determination that a particular party is exempt from the payment of property taxes or that a person is entitled to reduction in taxes as with a homestead exemption.

Exhibit: 1. Documentary or physical evidence submitted in a trial. 2. An attachment to a document.

Express: Stated in words, spoken or written. COMPARE: Implied.

F

Failure of Purpose: When the intended purpose of an agreement or arrangement can no longer be achieved; in most cases, this releases the parties from their obligations.

Fair Housing Laws: The common name for federal housing discrimination statutes.

Fair Market Value: SEE: Value, Fair Market.

Fannie Mae: The former FNMA. A private corporation that sells securities over the stock exchange to get money so that it can buy and sell conventional loans in addition to government-backed notes.

FDIC: Federal Deposit Insurance Corporation.

Fee: An estate of inheritance; title to real property that can be willed or descend to heirs.

Fee, Conditional: SEE: Fee Simple Defeasible; Fee Simple Subject to a Condition Subsequent.

Fee Simple Absolute: The greatest estate one can have in real property; freely transferable and inheritable, and of indefinite duration, with no conditions on the title. Often called fee simple or fee title.

Fee Simple Defeasible: A fee estate in real property that may be defeated or undone if certain events occur or certain conditions are not met. SEE: Fee, Conditional; Fee Simple Determinable.

Fee Simple Determinable: A defeasible fee that is terminated automatically if certain conditions occur.

Fee Simple Subject to a Condition Subsequent: SEE: Fee, Conditional.

FHA: Federal Housing Administration.

FHLMC: Federal Home Loan Mortgage Corporation; also known as "Freddie Mac." SEE: Secondary Marketing.

FICO Scores: A method of scoring consumer credit initially developed by Fair, Isaac and Company.

Fiduciary Relationship: A relationship of trust and confidence, where one party owes the other (or both parties owe each other) loyalty and a higher standard of good faith than they owe to third parties. For example, an agent is a fiduciary in relation to the principal.

Finance Charge: Any charge a borrower is assessed, directly or indirectly, in connection with the loan.

Financing Statement: A brief document that, when recorded, gives constructive notice of a creditor's security interest in an item of personal property.

First Lien Position: The spot held by the deed of trust with highest lien priority, when there's more than one deed of trust on the property. SEE: Deed of Trust, First.

Fixed Term: A period of time with a definite ending date.

Fixture: An item of personal property that has been attached to or closely associated with real property in such a way that it has legally become part of the real property. SEE: Annexation, Actual; Annexation, Constructive.

Floor Area Ratio Method: A flexible method of limiting the size of a building in relation to the size of a lot; used in some zoning ordinances as an alternative to strict size and coverage limits.

Forcible Entry and Detainer: Common name of the legal proceeding to institute eviction proceedings against a tenant in Texas.

Foreclosure: When a lienholder causes property to be sold, so that the unpaid lien can be satisfied from the sale proceeds.

Foreclosure, Judicial: A lawsuit filed by a mortgagee or deed of trust beneficiary to foreclose on the security property when the borrower has defaulted.

Foreclosure, Nonjudicial: Foreclosure by a trustee under the power of sale clause in a deed of trust.

Forfeiture: Loss of a right or something else of value as a result of failure to perform an obligation or condition.

Four Unities: SEE: Unities, Four.

Fraud: An intentional or negligent misrepresentation or concealment of a material fact.

Fraud, Actual: Intentional misrepresentation or concealment, or negligent misrepresentation, which is making a false statement without reasonable grounds for believing it is true.

Freddie Mac: The FHLMC.

Freehold: An ownership estate in real property; either a fee simple or a life estate. The holder of a freehold estate has title, whereas the holder of a less-than-freehold estate (leasehold estate) is merely a tenant, having a temporary right to possession, but no title.

Frontage: The distance a piece of property extends along a street or a body of water.

Fructus Industriales: Plants planted and cultivated by people, such as crops ("fruits of industry").

Fructus Naturales: Naturally occurring plants ("fruits of nature").

Future Interest: SEE: Interest, Future.

G

Gain: The portion of the proceeds from the sale of an asset that the IRS recognizes as taxable profit.

Gain, Capital: A gain realized on the sale of a capital asset. Real estate is considered a capital asset if it is income property, investment property, or property used in a trade or business.

Garnishment: A legal process by which a creditor gains access to the funds or personal property of a debtor that are in the hands of a third party. For example, if the debtor's wages are garnished, the employer is required to turn over part of each paycheck to the creditor.

General Lien: SEE: Lien, General.

Ginnie Mae: The GNMA.

GNMA: Government National Mortgage Association. SEE: Secondary Marketing.

Good and Indefeasible Title: The legal standard on which Texas title insurance policies guarantee title to the owner.

Government Survey: A system of land description that divides the land into squares called townships (each approximately six miles square, containing 36 square miles), which are divided into 36 sections (each approximately one mile square and containing approximately 640 acres). Also called the rectangular survey or the section, township, and range system.

Grace Period: A period of time allowed by a lender where a borrower may make a late payment without penalty. COMPARE: Default.

Grant: To transfer or convey an interest in real property by means of a written instrument.

Grantee: One who receives a grant of real property.

Granting Clause: Words in a deed that indicate the grantor's intent to transfer an interest in property.

Grantor: One who grants an interest in real property to another.

Grantor/Grantee Indexes: Indices of recorded documents, with each document listed in alphabetical order according to the last name of the grantor (in the grantor/grantee index) and grantee (in the grantee/grantor index). The recording number, or some other reference number of each document is given, so that they can be located in the public record.

GSA: General Services Administration.

Guardian: A person appointed by a court to administer the affairs of a minor or an incompetent person.

H-I

Habendum Clause: A clause included after the granting clause in many deeds; it begins "to have and to hold," and describes the type of estate the grantee will hold.

Heir: Someone entitled to inherit another's property under the laws of intestate succession. COMPARE: Bequest; Devise; Legacy.

HMDA: Home Mortgage Disclosure Act.

Holder: A person or entity who owns a negotiable instrument.

Holdover Tenant: A tenant who fails to surrender possession of the premises at the end of a tenancy.

Homeowner's Association: A nonprofit association made up of homeowners in a subdivision, responsible for enforcing the subdivision's CC&Rs and managing other community affairs.

Homestead Protection: In Texas, constitutional protection against the claims of certain creditors, for property used as the debtor's residence.

HUD: The Department of Housing and Urban Development.

Hypothecate: To make property security for a loan without giving up possession of it. COMPARE: Pledge.

Impact Fees: A fee charged by a municipality to developers and property owners in a new subdivision to fund or defray the cost of building facilities for water, sewage, drainage and roads.

Implied: Not expressed in words, but understood from actions or circumstances. COMPARE: Express.

Implied by Law: Required by law to be part of an agreement; read into an agreement even if it contradicts the express terms the parties agreed to.

Implied Warranty: SEE: Warranty, Implied.

Implied Warranty of Habitability: A warranty implied by law in every residential lease, that the property is safe and fit for habitation.

Impound Account: A bank account maintained by a lender for paying property taxes and insurance premiums on the security property; the lender requires the borrower to make regular deposits and pays the expenses out of the account. Also called a reserve account.

Improvements: Man-made additions to real property.

Income Property: Property that generates rent (or other income) for the owner, such as an apartment building.

Incompetent: Not legally competent; not of sound mind; mentally ill, senile, or feebleminded.

Independent Contractor: A person who contracts to do a job for another, but maintains control over how he or she will carry out the task, rather than following detailed instructions. COMPARE: Employee.

Ingress and Egress: Entering and exiting; usually refers to a road or other means of access to a piece of property. An easement for ingress and egress is one that gives the dominant tenant access to the dominant tenement.

Inherit: In strict legal usage, to acquire property by intestate succession, but commonly used to mean acquiring property either by intestate succession or by will.

Injunction: A court order prohibiting an act or compelling an act to be done. SEE: Enjoin; Equitable Remedy.

Inquiry Notice: SEE: Notice, Inquiry.

Installment Sale: A sale in which less than 100% of the sales price is received in the year the sale occurs.

Instrument: A document that transfers title, creates a lien, or gives a right to payment, such as a deed, deed of trust, or contract. SEE: Negotiable Instrument.

Insurance Hazard: Insurance against damage to real property caused by fire, flood, or other disasters.

Insurance, Homeowner's: Insurance against damage to the real property and the homeowner's personal property.

Insurance, Mortgage: Insurance that protects a lender against losses resulting from the borrower's default.

Insurance, Title: Insurance that protects against losses resulting from undiscovered title defects.

Insurance, Title, Extended Coverage: Title insurance that covers problems that should be discovered by an inspection of the property (such as encroachments and adverse possession) in addition to the problems covered by standard coverage policies.

Insurance, Title, Standard Coverage: Title insurance that protects against latent title defects (such as forged deeds) and undiscovered recorded encumbrances, but does not protect against problems that would only be discovered by an inspection of the property.

Integration Clause: A provision in a contract document stating that the document contains the entire agreement between the parties.

Intent, Objective: A person's manifested intention; what he or she appears to intend, whether or not that is what he or she actually intends.

Intent, Subjective: What a person actually intends, whether or not that is apparent to others.

Interest: 1. A right or share in something (such as a piece of real estate). 2. A charge a borrower pays to a lender for the use of the lender's money. COMPARE: Principal.

Interest, Future: An interest in property that will or may become possessory at some point in the future. SEE: Remainder; Reversion.

Interest, Prepaid: Interest on a new loan that must be paid at the time of closing; covers the interest due for the first month of the loan term. Also called interim interest.

Interest, Undivided: A co-tenant's interest, giving him or her the right to possession of the whole property, rather than to a particular section of it. SEE: Unity of Possession.

Intermediary: Under Texas law, a broker who is employed to negotiate a transaction between the parties (buyer-seller or landlord-tenant) of the transaction, and for that purpose may act as an agent of the parties.

Interpleader: A court action filed by someone who is holding funds that two or more people are claiming. The holder turns the funds over to the court; the court resolves the dispute and delivers the money to the party who is entitled to it.

Interrogatories: Written questions submitted to the opposing party in a lawsuit during discovery, which he or she is required to answer in writing and under oath.

Intestate: Dying without leaving a will.

Intestate Succession: Distribution of the property of a person who died intestate to his or her heirs.

Invalid: Not legally binding or legally effective; not valid.

Inverse Condemnation Action: A court action by a private landowner against the government, seeking compensation for damage to property that resulted from government action.

Inverted Pyramid: A way of visualizing ownership of real property; theoretically, a property owner owns all the earth, water, and air enclosed by a pyramid that has its tip at the center of the earth and extends up through the property boundaries out into the sky.

Investment Property: Unimproved property held as an investment because it is appreciating in value.

IRS: Internal Revenue Service.

J-L

Joinder Requirements: The rules requiring both husband and wife to consent to and sign agreements and conveyances concerning homestead property.

Joint Tenancy: SEE: Tenancy, Joint.

Joint Venture: Two or more individuals or companies joining together for one project or a related series of projects, but not as an ongoing business. COMPARE: Partnership.

Judgment: 1. A court's binding determination of the rights and duties of the parties in a lawsuit. 2. A court order requiring one party to pay the other damages.

Judgment Creditor: A person who is owed money as a result of a judgment in a lawsuit.

Judgment Debtor: A person who owes money as a result of a judgment in a lawsuit.

Judgment Lien: SEE: Lien, Judgment.

Judicial Foreclosure: SEE: Foreclosure, Judicial.

Judicial Review: When a court considers whether or not a statute or regulation is constitutional.

Jurisdiction: The extent of a particular court's authority; a court cannot hear a case that is outside its jurisdiction.

Just Compensation: SEE: Eminent Domain.

Land Contract: SEE: Contract, Land.

Landlocked Property: A parcel of land without access to a road or highway.

Landlord: A landowner who has leased his or her property to another. Also called a lessor.

Latent Defects: Defects that are not visible or apparent; hidden defects.

Lawful Object: A legal purpose.

Lease: A conveyance of a leasehold estate from the fee owner to a tenant; a contract in which one party pays the other rent in exchange for the possession of real estate.

Lease, Fixed: A lease in which the rent is set at a fixed amount, and the landlord pays most or all of the operating expenses (such as taxes, insurance, and repair costs). Also called a flat lease, gross lease, or straight lease.

Lease, Graduated: A lease in which it is agreed that the rental payments will increase at intervals by an agreed amount or according to an agreed formula.

Lease, Ground: A lease of the land only, usually for a long term, to a tenant who intends to construct a building on the property.

Lease, Net: A lease requiring the tenant to pay all the costs of maintaining the property (such as taxes, insurance, and repairs), in addition to the rent paid to the landlord. Sometimes also known as triple net.

Lease, Percentage: A lease in which the rent is based on a percentage of the tenant's monthly or annual gross sales.

Leasehold Estate: An estate that gives the holder (the tenant) only a temporary right to possession, without title. Also called a less-than-freehold estate.

Legacy: A gift of personal property by will. Also called a bequest. SEE: Legatee.

Legal Description: A precise description of a piece of property; may be a lot and block description, a metes and bounds description, or a government survey description.

Legatee: Someone who receives personal property (a legacy) under a will.

Legislature: The arm of a government that has primary responsibility for making new laws.

Lender, Institutional: A bank, savings and loan, or similar regulated lending institution; as opposed to an individual or private business that loans money.

Lessee: One who leases property from another; a tenant.

Lessor: One who leases property to another; a landlord.

Less-Than-Freehold Estate: A leasehold estate.

Levy: To impose a tax.

Liable: Legally responsible.

License: 1. Official permission to do a particular thing that the law doesn't allow everyone to do. 2. Revocable, nonassignable permission to enter another person's land for a particular purpose. COMPARE: Easement.

Lien: A nonpossessory interest in property, giving the lienholder the right to foreclose if the owner doesn't pay a debt owed to the lienholder; a financial encumbrance on the owner's title.

Lien, General: A lien against all the property of a debtor, rather than a particular piece of his or her property.

Lien, Involuntary: A lien that arises by operation of law, without the consent of the property owner. Also called a statutory lien.

Lien, Judgment: A general lien against a judgment debtor's property, which the judgment creditor creates by recording an abstract of judgment in the county where the property is located.

Lien, Materialman's: Similar to a mechanic's lien, but based on a debt owed to someone who supplied materials (as opposed to labor) for a project.

Lien, Mechanic's: A specific lien claimed by someone who performed work on the property (construction, repairs, or improvements) and has not been paid. This term is often used in a general sense, referring to materialmen's liens as well as actual mechanics' liens.

Lien, Property Tax: A specific lien on property to secure payment of the property taxes.

Lien, Specific: A lien that attaches only to a particular piece of property (as opposed to a general lien, which attaches to all of the debtor's property).

Lien, Statutory: SEE: Lien, Involuntary.

Lien, Tax: A lien on property to secure the payment of taxes.

Lien, Voluntary: A lien placed against property with the consent of the owner; a deed of trust or a mortgage.

Lienholder, Junior: A secured creditor whose lien is lower in priority than another's lien.

Lien Priority: The order in which liens are paid off out of the proceeds of a foreclosure sale.

Life Estate: A freehold estate that lasts only as long as a specified person lives. That person is referred to as the measuring life.

Life-Estate Pur Autre Vie: A life estate "for the life of another," where the measuring life is someone other than the life tenant.

Life Tenant: Someone who owns a life estate; the person entitled to possession of the property during the measuring life.

Limited Liability Company: A business entity where each owner has the limited liability of a corporate shareholder and the tax advantages of a partner.

Limited Partnerships: SEE: Partnership, Limited.

Liquidated Damages: SEE: Damages, Liquidated.

Lis Pendens: A recorded notice stating that there is a lawsuit pending that may affect title to the defendant's real estate.

Listing: A written agency contract between a seller and a real estate broker, stipulating that the broker will be paid a commission for finding (or attempting to find) a buyer for the seller's property.

Listing, Exclusive Agency: A listing agreement that entitles the broker to a commission if anyone other than the seller finds a buyer for the property during the listing term.

Listing, Exclusive Right to Sell: A listing agreement that entitles the broker to a commission if anyone—including the seller— finds a buyer for the property during the listing term.

Listing, Net: A listing agreement in which the seller sets a net amount he or she is willing to accept for the property; if the actual selling price exceeds that amount, the broker is entitled to keep the excess as his or her commission.

Listing, Open: A nonexclusive listing, given by a seller to as many brokers as he or she chooses. If the property is sold, a broker is only entitled to a commission if he or she is the procuring cause of the sale.

Litigant: A party to a lawsuit; a plaintiff or defendant.

Litigation: A lawsuit (or lawsuits).

Littoral Rights: The water rights of a landowner whose property is adjacent to a large body of water. COMPARE: Riparian Rights.

Loan, Carryback: When a seller extends credit to a buyer to finance the purchase of the property, accepting a deed of trust or mortgage instead of cash. Sometimes called a purchase money loan. SEE: Seller Financing.

Loan, Construction: A loan made to cover the cost of construction of a building, usually arranged so that the money is advanced in installments as the work progresses.

Loan, Conventional: Loan with only the property as security, without the government insuring (FHA) or guaranteeing (VA) the loan.

Loan, Guaranteed: A loan in which someone (the VA, for example) guarantees repayment; if the borrower defaults, the guarantor reimburses the lender for some or all of the loss.

Loan, Purchase Money: 1. A loan the borrower uses to buy the security property (as opposed to a loan secured by property the borrower already owns). 2. A carryback loan.

Loan Assumption Fee: A fee a lender charges a buyer in return for granting the buyer permission to assume an existing loan.

Loan Fee: A loan origination fee.

Loan Origination Fee: A fee a lender charges a borrower in exchange for issuing a loan; also called a loan fee.

Lock-in Clause: A clause in a promissory note or land contract that prohibits prepayment before a specified date, or prohibits it altogether.

Loss, Capital: A loss taken on the sale of a capital asset. Real estate is considered a capital asset if it is income property, investment property, or property used in a trade or business.

Loss, Passive: A loss taken in connection with income property. SEE: Passive Income.

Lot: A parcel of land; especially, a parcel in subdivision.

Lot and Block Description: The type of legal description used for platted property. The description states only the property's lot number and block number in a particular subdivision. To find out the exact location of the property's boundaries, a person consults the plat map for that subdivision at the county clerk's office.

M

Majority, Age of: The age at which a person gains legal capacity; in Texas, 18 years old. COMPARE: Minor.

Maker: A person who signs a promissory note; the borrower who promises to repay the debt.

Market Value: SEE: Value, Fair Market.

Material Breach: SEE: Breach, Material.

Material Fact: An important fact; one that is likely to influence a decision.

Materialman: Someone who supplies materials for a construction project. SEE: Lien, Materialman's. COMPARE: Mechanic.

Maturity Date: The date by which a loan is supposed to be paid off in full.

MCE: Mandatory Continuing Education.

Measuring Life: SEE: Life Estate.

Mechanic: Someone who performs work (construction, improvement, or repairs) on real property. SEE: Lien, Mechanic's. COMPARE: Materialman.

Mediation Clause: A clause in a contract requiring mediation in the even of a dispute.

Mediator: A person who helps the parties reach a voluntary agreement. COMPARE: Arbitrator.

Meeting of Minds: SEE: Mutual Consent.

Menace: Threatening physical harm to a person or threatening harm to a person's reputation to force someone to sign a document. COMPARE: Duress; Duress, Economic.

Merger: Uniting two or more separate properties by transferring ownership of all of them to one person.

Meridian, Principal: In the government survey system, the main north-south line in a particular grid, used as the starting point in numbering the ranges.

Metes: Measurements.

Metes and Bounds Description: A legal description that starts at an easily identifiable point of beginning, then describes the property's boundaries in terms of courses compass directions and distances, ultimately returning to the point of beginning.

Mineral Rights: Rights to the minerals located beneath the surface of a piece of property.

Minor: A person who has not yet reached the age of majority; in Texas, a person under 18.

Minor, Emancipated: A minor who is or has been married, is on active duty in the armed forces, or has a declaration of emancipation from a court. An emancipated minor has legal capacity to contract.

Misrepresentation: A false or misleading statement. SEE: Fraud.

Mistake, Mutual: When both parties to a contract were mistaken about a fact or a law.

Mistake, Unilateral: When only one of the parties to a contract was mistaken about a fact or a law.

Mitigation: When the nonbreaching party takes action to minimize the losses resulting from a breach of contract.

MLS: Multiple Listing Service.

Monument: A visible marker (natural or artificial) used in a survey or a metes and bounds description to establish the boundaries of a piece of property.

Mortgage: An instrument that creates a voluntary lien on real property to secure repayment of a debt. The parties to a mortgage are the mortgagor (borrower) and mortgagee (lender). Unlike a deed of trust, a mortgage does not include a power of sale, so it can only be foreclosed judicially.

Mortgagee: A lender who accepts a mortgage as security for repayment of the loan.

Mortgagee's Title Policy: A title insurance policy that is intended to protect the interest of the mortgagee. SEE: Mortgagee; Insurance, Title. COMPARE: Mortgagor's Title Policy.

Mortgagor: A person who borrows money and gives a mortgage to the lender as security.

Mortgagor's Title Policy: A title insurance policy that is intended to protect the interests of the mortgagor. SEE: Mortgagor; Insurance, Title. COMPARE: Mortgagee's Title Policy.

Multiple Listing Service (MLS): 1. An organization of brokers who share their exclusive listings. 2. A computerized database containing listing information which is shared by real estate licensees.

Mutual Consent: When all parties freely agree to the terms of a contract, without fraud, undue influence, duress, menace, or mistake. Mutual consent is achieved through offer and acceptance; it can be referred to as a "meeting of the minds."

Mutual Mistake: SEE: Mistake, Mutual.

N

NAR: National Association of REALTORS®.

Natural Person: A human being, an individual (as opposed to an artificial person, such as a corporation).

Negative Amortization: A loan repayment calculation where the monthly payments are insufficient to repay principal and interest cost; results in unpaid interested being added back to the amount of the loan thereby creating an increasingly larger loan balance.

Negligence: Conduct that falls below the standard of care that a reasonable person would exercise under the circumstances; carelessness or recklessness. Negligence that causes harm is a tort. Negligence refers to a legal duty of conduct, while neglect refers to a general omission or lack of care.

Negotiable Instrument: An instrument containing an unconditional promise to pay a certain sum of money bearer, on demand, or at a particular time. It can be a check, promissory note, bond, draft, or stock. SEE: Note, Promissory.

Nonbinding Arbitration: The decision of the arbitrator is reviewable by the court.

Nonconforming Use: A property use that doesn't conform to current zoning requirements, but is allowed because the property was being used in that way before the present zoning ordinance was enacted.

Nonpossessory Interest: An interest in property that does not include the right to possess and occupy the property; an encumbrance, such as a lien or an easement.

Nonrecognition Provision: A provision in the income tax law that allows a taxpayer to defer recognition and taxation of a gain until a later time or later transaction.

Nonrecourse Loan: A loan where the lender's only remedy will be to foreclose against the collateral used in the loan. Under this type of loan, the borrower will face no personal liability in the event the sale of the foreclosed property is insufficient to pay all amounts due under the loan.

Notario Publico: A Mexican public official often confused with a Texas notary public. COMPARE: Notary Public.

Notary Public: An official whose primary function is to witness and certify the acknowledgment made by someone signing a legal document in Texas. A notary public is not the same as a notario publico.

Note: SEE: Note, Promissory.

Note, Demand: A promissory note that is due whenever the holder of the note demands payment.

Note, Installment: A promissory note that calls for regular payments of principal and interest until the debt is fully paid. The note is fully amortized if the regular payments are enough to pay it off in full by the maturity date. The note is partially amortized if the payments won't pay it off, so that a balloon payment is due at the end of the term.

Note, Promissory: A written promise to repay a debt that is enforceable in a court of law. COMPARE: Note, Real Estate Lien.

Note, Real Estate Lien: A promissory note used in real estate financing. SEE: Note, Promissory.

Note, Straight: A promissory note that calls for regular payments of interest only, so that the entire principal amount is due in one lump sum at the end of the loan term.

Notice, Actual: Actual knowledge of a fact, as opposed to knowledge imputed by law.

Notice, Constructive: Knowledge of a fact imputed to a person by law. A person is held to have constructive notice of something when he or she should have known it, even if he or she didn't know it. Everyone has constructive notice of the contents of recorded documents, since everyone is expected to protect his or her interests by searching the public record.

Notice, Inquiry: When there were circumstances that should have alerted someone to a possible problem and caused him or her to investigate further, he or she may be held to have had notice of the problem.

Notice of Cessation: A notice recorded by a property owner when construction on the property has ceased, although the project hasn't been completed; it limits the period in which laborers and suppliers can file mechanics' liens.

Notice of Default: A notice issued by a trustee, stating that the deed of trust borrower has breached the loan agreement.

Notice of Sale: A notice issued by a trustee setting the date for the foreclosure sale.

Notice to Vacate: A notice to a tenant demanding that he or she vacate the leased property.

Novation: 1. When one party to a contract withdraws and a new party is substituted, relieving the withdrawing party of liability. 2. The substitution of a new obligation for an old one.

O

Objective Intent: SEE: Intent, Objective.

Offer: When one person proposes a contract to another; if the other person accepts the offer, a binding contract is formed. SEE: Acceptance.

Offeree: One to whom an offer is made.

Offeror: One who makes an offer.

Open space Appraisal: SEE: Rollback Taxes.

Opinion, Judicial: A judge's written statement of a decision in a court case, outlining the facts of the case and explaining the legal basis for the decision.

Option: A contract giving one party the right to do something, without obligating him or her to do it.

Optionee: The person to whom an option is given.

Optionor: The person who gives an option.

Option to Purchase: An option giving the optionee the right to buy property owned by the optionor at an agreed price during a specified period.

Ordinance: A law passed by a local legislative body, such as city council.

Ouster: One co-tenant refuses to allow occupancy by the other co-tenant.

Ownership: Title to property, dominion over property; the rights of possession and control.

Ownership in Severalty: Ownership by a single individual or entity. COMPARE: Concurrent Ownership.

P

Panic Peddling: SEE: Blockbusting.

Parcel: A lot or piece of real estate, particularly a specified part of a larger tract.

Parol Evidence: Evidence concerning negotiations or oral agreements that were not included in a written contract, often altering or contradicting the terms of the written contract.

Partition, Judicial: A court action to divide up a property among its co-owners, so that each owns part of it in severalty or, if it is not practical to divide the property physically, each gets a share of the sale proceeds.

Partition, Voluntary: When co-owners agree to terminate their co-ownership, dividing up the property so that each owns a piece of it in severalty.

Partner, General: A partner who has the authority to manage and contract for a general or limited partnership, and who is personally liable for the partnership's debts.

Partner, Limited: A partner in a limited partnership who is primarily an investor and does not participate in the management of the business, and who is not personally liable for the partnership's debts.

Partnership: An association of two or more persons to carry on a business for profit. The law regards a partnership as a group of individuals, not as an entity separate from its owners. COMPARE: Corporation.

Partnership, General: A partnership in which each member has an equal right to manage the business and share in the profits, as well as an equal responsibility for the partnership's debts. All of the partners are general partners.

Partnership, Limited: A partnership made up of one or more general partners and one or more limited partners.

Partnership Property: All property that partners bring into their business at the outset or later acquire for their business; property owned as tenants in partnership.

Passive Income: Income (rents) received from income property, as opposed to wages, salaries, interest, dividends, or royalties. An IRS term.

Payee: The person entitled to payment under a promissory note.

Personal Property: Any property that is not real property; movable property not affixed to land. Also called chattels or personalty.

Personalty: Personal property.

Petitioner: 1. An appellant. 2. A plaintiff (in some actions, such as a dissolution of marriage).

Plaintiff: The party who starts a civil lawsuit; the one who sues.

Planned Unit Development (PUD): A development (usually residential) with small, clustered lots designed to leave more open space than traditional subdivisions have.

Planning and Zoning Commission: A municipal board responsible for preparing the community's general plan for development and recommending zoning districts.

Plat: A detailed survey map of a subdivision, recorded in the county where the land is located. Subdivided property is often called platted property.

Plat Book: A large book containing subdivision plats, kept at the county clerk's office.

Pledge: When a debtor transfers possession of property to the creditor as security for repayment of the debt. COMPARE: Hypothecate.

Point of Beginning (POB): The starting point in a metes and bounds description; described by reference to a monument.

Points: SEE: Discount Point.

Police Power: The constitutional power of state and local governments to enact and enforce laws that protect the public's health, safety, morals, and general welfare.

Possession: 1. The holding and enjoyment of property. 2. Actual physical occupation of real property.

Possessory Interest: An interest in property that includes the right to possess and occupy the property; not necessarily ownership.

Power of Attorney: An instrument authorizing one person (the attorney in fact) to act as another's agent, to the extent stated in the instrument.

Power of Sale Clause: A clause in a deed of trust giving the trustee the right to foreclose nonjudicially (sell the debtor's property without a court action) if the borrower defaults.

Precedent: A published judicial opinion that serves as authority for determining a similar issue in a later case.

Precedent, Binding: A precedent that a particular court is required to follow.

Preemption: SEE: Right of Preemption.

Prepayment: Paying off part or all of a loan before payment is due.

Prepayment Penalty: A penalty charged to a borrower who prepays.

Prepayment Privilege: A provision in a promissory note allowing the borrower to prepay. COMPARE: Lock-in Clause.

Prescription: Acquiring an interest in real property (an easement) by using it openly and without the owner's permission for at least five years. In contrast to adverse possession, a prescriptive use does not have to be exclusive (the owner may be using the property, too), and the user does not acquire title to the property.

Principal: 1. One who grants another person (an agent) authority to represent him or her in dealings with third parties. 2. One of the parties to a transaction (such as a buyer or seller), as opposed to those who are involved as agents or employees (such as a broker or escrow agent). 3. In regard to a loan, the amount originally borrowed, as opposed to the interest.

Principal Meridian: SEE: Meridian, Principal.

Principal Residence Property: Real property that is the owner's home, his or her main dwelling. A person can only have one principal residence at a time. The term is most often used in connection with the income tax laws.

Probate: A judicial proceeding in which the validity of a will is established and the executor is authorized to distribute the estate property; or, when there is no valid will, in which an administrator is appointed to distribute the estate to the heirs.

Probate Court: A court that oversees the distribution of property under a will or by intestate succession.

Procedural Law: A law that establishes a legal procedure for enforcing a right. COMPARE: Substantive Law.

Procuring Cause: The real estate agent who is primarily responsible for bringing about a sale; for example, by introducing the buyer to the property, or by negotiating the agreement between the buyer and seller. SEE: Listing, Open.

Promisee: Someone who has been promised something; someone who is supposed to receive the benefit of a contractual promise.

Promisor: Someone who has made a contractual promise to another.

Proforma Statement: A financial statement projecting anticipated income, expenses and cash flow based upon specific assumptions,

Proof, Burden of: The responsibility for proving or disproving a particular issue in a lawsuit. In most cases, the plaintiff has the burden of proof.

Property: 1. The rights of ownership in a thing, such as the right to use, possess, transfer, or encumber the thing. 2. Something that is owned.

Property Held for Production of Income: SEE: Income Property.

Property Manager: A person hired by a property owner to administer, market, and maintain property, especially rental property.

Property Used in a Trade or Business: Property such as business sites and factories used in one's trade or business.

Proration: The process of dividing the expenses of sale fairly between buyer and seller.

Public Record: The official collection of legal documents that individuals have filed with the county clerk in order to make the information contained in them public. SEE: Constructive Notice; Recording.

Puffing: Superlative statements about a property that shouldn't be considered assertions of fact. "The best buy in town," or "It's a fabulous location" are examples of puffing.

Punitive Damages: SEE: Damages, Punitive.

Pur Autre Vie: A French phrase meaning "for the life of another." SEE: Life Estate Pur Autre Vie.

Q-R

Quiet Enjoyment: Use and possession of real property without interference from the previous owner, the lessor, or anyone else claiming title. SEE: Covenant of Quiet Enjoyment.

Quiet Title Action: A lawsuit to establish who has title to a piece of property, or to remove a cloud on the title.

Quitclaim Deed: SEE: Deed, Quitclaim.

Range: In the government survey system, a strip of land six miles wide, running north and south.

Range Lines: In the government survey system, the north-south lines located six miles apart.

Ratification: The later confirmation or approval of an act that was not authorized when it was performed.

Ready, Willing, and Able: Making an offer to purchase on terms acceptable to the seller, and having the financial ability to complete the purchase.

Real Estate Contract: 1. A land contract. 3. Any contract having to do with real property.

Real Estate Investment Trust (REIT): A real estate investment business, usually publicly traded, which purchases and manages real estate and/or real estate related loans for the benefit of its shareholders.

Realization: The point at which a gain or profit is actually obtained; for example, the value of a piece of property has been increasing steadily, but the owner's profit won't be realized until she sells the property.

Real Property: Land and everything attached to or appurtenant to it. COMPARE: Personal Property.

Realtor®: A broker or salesperson who is an active member of a state or local real estate board that is affiliated with the National Association of Realtors® or the Texas Association of Realtors®.

Realty: Real property.

Recognition: The point at which a gain is taxed (which is ordinarily in the year it was realized, but may be later if a nonrecognition provision applies).

Recording: Filing a document at the county clerk's office so that it will be placed in the public record.

Recording Number: The numbers stamped on documents when they are recorded, used to identify and locate the documents in the public record. (Each page is stamped with a consecutive number, but an entire document is often referred to by the number on the first page.)

Recovery Trust Account: Collectively refers to two large accounts created by state law and administered by TREC; used to reimburse persons who have been legally harmed by the acts of a real estate licensee, certificate holder and/or employees/agents.

Rectangular Survey: SEE: Government Survey.

Redemption: 1. When a defaulting borrower prevents foreclosure by paying the full amount of the debt, plus costs. 2. When a mortgagor regains the property after foreclosure by paying whatever the foreclosure sale purchaser paid for it, plus interest and expenses. COMPARE: Reinstatement.

Redemption, Equitable Right of: The right of a borrower to redeem property prior to the foreclosure sale.

Redemption, Statutory Right of: The right of a mortgagor to redeem property after a tax foreclosure sale. This right is so named because it is granted to borrowers in Texas by means of a statute.

Redlining: When a lender or insurance company refuses to do business with property owners living in a certain neighborhood because of the racial or ethnic composition of the neighborhood.

Reformation: A legal action to correct a mistake, such as a typographical error, in a deed or other document. The court will order the execution of a correction deed.

Regulation: 1. A rule adopted by an administrative agency. 2. Any governmental order having the force of law.

Regulation Z: The Federal Reserve Board's regulation that implements the Truth in Lending Act.

Reinstatement: Preventing foreclosure by curing the default. COMPARE: Redemption.

Relation: When a body of water gradually recedes, exposing land that was previously under water. Also called dereliction.

Relation Back: A legal doctrine that allows a court to rule that a party acquired title at some point before he or she actually received the deed. Applied in cases involving escrow or the exercise of an option to purchase.

Release: 1. To give up a legal right. 2. A document in which a legal right is given up.

Release, Lien: SEE: Release of Lien.

Release of Lien: A document provided by a lienholder providing evidence that a lien has been released.

Remainder: A future interest that becomes possessory when a life estate terminates, and that is held by someone other than the grantor of the life estate; as opposed to a reversion, which is a future interest held by the grantor.

Remainderman: The person who holds an estate in remainder.

Remand: When an appellate court orders further trial proceedings in a case, sending the case back to the court that originally tried it, or to a different trial court.

Rent: Compensation paid by a tenant to the landlord in exchange for the possession and use of the property.

Renunciation: When someone who has been granted something or has accepted something later gives it up or rejects it; as when an agent withdraws from the agency relationship. COMPARE: Revocation.

Rescission: When a contract is terminated and each party gives anything acquired under the contract back to the other party. (The verb form is rescind.) COMPARE: Cancellation.

Reservation: A right retained by a grantor when conveying property; for example, mineral rights, an easement, or a life estate can be reserved in the deed.

Reserve Account: SEE: Impound Account.

Residential Rental Locator: A Texas real estate licensee who offers, for consideration, to locate a unit in an apartment complex for lease to a prospective tenant. COMPARE: Broker; Salesperson; Certificate Holder.

Res Judicata: The legal doctrine holding that once a lawsuit between two parties has been tried and a final judgment has been issued, neither one can sue the other over the same dispute again.

RESPA: Real Estate Settlement Procedures Act.

Respondent: 1. An appellee. 2. In a dissolution of marriage, the party who did not file the action.

Restitution: Restoring something to a person that he or she was unjustly deprived of.

Restriction: A limitation on the use of real property.

Restriction, Deed: A restrictive covenant in a deed.

Restriction, Private: A restriction imposed on property by a previous owner, or the subdivision developer; a restriction covenant or a condition in a deed.

Restriction, Public: A law or regulation limiting or regulating the use of real property.

Restrictive Covenant: A promise to do or not do an act relating to real property; usually an owner's promise to not use property in a particular way. May or may not run with the land.

Reverse: To overturn a lower court's decision on appeal, ruling in favor of the appellant. COMPARE: Affirm.

Reversion: A future interest that becomes possessory when a temporary estate (such as a life estate) terminates, and that is held by the grantor (or his or her successors in interest). COMPARE: Remainder.

Revocation: When someone who granted or offered something withdraws it; as when a principal withdraws the authority granted to the agent, an offeror withdraws the offer, or the Real Estate Commissioner cancels a real estate agent's license. COMPARE: Renunciation.

Rezone: An amendment to a zoning ordinance, usually changing the uses allowed in a particular zone. Requires the approval of the local legislative body. Also called a zoning amendment.

Right of First Refusal: A right of preemption.

Right of Preemption: A right to have the first chance to buy or lease property if the owner decides to put it up for sale or make it available. Also called a right of first refusal. COMPARE: Option.

Right of Survivorship: A characteristic of joint tenancy; surviving joint tenants automatically acquire a deceased joint tenant's interest in the property.

Right of Way: An easement that gives the holder the right to cross another person's land.

Riparian Rights: The water rights of a landowner whose property is adjacent to or crossed by a stream or river. COMPARE: Littoral Rights.

Rollback Taxes: Real property taxes imposed when land no longer qualifies for an alternate (and lower) agricultural property valuation method such as Ag-Use Appraisal or Open Space Appraisal. Depending on the type of agricultural valuation method previously used, the rollback period may range from three to five years.

Rollover: When a taxpayer sells his or her principal residence and reinvests the sale proceeds in another home, deferring recognition of the gain on the sale.

RTC: Resolution Trust Corporation.

Rule of Capture: A legal doctrine followed in Texas that grants a landowner the right to all oil and gas produced from wells on his or her land, even if it migrated from underneath land belonging to someone else.

Running with the Land: Binding or benefiting the successive owners of a piece of property, rather than terminating when a particular owner transfers his or her interest. Usually said in reference to an easement or a restrictive covenant.

S

Salesperson: 1. A person who is licensed to represent one or more of the parties to a real estate transaction for compensation. 2. The entry-level Texas real estate license. COMPARE: Broker; Residential Rental Locator; Certificate Holder.

Secondary Marketing: Buying and selling existing promissory notes and deeds of trust. The primary market is the one in which lenders loan money to borrowers; the secondary market is the one in which the lenders sell their loans to the large secondary marketing agencies (FNMA, FHLMC, and GNMA) or to other investors.

Secret Profit: A financial benefit that an agent takes from a transaction without informing the principal; usually the result of self-dealing.

Section: In the government survey system, a section is one mile square and contains 640 acres. There are 36 sections in a township.

Security Agreement: An instrument that creates a voluntary lien on property to secure repayment of a loan. For debts secured by real property, a security agreement is either a deed of trust or a mortgage.

Security Deposit: Money a tenant gives a landlord at the beginning of the tenancy to ensure that the tenant will comply with the terms of the lease. The landlord may retain all or part of the deposit to cover unpaid rent or repair costs at the end of the tenancy.

Security Interest: The interest a creditor may acquire in the debtor's property to ensure that the debt will be paid.

Seisin: The possession of a freehold estate; ownership. Also spelled seizen or seizin.

Self Dealing: When a real estate agent buys the principal's property (or sells it to a relative, friend, or associate, or to a business he or she has an interest in), without disclosing that fact to the principal, and in violation of his or her fiduciary duties to the principal.

Seller Financing: When a seller extends credit to a buyer to finance the purchase of the property; as opposed to having the buyer obtain a loan from a third party, such as an institutional lender. SEE: Loan, Carryback.

Separate Property: Property owned by a married person in Texas that is not community property; includes property acquired before marriage, or by gift, by will or inheritance during marriage. COMPARE: Community Property.

Service of Process: Delivery of a legal document (especially a summons) to a person in accordance with the rules prescribed by statute, so that he or she is held to have received it (whether or not he or she actually did).

Setback Requirements: Provisions in a zoning ordinance that do not allow structures to be built within a certain distance of the property line.

Settlement: 1. An agreement between the parties to a civil lawsuit, in which the plaintiff agrees to drop the suit in exchange for money or the defendant's promise to do or refrain from doing something. 2. Closing.

Settlement Statement: A document that presents a final, detailed accounting for a real estate transaction, listing each party's debits and credits and the amount each will receive or be required to pay at closing. Also called a closing statement.

Severable: When one provision in a law or a contract can be held unenforceable, without making the entire law or contract unenforceable.

Severalty: SEE: Ownership in Severalty.

Severance: Termination of a joint tenancy, turning it into a tenancy in common.

Sheriff's Sale: A foreclosure sale held after a judicial foreclosure. Sometimes called an execution sale.

Special Assessment: A tax levied only against the properties that have benefited from a public improvement (such as a sewer or a street light), to cover the cost of the improvement; creates a special assessment lien.

Special Exception Permit: SEE: Conditional Use Permit.

Specific Performance: A legal remedy for breach of contract in which a court orders the breaching party to actually perform the contract as agreed, rather than simply paying money damages.

Statute: A law enacted by a state legislature or the U.S. Congress. SEE: Statutory Law. COMPARE: Ordinance.

Statute of Frauds: A Texas law that requires certain types of contracts to be in writing and signed in order to be enforceable.

Statute of Limitations: Law requiring a particular type of lawsuit to be filed within a specified time after the event giving rise to the suit occurred.

Statutory Law: Laws adopted by a legislative body (Congress, a state legislature, or a county or city council), as opposed to constitutional law, case law, or administrative regulations.

Statutory Retainage: A statute that protects subcontractors by requiring property owners to retain 10% of the entire construction amount for 30 days following the completion of the work.

Steering: Channeling prospective buyers or tenants to particular neighborhoods based on their race, religion, national origin, or ancestry.

Subagent: 1. Any person who serves as an agent of an agent. 2. A Texas real estate licensee who represent a principal through and with the consent of the principal's broker. SEE: Broker; Principal.

Subdivision: 1. A piece of land divided into two or more parcels. 2. A residential development.

Subdivision Plat: SEE: Plat.

Subdivision Regulations: State and local laws that must be complied with before land can be subdivided.

Subject to: When a purchaser takes property subject to a deed of trust or mortgage, he or she is not personally liable for paying off the loan; in case of default, however, the property can still be foreclosed on. COMPARE: Assumption.

Sublease: When a tenant grants someone else the right to possession of the leased property for part of the remainder of the lease term; as opposed to an assignment, where the tenant gives up possession for the entire remainder of the lease term.

Subordination Agreement: An agreement between lienholders to change, among themselves, the priority of a specific lien.

Subordination Clause: A provision in a mortgage or deed of trust that permits a later mortgage or deed of trust to have higher lien priority than the one containing the clause.

Subpoena: A legal command ordering a person to appear at a deposition, court hearing or administrative proceeding to testify or produce documentary or physical evidence. An order requiring a witness to attend.

Subpoena Duces Tecum: An order to produce books, records or other document.

Substantial Performance: When a promisor doesn't perform all of his or her contractual obligations, but does enough so that the promisee is required to fulfill his or her side of the bargain. COMPARE: Breach, Material.

Substantive Law: A law that establishes a right or a duty. COMPARE: Procedural Law.

Successor in Interest: A person who has acquired property previously held by someone else; for example, a buyer or an heir.

Summons: A document informing a defendant that a lawsuit has been filed against him or her, and ordering the defendant to file an answer to the plaintiff's complaint with the court.

Surrender: Giving up an estate (such as a life estate or leasehold) before it has expired.

Survey: The process of precisely measuring the boundaries and determining the area of a parcel of land.

Survivorship: SEE: Right of Survivorship.

Syndicate: An association formed to operate an investment business. A syndicate is not a recognized legal entity; it can be organized as a corporation, partnership, or trust.

T

Tacking: When successive periods of use or possession by more than one person are added together to make up the five years required for prescription or adverse possession.

Taking: When the government acquires private property for public use by condemnation, it's called "a taking." The term is also used in inverse condemnation lawsuits, when a government action has made private property useless.

TAR: Texas Association of REALTORS®.

Tax Increment Financing: A method of using only a portion of the property taxes generated from a designated geographic area for a stated period of time in order to finance municipal public improvements (i.e., roads, bridges, sidewalks) within that district. The funds used for this type of financing normally consist of only the increased amount of taxes generated from rising property values within that district.

Tax Sale: Sale of property after foreclosure of a tax lien.

Tenancy: Lawful possession of real property; an estate.

Tenancy, Joint: A form of concurrent ownership in which the co-owners have equal undivided interests and the right of survivorship. The right of survivorship means that when one joint tenant dies, the surviving tenants automatically acquire his or her interest in the property. SEE: Unities, Four. COMPARE: Tenancy in Common.

Tenancy, Periodic: A leasehold estate that continues for successive periods of equal length (such as from week to week or month to month), until terminated by proper notice from either party. Also called a month-to-month (or week-to-week, etc.) tenancy. COMPARE: Estate for Years.

Tenancy, Term: SEE: Estate for Years.

Tenancy at Will: When a tenant is in possession with the owner's permission, but there's no definite lease term; as when a landlord allows a holdover tenant to remain on the premises until another tenant is found.

Tenancy by the Entirety: A form of co-ownership of property by husband and wife (in states that don't use a community property system).

Tenancy in Common: A form of concurrent ownership in which two or more persons each have an undivided interest in the entire property (unity of possession), but no right of survivorship. COMPARE: Tenancy, Joint.

Tenancy in Partnership: SEE: Partnership Property.

Tenant: Someone in lawful possession of real property, especially someone who has leased property from the owner.

Tenant at Sufferance: A tenant who holds over beyond the expiration of the tenancy without the permission of the landlord.

Tenant, Dominant: A person who has easement rights on another's property; either the owner of a dominant tenement, or someone who has an easement in gross.

Tenant, Holdover: A lessee who remains in possession of the property after the lease term has expired.

Tenant, Life: Someone who owns a life estate.

Tenant, Servient: The owner of a servient tenement—that is, someone whose property is burdened by an easement.

Tenement, Dominant: Property that receives the benefit of an appurtenant easement.

Tenement, Servient: Property burdened by an easement. In other words, the owner of the servient tenement (the servient tenant) must allow someone who has an easement (the dominant tenant) to use the property.

Tenements: Everything of a permanent nature associated with a piece of land and ordinarily transferred with the land. Tenements are both tangible (buildings, for example) and intangible (air rights, for example).

Term: A prescribed period of time, especially the length of time a borrower has in which to pay off a loan, or the duration of a lease.

Testament: SEE: Will.

Testate: Refers to someone who has died leaving a will. COMPARE: Intestate.

Testator: A man who makes a will.

Testatrix: A woman who makes a will.

Tester: A person working with a fair housing organization who pretends to be interested in buying or renting property from someone suspected of unlawful discrimination.

Texas Real Estate Research Center: A research center located at Texas A & M University devoted to the study of real estate issues. Also known as the Real Estate Center.

Time is of the Essence: A clause in a contract that means performance on the exact dates specified is an essential element of the contract; failure to perform on time is a material breach.

Timeshare Use: A license that entitles the holder to possession of the property only for a specific, limited period each year.

Title: Lawful ownership of real property. Also, the deed or other document that is evidence of that ownership.

Title, After-Acquired: Title acquired by a grantor after he or she attempted to convey property he or she didn't own.

Title, Chain of: The chain of deeds (and other documents) transferring title to a piece of property from one owner to the next, as disclosed in the public record.

Title, Clear: Title that is free of encumbrances or defects: marketable title.

Title, Equitable: The vendee's interest in property under a land contract. Also called an equitable interest. COMPARE: Title, Legal.

Title, Legal: The vendor's interest in property under a land contract. COMPARE: Title, Equitable.

Title Commitment: A commitment by a title company, valid for 90 days, to issue a title insurance policy. A commitment contains a report that discloses the condition of title to a specific property as of the date of the report. The commitment contains the grounds upon which the policy of insurance will be issued to the buyer at closing.

Title Company: A title insurance company.

Title Insurance: SEE: Insurance, Title

Title Plant: A duplicate (usually microfilmed) of a county's public record, maintained by a title company at its offices for use in title searches.

Title Search: An inspection of the public record to determine all rights and encumbrances affecting title to a piece of property.

Tort: A breach of a duty imposed by law (as opposed to a duty voluntarily taken on in a contract) that causes harm to another person, giving the injured person the right to sue the one who breached the duty. Also called a civil wrong (in contrast to a criminal wrong, a crime). SEE: Negligence.

Township: In the government survey system, a parcel of land 6 miles square, containing 36 sections; the intersection of a range and a township tier.

Township Lines: Lines running east-west, spaced six miles apart, in the government survey system.

Township Tier: In the government survey system, a strip of land running east-west, six miles wide and bounded on the north and south by township lines.

Tract: 1. A piece of land of undefined size. 2. In the government survey system, an area made up of 16 townships, 24 miles on each side.

TREC: Texas Real Estate Commission.

TRELA: The Real Estate License Act.

Trade Fixtures: Articles of personal property annexed to real property by a tenant for use in his or her trade or business.

Trespass: An unlawful physical invasion of property owned by another.

Trial: The fundamental court proceeding in a lawsuit, in which a judge (and in some cases, a jury) hears evidence presented by both parties and issues a judgment. COMPARE: Appeal.

Trust: A legal arrangement in which title to property (or funds) is vested in one or more trustees who manage the property on behalf of the trust's beneficiaries, in accordance with instructions set forth in the document establishing the trust.

Trust Account: A bank account, separate from a real estate broker's personal and business accounts, used to segregate trust funds from the broker's own funds.

Trustee: 1. A person appointed to manage a trust on behalf of the beneficiaries. 2. A neutral third party appointed in a deed of trust to handle the nonjudicial foreclosure process in case of default.

Trustee's Sale: A nonjudicial foreclosure sale under a deed of trust.

Trust Funds: Money or things of value received by an agent, not belonging to the agent but being held for the benefit of others.

Trustor: The borrower on a deed of trust. Also called the grantor.

U

Unconstitutional: Violating a provision of the U.S. Constitution or a state constitution.

Undivided Interest: SEE: Interest, Undivided.

Undue Influence: Exerting excessive pressure on someone so as to overpower the person's free will and prevent him or her from making a rational or prudent decision; often involves abusing a relationship of trust.

Uniform Settlement Statement: A closing statement required for any transaction involving a loan that is subject to the Real Estate Settlement Procedures Act (RESPA).

Unilateral Contract: SEE: Contract, Unilateral.

Unilateral Mistake: SEE: Mistake, Unilateral.

Unincorporated Association: The legal designation for an organization that has recorded a statement listing the names of those who are authorized to execute conveyances on its behalf, which makes it possible for title to be held in the association's name.

Unities, Four: The unities of time, title, interest, and possession, required for a joint tenancy.

Unity of Interest: When each co-owner has an equal interest (equal share of ownership) in a piece of property.

Unity of Possession: When each co-owner is equally entitled to possession of the entire property, because the ownership interests are undivided.

Unity of Time: When each co-owner acquired title at the same time.

Unity of Title: When each co-owner acquired title through the same instrument (deed, will, or court order).

Unjust Enrichment: An undeserved benefit.

Untenantable: Not fit for occupancy.

Use Variance: SEE: Variance, Use.

Usury: Charging an interest rate that exceeds legal limits.

V

VA: Department of Veterans Affairs.

Valid: The legal classification of a contract that is binding and enforceable in a court of law.

Valuable Consideration: SEE: Consideration.

Valuation: SEE: Appraisal.

Value: The amount of goods or services offered in the marketplace in exchange for a given thing.

Value, Assessed: The value placed on property by the taxing authority (the county assessor, for example) for the purposes of taxation.

Value, Fair Market: The amount of money that a piece of property would bring if placed on the open market for a reasonable period of time, with a buyer willing (but not forced) to buy, and a seller willing (but not forced) to sell, if both buyer and seller were fully informed as to the possible use of the property. Also called market value.

Variable Interest Rate: An interest rate on a mortgage or deed of trust that is adjusted periodically, usually to reflect changes in a particular economic index. A loan with a variable interest rate is often called an adjustable-rate mortgage or ARM.

Variance: A permit obtained from the Zoning Board of Adjustment allowing the holder to use property or build a structure in a way that violates the zoning ordinance. COMPARE: Conditional Use Permit; Nonconforming Use.

Variance, Use: A variance that permits an owner to use the property in a way that isn't ordinarily allowed in that zone; for example, a commercial use in a residential zone.

Vendee: A buyer or purchaser, particularly someone buying property under a land contract.

Vendor: A seller, particularly someone selling property by means of a land contract.

Vested: When a person has a present, fixed right or interest in property, even though he or she may not have the right to possession until sometime in the future. For example, a remainderman's interest in property vests when it is granted, not when the life estate ends.

Void: Having no legal force or effect.

Voidable: SEE: Contract, Voidable.

W

Waiver: The voluntary relinquishment or surrender of a right.

Warranty, Implied: In the sale of property, a guarantee created by operation of law, whether or not the seller intended to offer it.

Warranty of Habitability: SEE: Implied Warranty of Habitability.

Waste: Destruction, damage, or material alteration of property by someone in possession who holds less than a fee estate (such as a life tenant or lessee), or by a co-tenant.

Water Rights: SEE: Littoral Rights; Riparian Rights.

Will: A person's stipulation regarding how his or her estate should be disposed of after he or she dies. Also called a testament.

Will, Formal: A written, witnessed will.

Will, Holographic: A will written entirely in the testator or testatrix's handwriting, which may be valid even if it was not witnessed.

Will, Nuncupative: An oral will made on the testator or testatrix's deathbed.

Writ of Execution: A court order directing a public officer (usually the sheriff) to seize and sell property to satisfy a debt.

Writ of Possession: A court order informing a tenant that he or she must vacate the landlord's property within a specified period or be forcibly removed by the sheriff or constable.

Zoning: Government regulation of the uses of property within specified areas. SEE: Conditional Use Permit; Nonconforming Use; Rezone; Variance.

Zoning Board of Adjustment: A panel of local residents empowered by law to hear and grant relief from the effects of zoning. SEE: Variance.

Zoning, Exclusionary: A zoning law that has the effect of preventing certain groups (such as minorities or poor people) from living in a community.

Zoning Amendment: SEE: Rezone.

W

Z

Appendix A: Matching Terminology Answers

Chapter 1

1. O
2. I
3. V
4. G
5. J
6. L
7. D
8. F
9. K
10. E
11. U
12. P
13. T
14. A
15. R
16. S
17. Q
18. B
19. C
20. N
21. H
22. M

Chapter 2

1. J
2. M
3. O
4. N
5. S
6. C
7. U
8. G
9. I
10. CC
11. L
12. A
13. V
14. H
15. R
16. E
17. AA
18. W
19. D
20. X
21. Z
22. DD
23. F
24. BB
25. T
26. Q
27. Y
28. K
29. B

Chapter 3

1. K
2. R
3. O
4. C
5. Y
6. D
7. S
8. X
9. F
10. G
11. BB
12. W
13. CC
14. B
15. V
16. I
17. H
18. E
19. P
20. A
21. U
22. N
23. L
24. J
25. DD
26. Z
27. M
28. T
29. Q
30. AA

Chapter 4

1. J
2. Q
3. A
4. E
5. D
6. X
7. U
8. K
9. H
10. L
11. R
12. S
13. T
14. P
15. I
16. F
17. G
18. O
19. N
20. M
21. C
22. W
23. V
24. B

Chapter 5

1. BB
2. H
3. N
4. X
5. I
6. S
7. T
8. D
9. B
10. Q
11. K
12. U
13. C
14. EE
15. P
16. DD
17. FF
18. W
19. V
20. A
21. J
22. F
23. AA
24. R
25. Y
26. Z
27. E
28. L
29. CC
30. M
31. O
32. G

Chapter 6

1. C
2. T
3. S
4. F
5. X
6. D
7. Y
8. B
9. P
10. M
11. H
12. U
13. N
14. Q
15. E
16. J
17. O
18. W
19. R
20. L
21. K
22. I
23. V
24. A
25. G

Chapter 7

1. L
2. J
3. M
4. Q
5. R
6. B
7. C
8. A
9. N
10. D
11. H
12. E
13. P
14. F
15. S
16. G
17. I
18. O
19. K
20. T

Chapter 8

1. Q
2. L
3. O

Appendix A: Matching Terminology Answers

4. J
5. M
6. H
7. N
8. U
9. G
10. C
11. E
12. S
13. R
14. A
15. D
16. I
17. B
18. P
19. F
20. T
21. V
22. K

Chapter 9

1. E
2. H
3. D
4. U
5. S
6. T
7. M
8. P
9. V
10. O
11. B
12. N
13. Q
14. C
15. J
16. R
17. A
18. I
19. F
20. G
21. L
22. K

Chapter 10

1. O
2. E
3. C
4. J
5. F
6. M

7. H
8. I
9. K
10. A
11. D
12. L
13. N
14. B
15. G

Chapter 11

1. CC
2. OO
3. K
4. Q
5. J
6. AA
7. F
8. BB
9. A
10. M
11. II
12. U
13. GG
14. C
15. X
16. P
17. MM
18. EE
19. LL
20. D
21. NN
22. W
23. V
24. Z
25. T
26. I
27. R
28. JJ
29. HH
30. H
31. N
32. G
33. FF
34. E
35. B
36. KK
37. S
38. L
39. Y
40. DD
41. 0

Chapter 12

1. R
2. G
3. L
4. H
5. T
6. Y
7. D
8. N
9. M
10. W
11. Z
12. K
13. J
14. I
15. P
16. V
17. C
18. O
19. B
20. Q
21. X
22. U
23. S
24. F
25. A
26. E

Chapter 13

1. D
2. L
3. O
4. N
5. K
6. P
7. F
8. A
9. J
10. M
11. B
12. S
13. E
14. U
15. H
16. G
17. I
18. V
19. T
20. C
21. Q
22. R

Chapter 14

1. X
2. D
3. T
4. N
5. M
6. E
7. J
8. G
9. O
10. W
11. R
12. S
13. U
14. C
15. B
16. H
17. V
18. P
19. K
20. F
21. Q
22. A
23. I
24. L

Chapter 15

1. N
2. O
3. B
4. S
5. X
6. U
7. R
8. Q
9. I
10. L
11. BB
12. W
13. E
14. D
15. P
16. G
17. A
18. T
19. H
20. M
21. CC
22. Z
23. F

24. Y
25. C
26. K
27. J
28. V
29. AA

Chapter 16

1. B
2. O
3. A
4. I
5. L
6. H
7. C
8. J
9. Q
10. E
11. D
12. R
13. F
14. S
15. G
16. M
17. P
18. K
19. N
20. N
21. U

Chapter 17

1. K
2. E
3. G
4. B
5. L
6. F
7. H
8. A
9. P
10. C
11. N
12. I
13. O
4. J
15. D
16. M